Divided Soul
The Life of Gogol

BOOKS BY HENRI TROYAT
(Published in English)

FICTION

ONE MINUS TWO
JUDITH MADRIER
MOUNTAIN
WHILE THE EARTH ENDURES
  MY FATHER'S HOUSE
  THE RED AND THE WHITE
  STRANGERS ON THE EARTH
THE SEED AND THE FRUIT
  AMELIE IN LOVE
  AMELIE AND PIERRE
  ELIZABETH
  TENDER AND VIOLENT ELIZABETH
  THE ENCOUNTER
THE LIGHT OF THE JUST
  BROTHERHOOD OF THE RED POPPY
  THE BARONESS
EXTREME FRIENDSHIP

NON-FICTION

FIREBRAND: THE LIFE OF DOSTOYEVSKY
DAILY LIFE IN RUSSIA UNDER THE LAST TSAR
PUSHKIN
TOLSTOY
DIVIDED SOUL: THE LIFE OF GOGOL

HENRI TROYAT

Divided Soul
The Life of Gogol

Translated from the French
by Nancy Amphoux

MINERVA PRESS
NEW YORK

Minerva Press Edition, 1975
(an imprint of Funk and Wagnalls)

GOGOL was published in France
by Flammarion et Cie
GOGOL by Henri Troyat © Flammarion et Cie 1971

Library of Congress Catalog Card Number 75-943
ISBN 0-308-10170-7

Contents

PART III

Divided Soul
The Life of Gogol

Part One

1. Childhood

When Marya Ivanovna Gogol-Yanovsky saw that she was pregnant again, her joy was soured by apprehension: after two ill-fated deliveries, which had nearly cost her her life, was she going to bring forth yet another stillborn child? Her husband, Vasily Afanasyevich, equally anxious, surrounded her with tremulous adoration. To placate the malevolent fates, they decided that if the child was a boy they would call him Nikolai, in honor of the miraculous icon of the saint of that name worshiped in the neighboring village of Dikanka. The village priest was asked to pray daily for a favorable outcome. A forest of propitiatory tapers grew up around the icon. And as the sweltering summer of 1808 drew to a close, the couple's unrelenting, agonizing vigil began, with its counterpoint of plans and prayers.

A peaceful, quiet, retiring pair, they lived on their property of Vasilyevka, in the government of Poltava, in the heart of the Ukraine. There was a low, wooden house with a semicircle of pillars in front, a garden, a pond, and a farmyard raucous with the cackling of geese; there were rosaries of finely sliced apples and pears drying on a fence-top in the sun; there were huts for the lazy, good-humored servants, about twenty-seven hundred acres of land, and some two hundred serfs working in the fields. What more could be desired by people for whom city lights held no appeal?

Vasily Afanasyevich Gogol-Yanovsky was descended from an old Ukrainian family ennobled under the Polish allegiance in the seventeenth century. One of his ancestors, Ostap Gogol, made a name for

himself around 1655 when he fought alongside the hetman Peter Doro-
shenko as a colonel of the Cossacks. His paternal grandfather, Damian,
had been a priest. His father, Afanasy Damyanovich, trained for the
church first at the Poltava Seminary and then at the Ecclesiastical
Academy of Kiev, but finally abandoned his religious vocation and
settled with his wife, the former Miss Lisogub—a woman of extremely
ancient and honorable Cossack lineage—on the little estate, Vasilyevka,
that she had brought as her dowry.[1] It was there that Vasily Afanasyevich
Gogol-Yanovsky first saw the light of day, in 1777. An only son, he, too,
had followed the family tradition and studied at the Poltava Theological
Seminary; but then, deciding in favor of a "civilian career," he took a position, in the postal administration, that did not require his physical presence. A few years later, he resigned with the rank of collegiate assessor
and retired to the country to help his parents run their estate. He was so
scantily endowed with business sense, however, that he was precious
little help to them. Respectably well educated, he knew Latin, appreciated
music, read a good deal, told stories well, and even wrote occasional verse
and comedies in Little Russian. These showed a thorough knowledge of
Ukrainian folk customs, and on their evidence the author would seem to
have been quite a gay dog: a lover of jest, practical jokes, and parties.
However, his character was essentially dreamy, sensitive, and feckless. Of
unprepossessing appearance and capricious will, he let himself be carried
along without seeking to impose any direction upon his thoughts or actions. He was very fond of nature and had built little kiosks and artificial
grottoes in his garden, and given poetic names to the paths. There was a
"vale of tranquillity," for instance, at Vasilyevka; and the local birds received special treatment: the laundresses were forbidden to wash in the
pond, lest the noise of their scrubbing boards frighten away the doves and
nightingales.

This tender plant, Vasily Afanasyevich, burst into full bloom when he
fell in love with Marya Ivanovna. According to her, it all began with a
childhood dream. One night the Blessed Virgin appeared to Vasily
Afanasyevich, then aged thirteen; pointing at an unidentified baby playing nearby, the Virgin said in a melodious voice, "Thou shalt marry,
and here is she who will be thy wife." Sometime later, calling on some
neighbors with his parents, Vasily Afanasyevich saw a seven-month-old
baby girl, identical in every respect to the one he had admired in his
dream, in the arms of a beribboned nanny. From that instant he knew
his destiny and had only to wait for the chosen one to reach an age at

which she might respond to his sentiments. Daughter of the landowner Kosyarovsky, her first name was Marya and she was being brought up by her aunt Anna Matveyevna Troshchinsky.

For the next few years, Vasily Afanasyevich lived happily with his secret, supervising his future fiancée's growing grace and intelligence. He often called upon her, listened rapturously to her childish babblings, brought her scores of little presents, taught her to build playing-card castles, and played dolls with her, while her good aunt wondered to see this serious, sober young man derive such intense pleasure from the company of a child. "My feelings for him were very special, but I remained quite composed," Marya Ivanovna later wrote. "He sometimes asked if I were not bored with him and did not find him trying. I would answer that I enjoyed his company, and indeed he was extremely kind and thoughtful from my earliest childhood."[2]

One day when Marya Ivanovna, escorted by a few servant women, was going for a walk on the banks of the Psel, she heard the sweet strains of a wind orchestra drifting across the stream. The Gogols were the only people in the neighborhood to possess such a thing; but how did it come to be there just in time to serenade her? Hidden behind the trees, the musicians played a series of increasingly languorous airs, while Marya Ivanovna's heart melted with culpable gratification. She could not tear herself away. At last it grew late, and the servants dragged her off; but the musicians followed them all the way home, taking cover in the thickets. The melody approached, wafted away, flowed nearer, hopped, skipped, wrapped around her. When she told her aunt about this wonderful thing that had happened, the aunt said with a smile, "How very fortunate that you chanced to be out just when he, who so loves nature and music, was also taking advantage of the fine weather! But, in future, do not go so far from the house."

On the eve of Marya's fourteenth birthday Vasily Afanasyevich, then twenty-seven and permanently settled at Vasilyevka, made bold to ask her if she loved him. Startled, not quite knowing why, she answered, "I love you as I love everybody else." And leaving him there in suspense, she scurried out of the drawing room. Mortified, Vasily Afanasyevich confided his plans and his disappointment to Aunt Anna Matveyevna; this energetic woman instantly promised to take matters in hand. She was sure, she said, that Marya loved her charming neighbor; why, whenever he went away, the poor thing fell into a decline; she was so young; she was afraid of men; she would make an excellent wife!

When he had gone home reassured, Anna Matveyevna undertook to interrogate her niece. The only thing the little girl could find to put forward in her defense was that if she got married all her girlfriends would laugh at her—an utterly insignificant objection, which the aunt swept aside with a word. Pushed and pulled, congratulated and embraced, Marya suddenly awoke with a fiancé in her heart. The parents were now consulted and hastened to give their blessing, so Marya returned to their home for the preparation of her trousseau. "My fiancé used to come often," Marya Ivanovna wrote. "When he could not come, he would write. Without unsealing the letters, I would hand them to my father, who, after reading them, would say with a smile, 'He has clearly read a great many novels!' And truly, the letters were filled with the most tender expressions. My father would dictate the replies. I always carried my fiancé's missives with me."

The wedding was held in the aunt's house at Zharesky, but after a day of festivities the husband returned home alone, for everyone agreed that Marya Ivanovna was too young to share a man's life. In a year, they would see. . . . The bride accepted the separation calmly, the bridegroom in despair.

At the end of a month they were both so miserable that the doting parents agreed to reconsider. In a shower of tears, blessings, cautions, and exhortations, Marya Ivanovna clambered into the coach and set off for Vasilyevka.

An hour later, she was in her new home. Vasily Afanasyevich's father and mother were awaiting their daughter-in-law on the threshold, with the bread and salt of hospitality. "They welcomed me as their own child," she wrote. "My mother-in-law dressed me according to her own taste, in old gowns dating from her youth. . . . My husband did not wish me to continue my studies. He spoke no foreign language except Latin and did not wish me to be more learned than he; so we read only Russian books, always together, whenever we had a moment of leisure alone, which was not often. . . . I never went to gatherings or balls, finding my happiness inside my own family. We were never apart, not even for a day, and when he went out to inspect his land he took me with him in the calèche. If I had to remain alone at home I was afraid for him; I felt as though I would never see him again. . . ."[3]

To spare his wife the anguish of waiting, Vasily Afanasyevich usually contrived to come home early. Once, he was actually a few minutes late, and she fell ill and lay in bed for several days, tossing with fever. These irrational anxieties were mixed with more tangible concerns. The property was rich in good land, yet failed to support its inhabitants. The trees in the orchard creaked with the weight of pears, plums, and cherries; massive milch cows grazed in the heavy, green meadow; the fields yielded an abundant harvest of stiff, golden wheat. But whenever he did his accounts, Vasily Afanasyevich would discover that his expenses were well in excess of his income. Then, in panic, he would organize a fair or build a little distillery in the hope of making some money from the sale of spirits, or, more simply, he would borrow from an easygoing neighbor, to tide them over until the next season.

Marya Ivanovna, who only yesterday had been playing with dolls, was now mistress of the household, scolding the servants and dazzling her husband with her youth and authority. Very soon, from the mild-tempered and affected little girl, there emerged a young woman with white skin, dark eyes, heavy arched eyebrows, chiseled features, a strongly drawn mouth, and a decided manner. Her nerves had been badly shaken by the arrival of two stillborn babies in rapid succession in the first year of her marriage. Now pregnant for the third time, she interpreted every heartbeat with anguish.

This time she did not want to have the baby at home. The family decided that she should go to Sorochinsk, a little town nearby in which Trakhimovsky, a physician renowned throughout the region, had his practice. It was there, in a little cubicle with a floor of beaten earth, that she gave birth, on March 20, 1809, to a boy, Nikolai. Item number 25 of the Sorochinsk parish records bears witness to the birth and baptism.[4]

As soon as she returned home, Marya Ivanovna's fears for the outcome of her pregnancy gave way to fears about her son's health. He was puny, pale, and sickly. She was permanently convinced that he was about to die, and this ever-present menace made him all the more precious. One moment she imagined him dead; the next, astounding the world with his genius.

To win the fates to her side, she decided to build a church at Vasilyevka—never mind the cost. The builder agreed to defer payment. The family silver was sold to purchase the sacred vessels. A heavy, embroidered altar cloth was ordered. But even that did not improve little Nikolai's health. He had asthma, he had fainting spells, and he had tantrums, which the doctors said were a by-product of scrofula. His pasty complexion refused to glow, whether from the sun or at play. His ears suppurated. A hundred times a day, his mother felt him to see whether he was not too hot or too cold, uncovered him, swathed him, kissed him, made the sign of the cross over his head; and he, in this atmosphere of mute adoration, eventually came to regard himself as a sort of household idol. His sense of his superiority was undimmed by the birth of his sister, Marya (1811) and brother, Ivan (1812). He was the first; he reigned by divine right. He was the center of the household, and consequently of the world as well. "I had no emotions at all, and treated the things around me as so many objects placed there for my pleasure and comfort," he later wrote to his mother. "I had no particular affection for anyone, except you, and even that feeling was dictated solely by nature."[5]

Beyond all doubt, his mother emerges as the most lively, active, worried, and worry-inspiring member of the little human group that formed his universe. She imposed her poetry upon the whole household. At the slightest provocation, she would sink to her knees before the icons. She began taking Nikolai to church when he was little more than a baby; at first, however, all he felt as he sat there asphyxiated between the adults, nauseated by the smell of incense, and deafened by "the ghastly noise of the sacristan,"[6] was boredom. He crossed himself because everybody else did; he let his mind drift limply among the holy images. But one day he took it into his head to ask his mother for a clarification of certain particulars regarding the Last Judgment, and she, a prophet new-inspired, painted so compelling a picture of the life to come in paradise and in hell that he had nightmares all night long and woke several times soaked in cold sweat and howling with terror. The vision of eternal hell-fire remained with him a long time; the mere thought of it set him shivering. "You painted for me so perfect, so clear, so moving a picture of the felicities awaiting the virtuous, and so striking and terrifying an image of the eternal torments of the sinners, that it shook me to the roots, aroused all my sensitivity, and sowed in me the seeds of the highest thoughts, which germinated later," he wrote.[7] From that day on, little Nikolai went to church every Sunday in a fever of mingled adoration and dread.

When his father took him out with his brother to inspect the fields, however, everything seemed light and gay: the scythes glinting through the yellow mass of wheat, the tanned faces of the harvesters, the songs of the girls tying up sheaves. . . . All his life he remembered the glorious summers of Little Russia with a deep sense of gratitude. "Not a cloud in the sky," he wrote in "The Fair at Sorochinsk." "Not a sound in the fields. Everything is as though dead. High in the heavenly gulf a single lark flutters, his silvery song climbing down the stairways of the air toward the enamored earth. . . . A myriad insects, like emeralds, topazes, rubies, rain down upon the many-hued vegetable patches shaded by giant sunflowers. Gray-streaked haystacks and sheaves of golden wheat stand ranged as in an encampment covering the endless plain. The boughs of cherry tree, plum, apple, and pear sag with the burden of their fruit. . . . What delight, what easy leisure lies in those summers of Little Russia!" When he returned from his outings, he would tell the rest of the family what he had seen, while they gaped at the acuteness of his observation and the extent of his vocabulary.

Now and then his father would throw in a comment or repeat a conversation he had had with some peasants. Vasily Afanasyevich was a round little body, smiling and soft-hearted, who spoke Russian and Ukrainian equally well but preferred the former for serious talk and the latter for matters of less consequence.

The third person of Nikolai's trinity was his grandmother, Tatyana Semyonovna, née Lisogub. She had lost her husband shortly after Vasily Afanasyevich's marriage and lived in a two-room pavilion adjoining the house. Nikolai loved to visit her domain, a clutter of old boxes, old clothes, and souvenirs. Her face was shriveled and pitted like a sponge. She undoubtedly told her grandson about the glorious days when the "Zaporog" Cossacks formed an independent brotherhood, with the *syech* electing their own leaders and defying the Pole. One of the last heroes of the epoch was Ostap Gogol, the fierce ancestor who had given his name to the family. After the Zaporogs' submission to Russia and the edict of Catherine II, the *syech* was dispersed, the last hetman abdicated, and legend gave way to history. Tatyana Semyonovna also knew old songs and terrifying folk tales, which Nikolai never tired of hearing. This fascination with the mysterious, this attraction with terror, would well up in an instant, just when he imagined himself safe and serene. One day, when his mother and father were away, the five-year-old child sat watching the darkness creep over the windowpane and was suddenly seized by anguish. "I huddled back into the corner of the sofa," he said, "and there, in the utter stillness, listened to the ticking pendulum of the wall clock. . . . Suddenly the miaow of a cat broke the calm that was oppressing me. I saw the animal moving slowly toward me as it cried. Never shall I forget its motion, its stretching, its soft paws with their claws that clicked on the floor boards, and its green eyes sparkling with an evil light. I was afraid. I climbed up the back of the sofa and clung to the wall. 'Kitty, kitty,' I murmured to give myself courage; and then I leaped down, grabbed the unresisting cat, ran into the garden, and threw the animal into the pond. Again and again, while the cat swam and tried to return to the surface, I pushed it under with a stick. I was terrified, trembling all over, and at the same time I felt a kind of satisfaction, perhaps because I was paying it back for the fright it had given me. But once it had drowned and the last ripples died away on the water, I suddenly felt sorry for it. I was stricken with remorse. I felt as though I had drowned a human being. . . ."[8]

Sometimes he heard the voices of the dead, too, in the midst of a silence, and their call chilled his blood. "No doubt you have known the same thing—a voice calling you by name," he wrote in *Old World Landowners*. "To hear simple folk talk, it is a soul yearning for you and announcing your imminent death. I confess that I have always dreaded these mysterious summonses. I often heard them in my childhood. Suddenly someone behind me would pronounce my name distinctly. Most often it happened on a beautiful, sunny day: not a leaf trembled in the trees, a deathly silence hung in the air, even the crickets had stopped singing, there was not a living creature in the garden. The most sinister stormy night, with all the fury of the elements unleashed, falling upon me unprepared in an impenetrable forest, would have produced less fear in me than that horrible silence beneath a cloudless sky. Usually I would take to my heels and run until I was exhausted and panic-stricken, and would not grow calm again until I met another human, the sight of whom would efface the agonizing sensation of the void that was gripping my heart."

Fortunately, the "agonizing sensation of the void" was as speedily forgotten as it was intensely experienced. After such hallucinations, the desire to play returned with renewed vigor, and Nikolai would join in games with his brother and sister without another thought. Best of all, however, he loved gardening. "Spring is coming," he wrote to his mother in 1827, "the jolliest time of year for anyone who knows how to enjoy it. It reminds me of my childhood and my passion for horticulture. For me—do you remember?—the spring meant a burst of activity; I was in my element. I can still see myself musing at the side of a twisting path, shovel in hand. . . ."

The house was always lively, warmhearted, and hospitable. Friends and relations filled it all year long. The rooms were small and low, with stoves rising to the ceiling; there were quantities of chests, creaking doors, and massive pieces of furniture. There was a swarm of girls in striped petticoats buzzing in the servants' hall, and all the abundance, sweetness, and rusticity of the life of the landed gentry of olden days. The Vasilyevka serfs were not ill-treated and .never so much as dreamed of desiring their freedom. No one, serf or master, thought to challenge the necessity of serfdom. It was natural for some individuals to be born free and others in slavery, just as it was natural for some men to be tall and others short, some blond and others brunette. God had not desired equality in nature, so it was wrong for a Christian to rebel against inequality in society.

Marya Ivanovna reigned over the servants with her bunch of keys at her waist—the cellar doors were forever having to be locked and unlocked. Food was an important matter in the household. Somebody was always cooking, brine-pickling, drying fruits and vegetables. The pantry bulged with mouth-watering provender, enough to withstand a six months' siege. "There," Nikolai Gogol wrote in *Old World Landowners,* "no desire reaches beyond the farmyard fence, the apple-orchard hedge, and the village isbas standing lopsided and forlorn among the willows, elders, and pear trees. The lives of these modest landowners pass so calmly and peaceably that in a moment of forgetfulness one surprises oneself doubting the very existence of passions and desires, all the futile agitations engendered by the evil spirit to trouble the poor world: all that, one can think, is out of a dream, just a glittering phantasmagoria."

Occasionally the Gogols would emerge from their Vasilyevka retreat for a brief visit to some neighboring gentleman-farmer. The most important of these, and the one they most often went to see, was a distant cousin of Marya Ivanovna, and the family's "benefactor" and "protector"—a man named Dmitri Prokofyevich Troshchinsky. He reigned over his Kibinsk estate like a little king. This personage, who had "come up from nothing," had ascended to the rank of secretary of state under Catherine II but was elbowed aside soon after Paul I came to the throne; he returned to favor, however, under Alexander I, who had thrown himself into Troshchinsky's arms, saying, "Be my guide." The young emperor made him a minister, and he served in the government for a few years; then, pleading age and fatigue, he retired to his estate. Once away from the capital, he consented to serve as marshal of nobil-

ity for the Poltava district. Rich, idle, and highly esteemed, Troshchinsky could not bear to be alone. According to contemporaries' accounts,
his house, which was everlastingly filled with guests, resembled a
labyrinthine gypsy encampment incessantly traversed by the ebb and
flow of arrivals and departures. There were never enough people at
table. Every day, he required some fresh diversion. He had a company
of actors recruited from among his serfs, an orchestra, jesters. The
story is told of how an artillery officer whom no one had ever seen before introduced himself to Troschinsky one morning with the idea of organizing a fireworks display. The master was so delighted that he kept
the man around for three years. When the Gogols came to visit, they
brought the whole family along. Nikolai adored the journey, which was
over forty versts.*

The moment the coach turned into the Kibinsk drive, the distant,
melodious strains of the serf-musician orchestra became audible. Then,
between two curtains of trees, the two-story wooden house rose up and
spread out like a palace. The luxury within left one gasping: paintings
everywhere, precious furniture, bronze statuettes and porcelaine figu-
rines, downy sofas, ancient weapons, collections of coins and snuffboxes, and rugs so soft one hardly dared step on them. A throng of
servants crowded into the anteroom. Scattered about the grounds were
little guesthouses for the more noteworthy visitors. The Gogols de-
posited their luggage in one of these and quickly changed out of their
traveling clothes. Servants, carriages, horses, a physician were placed at
their disposal. Well before the dinner hour, a diffident crowd assembled
in the drawing room and silently awaited the appearance of the master
of the house. At last he showed himself, in dress uniform decked out
with all his ribbons and decorations. Very old and bent, he had an eagle
beak and an icy countenance expressing boredom and disdain. During
the meal, the guests devised games—charades, guessing games, and
masquerades—to be played for their host's entertainment when they
left the table. The preparation of complete theatrical performances,
which Troshchinsky adored, required more time. He had built a theater
on the grounds, and the honor of producing plays in Little Russian fell
to Vasily Afanasyevich Gogol-Yanovsky. Occasionally he even wrote
one himself, on command. The roles were taken by the guests or by
serf-actors living on the estate. Vasily Afanasyevich and his wife often

* 1 verst=3,500 feet, or approximately .66 mile.

figured in the cast, while little Nikolai watched rehearsals with avid and delighted eyes. How he admired his father for making up the words other people were speaking on the stage, and how he roared with laughter at those tales of cunning females and doltish peasants.[9] Troshchinsky, seated in the front row, observed the action through his opera glasses, and whenever he deigned to smile, actors and audience alike heaved a sigh of grateful relief.

The other foolproof means of cheering up the old gentleman was to tease his clowns, Roman Ivanovich and Bartholomew. The latter was a defrocked priest and so remarkably filthy that he had to eat by himself behind a screen. When he had finished, someone would glue his beard to the table with sealing wax and the whole room would look on in delight as he winced and grimaced, tearing the hairs loose one by one. Another common entertainment at Kibinsk was the barrel game. After filling a huge wooden vat with water, the master would fling in a handful of gold coins and invite his guests to dive to the bottom for them. Anyone who could pick them all up in one dive was allowed to keep them, but if he left any at the bottom he had to throw back the ones he had fished out and let the next man have his turn. In this contest, some of the guests competed as fiercely as the clowns. Wringing wet and laughing uproariously, they were rewarded at the end of the match by a condescending twitch of the ex-minister's lips, from his vantage point on the veranda at the top of the steps.[10]

As a rule, Troshchinsky was rather rude to his guests, addressed them haughtily, and would turn abruptly away to lay out a game of solitaire. But the Gogols enjoyed preferential treatment. He appreciated the jollity, dreamy cheerfulness, and honesty of Vasily Afanasyevich and often turned to him for assistance with the management of his vast estate. In exchange, Vasily Afanasyevich, being regarded as an authority in both choice of entertainments and the supervision of accounts, knew he could always rely on Troshchinsky if times were bad. Whenever the household ran short of cash or needed a letter of recommendation to the governor, all eyes instantly turned to Kibinsk. "My husband and I," Marya Ivanovna wrote, "used to make lengthy visits to Troshchinsky's estate, and it was not easy to persuade him to let us go; toward the end, it made him so cross that he became ill when he was told that we wanted to go home. Guests usually found it difficult to take leave of him without putting him in a bad mood. He was always grouchy when he had to say good-by to anyone. But his house seldom remained for long without a great number of people. Very soon, another crowd would fill the place. . . . The double doors would open wide in room after room, and some orchestra or quartet would begin playing. . . ."[11]

Parting from the crochety and capricious old aristocrat, little Nikolai took away with him a vision of an enchanted world bursting with jokes and tricks, music, laughter, lights, and bowing and curtseying. On their return home, Vasilyevka seemed more shabby and small than before, but also more warmly familiar. Back in his everyday childhood he dreamed of Troshchinsky's theater and cursed fate for making him too young to appear on the stage himself. Emulating his elders, he tried to compose poetry and proudly read out his verses to his family. He also made drawings, and insisted that his works be framed. A theology student who had been hired as a tutor sought to instill what small learning he possessed into the minds of Nikolai and Ivan, but the results were so disappointing that the parents soon decided to send their two sons to the boarding school at Poltava.

In 1819, at the age of ten, Nikolai found himself plunged into a crowd of strangers. Here he was, the petted and pampered apple of every eye, suddenly become invisible in the mass of pupils, with no one to worry over his delicate constitution or applaud his dazzling gifts. How could it be that, despite all his efforts, he was not at the head of the class? Was he less brilliant than he had supposed? Or were his teachers blind?

"The holidays are approaching," he wrote his parents; "I have not yet managed to finish all my work. . . . I ought to have a tutor for mathematics. If you come through Poltava soon, I am sure you will arrange everything for my welfare. I kiss your inestimable hands and I have the honor to be, with filial respect, your obedient son, Nikolai Gogol-Yanovsky."[12]

Nikolai was looking forward to a joyful holiday, but he returned to a siege of mourning. To the immense despair of his parents, his brother, Ivan, died after a short illness; Nikolai was so grief-stricken that he had to be withdrawn from the school.

Now that he was back at Vasilyevka, he secretly hoped that he might never have to go to school again. But after lengthy deliberations his mother and father decided, with aching hearts, that he could not be properly taught at home and must be enrolled in an educational establishment of the highest quality. It happened that a "High School for

Advanced Study" had just been founded by Prince Bezborodko in Nye-zhin. The curriculum seemed satisfactorily solemn—nothing at all like the miserable little school in Poltava. Unfortunately, fees and board amounted to a thousand rubles a year.† The Gogols could not afford it. They turned to the heaven-sent Troshchinsky, who promised to arrange a grant.

† Monetary fluctuations being what they are, one might as well take Gogol's ruble to be something over $1.00—an accurate calculation would be meaningless.

2. The Nyezhin School

A heavy yellow carriage drawn by six horses pulled up before the steps of the "High School for Advanced Study," and the pupils who had come running at the sound of the harness bells watched "the new boy" emerge. Was this a human being or some nocturnal bird? Shivering, skinny, and small, he had on far too many clothes for the season. His small, pointed face stuck out of his wrappings like a buzzard's out of its plumage. He was flanked by his father and a servant. A sissy, for sure. His name was whispered around him—"Gogol-Yanovsky"—elbows jogged ribs, titters flew. He glanced timorously about. "He was more than simply wrapped up in his shawls, capes, and blankets," wrote Lyubich-Romanovich, one of his fellow pupils: "He was enveloped, hermetically sealed." "When they began to unswathe him, it took them a long time to uncover a feeble, extremely ugly boy, positively disfigured by scrofula. . . . He eyes were red-rimmed, his cheeks and nose were covered with pink spots, and his ears slowly suppurated. . . ." Nikolai Gogol felt totally lost, in a world even more hostile than that of the school at Poltava. Was it possible that he had to remain alone among all these enemies: pupils, proctors, teachers?

Having barely scraped through his entrance examination, he joined the ranks of the sloths sprawling on the benches at the rear of the class, half listening to the lesson and doodling to pass the time. Decidedly, nobody at Nyezhin liked him. After his father's departure, he felt a moment of sheer panic, as though fate had singled him out to be thrown to the lions. True, his old manservant, Simon, had stayed behind to console him, but the best muzhik in the world was unequal to the anguish of an aristocrat. Fortunately the summer holidays were approaching. It was spring 1821. Nikolai Gogol decided to grit his teeth and endure, until his liberation.

A few wonderful weeks at Vasilyevka and then back to the classroom in August, where despair overwhelmed him again, worse than before. He thirsted for his house and family as a man in the desert thirsts for water. What could he do to make his parents take him back again? If he said he was bored at Nyezhin and didn't care at all about his studies, the most he could hope for would be exhortations to diligence and patience. The only way to soften their hearts was to make them fully aware of the deplorable state of their son's health and the dangers he was running, far from their side. That his mother could survive carefree and happy was intolerable to one who had to endure the harsh discipline of the school. If he could not be happy, then she had no right to be either. With a mixture of sincerity and cunning, affection and calculation, Nikolai Gogol, aged twelve, wrote to his parents on August 14, 1821:

"Oh, my dearest parents, if you came here at this moment when I am writing to you, you would see what has become of your child! . . . Since the holiday, I have been so sad that my tears flow daily in spite of myself, and whenever I think of you they course down my face like a torrent. Also, my chest is so painful that it is hard for me to write for more than a few minutes at a time. . . . Farewell, dearest parents, tears prevent me from writing more. My good Simon is so concerned for me, not a single night goes by that he does not come urging me to cease weeping over being separated from you. Often he has spent the whole night at my bedside. I told him to go away and sleep, but couldn't make him go. . . .

"P.S. So far, scarcely half the pupils have returned!"

The last remark was designed to suggest that his parents had sent him back to school early. Alarmed by his portrayal of his sufferings, they retaliated with a battery of questions and may have even written to the head of the school to demand a medical examination. Fearing he had carried his deceit too far, Nikolai quickly shifted his ground:

"The day after my arrival at Nyezhin I felt a pain in my chest. That night it hurt so badly that I could hardly breathe. In the morning I felt better, but my chest was still sensitive. That explains my concern. Also,

I was very sad to be parted from you. But now, thanks be to God, it is gone. I am well and cheerful again . . ."[1]

The parents were reassured, and settled down to await the next crisis. They knew their son had a tendency to exaggerate but nonetheless worried to think of him being exposed to all sorts of influences and illnesses so far from home.

Nikolai Gogol, meanwhile, was growing used to his new life as a "recluse." Prince Bezborodko's school—a brand-new building with a colonnaded façade—stood in extensive grounds crossed by a stream. A thousand birds nested in the reeds along the banks, and the boarders awoke to their chorus at dawn. The boys rose at half past five. Half asleep, they washed and marched off in rows to church for morning prayers and then to the dining hall for tea. Classes followed, from nine until noon, and resumed after lunch until five. The boys spent most of their free time in the garden, and often, in good weather, sat under the trees to study and do their homework.

Lessons were taught in Russian, of course, which was the official language of the Ukraine as of every other province of the empire. Little Russian was considered a dialect and the pupils spoke it only occasionally, among themselves or in jest. Nikolai loved the fruity, earthy, untranslatable phrases and the customs, songs, dances, and terrifying or comical tales that made up the folklore of his native province. He was continually being corrected by his teachers for some Ukrainian or even Polish expression that had slipped into a composition, or for the faulty pronunciation of a Russian word,* as though it were impossible to be a Russian and remain a Ukrainian too.

The "High School for Advanced Study," hastily thrown together in obedience to the prince's will, was a pretentious establishment with a cumbersome, incoherent, and fragmentary curriculum. The classes were called "museums." The course lasted nine years and included lessons in religious education, Russian language and literature, Latin, Greek, German, French, physics, mathematics, political science, geography, history, military science, drawing, and dancing. The staff was a heteroclite body in which the most obtuse pedantry rubbed shoulders with a prudent liberalism. The pupils, too, were very dissimilar in nature and background. Those from the "aristocracy" looked firmly down

* The Polish domination in the Ukraine, and the many prolonged contacts between Ukrainians and Poles, had brought a number of slightly deformed Polish words into the Ukrainian language.

upon those from less exalted families. "We laughed at Gogol all the more," Lyubich-Romanovich wrote, "because he posed as a democrat among us, the sons of aristocrats. He hardly ever washed his hands or face in the morning, wore dirty underwear, and his clothes were all spotted and stained. His trouser pockets were stuffed with all kinds of sweets, chocolates, and gingerbread, which he would dig out and chew whenever he felt like it, even during lessons in school."

Lyubich-Romanovich was a sworn enemy of Nikolai Gogol. The other boarders at Nyezhin, less intransigent than he, sniffed around their fellow pupil as though he were some strange animal, trying to find out how he worked, torn between revulsion, uneasiness, mockery, and friendliness. To tell the truth, with his spavined appearance and withdrawn personality, Nikolai Gogol offered few footholds for friendship. If anyone asked him a personal question, he would parry with a lie. His amazed schoolmates often discovered that some simple little fact lay hidden beneath the absurd fabrication he had fed them. He acted as though he were trying at all costs to preserve a zone of darkness around himself. He felt free only to the extent that he could elude others. Divested of his secrets, he would have lost his vital force. His classmates named him "the mysterious dwarf," but they were intimidated by him, and not only by his aloofness: his gift for observation and mockery also held them at bay. For the scrawny paleface with the long, drooping nose and hollow chest was an expert at turning teachers and boys alike to ridicule. Woe unto anyone who fell into the clutches of his wit. He would mimic one boy's tics, give a hilarious nickname to another, and write satirical verses about a third. Zelder, the German teacher, a long stork of a man with an adipose face and dim-witted expression, would suddenly hear a song wafting up from the pupils' benches—attributable, no doubt, to Nikolai Gogol—in which he was likened to a boar on herons' legs. The bushy haircut of Borozhdin, a pupil, earned him a mordant epigram by Nikolai Gogol. Ritter, another pupil, wept with exasperation because Nikolai Gogol used to tell him every day, with an air of earnest conviction, "I assure you, you've got eyes like a heifer."

Coupled with a determined neglect of his studies, this fondness for levity prompted some of the teachers to deal harshly with "the mysterious dwarf." The warden's record book bears traces of the numerous penalties inflicted upon Gogol-Yanovsky. "December 13, to the corner for misconduct; December 19, no dinner for laziness; December 20, bread and water for dinner; same day, no tea because he was laughing during religious education. . . ."

"It is a pity," the headmaster wrote to his parents, "that your son is so lazy, for when he consents to work he can do as well as the rest, which proves his basic ability."

The months sped by, with their monotonous burden of lessons, homework, punishment, and laughter. The child was growing. The sleeves of his uniform had to be let out. He was fourteen, fifteen. . . . One day, threatened with a caning for misbehavior (caning was an exceptional punishment), he feigned hysterics. Screaming, foaming at the mouth, and stamping the ground, he so frightened the headmaster that he ordered Nikolai to be carried to the infirmary by the four disabled veterans employed by the school as watchmen. There was no further talk of punishment, and Nikolai Gogol "recovered" in a few weeks. In fact, the attack may only have been half simulated. He was easily upset and had been carried away by his own ruse. His response began in playacting and degenerated into a genuine nervous upheaval. Afterward he bragged to his classmates how he had fooled them all. In him, intense melancholy always alternated with a sudden need to clown.

"You know how I love everything gay," he wrote to his mother. "You alone have seen that beneath an exterior some would call cold, I hide a wild desire for fun (without going too far, of course)."[2] And to a friend, "I began with complaints, but now I feel quite cheerful again."[3] These sudden shifts of mood, switches from pink to black, contradictory emotions: he abandoned himself to his juggling act with the fervor of a maniac. He needed no particular reason to veer from optimism to despair, and when he had any real cause for woe, he sometimes remained curiously calm.

For the past four years his father had been insisting that he was ill. Vasily Afanasyevich had a tendency to hypochondria and always imagined himself at death's door. Early in 1825, however, he really did fall ill. He began coughing blood and went to Kibinsk to consult Troshchinsky's physician. Marya Ivanovna, about to give birth, could not join him and sat awaiting his return from one day to the next, but he never came back. When she heard that he had died, away from her, it was such a blow that she nearly lost her mind. She had to be fed by force. Incapable of writing to her son, she asked the headmaster to break the terrible news to him. Wild with grief, Nikolai's first impulse was to throw himself out the window.

Wasn't it enough to have lost a dearly beloved brother? And now God was taking his father from him. Why didn't the other children have to undergo such trials? The thought of death—the black, cold hole—horrified him. Then he mastered himself. The notion that he, at sixteen years of age, was now the master of the family revived his sense of responsibility and pleasingly added to his stature. His chief concern must be to comfort his mother, whose health might be undermined by grief; and to restore her zest for life his only weapon was his pen. He must therefore send her a letter at once poignant and well constructed, every phrase of which would pierce her heart. In addition, he might better alleviate her sufferings by shifting their forces to himself. If only he were a real writer, so that he could express in flawless style all the ideas swarming in his head. His composure returned as he prepared himself for his task. Literature magnified life. His sorrow was gradually transformed into a search for the right adjective. On April 23, 1825, he wrote to his mother:

"Do not worry, dearest Mother. I have borne up under this blow with Christian fortitude. Of course, at first I was dreadfully saddened by the news, although I did not let anyone see how sad I was. I even thought of ending my life, but God prevented me and, when evening came, I saw only a still sorrow within me, which finally turned into mild, scarcely perceptible melancholy coupled with a feeling of reverence for the Almighty. I bless thee, sacred faith! In thee alone my pain finds consolation and satisfaction. So it is, dear Mother, that I am calm now, although I cannot be happy, having lost the best of fathers, the most loyal of friends, all that was dear to my heart. But do I not still possess a sensitive, tender, virtuous mother, capable of replacing father, friend, and all that is sweetest and most dear? Yes, I still have you, and so fate has not abandoned me. . . . Ah, what worries me most is your pain. Be brave; make it as small as possible, as I have done with mine. Commit yourself, as I have done, to the Almighty. . . . The holiday begins in six weeks, and I shall be with you. Until then, calm your sorrow, if only a little. Do not forget that on your condition depends that of your respectful son, who loves you dearly. . . ."

The next day, April 24, brought a fresh supplication: "I beg you, dear Mother, not to despair; have pity upon us, poor orphans, whose happiness depends upon you. Have pity upon us, I say it again, do not destroy our last chance of felicity."

A few weeks later, having received no reply, Nikolai Gogol resorted

to his customary means of applying pressure—a threat to resort to some
dreadful extremity: "If I receive no reply to that letter, your silence
will be a fatal indication for me and I shall abandon myself to despair
and put an end to this cruel uncertainty. As you can see, my happiness
or wretchedness depends only on one sign from you. . . ."[4]

The "sign" finally came and Nikolai took heart. Contact being restored between himself and his mother, he was saved. She need only
be convinced that, in losing a husband, she had gained a son. During
the holiday she would be amazed to see how grief had matured him,
and what a beautiful soul he was bringing her as a gift. Persuaded
that this profound transformation had actually taken place, he now
bore his mourning with a kind of gratitude.

"Soon I shall see you," he wrote to his mother, "and I daily rejoice
at the prospect. I am already thinking about what kind of present to
bring you. But I know I can offer you nothing better than a good heart,
aflame with the most tender love for you. . . . I make bold to say that I
have aquired many good qualities which you will notice, I think; my
understanding of things has improved, become more penetrating and
profound. . . ."[5]

There was an element of truth in these rhetorical tirades. The years,
his grief, and communal life had indeed fortified Nikolai Gogol.

During the summer months at Vasilyevka he had the joy of seeing his
mother, grandmother, and sisters, and measuring the extent of his
authority over them. He returned to the school, now called a *lycée*, with
less apprehension than before. His mother had evidently surmounted
her grief and been delivered, without complications, of a baby girl,
Olga. So he was still the only son. Surrounded by women. This redoubled his energy. Also, although an unsociable type, he had managed to
make a few friends: fellow pupils sharing a love of literature. His best
friends were Alexander Danilevsky, whom he had known previously at
the Poltava school, and Gerasim Vysotsky, two years his senior, a boy
with a thoughtful and ironic mind. Other members of the school were
Nestor Kukolnik,[6] top boy in his class, Eugene Grebenka,[7] Konstantin
Bazili,[8] Prokopovich,[9] and Lyubich-Romanovich.[10] The youngsters
were voracious readers, and could not be content with the meager
school library. Troshchinsky, the benefactor, agreed to lend them some
items from his personal library, in which French authors predomi-
nated. Sometimes Nikolai Gogol bought books with his spending money.

"I refuse myself even the strictest minimum," he wrote to his mother, "in order to remain in my present state and at the same time satisfy my longing to see and feel Beauty. To that end I very painfully devote my entire year's allowance, setting aside only a tiny fraction for my needs. The Schiller that I sent for from Lemberg cost forty rubles, a considerable sum for a person in my circumstances; but my rewards far exceed the sacrifice, and I now spend a few hours each day in the greatest joy. Nor have I neglected the Russians, and immediately order all the best things published. . . . Sometimes in a periodical I read that some admirable work is now on sale. My heart begins to thud and, with a sigh, I put the magazine aside, remembering that it is impossible for me to purchase the book. The longing to possess it troubles my sleep, and if any money comes to me I exult like the most avaricious of misers."[11]

The boys began pooling their money to buy books and periodicals. The project was so successful that they soon needed a librarian, and Nikolai Gogol was the unanimous choice. He performed his office with sacerdotal solemnity, insisting that the text be read in his presence and, to prevent the pupil from soiling the pages as he turned them, placing a paper sheath upon his index finger before he began to read. Such fastidiousness was surprising in a boy who took so little care of himself; but all things literary were sacred. He himself was conspicuously dirty, but a spot in a margin or a scuffed binding caused him actual pain.

His position as librarian gave him first choice of the books. He wanted to know everything about contemporary authors—who, of course, were not in the curriculum. The literature teacher, a starched idiot named Nikolsky, held the writers of the previous century in the highest esteem and felt nothing but contempt for such newcomers as Pushkin, Zhukovsky, and Batyushkov, although these were the names the pupils admired. Just then, Pushkin was publishing the first chapters of his verse novel *Eugene Onegin,* whose fame stretched to the remotest provinces. Marveling at those singing lines, of a perfection that defied analysis, Gogol copied out *The Gypsies, Poltava, The Robber Brothers,* and passages from *Eugene Onegin* into a notebook. To impress Nikolsky, he dreamed up the idea of showing him one of his idol's most beautiful poems, *The Prophet,* and pretending he had written it himself. After reading it, Nikolsky frowned and sneered and criticized every line until the infuriated Gogol confessed. Without batting an eyelid, his teacher declared from the top of his lectern, "So you don't imagine that Pushkin can write badly? Well, there's proof of it!"[12] And he went on to accuse the poet of "triviality" of language and said he lacked "elevation." Such attacks only intensified Gogol's adoration of his favorite, however. In the past, he had imagined his talents lay in the field of painting only, but now he began to wonder if he had any literary gifts as well. During class time, the boy who had been scribbling drawings behind his classmates' backs now began to scribble verses. In his letters to his mother there was less talk of the paintings he was going to paint and more of the poems he was in the process of writing.

"I was intending to send a few of my poems and drawings to Papa for Christmas, but . . . Heaven did not want him to see them," he wrote on April 24, 1825.

On September 10 of the following year, "You ask me to bring you my latest poems for Christmas. That is still a long way off, but I shall try to have something ready."

On November 26, 1826, he proudly announced, "I think you will be surprised by the progress of which I shall bring you proof. You will not recognize my literary work, which has undergone a radical transformation. It is now of a completely different type."

His head buzzed with ideas; every style was right: in rapid succession he produced an epic poem, *Russia Under the Tartar Yoke;* a romantic drama à la Schiller, called *The Brigands;* and a satire on the inhabitants of Nyezhin, *A Few Words on Nyezhin, Where the Law Is Not Made for Fools*. This was a work in five parts: "(1) dedication of a chapel in the Greek cemetery, (2) election of a Greek magistrate, (3) the fair for gluttons, (4) dinner at the home of the marshal of nobility, (5) a students' gathering." In addition, there were "occasional" poems ridiculing students and teachers. But, increasingly, Nikolai and his "circle" were turning to the sentimental genre.

"All my early attempts at literature, my first exercises in composition, where I acquired some mastery during my last years in school, were lyrical and serious in character," Nikolai Gogol noted in his *Confession of an Author*. "Neither I nor any of my comrades, who were also trying to write, thought I would become a comic and satiric author. Yet, in spite of my basically serious nature, I often wanted to joke and even plagued my neighbors with my sarcasm. . . . They said I was less good at mocking my fellows than at guessing what they would say in any given situation, imitating their turn of thought and way of speaking."

Fired by emulation, the boys rhymed from dawn to dusk and met every Sunday to compare their output. Praise and criticism were equally without appeal. When Gogol tried his hand at prose, with a "Slav story" entitled "The Brothers Tverdoslavich," the fraternity demolished him. It was even decided, at a meeting of the group, that this effort deserved to be destroyed. "Gogol did not protest, did not resist," Lyubich-Romanovich wrote. "Very calmly, he picked up his manuscript, tore it into tiny pieces and threw them into the lighted stove. 'You should stick to poetry,' was Bazili's friendly advice. 'Don't write prose; it's not right for you at all. Besides, it's very plain that you will never be a writer.' "[13]

Notwithstanding the prophecy, Nikolai Gogol persisted in his attempts.† Since his friends did so too, some market for the output became necessary. Handwritten magazines were created to exhibit the school's literary production: *The Star, The Northern Dawn, The Literary Meteor, The Dunghill of Parnassus.* Of some of these endeavors (total circulation: one copy), Nikolai Gogol was the editor in chief. He inundated them with his poems and prose, and illustrated them with his drawings. His readership was composed of the remainder of his class. The magazine was borrowed back and forth, and passed from hand to hand; passages were read aloud.

Such readings were less successful, of course, than the performances of plays by the same group of pupils. From his earliest age Nikolai Gogol had had a passion for the theater, and now, at school, he remembered the comedies produced by his father at Kibinsk. At Nyezhin there was a captive audience asking only to applaud, and actors for every part. After some hesitation, the good-natured headmaster finally authorized performances in the school, whereupon Nikolai Gogol, at the summit of exultation, transformed himself into actor, director, and designer. The boys themselves made the costumes and painted the scenery, under his direction. They dunned their families for material and props: "Send me cloth and props for the theater. . . . If you could send me a few costumes or even one, it would be perfect."[14]

Then, in the gym—converted into a theater, with platform stage, curtain, rows of chairs and benches—a large audience would gather. In addition to the schoolboys sitting side by side in their gray uniforms, there were a few neighborhood landowners, local government officials, parents, and soldiers garrisoned at Nyezhin. Ozerov's *Oedipus in Athens,* Fonvizin's *Dadais,* Krylov's *Lesson to Young Ladies* were per-

---

† Nothing remains of all the early works mentioned above, whose titles alone have survived in the memoirs of his contemporaries.

formed there, together with some of Gogol's father's comedies and a few plays translated from French.

Every time Nikolai stepped onto the stage, the audience would split their sides. He was most extraordinary in character parts. His classmates screamed with laughter when they saw him walk on as a bent, toothless, irritable old man or raucous female busybody. "I have seen Fonvizin's *Dadais* in Moscow and St. Petersburg," Bazili wrote, "but I remain convinced that no actress has ever played Mrs. Prostakov as well as Gogol, who was then sixteen." Pashchenko, another schoolmate, agreed: "We all thought then that Gogol would become an actor, for he was enormously gifted, whether for imitations, make-up, voice changes, or the ability to put himself inside the character he was portraying. . . ." This game of changing skin and covering one's tracks, losing oneself in somebody else, suited Gogol's inner nature so well that on stage, protected by the footlights, the timid boy swelled with self-confidence. In disguise he feared no one, and the applause was doubly sweet to him because it was addressed to a false semblance of himself.

His greatest triumph, beyond any doubt, was during the pre-Lenten season of 1827. On February 1, then eighteen, he wrote to his mother: "I have never enjoyed myself so much! I even regret that time goes by so quickly. . . . Our theater is ready. What a source of delight!"

After the festivities, he sent this victorious dispatch to his friend Vysotsky: "Four days running, we gave theatrical performances. Everybody acted remarkably well. Our audience, most of them connoisseurs, acknowledged that they had never seen such a fine spectacle on a provincial stage. Our sets (there were four changes) were admirably painted. The background landscape was perfection, the lighting splendid, the music ideally played. We made up an orchestra of ten musicians, but they were placed in the most favorable location from an acoustical point of view and could easily rival a symphony orchestra. They played four overtures by Rossini, two by Mozart, one by Weber, and one by Sevryugin.[15] These are the plays we acted: Fonvizin's *Dadais,* Kniaznin's comedy *The Awkward Arbiter,* Kotzebue's *Riparian Right,* and a play by Florian. . . . And that isn't the end: For Easter we are preparing another set of plays. . . ."[16]

This unbridled passion for the theater and poetry was not to the liking of all the teachers. Some, such as Shapolinsky, the headmaster, and the young inspector, Byelusov, who taught "natural law," were in favor of them; but others, such as Bilyevich, the political-science teacher, saw them as a threat to discipline and the children's moral edification. When he failed to have the performances banned, Bilyevich took the refusal as a personal affront and set himself up as the guardian of tradition against a body of weak teachers "overrun by their pupils' demands."

The recent Decembrist uprising, fomented by a few liberal officers and quelled in blood on Senate Square, in St. Petersburg, on December 14, 1825, had unnerved every Russian. While the ringleaders, among whom figured some of the greatest names in the Russian aristocracy, were being hanged or marched off to Siberia, the new tsar, Nicholas I, was consolidating his authority and demanding the denunciation of all subversive tendencies as proof of his subjects' loyalty to the throne. The pupils at the Nyezhin School may not have talked much of such remote political events, but the teachers could not fail to be affected by them, each in his own way. The rigidly reactionary Bilyevich scented a camouflaged liberal in his colleague Byelusov. Defeated in the affair of the theatrical performances, he sought revenge elsewhere. Writing report after report, he accused some of the pupils, Gogol-Yanovsky among them, of insolence and of writing seditious poetry. "Some of our boarders," he wrote on October 25, 1826, "acting without the headmaster's knowledge, are writing highly unsuitable verse, reading books improper for their age, and even keeping in their possession works of Alexander Pushkin and other authors of that caliber." There was a simple explanation for this disorder, he wrote: the children had been corrupted by the instruction of their natural-law teacher, Byelusov. In front of the faculty senate he accused Byelusov of reading his lectures from personal notes "inspired by the dangerous philosophy of Kant." Didn't Byelusov claim that men were born free and had rights as well as duties? If that were so, where was the ancestral practice of serfdom? Could one pretend to serve the emperor while preaching the independence of the human mind? What lay ahead for Russia, nay, for the whole world, if people were not prevented from sowing these seeds of rebellion in young heads?

Shapolinsky, the headmaster, tried to hush up the matter, but the enraged Bilyevich would not desist. After a year of dithering and delay, a new headmaster, Yarnovsky, was appointed in Shapolinsky's place and sided against the natural-law teacher. An administrative inquiry was ordered into "the freethinking affair" at Nyezhin. Every pupil's ex-

ercise books were scrutinzed by the faculty council. Those of Nikolai
Gogol, among others, were found to contain compromising phrases, and
impounded as evidence for the prosecution. Gogol was summoned and
interrogated as a witness. He tried to save Byelusov by belittling the
effectiveness of his lessons, but the pupils' very sympathy for their
teacher made him suspect. Lurking behind these misguided school-
children, the investigating committee detected the grimacing scarecrow of the French Revolution. There must be tracts against the government in their drawers, or in their heads at least. Why, that was exactly
how the Russian secret societies had been founded. There was no time
to lose; the organization must be dismantled. Ex-headmaster Shapolinsky, and Landrazhin and Zinger, two of the teachers who had openly
supported Byelusov, were also denounced as having a pernicious influence upon the young. A report to this effect was sent to the minister
of education. Shapolinsky, Landrazhin, Zinger, and Byelusov were ultimately removed from the school. A decision by Nicholas I, dated
October 6, 1830, decreed that the convicted teachers of Russian na-
tionality would be placed under supervision in their birthplaces, and
aliens would be deported to their country of origin.

While this tempest was raging among the teachers, their pupils returned to their studies with ever-diminishing zeal. Dumb and indifferent, Nikolai Gogol memorized his lessons. Even Russian grammar
and syntax revolted him. He wrote instinctively, making unpardonable
errors and imitating the pretentious manner of certain contemporary
prosodists. Into his letters and essays he poured the full gamut of sentimental pathos made fashionable by Karamzin's *Poor Liza*. Whenever
he wanted to be sincere, his style swelled in step with his heart. But to
this infelicitous indulgence in phrase was allied a love of the unique
word, the unexpected adjective.

"I can still see him, a blond boy in a gray uniform with long hair
and the withdrawn look of someone guarding a secret—a lethargic expression and a graceless walk," wrote his Latin teacher Kulzhinsky.
"He never knew his lesson. He was my pupil for three years and I
never taught him a single thing except the translation of the first paragraph of the chrestomathy to Koshansky's grammar: *Universus mundus
plerumque distribuitur in duas partes, coelum et terram.* . . . In class
he habitually kept a book concealed on his knees under the desk, without giving a thought, naturally, to either *coelum* or *terram.* . . . I gave
him "0s" and "1s" for three years. . . . Nor did he learn anything from

my colleagues. During his years at school he acquired only a hint of formal discipline and a notion of the evaluation of knowledge and ideas. He owes nothing more to us. His talent went unrecognized at school, and he did nothing to reveal it to us. Some of his teachers might have encouraged and enriched his gifts though, if he had consented to open himself to them. Gogol was looked upon as a relatively talented boy, but lazy—so lazy that he would not even bother to learn to write Russian correctly. A pity we did not sense what was there. But, then, who knows? Maybe it's better this way. . . ."[17] The same teacher added, "He was *terra rudis et inculta*. As regards Gogol's mastery of grammar upon leaving the school, I can affirm without fear of contradiction that he was unable to conjugate his verbs in any language."[18]

In any event, as Gogol progressed in his school career his thoughts turned less and less upon scholastic amusements and more and more upon the adult life awaiting him beyond the school doors. Since his father's death, he had readily seen himself as the family protector and adviser. In every letter home he exhorted his mother to inform him of the smallest detail of her affairs, and put her on her guard against the malevolence of those she employed to defend her interests.

"I beg you to tell me everything you plan and carry out as regards the management of the estate," he wrote. "Above all, tell me about any new buildings and activities. . . . If you need plans for a façade and construction drawings, let me know immediately. Façade and drawings will both be painstakingly executed and sent by return post. The façade will definitely be beautiful and the cost small."[19]

Again: "Let me know when you are going to begin distilling the vodka and how much it will cost a pailful, according to the current price. Does the distilling go well at home, and will it bring in enough money?"[20]

And "Have you put in the windmill you wanted?"[21]

Nikolai was not unaware of his mother's financial difficulties. It occasionally pained him to be a burden to her, and he hoped one day to amaze her with his achievements.

"Now I am completely engrossed in my studies," he wrote on December 15, 1827. "Every day, from morning till night, my serious activities are not interrupted by the slightest distraction. Let us not regard the past. The object now is to make up for lost time. In the six short months to come I want to do much more than during the entire six years I have spent here. I want to and I shall succeed, for I have always got what I wanted before. To be sure, circumstances are against me, and especially our lack of money. At the first opportunity, you must send me at least sixty rubles before the new year, so I can buy the books I require for my studies. There are others I need just as badly, but with this first set and thanks to my iron patience, I hope to be able already to lay the foundations of the immense edifice I dream of, which nothing will be able to shake. At the moment, I am studying languages. Thank God, my efforts are meeting with success. But all that is nothing compared with my intentions: in six months I want to master three languages completely."

Always tomorrow! The more harshly he condemned his past laziness and ignorance, the more certain he was of future triumph. His errors and weaknesses themselves seemed to point to an exceptional destiny ahead. The lower one started, after all, the higher one could soar. His humility, thus, was simply an aspect of his conceit; his modesty fed his pride. He was stumbling through the valley but saw himself shining on the peaks. How was this glorious ascension to be brought about? He had as yet no idea, and hardly worried on that score. God would see that he did not remain in the shadow. In the meantime, the contradictions in his personality must, he surmised, render him incomprehensible to his fellows. He was proud to pose a living problem to their eyes, especially those of his mother.

"I have lost six years!" he wrote to her again, on March 1, 1828. "The amazing thing is that I was able to learn so much in this ridiculous establishment. . . . Whatever I may know, I owe to no one but myself. . . . But there is plenty of time ahead. I have the necessary strength and application. . . . I have suffered more from grief and penury than you imagine. . . . I doubt that anyone has felt as deeply as I the ingratitude of men, their injustice, imbecilic demands, chilling scorn, etc. I have endured them all without a murmur; no one has heard me complain. Better yet, I have praised those who were the cause of my misery. It is true that I am an enigma to everyone. No one has guessed what I am. At home I am considered a lunatic, an unbearable pedant who thinks himself more intelligent than the rest of the world, different from everybody else. Will you believe me if I tell you that, privately, I have joined you in laughing at myself? For the people here, I am a paragon of modesty, mildness, and patience. In one place I am taken to be the most peaceable, self-effacing, and courteous person imaginable; in another, the most moody, withdrawn, and uncivilized; in a third, the biggest chatterbox and bore. For some I am clever, for others a dolt. Judge me how you please, you will not know my real nature until I have set off on my true path. Do believe, in any event, that my heart is always filled with the most noble sentiments, that in myself I have never been humiliated, and that I have dedicated my entire life to the good. You say I am a dreamer who can't stick to anything; as if I didn't laugh at my dreams myself! No; I know men too well to be a dreamer. The lessons they have taught me will never fade, and will serve to ensure my happiness. You will see that in time I shall be able to return them good for all the evil they have done me; for within me that evil coming from them has changed into good. It is a certain truth that he who has been most sorely tried by life, constantly bearing the yoke of unhappiness, will be the happiest of men."

Writing these lines on the eve of his nineteenth birthday, Nikolai Gogol was assuredly convinced that he had greatly lived and greatly suffered. His predilection for extremes, combined with his exploration of the poets, incited him to overstatement. It didn't occur to him that school was only the anteroom of the world, that his alleged tribulations were no great matter compared with those awaiting him on the far side of the wall. Every human perfidy and every hostile caprice of fate he had already felt, or so he thought, piercing his flesh. They were so many proofs of the Almighty's special interest in him. The more he had to groan about, the more certain he was to be the chosen of God.

There was an element of sincerity in this literary pose. Pathologically oversensitive, he must very often have been hurt by the jibes of his schoolmates and the scolding of his teachers. He was tormented for nights on end by a jab any ordinary boy would forget without further ado. He knew some people thought him ugly, puny, scrawny, misshapen, unkempt, and dirty. His awareness of his relative poverty humiliated him and made him long to be rich and honored. At the same time, he had an uncommonly penetrating eye, which disclosed all the absurd or petty traits of those around him—as though a magnifying glass stood between his eye and the object of his attention. Faces sagged, noses grew, warts expanded into planets. In an instant, this teacher acquired the snout of a pig, that boy a badger's muzzle. Willy-nilly, Nikolai found himself in the midst of a zoo, where, with secret laughter, he took his revenge on all who had offended him.

His two best friends, Danilevsky and Vysotsky, had left the school. After completing his studies in 1826, Vysotsky had been given a job in the ministry of the interior in St. Petersburg. Nikolai Gogol dreamed of finding a place in the hierarchy too. Without totally abandoning the idea of becoming a great writer or painter, he now wanted to become a great statesman as well. Wasn't that the best way of all to serve mankind? When he closed his eyes, he saw himself at the pinnacle of glory, a senator, minister—a sort of Troshchinsky surrounded by supplicants and radiating benevolence.

The people of Nyezhin might be insignificant, but not so those in the rest of Russia. In St. Petersburg, in particular, there must be an absolute agglomeration of greatness. Living there, for sure, would be as good as living twice. To add weight to his desire to settle in the capital, he called, as usual, on the will of God. He was impelled by a supernatural force; his father's spirit was pointing the way. He wrote to his mother on March 24, 1827:

"That pure and noble being, my father, inspires and supports me on my arduous road; he has made it possible for me to know myself. Often, in moments of distress, he enters into me like the celestial fire and illuminates the thoughts that invade me. . . . And then I realize my strength, which I shall use in a great and noble work for the good of my country, the happiness of my fellow citizens, and the joy of my fellow men. Generally hesitant and inclined to self-doubt, I suddenly feel fired by a proud awareness of my powers, and my soul seems to see that angel pointing out the goal of my desperate search with firm and implacable hand. . . . In a year I shall enter into the service of the state! . . . My candle's going out; it is nearly midnight. . . ."

Having thus forewarned his mother that he might soon abandon her, Nikolai sought an ally in the person of his uncle Pyotr Petrovich Kosyarovsky. In view of Marya Ivanovna's probable reluctance, it was important to convince the largest possible number of members of the family that salvation, for an ambitious youth, lay not on the land of his forefathers, at Vasilyevka, but in a ministry at St. Petersburg.

"Yes," he wrote his uncle Kosyarovsky on October 3, 1827, "it may be that I shall spend the rest of my life in St. Petersburg; in any case, this is the aim I adopted long ago. Even in childhood, when I was hardly aware of my own existence, I was already burning with an inextinguishable desire to dedicate my life to the welfare of the state and to make myself, in some way or other, useful. The thought that I might not be able to do so—obstacles would be set in my way, I would somehow be prevented from devoting myself to my fellow men—would cast me into the deepest despair. I would break out in a cold sweat at the idea that I might be destined to return to dust without having attached my name to some admirable deed. To enter the world and leave it again without any trace of my passage seemed dreadful. I considered all the positions I might occupy and duties I might perform in the state and finally decided in favor of legal work. I saw that it was in this field I would find the most work; it was there alone I could do good and really make myself useful to mankind. Injustice, which is the worst thing in the world, has always wrenched my heart. I vowed then I would not lose another instant of my brief life without doing good. For two years my special subject of study has been the law of the various peoples, and in particular natural law, the basis of legislation. Now I am studying the law of our country. Will my noble designs be achieved? Or will they remain unknown and I myself sink into obscurity? . . . I have never confided in anyone, not even in my friends at school, although several of them are worthy of respect. I don't know why I am speaking to you so openly now. Is it because you have shown more interest in me than the others, or because of our family relationship? I do not know. An incomprehensible feeling drove my pen, an unknown force compelled me to act, and suddenly I had an intuition that you would not take for an inconsequential dreamer someone who has been pursuing the same goal for three years. . . ."

As he wrote these lines, Nikolai Gogol believed he really cared about the law, although his knowledge of the subject was virtually nil and he had not the slightest intention of augmenting it. But in reviewing the various possible careers, he saw, when he came to that of judge, that it fit him like a glove; and he thereupon determined, following his usual mental process, that he had been destined for this noble work for all eternity and had already digested all the books that would prepare him for it. In doing this, he had no sense that he was lying either to his uncle or to himself. Pen in hand, he honestly saw himself in the role of a judge, but the dream vanished almost before the glue had dried on the envelope, and he never again alluded to this desire to belong to his country's judicature. He was also sinning against truth when he claimed never to have told anyone of his wish to be a government official. Not only had he informed his mother, but he discussed the question daily with his schoolmates. His friend Vysotsky was the chief ear for his administrative aspirations.

"My thoughts fly to St. Petersburg," he wrote him on March 19, 1827.

"I sit beside you in your room, walk along the boulevards with you, admire the Neva, the sea. In a word, I become *you*. . . . My only thought now, the only favor I ask of God, is that we should be united as soon as possible. By the way, you have not told me much about life in St. Petersburg. What are prices like there? What are the most expensive things? . . . What are lodgings like? How much a year does one have to pay for two or three nice rooms? Which are the expensive parts of town? And the cheapest? How much do you have to reckon for heating, etc.? Ah, I was almost forgetting to ask about salaries, and how much you earn. How many hours do you spend in your office? What time do you get home?"

Vysotsky vainly sought to stem the tide of Gogol's enthusiasm, expaining all the difficulties of life in St. Petersburg, but Gogol would hear none of it. By comparison with Nyezhin, the distant capital gleamed in his eyes with the light of intelligence, riches, and power. He, clearly destined to amaze the world with his virtues and achievements, could no longer be content with such dingy, provincial surroundings. He sat and glared at his eternally identical soup, dreaming of fire and ice.

"Living here in utter isolation," he wrote Vysotsky again, on June 26, 1827, "and finding no one with whom to share my thoughts, I am like an orphan, a foreigner, in this deserted town of Nyezhin. . . . I can't bear to wait for the end of school and the blessed freedom it will bring! I do not know how it will be possible to endure these conditions for another whole year. What an awful thing it is to be buried in death and silence among base creatures condemned to remain in obscurity! You know all these Nyezhin people, these wretches who are content simply to exist. They have buried their lofty human destiny beneath the crust of their peasant natures and base self-satisfaction. And it is among such beings that I am forced to crawl. I count among them some of our beloved teachers. . . . Sometimes I feel that they are waiting for me there [in St. Petersburg]. . . . Especially since, in a way, I belong to your circle. I trust that my name occasionally crosses your lips. . . . I can already see myself in St. Petersburg, in a cheerful little room overlooking the Neva, for I have always hoped to find an apartment there. I do not know whether my hopes will ever materialize and I shall actually live in that paradisical place, or whether the implacable spindle of the Parcae will not plunge me with these complacent plebians (chilling thought!) into the depths of oblivion, consigning me to the bleak zone of the obscure. . . . I do not know whether anything can prevent me from coming to St. Petersburg, even though you have very rightly put me on guard against the cost of living there, and especially of food. . . ."

This vision of Petersburg life so inflamed Gogol that he, whose sartorial neglect had previously been a joke for all the Nyezhin school-boys, suddenly discovered that he was a dandy at heart. He was stifling in his gray school uniform. Social success was impossible without a well-cut coat.

"Couldn't you order a frock coat for me there, in St. Petersburg, from the best tailor in town?" he asked Vysotsky in the same letter. "Your own measurements could even be used, as we have the same height and girth. If you have put on weight, you can tell them to make it a little narrower, but we can see to that later. For the moment, find out how much a really good suit of evening clothes would cost, in the latest fashion, and write me the price in your letter so I will know how much money to send you. I will buy the cloth here, since you say it's so very dear in St. Petersburg. Tell me, too, what material is most in fashion for vests and trousers; give me the prices for both the material and making it up . . . What color is being worn for dress? I'd like to have blue, with metal buttons. I have so many black coats, I am tired of looking at them."

Shortly thereafter, he was writing to his mother:

"I have recently received a letter from St. Petersburg about the frock coat I should like to order. To make it up in the finest-quality cloth, with lining, buttons, and extras, the best tailor asks 120 rubles. Not daring to ask you for such a sum at the moment, as I am only too aware of your straitened circumstances, I shall wait until you are able to send it to me."[22]

In Nikolai Gogol these trivial vestimentary preoccupations alternated with spiritual upsurges of such violence that he thought his ribs must burst. He wanted to fly, soar higher and higher, stun the whole world, and, at the end of his ascension, wrest a smile from God. In the smallest events of his existence he glimpsed the will of the Almighty. A scolding in class, a poor grade, a cold in the head, a lost letter were so many tokens of supernatural regard. By treating him so badly, his fellows were unwittingly obeying the divine will. Hoping to harm him, they were actually helping him in his quest for perfection. In fact, it must have been necessary, from the standpoint of eternity, for him to lose his brother and his father.

This adherence to the edicts of Providence did not prevent him from aspiring to more tangible successes at the earliest possible date. Serving the state was still serving God. And serving God was protection against the hazards of the other world. To disappear "without leaving a trace," like a needle in a haystack, was the most harrowing threat possible to Gogol. Let his name, at least, survive! Yet a true Christian should contemplate the leap into the unknown with a tranquil mind or, at any rate, should not display such concern for the name he would leave behind. At this stage, however, the piety of Nikolai Gogol was purely conventional. He often recalled the ghastly picture of the Last Judgment his mother had painted years before. His flesh still cringed from that infant terror, and so his love of God sprang primarily from his fear of death. He knelt and crossed himself more as a precautionary measure than out of religious fervor. He transformed religion into recipes, and since the sauce was pleasing to his own taste, he advised his mother to apply the same method to his youngest sister, Olga. The more she could terrify the child with the picture of Hell she would lay before her, the straighter would be the path her daughter would tread in later life.

Just then, however, his terrors were confined principally to his final examinations. He was cramming at top speed. His excellent memory enabled him to skim off and retain snatches of learning here and there. He was reluctantly obliged to concede that it was not possible to learn a foreign language in a few weeks. His German was unintelligible and he could not read a French book without constant recourse to a dictionary. But the examiners proved compliant: he received good grades in every subject except mathematics. However, he was classed in the fourteenth *chini* on the table of civil rank of the empire.‡ Such a low rating, when less brilliant pupils had been placed higher up the scale, must be the price he had to pay for his open sympathy for the liberal teacher Byelusov. Well, never mind: the main thing was that he had finished school. At last he could shed his hideous gray students' uniform. According to his teachers, he was the first to appear in "civilian" dress. "I can see him now in a light-brown frock coat, the flaps lined with checkered red material," Kulzhinsky wrote. "This type of lining was considered the *ne plus ultra* of elegance by the young men of the day. And Gogol, strolling through the school, would spread the tails of his coat, as though by accident, to show off the lining."[23]

‡ There were fourteen degrees, or *chini*, in this table of ranks, inaugurated in 1722 for both civilians and members of the armed forces, and every one of the tsar's subjects progressed through them from the age of fifteen until death.

After bidding farewell to his classmates and teachers, he heaved a sigh of relief as he climbed into the carriage his mother had sent for him. This time, he thought, the holiday would last forever.

Climbing out again at Vasilyevka, on a luminous June morning in 1828, Nikolai fell into his mother's arms. She wept with joy, could not take her eyes off her son, who had now become a man, so far away, in so short a time. There was a shadow of mustache above his lip. His long blond hair was parted by a line as sharp as a knife stroke. His slanting eyes with the swollen tear ducts twinkled ironically. For Marya Ivanovna he was the most handsome, most intelligent, and most sensitive being ever born. The star of genius gleamed on his youthful brow. His very sighs merited immortality. She never wearied of praising his drawings and poems. And he wanted to leave her and live in St. Petersburg! It would be a second widowhood. In despair, she exhorted family and friends to behold her sufferings. She implored her son to alter his decision.

Privately, Nikolai saw that life at Vasilyevka was sweet. The round of visits with neighbors, impromptu suppers, excursions to the fair in the nearby village, picnics, gardening, and the interminable chats by the evening lamp—this, the charming side of country life, was balm to his soul after the promiscuity, the noise, and the senseless and inhuman discipline of the school. He liked the company of his four sisters, the eldest of whom was seventeen and the youngest just turned three. He listened with the same old pleasure to his grandmother Lisogub talking about the remote past, when the Ukraine had been free. He grew giddy with gratitude for all his mother's little attentions. Family cooking made his mouth water. But none of these attractions could weaken his determination. The Almighty had pointed out the road to the capital, and follow it he would though it meant wading through rivers of tears. The annoying thing was that his uncle Kosyarovsky had recently announced his intention to leave the Ukraine for Luga. How would Marya Ivanovna take the simultaneous departure of the two strong men of the family?

With the cool effrontery of his nineteen years, Nikolai wrote Kosyarovsky, on September 8, 1828, asking him to change his plans: "How can you forsake those who love you so much? . . . I pray, beg, adjure you, in the name of friendship and the bonds by which we are united, in the name of anything capable of moving your heart, do not abandon us, reconsider your cruel decision, come to Vasilyevka, be the guardian angel and comfort of our mother."

In the same letter, he informed Kosyarovsky that he himself had decided to go to St. Petersburg and that nothing would change his mind. Thus, what he asked of his uncle he neither could nor would ask of himself. "I shall be leaving for St. Petersburg, without fail, at the beginning of winter," he wrote. "From there, God alone knows where fate will take me. Perhaps I shall make my way abroad, and no more will be heard of me for years. . . . I confess, moreover, that I have wished never to come home again, on more than one occasion, ever since I have had to witness the despair and struggles of our incomparable mother, who is exhausting herself in her search for the money we need; this constant worry is ruining her health, but she will not give it up, and will do anything to satisfy our smallest whim. . . . Who will there be to watch over and comfort her in my absence, when fresh anxieties will augment her present torments, and in particular, her concern for her son?"

Nikolai had calculated that he would need a thousand rubles for the journey. Marya Ivanovna, ever short of cash, was alarmed by the enormity of the sum, but he continued to insist that she must find it. In return, he offered to transfer his share of his father's estate to her. The house, garden, woods, and pond that constituted his portion weighed little against his desire to flee the country. He insisted that the papers be drawn up and signed. He would not come back until he had made his fortune, and then it would be only to cover his family with presents. He would help to set up his sisters in life. And what if, peradventure, he should fail in the government administration? Well, he would do something else. "You are not yet familiar with all my capacities," he wrote to Kosyarovsky. "I have learned more than one trade. I am a fair tailor, I know how to paint frescoes on walls, I can work in a kitchen and have a respectable knowledge of the culinary art. You think I am joking? Ask Mother. But I rely mainly on my patience and perseverance, for which I thank God; in the past I did not have them, but today I am determined never to abandon what I undertake until I reach my goal. I do not say this as a boast, but in order to dispel your qualms about my future. I shall always have bread to eat in plenty. . . ."

In his list of the trades he could ply in order to keep body and soul together, Nikolai Gogol made no mention of writing; but he had never written as much as during these months at Vasilyevka.

First he wanted to polish off a verse idyl, *Hans Kuechelgarten* which he had begun at school. He had taken the subject from a work by Vos, *Louise,* translated by Teryaev in 1820. For style, he had consulted Pushkin and Zhukovsky. But no matter how he tried, his hand remained lethargic, his rhymes were like glue, the whole thing reeked of *ennui.* On one side the author described the patriarchal bliss of a German family illumined by the angelic Louise, who was in love with Hans. On the other, he set Hans, a tormented dreamer swimming in a romantic stew. Hans suffered from some undefined malaise:

> "In the tempest of his heart,
> Vaguely he wondered
> What he wanted, what he sought,
> To what goal tended his wild soul,
> Filled with love and impatience,
> As though seeking to embrace the whole earth."

Hans, a combination of Goethe's Werther, Pushkin's Lensky, and Chateaubriand's René, had several things in common with his creator too. At every turn, the private preoccupations of Nikolai Gogol invaded his work. What he had said in prose in his letters to his mother, his uncle Kosyarovsky, and his friend Vysotsky, was repeated in verse in the poem. Like Nikolai Gogol, Hans Kuechelgarten felt a sudden need to escape the confines of his narrow life and accomplish some magnificent deed, "to leave a trace of his passage on earth."

> "It's settled. Why should I
> Leave my soul to perish here,
> Seek no other goal,
> Not strive for the best,
> Condemn myself to obscurity unknown,
> A creature half alive to all?"

The scorn Nikolai Gogol felt for the petty people of Nyezhin, Hans Kuechelgarten extended to the rest of the universe:

> "How venomous their breath,
> How false the beating of their hearts,
> How perfidious their minds,
> And how hollow ring their words!"

Also, Hans Kuechelgarten's joy at the thought of returning home is
none other than that of Nikolai about to leave school for good:

> "So the imprisoned pupil
> Awaits his desired release.
> His studies are soon over.
> His mind floods with dreams.
> He is borne aloft by thoughts.
> Here he is, free, independent,
> Delighting in himself and the world.
> But as he parts from his companions,
> Whose efforts, laughter, and peaceful
> Nights he has shared,
> He muses, gloom invades him,
> And, weighted down by sadness,
> He sheds a furtive tear."

If the lyric passages of *Hans Kuechelgarten* are lacking in both
mastery and originality, certain descriptions are remarkable for their
audacity. Inspired by Pushkin's realism, Gogol did not hesitate to write
of a pink dressing gown, a steaming coffeepot, an appetizing yellow-
crusted cheese, or a strutting rooster among the farmyard hens.

These direct, candid notes were apparently effortless, but he attached
less importance to them than to the bombastic tirade. Art, for him, had
to be noble. He confused emotion with inflation.

He wrote another poem, *Italy,* in which, on the eve of his departure
for Russia's chill and foggy capital, he celebrated the Mediterranean
dolce vita, alluded to Raphael, and wondered whether it would one day
be given him to visit the "oasis" in "the desert of the world." Then he
reworked a little meditation composed at school and entitled *Woman,* a
delirious hymn to the being "whose divine features reflect eternity."
Borne aloft by his adolescent fantasies, he spoke of women with an
eloquence all the more assured for his having never been near one.
Separated from them all by the dizzying chasm of sexual dissimilarity,
not daring even to imagine the contact between two such different
epiderms, he placed them on a pedestal and worshiped from afar: "She
is Poetry! She is the Idea, we but realities incarnate. . . ." As for love,
". . . it is an instinctive desire impelling man to recover his eternal past,
the past of his immaculate conception, his childhood innocence. Love is
a search for the original birthplace. The soul of man wants to unite with

that of woman and become one with it, in order to find his father again, the eternal God, and his brothers, sensations and phenomena unknown on earth. . . ."

Here is the heroine of all these sighs: "Her marble arm, traversed by the blue of veins filled with divine ambrosia, floated freely; her bare foot, red-enribboned, released from the jealous fetter of her shoe, advanced majestically and seemed not to touch the earth; her high breast lifted to the rhythm of her sighs; the diaphanous drapery covering her breasts shivered, designing piquant folds. . . . Her curls, black as night, tossed carelessly back, fell upon her brow and cascaded down upon her shining shoulders. The lightning of her glance seared the soul. . . ."

Subjugated by this sculptural beauty his imagination had produced, Nikolai never tired of contemplating her in his dreams. His admiration for her took the place of mere desire. If he had met her in flesh and blood, he would have fainted with terror. Or run away. Perhaps he might encounter such a female in St. Petersburg? His blood froze at the thought of certain contacts his schoolmates used to talk about.

If only he could respond to women the way he responded to a plate of food! He was an enormously greedy eater. The thought of a creamcake or a stuffed turkey shook him to the core. He would have walked leagues to eat some of those little poppy-seed cakes. And had no appetite at all for the fair sex. His wisest course would be to leave it to God. At the moment chosen by the Almighty, the creature destined for him would cross his path. There would be a sign, and he would no longer be afraid.

The weeks passed, and Marya Ivanovna showed increasing unwillingness to let her son go off to the capital. Whenever he became too insistent, she confronted him, weeping, with her financial straits. On September 23, 1828, she wrote, "My little Nikolai is in a hurry to begin his service, and I am quite certain that I shall not be able to hold him beyond the end of October."[24] She then held him until mid-December. In the meantime she somehow managed to scrape the money together and to obtain from the dying Troshchinsky a letter of recommendation to L. I. Kutuzov, a senior official in the ministry of the interior. He had signed, with trembling hand, and Marya Ivanovna was partially reassured. With this paper, her Nicholas would find help and protection everywhere. He had decided to travel with his former schoolmate from Nyezhin, Alexander Danilevsky, who lived thirty versts from Vasilyevka and was also intending to settle in St. Petersburg, where he was to enter the guards officers' school.

To friends wishing him a good journey Nikolai solemnly replied: "Farewell! Either you will never hear of me again, or you will hear nothing but good!"[25] So great was his haste to begin his adult life that he would not spend another day with his family, refusing even to spend the Christmas holidays with them. It was cold. The roads vanished in the flying snow. At last, Danilevsky hove into view in a covered sledge, and the servants began loading the baggage.

3. First Steps in St. Petersburg

To travel from Vasilyevka to St. Petersburg in the winter, one had to allow at least three weeks. Gogol had chosen to go by way of Chernigov, Mogilev, and Vitebsk, avoiding Moscow. He wanted, he said, to preserve the full intensity of his first impressions of the capital by postponing a visit to the other city. The cold was intense. The postmasters made difficulties about supplying fresh horses at the posting stations. Travelers were not served in order of arrival but according to their rank or mission orders. Gogol had never felt so humiliated to be only a fourteenth-class "collegiate registrar," with all these important personages taking precedence over him. To console themselves for the delays and affronts, the two young men talked excitedly of their imminent arrival in St. Petersburg. The *kibitka** lurched between the drifts, the wind whirled in gusts about the shivering horses, one interminable, ghostly-white plain gave way to another. At long intervals villages came into view, huddled beneath a white carapace; one posting station followed another, all with the same smell of boots, hay, and tar. Sometimes it seemed to Nikolai that this jaunt across Russia would never end and he would find himself back where he had started without seeing anything but snow. However, the names of their latest stopping places gave him hope. They were nearing their goal. One evening, the lights of St. Petersburg appeared on the horizon—a great, starry constellation on the ground. Marveling, Danilevsky and Gogol told the

* A kind of covered sledge.

driver to stop and climbed out of the sledge; standing on tiptoe, fearful and thrilled, they gazed at the mirage of ice, stone, and fire.

The spire of the Admiralty towered over a dream city. A cripple stood guard at the black-and-white-striped barrier. Yakim, Gogol's man-servant—a stalwart lout of twenty-six—implored his master to get out of the cold and return to the sledge. Inside the *kibitka,* the two friends prepared themselves for further revelations. Slowly the barrier rose, and the team trotted into town. "My God, what a racket, what a din, and what lights!" exclaimed Gogol in "Christmas Eve." "Four-story façades rose up on both sides; clogs clumped and wheels creaked so loudly that the noise became a thunder reverberating off the walls; the houses grew larger and seemed to spring out of the ground at every step; bridges shook; carriages flew; cab drivers and postilions shouted; the snow squeaked under the thousands of sledge runners gliding in every direction; pedestrians crowded and bumped into each other at the foot of houses hung with lanterns, and their hugely magnified shadows danced along the walls and crept upward until their heads reached roofs and chimneys."

The dazzlement did not long endure. The friends stopped first in a working-class district: Gorokhovaya Street near Kokushkin Bridge, where they had been told cheap lodgings were to be had. Instead of waking up "in a cheerful little room overlooking the Neva," Nikolai Gogol opened his eyes the next morning in a sordid, icy attic whose windows gave onto the dirty yellow wall of the house across the street. He had caught cold on the trip and had to stay in bed; Yakim nursed him, drowning him in scalding tea and cupping him with leeches. Danilevsky vanished for the entire day and came back that night filled with tales of the people he had met.

The moment he was well enough, Gogol resolved to move. First, he and Danilevsky shared a little two-room apartment; then he parted from his friend and moved alone, with Yakim, into a more hospitable estab-lishment on Great Meshchanskaya Street.

He was still a long way from the scintillating quays, illuminated squares, and marble palaces of the capital. Most of the people living on Great Meshchanskaya Street were modest folk: struggling artisans, small shopkeepers and merchants, low-ranking civil servants—a large, gray, vulnerable, obsequious, silent, anxious horde. A gate opened in the yellow façade to reveal a courtyard piled high with rubble. All the workshops emptied their garbage there. "In the building I inhabit,"

Gogol wrote, "live two tailors, a woman who sells ladies' gowns, a shoe-maker, a sock manufacturer, a man who repairs porcelain, a cleaner and dyer, a chocolate maker, a milkman, a furrier, a tobacco seller, and a midwife. It is only natural that the edifice should be covered with gilt signs."[1]

Everything in this hard-working neighborhood might speak of con-finement and wretchedness, but one had only to stroll through the center of the city to send one's head spinning like a top. The lighted shop-windows displayed their costly wares, the cafés overflowed with elegant crowds, the theaters sported impressive marquees: so many mad temp-tations for the impecunious passer-by. In the provinces, poverty could be worn with dignity, in the solitude of the big estates; but here it was like a disease that set your blood boiling at every street corner. In the end, these visions of pleasures so near and so unattainable created a diabolical obsession in the brain. One lived on the fringe of a permanent festival, with hollow stomach and watering mouth. Occasionally one yielded, and paid for the weakness for weeks afterward.

He had no choice but to accept it when he first came to St. Peters-burg. Nobody could afford to live there! "One dress coat and a pair of trousers cost me two hundred rubles," Nikolai wrote; "one hundred went for a hat, pumps, and gloves and to remodel a winter coat and buy a fur collar. . . ."[2] Even dressed in the latest fashion, he still did not feel equal to the inhabitants of the capital. Everyone here seemed cast in the same mold. A horde of automatons, preoccupied solely with getting ahead. The hell of bureaucratic constraint, jaded emotions, and careful compromise.

"I can tell you that St. Petersburg is completely different from what I had imagined. I saw the city as more beautiful, more dazzling; every-thing other people say about it is lies," he wrote to his mother on January 3, 1829. A few weeks later, "St. Petersburg bears no resem-blance at all to the other European capitals, nor to Moscow. Every capi-tal is made unique by its inhabitants, who give it the stamp of their na-tionality. In St. Petersburg, there is no stamp. The foreigners living here have adapted themselves to our customs and there is nothing foreign about them; whereas the Russians have begun copying the foreigners and are neither one way nor the other. A most extraordinary silence reigns over the city: one cannot scent even the slightest whiff of spirit in anyone: everyone works in an office and talks of administrative ques-tions and relations with colleagues and nothing else; everything is stifled,

enmired in the infinitesimal preoccupations and petty labors that consti-
tute the sterile lives of these people. It is amusing to encounter some of
them in the streets: one is so engrossed in his thoughts that you will
hear him muttering and arguing with himself; the next will supplement
his mutterings by gesturing with his body and hands."[3]

Gogol became aware of this monstrous administrative tedium the first
time he set foot in the streets, before he ever entered an office. Behind
every set of features in their fish-belly flesh, he correctly imagined a
citadel of files, ink-stained fingers, ignoble intrigues, servile little coughs.
Was that the fate awaiting him? To reach the position of Troshchinsky,
one has to start somewhere. He had left his provincial domain bearing
two or three letters of recommendation, which were to open every door
for him—in particular, a note for L. I. Kutuzov. This person, one snap
of whose fingers, it appeared, would guarantee the future of Nikolai
Gogol, happened to be ill. The wise course would be to wait patiently
until he was well again, without wasting time on lesser figures. Kutuzov
duly recovered, received the young man most courteously, addressed
him familiarly, promised to see what he could do for him, and sent him
away without further defining his intentions. Other potential protectors,
behind their ormulu-frosted mahogany desks, proved equally evasive.
The only available positions were those of clerks in departments of
which one had never heard. One offer, more serious than the rest,
aroused all the indignation of Nikolai Gogol:

"I am offered one thousand rubles a year," he wrote to his mother.
"Must I then sell my health and precious time for a sum that will not
even suffice to pay my room and board? What an absurdity! I should
scarcely have two hours of leisure a day, and the rest of the time I
should be nailed to a table, recopying the inanities and old chimeras of
this Mr. Director and that. . . . I am at a crossroads, and I do not want
to take any decision until the fate of one or two of my expectations has
been settled. . . ."[4]

Having turned down this inglorious prospect, Nicholas felt no com-
punction about continuing to seek financial support from his mother. In
one letter he would pose as stoic, prepared to endure all privations for
the sake of his ideal: "I have been extremely hard up of late, but small
matter. Little would one suppose how trying it is to go without supper
for a week!"[5] Or he would complain that it was impossible for him to
live on less than 120 rubles a month: "For I do have to eat, and I do
not dine as sumptuously as all that."[6] Another time, he would simply

demand an emergency subsidy: "I am well aware that it will be almost impossible for you at this time, and so I shall do my utmost not to renew this request. . . . I have a most pressing need of three hundred rubles."[7]

Marya Ivanovna, terrified by the thought of her son starving or freezing to death in the great hostile city, borrowed right and left, mortgaged land, sold the copper cucurbit of her distilling alembic, and sent the money, accompanied by a chiding letter.

He, meanwhile, was already feeling less alone and disorientated in St. Petersburg. He had found a few old friends from the Nyezhin school, like himself shabbily housed and short of cash, but also sharing his soaring hopes. In addition to Danilevsky, who had entered the guards officers' school and was now free every Sunday, he often saw Mokritsky, a student at the Academy of Fine Arts, the Prokopovich brothers Nikolai and Vasily, Ivan Pashchenko; Grebenka, Kukolnik, Lyubich-Romanovich. They would meet at the lodgings of one or another of the group, where each in turn would prepare some Ukrainian dish; and they would share their reminiscences of their distant province. Although he was not sorry to have left Vasilyevka, Nikolai Gogol recalled with nostalgia the quiet life of the landed gentry, the simple ways of the peasants, and the luminous Ukrainian sky. His grandmother's tales and those of his mother and the old household servants came back to him. Why shouldn't he transcribe them and make a little money? People in the capital were wild for Ukrainian legends and folk songs. In any case, it would cost nothing to try. He wrote to his mother:

"You have a keen and perceptive mind, and you know the manners and customs of our Little Russians; I know therefore that you will not refuse to give me all the particulars I need on this subject in our correspondence. . . . In your next letter I shall expect a description of a village deacon's costume, from cassock to boots, and with the exact name of each piece of clothing in the language of the oldest, most traditional, and most reactionary of our compatriots. I also want the names of all the items of clothing of our young peasant girls, down to the last ribbon; same thing for the dress of married women and muzhiks. . . . Secondly, I need exact details of the costumes worn in the days of the hetmans. . . . Also an exact description of a wedding, omitting no detail. . . . A few words on the ritual Christmas songs, on Midsummer Night, on the undines. . . . If you should also hear talk of any spirits, any *domovoye,*† try to find out their names and characteristics. Among the common people there are many beliefs, frightening tales, superstitions, and assorted anecdotes.. . . . All of it will be of the greatest interest to me."[8]

He did not yet know exactly what he would make of all this information he was clamoring for so urgently: a tale, perhaps, or an ethnographical essay. . . . For the moment, his main idea was to publish the works he had brought with him: his short poem *Italy,* and the long one, *Hans Kuechelgarten.*

Since he could not step straight into the shoes of a great statesman and benefactor of mankind, and since he could not bear the thought of being locked up from morning to night in an office littered with paper, he would have to exploit this other aspect of his talent. He would have to sell his verse. There was no sin in that. But whom should he consult? He would so like to be sponsored by his idol Pushkin! One day, with fine effrontery, he marched up to the poet's home but was paralyzed by timidity at the door, and fled into a tea shop. There he gulped down a glass of spirits to revive his courage, and returned to the charge. He rang; a manservant opened. The master could not receive him. "He is resting," said the servant. "Of course, he has been working all night long!" murmured the gaping Nikolai. "And how!" the man replied, "at the card table!" Gogol retreated, keenly disappointed. He would never dare try there again. For his first attempt, he had aimed too high.

He sent *Italy* to the *Son of the Fatherland,* a periodical, asking the director, Thaddeus Bulgarin, to publish it anonymously. Bulgarin was a paid police informer, held in contempt by all his colleagues but in high esteem by the government. He acceded to the request of his unknown correspondent, and on March 23, 1829, Nikolai Gogol, who had just celebrated his twentieth birthday, read his poetry printed in black on white in a publication circulating in hundreds of copies. At the bottom were the words "No signature." No one mentioned the work in the press, but the young man swelled with pride. Since *Italy* had seen the light of day, the way was open for *Hans Kuechelgarten.* This time he would be his own publisher. He collected all the money his mother had sent him, toured the printers, bargained, and finally reached agreement with a certain Plyushar. But just as he was about to hand his manuscript over to the printer, doubt overcame him. He read it over for the hundredth

† A kind of household genie in Russian folklore.

time, changing a line here and there and adding a comma or two; he thrilled to think of the fame awaiting him, then suddenly quailed in fear of failure. Should he expose his name, which meant so much to him, to the shafts of a few envious journalists? Perhaps it would be better to wait, before signing himself Nikolai Gogol, until he had produced something really flawless. He had many friends, yet would ask advice of no one. He had kept secret the whole idea of publishing *Hans Kuechelgarten* and did not intend to lose the benefit of all that discretion out of mere cowardice. How sweet a thing was dissimulation! He chose a pseudonym, V. Alov; then he wrote a "Publisher's Note," to be prefaced to his "idyl in eighteen tableaux," that was both prudent and shrewd:

"This work would assuredly never have seen the light of day, had not imperative considerations led the author to publish it. The poem presented here is the work of a young man of eighteen; we make no claim to judge its merits or demerits, leaving that to the enlightened reader. Nevertheless, we would like to observe that several tableaux have unfortunately been lost, which undoubtedly gave greater unity to the whole and presented a fuller portrait of the chief character. We are, in any event, proud to have been of assistance in making the work of a young talent known to the public."

The censor's office gave its imprimatur on May 7, 1829, and very shortly thereafter Nikolai Gogol held the first copies of his work. He looked at this marvel: a real book—printed, not a manuscript—smelling of ink and new paper, with the author's name on the blue cover, and the title and price—five rubles. Who knows? Perhaps hundreds, even thousands of unknown readers would consent to spend that much to weep over his hero's romantic destiny. Perhaps Pushkin himself would read *Hans Kuechelgarten* and, charmed by the music of the lines, would ask to meet the mysterious Alov. The thought sent thrills of excitement through him. He had to make an effort to believe that he was not already the poet's intimate friend. Twitching with impatience, he went in and out of bookshops. Alas! Days passed and the stacks did not dwindle on the shelves. Pushkin gave no sign. Neither did the press. It was as though *Hans Kuechelgarten* had sunk like a stone beneath the waters. Then, suddenly, the critics awoke. One of them, N. Polevoy, whose views were highly respected, wrote in his paper, the Moscow *Telegraph*, "The publisher of this book says that Mr. Alov's poem was not intended for publication but that imperative considerations led the author to change his mind. We consider that considerations still more imperative should have restrained him. . . ."

The *Northern Bee* tolled the same knell; *"Hans Kuechelgarten* contains so many inanities, the tableaux are so monstrous, and the author's inventions—whether of poetical ornamentation, style, or prosody—so witless, that the world would have been none the poorer had this first attempt of a young talent remained hidden under its bushel."

Nikolai Gogol received every word like a slap in the face. What were the teasings of his schoolmates at Nyezhin compared with the trouncing he was receiving now? He had been well advised to hide behind a pseudonym! That way, at least, none of his associates would learn his shame. Even his closest friends were unaware that they were rubbing elbows with the unfortunate Alov. He who had dreamed of delighting Pushkin! It was a severe blow. And he could not even rise in protest against his critics. On the contrary! He thought they were absolutely right. Not one line of *Hans Kuechelgarten* now appeared worthy of survival. How could he live down the shame? Something radical was called for. July was ending. St. Petersburg lay panting in humid heat; the brackish smell of the canals seeped through the open windows. Nikolai Gogol hired a cab and, accompanied by his manservant, Yakim, made the rounds of the city's booksellers to buy up every remaining copy of *Hans Kuechelgarten.*

He piled the string-tied packages into the carriage, half furious and half in sorrow. There could obviously be no question of trundling this humiliating cargo back to the apartment he was sharing with Prokopovich, where their friends often gathered. Some hidden place was needed, far from all eyes. He took a room in a hotel on Vozhnesensky Street. There, with the help of his servant, he lit a fire in the stove and threw the new volumes into it, one by one. The pages would not burn; they crinkled and blackened, smoking. At last the purifying flames leaped up. More was consumed on that occasion than the author's illusions: it was his soul being regenerated in a divine combustion. He stood a long time staring at the miniature holocaust, fascinated. When it was all over, he felt relief, tempered by sorrow.

Back at the apartment, he told no one of the *auto-da-fé,* but his life suddenly seemed vain and empty. What could he do next, after such a searing setback? For some weeks he had been dreaming of following Hans Kuechelgarten's example, going abroad to blossom and flourish under foreign skies. He had begun preparing his mother for the idea of a journey long before, in a letter dated May 22. As always, he planned ahead, proposed a scheme only to reject it immediately, inventing extraordinary circumstances to justify his intentions. This time, to prevent Marya Ivanovna from taxing him with selfishness, he invented a mysterious friend prepared to assume all the expenses of the expedition:

"This journey, which would ordinarily entail considerable expense, would have cost me nothing; all my expenses would have been paid and my every wish fulfilled during the cruise. But imagine my bad luck! As though fate had willed it, the generous friend who had made all these promises to me has suddenly died! His intentions and plans have been reduced to nothing, and I am now tasting a poison of cruel bitterness. The cancellation in itself grieves me less than the loss of a being to whom I was attached for life. And there, heaven has snatched him away again. . . ."

Having thus interred the mythological creature his pen had engendered, Gogol told himself that the idea of his departure and the expense it would entail were now planted for good in his mother's mind. She knew that her son was drawn to foreign parts and would need money if he decided to go. During the ensuing days, he left her to fret and dreamed on, longing for escape.

"A strange fact," he wrote in his *Confession of an Author,* "how, even as a child, even at my desk at school, even at a time when I hoped to enter government service rather than make a career in literature, I always felt that some great personal sacrifice—I did not know what—lay in store for me, and that in order to serve my country I should have to complete my preparation far away from it. I did not know how it would happen, and never even thought about it; but I imagined myself so vividly, pining for my homeland on some foreign ground, and that vision haunted me so frequently that I was filled with sorrow."

In St. Petersburg, prose was the only thing. Perhaps poetry was flourishing beyond the frontier. There must be somewhere, far away, a country of love, reason, beauty. America. The land of pioneers and inventors. Virgin soil. Just what he needed! But it was at the other end of the world. It must be possible to expatriate oneself less expensively. Germany, for example—tender, romantic Germany. To think that he was prevented from going there by a few paltry rubles! At this point, Marya Ivanovna sent him quite a large sum of money, with which to pay the interest on the Vasilyevka mortgage. Contemplating this heaven-sent sheaf of bank notes, Nikolai sensed that God was with him. Wasn't it foolish to deposit so much money in the coffers of the authorities, when he needed it for his trip? The authorities could wait; he could not. Fingering the bundles of assignation rubles, he thought of Lübeck. Why Lübeck? He didn't know himself. He liked the name; it rang like a bell. He would go there, to forget and to meditate. All that remained was to inform his mother of his imminent departure and appropriation of the funds she had entrusted to him. From day to day, he put off the ordeal of confession. To ease his conscience, he decided to send Marya Ivanovna a formal authorization to dispose of his share of his inherit-ance. Having purchased a sheet of notarized stationery, he wrote:

"Beloved Mother, prompted by feelings of filial devotion, I can no better demonstrate my affection than by setting your welfare upon a solid foundation during the period of my absence." There followed de-tailed instructions entitling Marya Ivanovna to dispose of the goods and chattels and serfs belonging to her son. The document, dated July 23, 1829, was signed, "Nikolai Gogol-Yanovsky, government official 14th class." The next day, July 24, Gogol finally sat down at his table to write the letter of explanation. What pretext could he find to justify this need for new horizons? In the first place, of course, there was the will of the Almighty. That was a language the devout Marya Ivanovna must understand:

"The hand of the Almighty has been laid upon me, and inflicted upon me the most just of punishments. But how dire it is, that punishment. Madman that I was! I wanted to resist these aspirations of the soul, which God himself instilled in me, and which were filling me with a thirst never to be assuaged by an idle and dissipated life in society. He had shown me that I was to direct my steps toward a foreign land, there to learn, in silence, in solitude, and through ceaseless labor, how to dominate my passions so that gradually I should rise to a summit from which I could dispense felicity and make myself useful to the world. And I dared to play deaf to these divine solicitations and pre-ferred to go on crawling in this capital among all these civil servants living out their empty lives. . . . Heights of happiness indeed, to creep up at the age of fifty to the rank of state councilor, with a salary barely sufficient to provide a decent standard of living and no opportunity to perform the smallest service for mankind! . . . Nevertheless, to please you I was resolved to enter the service here, however trying it might be. But God did not wish it. Everywhere, I have encountered nothing but failure, even, oddly enough, where I least expected it. People with no ability and no patronage easily obtained what I could not get even with the aid of my protectors. Was this not a sign of divine intervention in my life? Was not God plainly punishing me, to return me to the right path? I continued, however, stubbornly, waiting months on end in the hope of some reward. . . ."

After reeling off this skein of mystical speculation, Nikolai Gogol felt on somewhat firmer ground. But when he read it over, his argument did not seem altogether convincing: he needed a supplementary motive for flight. In his previous letter he had invented the generous friend, cut off in the flower of his youth. This time he would proffer his love for a woman, supremely beautiful and sublimely inaccessible—first God, then one of his angels. In fact, he had not had a single sentimental adventure since his arrival in St. Petersburg, and felt no impulse to involve himself with a member of the fair sex. He was paralyzed by the mere sight of one of these creatures with the long hair and velvet smile. Now, however, pen in hand, he forgot the motive for his deceit and felt himself utterly in love. The more details he supplied of the torments he was enduring, the faster his heart throbbed. With gusto and despair, he announced to his mother, in the same letter:

"Oh, what a frightful punishment! None could be more painful or more cruel to me! I cannot . . . I have no strength to tell it. . . . Mother, my dear Mother, I know you are my only true friend! Will you believe me? . . . You know I have always been endowed with rare strength of character for a young man. . . . Who could have divined such a weakness in me? . . . But I have seen it . . . No, I shall not name her. . . . She is too far above me, above anyone. I might call her an angel, but that the term does not suit her. She is a divinity whom human passions hardly touch. Her radiant face imprints itself for all time on the heart; her eyes pierce your soul; no man could bear the burning, penetrating flame of her look! Oh, if you had seen me then! I know, it is true, how to hide my feelings from others, but can I hide them from myself? All the torments of infernal despair were boiling in my breast. Oh, what an appalling situation! I think that, if there be a hell for sinners, it must be less dreadful. No, it was not love! . . . Or in any case I have never heard tell of such a love. In my demented movements, with my racked soul, my only need was to see her, my only desire to capture a single glance from her. . . . To see her yet once more was my sole wish, which increased with every passing day, more bitter and inextinguishable. At last, I realized my hopeless state and withdrew in terror into myself again. Everything around me had lost its appeal, life and death seemed equally intolerable to me, my soul was unable to understand what was transpiring within it. I saw that I should have to flee myself if I wanted to go on living and restore even a semblance of peace to my devastated heart. Chastened, I recognized the invisible Right Hand protecting me, and blessed the road it pointed to. No, this creature He had sent to strip me of my rest and overturn the tottering world I had erected, this creature was no woman. Had she been one, all her powers of seduction could not have produced in me this agonizing, inexpressible impression. She was a divinity created by Him, a part of Himself. But in the name of heaven do not ask me her name; her station is too high!"

Upon receiving this epistle, in which the Almighty and a *femme fatale* combined forces to drive Nikolai Gogol from St. Petersburg, Marya Ivanovna must have wondered if her son had lost his mind. The letter concluded, by the way, with singularly precise considerations of an economic nature.

"And so," wrote Nikolai, "I determined to leave. But how? A journey abroad is difficult and demands much preparation. I had hardly commenced when, to my great amazement, everything seemed to fall into place of its own accord. My passport was easily obtained. Only one difficulty remained: money. I was about to give up in despair when I received from you the money for the deposit. I immediately went to see the authorities to ask how much extra time they would allow for the payment of the interest, and was told they would give up to four months, for payment of a fine of five rubles for each month's delay per thousand rubles borrowed. . . . To be sure, what I did was rash and not very sensible, but could I do otherwise? I have kept all the money for the mortgage interest and can now affirm that I shall not be asking you for more. . . . Do not grieve, dear Mother. I needed a crisis like this. This lesson will assuredly do me good. I have a bad character and have been spoiled (I confess it with all my heart). Laziness and the idle life I was leading here could well have magnified my failings still more. I must transform myself, regenerate myself, be reborn into a new life. My soul will blossom in work and activity, and, if I cannot achieve happiness (no, I never shall be personally happy, this divine being has gone from me and taken with her my soul's peace), I shall dedicate the rest of my life to the welfare and happiness of my fellow men. Do not fear the separation: I am not going far. Lübeck is the goal of my journey, a large German city on the seashore, renowned as a center of world trade. . . ."

The last lines of the letter were lost for Marya Ivanovna in a flood of tears: her money gone, her son flown. And would he not encounter a thousand dangers on the ship bearing him toward the German coast?

The sea was rough. The steamer creaked and heaved under the blows of tall green waves. Whipped by the spray, Nikolai Gogol staggered up and down the deck struggling with an insidious desire to vomit. He had left his friends the night before, without explanation. None of them understood his flight. To save money, he had not brought along his manservant; Yakim folded his arms in the apartment to await his return. All the passengers were sick. The hands chewed tobacco and spat. Two days later, the coast of Sweden appeared, and Bornholm Island, with its naked cliffs and verdant hinterland. Four more days between sky and water and the port of Lübeck ebbed through the dirty mist of dawn.

At first, upon disembarking, Gogol was dizzied by the noise and bustle of the wharfs. Then he conscientiously toured the town, admiring the high narrow houses roofed with red tiles, the spic-and-span little courtyards, the shops bursting with provender, the inns filled with fat pink Germans drinking beer, the young peasant girls in flowered blouses parading down the streets, even the Swiss, English, and American tourists he met in the hotel dining room. But what struck him most was the great age of the public buildings. By comparison with St. Petersburg, only a century old, even the most ordinary buildings seemed bowed down by history. With what emotion he stepped into the Gothic cathedral, a veritable forest of stone lit by the supernatural intensity of stained glass! Was not this tormented architecture the most perfect expression of human faith? And the monumental clock, which opened its doors at noon to let out the twelve Apostles parading around in a circle! And the paintings of the German and Italian masters! Gazing upon some of them, Nikolai Gogol, who had abandoned his brushes since leaving Nyezhin, dreamed of becoming a painter again.

His curiosity was quickly dampened, however, and a feeling of solitude chilled him to the bone. He wondered what he had come in search of in this place where he could not even speak the language. Lines from *Hans Kuechelgarten* ran through his memory:

> "An insuperable sadness
> Suddenly seizes the traveler.
> His soul is filled with reproach,
> With pain and with pity:
> Why has he come this way?"

Thus, like his hero, he had traveled the world, only to find himself face to face with his own image. Moreover, he had undoubtedly inflicted great pain on his mother. Ever since his arrival, he had been wanting to implore her pardon; he had quite forgotten "the will of the Almighty" and the woman with the "radiant face" whose cruelty had driven him into exile. Illness now became the reason for his departure.

"I may have forgotten to tell you the main thing that brought me to Lübeck," he wrote to her on August 13, 1829. "During the entire spring and summer in St. Petersburg, I was not at all well. Now I am better, but my hands and face are covered with eruptions. The doctors assure me that it is a consequence of the scrofula, that my blood is vitiated, that I should swallow purgative dococtions and take the waters at Travemünde—a little town 18 versts from Lübeck. . . ."

And indeed he went to Travemünde, but stayed only three days and never thought of the allegedly prescribed treatment; he proceeded to Hamburg and then returned to Lübeck, more unsettled and disorientated than ever. A letter from his mother awaited him there—a terrible letter: not only did she order him to remove himself to St. Petersburg without further ado, but her interpretation of his reasons for his trip was exceedingly disagreeable. Putting together his tale of illness and his fictitious romance, she concluded that he had contracted a venereal disease from the person whose beauty he had sung. This supposition plunged Nikolai into an abyss of horror. His lies were coming home to roost.

"How could you, dear Mother, think I was a victim of debauchery, that I had fallen to the lowest level of human baseness, that in a word I was suffering from an affliction the very thought of which makes my mind shudder with revulsion," he wrote to her. "This is the first time— and God let it be the last—that I have received a letter so horrifying. It seemed to me as I read it that I was hearing a curse upon myself. Could the son of such angelic parents be this monster, possessing no trace of their virtue? . . . I am ready to swear before God that I have committed no depraved act and that my morality here has been even more unimpeachable than during my residence at the school and at home. . . . I absolutely cannot comprehend what made you think I had contracted that particular disease. In my letter I do not recall saying anything in any way associated with such an indisposition. . . ."[9]

Forgetting that he had just recently justified his departure by the need to treat a severe case of scrofula complicated with eruptions on face and hands, he now pursued, imperturbably: "I believe I spoke to you of a chest ailment that made it difficult for me to breathe, and from which I have now, thank God, recovered. Ah, if you only knew how wretched I was! I never had a single night's uninterrupted sleep, never one happy dream. I never ceased to think of the distress, dismay, and worry I had caused you."

This time, he made up his mind to go home. Also, his money was running out.

In a Lübeck of forbidding cleanliness and cold, there was absolutely nothing for him to do. He set sail again, on the same ship that had brought him.

One evening Prokopovich was on his way home when he collided in the street with an overjoyed Yakim running to the bakery: his master was back! Prokopovich found the traveler sitting in the midst of his trunks, a bleak and weary expression on his face. To his friend's questions, Gogol replied evasively. He clearly did not want to talk about his journey to Germany. Prokopovich and his other friends respected his silence. The Lübeck episode remained a mystery to all, including, no doubt, its protagonist.

4. Civil Servant

St. Petersburg again: mist, rain, cold, and lack of money. How to pay the
interest on the mortgage? If the money was not received in time, the
Vasilyevka estate would be sold at auction. To top it all off, Dmitri
Prokofyevich Troshchinsky, the family benefactor, had died the previous
June. His heir and nephew, Andrey Andreyevich Troshchinsky, was
not so easy to approach. In desperation, Marya Ivanovna wrote to him
in St. Petersburg, where he had gone on business, to implore his help.
Andrey Andreyevich Troshchinsky summoned Nikolai Gogol, scolded
him roundly, but finally paid the debt in full. He even gave his young
relative some financial assistance and made him a present of a winter
coat. But, he added, Gogol would have to contemplate the future more
seriously thereafter, not as an artist. And he promised to help him find a
job in the administration.

Despite this promise, or perhaps because of it, Gogol had a sudden
urge to try his luck in the theater. The dread of ending his days as a
scribe emboldened him. He had been such a great success as an actor at
school, it would be a crime not to cultivate this God-given talent. He saw
himself celebrated, a Garrick, a Talma, a Dmitryevsky . . .

One gray and rainy morning he went down the English Quay to the
home of Prince Sergey Sergeyevich Gagarin, director of the imperial
theaters. He was dressed in his best, but a sudden toothache had forced
him to tie a black kerchief around his throbbing cheek. The prince, he
trusted, was sufficiently sophisticated not to be distracted by this small

detail. Young Mundt, Gagarin's personal secretary, received the visitor and asked him his business:

"I want to enter the theater as an actor," Gogol firmly replied.[1]

Mundt asked him to wait, as the prince was still dressing. Nikolai Gogol sat near a window and stared out at the Neva, flowing past below. Now and then he made a face and put his hand to his cheek.

"I believe you have the toothache," said Mundt. "Would you like some Cologne water?"

"Thank you," muttered Gogol. "It will go away by itself. . . ."

A little while later, Mundt suddenly became very busy, running about in all directions, opening door after door, and finally introducing the applicant into the directorial office. A religious awe welled up in Gogol at the sight of the smooth, cold face framed in side whiskers. Gagarin, a great balletomane, was said to feel nothing but contempt for Russian plays and confused Walter Scott with Voltaire. Nevertheless, a word from him could determine a career. He was clearly fond of intimidating visitors. Behind his back, Mundt observed the scene.

"What do you want?" the prince asked.

Nikolai Gogol, clutching his hat to his stomach, gathered all his courage and said, "I want to become an actor in the theater, in the Russian company."

"Your name?"

"Gogol-Yanovsky."

"Of what birth?"

"Noble."

"What leads you to want to go on the stage? As a gentleman, you could enter the government administration."

"I am not rich," stammered Gogol. "I doubt that a position in the administration could satisfy my requirements. Also, I do not think I am made for that type of work. And I feel a real attraction to the theater."

"Do not imagine that anybody can become an actor. It takes a certain talent."

"Perhaps I possess that very talent."

"Perhaps! What kind of parts do you intend to play?"

"I don't know exactly, to tell the truth. But I should think serious parts would suit me best."

The prince cast one ironic glance over his figure and said, with a thin smile:

"I think, Mr. Gogol, you would be more comfortable in comedy. But, after all, that is your business!"

He instructed Mundt to arrange for Khrapovitsky, inspector of the Russian Acting Company, to audition Nikolai Gogol a few days later.

The audition took place in the morning at the Grand Theater. Khrapovitsky was a believer in classical declamation. He received Gogol in his office, where the stage director and a few actors from the company were assembled. In front of this audience of specialists, the neophyte lost his remaining shreds of self-confidence. As he had not prepared anything, Khrapovitsky suggested that he read a soliloquy of Orestes from Racine's *Andromaque* in a translation by Khvostov. His nose buried in the script, Gogol reeled off Khvostov's heavy lines in a complete monotone, and the irritated Khrapovitsky stopped him after two minutes.

After tragedy, he tried comedy. But the apprentice was scarcely more at ease in the interpretation of the *School for Old Men*. He could read his sentence in the eyes of the judges. Did he really have no talent at all, or was it the atmosphere of St. Petersburg that paralyzed him? With one icily courteous phrase, Khrapovitsky dismissed him. A few months previously, Gogol had vainly sought to interest someone in performing two of his father's Ukrainian comedies, *The She-Dog in Lambs' Clothing* and *The Romance of Parasya*. Decidedly, he must give up all thought of the theater, in any form. The only goal permitted him was the clerk's desk.

Andrey Andreyevich Troshchinsky did not exert himself in vain. On November 15, 1829, Nikolai Gogol was appointed to a position in the department of public works of the ministry of the interior, with the less than modest salary of five hundred rubles a year. So, he was going to lose himself in the gray horde of little civil servants. All things considered, he preferred even this constraint and poverty to the prospect of returning to family life at Vasilyevka. He wrote to his mother:

"When I compare my situation with that of a good many other civil servants, I see that it is not a total loss; many of my colleagues would like to be in my place, and I need only increase my patience and hope for promotion. But of course, those colleagues of whom I speak receive enough money from home to provide for their basic needs, whereas I must live on my salary alone. Judge for yourself: entertaining no one, almost never going out, and giving up my favorite pastime, the theater, I can in no manner reduce my expenses to less than a hundred rubles a month. I exclude from that sum expenses for such things as the purchase of clothes, boots, a hat, gloves, handkerchiefs, etc., which alone amount to five hundred rubles. Now, consider that I receive five hundred rubles a year, even less. . . . Fortunately, until now I have had a benefactor as exceptional as Andrey Andreyevich Troshchinsky. Hitherto I have lived on subsidies. As proof of my efforts at economy, I remind you that I am still wearing today the suit I ordered upon my arrival in St. Petersburg. You can imagine how threadbare and worn is this coat, which I wear every day. I have not had the means to order another, or even to buy a warm coat, which is indispensable in the winter. Luckily I am accustomed to the cold, and went through the entire season in a summer coat. The money I requested from Andrey Andreyevich could not be used to buy clothing; it had to go on my food and lodging. And I did not want to ask him for any more, because I had already seen that I was a burden to him. He has told me, moreover, on several occasions that he would help me only until your own situation had at least partly improved, that he had a family of his own and his prospects were not always so bright. You will understand that it becomes difficult for me, in the circumstances, to lay my troubles before him. . . . Furthermore, he is preparing to leave St. Petersburg in May. What am I to do then? There is only one course remaining, dear Mother: to ask you whether you will be able to send me one hundred rubles a month?"

Having tossed out this figure, Gogol paused, his pen suspended. Wasn't he being a little greedy? He prudently considered reducing his demand; maybe eighty rubles would be enough. . . . But where anyone else would simply have altered a word or two, he invented a whole tale to justify his change of heart. Willy-nilly, lies flowed more naturally than truth from his pen:

"Just as I was about to end this letter, the head of my department came to see me and brought me some very pleasant news, namely that my salary was to be raised by twenty rubles a month. Now, therefore, dear Mother, I ask if you can send me eighty rubles a month?"[2]

In support of his application, he appended a table of his income and expenditure for the month of January 1830:

Income	Rubles	Expenditure	Rubles
January salary	30	Rent	25
Balance of sum from Andrey Andreyevich	50	Table	25
		Firewood	7

Income	Rubles	Expenditure	Rubles
From *Northern Archives*		Sugar, tea, bread	20
for translation of French		Candles	3
article on "Russian Trade		Water carrier	2
in the Late-16th and Early-		One pair gloves	3
17th centuries"	20	Laundress	5
Total	100	Food for manservant	10
		Two handkerchiefs	2
		Minor expenses, such as:	
		cab, barber, etc.	5
		One pair suspenders	4
		Total	111
		Plus public baths	1.50

To intensify the tragic dimensions of the situation, he added, with studied nonchalance: "Forgive me for writing so badly and illegibly. My hand is bandaged because I injured myself with a splinter of glass. Pain prevents me from saying any more to you. . . ."

Once again Marya Ivanovna yielded, fretfully, to the importunities of her cherished, her impossible, her worrisome "Nikosha."

He, meanwhile, had already changed jobs. On April 10, 1830, he started work in the department of appanage of the ministry of the court, with an annual salary of six hundred rubles. On June 3 he was "established," and on July 10 became deputy head; his salary then rose to 750 rubles per annum. It was neither riches nor even comfort, but it was some consolation to be able to tell himself that at last he was no longer living solely on other people.

His friends Prokopovich and Pashchenko shared his apartment, which reduced his expenses and enlivened his days. Three rooms, one for each, with Yakim sleeping in a cupboard. At nine in the morning Nikolai was at his desk, settling down to some tedious task: stitching leaflets together, copying a statement of accounts, penning a report, underlining titles. Bent over his desk, he observed his colleagues. Young and old, fat and thin, bald and hirsute, they all shared a deadly dullness caused by their work and the terror of criticism. Years of this discipline had broken their spirits, smoothed away every wart of their personalities, and lowered their ambitions. They nourished themselves on ink and paper and saw no further than the tip of their pen. When a superior asked their opinion on some matter relating to their work, it never occurred to them to say what they thought; they worriedly tried to guess what he wanted to hear. This was the kingdom of servility, of respectable poverty, intrigues for promotion, crude jests, and hollow stomachs. On Sunday mornings they went to Mass, to please their chiefs. On Sunday afternoons they drank. On Monday they resumed their work with heavy heads. Their only hope was an unexpected gratification, a small bribe. . . . But in the department of appanage, opportunities for that kind of enrichment were few. Direct contact with the public was necessary if one was to scrape up the old ruble here and there. Nikolai wrote to his mother:

"You tell me, dear Mother, that many people have come poor to St. Petersburg and, living on their salary alone, have earned fortunes by their zeal and application in the work. . . . But remember in what period these events took place. . . . In the time of Catherine the Great and Paul I, the Senate and government chancelleries were places where people could grow rich. Nowadays, opportunities for gratuities in such positions are much more restricted. At best, they are so insignificant that they are virtually no help at all in the mediocre lives of these civil servants."[3]

Gogol's superior, a man named Vladimir Ivanovich Panaev, had once been an amiable poet—a writer of "idyls"—and had enjoyed a small reputation. Today he was a fleshless government employee, punctual and meticulous, hostile to all forms of imagination. Was that the fate in store for people who betrayed their true vocation? The mere thought made Nikolai Gogol's flesh crawl. And yet, oddly enough, while he scorned the paltry creatures surrounding him in the office, he felt they were teaching him something. His understanding of the oppressed was increasing; he was collecting heads, twitches, retorts, grimaces, populating himself with a hundred humble or hideous creatures.

At last, three o'clock in the afternoon! Foreheads lifted, files closed, everyone hurried to the exit. Nikolai Gogol dined quickly and went to the Academy of Fine Arts. The number of people in the streets had suddenly quadrupled. The offices disgorged their population of mean and mighty officials onto the pavements. There was something fascinating in this crowd, in which the "collegiate registrar" walked side by side with the "titular councilor." One could not help thinking of a living pyramid, with men like himself, Gogol, at the base, and another Nikolai, the tsar, the master of every breathing thing in Russia, at the summit.

The Academy of Fine Arts was on Vasilyevsky Island. Gogol crossed the Dvortsovy Bridge and went along the stern façades of the university buildings. Across the water, he could see the enormous St. Isaac's Cathedral and the monument of the bronze horseman rearing up on its granite base.

The palace of the academy, an imposing two-story edifice, engulfed its visitors through a central portal. Gogol crossed the court of honor and slipped into the nature-drawing class. There he installed himself behind an easel and endeavored, charcoal in hand, to reproduce the pose of the model—some hulking, half-naked fellow perched high on a stool. Yegorov and Shebuev, the professors, moved among their pupils correcting the drawings. The classes lasted from five until seven in the evening. For those two hours, Nikolai Gogol forgot the exigencies of his desk and might almost believe himself an artist.

When he emerged, the oil lamps were already lit in the foggy city. He went home for dinner or to some gathering of former students of the Nyezhin School. In the Ukrainian atmosphere surrounding him in their company, his thoughts turned increasingly toward folklore. He continued to badger his mother and eldest sister, Marya, for information: customs, legends, sayings, songs, details of costume—he was never satisfied with what they told him. All the details he gleaned from them were transferred to a notebook entitled *Hold-All Notebook*. As its covers swelled, he became convinced that he was sitting on a gold mine. But would he be able to work it himself? Would he have enough skill and patience, or would he ruin his precious raw material?

The educated readers of St. Petersburg seemed to dote upon Ukrainian stories, whether comic, fantastic, or bloodcurdling. Aladin's *Kochubey,* Somov's *Haïdamaki,* Kulzhinsky's *Cossack Hat,* and the tales of Olin and Lugansky—all were read and praised. Why not a story by Nikolai Gogol in the same vein? His first experiences of the literary world had not, it is true, been particularly encouraging. He had published a few translations,[4] and then a Ukrainian short story, "Bisavryuk, or St. John's Eve," in the monthly *Annals of the Fatherland* (issue of February–March 1830), with no name.[5] Svinin, the director of the publication and an inferior journalist, had so altered his manuscript that Nikolai Gogol swore he would never give him another line of his prose. A few months later, in December 1830, it was the periodical *Northern Flowers* that received a chapter from his unfinished historical novel *The Hetman,** signed "oooo." The idea of this curious signature

---

* The author began the novel at Nyezhin, and later, dissatisfied with his work, destroyed most of it.

had been suggested to him by the four o's in his name, Nikolai Gogol-Yanovsky. On January 1, 1831, in the *Literary Gazette,* there appeared simultaneously a chapter entitled "The Master," from his story "A Terrible Vengeance" (under the pseudonym of Glaychik), and an article on teaching geography to children (under the pseudonym of Yanov).

Although he had had several manuscripts published, he still could not bring himself to tear off the mask. No doubt it was Anton Delvig, director of both the *Literary Gazette* and *Northern Flowers,* who forced his hand. The young author apprehensively gave the *Literary Gazette* his essay on *Woman,* written at school, and consented for the first time to have his real name appear at the bottom of a printed page. An odd name, moreover: *gogol* is the Russian word for grebe, that little aquatic bird with dull plumage, elongated crest, and pointed bill, that swims excellently, flies poorly, and cannot walk at all. In fact, as it happened, Nikolai Gogol was beginning to look increasingly like a bird.

At this point he rejected the second half of his name. Born Gogol-Yanovsky, he would succeed as Gogol. Now that he had revealed his identity to the public, he sat trembling and awaited results. *Woman,* a puerile and bombastic elucubration, went unnoticed, but its author had gained the good opinion of the director.

Anton Delvig, a friend of Pushkin and Zhukovsky, and himself a poet, was a man of taste, learning, and humanity. Tall and ponderous, with a domed forehead, and black-rimmed spectacles perched on his nose, he received in a dressing gown, lying across a sofa amid a mound of books and manuscripts. His idleness was proverbial, but the truth was that he had a weak heart, and the smallest physical effort exhausted him.

Looking at him, Gogol thought in awe that this gasping, benevolent figure was a close associate of Pushkin, that the hand he had just touched had touched the hand of Pushkin, that the mouth addressing him had lately spoken to Pushkin. Seated in the little study, he felt he was drawing closer to a star and already saw its light. No doubt they talked of Pushkin—of Pushkin the elusive, who, after being exiled to his family home by Alexander I for a few subversive lines, had been returned to favor by Nicholas I but scorned the capital and cared only for Moscow; of Pushkin who had published, one after another, such masterpieces as *Poltava,* the seventh canto of *Eugene Onegin,* and *Boris Godunov;* of Pushkin who, it appeared, was working "like an angel" far away in the country at his Boldino farm; of Pushkin who, after chasing so many petticoats, was now thinking of marrying a Muscovite beauty . . . Delvig was touched by the long-nosed young man's interest in Pushkin in particular and literature in general.

The visitor unquestionably merited something better than an obscure clerk's job in the department of appanage. It so happened that there was in St. Petersburg another poet, another friend of Pushkin, and the fairy godfather of all impecunious young men of letters: Vasily Andreyevich Zhukovsky. At the mere sound of his name Gogol went into raptures. Since his school days he had looked upon Zhukovsky as his second idol, only just overshadowed by Pushkin, and here was Anton Delvig offering to introduce him! Zhukovsky, who was a consecrated celebrity, the private tutor of the heir apparent Alexander Nikolayevich, and held in high esteem by the Sovereign, received a stipend of twenty-five thousand rubles a year and lived in the Shepelevsky Palace. Thither Anton Delvig proceeded, flanked by his young colleague. In the presence of the romantic cantor of *Svetlana,* Gogol felt himself smaller and more vulnerable than ever.

Zhukovsky had pallid skin, slanting dark eyes of oriental cast, and an indulgent smile. A hundred times, Pushkin and others had run to him to calm the tsar's wrath or wring a concession from the censor. He welcomed his guests cordially, appeared interested in the fate of his new fellow author, and promised to recommend him to Pyotr Alexandrovich Pletnyev—another of Pushkin's friends!—who, he said, could find him some more promising work. Years later, remembering his first encounter with Zhukovsky, Gogol wrote to him:

"When I was still a very young man, on the threshold of life, I came to see you. You had already accomplished half your achievements. It was at the Shepelevsky Palace. The room where we met no longer exists; but I see it as though I were still there, down to the smallest detail of the furniture and decorations. You held out your hand to me and expressed your desire to help your future emulator. How affectionate, how benevolent was your expression! What was it that united us despite the difference in our ages? It was art. . . . From the day of our first meeting, art became for me the essential, the prime element of my life; all the rest was secondary. It seemed to me that I must enter no other relationship on earth, whether of a family nature or as a citizen, for literature was in itself a service."[6]

Zhukovsky was a man of his word. He personally introduced Gogol to Pletnyev, who was at that time inspector of the Patriotic Institute for young ladies of the aristocracy. He was a poet, critic, and professor of literature, but above all, profoundly loyal to his friends, and he could refuse Zhukovsky nothing. This Gogol, moreover, was not without qualities. He had just published an article on the teaching of geography and had, therefore, the stuff of an educationist in him. They would find some private tutoring for him and try to get him—why not?—a position at the Institute. All these rosy hopes were dashed by Delvig's sudden death from influenza, on January 14, 1831.[7] But even though the initiator of the whole undertaking was gone, Zhukovsky and Pletnyev did not desert his protégé. On their advice he published, in the *Literary Gazette,* a dithyrambic article on Pushkin's *Boris Godunov:* "Sublime! When I turn the pages of the product of your genius, when your lines mutter and leap out at me in notes of fire, a sacred terror runs through my veins, my soul shudders in fear because it has discovered God in the depths of his eternity!"

Pushkin must have smiled when he read this grandiloquent rubbish littered with exclamation points. Gogol was sincere, however; but, as usual, he went too far.

On February 6, 1831, the headmistress of the Patriotic Institute addressed a report to the authorities notifying them that one Gogol, employee in the department of appanage, would agree to teach history to the junior classes for an annual salary of four hundred rubles: "the inspector himself [Pletnyev] recommending this employee and guaranteeing his competence and loyalty, Your Excellency may see fit to apply to the highest authority for approval of the choice of Mr. Gogol as professor of history at the Institute." Three days later, on February 9, the empress, patroness of the Institute, signed the appointment, and on February 10, Gogol was writing his mother a letter of victory. As was his wont, he exaggerated both the obstacles he had overcome and the triumphs he anticipated. The setbacks he shared with so many writers at the beginning of their careers constituted in his eyes a unique martyrdom in the history of the world. In exchange, the smallest word of encouragement blinded him like a ray of sunlight striking through the clouds. He thought solely in terms of disasters and conquests:

"How grateful I am to the divine Right Hand for the failures and troubles I have endured! I would not trade them for the most precious treasures in the world. . . . Many people have not experienced in their entire lives what I have already known. . . . On the other hand, what peace there is now in my heart! And what strength and courage in my soul! I am still consumed by the same desire: to be useful. What pleases me most is that it is no longer I who seek new aquaint- ances, but others who want to meet me."

Gogol began work at the Patriotic Institute on March 10, 1831, be- came "established" on April 1 of that year, and was simultaneously promoted from fourteenth to ninth *chin*. That made him, overnight, a "titular councilor." His head whirled. In his mind, so ready to stretch the truth, it was no longer Pletnyev who had got him his position, but the empress herself who had singled him out for advancement. He wrote his mother again: "Suffering from hemorrhoids, I had the foolish idea that it was some other and more dangerous ailment. Later I learned that there was not one man in St. Petersburg free from this nuisance. The doctors advised me to stay off my feet as much as pos- sible, and this situation led me to abandon a position that I have always deemed insignificant, although another man would have been perfectly satisfied by it. My true way lies elsewhere. It is straight, and I turn into it now determined to walk with a firm step. I might have remained without employment if I had not managed to become "known" in the meantime. Her Majesty the Empress has commanded me to read les- sons at the Institute for the young ladies placed under her protec- tion. . . . Instead of shutting myself up in an office forty-two hours a week, I have only six hours of classes and shall earn a little more money. Meanwhile, in the silence of my solitary room I am performing a labor that will bring me far greater fame than the other. At present I have all the time I need to devote to it. I am working harder than ever and am more cheerful than ever too. . . ."[8]

He would have been still more triumphant if he could have read a letter Pletnyev had written to Pushkin a few weeks before:

"I must introduce you to a young writer who is full of promise. You may have noticed in *Northern Flowers* an extract from a historical novel signed "oooo" and, in the *Literary Gazette,* some *Thoughts on the Teaching of Geography,* an essay on *Woman,* and a chapter from a Ukrainian short story, "The Master." They were written by Gogol- Yanovsky. He started a career in the administration, but his passion for education has enlisted him in my ranks. Now he is a teacher. Zhukovsky is delighted with him. I can't wait to bring him around to receive your blessing. He loves learning for its own sake, and as an artist is ready to suffer every privation. I am moved and marvel at that."[9]

At first, the new history teacher at the Patriotic Institute took his work very seriously indeed, but he soon wearied of reciting elementary principles of history to an audience of little girls in brown uniforms. He dreaded his classes and awaited the recreation period as impatiently as his pupils. To supplement his income, Pletnyev had found him work as a tutor in several great families: the Balabins, the Longinovs, the Vasilchikovs. Their children grew quite fond of this curious teacher with the avian profile. The Longinov boy (Mikhail Nikolayevich) was to remember him as a small, thin man "with his nose set on askew, crooked legs, a tuft of hair on his skull, the least elegant hair style imaginable, a jerky way of speaking, interrupted by little sniffs, a face shaken by tics. . . ." He dressed conspicuously, propping his chin up with a high cravat. His pupils, put off by his double name, wanted to call him Mr. Yanovsky, but he would not allow it: "Why do you call me Mr. Yanovsky?" he would say. "My family name is Gogol. Yanovsky is only an appendage stuck on by the Polish."[10]

Relying on his recollections of his school days at Nyezhin, he taught them a smattering of Russian, natural science, history, and geography. But he spent most of his time telling Ukrainian anecdotes that made them roar with laughter, and back at his apartment he continued, pen in hand. Now he was sure he was on the right track. From his *Hold-All Notebook* he would extract half a dozen fantastically funny short stories. What should he call the collection? *Little Russian Tales, Evenings on a Farm?* And should he sign his real name? To protect his professorial dignity, Pletnyev advised him to use a pseudonym. He chose "Ruby Panko, the beekeeper." But the printers were a long way off: in his eyes, every page of the manuscript demanded revision, amendment, total rewriting. When he considered one section finished, Yakim would deliver it to a copyist.

In May, a heat wave descended upon St. Petersburg. Voluminous white clouds sailed across the sky. Prosperous city dwellers were already longing for their villas buried in the greenery of Tsarskoye Selo, Pavlovsk, Krasnoye Selo, or Gachina, just outside the capital. Suddenly an electrifying news item arrived: Pushkin and his young bride had come to town and were staying at the Demuth Hotel. In a few days they would be leaving for Tsarskoye Selo, where they had rented Kitaev's house. Gogol absolutely had to see them before they went. One evening in late May, Pletnyev gave a reception for the poet in his home. The life of the party was their mutual friend Alexandra

Osipovna Rosset, who had also taken a liking to Gogol. She was a young woman of twenty-two, the daughter of a French émigré, dark-haired, refined, pretty, and unusually clever, and a maid of honor to the empress. She was wild about art, poetry, and politics; her eyes were intense and her tongue lively, and she set men afire, both young and old. Some of the finest minds in Russia were among her intimate friends, and she exerted her influence at court on their behalf. Zhukovsky had nicknamed her "the celestial imp. It was whispered that Grand Duke Mikhail Pavlovich and Emperor Nicholas I themselves were not insensitive to her charms. That evening, she appeared in all her grace and loveliness, but Gogol hardly saw her; no more did he notice the extremely young, beautiful, languid Natalya Nikolayevna Pushkin. He had eyes only for a little man with dark skin, thick lips, and great eyes glittering with intelligence. Thick chestnut side whiskers framed his cheeks. He was wearing an evening coat and wide cravat, its ends falling on his white shirt front. He was holding a glass in his hand. The hand that had written *Eugene Onegin*.

Pletnyev introduced the two men. From the outset, Pushkin was friendly. "How nice Pushkin is! He instantly tamed the mulish *Khokhol* [Little Russian]," Alexandra Rosset wrote in her diary[11]; and farther on, "I observed that he glowed whenever Pushkin spoke to him." Gogol and Pushkin must have had little opportunity to unbosom themselves, however, at that noisy reception. A few words of conventional politeness, a vague invitation to meet another time, a smile, and a handshake; and Gogol returned home in a trance. At last he was entering the Eden of literature. Men of the stature of Zhukovsky and Pushkin were treating him as a friend. How would they be when he had published *Evenings on a Farm?*

Summer came; people were leaving St. Petersburg, and there were a few cases of cholera, but not many fatalities except in the poor districts. Groups of ragged men and women collected here and there hurling invective at the doctors and apothecaries who were poisoning the people. Police patrols quartered the town. A few roughnecks were arrested as a warning. There was nothing to buy in the markets. All food was suspect. The overworked physicians advised people to drink hot milk, or egg white beaten with oil, or salt water, to guard against the disease.[12] The court had long since left for Tsarskoye Selo. The order came to cordon off St. Petersburg to prevent anyone from entering or leaving the city. Luckily Gogol's friends had found him a job in

Pavlovsk as a tutor in the family of Princess Vasilchikov. He hastened there, while the half-empty capital became transformed into a fortified camp.

Pavlovsk, one of the favorite watering places of St. Petersburg high society, was only two versts from the imperial residence at Tsarskoye Selo, where Pushkin, Zhukovsky, and Alexandra Rosset were staying. Princess Vasilchikov's home swarmed with servants, guests, and hangers-on. In particular, there was a group of little old women who had been living in their benefactress' shadow for years, housed and fed, doing nothing. After all, the greatness of a family was measured by the number of parasites it could maintain.

Every morning, Gogol struggled to teach the Princess' son—a retarded boy with long legs and globular eyes—to read. Holding the child on his knees, he would point to the pictures in a book and say, "There, Vasenka, that's a sheep—baaa, baaa! And there's a dog— woof, woof!" Vasenka got it all backward. And Gogol patiently began again.[13] As soon as the lesson was over, he rushed to his manuscript.

Sometimes he would go to see the Princess' favorite parasite, old Alexandra Stepanovna. In the low-ceilinged room furnished with a sofa, a few armchairs, a round table with a red cotton cloth, and a big lamp with a green shade, Alexandra Stepanovna's cronies sat around her, as ancient, wrinkled, and shrunken as herself, knitting stockings. They would invite Gogol to sit down and read them what he had written. One evening, as he was settling down before his audience, the Princess' nephew, young Count Sollogub, came in and asked if he might listen. He was wearing the uniform of the students of the University of Dorpat, fancied himself a versifier, and affected an air of worldly superiority.

"I lay back in my armchair," he wrote in his *Recollections,* "and began to listen. The little old women began moving their needles again. With the reader's first words, I sat bolt upright, stung to attention, wondering, amazed. . . . He was reading a description of a Ukrainian night: 'Do you know the Ukrainian night? Ah, no, the Ukrainian night, you don't know it! . . .' He gave such a distinct color to his text, by his informal manner of speaking and an indefinable ironic implication that was never quite realized but trembled in his voice and shaded his original and alert features! His gray eyes smiled as he shook his head, tossing back the hair falling over his forehead. . . . Suddenly he exclaimed, 'But that's not the way to dance the *hopak!'* The old parasites blurted out, 'What do you mean, that's not the way?' They thought the reader was talking to them. He smiled and continued the monologue of the drunken muzhik. I confess I was stupefied, devastated. When he finished reading, I flung myself upon him and wept. The young man's name was Nikolai Vasilyevich Gogol."

Gogol read passages from his tales at Alexandra Rosset's home too, and with the same success. "I found him gauche, shy, and melancholy,"[14] she wrote in her diary. He, on the other hand, was subjugated by the girl's grace, sweetness, and spontaneity. She was not disturbing or frightening, he thought, like the other creatures of her sex. With her he could relax a little. He could even see how people could fall in love with her. Not physically, of course; how disgusting! But with the heart, with the mind. Besides, she was soon going to be married, to a young diplomat named Smirnov. The emperor had already given his consent. Smirnov was rich but of less than average intelligence. Pushkin thought the marriage foolish. He, too, most likely, cherished tender feelings for the empress' maid of honor.

Gogol often went for a walk along the lanes of Pavlovsk, and on to Tsarskoye Selo. The park surrounding the imperial residence, with its heavy foliage, green and velvety lawns, marble statues, lake, swans, bridges, artificial ruins, and its old rococo chateau, invited daydreams. This walker's gaze, however, was not tempted by such conventional marvels. He was looking for one thing only, as he rounded every bend: a little man armed with a stick, wearing a high top hat, and striding energetically along.

At the sight of Pushkin, Gogol knew he had not wasted his day. An open friendship grew between the two men. Zhukovsky often joined them; they talked about their work, their plans. Alexandra Rosset wrote in her diary, "Zhukovsky is triumphant, having captured the mulish Khokhol. . . . I promised Pushkin to scold the poor Khokhol if he becomes too mournful in North Palmyra, where the sun always looks so sickly. Pushkin said that the northern summer is a caricature of a southern winter. They teased Gogol so much about his shyness and uncouthness, that at last they put him at his ease."[15]

Gogol was so proud of his new friendship with Pushkin that he wanted to tell all his friends about it. But perhaps they would take him for a name-dropping braggart. He instantly conceived a scheme. With his predilection for the most complicated solution possible, he told Pushkin that he had no fixed address in St. Petersburg and asked if he could have his mail sent to the poet's home. Pushkin was mildly startled, but agreed, and so it was that on July 21, 1831, Gogol was able to inform his mother, with feigned casualness, in the postscript to a letter containing no mention of his association with Pushkin, "Write to me in care of Pushkin, at Tsarskoye Selo. Don't forget to write on the envelope, 'To His High Nobility Alexander Sergeyevich Pushkin, for Mr. N. V. Gogol.'" Three days later he repeated his instructions: "Are you sure you have not forgotten the address? In care of Pushkin, at Tsarskoye Selo."

He was sorry to leave Pavlovsk, in mid-August, for St. Petersburg, where the proofs of the first volume of *Evenings on a Farm* were awaiting him. On Pletnyev's advice he had entrusted the manuscript to a printer on Bolshaya Morskaya Street. In a frenzy of impatience, he went to the print shop to oversee the work. Ah, if only his new friend Pushkin could be at his side! To make him a partner in his joy, he wrote to Tsarskoye Selo:

"The strangest thing of all was my visit to the printer's. The moment I opened the door, the typesetters, seeing me, began to snicker, turning toward the wall. I was somewhat taken aback and asked the man who set up the pages for an explanation. He, trying to evade the question, finally told me! 'The little stories you were good enough to send us from Pavlovsk to be printed are very funny and have greatly amused the typesetters.' From this I concluded that I was an author entirely to the taste of the common people."[16]

The typesetter episode may have been true, or it may have been made up by Gogol as a preparatory anecdote for his entrance into the world of letters. Perhaps he surprised a smile as he stepped into the workshop, and in an instant the whole fable was complete in his head. He ended his letter with his wishes for the happiness of Mrs. Pushkin, whom he inadvertently named Nadezhda Nikolayevna. "Your Nadezhda Nikolayevna, or in other words my Natalya Nikolayevna, thanks you for your kind regards," Pushkin replied. And he added, "I congratulate you upon your first triumph: the typesetters' snorts of laughter and the explanation of the page setter."

St. Petersburg was still half empty, but the cholera epidemic seemed to have abated. Rain and wind: autumn came early. There was even a hint of flood. The streets and passages of the Meshchansky district disappeared under a shallow layer of water. The rain continued to fall.

As everyone knows, bad weather is an incitement to read. So, Gogol thought, the conditions for the launching of *Evenings on a Farm* were ideal. As soon as he could obtain a complete set of proofs, he sent them to Pushkin for his opinion. The poet read them at one sitting and exploded with enthusiasm.

"I have just read *Evenings on a Farm,*" he wrote in late August 1831 to Voyekov, editor in chief of the *Literary Supplement* to *The Russian Veteran.* "I find them entrancing. Now, there is real gaiety, sincere and spontaneous, without affectation or gimmickry! And what poetry, too, in places! What sensitivity! It is all so new in our literature that I cannot believe my eyes. I am told that when the author went to the shop where they were working on *Evenings,* the typesetters burst out laughing and chuckling in front of him. The page setter explained their attitude by saying they had nearly died of laughter setting up his text. Molière and Fielding would have been happy to divert their typesetters as much. I congratulate the public upon the appearance of a frankly happy book, and I wish the author more success, with all my heart. But for heaven's sake defend him if the journalists, as is their usual practice, criticize the *impropriety* of his expressions, his want of *taste,* etc. It is high time the *précieuses ridicules* of our Russian literature got their comeuppance!"

At last, early in September 1831, St. Petersburg became an animated and elegant city again, and the book came off the presses. Its full title was *Evenings on a Farm near Dikanka,* "tales published by Rudy Panko, beekeeper." Gogol made the rounds of the booksellers to negotiate the commissions he would allow them for each copy sold, signed his press copies, and waited. The first echoes were so eulogistic that, sending a dedicated copy to his mother on September 19, he wrote:

"Here is the fruit of my leisure. Everyone here has liked it, beginning with the empress; I hope you, too, will derive some pleasure from it; that in itself will be enough to make me happy. Keep well and cheerful, as though every day of your life were a holiday."

He proceeded coolly to beg his sister Marya to send additional material for the second volume of *Evenings:*

"You recall, dear sister, how happy you were when you began to collect Little Russian tales and songs for me! Unfortunately, you didn't keep it up. Couldn't you begin again? I have the most urgent need of more."[17]

His concern for detail drove him to ask Marya to buy him some old Ukrainian costumes in the country: "I remember very clearly that we once saw, in our church, a girl wearing the old-fashioned costume. I am sure she would be glad to sell it. If you find a hat or some clothes of some far-off period in muzhik's hut that are at all unusual, buy them even if they are torn. . . . Pack it all up in a trunk or case and send it to me the first chance you have."[18]

Now he was certain he had found his true vocation. No more worries for the future. Fame would lead to fortune. Why did his mother persist in fussing about him? Soon he would no longer be asking her for money; it would be his turn to provide for her! In earnest of his intentions, he sent her a reticule and some gloves, and a bracelet and belt buckle to Marya. He asked them which colors suited their complexions best, and what size shoes they wore. "I need to know just in case, especially if I have any extra money."[19]

He also wrote, "For the moment, the Almighty has sent Andrey Andreyevich [Troshchinsky] to help you; next year He may give that privilege to me; and so you see we must be cheerful and lively, and work, and while we work, enjoy ourselves as much as possible."[20]

The second volume of *Evenings on a Farm* reached the booksellers in March 1832, and it enhanced the author's renown. "The devil take me if I'm not very nearly in seventh heaven," he wrote his friend Danilevsky in the Caucasus.[21]

The critics were divided. The young Belinsky, who did not yet have a column in any paper, trumpeted his admiration to the four winds: "What wit, what gaiety, what poetry, what a sense of the people!"[22] Nadezhdin wrote, in *The Telescope,* "As yet, no one has succeeded in portraying the customs of the Ukraine in as lively and winning a manner as the good beekeeper Rudy Panko." But the Big Three were not amused. In the Moscow *Telegraph,* Polevoy, defender of Hugoesque, Walter Scott romanticism, addressed himself to the author thus: "All your stories are so incoherent that, notwithstanding the flavorful details springing visibly from folk tradition, it is difficult to read on to the end. The wish to impose a Little Russian tone upon your writings has so thickened your tongue that it is often impossible to seize your meaning." In the *Northern Bee,* Ushakov complained that Gogol's descriptions were "lacking in accuracy, scope, and originality." In *The Reading Library,* Senkovsky claimed that both volumes formed one montonous whole, that the language was improper, even coarse, and that this type of literature was designed for a public "of a level inferior even to that of Paul de Kock."

But Pushkin had warned his young colleague that these vivid stories would shock some of the more "refined" members of society. A true storyteller, he had said, should listen to the voices of those who liked to read stories, not those who made a profession of dissecting them. So it was that Gogol, who had suffered so acutely at the critics' hands after the publication of *Hans Kuechelgarten,* now received the digs and pricks of the press with a serene and ironic smile. As though by chance, his literary enemies were the very ones who were forever reviling Pushkin. Some opprobrium, when it comes from the mire, is more precious than praise. As he went from bookseller to bookseller, he thought of the time, not so very long past, when he had brooded over the unsold sheets of his poem sleeping upon the shelves. What a change there had been since then, in his life! Now the booksellers welcomed him with broad smiles. He watched the stacks of *Evenings* dwindling day by day. The first edition, which he had set at twelve hundred copies, would be sold out in a few weeks. Even so, he felt that his work was still imperfect and that, to please God, he must aim higher.

5. *Evenings on a Farm near Dikanka*

When he came to ask himself what had led him to write a book, Gogol
was forced to admit that the decision was dictated chiefly by his need of
money, and he saw writing as a means of supplementing his income. The
same consideration had motivated his choice of subject and form: since
Ukrainian regional literature was in vogue and since, through his family,
he could obtain much previously unpublished lore, then this was the vein
he should mine to the exclusion of all others. Nevertheless, the moment
he began work on *Evenings on a Farm,* the enthusiasm of the artist
swept away the cool calculations of the businessman. He had imagined
he was going to slog away at a rather boring commission, and he found,
instead, that the best part of his day was the hours he spent with his fictitious characters. Alone in a chilly and sullen St. Petersburg, he luxuri-
ated in his re-creation of the rich earth of the sun-bathed Ukraine, the
lazy peasants—a whole universe of good health, easy life, and legend.
In his *Confession of an Author* he wrote:

"The merriment observed in my early works corresponded to a certain
spiritual need. I was subject to fits of melancholy which I could not even
explain to myself and which may have originated in my poor health. To
distract myself, I imagined every conceivable kind of funny story. I
dreamed up droll characters and figures out of thin air and purposely
placed them in the most comical circumstances, with never a thought
why I was doing it or what profit I could make from it. It was youth that
pushed me—youth, which, as everybody knows, never asks itself questions."

The eight tales in *Evenings on a Farm* swarm with comic incidents, it is true, but they also contain terrifying, hallucinating pages—not the work of an author whose sole aim is to amuse himself. It would seem that the hearty laughter of one passage is there only to offset the anguish in which Gogol indulges us—and himself—in another. Walking side by side with his heroes, he feels the need to jest like a child who reassures himself by laughing in the dark. The greater the fear, the louder the laugh. It is this mixture of superstitious dread and peasant joy that gives the work its particular flavor.

Nearly all the protagonists of *Evenings on a Farm* are painted with a palette knife in lurid hues. There are old, truculent, sententious Cossacks, tough young fellows ogling the girls, women past their prime who have the whip hand of their husbands and deceive them too, popes' sons, sacristans, witches, drunkards, innocents, buffoons, devils. The devil, moreover, is as much a member of the village as any of the other inhabitants. He is the same size as they are, and cut from the same cloth; the only difference is that he has more power and his thoughts are evil. In some cases he can be outwitted; in others it's you who lose, and then the jovial devilry changes into a life-and-death struggle between the Christian credo and the forces of darkness. Some stories, such as "The Fair at Sorochinsk," "The Lost Letter," and "A Bewitched Place," are no more than picturesque entertainments; with "A May Night" and "Christmas Eve," however, the negative powers enter the lists. One step farther into the supernatural and we arrive at the insane witchcraft of "St. John's Eve" and "A Terrible Vengeance."

In "St. John's Eve," poor Petro, who is in love with fair Pidorka and hasn't enough money to marry her, makes a pact with the devil: a treasure will be his if he sacrifices a child at the witches' Sabbath. The child produced by the witch is none other than his betrothed's little brother. Petro tries to back out, but the allure of gold is too great. For the love of Pidorka, he cuts off the little boy's head; grotesque monsters burst out cackling all around him, the witch laps up the fresh blood like a she-wolf; and the murderer, now rich, marries the girl of his dreams, but they are never to know a moment's peace.

Still more disturbing is "A Terrible Vengeance," with its old sorcerer —a traitor to his country; murderer of his wife, son-in-law, and grandson; and lover of his daughter, whom he also kills in the end. He goes to find a pious hermit and asks him to pray for his condemned soul, but the letters in the holy book drip blood and the good man refuses in terror to intercede with God for such a monstrous sinner, so the sorcerer murders the hermit too. From beginning to end the story is nothing but battle, ruse, premonitory dreams, magic ritual, and bloodless corpses rising from their graves with a long wail, "I'm suffocating, suffocating!" Evil has no limits here. Beneath the seemingly orderly face of nature writhe the forces of primal chaos.

But just as the author is naturally led to combine the burlesque and the horrifying, so he cannot launch into fantasy except from a spring-board of solid reality. Indeed, the more irrational the tale, the greater his need to fill it with authentic detail. Before setting to work, he con-scientiously read all sorts of books on the Ukraine—books by Kotlyar-evsky, Kvitka-Osnovyanenko, Artemovsky-Gulyak; he pored over lin-guistic and ethnographic studies of the southern provinces; he dug into his father's jolly comedies; he skimmed treatises on magic; he reviewed his *Hold-All Notebook* to extract the particulars supplied by his mother and sister; he examined the old gowns, bonnets, and fichus they had sent him. This mass of data and palpable objects allayed his anxiety about the credibility of his poetic lie. Even if he did not use them all, these documents served to build a solid foundation beneath his feet. Imagining something out of nothing was tantamount, for him, to throwing himself off a cliff. Fear clutched him at the very thought. Quick, quick: mate-rial! He could never find it in himself. He seems to have perceived life clearly only through other people. In his *Confession of an Author* he wrote: "I have never created anything out of my own imagination. It is an ability I have never possessed. I succeeded only when I could draw upon reality, using information available to me."

He did not invent even the subjects of his tales. He took them from traditional folklore and embellished them in his own way. Let others give him the canvas and they would see how magnificently he could embroider it!

His treatment of this raw material was amazingly complex. Armed with his magnifying glass, he isolated a detail—one feature of a face, dress, personality—which then leaped into the foreground. Proceeding thus with photographic precision, he arrived at hallucinatory distortion. The harder he tried to be exact, the further he receded from the truth. His fondness for simile accentuated the gap. When he mounted a meta-phor, it carried him a thousand leagues. Some were quaint or touching; others broke the story's charm. He didn't care: nothing intrigued Gogol more than to veer off the main road and lose himself in the byways.

Notwithstanding the systematic transformation that was characteristic of his art, it was the "realism" of *Evenings on a Farm* that first surprised and delighted his readers. To them, the minuteness of the description was proof of its authenticity. Reading the tales of Rudy Panko, they felt that they were hearing an incredible fantasy and, at the same time, learning about Ukrainian customs.

This author's Ukraine, moreover, is extremely reassuring. Completely engrossed in his picturesqueness and phantasmagoria, he blithely ignored the problem of serfdom. The abuses of autocracy did not shock him in the slightest; the wretchedness of the peasantry was none of his concern. One closed the book without a single social problem in one's mind.

As for the "triviality" of certain passages, by which some critics were annoyed: Gogol seems to have counterbalanced it intentionally with all the lyricism of which he was capable. There again we see the author's duality: not only did he combine panic and laughter, real and supernatural; he also switched from the rowdy and crude to quite unpredictable flights of poetry. Suddenly a passage in the grand manner erupts at the beginning of a chapter; a prose poem drifts through a farce:

"Divine night! Enchanting night! Immobile and inspired, the gloom-filled forests cast gigantic shadows before them. Silence and peace reign above the ponds. Their chill, dark waters are mournfully imprisoned between dark green garden walls. The virginal thickets of wild cherry and plum timidly dip their roots in the icy damp of the spring, and their foliage can be heard to murmur, near and then far away, as though it became angry and chiding whenever the night breezes crept flirting up to steal a kiss. . . . Infinite, marvelous spaces open up in the sky, and, in the soul, silver visions rise in hosts from the depths. Divine night! Enchanting night!"[1]

Note, however, that this painting of the Ukrainian night is not the prelude to a love scene, as might be expected, but to the stammerings and staggerings of a drunken peasant trying to dance a *hopak*.

When he wishes to suggest the beauty of some natural scene, Gogol is often swept away by his inspiration and, in his exaggeration, reverts to rhetoric. For example, speaking of a pond at night, he wrote: "Like some feeble old man, it clasped the dark and distant sky in its cold embrace and covered with icy kisses the stars of fire, which turned pale in the tepid night air as though they had sensed the approach of the dazzling ascension of the queen of night."[2] Here is a river: "It is capricious as a girl in those intoxicating hours when the faithful mirror reflects her features modeled in pride and light, her shoulders white as lilies, her marble throat shadowed by the dark wave of chestnut tresses. Just as the beauty disdainfully throws off one set of finery only to don another, following her never-ending whim, so does the river alter almost annually its course, choosing for itself a different channel and surrounding itself with new and varied scenes."[3]

Or take the Dnieper boiling in a storm: "The tall waves roar, striking the foot of the mountains and falling back, flashing and moaning, weeping and sobbing. So the old Cossack mother laments, watching her son set off to war. Valiant and reckless, he moves forward on his black horse, fist on hip and bonnet stuck rakishly askew on his head; she, meanwhile, runs sobbing after him, clutches at his stirrup, snatches at the bit, twists her hands, and weeps hot tears."[4]

It is in the portrayal of female characters that the author appears most prolix and uncomfortable, however. Paraska, in "The Fair at Soro- chinsk," is "a pretty child with a round face, her eyebrows arching evenly above her hazel eyes, and little pink lips in a careless smile." Another Cossack has "fresh cheeks tinted like a poppy of the most deli- cate pink when, bathed in the dew of the Lord, it is set alight, lifting up its petals and looking its best to face the rising sun; her eyebrows are like the black laces girls buy nowadays to string crosses and coins on; . . . her little mouth seems created to exhale the song of the nightingale."[5] Hannah, in "A May Night," has "bright eyes shining with welcome in the semidarkness, like little stars." Oksana, in "Christmas Eve," admires her reflection in the mirror and sighs, "Can it be that my black eyebrows and my eyes are so beautiful that there are none like them in all the world?"

Every one of these village beauties is seventeen years old and has jet-black irises, coral lips, and pearly teeth. Idealized out of sight by an author who has had little contact with women, they are the cold, smooth, precious, and mysterious objects for which young men damn themselves. Even the speech of these polished dolls is conventional. It is only the old, in *Evenings on a Farm,* who have living faces and talk like real Ukrainian peasants. One, speaking of women, exclaims, "God in Heaven, what have we done to you, poor sinners that we are, to de- serve this scourge? As if there weren't enough dirt of every kind here on earth, without you having to create women too!"[6]

That uncharitable sentence might be the subtitle of the last story but one in the collection, *Ivan Fyodorovich Shponka and His Aunt.* Unlike the other stories, this one is neither folklore nor fantasy. It has a sharpness of style and casual irony of observation that make it an introduction to the whole world of petty people, trivial drama, and unexalted oddity. In it, perhaps for the first time, the author shows us what nonentities some lives are, however much God made them. The subject of his scrutiny here is a gray, colorless little person, a character in an inside-out novel: instead of standing out in relief, everything in him recedes. He is less than a man—an anti-hero. The story relates the torments of a retired soldier, now a landowner, whose aunt wants to marry him off by force to a blond tub of lard living in the neighborhood. Ivan Fyodorovich is a weakling, a dreamer. His aunt, Vasilyevka Karpovna, is a robust and decided spinster who intimidates him: "It seemed that nature had committed an unpardonable error in assigning her a dark brown dress with little ruffles to wear, . . . when she was made for dragoons' mustaches and cavalry boots." Ivan Fyodorovich is hauled off by this redoubtable figure to meet his intended, and, that night, he has a nightmare.

"He dreamed that he was already married, and everything in the little house was most peculiar, extraordinary. In his room, in the place of a single bed, there was a double bed. His wife was sitting on a chair. He felt so odd, he didn't know how to speak to her, what to say to her, and then he saw that she had the head of a goose. Turning around by chance, he saw another woman, and she, too, had the head of a goose. He looked in another direction and saw a third. He glanced behind him, and there was a fourth! He was panic-stricken. He ran into the garden. It was terribly hot there. He took off his hat, and what did he see? There was a woman inside the hat. Perspiration streamed down his face. He went to pull a handkerchief from his pocket and found still another woman inside it. He pulled a cotton plug from his ear, and behind it there was a woman. He began hopping up and down. His aunt looked at him and solemnly declared, 'Yes, you'll have to hop now, because you're a married man.' He ran toward her. Too late; she had already changed into a church steeple. He felt himself being pulled up to the top by a rope. 'Who is pulling me?' he whimpered. 'It's I, your wife, pulling you up there, because you're such a dumbbell.' 'No, I'm not a bell, I am Ivan Fyodorovich!' he cried. 'Yes, you are a bell!' said Colonel P. of an infantry regiment, who was walking by. Then he dreamed that his wife was not a human being at all, but a kind of woolen material. He went into a shop in Mogilev. 'What material do you wish?' the salesman asked, and added, 'Try some wife, that is the most fashionable fabric now. Very durable! Everyone is having coats made of it these days.' The shopkeeper measured and cut off his wife. Ivan Fyodorovich took it under his arm and went to a Jewish tailor. 'No, no,' said the Jew, 'it's very poor stuff. Nobody is using that for coats any more. . . .'"

Was Ivan Fyodorovich's nightmare a comic transposition of the author's sick fear of the fair sex? That might be a presumptuous affirmation; yet he was undeniably paralyzed by the female phenomenon. Let a woman be young and pretty, and he could neither describe her in a story nor approach her in reality. At the time, however, none of his readers noticed the artificiality of the young lovers in *Evenings on a Farm*. There was the spiciness of the other characters—gossips, deacons, sorcerers, devils, distillers, and regimental sergeants—to enliven the insipid brew of rustic idyls. The readers enjoyed themselves enormously and were pleasantly terrified by this comic opera with the brightly colored costumes. There was local color in superabundance: every character's name was a joke, the odors of Ukrainian cooking— poppy-seed cakes and cheese patties—tickled the nose; the rough language peppered with dialect, droll diminutives, and Little Russian proverbs was in itself a guarantee of success. To be sure, some sentences are too long, and there are clumsy incidents, an excess of epithet, artificial lyricism, psychological inconsistency—but in some inexplicable way these very failings add to the charm of the book.

Encouraged by his readers' response, Gogol might have become a strictly regional author, grinding out *Evenings on a Farm* until he had exhausted the resources of Ukrainian folklore. The temptation was strong. But two months after *Evenings* went on sale, Pushkin published his *Byelkin's Tales,* a masterpiece of narrative conciseness and streamlining. The sentences were short and vivid, the vocabulary succinct; there were no metaphors; the story galloped from verb to verb; the author never showed himself and never explained his characters. Seen from without, they revealed themselves to us through their actions alone. In Gogol, everything was subjective and fanciful; in Pushkin, everything was objective and real.

The public which adored *Evenings on a Farm* was disappointed by *Byelkin's Tales,* mistaking their simplicity for paucity. Gogol, on the other hand, knelt down and worshiped. Once again, he told himself, Pushkin had shown him the way. He would not change his genre or style, of course, because his way of telling stories was attuned to his very heartbeat and the temperature of his blood. But perhaps he would be well advised to concern himself with less extravagant characters than the churls and termagants of the Ukraine.

While debating his literary future with himself, he candidly reveled in his new fame. Now everybody knew that the pseudonym of "Rudy Panko" hid a certain Gogol.

"In the future," he wrote to his mother, on February 6, 1832, "address your letters in the name of Gogol alone, for the second part of my family name has been mislaid somewhere along the way. Perhaps somebody picked it up on the highroad and is now wearing it as his own. In any case, nobody knows me by the name of Yanovsky any more. . . ."

On Friday, February 19, 1832, he and all the other men of letters of the capital attended a dinner party given by Smirdin the bookseller to celebrate the opening of his new shop, on the Nevsky Prospect. The table was set up in the big room with book-lined walls. Eighteen places were laid. The invitation was for six o'clock: Pushkin was there, Zhukovsky, the old fabulist Krylov, Dmitryev, Batyushkov, Bulgarin, Grech. The first toast was drunk to the emperor and was followed by a resounding hurrah. Champagne toasts followed, to the health of Krylov, Zhukovsky, Pushkin, and others. At one point, Pushkin, seeing his sworn enemies Grech and Bulgarin seated on either side of Semyonov the censor, called over, "Hey, Semyonov, you're like Christ on Golgotha!" Several guests laughed; Bulgarin and Grech scowled; but the incident was soon forgotten.[7] Eating and drinking among his illustrious colleagues, Gogol must have pinched himself to make certain he was really awake. He came home very late, with fuddled brain and jubilant heart.

In spite of the money from the sale of *Evenings on a Farm*—for which booksellers gave him a few rubles on every copy sold—his material circumstances could hardly be said to have improved. He was living near the Kokushkin Bridge in an icy and uncomfortable attic. As in the past, he sometimes assembled his friends to partake of a Ukrainian supper cooked by Yakim. One of the guests wrote in his diary, "I went to a dinner at Gogol-Yanovsky's[8]; he is the author of the jolly tales of the beekeeper Rudy Panko. He is a pleasant young man of twenty-three, but there is something deceitful in his physiognomy that puts one on one's guard. I met there some ten Little Russians, nearly all former pupils of the Nyezhin School."[9]

The presence of Gogol's best friend, Danilevsky, would have ensured the success of these fraternal feasts. But Danilevsky was still in the Caucasus.[10] Enamored of the very pretty Emily Alexandrovna Klingenberg, he wrote in his letters such fiery descriptions of his passion that Gogol, much as he himself tended to exaggerate, urged him to moderate his fervor. He who had never experienced any form of involvement proceeded to set out the characteristics of genuine love for his friend:

"Love before marriage is wonderful, exalting, terrifying, and totally inexplicable," he wrote to Danilevsky. "But he who has known no other form of emotion than this has known, at best, a spark, an attempt at love. . . . The second part of the book, however (or rather the book itself, the first part being only a prologue), is as a sea of calm delight, more clearly perceived with every passing day, and with every passing day more appreciatively savored, in astonishment to think that it had flowed so long unseen. . . . Love before marriage is like the verse of Yasykov."[11] Stirring and full of heat, it subjugates the senses. Love after marriage is the poetry of Pushkin: it does not immediately captivate you, but the more you read it, the deeper it goes, growing into an ocean. . . ."[12]

He later confessed to Danilevsky: "I fully understand, and even feel the state you are in, although I personally, heaven be thanked, have never known it. I say heaven be thanked, for such fire would have reduced me to ashes in a trice. . . . Fortunately, my strong will has twice dissuaded me from glancing into the abyss."[13]

Apropos, the beginning of 1832 was marked for Gogol by two weddings, that of his friend Alexandra Rosset, the "celestial imp," who married the rich and uninteresting Smirnov; and that of his sister Marya, who married a man called Trushkovsky, of Polish origin, a surveyor by trade, of less than modest means. The first of these saddened him somewhat, for he nursed a deep platonic affection for the brilliant maid of honor. And the second worried him, or at least the patriarch in him.

Marya Ivanovna, who had hoped her daughter would make a good match, could not hide her disappointment. Gogol considered that a man's true wealth lay in his brain; and on the strength of his vast experience, he gave his mother and the young fiancée lessons in domestic economy. First of all, the ceremony itself must be kept to an absolute minimum. "I have always disliked these solemnities and nuptial receptions," he wrote. "If I had decided to wed, my wife would have seen no one at all for at least two weeks."[14] He was asked to buy cloth and handkerchiefs for the trousseau. Pointless expenditure: "The fiancé, you say, is not a fool, and will therefore attach no importance to such trivia. . . . Remind my sister that she must display great frugality and give up many personal gratifications. She has elected this fate of her own free will!" In the end, scratching together the little money he had managed to save, Gogol sent five rubles toward the expenses of the new household. It was a big sum for someone in his circumstances, and it pleased him mightily to wave so much money in his family's face. To his mother, who was urging him to call upon somebody named Bagreyev, an influential personage "who could be useful to him," he haughtily replied:

"You persist, it seems to me, in looking upon me as a beggar for whom anyone with a little name and a few connections can do good. I beg you not to concern yourself with this. My road lies straight before me and I confess I do not see what good any man could do for me. I trust and hope only in God."[15]

This was just another swagger, for at the time he was eagerly seeking the company of highly placed persons to consolidate his budding fame. Besides, two months earlier this enemy of social climbing and patronage was proudly writing to his mother, when she complained of postal delays:

"Tell the postmaster of Poltava that I saw Prince Golitsyn a few days ago and complained to him about the wretched state of the mail. He immediately passed on my remarks to Bulgakov, the postmaster general. But I asked Bulgakov not to call the Poltava office to account until you yourself have given me more information about the matter."[16]

Thus, boasting of his connections while pretending to scorn them, lusting for vulgar fame while claiming to aspire only to the glory of God, he whirled about in the coils of his contradictory personality and lied to everyone in the hope that he could ultimately deceive himself with his own fabrications.

6. Marking Time

In St. Petersburg spring was dragging along, cold and sullen. Gogol, suffering from solar deprivation, dreamed nostalgically of the Ukraine. He suddenly decided to spend his summer at Vasilyevka. On the way, he could stop at Moscow, where *Evenings on a Farm* had been very successful, and make a few useful friends. At the beginning of a literary career, no support, no ally could be neglected. With two or three partisans in all the big cities, his future would be assured. He applied for a leave of absence from the Patriotic Institute and set out, with Yakim, toward the end of June 1832.

The stagecoach trip, under a driving rain, exhausted him. Moscow welcomed him with peals of bells. Throat contracted with emotion, he stared at the sights: the churches, palaces, Red Square, and the walls of the Kremlin with their swallowtail crenelations. He found it much more barbaric, and much gayer, than the noble official architecture of the capital. Even the people in the streets here looked happy and free, wonderfully Russian in color, noise, and variety. Shivering and weak, he staggered into the hotel and prepared to be ill. But the thought of all those people waiting to welcome him with open arms overcame his fear of a chill. He was like an actor with stage fright.

The first person he met was the celebrated historian and journalist Pogodin, former director of the Moscow *Messenger*. Heavily built, broad-lipped, and bearish in manner, Pogodin took Gogol under his wing. They discussed the history of the Ukraine, and Gogol told how the little girls at the Patriotic Institute loved him because he replaced

deadly chronology by an animated re-creation of the past. To hear him
talk, he had invented an entirely new approach to history. He discoursed on his teaching methods so confidently that his listener, although
himself an academic, sat gaping. However, when Pogodin asked to see
some of the pupils' exercise books so he could judge how well they had
digested the course, Gogol eluded the question, embarrassed.

Later they went to visit the poet and theater critic Sergey Timofeyevich Aksakov,[1] who lived on Afanasyevsky Street in the Arbat district.
Turning up unannounced, they found Aksakov in shirt sleeves playing
cards with a group of friends. Eyes looked up. "And here is Nikolai
Vasilyevich Gogol!" Pogodin cried triumphantly. There was a moment
of confusion. Aksakov's son Konstantin, a great admirer of *Evenings on
a Farm,* rushed up to Gogol and heaped compliments upon him, while
Aksakov himself, with an apology, sat down again to finish his game. As
he played, the master of the house observed his guest out of the corner
of his eye: "In those days," he wrote, "Gogol's outward appearance . . . was hardly prepossessing: a tuft of hair at the summit of his
skull, the rest cut short at the temples, neither beard nor mustache, and
a stiff shirt collar, too high—gave him a mild resemblance to some
crafty Ukrainian. His dress showed pretensions to elegance. I recall
that he wore a striped vest of rather loud hue, with a heavy chain across
it." After he left, those present came to the unanimous conclusion that
he had made an "unfavorable and unpleasant impression." Even young
Konstantin Aksakov, who had gone up to him so enthusiastically, deplored "his haughty airs, scornful and unsociable."[2]

A few days later, Gogol returned early one morning to see Aksakov,
who had promised to introduce him to Zagoskin, an author of historical
novels which were very popular just then. This time, to set the young
writer at ease, Aksakov himself told him how much he had enjoyed
Evenings on a Farm. But Gogol remained totally aloof. "There was
something intimidating about him," wrote Aksakov, "which prevented
me from opening myself in my usual way." They went outside and
walked in the direction of Zagoskin's home. As they went along, Gogol
sighed and lagged behind, complaining that he was suffering from
various incurable afflictions. "I looked at him in surprise, for he seemed
perfectly healthy to me," Aksakov wrote; "and I asked him, 'But exactly what is the matter with you?' He answered evasively and I gathered that the seat of his ailment was somewhere in the intestines. Then
we began talking of Zagoskin. Gogol praised the alacrity of his pen,

but remarked that he was not writing what he should, especially for the theater. I imprudently replied that it was difficult for us to write anything else because our world was so bleak and policed, so conventional and empty, that even its follies could not raise a laugh. He looked at me sharply and said, 'That is not true! The comic is hiding everywhere, but we do not see it any longer, because we have grown used to it! Let an author with real talent put it in his writings or on the stage, and we shall split our sides laughing and wonder how it was we never saw so much that was comical before. . . .' As we talked, I noticed that he seemed to take a particular interest in Russian comedy and to have some original ideas on the subject."[3]

Zagoskin welcomed Gogol with a loud rush, kissed him three times, whacked him on the back, vowed his admiration and eternal friendship, and, without pausing for breath, began talking about himself, his historical research, his discoveries in the archives, his travels, his plans, his readings, his collection of snuffboxes. His dazed guests soon beat a retreat. But Gogol still had not had his fill of intellectual lights. He also saw Ivan Ivanovich Dmitryev, the "patriarch of Russian poetry," a withered old gentleman, elegant and courteous; and, last but not least, the famous actor Shchepkin, who preached "anti-theatrical theater."

Mikhail Semyonovich Shchepkin had once been a household serf in the Volkenstein family; his masters had given him permission to study and then to act in plays at Kursk and Poltava. After every performance he would don his livery again and serve supper to their lordships. He was so successful as an actor, however, that at the age of thirty, thanks to a subscription initiated by Repnin, the governor general, he was able to purchase his freedom, for ten thousand rubles. Since that date, he had triumphed in every great theater of Russia. Gogol had applauded him in St. Petersburg. What a stroke it would be if this universally admired man would consent to act in one of his plays! He had not yet written any, true, but it might happen any day. He should prepare the way now. By wonderful coincidence, Shchepkin was also a Little Russian! One evening when the actor was giving a dinner for twenty-five guests, he looked through the dining-room doors, which had been left open, and saw an undistinguished-looking young man arguing with the servants in the antechamber. Suddenly the stranger burst into the room and joyfully intoned the opening lines of a Ukrainian song. Then he introduced himself. A "country": Nikolai Gogol. Shchepkin, who had read *Evenings on a Farm,* burst out laughing and asked the newcomer to be seated. Conversation resumed, noisy and gay. Between glasses of wine, the master of the house advised his guest to write for the theater. Gogol did not say no. No doubt he was amazed at his own audacity—he who was usually so timid—in walking into this house where he had not been invited. Perhaps it was his new reputation that had given him the confidence. Sometimes he had the impression that someone else was acting in his place. In any event, he had not wasted his time in Moscow. What a lot of new friends, in only ten days!

He continued his journey to Vasilyevka, filled with gratitude toward the ancient capital of the tsars, which had welcomed him so warmly. In comparison with St. Petersburg—a new, severe, cold, European city quartered by broad rectilinear avenues, stuffed with civil servants of every rank, and dominated by the omnipresent tsar—Moscow remained in his memory as the old city of prosperous merchants, nonchalant noblemen, colorful commoners, partriarchal tradition, and good food.

During the first part of his journey he was accompanied by rain. At posting station after posting station the sullen postmasters received him with the same words: "No horses; you'll have to wait!" To pass the time, he nagged at Yakim or read Richardson's *Clarissa Harlowe* sitting on a bench in the main room of the inn. At last, a team; off they went through the mud, with a lurch and jangle of bells. Now and then the traveler would stick his head out the window and peer at the sky. "I had had enough of it," he wrote to Dmitryev, "of that gray northern sky that was almost green, and those pines with their lugubrious and monotonous silhouettes, which had been chasing me all the way from St. Petersburg and Moscow."[4] The low, wooden towns crept past along the road: Podolsk, Tula, Orel, Kursk. The weather grew milder, the sky turned blue, announcing the verdant Ukraine.

On July 17, suffering from stomach troubles, Gogol stopped in Poltava to consult various physicians, who gave various contradictory opinions regarding the cause of his discomfort; convinced that none of them knew anything, he decided he would devise his own treatment. The last stop, in the middle of the vast steppe, was the little town of Mirgorod: whitewashed cottages, unsurfaced dirt roads, haystacks, wooden fences, and puddles of water. The next day he was at Vasilyevka, in the midst of his family.

The reunion was tearful, as he had expected. His mother, who had put on weight but lost none of her vivacity, brooded over him with covetous eye. His grandmother fired a volley of signs of the cross, thanking the Lord for bringing her grandson home safe and sound. His eldest sister, married since April, glowed with happiness as she hung upon the arm of her young husband, Trushkovsky, a handsome and amiable but unenterprising young man who worked in Poltava and lived at Vasilyevka to save money. His other sisters—Anna (eleven), Elizaveta (nine), and Olga (seven)—had grown so big he hardly recognized them. Nothing else had changed. The doors of the old home still creaked as before. The cupboards still gave out the same smell of overripe apples, the table groaned beneath the same preserves and sweets, the same flies and bees hummed above the dishes, the same servants rushed about doing nothing, the same trees bent beneath the weight of their fruit in the orchard, and in the courtyard the same hens and geese gravely perambulated.

Despite the charms of this beloved setting, Gogol was not recovering from his journey. His first meals, copious as always, aggravated his condition. He loved to eat and lost all self-control at the sight of dumplings and cream or cheese flans or marinated mushrooms. Attentive to every internal gurgle, he unblushingly reported on the phases of his digestion to his family, and even by letter to his newly acquired friends.

"Will you believe me if I tell you that the mere sight of a vehicle moving along the road gives me nausea," he wrote to Pogodin on July 20, 1832. "My health is exactly as it was when we met, except that my diarrhaea has stopped and I now have a tendency toward constipation. Sometimes I seem to feel a pain in the liver and back; at other times it is my head that hurts, and my chest too, a little. Such are my sufferings. The days here are beautiful. A mass of fruit, but I'm afraid to eat any. . . ."

Later, to Pogodin again: "I am a little better now, although I still have a pain in the chest and a heaviness in the stomach—perhaps because I am incapable of following a diet. . . . The Ukraine seduces me (with her fruit) continuously, and my stomach is continuously occupied by the digestion of pears and apples."[5]

While fussing over her son, who had lost his appetite in the capital, Marya Ivanovna also began very quickly to tell him of her financial troubles. She had not paid her taxes. She was in debt to half the people she knew. She did not know where she would find the money to educate her daughters. Gogol heard out her lamentations in mingled sorrow and annoyance. The day might come when he would earn enough to take care of the whole family. But until it did, what could he do? He absolutely must persuade the booksellers to buy a second edition of *Evenings on a Farm.*

"A good many landowners hereabouts have tried to get my book by writing to Moscow or St. Petersburg, but could not get hold of a copy anywhere!" he wrote to Pogodin. "Those booksellers are such stupid fools. Don't they realize there is a demand? I would be willing to let them have the whole edition for 3,000 rubles, if they won't give more. That will make less than three rubles per copy for me, whereas they will sell them at fifteen and make a profit of twelve rubles on every copy. . . . I would even accept 1,500 rubles immediately, for I need it badly, and the rest could be paid in two or three months. . . ."[6]

Although he was begging Pogodin to carry out these negotiations for him, he did not really expect anything to come of them in the immediate future. Oh, well, he would take care of things himself when he went back to St. Petersburg. For the moment, all he wanted was to rest and enjoy himself in his family. He rose late, read, puttered in the garden, and then would be suddenly galvanized into action: donning a white overall, he would seize a brush and a bucket of paint and repaint the dining room and the drawing room, decorating the plinths and the door frames with little bouquets of flowers and curlicues.[7] He saw the neighbors, too, and questioned the peasants in search of subjects for more tales like "A Terrible Vengeance" or "Ivan Fyodorovich Shponka and His Aunt." The *Hold-All Notebook* swelled with notes, impressions, outlines, plans. . . . He was full of confidence and preened himself in front of his mother, who was fiercely proud of his success. She knew all the stories in *Evenings on a Farm* by heart. He, though, would smile a very superior smile and say that they were nothing; people would see, very soon, what he was capable of. He liked to talk about his important connections—Pushkin, Zhukovsky, and Krylov, the greatest names in Russian literature—but also the princes, generals, ladies in waiting, ministers. For example, he boasted that he could get his sisters Anna and Elizaveta admitted as boarders to the Patriotic Institute at no cost to the family. The best possible education, at a bargain price. Marya Ivanovna leaped at the proposal, and it was decided that the two girls would go to St. Petersburg with their brother. But the children would have to have a chambermaid. What a pity Yakim wasn't married! But it was not too late to fix that. Having consulted her son, Marya Ivanovna summoned Yakim and, without further preliminaries, suggested that he should marry one of her serving-women, Matryona, whom she had selected just for him on account of her excellent qualities: she was hard-working, orderly, and clean. Of course she did not want to force him into the marriage, she continued, in a tone that would brook no opposition; she was only asking his opinion in the matter. Under his mistress' piercing stare, Yakim, blushing and giggling, swayed back and forth and stammered, "It's all the same to me. . . . Do as you please. . . ." Delighted by his tractability, Marya Ivanovna ordered everything to be prepared for their wedding.[8] Yakim now found himself with a wife he hadn't wanted, and the little girls with a chambermaid in tears.

Proceedings had reached this stage when all the children came down with measles. The departure had to be postponed. The month of August crept past, its hot, dry days vibrating with mosquitoes.

"I am happy here," Gogol wrote to Dmitryev. "I think there is no one in the world who loves nature as passionately as I do. I am afraid to turn away from the country even for an instant; I watch every shimmer of it and discover beauties I never even dreamed of before."[9]

In another letter to the same correspondent: "This land seems to lack nothing! A splendid summer. Wheat, fruit, everything grows in heaps and piles. And yet the people are poor, estates are falling in ruins, debts are unpaid. The lack of means of communication is responsible. That is why the inhabitants have become lazy and somnolent. The landowners are seeing for themselves now that growing wheat and manufacturing spirits are not enough to raise incomes sufficiently and they will have to consider setting up factories and shops."[10]

This was exactly the opinion of Marya Ivanovna, who had already vainly attempted to make a fortune planting tobacco. Her son-in-law, Trushkovsky, was now urging her to install a tannery. A specialist from Austria had offered to set up and direct the works. He guaranteed an income of eight thousand rubles the first year. But twenty-five employees had to be hired. Gogol would have preferred a more modest beginning. His mother, his brother-in-law, and the Austrian expert said he was too cautious. Reluctantly he gave way. What was the good of arguing with them? In any case, after he left they would do as they pleased. Anna and Elizaveta were convalescing, wan and gaunt after weeks in bed. They were being crammed with food to build up their strength.

At last, on September 29, they climbed into the old yellow family rattletrap, tearful and sniffling, with their brother beside them. Yakim and Matryona sat next to the coachman, outside. Marya Ivanovna and her eldest daughter accompanied the travelers as far as Poltava in an open calèche. There the ultimate parting took place. After forty-eight hours at an inn, Gogol, his two little sisters, Yakim, and Matryona all turned northward behind hired horses, while Marya and her daughter went back to Vasilyevka.

The trunks lurched, the axles groaned as though they would snap, Gogol tried to amuse the little girls, who were perpetually in tears. But the stages were long, there were no horses to be had at the stations, and the carriage suffered several injuries before breaking down irrevocably on the road into Kursk, where they had to stay a week for repairs. Gogol impatiently wrote to Pletnyev:

"May God preserve you from ever learning what a long journey is. The worst thing of all is arguing with the foul beasts of stationmasters, who, when the traveler is a mere craftsman like you and me and not a general, do their utmost to humiliate us incessantly and make us poor devils pay for the generals' tongue-lashings."[11]

The little girls, meanwhile, having dried their tears, began to take an interest in their new life. "They are not thinking about home at all any more," Gogol wrote to his mother. "I am astonished that they could forget so quickly. Only Anna still remembers, especially when we have a long wait for fresh horses."[12]

As soon as the carriage was patched up and greased, the journey resumed under a warm sky, through an autumnal landscape.

They reached Moscow on October 18. The pavements were heaped with dead leaves. Hundreds of crows had stationed themselves on the crucifixes and cupolas of the churches. A heavy gray sky was pressing down upon the roofs. Gogol ordered a large umbrella attached to the carriage to supplement the inadequate hood, which was deformed and full of holes.[13] He could not possibly leave town without visiting the friends he had previously acquired and making some new ones. Parking his sisters in a hotel with Yakim and Matryona, he ran to see Aksakov and Zagoskin, became acquainted with Mikhail Maximovich, professor of botany at the university and collector of Ukrainian legends, and Osip Bodyansky, professor of Slavic studies and also an impassioned Ukrainist. Four days of rushing hither and thither, visits and exalting conversations, and he set out for St. Petersburg.

As soon as he reached the capital, Gogol went to the Patriotic Institute to see about having his sisters admitted as boarders. Mrs. Wistinghouse, the director, a hunchbacked old woman who weighed every word, received him coldly and demanded why he had shown no signs of life during the four months of his absence. Besides, enrollment had reached capacity, she said, and the Institute accepted only the daughters of officers. After listening to the apologies and insistent explanations of her petitioner, however, she agreed to pass on his request to the empress. The application, dated November 13, 1832, stipulated that Mr. Gogol would give up his professorial salary, of twelve hundred rubles per annum, if his sisters could be enrolled in the institution.

Pending the supreme decision, Gogol, taking very seriously his role of older brother, selected books for Anna and Elizaveta to read, took them for walks and to the theater and the zoo, and bought them toys and sweets. Matryona was very good with them, but Yakim had begun to drink. His master noticed and gave him a beating. "I hit him very hard," he confessed in a letter to his mother.[14] He had grown very nervous, striking the servant increasingly often and shouting, "I'll smash your face in if you don't stop!"[15]

When he had almost given up hope of finding a place for his sisters, the empress granted his request. He took the little girls to the Institute, where classes had already begun. Matryona had curled their hair and dressed them in the boarders' gown, of chocolate-colored "ladies' cloth." She, too, was in her Sunday best: following the custom, she would remain to serve the young ladies and, being housed and fed in the school, would see Yakim very infrequently. Neither complained much, however: the will of the gentry was sacred.

It seemed most odd to Anna and Elizaveta to have their own brother for a teacher. As they watched him solemnly discoursing behind the podium, they thought he was playing a part he didn't really believe in. If he called on them, however, they were paralyzed by the whisperings and snickerings of the class, and usually refused to answer. He would stay with them after lessons, sharing their tea and polishing off their jam jars, for he had the sweetest tooth of the three. He began coming less and less often to the Institute, however; every other day he would pretend to be ill. After all, he was not being paid. The director magnanimously agreed to keep the little girls on despite their brother's inadequacies.

He moved, about this time, into an apartment on Little Morskaya Street. Assisted only by Yakim, he did all the decorating himself, painting doors, nailing up shelves, cutting and sewing curtains—to save money, but also because he wanted to. There was a steep and gloomy staircase, a tiny entrance hall, and two rooms overlooking the courtyard. One of the rooms was bedroom, dining room, and drawing room, and the other was the study, furnished with sofa, chair, table stacked with books, and high writing desk. The walls were garnished with English steel-plate engravings showing views of Greece, India, and Persia; Gogol was very proud of them. In this modest domain he entertained his friends from the Nyezhin School as before, but now Pushkin came too, and Pletnyev and other new acquaintances, including the young Annenkov, a lynx-eyed observer equally enamored of literature. His usual offering to his guests was very strong tea, sponge cake, and cracknels. He also gave dinner parties now and then, the cost of which was shared by all present. On these occasions he himself would cook curd doughnuts, dumplings and cream, or some other Ukrainian dish whose heavy odor would embalm the room. With his top hair standing on end, a lurid cravat around his neck, and an apron over his stomach, he looked, his friends said, like a rooster perched upon his spurs at the kitchen door.

He had amused himself by giving all his friends the names of French authors. There were Victor Hugo, Alexandre Dumas, and Honoré de Balzac. One bashful young pup was called Sophie Gay;[16] and Annenkov he had baptized, although he never knew why himself, Jules Janin.[17] Yet Gogol cared little for French literature. To him the French were superficial, forever pulling down one government only to replace it by another. They had just proved it again, in July 1830, when they drove out that poor Charles X. The writers of such a nation could not, he thought, be serious. In particular, he made a point of looking down on Molière, criticizing the weakness of his plots, the banality of his denouements. Pushkin, hearing him demolish the author of *The Misanthrope,* indignantly retorted that an author's genius did not lie in the dramatic tricks he used but in the humanity his work contained. After this conversation Gogol reread Molière and saw more of his significance. He had complete faith in Pushkin's judgment. With Pushkin, and him alone, Gogol felt at once dominated and guided. And yet everything about the poet—a man of passion, courage, generosity, a lover of women and gambling, who lived at breakneck, daredevil pace—should have repelled him. How could such a poet cling so strongly to earthly pleasures? What mysterious link bound the tranquil assurance of his work to the wild disorder of his life? Why did so many people understand and love him? Gogol, exactly the contrary of Pushkin, never abandoned himself to his natural impulses. He was always on guard, scrutinizing his surroundings, giving nothing of himself.

"He never unbuttoned himself, one might say," Annenkov wrote, "and it was impossible to find him disarmed. His piercing eye constantly followed the states of mind and characteristic reactions of other people; he wanted to *see* even those things he might easily have guessed."[18]

When someone related some interesting fact in his presence, he would freeze in an attitude of remarkable intentness. His whole being became a suction pump. Annenkov had seen this expression of intellectual greed on his face when one of his guests, probably a doctor, spoke of the behavior of the insane and the inflexible logic they applied in developing their wild ideas. Another guest then told a story of an insignificant office worker who had saved and saved to buy the English hunting gun of his dreams and had lost it his first time out shooting, in the marshes of the Gulf of Finland. The man was so afflicted by the loss that his colleagues had taken up a collection to buy him another. "Everyone in the room laughed at this anecdote, based on a true story," Annenkov wrote. "Gogol alone listened, thoughtful, staring at the floor."

Forever ferreting about in search of new ideas, ideas he could "use," he was not satisfied with those served up to him at home; he often made the rounds of the drawing rooms, culling more material here, there, everywhere. He could be seen, with eager eyes, vibrating ears, and ostentatious cravat, at the Karamzins', Zhukovskys', Pletnyevs', Pushkins', in the dressing room of the actor Sosnitsky, and at the bedside of Alexandra Smirnov, slowly convalescing from a difficult confinement. When he returned home at night, he would go to his desk and jot down all the thoughts and notions whirling in his head, however they came to him. He liked to work in big office record books. His tiny, close, feminine writing completely covered the page, leaving neither margins nor blanks. The letters, in pale brownish ink, collided with one another, the words ran together, lines waved up and down, and microscopic corrections were squeezed between the barely legible lines of the original. The draft of an article on "Sculpture, Painting, and Music" shared a page with a short story of a mysterious street, on Vasilyevsky Island, lit by a single lantern. The first sentence of one story, "There is nothing more handsome than the Nevsky Prospect, at least not in St. Petersburg,"[19] was followed by a study on Herder. Personal reactions invaded notes on historical readings: *The Varangians, Alliances Between European Kings and Russian Emperors, The Century of Louis XIV, The Norman Conquests.*

This diversity and confusion of subjects is evidence of the author's acute perplexity. He really didn't know which way to turn. After delighting him, the success of *Evenings on a Farm* now began to frighten him. He saw the shortcomings of his collection and could not bear to hear people speak well of it. He even thought that his readers, by insisting upon praising such a mediocre product, were implicitly deprecating whatever he might write thereafter. He had far too high an opinion of himself to consent to be a mere entertainer. He was born to bring light to the human race, and it was his duty to progress with each book until he attained the perfection desired by God.

"You talk about *Evenings,*" he wrote to Pogodin. "The devil take them! I will not put out another edition. Certainly I have nothing against making money, but to write for that alone, to pile up story on story, that I cannot do. . . . I was almost forgetting that I ever wrote those *Evenings,* and you go and remind me. . . . Let them sink into oblivion until the day I have produced something important, great, truly artistic. I remain idle and immobile. I do not want to give anything small, and nothing big will come out. In a word, I am suffering from intellectual constipation."[20]

As the weeks went by, he grew increasingly worried by this inability to conceive a work worthy of the destiny he had assigned to himself. His letters to his friends were one long lament: "The most annoying thing of all is that my creative power continues to elude me."[21] "I am doing absolutely nothing. Was total sloth the only thing I brought back with me from home?"[22] "I have grown so cold, hard, so ordinary, that I don't know myself any more. It will soon be a whole year since I wrote a single line. Try as I like, it's wasted effort."[23] "I do not know if the Almighty will deign to send me inspiration."[24]

Late in 1832, however, he thought he had found the answer. It would be a comedy, *The Vladimir Cross.* The subject, as he explained it to a few friends, was the mania for decorations and honors. A senior government official, impelled by his longing to possess a particular decoration —the Order of St. Vladimir, which raised its recipient to the rank of "gentleman"—consecrates his entire life to that obsession, and eventually goes mad, believing himself to *be* a Vladimir Cross (third degree)!

"Gogol has an idea for a comedy," Pletnyev wrote to Zhukovsky on December 8, 1832. "I don't know if he will manage to produce it this winter, but I expect something quite out of the ordinary from him in this form. I have always been struck by the dialogue in his tales."

Gogol himself was writing, to Pogodin on February 20, 1833:

"I have always been infatuated with comedy. I was obsessed by the idea in Moscow, on my travels, and when I got here, but as yet nothing has materialized. The subject was beginning to emerge though, and the title even wrote itself on the first page of a big blank notebook, *The Vladimir Cross.* Tons of bile, pepper, and laughs! But I stopped short when I saw my pen stumbling over passages the censor would never pass. And what good is a play that will never be performed? Drama only lives on the stage. Otherwise it is a soul without a body. All that remains for me to do, therefore, is to invent a subject so innocuous that even a police commissioner would not be upset by it. But what sort of comedy is that, when there is neither truth nor malice?"

A few days later, Pletnyev confirmed the situation in a letter to Zhukovsky: "Nothing new from Gogol. His comedy is still in his head. He wanted to put too much in it, was continually coming up against the problems of expression for the stage and, in a temper, finally wrote nothing."

He did, in fact, finish a few scenes of *The Vladimir Cross* and buried them in his stack of experiments.[25] He also outlined a comedy with an "innocuous subject," as he put it himself, called *The Suitors,* but he found it so insipid that he laid it aside, intending to rework it when inspiration should return. Finally he began work on some short stories: "The Nose," "Diary of a Madman," "The Quarrel of the Two Ivans,"[26] but he wrote reluctantly, with an unpleasant feeling that he was repeating himself, not moving forward. Perhaps it would be better if he turned away from both theater and short stories and devoted himself to history. He had always had a fondness for the past. He dived headfirst into research. Sometimes, however, he felt a twinge of regret at having given up the idea of direct contact with the public.

"I set to work on a historical study," he wrote to Pogodin, "but immediately see the scene on stage; I hear the applause, see the faces leaning over the boxes, down from the balconies, and up from the stalls, laughing, showing their teeth, and I send my historical study to the devil."[27]

It would soon return, however: a historical study was security, whereas all other literary forms were hazardous mental undertakings. In a play or short story one could go completely off the track, but not when simply re-creating the past on the basis of reliable documents. And then, as far as fame and fortune were concerned, those of the historian were in no way inferior to those of the novelist or playwright. Besides, Pushkin himself had turned to history, with his Pugachev.

At first, Gogol naturally thought of a history of the Ukraine. He collected material, pored over archives, annotated the works of contemporary chroniclers. But he was soon bored to death by the drudgery of compilation. The printed page exhaled a graveyard odor. He could not bring himself to apply the desiccating methods of the "barbarian academics" to past events. His aim was to reawaken the dead and endow them with all their living warmth, and for that the chronology of events was less important than the hum of everyday existence. To re-create the past, one needed to discard official evidence and immerse oneself in legend and folklore. The more one knew of that, the better chance one had of bringing back the past as it actually was. On November 9, 1833, Gogol wrote to Maximovich:

"I have harnessed myself to a history of our incomparable, our ill-starred Ukraine. Nothing is more soothing than history. My thoughts begin to flow, to become organized. I believe I shall write this work and say quite a few things in it that have not been said before. I was very glad to hear you have picked up some new songs. Please make copies of everything you have, and send them to me. I can't live without songs. You can't imagine how they help me in my work. Not just historical songs, but the obscene ones too. All add touches of color to my history and make increasingly clear to me the times and men that are—alas!— no more."

He reiterated his point in a letter to the Slavic philologist Srezhnevsky:

"One note of a song tells me more about the past than all those dreary-bareboned chronicles—if you can call a study written *a posteriori* a chronicle, that is; or comments made when memory has already given way to oblivion. Those chroniclers make me think of a landowner locking his stable door after the horse has been stolen."[28]

Although he regarded his decision to write a living history of the Ukraine as a sacred oath, he was already wondering if he had not been mistaken to restrict himself to a single region. After the publication of *Evenings on a Farm* he had been afraid of being classified as a regional author; now, with this work on Little Russia, he would no doubt be pigeonholed as a Cossack historian. Whereas his significance must be no less than universal. To fulfill his destiny, he would have to follow up his history of the Ukraine with a history of the world. The magnitude of the task made his head reel. He quailed, but did not doubt his powers. It was all a question of construction. Let's see: eight or nine volumes. He jubilantly fired off a *Plan for Teaching World History* to Uvarov, the minister of education:

"Properly understood, world history is not a collection of unrelated histories of individual states and nations having no over-all plan or common objective. It is not the accumulation of inert, dry facts it is generally supposed to be. Its scope is immense: it must embrace all mankind at a single glance, and show how it has developed and improved from its feeble beginnings to the present day."[29]

On December 23, 1833, he wrote to Pushkin:

"I will finish the history of the Ukraine and southern Russia, and then I will write a history of the world, of which there is no truthful version yet, not only in Russia but even in Europe. What a storehouse of tradition, belief, and song I shall bring together there!"

His determination to become a great historian had grown so strong that he suddenly decided, on Maximovich's advice, to apply for the chair of world history at the recently founded University of St. Vladimir, at Kiev. True, he possessed no degrees, his erudition was by no means limitless, and his teaching experience was virtually nil; but there was a shortage of professors in Russia, and the minister of education would not quibble over such trivial things as qualifications. After all, Maximovich, who had been teaching botany at Moscow, was going to be professor of literature at Kiev, at his own request. In "the mother of Russian cities," Gogol and he would be together again. They would do research in the archives, they would dine and sup on folksong and legend; they would teach the world a new approach to history.

"To Kiev; let's go to Kiev! Our ancient and admirable Kiev!" Gogol wrote to Maximovich. "It's ours, not theirs; all our ancient history began there. St. Petersburg bores me; or, rather, I am overcome by its abominable climate. It will be wonderful if you and I can get jobs in Kiev; we can do much good."[30]

There remained the obstacle of the minister. Gogol's report on the teaching of world history must have left him favorably disposed, and to banish any remaining hesitations they would simply mobilize their friends. First on the list came good old Zhukovsky, the tutor of the heir apparent; but Pushkin must not be neglected, as he was on good terms with some of the bigwigs and knew Uvarov personally. Gogol accordingly sent him a letter carefully calculated to flatter the minister if it were shown to him:

"If Uvarov were of that race of whom so many are to be found in high office here, I should not have decided to appeal to him or lay my ideas before him, and would have given the same answer as I did three years ago when I was offered a chair at the University of Moscow.[31] But at that time Baron Lieven, a man of no vast intelligence, was in charge of the ministry of education. It is sad to think that no one can appreciate our work. Uvarov knows his stuff, however; I have realized that clearly from his views and comments and his ideas on Goethe, not to mention his work on hexameters, which shows such extensive philosophical knowledge of the language and such alertness of mind. I am convinced he will accomplish far more here than Guizot did in France. And I am certain that if he deigns to look closely at my plan, he will single me out from the swarm of nonentities with which our university faculties are overrun."[32]

If that wasn't spreading it thick enough to convince Uvarov, then there was no hope for diplomacy! But one had to have patience. Decisions were always a long time ripening in the higher spheres of the administration. At the approach of the new year, Gogol's enthusiasm took on a mystical hue. Since he had not achieved anything transcendent in 1833, God must have designated 1834 as his year of glory. One glacial night, bending over his desk, he drew up a balance sheet of the past twelve months. Not one major publication, no money, debts galore, his mother forced to reorganize her tannery and dismiss the "Austrian expert" who had so expertly fleeced her, Vasilyevka mortgaged again. But that was all drowned in the flood of hope welling within him.

"A great, a solemn minute," he wrote. "The past murmurs at my feet; above me, through a mist, glows the indecipherable future. I implore you, life of my soul, my Genius! Oh, do not hide from me! Watch over me in this minute and do not leave me all this year, which looks so promising for me. What will you be, my future? Oh, be brilliant, be filled with activity, wholly dedicated to work and tranquillity. Mysterious and impenetrable 1834! Shall I mark you by some eminent work, and in what place shall I accomplish it? Will it be here, among these tall houses crowding together, these raucous streets, this febrile buying and selling, this shapeless mass of fashion, ostentation, civil servants, savage Nordic nights, tinsel and base mediocrity? Or in my fair, my antique Kiev, my

Promised Land, crowned with fertile gardens, girdled by its magnificent southern sky, with its intoxicating nights, its brush-covered hills, its gorges like harmonious goblets, and my Dnieper, whose pure, swift waters bathe the mountains' feet? Out there? Oh, I do not know how to summon you, my Genius! You who filled my ears even in my cradle with those winged, melodious songs that gave birth within me to such marvelous thoughts, still undimmed, who lulled me with dreams so vast and so entrancing! Oh, see me! Let your celestial gaze fall upon me. I kneel. I lie at your feet; oh, do not leave me. Stay with me, on earth, like some admirable brother, even if only for two hours each day. I shall achieve. . . . I shall achieve. . . . Life boils within me. My word will be inspired. Above it, inaccessible divinity will hover. I shall achieve. Oh, give me one kiss and grant your blessing upon me."

This solemn invocation, issued during the night of December 31, 1833, was sincere despite its grandiloquence. Whenever he was in the grip of a lofty emotion, Gogol became incapable of simplicity. He shed words as other people shed tears.

At the beginning of the new year, he was so certain he would be given the coveted professorship that he wrote to Maximovich:

"In your letter you speak of Kiev. I still plan to go there. The matter will be settled any day now."[33]

And although the history of the Ukraine existed only in outline, he put an announcement in the *Northern Bee* of January 30, 1834:

"New books. Publication of a *History of the Little Russian Cossacks,* by N. Gogol, author of *Evenings on a Farm.* As yet there has been no full and adequate history of Little Russia and its people. I have decided to take on the task of providing one. For nearly five years I have been assiduously collecting material concerning the history of this region. One half of my book is almost ready, but I am delaying publication of the first volumes, as I suspect there are numerous sources of documents still unknown to me, which must be in the possession of private persons. That is why I make this general appeal to those who have any material at all, in the form of chronicles, memoirs, songs, *bandura* stories,* business papers, etc., to send them to me, either the originals or copies, at the address below."

There were no replies. But, and this was a considerable compensation for his pride, Minister Uvarov published his *Plan for Teaching World History* in the *Ministry of Education Rewiew,* and the empress rewarded

* Tales told by the players of the *bandura,* a kind of lute.

him with a diamond ring "for his excellent work." This time he was sure
he had won. He began preparing himself and Yakim for their imminent
departure.

The news struck like thunder: despite all promises, it was some person
named Vladimir Zish, the candidate of the chancellor at Kiev, who had
been appointed to the chair for which Gogol had applied. As soon as the
shock had worn off, he riposted energetically, with imprecations, questions, and supplications to all and sundry.

"What can you tell me about Zish?" he wrote Maximovich on March
29, 1834. "Is there official confirmation? The minister himself had
promised me that place."

A few days later he was suggesting that Maximovich should write to
Bradke, the chancellor, to see if something could be done: "When you
write to Bradke, slip in a few allusions along these lines: he should get
Gogol into his university, because you know no one who has a more
exhaustive knowledge of history or is able to display it better. Add a few
more compliments of the sort, as though incidentally. This is most essential, for the minister will do anything in his power if the chancellor gives
his consent."

To Pushkin: "I am going to importune you with a request: if you
speak of me to Uvarov [the minister of education], tell him you have
been to see me and found me practically at death's door. Tell him, too,
that you are furious because I continue to stay on in town when I am
under doctors' orders to leave at once. After making it clear that I might
well give up the ghost within the next month, change the subject and talk
about the weather or anything else that comes to mind. I think it will not
be without some effect."[34]

"Count on me," Pushkin replied the same day. "I'll go shake my
finger at Uvarov today; will tell him of your approaching demise and
then, by means of a subtle and imperceptible transition, I shall turn to
the immortality awaiting him. Who knows? Maybe we will get something out of him!"

Pushkin's campaign produced no immediate results. The minister said
he would think it over, he would look at the file, he would reconsider if
another opportunity arose. . . . Then, Pogodin offered Gogol a position
as assistant professor at the University of Moscow. The postulant's
response was a categorical refusal. Assistant to whom? Assistant in what?
Did they think world history could be taught anywhere except from the
height of a professorial chair? Furthermore, the climate of Moscow was

no better suited to him than that of St. Petersburg. It was Kiev he needed, with its sun and its students. Why was God not helping him in this struggle? Only recently he had written to his mother: "Have you thought to have a mass said for the success of the tannery? If not, order Father Ivan to say one so that your activities may prosper, and mine too."[35]

The mass bore no fruit, either for the tannery, profits from which were virtually non-existent, or for his professorial dream, which was growing increasingly faint. Perhaps he should have ordered the mass himself, instead of acting through his mother? He was religious, but seldom set foot inside a church. No: God could not be punishing him for the infrequency of his attendance; his relations with the Almight were so very unconstrained, he consulted Him on any subject, anytime, anywhere. When his mother told him he ought to go to church more often, he retorted:

"I venerate God's apostles and his ministers, but the place in which one prays to Him is of no consequence. He is everywhere; therefore He hears our prayers."[36]

Fuming, he continued to teach, very irregularly, the rudiments of history to the little girls at the Patriotic Institute. These eternal brats in brown uniform; those bird-brains; and his own sisters would have to be among them! What a comedown from the vast public he had aspired to conquer in Kiev! At his request, his twelve-hundred-ruble salary was restored with retroactive effect from January 1, and the Misses Gogol were allowed to stay as a "special reward." At last, the minister offered him a lectureship in medieval history at the University of St. Petersburg. Unfortunately, he would again have to be listed as an assistant, not as a full professor. Were they all in a plot to belittle him? Lucky for them he needed the money! Swallowing his resentment, he accepted; his appointment was confirmed in a decree dated July 24, 1834. He did not tell his friends his real title, however: when he eventually announced the new job, "assistant" remained in his inkwell, while "chair" flowed automatically into his pen.

"I have decided to accept, temporarily, a chair at St. Petersburg," he wrote to Pogodin. "I will be lecturing on the Middle Ages."[37]

To his mother: "I have thrown off all trivial encumbrances and given up my other occupations. At the moment, I am contenting myself with a position as professor at the University of St. Petersburg and nothing more. I have neither time nor desire to do anything else."[38]

But he had not given up the fight for Kiev. There could be no problem in getting a transfer there: once the minister learned of his success in the capital, he could not refuse him a chair in whatever university he might choose. "So I have decided to accept a chair here, for a year, which will put me in an even better position to be appointed to Kiev,"[39] he told Maximovich.

He even asked his friend, who had just arrived there himself, to find him a house, "if possible with a little garden, somewhere on a hill with a little glimpse of the Dnieper." Maximovich, meanwhile, was feeling lost in a new city and a new job, and wondering whether, having interested himself in literary history only incidentally and for his own pleasure, he was going to be able to teach the subject. Was it right for him to pass himself off as an authority in front of an over-trusting audience of young people? Wouldn't he have done better to remain in his field of real expertise—botany? The prickings of his conscience, detailed in every letter, positively bewildered Gogol, who personally felt nothing of the sort.

"In the name of friendship, in the name of our Ukraine, in the name of the tombs of our fathers, don't sit there sweating over books," he wrote to Maximovich. "The devil take me if they can do anything except befuddle your brain. Remain as you are and express your own thoughts, and as little as possible of them. Students, especially at first, are so stupid that it would be simply criminal to exert oneself for their sakes. The best thing is to have conversations with them on aesthetic questions. That is what Pletnyev does; he has very sensibly decided that all theories are absurd and lead nowhere. He has stopped lecturing at all, and simply engages in explanations and discussions with his students, actually rubbing their noses in beauty. You have taste, you know more about Russian literature than any pedagogue-elucidator; what more do you want? I beg of you, in the name of heaven, spend the smallest possible amount of time on this nonsense."[40]

He was about to have to spend some time on that "nonsense" himself, however, for the academic year at his university began in September. Notwithstanding his sublime contempt for his future auditors, his chest constricted in a panic, identical in every respect to that of Maximovich, at the thought of the ordeal ahead. It was so stimulating to cut broad swathes through the forest of historical events, and so tedious to concern oneself with the paltry details of time and place. In the domain of plans and projects he felt like a king, but like a slave when it came to carrying them out. Neither his history of the Ukraine nor his history of the world had emerged from the primeval limbo, and here he was about to have to scrape away at the history of the Middle Ages.

And wasn't it just his luck, exactly when he was beginning to feel like writing fiction again! That spring he finished a few stories, "The Portrait," "Viy," "Taras Bulba," and ideas for others were going through his head. But the creations of his mind must now be stifled for the sake of a few stupid popes, Genghis Khan, Frederick Barbarossa, and Alexander Nevsky.

7.   Assistant Professor

It was two o'clock in the afternoon when Gogol entered the lecture hall.
It was packed. Having learned that the new lecturer in medieval history
was the author of *Evenings on a Farm,* students from other departments
had joined those in the philology section to hear the opening lecture.
They rose noisily, in a body. Gogol bowed awkwardly, very pale, and
walked to the lectern. His hat rim twisted in his hands. His stomach
was hollow with stage fright. Slowly he climbed up to the platform. The
rector came in, welcomed the new assistant professor, and seated himself
heavily in his special armchair.

Gogol stood alone before a sea of unfamiliar faces. The youth of his
audience intimidated him. Hundreds of pairs of eyes converged upon
him with expressions of insistent curiosity. The coughing died away, feet
ceased shuffling, the silence deepened. For safety's sake, Gogol had
learned his first lecture by heart. He uttered a private prayer, and began. The tone of his own voice, ringing high and clear, immediately
reassured him, and the students were as quickly conquered by the little,
white, sickly-looking person with the quick eye. This was no professor
lecturing at them: it was a visionary, a poet. He was re-creating the
dark days of the Middle Ages, the armored hosts of the Crusades, the
saintly arrogance of the chivalric orders, the horrors of the Inquisition,
the mysterious doings of the alchemists. Not a single name, not one
date: a sheaf of general ideas, a sort of mirage, in some places glittering and in others very misty.[1] After forty-five minutes, the orator fell
silent before his mesmerized audience. They exploded into applause.

As he stepped down from the platform he was surrounded by a crowd of enthusiastic students. Delighted with his success, he told them: "For this first lecture, gentlemen, I tried to give you only the general feeling of the Middle Ages. Next time, we shall attack the particular, and must arm ourselves with the anatomist's scalpel."

Their appetites whetted, the students impatiently awaited the following lecture; Gogol arrived late, clambered up to the lectern, and began talking about the great migratory movements. This time he had not memorized his speech; he could not find his words, he halted and stumbled, looking like a bewildered sleepwalker. "He spoke so uncertainly, and in such a monotone, and he got into such a muddle, that we grew bored listening," one student wrote. "We could not believe this was the same Gogol who had given such a brilliant lecture the week before."[2] After talking for thirty minutes, he suddenly looked very upset, as though he could think of nothing more to say, announced that he had to abridge his lecture because some relatives had just returned from a trip and were awaiting him at home, and referred those who desired further particulars to certain books whose titles he quoted. At his third appearance, they asked for dates; he was unable to supply them, but promised to bring a full chronology to his next class. The chronology was copied from a book, and his students recognized it. Their infatuation for the new professor diminished weekly; fewer and fewer students attended his lectures, and Gogol felt increasingly less inclined to do any serious preparation for such a small audience. His learning and his enthusiasm alike had been exhausted in his opening lecture. Now he was merely paraphrasing other historians and diluting his own sauce. As usual, he often claimed ill health as an excuse to stay away or shorten the lecture. "Whether because he suffered from toothache, or for some other reason, we quite often saw him with his head wrapped in a white handkerchief," wrote another student. "His appearance was sickly, pitiful. And what a nose he had! Long, pointed, a veritable beak. I could not look at him close up without thinking, he's going to peck me and gouge out my eyes."[3]

In October 1834, however, his sense of dedication briefly returned, because Pushkin and Zhukovsky had promised to attend one of his lectures. For them he wrote a brilliant study of Caliph al-Mamun and his period. When he reached the university, he found the two poets mingling with the students in the hall outside. They went into the amphitheater together. The eminent guests sat to one side, the scattering of students flopped onto their benches, and the assistant professor, sick with fright and nerves, climbed to the lectern as though mounting the scaffold.

Discipline among the students had relaxed; they had been showing a definite tendency to chatter and snicker during lectures. Please God they would keep quiet for once! What a humiliation it would be, otherwise, in front of Pushkin and Zhukovsky! For some reason, everything went well. The text, supported by facts and poetically presented, flowed easily from Gogol's lips. The colorful figure of al-Mamun caught the young people's interest. At the end, Pushkin and Zhukovsky congratulated the speaker, now voiceless and weak-kneed.

But this was only a dying spark. At the very next lecture, the dismayed students found their same old Gogol, hemming and hawing, focusing on nothing, gesturing vaguely and returning with deadly monotony to his "migration of peoples." The other members of the faculty felt no friendship for him and actually looked upon him as an intruder in the university, to which he had gained access, they said, by his connections alone.

"A man of letters, who had been made a celebrity among the public by his stories entitled *Evenings on a Farm*," wrote Professor Nikitenko. "A talent like Teniers'.* But when he moves from actual to ideal life, he becomes inflated and pedantic. Whenever he touches upon spiritual matters, his thought, sentiment, and tongue lose all originality. He does not realize this, however, and struts about pretending to be a man of genius. Gogol imagines that his alleged genius entitles him to the most lofty pretensions. What has happened? His lectures are so bad that he has become the laughingstock of the students. The authorities are afraid they will play some trick on him—inevitable in the circumstances; but the consequences might be very unpleasant. The rector called him in and courteously informed him of the disagreeable rumors that were circulating about his lectures. For an instant his conceit failed him, and he admitted his incompetence and impotence. He also came to see me, and confessed that he was too inexperienced for this position in the university."

Rejected by the faculty and abandoned by the students, Gogol reluctantly went on with the purgatory of his course. On December 14,

* David Teniers (1610–90) was a Flemish artist noted for his paintings of village festivities, folklore, people smoking and drinking in taverns, alchemists' laboratories, witches' Sabbaths, etc.

1834, he wrote to Pogodin: "I am alone, absolutely alone in this university. Nobody listens to me; I have met no one who has been struck by the luminous truth I speak. That is why I have given up artistic refinements and my desire to arouse my sleeping auditors as well. Ah, if there were even one who understood me! But like every other living thing in St. Petersburg, they are a generation of dullards."

The "generation of dullards" happened to include one or two young people of no little merit, however, such as the future historian Granovsky and the future novelist Turgenev. The latter was to recall Gogol's efforts to interest his public with amused melancholy:

"I heard him in 1835, when he was teaching history at the University of St. Petersburg," he wrote. "His lessons were delivered, it must be said, in a most original manner. To begin with, Gogol missed two out of three classes on general principles; then, when he did deign to appear, he did not speak but muttered indistinct sounds, showed us little engravings of scenes in Palestine or other eastern lands, and seemed dreadfully confused. We were all convinced (and can hardly have been mistaken) that he had absolutely no idea of history. On examination day he appeared with bandaged head, as though suffering from toothache and at the end of his strength, and never opened his mouth. It was Professor Shulgin who interrogated the students. I can still see Gogol's narrow face with its long nose and the two ends of his black silk kerchief standing up like ears on top of his head."[4]

The students soon understood that if someone else was examining them in their professor's place, it was because Gogol was afraid to be shown up in all his ignorance if he led the questioning himself. "He's afraid Shulgin will catch him out!" they whispered. "That's why he's pretending he can't open his mouth!"[5] They did not know whether to feel pity or contempt for the weird figure with the long-suffering expression and bandaged face, who looked more like a student than a professor. In any case, it was hard to believe he was an author. Some thought it must be a coincidence and their professor simply happened to have the same name as the author of *Evenings on a Farm.*

In reality, however, literature was occupying an increasingly large place in his life. Between classes at the university and classes at the Patriotic Institute, he was working fast and furiously for himself. In January 1835 he published *Arabesques* in two volumes, including "Nevsky Prospect," "The Portrait," "Diary of a Madman," fragments of Ukrainian short stories, the texts of his history lectures, and various articles. A few weeks later, in March, the bookshops put a second work by the same author into their windows. This was *Mirgorod,* also in two volumes, containing "Old World Landowners," "Taras Bulba," "Viy," and "The Quarrel of the Two Ivans." The second collection, appearing so soon after the first, was praised by the critics but did not sell: *Arabesques,* a boring conglomeration of odds and ends, had discouraged readers from buying *Mirgorod,* which was a rich and varied collection they might have appreciated.

About the same time, after reworking and polishing his short story "The Nose," Gogol offered it to Pogodin for the *Muscovite Observer.* Then he changed his mind and decided it should be published in Pushkin's *Contemporary,* and asked Pogodin to return the manuscript.[6] He was expecting an argument and was surprised by the alacrity with which Pogodin granted his request. In fact, the editors of the *Muscovite Observer* had already turned down the story, calling it "dirty and trivial."

Disappointed by his failure as professor and by the poor sale of *Arabesques,* Gogol began longing to get away from St. Petersburg again. "Tell me about our springtime!" he wrote to Maximovich on March 22, 1835. "I thirst, I thirst for that spring! Do you even know your own good fortune? You are there when the spring unfolds, you can breathe it . . . and after that, you dare to tell me you have nobody in whom you can confide?"

On April 3, in a frenzy of impatience, he applied to the rector of the university for a four-month leave of absence on grounds of ill health; and on May 1, after those examinations in which he cut such a sorry figure with his kerchief around his head, he left for the Caucasus. Neither Yakim nor his sisters, of course, were to accompany him on this long tour in which nothing could be planned in advance. At first, he intended to go to the hot springs for treatment. But after a brief stay in Moscow, he calculated that he could not afford such a long journey, and, substituting the Ukrainian steppe for the Caucasian mountains, proceeded to Vasilyevka. From there, however, as he was still worried about his health, he continued to the Crimea, for sea and mud baths. Then he returned home for a dose of family adoration. His two latest books had confirmed his mother's conviction that he was a superman. Embarrassed by the hyperbolic praise she lavished upon him, he had written her a few weeks previously:

"Speaking of my work, you call me a genius. However that may be, this seems strange to me. Can I be called a genius, who am a good-hearted, simple man, not altogether an idiot, perhaps, and having a little sense? I beg of you, dear Mother, do not use that term again in reference to me, especially when you are talking to other people. Do not give opinions about my books, and do not broadcast flattering speeches about my qualities. If you knew how disagreeable, how repugnant it is to hear parents endlessly singing their children's praises!"[7]

Marya Ivanovna was untouched by these exhortations: she knew full well that modesty was the first sign of genius. In her son's presence she struggled bravely to hold her tongue. But the moment his back was turned, she relieved herself of her excess affection. With radiant assurance, she claimed he was the author of every successful novel published in Russia. "Her adoration for him led her to the Pillars of Hercules," Danilevsky related. "She attributed every new invention to him (the steamboat, the railroad), and, to her son's acute discomfort, told everyone she saw about it at every opportunity. No human force could have undeceived her."

At Vasilyevka, Gogol rested and dreamed, as always. Impossible to write under that blue heaven!

"My head feels so empty and stupid that I don't know what to do," he told Maximovich. "As long as I keep talking, everything is fine; but the moment I pick up a pen, I am stricken with paralysis."[8]

To Zhukovsky:

"I have a headful of ideas and subjects, and if we had not had such a hot summer I should have used up a quantity of pens and paper; but the heat makes me frightfully lazy. Only a tenth of what I might have written actually was, and is impatiently waiting to be read by you. In a month I shall ring your bell, groaning under the weight of my notebooks."[9]

This was not an idle threat. Gogol had just heard that the director of the Patriotic Institute was thinking of hiring another teacher to replace him, and however much he disdained his work in that establishment, he could not give up the money it brought in without a struggle. If he told Zhukovsky about his great schemes, the poet might be more concerned to intercede with the empress on his behalf, so that he would not lose his salary just when he needed peace of mind so badly in order to create.

"Yesterday," he added in the same letter, "I learned a strange piece of news. It seems that some other monster is to occupy my place at the Patriotic Institute, which is very irksome for me because, for one thing, that work provided my subsistence, and, for another, I enjoyed the teaching. I was accustomed to thinking myself among friends there, in a family. However, Pletnyev writes that usurper's application will not go in until the beginning of August and, if the empress does not agree to hand over my place to the new teacher, it will remain mine. That is why I am turning to you: can you contrive it so that the empress refuses? She is kind and will undoubtedly not wish to grieve me."

Still relying on his sovereign's good will, he even contemplated taking his youngest sister, Olga, back to Petersburg and enrolling her in the Patriotic Institute along with the other two girls. But the child was hard of hearing and somewhat retarded, and the boarding-school atmosphere was likely to do her more harm than good. After a family debate it was decided that she should remain in the country, where she would glean what learning she could and eventually find a husband.

At the end of July Gogol set out for St. Petersburg again, stopping to see Maximovich in Kiev. Five days of conversation, walks through the holy city, meditation in front of the Andrey Pervozvanny Church, at the summit of Mount Andreyevsky, and he left for Moscow in a hired coach. His friends Danilevsky and Pashchenko went with him. For a joke, he passed himself off as a "professor/aide-de-camp" at the posting stations, which impressed the stationmasters and got them better horses more quickly.

Moscow, as always, welcomed him warmly. One Saturday evening he read his comedy *Marriage* (a reworking of *The Suitor*) to a large audience at the Pogodins'. Whenever he could hide in the skin of some other character, his natural shyness vanished, and then he was positively stimulated by an audience. Without ever stirring from his chair, he became by turns the blushing bride, the arrogant marquis, and the dithering suitor.

"He read so well, or rather, he acted so well," Aksakov wrote, "that many people who have heard him read now say that even with an excellent cast of actors the play is less rounded, less unified and funny on the stage than it was when the author read it alone. The people laughed so much that some of them were almost ill."

Mrs. Nashchokin, who met Gogol at the Aksakovs', noted that he had a slight Ukrainian accent and drawled his o's. "His hair was long, worn back from his temples, and he often shook his head."[10]

Gogol was back in St. Petersburg at the beginning of September, gloomily resuming his lectures at the university. Despite Zhukovsky's efforts, he had been relieved of his position at the Patriotic Institute and expected to see his professorial career similarly curtailed: a ministerial circular had just been issued stipulating that henceforth a professor must be at least a Ph.D. before he could hold a chair of history. His colleagues advised him to resign without waiting for a decision from above, but he was unwilling to condemn himself. At last he took the initiative.

"I have spat my farewell upon the university," he wrote to Pogodin, "and in a month I shall be a carefree Cossack again. Misunderstood I mounted the platform, and misunderstood I descend. But during these eighteen unrewarding months—for the general opinion is that I was poking my nose into something that was not my business—I have learned a great deal and added to the treasures in my soul. My mind is no longer visited by childish notions and partial learning; it is overwhelmed by lofty thoughts, full of truth and terrifying immensity. To you and you alone I say this, for anyone else would call it boasting."[11]

It was true that for Gogol the last months of 1835 were exceptionally rich in plans and achievements. He revised *Marriage,* wrote a short story, "The Coach," began a drama of medieval England called *Alfred the Great,*[12] and also became suddenly fascinated with a subject Pushkin had once mentioned in passing. It concerned a true story the poet was thinking of transforming into a verse comedy. The event had taken place not far from his estate at Mikhailovskoye, in the province of Pskov, but his friend Dahl, the author and lexicographer, had told him of a second and similar case, strengthening his conviction that the most outrageous knavery and skulduggery were practiced in Russia.[13]

The scheme was ingenious, to say the least: in those days a landowner's wealth was reckoned by the number of male serfs listed in the census return for the head tax. Now, peasants often died between two returns, but their names were not always taken off the lists. Having pondered this circumstance, an astute swindler began to buy up the departed souls for a pittance and mortgage them to the State Bank at the going rate for live souls, producing a deed of purchase as evidence of ownership.

The tale delighted Gogol, who instantly imagined the macabre hilarity of this nationwide quest for souls: zigzag journeys, plots within plots, and behind every door a twisted, comical, unforgettable face—just what he needed. Even the title was made to order: *Dead Souls.* In the face of such enthusiasm, Pushkin smilingly relinquished his subject. After all, it was better suited to the talent of this little Ukrainian schemer than to himself.

"For some time," Gogol later wrote, "Pushkin had been urging me to undertake something bigger; at last, after I had read him one short scene which appealed to him more than the rest, he said to me: 'Why, when you have the gift of seeing into a man and painting his whole portrait in a few strokes, making him as though he were alive, don't you begin some really big piece of work? It is really a sin!' Then he pointed to my haggard appearance and the infirmities that might put an early end to my days. He cited the example of Cervantes, who, although he had written some admirable short stories, would never have held his present rank among writers if he had not embarked upon *Don Quixote*. In conclusion, he gave me a subject of his own, upon which he had wanted to base a kind of poem, and which, according to him, he would never have given to anyone else."[14]

Alexandra Smirnov also wrote in her diary, "Pushkin spent four hours at Gogol's place and gave him the subject for a novel which, like *Don Quixote,* will be divided into cantos. The hero will travel all over the provinces. Gogol will use his own travel notes."[15]

Faint with gratitude, Gogol bore his booty back to his attic and set to work. The story started off at full gallop; but at the end of a few pages, the problems began. This novel was deeper and more complex than he had supposed. Every line opened up new avenues for exploration. Tossing it off in a few days was out of the question. But he needed money, and in a hurry! Perhaps Pushkin, who was so generous, would give him another idea. It would cost nothing to ask. He wrote, on October 7, 1835:

"I have begun *Dead Souls*. The subject is expanding into a very long novel, which I think will be very funny. But I have stopped with the third chapter. In this novel I should like to portray all of Russia, if only from one point of view. Do me a favor, give me a subject, any subject, funny or not, provided it is a purely Russian anecdote. My hand shakes with impatience to write a comedy for the stage. If I cannot do it, I shall be wasting my time and I don't know how I shall ever improve my situation. All I have, but really all, is my wretched 600 rubles from the university. Do me the favor of giving me a subject and I shall instantly write a five-act comedy which, I promise you, will be diabolically droll. In the name of heaven, my mind and my stomach are both famished. *Arabesques* and *Mirgorod* are not selling at all. The devil alone knows what that means. Booksellers are such foul creatures that they should all be hanged without remorse from the nearest tree!"

The commercial failure of *Arabesques* and *Mirgorod* was offset, for Gogol, by the praise lavished upon both books by the young critic Belinsky, writing in the Moscow *Telegraph.* While the official reviewers, Bulgarin and Senkovsky, were treating the author with condescension and deprecating the triviality of his portraits and heaviness of his style, Belinsky dared to write: "Mr. Gogol is now at the summit of our literature. He is taking the place vacated by Pushkin." Of course, Belinsky—a liberal protester—was preaching Pushkin's downfall because the poet had been returned to favor with the tsar after his long years of exile and rebellion; but even making allowances for political bias, Gogol squirmed to see himself placed, and by a critic of taste, higher than the man he looked upon as his master, especially when he was begging that master for help. Wouldn't Pushkin be furious to see the critics ranking him beneath a writer to whom he had just supplied the subject for a novel, and who was now demanding an idea for a play? Anything, sooner than the wrath of that angel whose head was so well stocked! But no; Pushkin was too great and generous to stoop to professional jealousy. He could turn a deaf ear to the twitterings of the literary sparrows. And he, Gogol, should do the same, if he wished to pursue his career with dignity. He must keep a cool head. Fix his eyes upon the ultimate goal. In future, no doubt, he would deserve the compliments being paid him now. For the time being, however, he did not have the right to bask in them. No matter what he read or heard about himself, he could not forget that he had written *Evenings on a Farm, Arabesques,* and *Mirgorod,* and that was all.

8. *Arabesques* and *Mirgorod*

Gogol adored prefaces, forewords, and marginal notes. They were like so many shields behind which a writer could hide to fend off the blows. Reading the curious "Notice" at the beginning of *Arabesques,* one would think we were still in the days of *Hans Kuechelgarten,* published at the author's expense:

"This collection [*Arabesques*] contains texts written at various times in my life. The reader will undoubtedly find many flaws attributable to youth. I must add that when I read the proofs at the printer's, I was often horrified by inaccuracies in syntax, tedious passages, and other signs of carelessness. Lack of time and sometimes highly unpleasant circumstances have prevented me from going over my manuscript with a clear head. I dare to hope my readers will have the charity to forgive me."

He sent a copy to Pogodin with this confession:

"Herewith my bric-a-brac. There are some mighty childish things in it. I hurried to have them published in order to clean all the old stuff out of my drawers and begin a new life."[1]

Indeed these *Arabesques* are a motley assortment. Stories, fragments of historical studies, considerations on art and literature. In passing, Gogol hails Pushkin as the greatest Russian poet, for whom "the nation's truth is in the soul of the people, not in the description of a *sarafan.*" He also wrote that Pushkin was "the Russian man at the culmination of his development, the Russian man as he may be two hundred years from now." And he defended inspired realism against conventional poetry: "It is beyond doubt true that an uncivilized mountaineer, free as the air . . . is far more picturesque than a justice of the peace in his frayed, tobacco-stained gown. But both belong to our universe, both deserve our attention, even though, for natural reasons, that which we see least often impresses us more. I have always had a passion for painting. I was especially fond of one of my landscapes, with a dead tree standing in the foreground. In those days I lived in the country and my neighbors were my judges. After looking at the picture, one of them shook his head and said, 'A good painter chooses a fine, strong tree covered with bright green leaves, not a dead one!' I was very young and his criticism annoyed me. Later, I understood why; and I also understood what the public liked and did not like."

In fact, in pretending to defend Pushkin, Gogol was pleading his own cause. Peering over the poet's head, he was answering those critics who had reproached him for the "triviality" of *Evenings on a Farm*. He wanted to convince them, and the public with them, that commonplace sorrows, mediocre ugliness, and everyday banality could furnish the elements of a work of art. The important thing was to avoid a servile copy. To magnify the raw material by the mind. Not to transform reality, but to illuminate it from within. "The more ordinary his subject," he wrote, "the higher the poet must rise, for he must extract what is extraordinary from it and yet contrive to make that extraordinary true."

He enlarged upon this idea in an article on a painting by Brulov, *The Last Days of Pompeii*. To him, the cold and academic composition was marvelous, and he tried to see in it truth transfigured by talent. In spite of the horror of the scene, he said, the observer is filled with a sense of beauty. The miracle lay in this transfiguration of terror into loveliness, of a momentary catastrophe into eternal harmony. He hoped with all his strength that his paintings of dead trees would also transcend their subjects and achieve the perfection of a Raphael or a Pushkin. Thinking of himself, no doubt, he wrote in his short story "The Portrait":

"Why does lowly, simple nature appear as though illuminated in one painter's work; why does it procure a sensation of exquisite delight, as though everything around one were flowing and moving in a more regular, more peaceful rhythm? And why, in some other painter who has been equally faithful to nature, does that same nature seem abject and sordid? The fault is in the lack of light. The most wonderful landscape in the world seems unfinished when there is no sun shining on it."

In this story, the longest of the group, art and evil intersect in a singular way, almost as though the two phenomena were fatally joined; as though, by exercising a talent in any form whatever, man falls more easily prey to the devil. Inspired, and therefore vulnerable, he fights on open ground. His sense of beauty is his Achilles heel, upturned to the arrows of the Other.

The first part of the work concerns the adventures of a poor and gifted young painter named Chartkov, who buys, in an antique shop, a portrait of an old man whose eyes shine with malevolent power. Back in his attic, he cannot contemplate the painting without a dreadful sense of uneasiness. He is fascinated by the stranger he has brought under his roof. "The painter seemed to have embedded in his canvas a pair of eyes torn from a human head." At night, Chartkov has such violent and realistic nightmares that he becomes unable to tell dream from reality. "He saw the old man's features move, his lips reach out as though to suck him in." Finally, Chartkov discovers a roll of gold coin hidden in the frame. From that day forth, he is poisoned by his own good fortune. He thinks only of money, success. He becomes a fashionable portrait artist, wielding his brushes mechanically and destroying his own genius, while the praises of the sophisticated hum about him. "He dined left and right, escorted ladies to exhibitions and even out walking, dressed as a dandy, publicly declared that a painter belonged to society and must maintain his station in life." Called one day to the academy of fine arts to give his opinion of the work of a young Russian painter living in Italy, he suddenly realizes, by comparison, how far he has fallen. He goes home and sets to work, desperately searching for his former talent, but to no avail. "The simple exercise of technique chilled his ardor, set up an insurmountable barrier to his imagination." Then, possessed by a demon of demented jealousy, he seeks out the most beautiful paintings, buys them at any price, and tears them to shreds, tramples upon them, "laughing with pleasure." Then he dies, in a fit of madness.

The second part of the story, considerably revised in 1841, explains the curse of the old man's portrait. He was none other than the devil, in the guise of a usurer of the reign of Catherine II. On the eve of his death, he asks a painter to record his features on canvas, hoping that his soul will remain trapped between the layers of pigment and will continue to

exert its evil influence upon men: for Satan must have a physical medium through which he can operate in the world, and only the artist
can supply it. The mesmerized painter never guesses to what depths
his act will plunge him. Mastering his aversion, he succeeds in capturing
the usurer's burning expression. Later, realizing that he has become
involved in a pact with the devil, he renounces his art, enters a monastery, and expiates his sin through prayer. After long years of fasting
and meditation, he at last feels pardoned and purified, takes up his
palette again, and paints a Nativity so beautiful that the monks fall to
their knees upon sight of it.

This anguish that leads one painter to suicide and another to the
monastery is experienced by the hero of "Diary of a Madman" as
well, and perhaps more intensely than by the former. Gradually, an obscure civil servant feels his reason escaping him. He is in love with his
boss's daughter, and extremely conscious of his congenital nullity. However, he has one advantage over the rest of the world: he understands
the language of dogs; he is also King Ferdinand of Spain. The woman
who marries him will be queen. But why is he suffering so? His chest is
bursting. His brain is on fire. "Mother! Save your unfortunate son!
Shed one tear upon his painful head! Behold how they torment him!
Clasp him to your breast, the poor orphan! There is no place for him on
earth! Everywhere, they drive him away! Mother, have pity upon your
poor, sick child. By the way, do you know the Dey of Algiers has a
wart just beneath his nose?"

More than once, Gogol himself knew that desperate appeal to the
mother, that visceral longing for protection, for the primal union, the
return to the womb. In his letters, otherwise filled with reproach, fury,
and falsehood, there shines an intransigent love for the woman who
gave him life. He unconsciously blamed her for all the nastiness meted
out to him by the world into which she had brought him; but she was
the only woman in his life. All the rest were snares. In a moment of terrifying lucidity, the hero of "Diary of a Madman" writes:

"Oh, what a cunning creature is woman! It is only now that I understand what woman is! Until this day, no one knew the object of her
love. I am the first to discover it. She is in love with the devil. Yes, I am
not joking. The learned men write nonsense, they say she is this or that.
She loves only the devil. See, over there, that one aiming her opera glass
in the front box of the balcony. You think she is looking at the potbellied
person covered with decorations? Far from it: she is looking at the

devil behind him. Look! There he is, hiding. He's beckoning to her. And she will marry him! She will marry him!"

Woman's allegiance to Satan erupts in another item in the collection, "Nevsky Prospect," made up of two stories with contrasting endings. The hero of the first, like that of "The Portrait," is a young painter full of talent and innocence, Piskarev. On the Nevsky Prospect he encounters an incredibly beautiful woman with hair "brilliant as agate" and a brow "of luminous whiteness," whose lips "seemed to enclose the secret of a whole swarm of exquisite dreams." Dazzled, he approaches her, in an impulse of incorporeal adoration: "In that moment he was as pure as the virgin adolescent who as yet feels only an indistinct, wholly spiritual aspiration toward love." She leads him to a whore house filled with prostitutes, and he flees, appalled. However, he cannot believe that a degraded soul can lurk behind those perfect features. He sees her again in his dreams, and persuades himself that it is his duty to marry her and save her from a life of debauchery. But when he finds her again to make his proposal, she is drunk and scornfully rejects him. In despair, Piskarev goes home and cuts his throat. Reality has killed the dream; the woman has killed the artist.

He has a friend, Lieutenant Pirogov, who has a very different adventure, also initiated on the Nevsky Prospect. He follows an alluring young German girl, engages her in conversation, succeeds in forcing her door, and is covering her with kisses and already imagining himself her lover when the fair lady's husband bursts in flanked by two stout friends, who beat him and throw him out into the street. Such a rude awakening might have prompted Pirogov, like the poor Piskarev, to begin asking questions about the way of the world, but he has neither the painter's sensitivity nor his pride. At first he thinks of lodging a complaint with his superiors; then he changes his mind, goes into a pastry shop, eats two creamcakes, and ends the evening with some friends. Thus, the practical man digests a humiliation and takes the good things of life as they come. In so doing, he unwittingly plays into the devil's hands; and the devil's hands are never more busy than on the Nevsky Prospect, where there are so many women to be found.

"Oh, do not trust that Nevsky Prospect!" Gogol writes. "Everything you see there is falsehood, illusion; nothing is what it seems. You imagine that *these* women . . . But trust them least of all. Above all, God save you from glancing once under their hats. However appealing the swirl of a beauty's cloak rippling in the distance, I will not be curious enough to follow her. Keep as far as possible from the street lamps too, and go your way as quickly as you can. Consider yourself fortunate if nothing worse happens to you than that one of them douses your elegant overcoat with its foul-smelling oil. That street lamp is a liar, too, like everything that lives and breathes here. It is lying every instant, that Nevsky Prospect; and most of all when night thickens above it, throwing the white and pale-yellow walls into relief, when the whole city is nothing but roar and illumination, when throngs of coaches speed across the bridges, the postilions shout as they bump up and down on the horses' backs, and the devil himself lights the lamps to show the world in a mask."

Gogol gave to *Mirgorod* the subtitle *More Evenings on a Farm,* presumably hoping, by this reference to a work that had been highly successful, to attract more readers to the new book. But although the four stories in *Mirgorod* do take place in the Ukraine, they bear no resemblance to the tales of *Evenings on a Farm* in theme, intention, or even style.

The group opens with a soft, sad tale of "Old World Landowners." An elderly couple, Afanasy Ivanovich and Pulcheria Ivanovna, alias Philemon and Baucis, spin out their idle lives in the country, wholly dedicated to their affection for each other, and to food. They gaze fondly upon each other, they eat, and they let their minds turn on the monotonous wheel of the hours. Contemplating this humble earthly bliss, Gogol forgot his habitual irony and yielded to tenderness. The house he describes in "Old World Landowners" is the house of his childhood, with the creaking doors, the pantry bursting with provender, the windows opening onto the orchard, where the boughs are sagging under the weight of their ripe fruit. He based his portraits of Afanasy Ivanovich and Pulcheria Ivanovna on his paternal grandparents. Other parts of the painting are borrowed from neighboring landowners. The Ukrainian sun smiles over all. The clamor of the outside world dies at the garden fence. Unhappiness would seem unthinkable in such a tranquil setting; but Pulcheria Ivanovna dies, leaving her husband positively amazed with grief. In telling this simple story, Gogol instinctively abandoned his usual needling analysis of emotion and bombastic style. His heroes' inner states are revealed by their smallest gestures, looks, and words. When we think we are seeing them from without, their inner lives creep into us. To express Afanasy Ivanovich's collapse after the death of his spouse, he avoids any exploration of his character's soul and simply shows him at the dinner table:

"A maid tied a napkin under Afanasy Ivanovich's chin, and it was a good thing she did, for otherwise he would have spilled gravy all over his dressing gown. I tried to arouse him and told him all kinds of news; he listened, always smiling, but at times his expression lost all interest and became completely vacant. Sometimes he would raise his spoon full of porridge and put it on his nose instead of into his mouth. Or he would reach the wrong way and poke his fork at the water jug, and the maid would have to guide his hand back to a roast chicken. When the curd cakes and cream were brought, Afanasy Ivanovich said, 'This is a dish . . .', and I saw that his voice was breaking and a tear was about to spring from his lead-colored eyes, although he was trying to hold it back. 'Here is a dish,' he went on, 'that my de . . . my de . . . my departed . . .' And suddenly he burst into tears, his hand dropped onto his plate, the plate rolled to the floor and broke, the sauce spread all over him. He just sat there, unconscious of anything, holding his spoon, and his tears poured out like a soundless fountain, poured in floods on the napkin protecting his front."

Considering this old man wracked by a grief he cannot master, the author asks, "Which has more power over us, passion or habit?" A little later, Afanasy Ivanovich hears a voice from the other world calling him in broad daylight, realizes that his hour has come, resigns himself to the idea "as obediently as a child," and is extinguished "like a taper when there is no more fuel to feed its puny flame."

The heroes of "The Quarrel of the Two Ivans"[2] are also people of no importance; but in this case the touch is that of a caricaturist. The idea for the story is said to have been suggested by the actual shenanigans of a pair of citizens of Mirgorod who were notorious for their quarrels and reconciliations. The author may also have been inspired by a book written by his Ukrainian compatriot Narezhny, called *The Two Ivans, or, A Passion for Quibbling,* published in 1825. The tone, style, and incidents of Gogol's tale, however, belong to no one but himself; it is heavily marked by his personal brand of irony and sourness.

There is, of course, a world of difference between his two Ivans: "Ivan Ivanovich possesses to an extraordinary degree the art of speaking agreeably. Ivan Nikiforovich, on the other hand, is usually silent. Ivan Ivanovich is tall and spare; Ivan Nikiforovich is slightly shorter but extends horizontally. The head of Ivan Ivanovich is like a turnip, root down; that of Ivan Nikiforovich is like a turnip, root up."

The quarrel breaks out between them because Ivan Nikioforovich will not trade his gun to Ivan Ivanovich for a sow and two sacks of oats, and because, in his anger, he calls Ivan Ivanovich a "gander." It soon reaches fever pitch, leading to lawsuits and preparations for hearings that drag on for decades; the adversaries grow old, and at the moment when a reconciliation seems possible at last, the dispute flares up again and the two Ivans will take nothing less than a judge's decree to settle it. In this protracted farce the author constantly intervenes, accentuating the grotesqueness of his characters with heavy metaphor and winking at the reader to join in the amusement. A woman named Agafya Fyodosyevna "wears a bonnet on her head, three warts on her nose, and a dun-colored cloak printed with yellow flowers. . . . Her body had grown in the shape of a tub." The judge's nose "was so close to his mouth that he could easily sniff his upper lip, so he used it as a snuffbox, since the tobacco intended to enter the nostrils invariably landed upon it." A court clerk "took his quill up in his teeth" in astonishment. At the high point of the proceedings, a brown sow bolts into the courtroom and carries off the documents of the case. Ivan Nikiforovich is so fat that he gets stuck in a door and cannot be worked loose until his arms have been crossed in front of him and a knee applied to his stomach. The breaths of the clerk and veteran who free him smell so strongly "that the courtroom seemed to have been transformed into a tavern."

Behind the parade of grins, however, a bitterness remains. When his laughter fades, Gogol seems suddenly overwhelmed by the platitude of the world he has portrayed. As the narrator leaves the town of Mirgorod, where the two Ivans—now "white-crowned," their brows "strewn with wrinkles"—still await the outcome of their suit, he watches the landscape dissolve into grayness and rain: "The damp went right through me. The dreary barrier and sentry box, inside which a veteran was patching his gray gear, passed slowly before my eyes. And the plains came again, here black and furrowed, there covered with green, and the same ravens, the same jackdaws with sodden wings, the same unvarying rain, the same leaden, tearful sky. Ah, my friends, life here below is so tedious!"

This disenchanted conclusion is in turn negated by the epic grandeur and reckless range of "Taras Bulba," another story in this collection. Gogol later revised and expanded the work,[3] in which he recalls the troubled times when the community of Zaporog Cossacks, formed around the middle of the fifteenth century in the islands below the Dnieper rapids, was defending its independence against the inroads of the Polish barons. The presence of two idioms, two religions, and two races in the frontier region provoked virtually continuous warfare.

Before writing this tale the author must have consulted numerous scholarly works on the history of the Ukraine, but the bulk of his information he owed to the folk legends and *bandura* players' songs collected by Tsertelev, Maximovich, and Srezhnevsky, and so he paid little heed to historical accuracy; also, his chronology is by no means rigorous. But the faithful presentation of facts interested him less than the psychology of his characters and the picturesqueness of their surroundings.

Clearly inspired by the novels of Walter Scott, who was then having a huge vogue in Russia, Gogol outdistanced his master in violence of touch and brashness of color. The drama is built in large, simple blocks, with a myriad details of sparkling sharpness embedded like gems in the cement of the narrative. This is some great barbarian jewel, crudely incised and overloaded with multicolored stones, all of them aglint. The barbarousness of customs, the torture, the drinking bouts, the massacre of the Jews, the fights, the pillage: every image is fiercely drawn, but not so fiercely that the characters are overpowered by their setting.

Of the entire cast, Taras Bulba, the father, is the most complete figure, with his rough vitality, primitive sense of loyalty, appetite, and intransigence. On either side are his two sons: Ostap, the warrior, all of a piece, inflexible and unapproachable; and Andrey, more sensitive and complicated, who betrays the Zaporogs for the love of a Polish woman. Naturally, like every other Gogolian heroine, she has "black eyes and a skin white as snow illuminated by the pink of the morning sun." She laughs, "and her laughter gives a radiant power to her blinding beauty." She speaks "with a silvery voice." In the wink of an eye she corrupts the valorous Andrey, who cries out: "What are my father, my companions, my country to me? My country . . . is you!" In return for which, the Polish woman—another she-devil—folds him in "her lovely arms of snow."

This sentimental intrigue weakens the structure of the story, but the author needed it to force Andrey to deny his birth and faith. Announcing the dreadful news to old Taras Bulba, Yankel the Jew utters this bitter phrase: "When a man's in love, he's not worth much more than a soaked boot sole: twist it and it bends." Taras Bulba is shattered, and his only thought now is to punish his son, the traitor and renegade. He finds him in a battle among the enemy ranks and kills him with his own hand. Then he sneaks into Warsaw in disguise to watch the torture of his other son, Ostap, who has been captured. Then he is taken himself, nailed to a tree, and burned alive. But his last utterance is a shout of encouragement to his decimated band. One day, he says, the tsar of Russia, who also fights for the Orthodox faith, will take them under his protection.

Despite all the horror, this tale, drenched in blood from start to finish, exhales a kind of optimism. The reader is reassured by the robust good health of the protagonists, the simplicity of their passions, the Homeric grandeur of their deeds, and the beauty of the country they traverse. He is invigorated by their prodigious energy. He does not feel that their suffering is futile, but rather that all this sacrifice corresponds to some profound historical necessity. It is as though their very defeats, magnified by art, are a kind of apotheosis. "Taras Bulba" is truly a painter's tale.

After congratulating Brulov on the mastery with which, in *The Last Days of Pompeii,* he transformed a scene of collective agony into a thing of beauty, Gogol applied his own aesthetic principle to himself, transcending reality to such a degree that this mountain of cadavers gives anyone who sees it a taste for life. "It is for the pacification and reconciliation of all that the high creation of art descends upon earth," he wrote in "The Portrait."

Notwithstanding the violence of its subject, "Taras Bulba" does, perhaps, leave the reader with a sense of "pacification" and "reconciliation," but its author never recaptured that tranquil confidence of the historical novelist again.

In "Viy" we are back with the devil, exacting and terrorizing. Through another, female character, he attacks the philosophy student Thomas Brutus, who, with a couple of friends, has set off on foot from the theological seminary to spend the summer holiday with his parents. At nightfall the three young men, wearied by their long march, stop in a village and ask a very old woman for hospitality. She reluctantly agrees, and installs one of them in her hut, another in an empty shed, and the third in the sheep pen. The moment Thomas Brutus lies down to sleep, he sees the old woman coming toward him with arms outstretched. Paralyzed by the forces of hell, he cannot push her away. She leaps upon his back and, thus bestridden and beleaguered by the blows of her broomstick, he carries her up to the sky. But as he flies, he retains sufficient presence of mind to recite some prayers, and the witch, her power inhibited by the holy words, begins to tremble, moan, and lose altitude. Then, when he touches earth again, it is his turn to straddle and thrash her. He thinks he has slain a monster, but in the light of dawn, "shining upon the gilded cupolas of the churches of Kiev in the distance," Thomas Brutus discovers to his stupefaction "a lovely girl with magnificent tresses hanging loose and lashes long as arrows" lying at his feet; "with white, bare arms outstretched, she moaned, raising to heaven her tear-filled eyes". Terror-stricken, he bolts. Later he is ordered by his rector to keep a deathwatch over the body of a woman in the church. Alone with the open coffin, he recognizes—more beautiful and desirable and disturbing than before—the witch he had beaten. Drawing a circle of chalk around his feet, he tries for three nights to ward off the forces of evil. The corpse, reanimated by lust, rises, walks toward him, returns to her coffin; but then the coffin itself begins to fly through the church "with piercing, whistling sounds." The windowpanes shatter, the icons crash to the ground, the doors are wrenched from their hinges, while Thomas Brutus sweats and recites his exorcisms in a failing voice. Then the demons summon Viy, an abominable gnome, chief of the earth spirits, who is covered with clay, has feet shaped like tree roots and eyelids that drag on the ground. The student instinctively senses that he must not look at him if he is to survive. But the temptation is too great; he takes one quick glance and is frightened literally to death. The cock crows for the second time and the spirits try to fly away, but it is too late, and some are trapped and remain stuck around the doors and windows of the church. "When the priest came that morning, he recoiled at the sight of such profanation of the holy sanctuary and did not dare sing the requiem."

Yet again, the Evil One has assumed the form of a pretty woman in Gogol's work. How many men, he thought, give way to temptation and become Thomas Brutuses scourged by witches! The soul is a fiend; the face, an angel. They work their evil at night and glow with candor in the rising sun. One should always draw a chalk circle around one's feet before looking at women.

"I own, I do not understand how it happens," Gogol wrote in "The Quarrel of the Two Ivans," "that women catch us by the end of the nose as lightly as they seize the handle of the teapot; was that what their hands were made for, is that all our noses are good for? Even though the nose of Ivan Nikiforovich looked like a prune, Agafya Fyodosyevna got hold of it and led our hero around like a poodle."

In "Nevsky Prospect" a drunken German cries, "I don't need a nose! For that nose I use three pound of tobacco every month. My nose alone costs me fourteen rubles and forty kopecks!"

And the poignant hero of "Diary of a Madman" solemnly notes: "At the present time the moon is inhabited solely by noses. And it is for that reason we cannot see our noses: they are all on the moon."

Throughout both *Arabesques* and *Mirgorod,* the leitmotif of the nose forms a counterpoint to the leitmotif of the woman / devil's accomplice. True enough, the author could hardly look in a mirror without being surprised by the length, the slenderness, and the cartilaginous autonomy, so to speak, of his own nasal appendage. They say that when he made a face like a nutcracker, he could actually touch it with his lower lip. He was hypersensitive to smells and analyzed and described them voluptuously. His heroes move about in a heavily olfactory atmosphere. They sneeze, snore, and snort. After all these tentative allusions, Gogol finally decided to give the nose a monument of its own. This story, "The Nose," was written in 1834 but not included in *Mirgorod.* After the editorial board of the *Muscovite Observer* had rejected it, it was published in *The Contemporary* under a note by Pushkin: "N. V. Gogol withheld publication of this sketch for a long time, but we found it so out of the ordinary, fantastical, droll, and original that we have persuaded him to allow us to share with the public the pleasure his manuscript has given us."[4]

For once, Pushkin had underestimated his protégé. The "sketch" is stranger than appears at first glance. Inspired by the fantasies of Hoffmann and Chamisso, the author's first impulse was certainly to create nothing more than a great hoax; but without his willing it, the farce acquired more sinister overtones.

One morning a barber finds the nose of one of his customers, collegiate assessor Kovalev, inside the loaf of bread he is about to eat. Startled by his discovery, he seizes the piece of flesh with some distaste and goes to throw it into the Neva. But the nose reappears and begins parading about St. Petersburg. "This time it was wearing a gold-embroidered uniform with a huge high collar, thin leather breeches, and a sword at its side. Its plumed officers' hat showed that it was a state councilor." The hapless Kovalev approaches this essential adornment of his person, speaks to it, and tries to persuade it to return to its proper place; but the nose, very haughty, replies, "You are mistaken, sir; I belong only to myself. Moreover, there could be no close connection between us. Judging from the buttons on your uniform, we are in different departments." And it disappears, leaving Kovalev utterly at a loss.

In the end, a policeman returns his nose, but the doctor he asks to restore it to his face refuses to attempt the operation. The whole business is beginning to be bruited about town. The gazettes are full of it. And then one morning Kovalev wakes up with his nose in the middle of his face.

The most extraordinary thing about this incident is that none of the characters find it in the least extraordinary, and the reader himself is asked not to be very surprised. The barber takes fright when he sees a nose in his bread, but his wife is only dreading a visit from the police. The employee of the newspaper in which Kovalev wants to place an advertisement finds the occurrence odd but nothing more, and refuses the advertisement on the ground that his paper might be accused of facetiousness. He nonetheless observes quite sympathetically that his customer's face is indeed incomplete. "What a strange thing to happen!" he says. "The place is quite bare, and flat as a pancake fresh from the pan." The police commissioner, to whom Kovalev turns next, receives him coldly and suggests, that "a respectable man does not have his nose pulled off." The policeman who returns the nose to its owner placidly announces, "Your nose is perfectly intact." The doctor summoned to attach the appendage examines his patient and decides: "I could, of course, put your nose back in place, but I promise on my honor that you would be even worse off than before. Let nature take its course. Wash often in cold water and, I assure you, you will be just as healthy without a nose as if you had one." The townspeople see nothing more than an entertaining oddity in the uniformed nose. "These events were highly diverting to the habitués of society drawing rooms, who happened just then to be short of anecdotes to amuse the ladies."

And Gogol concluded, "The whole thing doesn't make sense: I absolutely do not understand it. And the strangest and most incomprehensible thing of all is that authors should choose to write about such subjects. I confess, really, come to think of it, it is absolutely inconceivable. But when you do come to think about it, there is something in it after all. Say what you will, such things happen in the world; seldom, I agree, but they do happen."

Another comment: In the newspaper office, Kovalev says, referring to his lost nose, "It's the devil playing a trick on me." It is the devil, too, no doubt, who turns everything topsy-turvy in St. Petersburg, thickens the fog in the streets, freezes hearts, afflicts people with blindness. Even more disturbing than the profaned church in "Viy" is this "northern capital of the empire," in which the mystery grows and spreads in the evil light of the street lamps. No flying coffins this time, but a nose walking around on two legs. No funereal horror, but a chuckling nonsense. No hideous gnomes, but respectable passers-by and cautious civil servants. The line between real and unreal gently melts in a world of chiaroscuro. Satan takes faces apart, plants a plumed hat on a piece of flesh, sets a pair of nostrils in a coach-and-four, gives a high rank to an amputation, and so muddles the minds of honest citizens that no one even protests.

The moment he regains possession of his nose, Kovalev resumes his favorite pastime, which is "the smiling pursuit of every pretty woman he sees." Ah! so he's only a rogue, an ally of the Great Tempter. When the devil gives him back his nose, he has undoubtedly hidden himself inside it, and will stay there forever.

This nasal appendage, suddenly endowed with an independent existence, may well have a sexual significance that escaped the author. An impotent Gogol chose to imagine a part of himself, oblong and detached, vibrating and scouring the world in search of high adventure. He projected his intimate protuberance into the crowd, where its turgescent nakedness rubs against the uniforms of lords and gowns of ladies. He was unconsciously liberating himself from an obsession in the incoherence of a dream.

In the first version, the state councilor-nose goes into the Cathedral of Our Lady of Kazan. Foreseeing the censor's reaction to this, Gogol declared himself willing to send his curious hero to a Roman Catholic church rather than an Orthodox place of worship. In the end, the censor opted for the bazaar (Gostiny Dvor) as the meeting place between Kovalev and the most precious part of his anatomy. A passage in which Kovalev bribes a policeman was also deleted. Gogol had already been scolded for depicting, in "Nevsky Prospect," a lieutenant being beaten by two Germans. To justify such a crime, the author was obliged to make it clear that Pirogov was not in uniform, "but arrived dressed in civilian clothes, with a simple overcoat and no epaulets."

To obtain permission to publish "Diary of a Madman," he had had to cut a long passage from a letter written by one dog to another concerning her master, who was obsessed by his longing for a decoration: "He seldom opens his mouth, but a week ago he was constantly repeating, 'Will they give it to me or not?' Then, triumph. All morning, gentlemen in uniform were coming to congratulate him. After dinner he lifted me up to his neck and said, 'Look, Madgie, what have I got here?' I saw a ribbon. I sniffed it, but could discover no scent at all. Finally, I licked it, discreetly. It was slightly salty." To speak in such terms of a decoration awarded by the emperor was bordering on sacrilege. A decoration without a smell. And salty, what's more. And soiled by the insolent lick of a dog. The whole paragraph was crossed out by a censor's furious quill.

But no administrative exorcism can prevail against certain forces of the mind. It was as though the amputated sentences had left their roots in the text. Despite the scrupulous cleansing and scouring, a strong smell of sulphur rises from Gogol's stories, whether Ukrainian or Petersburgian, macabre or bawdy, satanical or modestly ordinary.

9. *The Inspector General*

There was no word of Pushkin, who had gone to earth on his Mikhailo-vskoye farm; perhaps he was annoyed by that letter asking him for a subject for a comedy. At last, on October 23, 1835, the news came that he was back in Petersburg. He had hardly moved into his apartment overlooking the Neva near the Prachechny Bridge when Gogol returned to the charge. Pushkin seemed worried. There had never been any real intimacy between the two men, and it would not have occurred to Gogol to question his illustrious friend about his private life. He knew, of course, as everyone knew, that Pushkin was jealous of his excessively pretty young wife, that it had infuriated him to be appointed—at his age!—a gentleman of the chamber, that he fumed and fretted whenever he had to appear at palace balls, that he was living well beyond his means, that his slightest initiative provoked a government remonstrance, that he was at once the tsar's pet and his prisoner. But all of that lay be-hind an invisible line which the poet guarded with dignity. Firm and courteous, he talked only literature with his young colleague, who soon recovered his nerve and made bold to repeat his demand. Pushkin laughed. A subject for a comedy? Yes, he had just made a note of one. A few lines of his quick script: "Krispin comes to a county town for the fair and is mistaken for . . . The mayor is an imbecile; the mayor's wife flirts with him; Krispin becomes engaged to the daughter." This was based on something which had actually happened to Paul Svinin, editor of a periodical,[1] who had gone to Bessarabia and been mistaken for an inspector general on a tour of duty. Welcomed with open arms by the mayor's family, he posed as a great dignitary, courted the ladies, made promises to the gentlemen, and received petitioners. Pushkin himself, moreover, had been involved in a similar case of mistaken identity when he was passing through Nizhny Novgorod in August 1833 and the governor there was informed that he was an envoy from the capital on a secret mission.

As he listened, Gogol almost began to bounce up and down in his chair. This was the very thing he needed. A little provincial town. A conceited impostor. Idiots who take him at his word. The administration ridiculed. The faults of all laid bare in broad daylight. A tempest in a teapot. Now, if Pushkin would only agree to give this little gem to him. Once again, the poet yielded to his pleading, and was later heard to say, with a wry grin, "You must be on your guard with that Little Russian; he skins me so adroitly that I never even have time to call for help."[2]

In fact, the subject of the traveling man-in-the-street mistaken for a VIP had already been treated in a comedy by Kotzebue, *The Little German Town,* and in another by the Ukrainian author Kvitka-Osnovyanenko, *The Visitor from the Capital, or, Tumult in the County Town.*[3] There had even been a comedy by Polevoy entitled *The Inspectors General, or, Who Comes from Afar May Lie All He Likes* (1832). None of these precursors, however, could have inspired Gogol: he refused patronage from any source other than Pushkin. The creative spark had to come from the top.

Abandoning *Dead Souls,* he plunged into *The Inspector General.* He had not been wrong about the quality of the subject: scenes virtually wrote themselves; characters emerged, each with his particular frown or tic; and the lines clattered merrily. In the fever of creation, Gogol hardly left his room except for an occasional visit to the Patriotic Institute to see his sisters, or to call on a few friends for a change of scene. This time, he was certain of success. On November 10, 1835, he wrote to his mother:

"We are all in good health here. My sisters are growing, studying, and enjoying themselves. I personally am anticipating something extremely pleasant. I think that within two years at most I shall be able to invite you to come to St. Petersburg for a visit with your daughters. In the meanwhile, we must not complain."

On December 4, 1835, he finished the comedy and gave it to a copyist, but instantly took it back again and began revising, cutting, tightening, sharpening. "The comedy is finished and copied," he wrote to Pogodin on January 18, 1836, "but I have just realized that I absolutely must make a few changes. This will not take long, as I have decided to produce the play for Easter; it will be completely ready by the beginning of Lent, and the actors will have ample time to learn their parts."

That same day, January 18, he read *The Inspector General* to a group of friends at Zhukovsky's: Pushkin was there, and Vyazemsky,[4] and Vyelgorsky. Peals of laughter greeted the very first scene. The listeners exchanged occasional glances of mischievous delight. At the end, there was nothing but praise, and a jubilant Gogol.

"He reads masterfully and provokes wave upon wave of laughter," Vyazemsky wrote to A. I. Turgenev the following day. "I am not sure the play will not lose something in performance, for few actors will be able to play it as he reads it. There is a kind of excess of glee in Gogol, which often leads him to go too far, and then his mockery is out of place."[5]

There were other drawing-room readings, all equally successful. The hard part, however, remained: As the play ridiculed provincial officials, the censor was not likely to allow it to be either published or performed. Unless, of course, an order should come from on high and smooth out all the obstacles. As though on the eve of a bloody combat, the friends drew up their plan of battle. Pushkin suggested that pretty Alexandra Smirnov should speak directly to the emperor, as she had previously and successfully done on behalf of his *Boris Godunov*. After all, Nicholas I had only recently authorized publication of Griboedov's *Wit Works Woe,* which had been prohibited throughout his father's reign. Perhaps he would let himself be tempted into a second display of literary liberalism. Zhukovsky undertook to win over the heir apparent. Count Vyelgorsky and Prince Vyazemsky planned other campaigns of seduction in the monarch's circle. Upon getting wind of an unfavorable first reaction from the censor's office, the conspirators took the offensive. As agreed, Mrs. Smirnov pleaded the author's cause to Nicholas I; she alluded to Molière, whose *Tartuffe* would never have been performed but for the enlightened protection of Louis XIV; she stressed the posthumous glory accruing to sovereigns who were also patrons of literature and the arts.

The emperor heard her out with a smile. He was a military man to the marrow of his bones, with a passion for discipline, mathematics, and symmetry. His fondest wish was to see everyone in Russia in uniform, physically and morally. Literature he regarded as an inoffensive pastime.

In his opinion, the best books were the ones you didn't have to think about. Paul de Kock was and remained his favorite author. With rare exceptions, he said, authors were nothing but agitators, better kept on a tight rein. Ah, but there was so much merry mischief in Mrs. Smirnov's black eyes that it was hard to refuse her a favor. Nicholas I was ever sensitive to feminine beauty, and so he agreed to˚ consider *The Inspector General*. Count Vyelgorsky read him the play. Either the tsar did not see the danger lurking in this scathing satire of administrative corruption, or he thought the majesty of the central government could not be compromised by a little mud thrown at a few provincial officials, or he took the whole thing to be innocent clowning—this last being the most likely hypothesis. Nicholas I was a great lover of vaudeville, and all he saw in *The Inspector General* was a series of preposterous situations calculated to give rise to loud and healthy guffaws; and so long as the people are laughing, they are not to be feared. In a gesture of amused benevolence, the emperor expressed his satisfaction with the comedy.

Events now followed with miraculous ease. The locked gears were released and wheels began to turn. Obedient to instructions from the palace, Oldekop, the censor, ordered only a few insignificant cuts; no mention should be made of the church that had been begun and left unfinished, or of the Order of Vladimir, for which the judge was yearning, or of the non-commissioned officer's wife who had been flogged by mistake. Subjects to these amendments, the report concluded, "The play is witty and admirably written. It contains nothing reprehensible." General Dubelt, chief of the constabulary, wrote in the margin, "Authorized." Gedeonov, director of the imperial theaters, received orders to begin rehearsals of *The Inspector General* at once, in the Alexandra Theater.

Upon seeing himself so swiftly and liberally gratified, Gogol was positively in the clouds. Some of the best actors in the capital were in the cast: Sosnitsky was to play the mayor, Dür would be Khlestakov, Afanasyev was cast as Osip—a promise of success, but a cause for concern as well, for these gentlemen thought extremely well of themselves and were very hard to handle. Khrapovitsky, the director, moreover, made no secret of his disgruntlement at being forced to produce a play he had had no say in selecting.

The play was read to the cast for the first time at Sosnitsky's home. Facing the assembled company, Gogol felt shrouded in ice. These were not friends who had come to hear him; they were judges wearing expressions of artificially polite interest. They had all heard of the author of *Evenings on a Farm,* of course, but the figure that had just walked into the room possessed nothing to inspire confidence, let alone respect. Was it a human being or a stork in disguise?

"Short and fair, with an enormous crest on top of his head, he wore gold-rimmed pince-nez on his bird beak, wrinkled up his eyes, and pursed his lips tightly together as though he had bitten them on the inside," Karatygin, one of the actors, related. "His green coat with the long tails and tiny mother-of-pearl buttons, his brown trousers, his way of taking off his top hat and turning it around and around in his hands, then nervously running his fingers through his crest: all of these together transformed him into a caricature."

The reading began. As usual, Gogol changed intonation, and almost his whole face, with every character, but his speech was always natural. He was funny without "hamming"—this the actors saw from the opening lines. But they were perplexed by the play. Brought up in the tradition of Knyazhnin, Shakovskoy, Marivaux, and Ducis, they balked at the triviality of some of the passages. How would the public react to such "platitude"? Wouldn't they lump actors and author together and reject the lot? Looks were exchanged under the author's nose, sometimes amused, sometimes startled. At the end, there was a ruffle of preoccupied and unconvinced applause, a few self-conscious compliments. Sosnitsky alone seemed pleased with the play. While he and Gogol stood talking together, the other actors drew aside and whispered: "What does it mean? Is this a comedy? He reads well enough, no doubt about that, but what language! His lackey talks exactly like a lackey, and Poshlyopkina, the locksmith's wife, is a proper matron from the haymarket! What is Sosnitsky raving about? What do Pushkin and Zhukovsky find so wonderful about it?"[6]

Rehearsals began, and the hostility increased. The actors had no faith in the play and acted their parts unwillingly. They felt dishonored by this vulgar rag being thrust upon them after their years of loyal service to the classical repertory. Some called for cuts or changes in the dialogue on grounds of propriety. Others, who would go to any lengths for a laugh, exaggerated the comic aspect of their parts by conventional posturing. Exasperated by their lack of understanding, Gogol struggled to prevent them from turning the play into a complete buffoonery. He issued written instructions, urging them to act naturally and simply. "The less the actor works for laughs, the funnier his part will be," he said. The

actors sulked and shrugged; Karatygin drew on his script a caricature of
the author, standing in the wings with his top hat in his hands and with
the expression of a rejected suitor on his face. As the weeks passed, the
atmosphere became increasingly charged. Wrestling with the scores of
little practical problems that kept cropping up, Gogol almost began to
wish some natural disaster would destroy the whole theater. What a gulf
between the play he had written and the play that was now taking
shape before his eyes!

The first line explodes like a firecracker: "I have called you together,
gentlemen, to announce a most unpleasant piece of news: an inspector
general is coming to visit us." The listeners are paralyzed by the mayor's
words, and the whole action proceeds from there. "Yes, an inspector
general," he goes on, "an inspector general from St. Petersburg, incognito. And with secret orders too." Faced with this imminent peril, of
which the first inkling has arrived in a confidential letter from a "reliable
source," everyone suddenly feels shabby and unclean and starts looking
around for a clothesbrush. In a few sentences the characters create the
whole little provincial town, in which they are both product and parasite.
An obscure backwater, from which "you can gallop for three years
without reaching the frontier." The dignitaries of the little town have
neither the appetite nor the resources of their powerful colleagues in St.
Petersburg. They steal money, of course; they coerce the townspeople,
open letters, neglect their duties, and fiddle with their influence, but
they do it cheerfully and in moderation. None of your spectacular
swindles or blatant thievery; at most, a kind of amiable corruption—
tolerated by some, encouraged by others, and providing the substance of
daily life for all. And now this easygoing *modus vivendi* compounded of
the spineless torpor of the victims and the unambitious knavery of their
exploiters is about to be challenged by the unexpected arrival of an inspector general, a brick thrown into the stagnant swamp. Steps must be
taken, and quickly, to ensure that the visitor does not see how dilapidated the town's affairs have become. The mayor, a ponderous, tough-
minded prevaricator, issues orders like an admiral on the bridge of his
sinking ship. He addresses each of his subalterns in turn.
Their names alone, in Russian, are like outrageous masks stuck on
their faces: Zemlyanika (Mr. Strawberry), Lyapkin-Tyapkin (Alley-
Oop!), Khlopov (Mr. Slap), etc. Let Master Zemlyanika, director of the
welfare institution, have clean bonnets put on his patients and hang

charts in Latin at the foot of their beds. Let Mr. Lyapkin-Tyapkin, the judge, drive the geese out of the waiting room and remove the clothes drying in the courtroom. And Khlopov, the superintendent of schools: he must see that his teachers behave themselves; some of them have the most peculiar habits. And Shpekin, the postmaster: he is not to open just one or two letters now and then, but every envelope that comes through the office, to discover if there are not a few actionable statements being made by discontented tradespeople. And the streets must be cleaned, and the garbage must be picked up, and a rickety old fence torn down. . . . Will they ever have time to get it all done before the inspector general reaches town?

Too late! Two local landowners, Bobchinsky and Dobchinsky, arrive bearing grim tidings: a mysterious young man named Khlestakov has taken rooms in the inn. According to his passport he is a government official, comes from St. Petersburg, and is en route for Saratov. He has been in town for two weeks, watching everything, dining on credit and never paying a kopeck. There can be no doubt: he must be the inspector general himself, traveling incognito and bearing secret orders. Without further ado, the mayor decides to confront him, inventing an investigation into the facilities provided for travelers as a pretext. He will try to soften him up, move him into his own house, and all the time pretend—there's the real trick—not to have guessed his true identity.

While he prepares for his expedition, we meet young Khlestakov and his manservant, Osip, at the inn. In reality, Khlestakov is a very junior official in the capital on his way to visit his family. The reason he has remained in this sordid flea bag for the past fortnight is that he has lost all his money at cards and hasn't a penny to pay the bill. The innkeeper is begrudging him even the short rations he gets, and threatening to prosecute. And suddenly, here comes the mayor in person.

This time, Khlestakov thinks he's in for it. He stands there, believing he is about to be thrown in jail for non-payment of debt, facing the mayor, who believes *he* is about to be relieved of office by an inspector general in disguise: the confrontation of two terrors, each growing with every word uttered by the other. Face to face, the adversaries size each other up, advance, extend antennae, and recoil in a protozoan ballet of vibrating pseudopods. As the misinterpretations accumulate, the quavering Khlestakov's defenses are reduced to vague threats: Don't anyone try to get him out of that room! "I wouldn't go with you if you brought a regiment. I shall go straight to the minister. . . . The only reason I'm hanging on in this hole is that I haven't got a kopeck to my name!"

The words do not fall on deaf ears. On one side "the minister," on the other "kopeck": clearly, thinks the mayor, the inspector general is waiting for a "gesture" on the part of those he has come to inspect. What a relief! The avenging angel assumes human form: he is part of the system of generalized corruption. With trembling hand and uneasy eye, the mayor holds out four hundred rubles. Khlestakov takes them. He then invites the traveler to be a guest in his own home.

Without the foggiest notion of what has earned him this privileged treatment, Khlestakov settles comfortably into the mayor's household. His wife and daughter cast flatteringly admiring glances at him. The local worthies do not dare sit in his presence. A succulent lunch has been set before him. Good food and strong wine heat his brain; giving his imagination free rein, he begins to talk, making himself more drunk with words. Nothing is compelling him to lie; he reckons neither the risk nor the advantage to be gained by his fabulations: he simply flings himself into them as an artist yields to and luxuriates in his inspiration— for the sheer pleasure of gratuitous deceit, loss of identity in the unreal; and the more unlikely his affirmations, the greater his fervor in propounding them.

Gogol was well acquainted with the temptation of lying for the sake of lying. All his letters to his mother and friends express his seething mythomania. In the character of Khlestakov, he simply carries his own tendency to deceive his fellow man to the point of madness. For a Russian reader, the very name of Khlestakov connotes swiftness and levity, the sound of cloven air, the hiss of a slim-thonged whip.[7] Khlestakov lashes out right and left, sets all the tops aspin, claims to be the kingpin of several ministries, feared by generals, with actresses at his feet, dining in Petersburg on soup sent straight from Paris "by steamship"; he has written mountains of books, including *Manon Lescaut* and *Robinson Crusoe,* and is an intimate friend of Pushkin. "I often say to him, 'Well, now, Pushkin, old chap, how's it going?' 'Well, old man,' he sometimes replies, 'oh, not too badly, not too well, got to make the best of it!' Most original chap!" And, watching the rapt faces of his audience, he becomes still more inflated. The less anchored he is in reality, the higher he soars. He even says of himself, "My thoughts are of an extraordinary lightness." Here is the chance of a lifetime offered to a wisp of vapor, an empty husk, zero gravity.

"Every day, I go to a ball. We play whist, the foreign minister, the French ambassador, the English ambassador, the German ambassador, and I. One of the most curious things is to look into my hall before I get up in the morning: counts and princes pushing and shoving and buzzing like hornets, that's all you can hear is bzzzz, bzzz. Sometimes even a minister. They mark 'Your Excellency' on the packages they send me. When I walk through the ministry, everyone trembles and shivers. Oh, they know I don't fool around; I've scared the living daylights out of them! Even the State Council fear me. That's the way I am, by George; I am not afraid of anyone. I tell the lot of them, 'I know what I'm worth.' I am everywhere, everywhere. Every day I go to the palace. Tomorrow, if not today, I'll be made a marshal." At this point, gesticulating wildly, Khlestakov slips and nearly falls, but the local officials tenderly bear him up. The entire social system flies to the impostor's aid. In another minute he would be calling himself the tsar—like poor Popryshchin in "Diary of a Madman," who imagined he was King of Spain.

The strangest thing of all is that Khlestakov's audience is utterly hypnotized by his extravagant pronouncements—as though, in that fantastic St. Petersburg from which he comes, the improbable were the rule, and the mist that shrouds the capital had spread into the provinces and befuddled everyone's wits. He shouts and threats, and therefore the local officials see him as the authentic delegate of authority. Their ancient instinct of servility bows their heads to anyone who knows how to raise his voice. "What do you think of him, Pyotr Ivanovich, what rank can he have?" whispers Bobchinsky. "My soul, he might well be a general!" Dobchinsky replies. "Well, I think," cries the inspired Bobchinsky, "I think he's miles above a general!"

The mayor himself suspects Khlestakov of some exaggeration, but is nevertheless persuaded that he holds a high position in the administration. One after the other, the local officials troop in to bribe the man from the big city and secure his good opinion. Finally realizing that they have taken him for some government eminence, Khlestakov pockets their cash without batting an eyelid, and with similar nonchalance pockets the money of a few shopkeepers who have come to complain about the mayor. He promises his protection to one and all. His manservant, Osip, is growing alarmed at the turn of events, and counsels Khlestakov to clear out at top speed. Khlestakov, with customary *sang-froid,* takes time to write a letter to his friend Tryapichkin,[8] to tell him about his adventure.

Then his eye falls upon the mayor's daughter Marya; he gives her a little whirl to pass the time and then flits over to her mother. "But she's quite a tasty morsel, the mother; not bad at all!" And when that lady feebly objects: "Pray permit me to point out to you that I am—in a manner of speaking—married . . . ," he overpowers her with, "No matter. Love knows no distinctions. Karamzin said, 'If the laws condemn us we will take refuge among the forest ferns.' " Thus he does not bother himself with any form of morality and means to live from day to day— picking, as he puts it himself, "the flower of pleasure." Why complicate life? There is no more line between good and evil than there is between truth and lie. Anyone who has a desire is forgiven a priori for seeking to satisfy it. When one has, like Khlestakov, the gift of lightness, one does not challenge the law: one flies over it. But Marya catches him at her mother's feet: "Ah, what a picture!" Never mind; he turns another somersault and asks the speechless mother for the hand of her daughter, who can't believe her ears.

Thereupon the woebegone mayor himself enters, having just learned that the shopkeepers have discovered all and have come to complain about him to the inspector general. But all is well: there is no more inspector general in his house, there is a future son-in-law. To become the father-in-law of such a great man is like having one of the ancient legends come true: the glorious union of the god from Olympus and the mortal maiden.

But the horses are now harnessed and Khlestakov hastily excuses himself: he must spend one day with his uncle, "a very rich old man." He'll be back on the morrow, cross his heart. Sighs, hand kissings, protestations of love. Khlestakov borrows another four hundred rubles from his father-in-law-to-be, climbs into the troika, and whirls off in a tinkle of little bells. A winged troika, carrying him off to fresh falsehoods elsewhere, an opalescent soap bubble about to vanish into thin air. That's how the Olympians behaved, after all.

The mayor's good fortune is beginning to go to his head; as though infected by Khlestakov's verbal spell, he now plunges headlong into his own dreams, seeing himself a general with a red (or maybe blue) ribbon across his chest, preceded everywhere by a squadron of mounted orderlies galloping like the wind. And in the meantime, he summons those shopkeepers who dared to denounce him and gives them a good drubbing: "Take care! I have my eye on you! I am not marrying my daughter to any old country squire! Let your presents be worthy of the circumstances! Don't think you're going to get away with a sturgeon and a few loaves of sugar!" Into the procession of friends and sycophants who have come to congratulate the lucky family bursts the postmaster, white as a sheet, with a letter in his hand. As usual, he has unsealed it. And now reads it aloud. It is from Khlestakov, and in it he tells his friend Tryapichkin about the mistake that has been made and how heartily he has laughed at all these idiots for supposing he was somebody else. The letter gets down to personalities, dealing out one or two prime insults to everyone present. The entire town is ridiculed. The stricken mayor suddenly grasps the vast swindle that has now stripped him naked before his electorate.

"I'm assassinated, slaughtered, butchered!" he stammers. "I can't even see straight. Instead of faces, all I see around me are pigs' snouts!" Suddenly he begins to berate himself, as though looking in a mirror: "You old animal, go on! Triple animal! Great fat fool, to take a whippersnapper, a sparrow, for a person of consequence! And there he is galloping down the road ringing his bells! He'll tell the whole world his story. Not only you will become an object of sneers and laughter; but worse, some scribbler, some ink spiller will come along and stuff you into a comedy! He won't take any notice of your title or your rank! That's the most unbearable thing of all! And they'll all start giggling and clapping their hands like a bunch of boobies! What are you laughing at? It's yourselves you're laughing at!"

Zemlyanika remarks, in a daze, "To save my soul, I couldn't explain how it happened. It was as though we were walking in a fog; the devil must have bewitched us." That is a line that has a familiar ring: almost every one of Gogol's creations has been affected in one way or another by the "fog" from the north, the devil in a frock coat "bewitching" minds until they can no longer distinguish between palpable and impalpable.

At this point the mayor supposes he has reached the bottom of the pit; but into the midst of the dozen pigs' snouts surrounding him erupts a new pig's snout: a policeman, the instrument of destiny. He says, "Sent by order of the imperial government, a senior official from St. Petersburg requests you to appear before him at once. He is staying at the inn." As though it were the Last Judgment to which he has just been summoned, everyone on stage freezes in a circle around the mayor. There is no one left but the guilty.

On this tableau the curtain falls. Another play is about to begin, and the spectator can imagine it clearly. The one he has just seen, however, passes as swiftly as a dream. From the first scene to the last, the pace never falters. An irresistible logic dictates the sequence of events in such a way that the audience, moving from one surprise to the next, feels convinced that things could not happen otherwise. It is this combination of grotesque phantasmagoria and mechanical perfection that gives the text its unique and original quality. An implacable mechanism propels the specters of a nightmare. There is not one extra word, not one instant of dead time, not one character without a point. Even the walk-ons are etched in unforgettable comic relief. Zemlyanika, Tyapkin-Lyapkin, the postmaster, Bobchinsky and Dobchinsky—each one, by his very presence, summons up some fragment of his private world. By allusion, the mayor's family is all families. Avenues open out on all sides: homes take form; mothers, husbands, children, schoolmasters, feuding landowners, wild-eyed scribes surge into view in the background. Fitting them together like pieces in a jigsaw puzzle, we recreate the town. A fenced-in, mediocre, stagnant, stifling little hell.

"With *The Inspector General*," Gogol later wrote, "I resolved to put together everything I knew about Russia at that time that was evil— all the injustices perpetrated in the places and circumstances in which a man is expected to display the highest degree of justice—and to have a good laugh at it all, once and for all."[9]

There is no doubt that he laughed as he wrote his play. Every character has a particular way of talking. Some lines are more revealing of a weakness of character or moral corruption than a hundred pages of courtroom testimony. There is the mayor shouting about an officer's wife he had flogged by mistake: "She lied; I swear she lied! She flogged herself!"[10] There is Zemlyanika, director of welfare, talking about his patients: "Since I have been at the hospital, they've been getting better like flies!" There is the judge, speaking of his clerk, who exudes a strong smell of alcohol: "He says his nurse dropped him in it when he was little and he has had a faint smell of vodka about him ever since." Or Bobchinsky requesting Khlestakov, when he next sees the emperor, to say, "Now, Sire, in such a town there lives a certain Pyotr Ivanovich Bobchinsky." And the mayor again, imagining how the inspector general will summon the officials: " 'Who is the judge here? Lyapkin-Tyapkin? Send in Lyapkin-Tyapkin! And who is director of welfare? Zemlyanika? Send in Zemlyanika!' "

The whole play is like this—big, violent, succulent. A strong dish that burns the roof of your mouth when you taste it; but when the laughter fades, sadness remains, and uneasiness, and a supernatural anguish. Khlestakov, flying down the road in his troika, has duped us as much as he has duped the mayor.

10. Performance

The day of the first performance was drawing near. The actors were rehearsing feverishly, script in hand, at the Alexandra. As usual, the management had not seen fit to schedule rehearsals for costumes or props. They were experienced: no one was going to bother them with trivial technical details. When the audience was there, they always managed somehow.

Notwithstanding these powerful arguments, Gogol insisted on seeing the sets on the day before opening night, and it was a good thing he did, for a plush, opulent décor had been ordered for the mayor's house, which Gogol replaced with a less pretentious interior, adding a cage and some canaries in a corner and a bottle of "white" liquor on the window sill. Khlestakov's valet, Osip, had been decked out in superb livery with gold braid, although his master's lack of funds was one of the mainsprings of the plot. Gogol rejected the costume, appropriated the oil-smeared garb of the theater lamplighter, and transferred it to Afanasyev, who was playing the part of Osip. Gogol also contested the wigs some of the actors were determined to wear on the grounds that they made them look funnier—but on that point he lost. After all, he was only a novice at this business, and the actors knew much better than he what the audience wanted.

He received some encouragement in that month of April 1836, however, from Pushkin, who introduced him to readers of the first issue of his periodical *The Contemporary* in the following terms: "Our readers will certainly not have forgotten the impression made upon them by

Evenings on a Farm. Everyone joyfully welcomed this lively presentation of a dancing, singing people, those fresh images of the Little Russian character, that gaiety at once naïve and mischievous. We gaped
at the sight of a Russian book that could make us laugh, we who have
not laughed since Fonvizin! We were so grateful to the young author
that we gladly forgave him the irregularities and infelicities of his style,
the patchy construction and improbability of some of the stories, leaving such shortcomings for the critics to gorge upon. The author has
now justified our indulgence, for he has steadily developed and improved since that time. He published *Arabesques,* containing his most
polished story, "Nevsky Prospect"; then the booksellers gave us his
collection *Mirgorod,* in which everyone has read the story of "Old
World Landowners," an idyl at once satirical and touching, which com-
pels one to laugh through tears of melancholy and sorrow; and "Taras
Bulba," the opening of which is as good as anything Walter Scott ever
wrote. And Mr. Gogol continues to forge ahead." A footnote announced, "His comedy, *The Inspector General,* will be performed in
the very near future at a St. Petersburg theater."

The St. Petersburg *News* published the following notice in the issue
of Sunday, April 19, 1836: "Today, April 19, first performance of
The Inspector General, original comedy in five acts, at the Alexandra
Theater."

Gogol left for the theater that day with jangling nerves and constricted diaphragm. It was rumored that the tsar himself might come to
the performance; and he did, with the heir apparent and all his retinue.
The entire audience rose when they entered the imperial box. Nicholas
I, in uniform, his shoulders broadened by heavy gold epaulets, bowed
to the public, who replied with cheers and applause. Then he sat and
the people followed suit, in a murmur like grass bowing in the wind.
Hidden behind a flat, Gogol peered tensely out at the glittering crowd:
what an amazing concentration of bald pates, black evening coats,
tiaras, bare shoulders, aiguillettes, white starched bibs, military dress
starred with decorations, limply waving fans, and bunches of flowers!
A sequined, sparkling, rustling world enclosed in the great basin of the
theater. "The ministers were in the first row," Alexandra Smirnov
wrote. "They were to applaud whenever the emperor, who sat with
both hands on the top of his box rail, would give the signal." Behind
the ministers crowded the representatives of the high aristocracy, the
senior officials, the lions of society. Here and there Gogol picked out a

friendly face: the old fable writer Krylov had come and was sitting, huge and gray and drowsy, in the stalls. Also present, in their season subscriber boxes, were the Vyelgorskys, Vyazemskys, Odoevskys, Annenkovs, Smirnovs—but Pushkin was not in St. Petersburg, unfortunately, and so could not be there. Representing the enemy camp, there were the critics Bulgarin, Senkovsky, and Grech, and so many more! Gogol suddenly saw that the great majority of these people could not possibly like his savage comedy. Those people up in the peanut gallery, perhaps; they might really laugh. But all the elite would be offended. What demon had driven him to write the play? He would have done better to leave it in his drawer. He fled to the manager's box, where he could watch the performance unseen.

The curtain rose with a swish of heavy material. And in the glow of the gas lamps the actors appeared, made up, costumed, bewigged, unrecognizable, speaking more loudly and falsely than ever before. All the author's good advice had been forgotten. Facing the footlights, a fierce contest ensued to see who could ham the most and get the most applause. Bobchinsky and Dobchinsky were all contortions, Khlestakov rolled his r's, grimaced, and fluttered about like a butterfly. The mayor, tall and lean, looked like some crafty old colonel. Osip was playing a music-hall valet. Watching and listening to them, Gogol did not recognize his play. His favorite lines hurt his ears like so many wrong notes. His ribs contracted in shame, rage, and resentment, and it grew worse when he looked at the audience, for it was just as he had feared: everyone in the cheap seats was having a splendid time, but in the stalls and boxes all was consternation.

Riveted to their chairs, the dignitaries blinked as the wild mockery of the provincial administration splattered in their faces like mud. Gogol could feel their indignation, though they never twitched a muscle. If they forbore to show their displeasure, it could only be on the emperor's account, since he had authorized the play. The emperor himself, meanwhile, must be wondering if he had made a mistake. Perhaps he would rise and march ostentatiously out of the theater. No: the loyal man, he was laughing and clapping his large, white-gloved hands. And the lords and ladies beneath him obediently applauded too—less and less energetically, it was true, as the play progressed.

"As a witness of that first performance," Annenkov wrote, "I can say what the auditorium of that theater was like during those four hours of the most remarkable play ever presented there. At the end of the first act, every face was a picture of bewilderment (the audience was most select), as though no one knew what he was supposed to think. The bewilderment increased with each succeeding act. Most people, having very different expectations and habits of the theater, were disconcerted and made up their minds that this was a farce, a conclusion that appeared to reassure them. The farce, however, contained such lifelike characterizations and tableaux that on two occasions, I believe, there was a general outburst of laughter, especially in the parts corresponding most closely to the notion of comedy held by a majority of the spectators. In the fourth act, however, the position changed completely: now and then a wave of laughter would roll across the house, but it was uncertain laughter that faded as soon as it began. There was almost no applause; but the whole house followed every twist and turn of the play with close, strained attention, sometimes in utter silence, which showed how completely they were involved in what was happening on stage. At the end of that act the bewilderment was transformed into virtually unanimous indignation, increasing in Act V. The upper-class portion of the public concluded with one voice, 'It's preposterous, a calumny, a farce!' "[1]

Similar judgments were being whispered along the rows of stalls: "A farce, not worthy of the name of art," Kukolnik lisped. "An intolerable insult to the nobility, the civil service, and the merchants," added Khrapovitsky. Some witnesses reported that the tsar's chuckling verdict was, "Now, there's a play! Everyone has taken a drubbing, and myself worse than anyone else!" When the curtain rose for the last curtain call, friends scattered through the audience began calling "Author!" and the balconies joined in; but Gogol had already run away, blown out of the building by a gust of hatred. He had never yet experienced so strongly the almost physical sensation of being detested by such a vast number of human beings. But it had never been his intention to wound them deliberately; couldn't one make fun of a few officials and still respect the administration? Why, it was doing the government a favor, to denounce the abuses committed by those who neglected the dignity of their office. He wandered through the streets, his head whirling, and eventually knocked at the door of his friend Prokopovich, who tried to cheer him up by showing him a copy of *The Inspector General,* which had gone on sale that day: "Here, admire your offspring!" Gogol threw the book on the floor, leaned on the table, and sadly intoned,

"Good God, if one or two of them had cursed me, one might have borne it; but the whole house, every last one of them."[2]

The following performances confirmed his fears. People rushed to the theater, there was a black market for tickets, prices soared, but the controversy over the play raged more and more fiercely. Conservative circles accused the author of seeking to undermine the established order. Nothing, they said, was sacred to him. He was a revolutionary at heart, pretending to confine his satire to provincial officials but, through them, striking out at the most important people in the empire. In liberal circles, on the other hand, the author was praised for his daring exposure of corruption in the tsarist regime. Gogol was more terrified by the applause of the latter than by the vituperation of the former, for however badly he needed to regain his confidence, he could not side with those who praised him. What they liked in the play he had never meant to put there. He was the tsar's man, body and soul. The only conceivable government for Russia, in his opinion, was a monarchy. He believed in control by administration, the table of ranks, serfdom . . . He only wished the agents of the state were more honest. The institutions were good; it was the men who, sometimes, were not. Society did not need reform, people did. By showing up their vices, a play like *The Inspector General* should have helped them gradually to mend their ways. The object of the whole exercise was moral, not political; how was it they had not seen it?

Every day brought fresh echoes of the altercation muttering around him. Count Fyodor Ivanovich Tolstoy (nicknamed "the American"), a notorious gambler and playboy, was saying in every drawing room that the author of the play was "an enemy of Russia" and out to be "put in chains and sent to Siberia." Vigel wrote to Zagoskin, "I know the author of *The Inspector General.* He is young Russia in all her insolence and cynicism." Lazhechnikov told Belinsky, "I would not give one kopeck to have written *The Inspector General,* that farce fit only for a Russian rabble."* Prince Chernyshev, minister of war, openly regretted he had bothered to see "that stupid farce."

Vyazemsky gave the following analysis of the row stirred up by his friend's play, in a letter to A. I. Turgenev: "Everyone here is trying to be more monarchist than the king, snorting with indignation that this play should be allowed on the stage, where, it so happens, it has been

* Vigel, Zagoskin, and Lazhechnikov were members of the Russian literary scene at this time.

wildly if not universally successful. You cannot imagine the absurd judgments it has provoked, principally among the upper crust: 'As if such a town could exist in Russia!' 'Why does he not show a single decent man, just one honest person? Don't we have any?' "

The journalists aggravated the dispute. In the *Northern Bee* Bulgarin accused Gogol of "building his comedy upon improbability and impossibility rather than upon probability and resemblance. The mayor, judge, postmaster, welfare director are portrayed as crooks and dolts," he went on. "The landowners and retired civil servants have subhuman intelligence. No true comedy can be based on administrative abuse, for it does not show the customs of a people or the features of even a section of society, but only the crimes of a few isolated persons which should arouse indignation, not laughter." Senkovsky, in *The Reading Library,* proclaimed: "In this comedy there is neither plot nor denouement, the story is old as the hills, and no masterpiece. All the characters are either swine or fools. Administrative abuse exists all over the world, and there is no reason to attribute it to Russia alone by transporting these activities to our land and choosing our compatriots for protagonists."

In a review called *Renown* the young critic Belinsky replied anonymously to the attacks: "Those who believe the comedy is purely funny are mistaken. It is funny, true, on the surface as it were; but beneath, what bitterness!" In his opinion, high society was incapable of taking an interest in the tale of these petty provincial officials, and still less of understanding the tyrannical influence they could exert upon the population. "As we sat watching an audience of state councilors, actual privy councilors, and all manner of other gentlemen—each possessing several thousand souls—assemble in the theater, we could not help thinking: it is most unlikely that *The Inspector General* will please them, most unlikely that they will feel gratified by the sight of these characters, which are so intimidating to us, being reduced to life size." Belinsky also said that the names of the characters in the play had already become bywords and the streets were filled with Khlestakovs, Zemlyanikas and Tyapkin-Lyapkins. To him, the author was "a great comic painter of real life."

In the eye of the storm, the "great comic painter" was shuddering to see himself transformed into a subject for scandal. It pained him to think he had unintentionally offended respectable people, important officials, and good Christians, almost more than it pained him to know he had, just as unintentionally, delighted the freethinkers. Both praise and blame were equally likely to cast him from the emperor's good graces. If this campaign continued, perhaps they would stop the performances. The publicity and noise made him so miserable that he finally came to hope they would. He was no man for the masses, he did not have a fighter's nerve, and here he was forced to feel the weight of thousands of strangers crowding around the fringes of his existence. He neither saw nor heard them, but he sensed their murmuring presence behind the walls of his room. Hiding in his attic, he imagined countless millions of Russians concerned exclusively with him, praising, damning, trampling, celebrating, consuming, digesting, and regurgitating him. He would never be alone again. One month after the first performance he wrote:

"*The Inspector General* is being performed, and I feel something so strange and uncomfortable! I had anticipated it, I knew in advance what it would be like, but even so I am depressed, gloomy, and bitter. My own work seemed repellent to me, unnatural and as though foreign to me. The leading part doesn't work: I had guessed as much. Dür has completely failed to grasp the character of Khlestakov. He has made him into an anthology of music-hall rogues, imported from the Parisian theaters to prance around here. Khlestakov is not a villain, he is not a professional liar: he forgets he is lying, he almost believes what he says. From the beginning of the performance, I sat there in the theater depressed. Little I cared for the applause and enthusiasm of the audience. I feared only one judge among all those who were there, and that judge was myself. I saw reproach in myself and dissatisfaction with my own work, and that spoiled everything else. On the whole, the audience was pleased. The mayor seems to be the part that reconciles them to the play. Bobchinsky and Dobchinsky, however, were worse than I feared. Pure caricature. Most of the costumes were hideous and burlesqued. One last word about the final scene. It was completely ruined. The curtain fell on nothing conclusive, as though the play had not ended. It is not my fault. They wouldn't listen to me. I persist in saying that the last scene will not work until people understand that it is a tableau. But I am told the actors would feel uncomfortable, they would have to hire a ballet master to pose the group, it would be humiliating for the actors, etc. I haven't the strength to argue any more, or try to do anything about it. I am weary in body and soul. I swear no one knows or hears my unhappiness. I want nothing more to do with them! My play repels me! I'd like to run away, God knows where!"[3]

Now, after the success of *The Inspector General,* Gogol was seized by the same wild urge to roam as after the failure of *Hans Kuechelgarten.* He had to put as many miles as possible, as quickly as possible, between himself and the public. Keep his distance. Recover his privacy. Abroad, if possible. But the play was to be produced in Moscow, at the Maly Theater, with Shchepkin playing the mayor. They were insisting that he attend rehearsals. Well, let them! He wrote to Shchepkin:

"I have acquired such a dislike for the theater that the mere thought of the unpleasantness awaiting me in Moscow is enough to keep me from becoming involved in any manner whatever. I can't take any more of it! Do whatever you please with the play, I shall not care. I have had enough of both the play and the worry it has caused me. Everyone is against me. Elderly and honorable officials proclaim that I hold nothing sacred, because I have dared to speak slightingly of the employees of the administration. The police are against me, the shopkeepers are against me, the men of letters are against me. They insult me, but they go to my play. There were no tickets for the fourth performance. Without the high protection of the emperor, my play would never have been performed on a stage; besides, some people are already doing their best to have it withdrawn. Now I see what it is to be a comic author. The faintest shadow of truth, and you see rise against you not one person but whole corporate bodies. For someone who, like me, loves people with brotherly love, it is hard to endure their hostility."[4]

Shchepkin, distressed by this missive, tried to make Gogol change his mind. "It is positively criminal to abandon your comedy to its fate," he wrote. "And where? In Moscow, which awaits you with open arms. You know full well that your play needs to be read aloud, by its author, more than any other play, to both the production staff and the actors. You know that and yet you won't come! Change your mind, for God's sake!"

Gogol would not change his mind. They could put on the play without him in Moscow. Shchepkin could direct it. Anyway, the result could hardly be worse than in St. Petersburg. "If I did come," he wrote back, "I would read badly, without any sympathy for my own characters."[5]

For him, *The Inspector General* already belonged to the past. The future began on the other side of the frontier. A tempting route: Germany, Switzerland, Italy . . . He planned to be away a long time. A year, maybe more. As long as it would take him to "forget," to be "cured."

"I am going abroad," he wrote to Pogodin. "There I shall masticate the disgust my contemporaries feed me daily. An author of our time, a comic author, an author who wants to portray the people of his time, must live far from his native land. No one is a prophet in his own country. I little care that every class of society is now hostile to me, but it pains and saddens me to see my fellow citizens wrongly up in arms against me when I love them with all my soul, and to see how they misinterpret everything. Put two or three scalawags on the stage: a thousand decent folk howl and protest, 'We are not scalawags!' God grant them peace! I am going abroad, not because I am unable to bear the discomfort, but for my health, and to divert myself; and, after selecting some at least halfway stable place of residence, to meditate upon my future work. It is high time I began to create and to know what I am doing when I do it."[6]

Pogodin was annoyed by this, and retorted: "It seems you've been upset by all the fuss [about *The Inspector General*]. You should be ashamed, old man; you're becoming a comic character yourself. Imagine an author who sets out to bite people—not just a nibble on the eyebrow, but a chunk right out of the eye—and does so; and then the people wince, turn away, snarl some insults, and, naturally enough, protest, 'There are no such people among us!' You should be glad to have hit the mark so well. But no, you're hurt. Well: doesn't that make you laughable too?"

Gogol displayed injured dignity: "I am not, as you put it, upset by all the fuss; I am not upset by the anger of those who recognize their own features in my creations and turn away from me, nor am I upset by the insults of literary enemies and petty talents; but I am saddened by the universal ignorance reigning in our capital; I am saddened by the wretched position of the man of letters in our country. All are against him, and he cannot summon strength in his defense to equal that of his assailants. 'A firebrand! A revolutionary!' Who says so? Those who say so are in the service of the empire, people of high position, people with long experience, people who should be intelligent enough to understand how things really are in this day, people of culture, or at least thought to be such in Russian society. Let numskulls protest and I would understand; but these are people I did not take for numskulls at all. The capital is offended because I described the behavior of six provincial officials; what would the capital say if I had described, however benignly, its own behavior? Farewell! I am leaving to drown my sorrows. Everything that has happened has been good for me. All the vexation and nastiness have been sent by almighty Providence for my edification, and I feel now that some superterrestrial will is showing me the way."[7]

The previous month, *The Contemporary* published "An Official's Morning" (a scene from Gogol's unfinished play *The Vladimir Cross*) under Gogol's name, together with a "review of reviews" (an article denouncing the literary tyranny of the Bulgarin-Grech-Senkovsky triumvirate) and a short story called "The Carriage" (a lighthearted and dancing sketch of provincial life). A real-life anecdote had given Gogol the idea for the latter,† in which Chertokutsky, a landowner, offers to sell his carriage to a general and invites him and some of his officers to dinner the following day, then gets drunk, arrives home very late at night, and forgets to warn his wife of the invitation. When the general and his retinue turn up, nothing has been prepared. Chertokutsky is startled out of a deep sleep, loses his head, sends his servant to say he is away from home, and runs to hide in his carriage. The indignant general determines to see the vehicle for which he has made a special trip, however, and naturally discovers Chertokutsky huddled inside it in his dressing gown.

With the authorities being so touchy, this joke about a landowner making insufficient obeisance to a general might well have been seen as an insult to the army. Fortunately, however, the censor demanded only insignificant cuts; and the readers themselves took little notice of this series of exceptionally clear-cut, realistic miniatures. The quarrel over *The Inspector General* overshadowed everything else.

After hurried and chaotic rehearsals, *The Inspector General* opened at the Maly Theater, in Moscow, on May 25, 1836. Shchepkin (the mayor) and Lensky (Khlestakov) were highly praised for their performances; but in Moscow too, and for the same reasons, the play was fiercely contested. "The young people were wild over *The Inspector General,*" wrote Stasov. "We used to recite whole scenes and passages by heart, correcting one another and picking up where the last person left off. Both at home and in society we became involved in violent

---

† Count Mikhail Vyelgorsky, famous for both his love of art and his incurable absent-mindedness, once invited the entire diplomatic corps to his home, forgot the invitation, and spent the evening at his club.

arguments with elderly (and sometimes not so elderly) persons, who were resentful of this new idol of the young and claimed that there was nothing true in Gogol, everything he wrote was pure fairy tale or caricature, there were no such people as his characters, or even if there were, there were fewer of them in the entire city than in his one little comedy. These skirmishes were heated and lengthy, but the old folk could not budge us at all, and our fanatical adoration of Gogol only increased."[8]

Despite Shchepkin's prayers, Gogol had not gone to Moscow for the opening night. He was not interested in the response of this new public, or rather, he dreaded it, hostile or favorable. He was wholly absorbed by his preparations for the great departure, "willed by the Almighty." First of all, he had to get the money together. He had sold *The Inspector General* outright to the management of the imperial theaters, for 2,500 assignation rubles; he also sold, in advance, the entire edition of the play in book form, giving the booksellers a large discount in order to get the cash more quickly. He probably borrowed here and there from his friends too. And lastly, he asked Zhukovsky to approach the emperor for a subsidy.

After paying his debts, he had more than 2,000 rubles left—enough to last him several months. In October, Smirdin the publisher would send more. He bought presents for his mother and sisters: cloth for a gown, fashionable hats, ribbons, shawls, books, an engraving of the Nevsky Prospect, a whole heap of trinkets to lessen the sorrow of parting. "No doubt I shall remain abroad more than a year," he wrote to his mother. Then he dealt with his manservant, Yakim. Taking him along would increase his expenses considerably, so he decided to free him; but Yakim wanted no part of this liberty, suddenly thrust upon him. A masterless man has no protection against the difficulties of life. No one would think of feeding or looking after him. He preferred to remain a serf. Gogol decided to send both Yakim and Matryona back to Vasilyevka. His mother would find something for them to do there. Anna and Elizaveta would stay at the Patriotic Institute during the summer holiday. A few days before leaving, he went to see them and exhorted them to be of good cheer and possess themselves in patience. Friends would call on them from time to time. He himself would write, often.

He also divested himself of some furniture. Heaving great sighs, Yakim moved to and fro in the half-empty rooms, rooms with stained wallpaper. At the last moment Gogol had found a traveling companion: Alexander Danilevsky, a fellow pupil at the Nyezhin School and the boy in whose company Gogol had first set foot in the capital, eight years earlier. After studying for a year at the guards junior officers' school and wandering in the Caucasus for a few months, the slender, elegant, and nonchalant Alexander had found himself a job in the ministry of the interior. But work bored him; he, too, was eager for new horizons.

The steamship on which the two friends had booked passage was not due to leave St. Petersburg until June 6, 1836. It was already hot in town. Wealthy families had fled the sweltering heat and were settled in their suburban villas. The unnatural light of the pallid northern nights disturbed Gogol: in that ghostly illumination the most ordinary objects took on a spectral allure. One evening, as he was sorting papers in preparation for departure, he received an unexpected visit from Pushkin. The poet had left his family at Kamenny Ostrov, where he had rented a villa, and come through the half-empty city on foot. On May 23, his wife had given birth to a baby girl, and on that subject he made a show of forced cheerfulness; but somehow, his face no longer knew how to smile. A few silver hairs striped his bushy brown whiskers. There was a bitter pinch to his thick lips, and his expression was darkened by an air of weariness, grief, and ill-humor. The drawing-room gossip left him no peace. It was said that his wife, the lovely Natalya, was not indifferent to the attentions of a young and appetizing horse guardsman, a French émigré named Georges d'Anthès, who was also the adopted son of Baron Heckeren, the Dutch ambassador. Gogol himself had heard this rumor several times without believing it. As always, he avoided private matters in conversation with Pushkin. They lived in such different worlds. Gogol undoubtedly told his caller the reasons behind his departure; and Pushkin, sick to death of St. Petersburg, could only encourage him. As a parting gift, he asked Gogol to read him the beginning of *Dead Souls*. Years later, Yakim related how the reading went on half the night. According to Gogol, Pushkin had been prepared to laugh, but his features soon altered. "Gradually his face lengthened, and by the end he was positively bleak," he wrote. "When I had finished, he spoke sorrowfully: 'My God, how sad our Russia is!' I was stupefied. Pushkin, who knew Russia so well, had not seen that the whole thing was pure caricature and invention! I then realized what a work could be, that rises from the depths of the soul filled with spiritual truth, and in what terrifying forms the shadows and darkness can be shown to us."[9]

A stale, uncertain dawn. The yellow glow of a candle. Open suitcases. Two hopeless men sitting face to face: the one soured by his marital worries, his debts, and the vicious tongues of his circle, the other by the idiotic fuss provoked by a play he had written. At thirty-seven, Pushkin was tired of living and of writing, but he could still inspire a longing to create a great work of art in the colleague ten years his junior. What was actually said that night? Did Pushkin really pronounce those fatal words about the sadness of Russia? Or were they another of Gogol's inventions, intended to reinforce his own theory of the deeper meaning of *Dead Souls?*

Yakim said it was after daybreak when they parted. Pushkin's slight figure, cane in hand and top hat on head, disappeared into the shadows of the staircase. Gogol made no attempt to see him again before leaving; nor did he seek out Zhukovsky, "the savior," to whom he was so deeply indebted. Most of his friends were unaware that he was going.

On June 6, 1836, Prince Vyazemsky accompanied the two travelers to the port, handed Gogol a few letters of recommendation to friends abroad, gave him a mighty hug, and wished him a good crossing. Danilevsky was beside himself with excitement. Everything amused him: the crowded pier, the longshoremen weighted down with baggage, the anxious air of the ladies. Thick black smoke rolled up from the smokestacks of the ship. A group of curious onlookers were examining the great paddle wheels. Deck hands in blue blouses and round straw hats with ribbons trotted along the deck. Gogol started up the ramp.

Part Two

1. *En Voyage*

The sky was overcast, the sea a little choppy. Standing on the deck, Gogol felt as if he were reliving, step by step, his former adventure: he was twenty years old and had just burned every copy of *Hans Kuechelgarten,* and was sailing toward the German coast to forget, far from his ungrateful fatherland, the failure of his poem. Only Danilevsky's presence prevented him from believing completely in his delusion. Then, too, it would require more than a touch of hypocrisy to feel any actual regret for those days of obscurity and poverty.

Unluckily, the intervening years had not given him sea legs. No sooner had he strolled once around the ship, bowed to the captain, and been introduced to a few passengers in the dining room, than the pitching and yawing began. The paddle wheels bit into the waves with mechanical obstinacy, but whenever the ship rolled over to one side, only the lower wheel worked, which made the whole craft lurch. The wind freshened, beating a pestilential, sooty smoke down onto the deck. The hull creaked, the engines wheezed and throbbed, and the horizon disappeared from view.

The following days brought rougher weather, and the passengers began to be alarmed. Mme. de Barante, the French ambassador's wife, uttered shrill cries at the sight of the mountains of green water that rose and fell in vertical walls as far as the eye could see. One of the distinguished passengers, Count Musin-Pushkin, suddenly died. Something in the ship was damaged and it lost speed, so the waves battered it with redoubled force. Gogol sought refuge in his cabin; lying nauseated on his bunk, he inhaled the odors of varnish, brine, tar, and bad cooking, and stared dully through the dripping porthole at the eternally rising and falling horizon. Instead of the scheduled four days, it took the ship ten days to cross the Gulf of Finland and the Baltic Sea. Gogol thought his hour had come at least a hundred times, and cursed the whole trip. But the instant he and Danilevsky stepped ashore at Travemünde, his health and good humor returned.

They took a stagecoach through Lübeck to Hamburg. There Gogol drew up a balance sheet of his past activities, and decided that the Almighty had done well to send him abroad. In some miraculous way, his worries lost their sting in this German city. The conflict over *The Inspector General* no longer made him wince. He cared no more about the play's success or failure than if it had been written by someone else. Besides, all his past work deserved nothing better than oblivion: his real career was about to begin, now. He moved into a hotel and sat down to write Zhukovsky:

"I swear I shall achieve something beyond the capacities of ordinary men. I feel the strength of a lion within me. If everything I have written so far were subjected to a close and critical scrutiny, what would remain? I leaf through old schoolboy notebooks, noting lack of concentration, carelessness on one page, haste and impatience on another. It is time, it is high time I set seriously to work. How helpful all this unpleasantness and vexation have been! I can say I have never sacrificed to the demands of fashion. No pleasure or passion could ever for one minute master my soul or divert me from my duty. There is no life for me outside my life, and my present removal from my homeland has been imposed upon me from above, by that same Providence which has set every other obstacle in my path for my edification. I shall remain away a long time, a very long time, as long as possible on foreign soil. My thoughts, my name, my work shall belong to Russia, but my perishable body shall stay far from her."[1]

His certainty of the divine mission devolving upon him relieved Gogol's mind about his final destination; since his fate was preordained, a brief period of relaxation would do nothing to alter it. With Danilevsky at his side, he saw the sights of the city, admired the narrow streets edged with ancient houses, visited the Gothic churches, spent an evening in an open-air theater, where sedate German women knitted stockings while watching the play; he even strayed into a street carnival in the suburbs. "They were dancing the waltz," he wrote to his sisters Anna and Elizaveta. "But you have never seen such a waltz. One dancer turns his partner in one direction, another in the opposite direction, and a third does not turn at all, but stands holding her with both hands, and, staring deep into her eyes, jumps up and down like a goat, paying no attention to the rhythm."[2]

As the weather was very hot, he decided, to Danilevsky's horror, to order himself a duck suit, which made him look like a scarecrow draped in mattress ticking. "Why do you find it so laughable?" he queried. "It's cheap, washable, and easy to wear!"[3]

From Hamburg they went to Bremen, glanced at the cathedral, descended into one cellar where they surprised a long row of cadavers sleeping their last sleep in a remarkable state of preservation, and then another where they paid reverent homage to century-old casks of Rhenish wine. "This wine is not for sale," Gogol wrote his mother. "It is kept for people who are very ill, or for distinguished visitors. Since I belong to neither category, I forbore to trouble the citizens of Bremen, who settle such issues by public referendum, with an application to consume some of it."[4] At the hotel, however, he ordered one bottle of "very old Rhenish" as a special treat for his palate, which was accustomed to far cruder fare. It was not a success: the wine was too heady for him, and when the time came to pay for it, he and Danilevsky exchanged a look of consternation: the hotelkeeper wanted "one gold napoleon." At that rate, they would not travel far or long. They swore to restrain themselves thereafter, and set off for Aachen.

There they dragged their feet in the dusty streets, duly admired the Palatine chapel and town hall, looked in on the baths, raised eyebrows at the numbers of old people in the resort, and decided to part company. Danilevsky wanted to go on to Paris, while Gogol was keen to explore the Rhine; an overloaded stagecoach carried him off to Cologne.

Alone of his kind. Not one compatriot with whom he could share his impressions. Perhaps he would have done better to follow Danilevsky. A straight road running through fields of wheat, inns containing identical hot sausages, identical beer in pottery mugs, tidy, tedious villages, pipe smokers, the harsh sounds of the German tongue: what monotony! In Cologne he boarded a ship, this time fearing neither storm nor breakdown. The slow voyage began, through the watery, historic, restful landscape.

"Our boat traveled for two days," he wrote to his mother, "and in the end, I became excessively bored by the landscape. The eyes weary as

when looking at a panorama. Towns, rocks, mountains, and ruins of
feudal castles pass beyond the porthole. At Mainz, a large and ancient
town, I went ashore but did not linger, although the town deserved a
visit, and found a seat in the coach for Frankfurt."[5]

From Frankfurt he slowly made his way to Baden-Baden. "There are
no really sick people here," he wrote his mother. "People come only to
enjoy themselves. The town is admirably situated, built along a ridge,
with mountains on all sides. The shops, ballroom, theater, and everything else are in the garden. Nobody stays in his room; one spends the
day seated at a little table beneath the trees. The mountains, even the
nearest, have a violet hue."[6]

In themselves, the beauty of the site and the amenities of the place
would not have kept Gogol in this little bourg he called "the villa of
Europe"; but he met a few Petersburg families there with whom he was
already acquainted, and was beguiled by their kindness and amiability.
There were the Repnins and the Balabins, whose daughter Marya
Petrovna had been his pupil. She had now grown into a graceful, ingenuous girl, natural and gay. Her mother, Varvara Osipovna, (of
French origin) had always been favorably disposed toward the peculiar
little tutor Pletnyev had recommended to her.

He became better acquainted with the ladies and their daughters at
Baden-Baden. They saw him every day in the park or restaurant, or out
walking. "He was most entertaining," Princess Repnin said; "very
obliging, and he was forever making us laugh." His new fame aroused
the curiosity of the aristocratic tourists of the little town; and he felt very
much at ease in their company. His firmly conservative views coincided
with those of the people there, and he took a genuine pleasure in female
company when friendship alone was involved—however much he
dreaded a woman's approach when he could feel the least physical
emanation from her. In friendship, he thought, feminine beauty lost its
evil influence and contributed to the pleasure of conversation. Once he
had lost his fear of their designs upon him, women gave him a sense of
pride, by admiring his talent and asking him for advice. Whenever he
found himself in a circle of affable lady listeners, his professorial vocation rose to the surface: he longed to nourish young minds, win over
trusting hearts, set an example. He meant to spend three days in Baden-
Baden, but was still there at the end of three weeks. Then his wander-
lust seized him again. He had to go. Why? Where? Perhaps it was himself he was running away from. He packed his bags, took his leave of

the Repnins and Balabins, who were disconcerted by the suddenness of his departure, and climbed into another stagecoach.

This time he headed for Switzerland. Berne, Basel, and Lausanne made little impression upon him. His first sight of the mountains, however, was like a physical blow: those white masses incrusted in the sapphire sky, then pink and blushing in the setting sun. He stopped in Geneva, took a room in a pension, strolled along the shore of the lake, walked through the old town, watched the clockmakers with interest, read some Molière, Shakespeare, and Walter Scott but was not inspired to take up his pen himself, worked half-heartedly on his faulty French by conversing with his neighbors in the pension dining room, and made a pilgrimage to Ferney, where the ghost of Voltaire awaited him. "The old fellow lived well," he wrote to Prokopovich after his visit. "A long and beautiful avenue leads to the house, a three-story building in gray stone. The drawing room is next to his bedroom, which was also his study. The bed is made; the old muslin coverlet is about to fall apart. It seemed to me that the door must open any minute to admit the little old man with his famous wig and straggling ribbon, who would ask, 'What do you wish?' I sighed and scribbled my name in Russian characters, for no reason."[7] It was indeed strange, to say the least, this visit of the most irrational and secretive of Russian writers, a dweller in mist and darkness, a friend of devils and witches, to the great French ironist, the sworn enemy of superstition and champion of science, justice, and clarity. If they had met, they would assuredly not have been able to find one subject on which they could agree. However, Gogol did not feel a complete spiritual alien at Ferney—perhaps because his goal, like Voltaire's, was to arouse his contemporaries with laughter. But what a difference between the light, tingling chuckle of *Candide* and the twisted, uncertain sneer of *Dead Souls!* After paying homage to the patriarch of French letters, he felt he must make obeisance to another local pinnacle: Mont Blanc. Hiring a guide, he ventured up the lower slopes to the snow line, walked along a row of *séracs,* turned back, and reached his pension exhausted. He wrote to his mother:

"It takes four days to reach the summit of Mont Blanc. The snow begins all of a sudden—there you are in the midst of winter. Snow ahead, snow behind, and snow all around, you no longer see the valley below, only several layers of cloud. Mountains of ice surround you, pierced by rays of sunlight. Sometimes there is a loud crack, like a thunderclap, an avalanche hurtles down, you hear the din it makes rolling down to the valley. It was cold, the snow seemed sprinkled with live sparks, I changed my light coat for a heavy winter one. As I was coming down, it grew warmer and warmer; I was in the clouds, and finally ended up in the rain; I opened my umbrella and so reached the valley again."[8]

Marya Ivanovna undoubtedly shivered with terror at the vision of her intrepid son scaling the Alps, edging along glaciers, leaping over chasms, and slipping between two boulders to get out of the path of avalanches, while in reality that same son was gazing down at the awesome scene and dreaming of the monotonous Russian winter. His whole being yielded to a gentle nostalgia for the horizontal. At a distance, the country he had fled in horror began to glow with fascinating allure. "What can I say to you of Switzerland?" he wrote Prokopovich. "Splendid views, more and ever more views. I begin to be sickened by them, and if I were now to happen upon one of our Russian landscapes, common and flat, with its wooden isba and gray sky, I could wonder at it as though I had never seen such a thing before."[9]

But at that point he was still able to distinguish between the unchanging landscape so dear to his heart, and the people who lived in the capital, all of whom were more or less guilty of having misunderstood his play. Russia without Russians: what a paradise! Or at least, without some of them. On the other hand, he missed his friends. At the beginning of his travels, he had forgotten all about them; today, surrounded by foreigners, he thought of them with a real pang: Pushkin, Zhukovsky, Prokopovich, Pogodin. To the latter he wrote: "There is in Russia such a collection of ugly mugs that the sight of them had become unbearable to me. Even now I want to spit whenever I think of them. At present everything I see is foreign, everything around me is foreign, but Russia is in my heart—not the ugly Russia I knew, but the beautiful Russia, and you and a few relatives and a small number of friends endowed with reliable tastes and noble souls."[10]

"The beautiful Russia" was also, of course, his mother and sisters. The letters he received from Marya Ivanovna at very irregular intervals were, as always, a tissue of laments and reproaches. She bemoaned her desperate financial straits and implored her son to come home. Most perilous of the dangers threatening him abroad was—women. And most perilous of women were Italian women. Marya Ivanovna's exhortations were so insistent that Gogol finally replied, "With regard to your remarks on the subject of Italian women, I would have you observe that I shall soon be thirty years old!"[11] (He was actually twenty-seven.) Another letter caused him deeper distress: it announced the death of his eldest sister's husband, Trushkovsky, leaving her pregnant as well as widowed. Faced with an event of such consequence, Gogol instinctively recovered his flair for sermonizing. The desire to edify his fellow man stifled any hint of spontaneity in him. Instead of allowing his sorrow to speak, he draped himself in orotund periods—the same ones, give or take a word, he had employed eleven years earlier, after the death of his father.

"I was dumfounded by the news in your last letter," he wrote to his mother. "It is always sad to see a man cut down by death in the flower of youth. Still more so, when he is a close relation. But we must be firm and hold our woes as nothing if we are to remain true Christians. We must remember that nothing is eternal here below, that joys and griefs intermingle, and that if we knew no sorrows we should not recognize happiness, and thus there would be no happiness for us."

And forgetting how readily he complained of his own most trivial personal problems, he sententiously concluded: "We must remain ever valiant and serene, whispering no word of our misfortunes. I know many joys still lie ahead for you. My sister, too, must not despair, if she wants to deserve the name of Christian."[12]

Not one shadow of anxiety for Marya's health or the possible difficulties of life with a newly orphaned son of three,[13] not one affectionate query, not one word of brotherly encouragement. A few months later, he showed the same indifference toward the birth of the new baby: "I am very pleased to hear my sister has been safely delivered of a son. But what a shame you are having such bad luck with the property!"[14]

Nor was he more deeply touched when, six weeks later, the infant died. These little incidents were willed by God and so had their usefulness. All things were gifts to those of lofty soul. He was more easily convinced of this, to be sure, when envisaging the misfortunes of others than when contemplating his own; but this nuance in no way detracted from the value of his principle.

The damp and chill drove Gogol out of Geneva in October. He went to Vevey, to a cozy family pension recommended by Zhukovsky, who had stayed there a few years before. The owner, a man named Blanchet, treated his guests—very few in that season—with fatherly solicitude. Although antisocial by nature, Gogol exchanged a few words of French every day with the other boarders or the master of the house, in the hope of increasing his vocabulary. He read French and could make himself understood in simple situations, but was still incapable of holding a conversation of any length. His timetable was restfully monotonous. He rose late and lounged about his room. The meals were too copious and made him feel heavy. Sometimes he thought there was "a whole herd of horned animals"[15] in his stomach. For a little exercise, he would stroll down the avenue of chestnut trees. Then, seated on a bench on the shore of the excessively blue, excessively calm lake, he waited for the boat that might bring some compatriot ashore. But the only people who disembarked were phlegmatic Swiss and bony Englishmen "with long legs." Disappointed, Gogol went back to the pension and sat yawning until dinnertime. Out of sheer boredom, he began to think of writing again. Suddenly he wanted to work on *Dead Souls,* the first chapters of which were in his suitcases.

"I have revised the whole beginning, expanded the plan, and am now working easily, as though I were writing a chronicle," he told Zhukovsky. "As a result, Switzerland has become more clement to me; its gray, mauve, blue, and pink mountains have become somehow less oppressive. If only I could make the book what it ought to be! What a vast and original subject! What scope, and what diversity! The whole of Russia will be in it. This will be my first major work, the work that will rescue me from oblivion. Every morning, as a kind of second breakfast, I add three pages to my 'poem' and laugh so hard myself that it relieves my solitary day."[16]

But the weather was turning: a melancholy mist shrouded the horizon, and his room was becoming increasingly chilly. As winter drew on, there seemed to be something mysterious the matter with him. He saw a physician, who examined and questioned him, decided he was suffering from "hypochondria resulting from hemorrhoids," and advised a change of air. Gogol would have liked to go to Italy, to that hot blue sky he had praised long before but never seen. But Italy was rife with cholera and the roads were cordoned off. Also, after several weeks of silence, Danilevsky had finally shown signs of life. He was in Paris, and invited his friend to join him there. Gogol let himself be tempted.

2. Paris

Upon reaching Paris, Gogol had himself driven straight to Danilevsky's room, on the rue Marivaux, fell into the arms of the "unpardonable forsaker," and provisionally accepted his hospitality. He soon transferred to a hotel, but there was only one fireplace and no stove in his room, and he could not long endure the damp chill that dripped down the walls. He moved again; this time Danilevsky and he shared a small furnished apartment at 12, Place de la Bourse, on the corner of the rue Vivienne. Here there were stoves, and the well-placed windows caught every ray of sunlight. Warm at last, Gogol revived, spread out his papers, and relaxed. He was much impressed by his first encounter with Paris.

"Paris is not so ugly as I had imagined, and—which is wonderful for me—has many pleasant walks," he wrote to Zhukovsky on November 12, 1836. "The Tuileries garden and the Champs-Elysées alone would satisfy anyone who wanted to walk all day long." To his mother, around the same date, "Yesterday I went to the Louvre for the second time and was unable to tear myself away. The most beautiful paintings in the world are gathered there. Last week I went to the famous Jardin des Plantes, where the rarest plants from every part of the world have been collected and are displayed in the open air. Elephants, camels, ostriches, and monkeys move about as though at home. It is the first place of this type in the world. At the moment, Paris is filled with musicians, singers, painters, and every other kind of artist. The streets are all lit by gas lamps. Many are like galleries or arcades, lit from above through glazed ceilings. The floors are marble; you could dance on them."

He also admired the obelisk of Luxor, which had just been erected in the Place de la Concorde, went to Versailles and visited the château and park, and watched the waterworks display, the long sparkling plumes of water crossing and recrossing. But it was the stir and bustle of the streets that entertained him most. He never tired of prowling the district, staring at people, inspecting shopwindows, catching on the wing a woman's smile or the graceful gesture of a salesgirl in a shop, musing over a bookshop display, stopping in fascination to watch "an enormous cylindrical machine grinding chocolate across the entire width of a shop-window," swallowing his saliva at the sight of a gigantic lobster or a turkey stuffed with truffles, pushing on to the broad boulevards," where fine trees raise their tall trunks in the heart of the city like seven-story buildings and crowds of foreigners jostle along the asphalt pavements together with a few of those 'lions' and 'tigers' of fashion, who are never accurately portrayed in French novels."[1] The swift melody of the French tongue, the pastel sky, the teams of horses rushing to and fro, harness glinting and hoofs ringing; the smell of frangipani and hot chestnuts, the atmosphere charged with nervous gaiety, the insolent stare, the slicing retort: it all made a strange concoction, which he inhaled, half delighted, half irritated. In this scene of swift sparkle and weightlessness, he felt more slow and lumpish than ever.

After wandering through the streets, he would drift into some huge café "with walls covered with frescoes under glass" and daydream, slouched upon a pillowy booth among the clink of saucers and surf of conversation. His favorite discoveries were the ice creams at the Café Anglais and Tortoni's, but he wanted more substantial·fare too. Quickly conquered by French cuisine, he could seldom resist the temptation of a good meal. He called restaurants "temples" and waiters "priests," and said he was enchanted by "the exquisite smell and taste of the victims sacrificed in these places." As often as not, unfortunately, his stomach would rebel after one of these gargantuan meals, and the extremely commonplace distress that ensued assumed gigantic proportions in his mind. He would expatiate upon it to Danilevsky in such detail that his exasperated friend would turn away. Then he consulted a certain Doctor Marjolin, who prescribed "Indian pills" for him; and as soon as he could bear the pain, back he went, with his friend, to another restaurant.

After dining they would play billiards until late at night or go to the theater. At the Opera Italien he heard Grisi, Leblache, Tamburini, and Rubini. At the Théâtre Français he applauded *Tartuffe, Le Malade Imaginaire,* and three other plays, all performed to perfection. He called Ligier "Talma's successor," an outstanding talent. As for Mlle Mars, she was still playing ingénues with great success, notwithstanding her sixty years: "At first it seems a little absurd," Gogol wrote to Prokopovich, "but in the later acts, when the child becomes a woman, one forgives her her years. Her voice is still sweet, and if you squint you can believe you are looking at an adolescent of eighteen. Everything about her is simple and alive; she is nature in a pure state. In the sad parts, the words seem to come from the depths of her very soul; nothing jarring, not one false or artificial note. Our Russian theater is badly in need of a Mlle Mars."[2]

Mlle George, on the other hand, who was playing at the Porte St. Martin, he found "monotonous and conventional." The ballet was entirely satisfactory: choreography, sets, costumes, everything was exemplary. "Fairy-tale opulence. On stage you see a profusion of gold, satin, and velvet. Here all the dancers, even the corps de ballet, wear the kind of costumes they give only to prima ballerinas at home. La Taglioni, a breath of air! No one has ever danced before with such unearthly lightness."[3]

In the end, however, this giddy, brilliant life aroused Gogol's suspicions. If external appearances were so alluring, he thought, perhaps there was nothing behind them. He was not far from wondering if the French had no souls, or else neglected them for the sake of a million superficial activities—the most foolish and noxious of which was assuredly politics. As the subject of an autocrat, brought up to respect order and love the tsar, he was appalled to hear affairs of state discussed openly in the marketplace, instead of being reserved for specialists. Too many people in Paris were still feeling the effects of the revolution of 1830. Several attempts had been made on the life of King Louis-Philippe. The previous year, Fieschi; in June 1836, Alibaud; in December, Meunier . . . Only recently, Prince Louis-Napoléon Bonaparte had vainly tried to start an insurrection in the Strasbourg garrison. Ministries changed at the drop of a hat: today Mr. Molé replaced Mr. Thiers. Who would replace Mr. Molé tomorrow? At the inauguration of the Arc de Triomphe, people were said to have shouted, "Vive l'Empereur!" No healthy and well-balanced state could behave like this. Gogol never tried to meet a single Frenchman, but condemned the entire nation for their emotional instability. The country might be a monarchy now, but the republic oozed through every crack. Every person had his own ideas of how it should be run. The newspapers were at one another's throats. How was such a crowd of magpies and hotheads to be governed?

"Everything here is politics," Gogol wrote to Prokopovich. "There is a shop selling newspapers on every street corner. You stop in the road to have your boots polished and before you know it someone has slipped a newspaper into your hand. You go somewhere to relieve yourself and there, too, they hand you a newspaper. People here care more about what is going on in Spain than about what is going on in their own homes."[4]

He expanded these views in his short story "Rome," whose hero, a young Italian who comes to Paris to study, soon concludes that France is "the kingdom of words without deeds."

"No Frenchman," wrote Gogol, "seemed to work at all except inside his feverish head; the digesting of interminable newspapers consumed his entire day, leaving him no time at all for the practical side of life. Without any clear idea of his rights, duties, or the social class to which he belonged, every Frenchman, brought up in the midst of this weird whirlwind of book-and-print politics, joined some party or other and instantly made all its interests his own, passionately attacking his adversaries before he knew who they were or what they wanted. Hence the word 'politics' ultimately became odious to our Italian. Everywhere, in business as well as in matters of the mind, he could see nothing but convulsive striving and a search for novelty at any price."

According to the young Italian-alias-Gogol, it was the academics who, by struggling "to give importance to things that were previously held to have none, and to exaggerate their influence at the expense of the natural order of things," showed the worst symptoms of this French exhibitionism; but the novelists, "devoting themselves exclusively to the study of bizarre and unlikely passions and monstrous and exceptional cases," were even more severely afflicted.

That year Victor Hugo was publishing *Notre-Dame de Paris,* Alfred de Vigny brought out *Stello,* Lamartine *Jocelyn,* Théophile Gautier *Les Grotesques,* Balzac *Le Lys dans la Vallée.* The previous year had seen *Les Chants du Crépuscule, Servitude et Grandeur militaires, Mademoiselle de Maupin,* and *Old Goriot.* Utterly impermeable to the capital's literary life, it never occurred to Gogol to meet any of the writers whose names were buzzing in his ears. He had not come to France to mingle with the French, but to feel himself more Russian in their midst. He was fiercely determined to remain a foreigner, a tourist in this country of chameleons. You did not need to see people in order to judge them. On the contrary: it was by observing them from afar that their true features could best be appreciated. Besides, a genuine author had no need of experience, because he had the gift of intuition. Serene in his ignorance, Gogol condemned Parisian superficiality, through the medium of his Italian student:

"At last he saw that despite its air of brilliance, bursts of nobility and surges of chivalry, the entire pale and imperfect nation was in reality nothing but a little music-hall farce composed by itself. There was no serious or sublime idea embedded deep in its heart; allusions to ideas everywhere, but no ideas; half passions everywhere, but no passion; everything about it was unfinished, imprecisely hinted at, sketched in with hasty hand. The nation as a whole was a clever drawing, not a masterpiece."

This contempt for Western civilization discouraged Gogol even more from associating with the French, especially now that he had found a little group of Russians in Paris: Mrs. Svechin, the Smirnovs, the Balabins, who had come on from Switzerland; his leisure time was amply occupied by them. He often went for tea to Alexandra Smirnov's house at 21, rue du Mont-Blanc; there he would listen to someone playing the pianoforte, or a discussion of the social and political events of the capital. Then he would describe his walks through Paris, his dinners, evenings, the throngs of people queuing outside the theaters, and how he bought his place in the line from someone who had got there ahead of him. Sometimes, carried away on the wings of his imagination, he would pretend to have visited countries he had never set foot in. For example, he claimed in Alexandra Smirnov's presence that he had been to Spain and Portugal. "I retorted that he had never gone to Spain," she wrote, "that it was impossible because there was trouble in that country, they were fighting at every crossroads, and those who had returned always had a great deal to tell about what they had seen, whereas he had never even mentioned the place before. To this he coldly replied, 'What is the good of saying everything, just to attract people's attention? All the people you know are forever talking, talking, telling everything they know and everything they don't, and all about their private affairs too!' "

With all his bravado, he never quite convinced her he had crossed the

Pyrenees. She knew he was quick to lie, and she did not mind; she interpreted his fabulations as the defenses of a timid soul against the pressures of reality. Admiring Gogol as an author, she invested him with profound psychological insights, confided in him increasingly, and readily sought his advice. His very ugliness and puniness reassured her: weary of her triumphs at court, disappointed by her marriage to a silly, garrulous man she did not love, she was fast approaching her thirtieth birthday, bidding farewell to the vain pleasures of youth and beginning to inquire into the meaning of life. Occasionally her natural high spirits would break through her mournful mask, and then the company would discover with delight the "celestial imp" celebrated by Pushkin and Zhukovsky.

"Three days ago I dined at the Smirnovs' with Princess Trubetskoy, Sollogub, and Gogol," young Andrey Karamzin wrote to his mother on February 11, 1837. "Gogol has made progress in French and now understands the language well enough to go to the theater and talk—extremely well—about what he has seen there. But it is not easy to talk at the Smirnovs', because Nikolai Mikhailovich [Alexandra's husband] interrupts as soon as you open your mouth, contradicting everybody and uttering inanities."

To work on his languages, Gogol often went to a young Frenchman named Noël, who lived in an attic in the Latin Quarter. He practiced his French there and also began to learn Italian in preparation for the trip he was still planning to that country. He was in no hurry, however. In his cozy little room on the corner of the Place de la Bourse, he was working happily away at *Dead Souls*.

When he picked up his pen, the noise from the street below faded away: Paris and its cafés, theaters, shops, sidewalks thronged with idlers, its congested carriageways, gas lamps, and rain all vanished, and there was not a single Frenchman in the world. Nothing but Russians, and in their midst: Chichikov, the cunning collector of dead souls.

"God has reached out his hand to me here and made a miracle, by leading me to a nice, warm, sunny apartment with a stove," Gogol wrote to Zhukovsky. "I wallow in it. My good humor has returned. I am writing *Dead Souls* with greater energy and optimism than at Vevey. I feel as though I were in Russia. Everything I see is Russian: landowners, civil servants, officers, muzhiks, isbas—in a word, the whole of Orthodox Russia. It actually makes me laugh, to think I am writing *Dead Souls* in Paris. The novel is huge, gigantic, and will not be finished

for a long time. It will create a host of new enemies for me, both individuals and social groups. But what can I do about it? It is my destiny
to be on bad terms with my compatriots. Patience! An invisible hand
etches the words before my eyes with the tip of its omnipotent scepter.
I know my name will fare better in posterity than in my lifetime, and
the weeping descendants of those same compatriots may be reunited
with my spirit."

In a postscript, he addressed his usual appeal to his friends for material for his book: "Can you not think of some incidents that might
arise over the purchase of dead souls? I would like it very much, for
your imagination surely perceives things which escape mine. Speak to
Pushkin about it; maybe he will think of something. I should like to
exhaust the subject utterly, from every angle. I possess a wealth of material of which I never dreamed before. Nevertheless you can still give
me more, for everyone sees things differently. Don't tell anyone the
subject of *Dead Souls*. You can tell them the title, but the only people
who can know what it is about are you, Pushkin, and Pletnyev."[5]

The more exceptional his new work appeared to him, the more it irritated him to hear the old ones praised. Prokopovich was ill-advised
enough to tell him that *The Inspector General* was still playing to full
houses in Russia; Gogol replied in a rage, on January 25, 1837:

"Please, I beg of you, tell me why you are all writing me about *The
Inspector General*. Both your letter and one Danilevsky had yesterday
from Pashchenko say that *The Inspector* is performed every week, the
theater is full, etc. What is the meaning of this mincing and affectation?
I absolutely do not understand what you are trying to achieve by it. In
the first place, I spit upon *The Inspector General*. In the second, I regard all that as pointless. I shudder to think of all my puerile scribblings.
They stand like accusing judges before my eyes. Oblivion, a long oblivion, is what my soul demands. And if some termite would devour
every copy of *The Inspector General* at a gulp, and *Arabesques* and
Evenings on a Farm along with it—all that nonsense I wrote; if no one
ever mentioned my name again, and nothing were written about me for
a long, long time, I should thank my lucky star. The true poet thinks
only of fame after death (and so far, alas, I have done nothing to
merit that). The renown one can have in one's lifetime is not worth a
kopeck."

He could indulge his aspirations to immortality by associating with
the exiled Polish poets Adam Mickiewicz and Bogdan Zalesky. The

politics of the former—a rabid nationalist who hated the Russian oc-
cupation of Poland, and a revolutionary at heart—could not fail to clash
with Gogol's prudent conservatism, of course; but the man's mind was
so noble and lofty that it was perfectly possible to respect his opinions
without sharing them. He was also a fervent mystic, and he intimidated
all his friends. Through him, Gogol began to take an interest in Roman
Catholicism. He thought of Rome again and the Vatican in particular.
Should he stay or go? It was carnival time: masks, streamers, confetti,
floats, street dances, Chinese lanterns, and oom-pah bands. The whole
city had St. Vitus' dance.

Suddenly the news came from Russia: Pushkin had been shot in a
duel with the horse guardsman Georges d'Anthès and had died on
January 29, 1837.

Gogol was dazed, as though the sky had fallen on his head and buried
him in the rubble. His friends talked of amorous intrigues, anonymous
letters, and aristocratic conspiracies. They said the poet had gone into
the field to defend his wife's honor. Two shots, and Russia's genius had
ceased to live. How could God have allowed a French turkey cock to be
the instrument of this tragic death? Was it just, for a nation's idol to
perish at the hands of a foreigner who had wormed his way into the
Imperial Army on the strength of his connections?

Gogol was unmoved by the talk. Little he cared why or how his friend
had disappeared. All that mattered was this impossible result: a world
without Pushkin, himself without Pushkin. To Danilevsky he said, "You
know how I love my mother; but I should not suffer more by her death
than I do now."[6] Young Andrey Karamzin wrote to his family: "I met
Gogol at dinner at the Smirnovs'. It is touching and sad to see the effect
Pushkin's death has had upon that man. He is utterly transformed. He
has abandoned his work and is horrified to think of returning to Petersburg, henceforth empty for him."

In truth, he was thinking very little about St. Petersburg at all. Another trip beckoned, an escape from his sorrow: in the first days of
March he set out for Italy. His *idée fixe* was to be in Rome for Easter.
He arrived just in time—after a short stay in Genoa and Florence—to
attend the pontifical mass in St. Peter's Basilica. The solemnity of the
ceremony left him gaping. "The pope is sixty," he wrote to his mother;
"he was carried into the church on a sumptuous litter surmounted by a
canopy. Several times, the porters had to stop because he was feeling
dizzy."[7] Not a word of his grief over Pushkin.

But what he did not say to his mother—who was too far removed from his literary and social preoccupations to understand it—he wrote to Pletnyev the same day: "No worse news could come to me from Russia. With him disappears the supreme joy of my life. I began nothing without his advice. I did not write a line without imagining him at my side. What would he say, what would he notice in particular, what would make him laugh, what would he approve of most? That is what I used to ask myself, and it encouraged me to go on. The secret thrill of a higher pleasure animated my soul. Dear God! my present book, inspired by him, his creation—I have not strength to continue. Several times I have tried to pick up my pen, but it fell from my hand. Sadness beyond words."[8]

Two days later, to Pogodin: "I shall say nothing to you of the immensity of our loss. But it is greater for me than for others. You speak as a Russian, a writer—and I, I cannot express the hundredth part of my anguish. It is my very life, my greatest joy, that has died with him. My only minutes of happiness were those when I was creating. And when I was creating, it was Pushkin alone who stood before my eyes. Whatever they said about me, I cared not; I spat upon that contemptible rabble they call a public. The only thing that mattered to me was the infallible word of Pushkin. I began nothing, wrote nothing without his advice. I owe every decent thing I have done to him. And my present work is his creature. He made me promise to write it and I have not penned one line without seeing him beside me. I rejoiced in the thought that he would be pleased with it, I tried to guess what he would like best; that would have been my most precious and keenly anticipated reward. Now I shall never receive that reward. What is my work now? What is my life? You invite me to return among you. To do what? Would it not be solely in order that the eternal destiny of the poet in our country might be enacted once again? Haven't I seen enough of our mob of enlightened illiterates? Don't I know what a councilor is, whether titular or privy? You write that everyone, however coldhearted, was moved by this loss. But what did 'everyone' do for him while he lived? Have I not witnessed the bitterness Pushkin had to endure, even though the monarch himself (may his name be blessed for that) valued his ability? Oh, when I think of our judges, our patrons, our knowing intellectuals, our honorable aristocracy. My heart fails at the mere thought! The reasons that impelled me to make a decision so contrary to my desires must have been imperative. Do you think I do not suffer to be mountain ranges apart from my friends? Do you suppose I do not love our limitless Russia?

"Soon I shall have spent a whole year on foreign soil, gazing at fair skies, in a world rich in men and works of art. But has my pen once tried to express these wonders, by which no one could fail to be impressed? I have not been able to devote one line to this foreign world. I am bound to my own, by indestructible ties. I have preferred our world, so poor and dull, with its chimneyless isbas and naked spaces, to these more radiant skies which have spread over me so hospitably. Can it be said that such a man as this does not love his country? But to return; to submit to the arrogant conceit of a class of stupid people who will look down upon me or try to injure me—no, really, thank you very much! Abroad, I can put up with anything; I am ready to beg with outstretched hand if need be. But in my own land, never. You can't fully comprehend my sufferings. You are sheltered in the port, you calmly rise above affronts and laugh at them. I have no harbor, the waves beat against and shatter me, the only anchor I can lean upon is the pride some higher power has lodged in my heart."[9]

To Prokopovich, the same day: "The all-great is no more. My life is poisoned from this day. Write to me, for the love of God! Remind me often that all is not dead for me in that Russia which already seems a tomb to me, mercilessly engulfing all that is dear to my heart. You know, you understand the importance of this loss for me."

These epistolary lamentations were heavily "literary": in pouring out his grief, Gogol could not prevent himself from posing as one great author bemoaning, in deathless prose, the passing of another. Over his correspondents' shoulders, he was addressing his attentive posterity. Nevertheless his sorrow was not feigned. There was in him, now as always, the mixture of despair and comedy, spontaneity and bombast. Pen in hand, he yielded to the intoxication of his own phrases. The more sincere he was, the less he sounded it. When he looked closely, moreover, he had to admit that what hurt him most in the poet's death was the loss of the irreplaceable poet and critic, not that of a friend. They had nothing in common: age, education, literary status, social position, or personality. Gogol had not written once to Pushkin during his entire voyage, although he had often corresponded with Zhukovsky. Pushkin was someone outside his world, a pure genius, the incarnation of his own artistic conscience. In moments of doubt he looked to his illustrious elder for reassurance. He asked more of him than ideas and advice: he wanted the vague encouragement conferred by the mere existence of a transcendent figure in one's chosen career.

Measure, harmony, serenity, lucidity, perfection of form: Pushkin was all that. More: Although his limpid and balanced art was the exact opposite of his younger colleague's bizarre and ambiguous creations, he had never tried to influence him. He suggested books to read, criticized what he wrote, but left him completely free—he helped him to become more truly himself.

Now, after becoming accustomed to this kind of support, Gogol suddenly found himself in a vacuum. Panic welled up in him. Would he ever be able to write without Pushkin? At first he had no desire to continue. It was as though his whole public had vanished at one stroke. His dejection did not last long, however, for it is an old and hoary truth that a creation carries demands within itself that can overcome any external reticence. The need to create returned to the writer, powerful as the instinct of self-preservation in a wounded animal. It was not Pushkin that *Dead Souls* needed; it was he, Gogol. His head was so full of the book that he thought it must burst. He could not carry it any longer. Feverishly he returned to his manuscript.

"I must continue the great work I have begun," he wrote to Zhukovsky. "Pushkin made me promise to write it; the idea belongs to him. Therefore this book has become for me a sacred testament. Every minute is precious to me now, but I do not think I have much time left."[10]

Later, also to Zhukovsky: "Oh, Pushkin, Pushkin! What a beautiful dream I had and what a sad awakening! What would life have been for me in St. Petersburg, now? But the all-powerful hand of Providence sent me here beneath the radiant Italian sky to forget sorrow, men, and the world, and become obsessed with its magnificent beauty. Italy has taken the place of everything else."[11]

Already, Pushkin was becoming a pretext for poetry, an elegant excuse, a name to write on the title page of the new book to underline its exceptional importance.

3. Rome

The trip, to Genoa by sea and then overland to Rome, did not improve Gogol's health. "I am feeling unwell in the most noble part of my person: the stomach," he wrote to Prokopovich upon arrival. "It will hardly digest at all any more, the beast! I am so constipated that sometimes I don't know what to do. It is all the fault of the bad climate of Paris, which, although there is no winter, is scarcely better than that of St. Petersburg."[1]

Lack of money—he arrived with two hundred francs in his pockets—compelled him to keep a close watch on his expenditures. He lodged, for thirty francs a month, at via Isidoro 17, in a room filled with smoke-glazed paintings and white statuary; every morning he drank a cup of chocolate costing four sous, but dined copiously for only six sous, and permitted himself the luxury of one postprandial ice cream, velvety, creamy, melting, in comparison with which Tortoni's ices were, as he put it, "dirt." Despite this singular diet, his digestive troubles abated. He attributed his improved condition to the miraculous Italian climate. He had been dreaming of the country for so long that he might easily have been disappointed by actual contact with the place and people, but no: reality exceeded his expectations. What he had proclaimed in verse in his early youth, when he knew nothing of Rome, he now repeated in prose in his letters to his friends:

"What can I say of Italy? It is admirable. Its effect is less immediate than gradual. The more you look, the deeper you penetrate its mysterious beauty. The clouds in the sky have a strange, silvery glint. The sun sets the distant horizon on fire. And the nights! They are magnificent. The stars shine more brightly than at home and even look larger, like planets. And the air! It is so pure that distant objects seem close at hand."[2]

"One falls in love with Rome very slowly, little by little, but for life. In short, the rest of Europe exists only to be visited; Italy, to be lived in."[3]

"Whoever has been to Italy can only bid adieu to other lands. He who has been to heaven has no more desire to return to earth."[4]

"My beautiful Italy! She is mine! No one will ever take her away from me. I was born here. Russia, Petersburg, snow, scoundrels, ministries, professorships, theater, it was all a dream. I have awakened in my homeland."[5]

"There can be no finer fate than to die in Rome. Here man is a good verst closer to God than anywhere else."[6]

"It is the land of my soul I have found again, the land where my soul lived before birth. What air! Inhale deeply; it is as though at least seven hundred angels had come flying in your nostrils. I assure you, sometimes I feel an irresistible urge to transform myself into an immense nose, no more eyes, arms, or legs, nothing but a gigantic nose with nostrils big as buckets, in order to inhale as much as possible of the scented emanations of the spring."[7]

His old obsession of the nose—detached from the person, transformed into a complete entity, now stalking the streets in search of good things to smell! The climate of Rome suited Gogol perfectly, for although he came from a part of Russia where winters were severe, he had never grown used to the cold. The sun revived his sluggish limbs and drove away his morbid thoughts. Acting and thinking seemed equally pleasant beneath the sapphire sky. Even the landscape here, with its carefully balanced masses, was as restful as a painting by some old master. The whole of Switzerland, with its chaotic mountains, glaciers, and boulders, was not worth one glimpse of the gentle Roman countryside. From this land of balance and light could spring only a transparent work of art.

Gogol, the tormented spirit, the inventor of gaping monsters, was struck dumb with admiration by Raphael. Raphael outstripped all the painters of the quattrocento, High Renaissance, and baroque put together. Similarly, Gogol thought nothing could surpass classical architecture, whose ruins inspired him to tranquil meditation. His mind, accustomed to shadowy labyrinths, irregularities, and chasms, wondered at the noble geometry of the Roman monuments. As he moved from one to the other, he detected in their stones "the encounter of two ages, pagan and Christian, representing the two greatest inspirations of the world."[8] He even thought that if God had given him the choice, for his life and home, between the "noble and magnificent grandeur" of ancient Rome, and modern Rome "with its ruins," he would have preferred the latter, so entrancing did he find the alliance of the two. It was not only that a truncated, ivy-covered column carved into the blue sky with the sun behind it was more picturesque than a new construction, but he felt so profound a sense of peace among the vestiges of a lost civilization that he quite forgot the contemporary world.

The more shaken he was by the bustle and noise of real life, the more closely he clung to the reassuring immobility of the past. All that moved and changed and pressed ahead in the world of art or politics was a manifestation of evil, he told himself. People chasing after the future had nothing but nonsense and ugliness in their heads; their disconnected movements were grotesque. The only music that could console the soul rose up from the depths of bygone ages. In Rome, the stream of days turned aside from the sacred oasis. The city truly deserved the name "eternal," for it lived outside time.

"Everywhere else," Gogol wrote to Danilevsky, "I have seen only pictures of change. Here everything has stopped where it is and is going no farther."[9]

With an insatiable thirst for discovery he attacked museums, churches, palaces, and ruins, dreamed in the Coliseum by moonlight, exclaimed over a porphyry column lost in the middle of a stinking fish market, fell upon the remains of the baths, temples, and tombs scattered about the countryside, adored the panorama at sunset from the height of a terrace in Frascati or Albano, bowed down to shattered statues, worshiped with the same veneration a triumphal arch, a smoke-encrusted pediment, a tree with its roots buried in ancient walls, a garish market guarded by silent stone colossi, the flimsy shanty of a lemonade hawker outside the Pantheon.[10] In his exaltation he began to date his letters "2588," counting from the founding of the city. Even modern Rome, grafted upon the ancient and medieval cities, filled him with joy. He delved delightedly into the twisting, narrow streets, sniffed the spicy odors of shops, smiled to see a flock of goats munching grass between the paving stones or a group of ragged urchins lying in the sun near a murmuring fountain, respectfully observed the progress of an abbot in a three-cornered hat and black shoes and stockings, bowed to a Capuchin "whose camel-colored gown suddenly flamed in the sunset," stood aside for a cardinal's carriage with gilded coat of arms. Here filth and poverty became so incomparably aesthetic. An alleyway caparisoned with multicolored laundry was a masterwork. A market display of bladders, lemons, leaves, and candles made him want to seize a brush and paint. The conversations outdoors, on the squares, and in the cafés rang gaily in the foreigner's ears. "The emptying of treasuries, debates in the Houses, and affairs of Spain have no importance here," he wrote. "On the other hand, feeling runs high over the recent discovery of an antique statue, the qualities of the great painters, the much-debated merits of the work of a new artist, and street carnivals. It is all that friendly sort of talk in which a man shows all of himself at once, and which has been replaced in other European countries by political arguments and the tedious social chatter that wipes all heartfelt feeling from every face."[11]

Gogol liked the Roman people for their innate sense of beauty, their essential dignity, their scorn for superficial wealth, their indolence comparable to that of the Ukrainian. He praised these descendants of the ancient Quirites for having escaped the "icy poison" of modern civilizations. Their good fortune, which they never guessed, was to live under the despotic authority of Pope Gregory XVI. Dominated by an interfering and finical administration, deprived of political rights, closely watched by the police, their compensation was to be relieved of the tedious obsession with public affairs. What could be more enviable in this day and age, thought Gogol, than the childlike irresponsibility of an oppressed nation?

"The ecclesiastical government itself," he wrote, "that ghostly survival of bygone days, has undoubtedly been maintained here only to preserve the people from foreign influences, to prevent any attempt by ambitious neighbors to break their proud character, so that they may flourish in the shadows."[12]

This homage to the immobility of the Romans was strange indeed, as Gogol could not be unaware of the growing nationwide resentment of Austrian domination. Pope Gregory XVI had appealed to foreign powers at the time of the Papal States uprisings. He was rabidly opposed to republicanism and loathed Mazzini, the apostle of emancipation and founder, in exile, of Young Italy. He had likewise condemned Lamennais and his paper *The Future*. European liberalism seemed no less dangerous to him than Italian patriotism. But the insurrectionary movement was launched. One conspiracy engendered another. Theoreticians, poets, and men of action were secretly gathering to support the cause of independence. With the facts staring him in the face, Gogol chose to ignore this agitation, which would have conflicted with his concept of the happy nation protected from the roar of history. Only the intellectuals, he thought, had caught the political disease, like those in Paris. The common people were wise enough to drowse in patriarchal calm. "I am now filled with the desire to know this people thoroughly," he wrote to Marya Balabin, "to probe the depths of its character; I watch its every manisfestation closely; I read all the publications reflecting it; and I can say it is the first people in the world to be endowed with such high aesthetic sense."[13]

He had moved, and was now living at strada Felice 126, in an apartment "right in the sun."[14] Determined not to live like a tourist, he was enlarging his Italian vocabulary, practicing writing letters in the language, studying the literature, talking to local people who knew him well and called him *il signor Niccolo*. From his contact with them he became persuaded that Italy, by remaining remote from the rest of Europe, would play a brilliant role in the future. Now it was true the country was divided and weakened; nothing of its former splendor and power had survived. But its failure in humdrum reality was offset by its crucial mission in the realm of morality. It was a living rampart against the "cold materialism" threatening other nations. Its radiant permanence reminded the French, Germans, and English that they had been wrong to abandon themselves to the trivialities of politics instead of fixing their sights upon art and faith. From this point of view, the Italians had several things in common with the Russians, who had also, according to Gogol, escaped the affliction of progress. There was no doubt, he told himself, that Providence had entrusted a similar mission of salvation to the great northern nation and the little southern one. That must be why he felt so much at home in the streets of Rome.

It was curious: as a Ukrainian, for whom the Poles were the hereditary foe, he should have felt nothing but mistrust for the Roman Catholic Church; but although he was both patriot and Orthodox, he was attracted by the grace and moderation of the Roman faith. At first it was the beauty of the works of art that drew him to the churches. His infatuation with classical and papal Rome predisposed him to feel the majesty of the places of worship. He wrote to his young friend Marya Balabin:

"Today I decided to enter one of those beautiful Roman churches you know so well, steeped in holy shadow, where the sun shines through the top of an oval cupola and down upon the nave like the Holy Ghost. Two or three kneeling figures in no way distract one's attention, and indeed give wings to prayer and meditation. There I prayed for you, for it is in Rome that one can truly pray. In other cities one can only pretend. Prayer in Paris, London, or St. Petersburg is prayer in the marketplace."[15]

Gradually, however, his thoughts became clearer and he saw what separated Russian from Roman Christianity. The Orthodox Church was a sort of solemn administration, petrified in immemorial ritual, having no direct power over souls; whereas the Roman Church, by virtue of its priesthood, was an active, militant, ubiquitous institution whose influence reached far beyond the holy precincts, penetrating into homes and directing individual lives. Both claimed descendance from Christ: the first aimed to preserve his mystery, the second to render him comprehensible to all. Which was more valuable? Absurd question; Gogol refused to choose. His anxious mother, informed of this flirtation with Roman Catholicism, adjured him to remain loyal to the faith of his fathers. He replied: "You were perfectly right to tell those people I would never change my religion. That is quite correct. Because our religion and the Roman Catholic faith are all one, and there is no reason to change from one to the other. Both are true."[16]

Nevertheless, while revising "Taras Bulba" in preparation for a new edition, he added a description of a prayer for divine intercession sung by the besieged Poles, and in the passage he spoke of the nobility of the service, the play of morning light through the stained-glass windows, and the majestic music of the organ: "Andrey stood open-mouthed, speechless with admiration." There, again, he unconsciously confessed how important externals were in his faith. His mysticism was primarily aesthetic: a kind of predisposition to respond to the mysteries of the extraterrestrial, having nothing to do with questions of doctrine.

This sensitivity to the divine presence was much appreciated by some of his lady friends. Varvara Osipovna Balabin had a Jesuit son. Her daughter Marya, although Orthodox, assiduously frequented Roman churches. Then, shortly after his arrival in Rome, Gogol met Princess Zenaida Volkonsky, once called "the Corinna of the North" by her admirers: a woman of talent and culture, a poet, musician, and singer, who, at forty-five, had preserved both her handsome features and her fiery temperament. Alexander I had had a soft spot for her; Pushkin had celebrated her in verse. After shining at court and at every gathering where the fate of Europe was being decided, she had retired to Moscow and adopted the Roman faith. Upon his accession, Nicholas I had instantly dispatched an Orthodox priest to return her to his fold. His remonstrations upset her and made her ill, but did not change her mind. When she recovered, she left Russia and settled permanently in Rome, in a splendid villa on the heights behind St. John Lateran. A Roman aqueduct crossed her garden; the house was surrounded by vines and cypresses and was built against an old tower. The view stretched far over the Eternal City, whose monuments floated, baseless, in a bluish haze. Beneath a tree stood a bust bearing the stern likeness of Alexander I, who had honored the princess with his friendship. Nearby, in a bed of flowers, stood a funerary urn in memory of the young poet Venevitinov, and marble slabs for Pushkin and Karamzin: the little personal pantheon of the lady of the house. It was in her home that Gogol became friendly with Stephan Shevyrev, professor of Russian literature, Slavophile critic, and friend of Pogodin. She liked to bring strong minds together and watch the sparks struck from their confrontation. Her Roman friends nicknamed her *Beata* on account of the intense fervor with which she had embraced her new faith. Her drawing room was likened to a branch office of the Vatican. Members of the Russian aristocracy who came there were sure to meet a few Roman ecclesiastics, patient and unctuous fishers of souls. Zenaida Volkonsky also protected Polish priests who had fled following the uprising of 1830. Two of them, Peter Semenenko and Jerome Kajciewicz, took it into their heads to convert Gogol. They saw him often at dinner parties in the princess' villa. The warmth of the welcome given him and the abundance of good things on the table appealed powerfully to him. Living in poverty, it was a source of some comfort to him to feel the supporting presence of this opulent and authoritarian benefactress.

"We are most pleased by Gogol's conversation," Semenenko wrote. "He has a noble heart, and what is more, he is young. If it were possible for us, in time, to increase our influence over him, he would not remain deaf to the truth and would give himself to it with all his soul. The princess cherishes this hope, and today we have seen for ourselves that it can be realized."[17]

Kajciewicz noted in his diary, "We have become acquainted with Gogol, a gifted Russian writer of Ikrainian origin, who, from the very first, showed a strong leaning toward Catholicism."

Not content with seeing Gogol at Princess Volkonsky's table, the pious Poles carried their campaign to his doorstep. He welcomed them gratefully and talked to them for hours about the role of Christianity in the society of the future. Soon, however, the priests changed tactics and began calling on him separately, for, as Semenenko wrote, "A conversation *à deux* is more conducive to self-revelation on both sides."[18] Kajciewicz even wrote a sonnet in Gogol's honor, the last line of which read, "Do not close thy soul to heaven's dew."

Despite all this urging, Gogol would not take the plunge. Princess Volkonsky became annoyed by his procrastination. Proselytizing was her passion; she had to save souls, as other women have to win hearts. She had already begun to ensnare her son, who was hanging to Orthodoxy by a thread. And Gogol had approved her in this undertaking. "She told us," Semenenko wrote, "that when she informed Gogol of her intentions regarding her son, he had taken a keen interest in the matter and encouraged her, hoping the boy would become a convert."[19] Why did this obstinate young Ukrainian think it wise for the young prince to adopt the Catholic faith, when he refused to come into the fold himself? Zenaida Volkonsky could not solve this enigma and urged the two priests to intensify their campaign. But they held that the feelings of a catechumen should never be forced. Gogol moved about quite comfortably in this atmosphere of pious conspiracy. As the pawn in these loving negotiations, he savored the covert allusions, discreet suggestions, and group meditations on Holy Writ. It would have been hard to give up his upbringing, his past, and his faith at one stroke. But to remain an Orthodox while playing at becoming a Catholic, to dabble in another religion without forsaking his own; what could be more titillating to a mind forever in search of novelty? He answered the insistent Zenaida Volkonsky and her henchmen with soft, pliable immovability.

As though to counterbalance this rather exalted side of his social life, Gogol often went to the loud and smoke-filled Café Greco, to meet the young Russian painters studying on grants from the Petersburg Academy of Fine Arts. The café served as post office for these gentlemen, and its walls were covered with the work of the more impecunious among them, in payment of their debt. Some drank chianti, others pitch-black coffee; all argued passionately, with their elbows on the tables.

These tall, long-haired, bearded youths in capes and broad-brimmed felt hats sacrificed on the altar of Beauty. There, among others, was the quiet, hard-working Yordan, the elegant and charming Moller, son of the minister of the navy; and above all, the intransigent Alexander Ivanov, with whom Gogol very quickly struck up a friendship. For Ivanov, art was a cult of asceticism. With famished stomach and feverish brain, he refused commissions, money, easy success, to devote himself to a single huge painting, *Christ Appearing to the People*. A philosophical summa, a pictorial synthesis, this enormous labor was devouring him alive. The conception was inspired by God; the execution, by Raphael, Veronese, Titian, and Tintoretto. He considered himself invested with a holy mission; for him, time did not count. He was never satisfied with his work and kept starting over and over again, accumulating drawings, pursuing perfection in a thousand preliminary studies, which alone would have filled a large gallery. He went to the Roman synagogue every Friday, for instance, to observe Jewish faces; he set up his easel in the disease-ridden Pontine Marshes, whose bleak landscape was to serve as a background for the group; he made countless copies of the heads of the Apollo of Belvedere and a Byzantine Christ he had unearthed in Palermo, hoping that the juxtaposition of the two physiognomies would give him the features of his John the Baptist.

Gogol liked to visit his studio, a large room lit by a skylight, its white walls covered with charcoal and pastel drawings. On the floor lay sheets of sketches, flattened tubes of paint, brushes, and oily rags. In every corner were boxes overflowing with paper. And on an enormous scaffolding, built specially for the purpose, the painting: it measured about 17¾ by 24½ feet. In the foreground, John the Baptist preached and baptized with upraised arms. Around him was a crowd of naked men emerging from the waters of the Jordan or preparing to immerse themselves. Among them were a few men wearing robes: the future apostles. And in the distance, walking on an arid plain, Christ. A few had already seen him. Others sensed his coming. Still others were wondering what the Precursor had meant by his strange words, "Behold the Lamb of God, which taketh away the sin of the world."[20] The figures were already there, strongly outlined, with a few touches of color. Ivanov wore a paint-stained smock. His long, unkept hair fell over his shoulders. His bushy beard, stippled with paint, invaded his cheeks. He must not have shaved for a fortnight. Palette in his left hand, brush in the right, he stared at his painting in despair.[21]

Gogol would wait for Ivanov to emerge from his meditation before speaking. He understood the torments of his soul, for he himself, working on *Dead Souls,* had experienced this same search for perfection. He was alluding to himself when he later wrote, "An artist whose work has been transformed by the will of God into a truly spiritual effort is incapable of any other task, he knows no intermittence in his labors, his thoughts could stray to no other subject, however he tried to coerce or compel them. In the same way a faithful wife, genuinely devoted to her husband, could never love another man thereafter, or sell her love to anyone for money, even if by doing so she might save herself and her husband from want."[22]

With Ivanov, Gogol discussed their respective scruples and the need of a long preparation for any act of artistic creation. But although the spirit of sacrifice was strong in both, they often differed on minor issues, for it would be hard to find two personalities more dissimilar than this frank, exigent, irascible painter, and the devious and sickly author. Following the example of Ivanov, Moller, and Yordan, Gogol began painting too. He prowled the streets of Rome with sketchbook and water colors. When he was copying a landscape or an ancient ruin, he did not feel guilty for stealing time from *Dead Souls.*

The book was progressing fitfully. Gogol usually worked on it in the mornings, standing at his high desk. Soon the sun beating through the shutters, his vociferous neighbors, the hawking sellers and bleating goats outside lured him out of doors; he would abandon his pen on any pretext. Besides, speed was irrelevant to a work of this significance. Solidity, he thought, was the fruit of long reflection. Like Ivanov, he could not see the end of his task. Like Ivanov, he refused to let himself be turned aside from his grand design by the pursuit of lucre. Like Ivanov, he believed himself inspired by God. To his friends in St. Petersburg and Moscow, who were exhorting him to write for their periodicals, he proudly replied that it was a sin to ask such things of him. At the same time, he begged them to send money. His financial difficulties were growing acute. The books he had published in Russia were bringing in nothing. He had sold all rights to his play forever. Having run out of other expedients, he turned to his Roman friends, borrowing from Peter to pay Paul. His association with the young painters living on government grants suddenly gave him the idea of asking for a pension himself. Was he not also an artist to whom the Italian climate was necessary for his intellectual development? Already in April 1837 he was writing to Zhukovsky:

"If I were a painter, even a mediocre one, my livelihood would be ensured. Here in Rome are fifteen of them, who have just been sent from Russia by the academy, and some of them don't draw as well as I do. They get three thousand rubles a year. If I were an actor, I should also have nothing to worry about. Actors receive ten thousand rubles and more a year, and you know quite well I should not have been a bad one. But I am a writer, and consequently must starve. I have thought and thought and can come up with nothing better than to ask the emperor. He is well disposed. I shall remember until my dying day the interest he took in my *Inspector General*. I have written a letter, which I enclose in yours. If you think it is properly worded, present it yourself, intercede for me! If you think it is badly written, I count on his magnanimity; he will forgive his humble subject. Tell him I am uneducated, I do not know how to write to such a lofty person, but I am filled with the sort of love for him that only a Russian can feel for his sovereign, and if I have dared to importune him with my request it is only because I know he cherishes us all like his own children. If I could have a pension like those of the pupils at the Academy of Fine Arts living in Italy, or that of the deacons serving in our church in Rome, I could stay here longer, for life in this country is very inexpensive. Find an opportunity and the means of speaking to the emperor about my stories "Old World Landowners" and "Taras Bulba." They are pleasant tales, liked by everyone and appropriate to every faction. The multitude of flaws in both texts went unnoticed by everyone except yourself, me, and Pushkin. If the tsar could read them! He is so responsive to works that express warmth of feeling and come from the soul! Oh, something tells me he will take an interest in my fate. But let it be as the will of God decides. In Him and in you I place my hopes."[23]

Zhukovsky was unable to obtain the much-desired pension, but on his appeal the emperor sent five thousand rubles to Gogol, who promptly burst into song: "I have received the grant accorded to me by our generous emperor," he wrote to Zhukovsky. "Gratitude is strong within my breast but will not overflow all the way to his throne. As a god, our tsar strews his bounty wide with both hands and will not hear our thanks. But perhaps the work of a poor poet will reach down to posterity, adding one more endearing stroke to the sovereign's glory. In any case, my gratitude can extend as far as you. You, always you! Your affectionate eyes watch over me."[24]

With the financial screws temporarily loosened, he abandoned himself to idleness with even fewer scruples than before. His "Ukrainian sloth" blossomed in the Roman sun. *Dead Souls* sank into the swamp. When his resources dried up again, he appealed to Pogodin: "If you're in funds, please send me a bill of exchange for 2,000 rubles. I'll pay you back in a year or eighteen months."[25]

Pogodin, Aksakov and a few other Moscow friends pooled their resources and, not without difficulty, raised and sent off the sum. Moved to tears, Gogol wrote to Pogodin: "I thank you, my dear friend, my loyal friend! Your concern for me has touched me to the bottom of my soul! So much love, so much care! Why does God love me so much? God! I am unworthy of such love! What have I done to deserve it? My talent is so feeble! Why was I not given health? Something has grown in this head and heart; is it possible I will not be given time to express even half of what I have conceived? I confess I am worried about my health."[26]

He resented his body's unwillingness to let him forget it. If only he could be pure spirit; but at every moment suspicious gurglings, twinges, and burnings were forcing him to attend to the realities of the flesh. He was clearly not made like the rest of the world. His entrails, nerves, veins, and bones must be arranged in some remarkable and unique fashion—a challenge to the medical profession. Ordinary drugs had no effect on him. He had to invent his own therapy. Not a day went by without suffering. The most unpleasant thing of all was his inability to perspire. In the midday heat his skin remained dry. And his intestines boiled. The doctors kept talking about ailments caused by hemorrhoids. What did they know about it?

"I fear hypochondria, which is now lurking," he wrote to Prokopovich. "My stomach could not be in worse shape and absolutely refuses to digest, even though I eat very moderately. My hemorrhoidal constipation has returned. And if I do not go out, my brain feels as though there were a sort of shroud over it the whole day long, preventing me from thinking and making my thoughts all hazy. My stomach is heavy and my pocket light."[27]

And to Danilevsky: "Help me to choose or order a wig. I feel like shaving off my hair—not in order to make it grow, but because that might help with my perspiration and, by liberating my head, my inspiration! My inspiration languishes! My head often feels covered by a thick cloud which I am continually struggling to dissipate, and there is so much still to be done."[28]

To Prince Vyazemsky: "Italy has prolonged my life but has been unable to destroy the evil that reigns so despotically over my body and has become a second nature to me. And what if I could not finish my work? Oh, perish the dreadful thought! It plunges me into such torment that I pray no mortal may ever know the like."[29]

Between two attacks of his affliction, however, he put up a good front: one moment he could be seen silent and strained, with tragic eye and hand on stomach, and the next, radiant with optimism, eccentrically attired, light of step, alert of speech, his laughter a peal and his appetite extravagant. He was a habitué of the *trattorie,* his long nose ferreting out the smell of good cooking and quivering in anticipation of the dishes he would soon select.

"Now I dine at Falcone's, near the Pantheon, where the broiled lamb is as good as that of the Caucasus and the veal more nourishing than anywhere else; they also serve a *crostata* with cherries that could make the most consummate gastronome salivate for three days running," he wrote to Danilevsky.[30]

At the end of his own placid and copious dinner he would sometimes descry another customer just beginning his meal. Thereupon, his mouth watering, he would order the same dishes as his neighbor and begin all over again.[31] Often he made himself a little "treat" when he got home again, to enliven his evening: boiled goat's milk mixed with sugar and rum. An upset stomach would follow these gastronomic orgies, and he would swear to keep a strict diet thereafter; but once the pain subsided, he returned to his gluttony. So he went, torn between his love of great ideas and his love of tasty dishes, his veneration of timeless Italy and his nostalgia for loathsome Russia, his worship of the beautiful and his penchant to depict the ugly, his pretensions to sincerity and his need to complain, lie, and elude the judgment of his contemporaries. His friends, who thought they knew him, were never sure which they would see that day, the high liver or the ascetic, the preacher or the billiard shark.

He could not bear solitude; the moment he reached Rome, he bullied Danilevsky into joining him. Next it was young Zolotarev who briefly shared his apartment at strada Felice 126. And although he regarded the Eternal City as his second home, Gogol often ran away from it. In July 1837 he rejoined a group of friends, including Alexandra Smirnov, in Baden-Baden, drank a vast number of glasses of iced water, ambled down the avenues in the park at the young woman's side, and consented to give a public reading of the opening chapters of *Dead Souls*.

He was about to begin reading to a circle of acquaintances, when a fierce thunderstorm burst. Lightning rent the sky, rain pounded at the windows, a torrent raced down the slopes above the house. Gogol paused worriedly, resumed reading, and then gave up and asked Andrey Karamzin to accompany him home—on account, he said, of the wild dogs prowling the streets. "There were no dogs there," Mrs. Smirnov wrote, "but I suppose the storm had deranged Gogol's weak nerves, and he was subject to those unbearable anxieties which are the lot of nervous people."

From Baden-Baden he went to Strasbourg, Karlsruhe, Frankfurt, and Geneva, where he met Danilevsky and Mickiewicz. Then he took a stage sleigh over the Simplon Pass back to Italy.

"The masses of those wild, terrifying mountains rolled past all along the road beyond the coach windows," he wrote his mother; "glittering waterfalls deafened us and buried us in a mist of droplets. For half a day we climbed up toward the Simplon, one of the highest passes, by a road of hairpin bends looking out to other chains of mountains. Suddenly everything was beneath us, and the summits we had been able to see before only by craning our necks now shrank away; the peaks, chasms, and waterfalls lay at our feet. The road often went right through the mountain, along corridors cut into the rock."[32]

They left the snow behind and transferred to a four-wheeled vehicle. The sleek majesty of Lake Maggiore dazzled Gogol; the animation of Milan reminded him of Paris. He paid a flying visit to Florence, "a small city of severe beauty,"[33] and finally reached Rome feeling that he had chosen to live in the only place in the world whose inhabitants had no cause to envy anyone else.

The following year, nevertheless, he went to Naples, where he dutifully admired the calm bay and its vaporous mountains, smoking Vesuvius, and the surrounding countryside; strolled through the narrow streets; went to Capri and took a boat trip into the Blue Grotto: "We edged into it in the boat, heads down, and suddenly found ourselves under a huge vault. We were in almost total darkness, but the water, an extremely deep sapphire, seemed illuminated from below by some blue flame."[34] He stayed at Princess Repnin's villa at Castellammare, but soon tired of the dust, dirt, clamor, and thieving urchins of Naples. From there he went to Livorno; then, in September 1838, he took a little run up to Paris, where Danilevsky, who had been stripped of his last penny by sharks, was calling him to the rescue. He managed to reline his friend's pockets, with the help of Pogodin and the Repnins, and they spent a few days together hanging about the cafés and restaurants.

From Paris he returned to Rome, via Lyon, Marseilles, and Genoa. He claimed his inspiration was never stronger than when traveling. His imagination was stimulated by the changing scene, disruption of his habits, and jerks and jolts of the road. He told, for instance, how he had had a positive fit of creativity in a little inn between Genzano and Albano: "I don't know why, but the instant I entered that inn I wanted to write. I called for a table, sat down in a corner, opened my briefcase, and there in the smoke-filled and stifling atmosphere with all the racket of the travelers going on around me, and the noise of colliding billiard balls and the bustle of waiters, I sealed myself off in a strange dream and wrote a whole chapter without once leaving my seat. I place those lines among the best I have ever written. It has seldom been given me to create with such gusto."[35]

As on his return from his previous voyage, he greeted Rome with relief. The only thing he missed were the Paris restaurants. But his excessive indulgence in them had upset his stomach again. "Wherever I turn my eyes, I seem to see more temples [restaurants]," he wrote to Danilevsky. "My mind has not been able to tear itself completely away from Montmartre and the boulevard des Italiens. Unfortunately, some fiend dwelling in my stomach will not let me see things as I would like, and is forever reminding me of some luncheon or dinner, in short of some sinful act, despite the holiness of the places I frequent, the admirable sun, and the fine weather."[36]

The end of that year brought him a great joy. On December 18, 1838, the heir apparent, Grand Duke Alexander Nikolayevich, arrived in Rome escorted by his tutor, Zhukovsky, and a full retinue. Another member of his entourage, young Count Joseph Vyelgorsky, whom the emperor had given to his son as a companion in his studies, was consumptive and had been forced to leave the group earlier, making his way southward alone, from one spa to another. Reaching Rome shortly before the grand duke, he went to live at the home of the very charitable Princess Volkonsky, and it was there Gogol saw him, exhausted and coughing blood. They had met before, in St. Petersburg at the beginning of the decade; but Gogol only really discovered Vyelgorsky in his illness. He was charmed by the diaphanous face, the eyes burning with fever. But he was too overjoyed to see Zhukovsky again to give very much attention to the newcomer just then.

Naturally Zhukovsky told Gogol all about Pushkin's agony. Together they wept over Pushkin's senseless demise, which had deprived the world of its greatest poet and themselves of the best of friends. Then they talked of their respective work, their mutual friends, the latest literary news from Russia, and *Dead Souls,* which was advancing slowly but surely. During the days that followed, Gogol took Zhukovsky on an exhaustive tour of the city. He was a tireless walker and guide, and managed to communicate his enthusiasm to the poet. Forum, Coliseum, Pantheon, churches, museums, picturesque alleys: they saw them all. Both men always carried paper and water colors on their outings, stopping often to paint a landscape, a ruin, or a ragged urchin with mocking eye. Gogol wondered how an official personage of Zhukovsky's stature could remain so simple in manner and warm in feeling. He called him "the envoy from heaven," and when "the envoy from heaven" abandoned him to go back to Russia, he wrote to Danilevsky, "He has left me here like an orphan and, for the first time, I am feeling sad in Rome."[37]

Three weeks after this parting, however, there came another surprise: this time it was Pogodin announcing his imminent arrival. He and his wife reached Rome on March 8, 1839, and Gogol promptly took them in hand as he had done with Zhukovsky. With childish glee he showed them *his* capital, hurrying them down the dusty, noisy streets until his exhausted and surfeited guests begged for mercy. At two in the afternoon he would lead them into a restaurant near the piazza di Spagna but would eat nothing himself, saying his stomach troubles had ruined his appetite and that he contented himself with a light snack around six in the evening. Pogodin decided to witness one of these "light snacks." Unknown to Gogol, a few of his friends in Rome foregathered in the back room of the trattoria Falcone, where he regularly took his meals, to spy on him. He came in, sat down, and was immediately encircled by *camerieri.* "He orders: macaroni, cheese, butter, vinegar, sugar, mustard, ravioli, broccoli . . . ," Pogodin wrote. "The waiters go running all over the place, fetching this and that. Gogol, his face aglow, takes the ingredients from the waiters' hands and issues his instructions with jubilant intensity. Now before him stand mountains of greenery, flagons filled with pale liquids. An enormous plate of macaroni is set before him, from which thick steam escapes as the lid is removed. Gogol throws a lump of butter onto the noodles, liberally powders the mound with cheese, assumes the pose of a priest about to offer a sacrifice, seizes a knife and prepares to cut. At that moment, our door flies open. We run out to him laughing. I call out, 'Aha, old man, so your appetite is ruined and your stomach all upset? For whom have you prepared all that, then?' At first disconcerted, Gogol quickly regains his aplomb and snaps back: 'Why are you making so much noise? I have no real appetite, of course; what you see is artificial. I am trying to stimulate it by eating some decent food. But the devil take me if I can finish it! I will eat without wanting to, and it will be as though I had eaten nothing. Come, sit here, I'll give you a treat. Hey, waiter, bring the next course.' The feast began with much gaiety. Gogol ate like four men, explaining throughout that it was all untrue and he really and truly did have an ailing stomach."[38]

Eventually, Pogodin and his wife left for Paris, where Danilevsky was awaiting them. "By the way," Gogol wrote to him, "I have heard that some spies have turned up to see you in Paris. Of course, this was to be expected, in view of the numbers of Russians living more or less legally in that city. Take care. I am certain the name of almost every Russian there has been noted in the black book of the secret police."[39]

After wishing the travelers a safe journey, he returned to Princess Volkonsky, who now seemed less anxious to convert him to the Roman persuasion. She had finally realized, no doubt, that no one could force him in this matter, and although she still received him as graciously as before, she could not forgive him for leading her on for so long. In her home he saw young Count Vyelgorsky, whose illness had progressed alarmingly. Pale, with drawn features and an expression of gentle melancholy, the twenty-three-year-old boy lounged in the garden "breathing pure air" as the doctors advised, or else hid in a little grotto with a book. He was keenly interested in history and literature and often talked to Gogol about Russia's past. Through their conversations, the writer began to see something enticingly fresh, noble, serenely courageous in this young man. Soon Vyelgorsky's strength declined even further, and he could no longer get up; then Gogol moved to his bedside, remaining for hours on end in tender contemplation of his face.

"I believe Joseph Vyelgorsky is definitely dying," he wrote to Pogodin. "Poor, gentle, noble Joseph! There is no room in Russia for admirable people. Only swine can live there!"[40]

To Marya Balabin: "I am now spending sleepless nights at the bedside of my poor friend Joseph Vyelgorsky, who is dying. You did not know his admirable soul, his fine feelings, his character, which is almost too strong for one of his age, or his remarkably profound intelligence. And soon it will all be death's prey. Now I live only for him; I watch over his final minutes. A fleeting smile or more cheerful expression on his face is the only event in my monotonous days. Strange and incomprehensible, I swear it, is the destiny of any Russian of real quality. The moment such a one appears, death takes him from us. I no longer believe in anything now, and if I catch a glimpse of anything beautiful I close my eyes and try to look away, for there is always a smell of the tomb around it. A low voice whispers to me. 'That will not live long. It is only shown to you so that you will know the eternal anguish of regret, so that your soul may suffer and be tormented.' "[41]

With this youth, who was wasting away before his very eyes, Gogol felt as never before the need to give himself to another human. In a way, the ineluctable march of death made it easier for him to give free rein to his most secret feelings. What he had never dared show to a person destined to survive, he could both think and utter to one who was about to disappear forever. The chill light of the tomb purified and justified everything. Freed from his usual constraint by the very pathos of the situation, he could feel a tenderness that no woman had yet inspired in him. With those he most admired he was always on his guard, as though fearing their friendship would be imperceptibly degraded, transformed into flirtation, even love. Never, with one of them, would he have abandoned himself to the trembling devotion he displayed in the sickroom. Never would he have opened his heart to them as he did here, for he knew they were creatures of the flesh, greedy for conquest and sin. Even the most devout, even those who seemed most detached from earthly pleasures! In the presence of Joseph Vyelgorsky, on the other hand, he could yield to the human urge to commune, to unite, and yet remain morally and physically uncompromised. He could be safe, and in love: for what had grown between them was love. Not friendship: a fraternal, immaterial, and despairing love, all the stages of which Gogol feverishly recorded in *Nights in the Villa:*

"They were tender and devastating, those sleepless nights. He sat, ill, in an armchair. How sweet to be near him and to look at him. For two nights already, we had been calling each other 'thou.' He had become so much closer to me."

Later: "I was not with him that night. The next morning I hurried, and came to him like a criminal. He was in bed when he saw me. He smiled at me with that angelic smile which had become his. He held out his hand and pressed mine affectionately. 'Traitor,' he said, 'you betrayed me!' 'Angel,' I said, 'forgive me. I suffered myself from your suffering, I was on the rack this night. My rest was all anxiety. Forgive me!' Oh, his sweetness. He pressed my hand. I began to fan him with a branch of laurel. 'Ah, so cool, so pleasant!' he said. At ten o'clock I came back to see him again. I had left him three hours before, to get some rest. He was sitting, alone. The dejection of boredom showed on his face. Seeing me, he gave a small wave of his hand. 'You are my savior,' he said. Those words still ring in my ears. 'Angel, were you bored?' I asked. 'Oh, so very bored!' he answered. I kissed his shoulder. He held out his cheek. We kissed. He was still holding my hand."

Later still, on the "eighth night": "That night, the doctor had ordered him to rest. He rose unwillingly and, leaning on my shoulder, moved to his bed. My darling! His weary look, his bright dressing gown, his slow steps. Leaning over my shoulder and pointing to the bed, he spoke in my ear: 'Now I am a lost man.' 'We'll just stay half an hour in bed,' I told him. 'Then we'll go back to your chair.' I watched you, my dear, my tender flower! All the while you were sleeping or dozing on your bed or in your chair I followed your movements, your changes of expression, bound to you by some incomprehensible force. My life was strangely new then, and yet it was also like a repetition of something far away, a long time ago. But I can see how hard it is to give any idea of it: the return of that fresh and fleeting moment of youth, that time when the novice seeks a fraternal friendship among others of his age— one of those purely juvenile friendships filled with childish and charming little nothings, a contest to see who can offer the most tokens of tender attachment. Oh, God! Why? I watched you. My darling young flower! Has this fresh breath of youth enveloped me only to let me sink again into the great cold where all feelings freeze; to age forty years in one day; to watch in even greater distress and despair the fading of my own existence?"

Hearing of the tender attachment that had been formed between Gogol and the dying youth, Alexandra Smirnov wrote, "I did not try to find out when and how the relationship was formed. I found their association perfectly correct, quite natural and simple."[42] Her insistence upon the "correctness" of the relationship between the two men probably means that other observers held a different opinion. But, for once in his life, blind with grief and anxiety, Gogol was indifferent to gossip.

At one point, when Vyelgorsky was failing rapidly, Gogol ran to fetch an Orthodox priest at his friend's request. Vyelgorsky confessed and received extreme unction in the garden, then was carried to his room. He was scarcely breathing, but still conscious enough to thank his friends and smile. Just as he was about to sink into a coma, Princess Volkonsky—who was single-minded if anything—sent for Father Gervais, a Roman Catholic priest, and whispered urgently to him, "Now is the moment to convert him." The priest firmly refused. "In the room of a dying man," he said, "there must be silence and peace." The frustrated princess did not insist; but on May 21, 1839, when Vyelgorsky breathed his last, she could not refrain from exclaiming, "I saw the soul flying out of him; it was Catholic!"[43] From that moment, she gave Gogol the cold shoulder.

He, however, was so shaken by this death that the princess' wrath left him quite unmoved. This was the first time he, as impotent onlooker, had witnessed the agony of someone dear to him. Pushkin had died leagues away; his loss was as abstract as a mathematical equation. It required a mental effort to imagine him suffering. But with Vyelgorsky, death entered Gogol's experience. He had seen it at work in this struggling body. He had felt its chill in his own veins. Was not human activity grotesque, when all it led to was the prodigious silence of the grave? What was the point of the baubles of fame, the struggles of painter and poet, the sweetness and rages of love, the blessings of the table, when every one of us would one day end up alone in a hole in the ground?

"I have just buried the friend fate gave me in a period of my life when one is no longer making new friends," Gogol wrote to Danilevsky. "I mean my dear Joseph Vyelgorsky. We have known and respected each other for many years, but became intimately, indissolubly, and definitively joined in fraternal affection only during his last illness."[44]

In the depths of despair, Gogol soon convinced himself that his only chance of recovery lay in fleeing the place of his pain. He embarked at Civitavecchia for Marseilles, where he was to meet Vyelgorsky's mother. Sainte-Beuve happened to be on the same ship. Sainte-Beuve spoke no Russian, and Gogol's French was very limited; how could they possibly have communicated? Nevertheless, the critic wrote some years later that their conversation had been "forceful, precise, and filled with lightning observations of society," and had given him a "foretaste of what was to be so original and true to life in the author's works."[45] He also said, in a letter to Prince Augustin Petrovich Golitsyn, "I found myself on the steamer in the company of Gogol, and in those two days I was able to perceive, despite his somewhat labored French, his rare distinction, originality, and artistic powers."[46]

In Marseilles, after performing his painful duty of relating her son's last days to Joseph Vyelgorsky's mother, Gogol turned to a stagecoach to wear out his grief in the fatigue and novelty of travel. He went first to Vienna; then to Hanau, where he met the Slavophile poet Yasykov; then to Marienbad, where he joined the Pogodins. They introduced him to a man named D. E. Benardaki, a curious character who had speculated brilliantly in wheat, bought land and factories, and amassed an immense fortune, which he administered with great intelligence. He belonged to the new school of landowners: he was a shrewd businessman, with clear ideas about farming, industrial development, the good and bad features of serfdom, urban administration, the workings of the courts, the control of credit, and the progress of state education. From his conversation, sprinkled with aphorisms and anecdotes, Gogol discovered the ruthless world of competition and profit, and the struggle for market control. The eloquent and astute Benardaki became for him a personification of the practical man. The Russian of the future must be modeled upon this man: farseeing, bold, and all of a piece. What a fine character for a novel this Christian millionaire would make![47] Every day after their baths, Gogol and Pogodin would go for a walk in the country with him.

However edifying Benardaki's conversation may have been, the Marienbad waters had no effect at all upon Gogol's system, and so he went back to Vienna in disappointment.

On his second visit to that large, populous, jolly city, the beauty of the palaces, the cool forests, and the good humor of the inhabitants left him equally untouched. "Oh, Rome! Rome!" he wrote to Shevyrev. "I feel as though I have been gone five years. There is no other place on earth." He was as worried as ever about his health. When he looked in the mirror, he saw how thin he was: perhaps he had drunk too much of that mineral water. "I look like a mummy," he wrote to Marya Balabin, "or rather, like an ancient German professor with his socks falling down around his toothpick ankles."[48] After further thought, he decided it was grief that was undermining him. He no longer had strength to hope or desire to live. "It is painful," he went on, "to find oneself old at an age still considered young; horrible to find in oneself a heap of ashes instead of flames, and to realize the impotence of enthusiasm. My soul, deprived of all that once uplifted it (what an atrocious loss!) can feel nothing now but the wretchedness of its own state. When you have read my letter, please tear it up. No one else must read this!"

He did not like the Austrians. Or rather, he lumped them in the same category as the Germans, and he could not forgive the Germans for having excited his admiration in his youth. "In those days, I confused German science, philosophy, and literature with the German people," he wrote.[49] Furthermore, "Vienna is one continual party; the Germans here spend all their time amusing themselves. But, as everybody knows, they have the most tedious amusements on earth: drinking beer and sitting at wooden tables under chestnut trees—and that is all!"[50] If only he could write! But he was paralyzed by loneliness. He needed a friendly atmosphere, distractions, the motion of travel to warm up his sluggish inspiration.

"It is very odd," he wrote Shevyrev, "but I am absolutely incapable of working when I am condemned to solitude, when I have no one to talk to and no secondary occupations, when there is only limitless and indefinite time before me. I was always amazed by Pushkin, who had to cloister himself, to withdraw alone to some village, in order to write. I am just the opposite: I have never been able to do anything in the country, and as a rule I can do nothing when I am isolated and bored. For I am bored in Vienna. All the sins of youth I have published so far were written in St. Petersburg, when I had a job and no spare time, and was beleaguered by the demands and diversity of my occupations. The work I have begun is not progressing. Yet I feel it could be important. Travel is my only hope. It is when I am traveling that the substance of what I write generally takes form. I develop almost all my subjects on the road."[51]

Despite his reluctance to take pen in hand, he had, in the previous months, revised "Taras Bulba," "The Portrait," "The Nose," "Viy," and *The Inspector General,* polished "The Lawsuit" and "The Servants' Hall" (scenes from the unfinished play *The Vladimir Cross*), and begun *Annunziata,* a Roman story that was never completed except for the fragment entitled "Rome." He had also rewritten his comedy *Marriage* for the third time but still could not find a satisfactory ending for it, and had conceived an idea for a heroic drama based on the history of the Zaporog Cossacks. From Rome to Marienbad and Marienbad to Vienna, these fragments came between him and *Dead Souls*. Could Italy alone revive his desire to carry on the great task? He believed it could; but family problems prevented him from going back there. His mother's letters were becoming desperate: she had exhausted all her resources, the creditors were threatening to sell Vasilyevka. His youngest sister, Olga, hard of hearing, was getting no kind of education at home. The eldest, Marya, widow of Trushkovsky, had taken it into her head to remarry the previous year. The match did not look brilliant, so Gogol had written a stern letter: "You must arm yourself with greater wisdom, consider that you are no longer a little girl, and realize that only a truly advantageous match would be worth a change of situation and the loss of your freedom."[52]

To his mother: "If her suitor's financial situation is no better than her own, he can't be worth much. She must realize that she will have children, they will give her endless worry and make innumerable demands, and she must not come to regret the state she has forsaken. It is understandable that a girl of eighteen will prefer good looks, a kind heart, and a sensitive nature above all else, and will scorn a fortune and the means of subsistence it offers. But it is unpardonable in a penniless widow of twenty-five to think no further than that."[53]

Thus chastised, Marya eventually rejected her suitor. But she might change her mind; such sudden reversals were common among lovers. Especially in the provinces, where there was so little distraction. It was essential that he take the poor goose in hand, shake her out of her daydreams, explain to her in person that she would never have a more peaceful life than at Vasilyevka, with her mother and son and her memories of her husband. The most serious problem of all, however, was that of the other two sisters, Anna and Elizaveta, who were about to end their careers at the Patriotic Institute. When they emerged from that hall of learning, they would be on their own. Whether he liked it or not, Gogol really ought to return to Russia and make arrangements for their future. A brief sojourn would suffice. And then back to Italy. Although he had made up his mind to go, he kept putting off his departure. He sat in his room, number 27 in the Römischen Kaiser, waiting for the Pogodins, who had promised to pass through Vienna on their way to Moscow. He thought the return might be less abhorrent in the company of this friendly pair.

"Is it possible that I am about to return to Russia?" he wrote to Shevyrev. "I can hardly believe it. I fear for my health. By now, I have grown completely unused to real cold. How shall I endure it? My circumstances are such, however, that I absolutely must go back; my sisters are coming out of the Institute and I have to do something about them, for there is no one I can ask to do it in my place. But as soon as I have settled my affairs, I shall fly to Rome again!"[54]

To his sisters Anna and Elizaveta: "Because of you I have decided to come to St. Petersburg. Do you even begin to realize the sacrifice I am making? Do you know that if it weren't for you I should not make the trip for a king's ransom?"[55]

He prudently refrained from giving his mother the exact date of his arrival. Even at a distance, he could not help being irritated by her. He respected her, he pitied her, he accused himself of being a bad son because he was not able to support her; but still he kept pecking away at her in his letters, as though to punish her for loving him too much. If she wanted to tell him how she had praised his talent to the neighbors, he ordered her never to engage in literary conversations but simply to say, "'I cannot judge his work; my verdict would be partial because I am his mother; all I can tell you is that he is a good and loving son and that is enough for me.'"[56]

If she tried to stir his affection by telling him she had had some shirts made especially for him, he expressed amazement at such an aberrant idea: "You were wrong to have those shirts made for me. I am sure I shall not be able to wear them, because they won't be what I am used to. You would have done better to wait until you had one of my shirts to use as a pattern."[57]

If she alluded to a "wonderful match" she had in mind for Anna when she came home from the Institute, he launched into one of his stern tirades: "Marriages are made between people of the same rank, and one would have to be an imbecile or a confirmed eccentric to defy parents, interests, and social position and choose some poor unknown girl for a wife; or else, the girl would have to be a paragon of beauty and intelligence, which is plainly not the case of our Anna, although she is a good girl and could make a good wife."[58]

And then, speaking of his sisters' pathological shyness, which his mother attributed to their sudden removal to such a different environment: "How can you be so unfair? On the contrary, that is the only

thing that could improve them. When they came up from the village
they were perfect savages; a stranger could not get a word out of them.
Today, at least, they know how to open their mouths and utter one or
two sensible words."[59]

For Gogol, and despite her forty-eight years, Marya Ivanovna was
obviously a retarded adolescent filled with unreasonable dreams, incapable of setting one foot in front of the other; and Anna, Elizaveta,
Olga, and Marya were even less able to cope with the storms and
stresses of life. He alone could save them from shipwreck. Five women
on his hands. And the responsibility of creating a great work. Savior
and creator. Perhaps this double God-imposed task would be beyond
his strength. However often he counted and recounted his money, including whatever he might receive from the new editions of his works,
he could not make up a total large enough to cover the cost of providing
for his sisters.

His anxieties were partially dispelled by Pogodin's arrival. Thank
God, he did have some good friends; they would not abandon him,
whatever happened. They pooled their money to buy two carriages.
Mrs. Pogodin and Mrs. Shevyrev, who was also staying in Vienna,
traveled in one; and Pogodin and Gogol in the other. They set out in
the middle of the night, on September 22, 1839.[60] Six days later, after
passing through Olmütz and Cracow, the travelers reached Warsaw.
There Gogol wrote to Zhukovsky:

"My sisters are coming out [of the Institute], and this absolutely
necessitates my physical presence. One thing torments me now. To set
them up, pay the music teacher who has been giving them lessons all
the time they have been there, etc. etc., I need around five thousand
rubles, and I confess that this is utterly beyond me. Once again, I am
compelled to turn to you. Perhaps the empress, at whose expense my
sisters have been educated, will be gracious enough to drop a few
crumbs, in some form or other, from her munificent hand? I know it is
shameful and outrageous of me to apply again to someone who has already laid such a burden of gratitude upon my heart that I am powerless to express it; but I can think of, I know of, I can see and imagine
no other means of extricating myself, and I know I should suffer remorse if I were *not* guilty of some impudence in this matter."[61]

The next day, September 17, 1839, the travelers set out again, still in
two vehicles, for Byalystock, which they reached the same evening.

They were in Smolensk on September 23, and at dusk three days later the dirt-encrusted coaches pulled up side by side in front of the gate to Moscow. A pale lantern lit up a striped guardhouse, a guard with his halberd, a puddle of water. Russian voices surrounded the coach. Where was Rome and its azure sky?

4. Home Again

In Moscow, Gogol stayed with the Pogodins, who lived in a huge white house at the back of an immense garden bordering the Virgins' Field. His room was on the second floor, very spacious and comfortably furnished, with five windows giving onto the street. He wrote to his mother on the evening of his arrival, but not to tell her he was there: he was too frightened that she might turn up to join him. He was fond of her—but in no hurry to see her again. With her, he knew he would find himself back in the atmosphere of financial problems, country gossip, brainless adoration, and absurd matrimonial projects. And so he resorted to yet another mystification, to discourage her from coming to town. Other people might find relief in the truth; but he was comfortable only when he was lying. Instead of heading his letter "Moscow," he wrote "Trieste, September 26, 1839." Then his pen began to skim along the page:

"I have not yet made arrangements for my return to Russia. I am in Trieste, where I began to take baths in the sea. They seem to have had a very good effect, but I have to stop now, because I started too late in the season; I shall continue next spring. If I do come to Russia, it will certainly not be before November, and then only if an opportunity arises and the trip is not ruinously expensive. But for my obligation to provide as well as possible for my sisters when they leave the Institute, I should not commit such an imprudence or risk compromising my health—for which you, a wise mother, would be the first to scold me. So I do not want you to cherish vain hopes. Perhaps we will see each other this winter, perhaps not. If we do—you must not mind this—it will be only briefly. Tomorrow I leave for Vienna, to be a little closer to you."

Having got this far, he encountered a tricky problem: what address should he give Marya Ivanovna? Why, Pogodin's, of course! The first lie is the hardest; the rest flow easily, like untangling a skein of wool. "Send your letter to Professor Pogodin, Virgins' Field, Moscow. But do not interpret this as a sign that I will soon be in Moscow myself. It is only so that your letters may reach me more quickly; from Moscow they will be sent by official courier."

Now, to give a little seasoning to his salad, he must describe the place in which he was pretending to be: "Trieste is a very animated commercial town—half the people are Italian, the other half Slavs who almost speak Russian, or in any event, a language similar to Ukrainian. The glorious Adriatic stretches before me with its health-giving waves. What a pity I began my treatment so late. Farewell, darling Mother. You can write more often now, as your letters will reach me more quickly. Your loving and grateful son, Nikolai."[1]

A few weeks later—still in Moscow—he sent another letter, this time as from Vienna, to announce his forthcoming departure for Russia. He did not expect to see her, he said, for another two months, as the trip was sure to be very long. But she could already forward the shirts she had had made to Pogodin's house. "If they aren't right, I shall use them for nightshirts."[2]

There was a risk in this tale, of course: some chance remark might inform Marya Ivanovna that her son had long since returned to the homeland. Oh, well, if he were unmasked he would simply improvise another story. His mother was so gullible, and he had so much imagination! As a precaution, however, he asked his friends to keep his return a secret. "I am in Moscow," he wrote to Pletnyev. "For the time being, don't tell anybody."

Since Pletnyev had recently lost his wife, Gogol went on: "I have learned of your loss and was saddened by it. Do you know that I had a premonition of her death? When I last parted from you, something told me in some vague way that you would be alone when I saw you next. I do not know why, but I have now acquired the gift of prophecy. There was one event, however, I could not predict: Pushkin's death. I parted from him as though for two days. How strange; good Lord, how strange! Russia without Pushkin! I shall come to Petersburg and Pushkin will not be there! I shall see you, and I shall not see Pushkin!"[3]

Indeed Pushkin's absence was more noticeable in the setting in which he had lived than it had been in Italy, where he had never been allowed to go. Gogol was constantly seeing people who had been friends of both men, and felt that absence keenly: it was like looking at a puzzle in which the central piece was missing. His acquaintances were worried by his moods: it was impossible to tell in advance whether he would be jovial and loquacious, or withdrawn, mute, and spiteful. He did not like new faces and was often sullen in the presence of ladies. Yet the Pogodins showed their guest every mark of consideration. If it were possible, they would have filed off the corners of the furniture so he should not bruise himself bumping into it.

He spent the morning in his room, writing, reading, or knitting a scarf to calm his nerves. At lunchtime he came down, rested and alert, and asked what was for dinner. If macaroni was on the menu, he would insist upon preparing it himself, while the doting family watched him officiate. Then he retired upstairs for a nap. At seven in the evening he reappeared, opened the doors of the ground-floor rooms, which were all laid out in a row—including those of the study in which Pogodin was working—and began to walk. At either end of the wing in which this exercise took place, a jug of cool water was placed on a stand by order of the mistress of the house. Every ten minutes, he would stop and drink a glass. This pacing did not disturb Pogodin, who never raised his head from his papers. And their son, then hardly more than a baby, merely looked on in bewilderment while this peculiar personage, dry and angular, strode along in the candlelight, hastening nowhere, his avian shadow racing along the moldings. "He always walked jerkily and at top speed," he later wrote, "making such a breeze that the stearin candles dripped, to my grandmother's intense annoyance. Sometimes she would shout at her maid, 'Grusha! Grusha! Bring me a shawl! The Italian (for so she called Gogol) is making such a wind that I can't bear it!' 'Don't be angry, Grandmother,' Gogol would say. 'I'll just finish the jug of water and then I'll be gone.' And so it was: when both jugs were empty, back he would go to his room. On these walks, and indeed at all times, he carried his head to one side. As far as dress was concerned, vests were his main interest, and those he wore were always in velvet, red or blue. He seldom went out and did not like to entertain, although he had a hospitable nature. I think celebrity tired him and it was unpleasant for him to see everyone hanging on his words and trying to draw him into conversation."[4]

In fact, "the Italian" was morbidly afraid of society. He longed for praise and yet snapped at people who gave him any. Despite his insistence upon secrecy, the news of his arrival quickly leaked out. The first person to see him after he moved into the Pogodin home was his dedicated admirer Shchepkin, the actor, who had been triumphing in *The Inspector General* for months. On October 2, the two men went to see Sergey Timofeyevich Aksakov, who had also just come to Moscow. The two Aksakovs, father and son, virtually worshiped the man whom the rather excitable Sergey Timofeyevich had christened "the Russian Homer." When the guests were announced, the entire family rose from the table in transports of joy. Gogol had not been expected for lunch. A place was laid, the best portions urged upon him. All eyes were fixed on him in gratitude. In his enthusiasm, Aksakov painted this flattering portrait:

"Physically he was so altered as to be scarcely recognizable. He had lost all trace of the close-shaven, elegant young man who had used to wear his hair short except for the tuft over the forehead, and dressed in the latest fashion. Now his magnificent, thick, fair hair reached almost to his shoulders. A handsome mustache and a little goatee on his chin completed the transformation. Every feature in his face had assumed a different significance. When he spoke, his eyes expressed gaiety, kindliness, and love of mankind; and when he was silent or lost in his thoughts one could read in him a grave aspiration toward something high and elevated. A wide-skirted coat resembling an overcoat had taken the place of the frock coat he no longer donned except on rare occasions. His whole appearance had become more dignified. His jokes—impossible to retell—were so original and comical that they sent everyone into fits of hilarious laughter while he, in relating them, never so much as smiled."[5]

But when Aksakov's son Konstantin asked if he had brought any new writing back from his sojourn in Italy, the reply was almost a snarl: "Nothing."

After her first interview with the great man, Panaev's wife[6] pronounced him "raving and moody." He took to dining almost every day at the Aksakovs', where he was greeted like the Messiah. Sitting in a high-backed armchair, it was he who presided at the table.

"At his place there was a cut-crystal glass and a jug of red wine," Mrs. Panaev wrote. "He was served a special cold meat pie and a roast which no one else could touch. The mistress of the house would offer him one thing after another, but he ate little and spoke to her almost sharply. He sat there, hunched and taciturn, glowering at the others. Sometimes a sarcastic smile would flit across his face. When we left the table, he would go off to the study alone, for his siesta. We would drink our coffee on the terrace; the mistress of the house ordered the servants not to make any noise when they cleared the table."[7]

The narrator's husband wrote:

"Gogol's physique had a disagreeable effect upon me. What struck me first was his long, thin nose, pointed like the beak of a bird of prey. He dressed with some pretensions to elegance, his hair was curled and he wore a toupet which puffed quite high over his forehead, as was the fashion in those days. As I watched, I became more and more unfavorably impressed, for I had constructed an ideal mental image of the author of *Mirgorod,* and Gogol bore no resemblance to it. I even disliked his eyes, which were small, piercing and intelligent, but had a cunning and rather unfriendly expression."[8]

Further, "Gogol spoke little, in monotones, and unwillingly. He seemed sad and pensive. He could not fail to see the admiration and veneration with which he was treated; and he accepted it all as his due, trying to hide his flattered conceit behind a mask of indifference. There was something forced and artificial in his manner, and those who regarded him as a man instead of a genius did not like it. This boundless deference to Gogol's talent was displayed by the Aksakov family with almost childish spontaneity and naïveté; occasionally they were positively absurd."[9]

Aksakov finally extracted a promise from Gogol to read one of his recent works in his home, on October 14, after a luncheon among friends. When the day came, the guests—among whom were Nashchokin, Panaev, and Shchepkin—assembled in the drawing room in a state of affectionate anticipation. The minutes passed; anxiety spread to the kitchen; the mistress of the house paled, blushed, and stared the door down; and still there was no Gogol. He turned up at four in the afternoon and, as usual, offered a perfunctory excuse for his lateness. In the dining room he sat, as was his wont, in the high-backed armchair, the seat of honor. He consented to be served before anyone else, drank his personal wine from his pink crystal glass without raising an eyebrow, listened to the conversation with a bored air, and spoke not a word. After the meal, he stretched out on Aksakov's sofa, lowered his head, and dozed off. Beckoning to his guests and imploring them to lower their voices, the master of the house tiptoed to the drawing room. The ladies wrung their handkerchiefs in anguish: When he woke, would he be cheerful or depressed? Would he consent to read, or not? Aksakov kept watch on the sleeper through a crack in the door. At last Gogol yawned, stretched, rose, and joined the group.

"I do believe I have been sleeping!" he said, yawning again.

After several attempts, Aksakov finally brought out: "You made us, I believe, a promise. Haven't you forgotten it?"

"What promise?" Gogol returned. "Ah, yes; no, I'm not in form today. I would read badly. Spare me the ordeal."

Aksakov renewed his entreaty, however, with such a tremor in his voice that Gogol relented. Every face came to life. The ladies whispered, "He's going to read, he's going to read!" The hero of the hour flopped down upon a divan in front of an oval table, bestowed one mournful glance upon his listeners, and suddenly released a loud belch, then another, then a third. The ladies started, the embarrassed gentlemen looked away.

"What's the matter with me?" the author muttered. "I declare, it sounds like the belches. It's yesterday's dinner: I couldn't digest it. Those mushrooms and that cold soup with kvass and fish. Eating and eating. That's simple enough: the devil knows what one doesn't eat!"

To the consternation of his entire audience, he belched again, then pulled a manuscript from his pocket, flattened it, and went on, reading:

"Here it comes again! Again! Another one! Let's see, maybe if I took a look at the *Northern Bee* . . ."

At last the audience understood that belches and comments were the beginning of a scene from a new play, and relief flooded every face. They dared to exchange a few admiring glances. At the end, there was a loud burst of applause.[10]

Satisfied with the reception given to this comic scene entitled "The Lawsuit," Gogol announced that he would now read "a great chapter" from *Dead Souls.*

This time, the room was practically hysterical. The author's talent was even greater than the reader's. With every sentence, a universe both ultratrue and grotesque, deadly dull and hallucinating, opened up in front of the dazed listeners. "After the reading," Panaev wrote, "Sergey Timofeyevich Aksakov, utterly overwhelmed, strode up and down the room, marched up to Gogol, clasped both hands in his own, cast little meaningful glances at us all, and kept repeating, 'Prodigious! Prodigious!' Konstantin Aksakov's little eyes were sparkling, he was pounding his fist on the table saying, 'There's Homeric power, truly Homeric!' The ladies were in ecstasies, sighing and uttering little cries."[11]

Gogol's friends wanted some yet more public homage for him, however. Since the day of his arrival they had been urging him to attend a performance of *The Inspector General* at the Moscow Bolshoy Theater. The actors, they said, were offended that he should be actually staying in town without even deigning to see them perform his play. The management offered to schedule a performance any day he liked. Could he withstand all this enticement without passing for a conceited boor? Mastering his distaste, he yielded, and went to the theater for the evening performance of October 17, 1839, hoping to remain unobserved.

But all Moscow already knew the author would be present. Long before the curtain rose, the huge white and gold hall was packed from stalls to balconies. Gogol slipped surreptitiously into the Chertkov box[12] (the first on the left), and huddled in a seat in the shadows behind the other occupants. The entire Aksakov family sat in another box, nearby. The play began; the atmosphere was electric. Knowing Gogol was there, the actors were determined to outdo themselves. Shchepkin, playing the mayor, and Samarin, as Khlestakov, gave their all to every line. The public guffawed and applauded. But all this clamorous jollity offended Gogol: he was watching a vaudeville act. Its success was founded upon a misunderstanding. He himself was a misunderstanding, a lost sheep in the literature of his age, an intruder among men. Why had he come?

During the first and second intermissions he crouched down to escape the searching eyes of the spectators. But in the third intermission Pavlov, a critic, spied him in the Chertkov box and pointed him out, calling for an ovation. Every voice thundered, "Author! Author!" Konstantin Aksakov shouted louder than the rest. It was a mob: its enthusiasm was the roar of a mob; Gogol was suddenly panic-stricken. He had never been able to bear crowds; they made him as dizzy as the unleashed ocean seen from a clifftop. Admiration was his lifeblood, yes; but it was always the wrong kind. This was not how he wanted to be praised. Compliments were either too fulsome or too feeble; they came too soon or too late; they were never aimed at the right place; they referred to a work he now despised; their caress stung instead of soothing. Enough! Enough! The roar in the theater grew louder. Hands clapped, mouths gaped in the pink broken mass of faces. Trembling with fright, Gogol edged from the box. Aksakov caught him and begged him to show himself to the public. He refused: he would sooner leap into the sea. While he was taking cover outside in the night, an actor came on stage in front of the curtain and announced that "the author was not in the house." There was a discontented murmur. Never had an author shown such contempt for the admiration of his public and the affection of his actors. What an insult for both!

"Your Gogol acts far too high and mighty!" said Pavlov to Konstantin Aksakov. "You've spoiled him!"[13]

The next day, fully aware how badly he had offended many of his admirers, Gogol drafted a letter to Zagoskin, the theater manager. The letter, which he asked Zagoskin to publish, was filled with excuses and justifications, equally lame. If he had run away on the evening of the performance it was, he said, because he had received particularly afflicting news of his mother only a few hours earlier. Hence, despite the applause, he had not felt able to stand before the curtain in triumph. Pogodin and Aksakov, having heard his explanation, judged them so plausible that they dissuaded him from tendering them. What was this mysterious communication from his mother, which had not prevented him from attending the performance but had caused him too much grief to respond to the acclamations of the crowd? No one would believe his story. Besides, he didn't believe it himself. He grumblingly agreed and gave up the idea of sending the letter. Anyway, Moscow was already fading from his thoughts.

According to the plan he had adopted, he should now go to St. Petersburg to fetch his sisters, but he had no money. Aksakov, however, was about to go to the capital to enroll his fourteen-year-old son, Mikhail, in His Majesty's page corps. His elder daughter, Vera, was to go with them. Where there was room for three, they could always squeeze in a fourth.

On Thursday, October 26, 1829, they set out. Aksakov had hired a "private stagecoach" with two compartments. Aksakov and Vera sat behind, Gogol and Mikhail in front. One half could communicate with the other by means of a little sliding window in a wooden frame. Gogol, huddled in his corner, had pulled the collar of his coat up over his chilly ears, encased his shoes in heavy woolen stockings, and put bearskin boots on top of those. Most of the time, he read (Shakespeare, in French) or dozed, leaning against a traveling case. This case, which he kept beside him even in the posting stations, contained his toilet articles.

"In it there were," wrote Aksakov, "a pomade which he put on his hair, mustache, beard; several brushes, one of which, long and curved, was for his long hair; scissors, nail clippers. . . ." Sometimes he would open the hatch to the back compartment and exchange impassioned considerations with Aksakov on the proper way to perform *The Inspector General,* the divine significance of art, or the beauties of Italy. In the Torzhok station the travelers ordered a dinner of a dozen "cutlets Pozharsky,"[14] and discovered, upon cutting into them, blond hairs mixed with the flesh. While the cook was being summoned, Gogol prophetically declared: "I know what he'll say: 'Hair? Where do you see any hair? How could there be any hair in a cutlet? It's nothing, absolutely nothing, chicken feathers maybe, a bit of down . . .'"

The cook appeared and repeated Gogol's little speech almost word for word. The travelers burst out laughing and the cook crossly withdrew. Vera nearly made herself ill, she laughed so hard.

At every stop, Gogol invented some similar diversion. He chattered with the waiters, travelers, coachmen. The extreme monotony of the trip had a beneficial effect upon him. The long, straight road between Moscow and St. Petersburg was the same one Pushkin had so often followed and described. The bells jingled. Striped mileposts whipped past at regular intervals. Behind the steamy windows sped smooth, gray plains, a village with its isbas bogged down in the thick autumn mud, ragged children playing around a manure heap, a telega driven by a muzhik with heavy, unkempt beard, and then more fields, as far as the eye could see, beneath a layer of fog. So it went, for five days.

At eight o'clock in the evening of October 30, the carriage finally rolled into the capital, where lamps glowed here and there on the ends of their poles. Gogol took his leave of the Aksakovs, grasped his traveling bag filled with his books and brushes, and went to the Pletnyevs, where he had been invited; but after a few days he moved into Zhukovsky's official apartment in the Winter Palace.

This dwelling had the solemn and glacial sumptuousness of a museum. The entrance was at the top of a marble staircase lined with statuary. Liveried lackeys stood guard on the landings. Visitors to the lofty rooms instinctively walked softly and lowered their voices.

Three fourths of Zhukovsky's time was taken up with official duties. As tutor to the heir apparent, he had to attend every formal dinner, ball, and ceremony. But whenever he found a free hour, he shrugged into his slippers and Chinese dressing gown and sat down at his desk to dash off a few lines of poetry.

The day of Gogol's arrival, he wrote in his diary, "Gogol is staying with me," alongside a note on his interview with Grand Duke Konstantin Nikolayevich, a cup of tea with the heir apparent, and a dinner with the grand duchess. In spite of his host's warm welcome, Gogol felt ill at ease in the gilded paneling of the Winter Palace. As soon as he had unpacked, he hurried off to the Patriotic Institute to see his sisters.

He found them in their brown dresses, like two novitiates in a convent. After six and a half years at the Institute, which they had never left, not even for holidays, they were so ignorant of the outside world that the mere thought of stepping through the school door paralyzed them. Their world was the classroom, the playground, the dormitory, their little schoolmates, the teachers, the inspectors. Anna, at eighteen, was even more immature than sixteen-year-old Elizaveta. Both were afraid of new faces, noise in the streets, mice, darkness, and storms. Once their joy at seeing their brother again had worn off, they began to worry about the life he was proposing to them. With the little money he had left, he bought them dresses, lingerie, combs, and shoes, touring the shops, following his own ideas of the mode, making mistakes, exchanging one article for another, and cursing the complexity of female fashion as he stood surrounded by cascades of fabrics and ribbons. At last, he extracted the girls from their retreat and installed them in the home of his friend Princess Elizaveta Petrovna Repnin, née Balabin, until he could take them back to Moscow.

In this strange home, Elizaveta and Anna felt irretrievably lost. Clinging together, they rolled frightened eyes, spoke to nobody, refused to put their heads out of doors, and scarcely ate. "They asked us if we wanted dinner and we refused, although we were very hungry," Elizaveta related. "But when we were alone we would creep up to the stove, steal a piece of charcoal, and gnaw at it because we were so famished—all because of our ridiculous shyness. Supper was another ordeal. I ate nothing, especially since I was seated next to one of the Balabin boys. I took what was in the platter without looking. One day Balabin pointed out that I had served myself a bone; I dropped my fork and burst into tears."[15] Elizaveta, the younger of the two, had a lively manner and pleasing countenance, but Anna, with her plunging nose, low brow, and little birds' eyes, was a living portrait of her brother. When she came into a room, people thought it was Gogol in disguise. Aksakov described the lamentable figures they cut in their new finery: "They did not know how to wear their long gowns," he wrote, "and were forever tripping over them, stumbling and falling; and these incidents only added to their confusion. They would not answer questions. It was painful, just then, to watch poor Gogol."[16]

Gogol had come to St. Petersburg hoping that Zhukovsky would be able to obtain a small annuity for him from the empress. But she was ill, so there was no possibility of applying to that source now. Seeing his "brilliant friend" in distress, Aksakov did not hesitate to offer him two thousand rubles, which he himself had borrowed from the multimillionaire Benardaki. Gogol was overwhelmed by such generosity, silently pressing Aksakov's hands until he nearly crushed them and gazing long and tenderly into his eyes. Now, he thought, he could go to Moscow with his sisters. After paying his debts, however, there was not enough left for the trip. Like it or not, he would have to wait until he could take advantage of Aksakov's coach again. But Aksakov still had business to transact in Petersburg and was in no hurry to leave.

Gogol was bored and exasperated by the delay; he sat and cursed the weather in his huge, badly heated room in the Winter Palace. One day Aksakov surprised him there wrapped in shawls from jaw to anklebone, with a mauve Lapland cap on his head. He was in a foul temper, inspiration would not come, his throat was burning, his nose was running, his sisters were uneducated, he needed money, he wanted to die, he longed for Rome. "I don't understand what is the matter with me," he wrote to Pogodin, "or what I am doing in Petersburg. I can think of nothing; nothing comes to my head. To think that I have already wasted a whole month here, horrors! It is all Aksakov's fault! He has gotten me out of one scrape and into another. I should have liked to go back to Moscow with him. I have begun to love him sincerely, with all my heart. Moreover, my sisters have all the company and service they could desire in his home. In short, it was sensible to wait for him; besides, he led me to hope he would soon be leaving: a week, then another week. But now a month has gone by. Everything on my side is ready, my sisters are dressed, their bags are packed. Ah, what misery! I have already found time to fall ill. I have caught cold, my throat is sore, my teeth ache, my cheeks. I can't keep still. Oh, God, God! When will I leave St. Petersburg?"[17]

To pass the time, he went to see a few of his former comrades. At Prokopovich's he read four chapters of *Dead Souls;* elsewhere, he met the young critic Belinsky, who had long admired him as an author but who, upon seeing him, remained rather distant, as though disappointed by the man. One evening, his friends tried to persuade him to go to a performance of *The Inspector General* by the Petersburg company. He raised his hands in horror: Moscow had been enough.

At last, having enrolled his son Mikhail in the page corps, Aksakov announced that he was ready to depart. This time, there being more passengers, he hired two "stages"—one four-seater, in which he traveled with his daughter Vera, and Anna and Elizaveta; and a two-seater for Gogol and a friend of the Aksakov family named Vaskov. Gogol often changed places with Aksakov, to be with his sisters in the larger coach; and indeed, they needed his supervision: the giddy, unstable creatures shrieked in fear at every jolt, shivered with cold or complained of being too warmly wrapped, wept with fatigue and felt sick to their stomachs; then, forgetting their nausea, they would begin bickering over nothing. At the posting stations they refused the food, because it was different from the genteel fare they had been accustomed to at the Patriotic Institute. The amenable Aksakov swallowed his annoyance and looked away from these creatures whom he had teasingly nicknamed "the patriots." Gogol, assisted by Vera, struggled to reason with the silly girls between fits of tears. "It was sad and comical to see Gogol," Aksakov wrote. "He simply could not cope with the situation, and all his efforts and advice proved ineffectual, irrelevant, or ill-timed, so that in this setting the brilliant poet was more incompetent than the greatest dolt on earth."[18]

Having left St. Petersburg on December 17, 1839, they reached Moscow four days later. After spending one night with the Aksakovs, the author and his sisters went to the Pogodins'. Gogol intended to place Anna and Elizaveta with some reliable person who could teach them how to behave in society, and then, his conscience at ease, hurry back to Italy. But who, alas, would want to take responsibility for these two savages? At the moment, they were all living comfortably in the rooms on the second floor of the handsome house on Virgins' Field. It was his fate, it seemed, to live in other people's homes, travel at other people's expense, and eat at other people's tables. A parasite, that's all he was! But by refusing to write for money, he was at least preserving the purity of his genius. Everything, even self-respect, must be sacrificed to the majesty of art. If only he could finish *Dead Souls* in peace—but living souls were preventing him.

He, ordinarily so irritable, showed infinite patience with Anna and Elizaveta. He would set them exercises in Russian or arithmetic, encourage them to take up a piece of embroidery, and reward them with bonbons, nuts, candied plums, a little vial, a sewing box. Often they would come into his room unannounced, open his drawers, and leaf through his manuscripts; and although shocked by their indiscretion, he let them do it, with feelings of mingled resentment and affection. If Elizaveta were frightened at night and could not sleep, he would sit by her bedside until she dropped off.

To cultivate the girls' minds and taste, he sometimes took them to Pogodin's study, a huge circular room lit by a glass cupola overhead. The walls of the room were lined from floor to ceiling with old books and precious bindings. A collection of ancient manuscripts slept on shelves or lay about on tables. Speaking in a low voice, Gogol would explain and discourse upon these treasures to his two dumfounded ninnies. Or he would take them to literary gatherings in the homes of the Khomyakovs, Elagins, and Kireyevskys,[19] where they sat bored to extinction in the white muslin gowns with which he seemed to have clothed them for eternity. Seeing them so gauche and graceless in that assembly of intelligentsia, their arms limp and their expressions dazed, he asked himself what man could conceivably be interested in them.

"They will live in Moscow," he wrote to Danilevsky; "I shall place them somewhere with friends, but at all costs they must stay away from home [Vasilyevka], where they would be finished for life. You know how my mother, without realizing it, always does the opposite of what she wants to do. Hoping to make her daughters happy, she would plunge them into despair and then blame God for the result, saying that everything that happens is willed by Him. In view of our impecunious situation, it is futile to think of finding husbands for them there, whereas here they have some hope. In any case, they have more chance here of meeting a decent man who is not looking only for a fortune, than they would anywhere else. I don't know what to do about our property, which is on the verge of total ruin; and it is very hard to see why this is so, since the estate is a good one in every respect. The muzhiks are prosperous, there is plenty of land, we have four fairs a year, one being the March livestock fair, which is one of the biggest in the district. It really requires effort to ruin such an excellent holding so completely."[20]

Having laid the blame for the family's misfortunes squarely on his mother's shoulders, it never occurred to him to go there and see what he could do to help. Criticism, not action, was his function. Besides, he couldn't be everywhere at once.

He had worked out a routine at the Pogodins', where he was living, and the Aksakovs', where he lunched at least three times a week. He would usually turn up unannounced, bringing a package of macaroni and preparing it himself—butter, salt, pepper, parmesan cheese—in front of the impressed company. One day he arrived announcing that he had taken the liberty of bringing Count Vladimir Sollogub along. Despite his imperturbable goodwill, the master of the house permitted himself a frown: he did not care for Sollogub and found the gesture in rather poor taste. "If any other friend of mine had done as much, I should have been angry," Aksakov wrote. "But whatever pleased Gogol could but please me too. Presumably he did not see the tactlessness of his act."[21] Out of love for Gogol, he welcomed Sollogub to his table— where they dined, for a change, on macaroni.

But macaroni, even *à l'italienne,* could not replace Italy; increasingly, Gogol was longing for Rome the irreplaceable. "Oh, let me escape quickly, for the love of God and all his saints, let me go to Rome, my soul will be at rest there," he said to Pogodin. "Quickly, quickly! I shall die here!"[22]

Where to find the money for the trip? The simplest way would be to publish something. But his drawers contained nothing but works in progress which he would not part with, so he settled down to revise his previously published work with a view to a complete new edition. Smirdin, the Petersburg bookseller-publisher with whom he initially sought to negotiate, offered him a pittance. Then he turned to the Moscow booksellers, who, knowing he was hard up, also proposed unacceptable terms.

The problem was simple: to earn enough to provide for his future and that of his family, he had to finish *Dead Souls;* to finish *Dead Souls* he had to go to Rome; to go to Rome, he had somehow or other to lay his hands on four thousand rubles; and to lay hands on four thousand rubles, he had his friends—period. If they had faith in his talent, they would certainly not refuse to form a sort of welfare society whose sole beneficiary would be himself. He was delighted by the idea, and wrote to Zhukovsky on January 4, 1840, portraying his circumstances in tones of deepest ebony:

"Everything is going badly! Our poor bit of ground, my mother's only refuge, will soon be sold at auction and then I do not know where she will lay her head. My hope of placing my sisters is also collapsing. I myself am in a state the horrors of which render me numb and inert as never before. One way or another, I must get back to Rome as soon as possible, where my mortally wounded soul will revive as it did before; and there I must set to work with a will and, if possible, finish my novel within a year. Here is what I have thought of: you get the money together; all of you who really care about me can contribute something, and make up a sum of four thousand rubles and lend it to me for a year. I give you my word that if in a year my strength has not failed me and I am not dead, I will pay it all back with interest."

Upon receipt of this appeal, Zhukovsky declined to take up a collection among his friends, few of whom were much better off themselves, and went directly to his pupil, the heir apparent, Alexander Nikolayevich.

"Gogol is on his uppers," he wrote. "He has taken back his sisters, who were boarders at the Institute. His little family estate is going down the drain. He needs four thousand rubles. I should have liked to find them for him elsewhere, but cannot manage it. Could you not lend me the amount? I would send it to Gogol and repay you at the first opportunity; that is to say, before the year is out or in a year's time at most."[23]

After allowing his arm to be slightly twisted, the grand duke agreed to release the money from his personal allowance. Victory! The vise was loosening around Gogol's head. Now that he was certain to return to Italy, he decided to bring his mother to Moscow for a short visit. When she left, she could take Anna with her, for he judged that she was definitely uncivilizable, and living in town only made matters worse. He did not despair of finding a place for Elizaveta in some hospitable family. His choice first fell upon Mrs. Elagin, Zhukovsky's niece; but the thought of such responsibility rather intimidated her and she turned to her uncle for advice. Zhukovsky, well-disposed as he was toward the author of *Dead Souls,* angrily replied: "You must on no account accept such a proposal; it would be weak and inconsistent of you. Gogol often behaves like a capricious egotist. Pogodin has offered to take his sisters, and so has Aksakov; but no, our fellow must have everything his own way and, without the smallest shred of tact, tries to unload his girls on you, who already have a family and possess neither the health nor the means to assume such a heavy burden."[24]

Fortified by this reprimand, Mrs. Elagin summoned the courage to refuse Gogol herself, but she pleaded his cause to a friend of hers, Mrs.

Raevsky, a wealthy and devout woman of fifty who had no children of her own and so lavished her affections upon deserving young women she took in out of charity. Mrs. Raevsky agreed to take Elizaveta under her wing, so from that angle, all was well. She could move into her new home whenever it suited her brother; but of course, they would wait until she had seen her mother.

Marya Ivanovna Gogol and her youngest daughter, Olga, then fourteen, reached town a little before Easter week and duly joined the rest of the family at the Pogodin pension. Her eldest daughter, Marya, had remained at Vasilyevka with her child.

Gogol had undoubtedly reminded his friends to keep the date of his return to Russia a secret, and his mother never suspected the subterfuge. It is true that her faith in him could overcome the evidence of her own eyes. Everyone was amazed at her youthfulness and poise. Plump, with regular features and a lively expression, she seemed, at fifty, like "an older sister of her son." Unobserved, she contemplated him with amorous voracity, while he treated her with deference, protectiveness, and affection, but visibly could not put up with either her praise or her complaints for very long. When he went out in the evenings to see his friends, she would remain seated by the samovar with Pogodin's mother, and the two women would descant upon the virtues of their respective offspring until they were hoarse.

If Marya Ivanovna had ever had the slightest doubt about her son's genius, the atmosphere of adulation surrounding him at the Aksakovs' and Pogodins' must instantly have dispelled it. She must have attended at least one of his numerous readings to groups of friends, such as the one he gave in Pogodin's study on April 17, the day before Easter, when he read Chapter VI of *Dead Souls,* in which Plyushkin the miser makes his first appearance. It was a triumph. Everyone congratulated the author and predicted a great future for a book so brilliantly commenced. The most enthusiastic of all was a newcomer, the young Slavophile writer Vasily Panov, who seemed as though blinded by divine revelation. Upon learning that Gogol was soon to set out for Italy, he spontaneously offered to accompany him and share the cost of the trip.

Gogol had just placed a notice in the *Muscovite News* in the following terms: "Owning no team or vehicle, seek traveling companion who does, to share expenses as far as Vienna. Virgins' Field, at the home of Professor Pogodin; ask for Nikolai Vasilyevich Gogol."

Vasily Panov's proposal could not have been better timed. The young man, pale, slender, and sickly looking, with long straight hair hanging down his neck and a naïve expression behind his spectacles, seemed a likely candidate. Gogol accepted. The pact was sealed by a group excursion to watch the midnight Easter processions emerging simultaneously from the Kremlin churches. A huge crowd, dotted with the flames of a thousand little tapers, stood shuffling, dense and quiet, in the square. Each cortege, with sparkling banners and gilded chasubles, wound along its special route through the mass of the faithful, who crossed themselves as it passed. The choirs sang lustily. Suddenly the great bells of Ivan Veliky began to peal, giving the signal for all Christians to rejoice. An overpowering, harmonious din assailed the ears. The ground began to shake. In the distance, other bells replied, adding their treble and bass bronze tongues to the chorus. In the crowd people began to embrace, relatives and total strangers.

"Christ is risen."

"Truly, he is risen."

Gogol exchanged the triple Paschal kiss with his friends. There was jubilation in his heart; Christ really was risen, now that he was going to Italy.

After shedding many tears, Marya Ivanovna left St. Petersburg on April 27, taking Anna and Olga with her. Elizaveta was entrusted to Mrs. Raevsky. And Gogol plunged into preparations for his own departure. Concerned as always with the material side of his life in Itay, it came to his notice that a person named Krivtsov, a relative of the Repnins, had been appointed director of the academy of young Russian artists living in Rome. A light switched on in his brain. Once more he turned to Zhukovsky, his official mediator with all earthly powers:

"Directors always have secretaries; so why should I not be his [Krivtsov's]? It would be most useful for me, as I would probably get about a thousand a year. Oh, how that would drive away those black, tormenting thoughts! Why, when most people earn something in the service of the state, can I, poor devil, not do the same? You could explain my position to the heir apparent, bring him around, and write to Krivtsov yourself."[25]

He did not really think anything would come of this scheme, but it cost nothing to try. One appeal more or less, after all, could make no difference to Zhukovsky.

To thank the friends and acquaintances who had shown such good will toward him during his stay in Moscow, he decided to invite them all to a party on May 9, the day of St. Nicholas. Every year, he tried to celebrate his patron saint's feast day in congenial company. This time, he decided with Pogodin to give a big luncheon in the garden, despite the cool weather and risk of rain. Simon, the old family cook, being manifestly incapable of meeting such demands, they had recourse to the celebrated Porphyry, chef at the Moscow Merchants' Club, who had a wide knowledge of Ukrainian specialties. Early in the morning, long tables were set out along the avenue of lindens. Porphyry officiated in the kitchens—watched over by Gogol, who lifted lids, sniffed delightedly at the steam rising from pans, lovingly supervised the preparation of capons and quails, gravely tasted a sauce, nibbled a sample of flaky pastry, and gave advice. The guests arrived early, their faces expressing affection and a hearty appetite. Shchepkin and his son were there, and Prince Vyazemsky, Nashchokin, Kireyevsky, Shevyrev, Zagoskin, Professor Armfeld, Pavlov, Dmitryev, Sadovsky, Redkin, and many more. Aksakov had come, too, in spite of a raging toothache.

The figure of a young infantry officer, "small in stature, in campaign dress, with a red collar devoid of insignia,"[26] stood out sharply among all these dark-garbed civilians. He was the poet Mikhail Lermontov. Exiled from St. Petersburg for the second time, following a duel with Ernest de Brabante (son of the French ambassador), he was stopping in Moscow on his way to rejoin his regiment in the Caucasus. The cause of his first exile, in 1837, was the poem he had written after Pushkin's death, a veritable cry of hatred of the high society which had destroyed the great poet.[27] All Pushkin's friends had been grateful to him for his courage; and Gogol further admired him as a writer of both prose and poetry. He had just read *A Hero of Our Time* and regarded it as one of the foremost works of Russian literature. But this was no time for compliments: the guests were growing impatient. When they sat down to eat, the noise and animation increased with every dish brought out. Each guest in turn proposed a toast. They drank to the hero of the feast, to the master of the house, to Russian writers in general and present company in particular.

After the meal, groups formed in the garden. At the request of his friends, Lermontov read a passage from his poem *The Novice,* which delighted the audience. Then Gogol made punch under the arbor. He was very merry and busy, but his gaiety seemed slightly forced. In the evening, a few ladies came for tea inside the house. The gathering ended shortly before midnight. Exhausted but happy, Gogol felt that he had now paid his debt of gratitude to all who wished him well.

The day of departure was rapidly drawing near. Mrs. Aksakov was already preparing provisions for the travelers: cold meat pies, shortbread, sausages, cold smoked sturgeon. Gogol instructed his sister Elizaveta to buy him three pounds of sugar, which she was to break into pieces, two pounds of candles, and a pound of coffee.[28]

On May 18 he and Vasily Panov climbed into a tarantass heavily laden with trunks and bundles; Aksakov and his son, Shchepkin and his son, and Pogodin and his son-in-law piled into two other carriages to accompany the travelers as far as the first posting station outside Moscow. When they reached the top of the Poklonny rise, everyone dismounted. Moscow lay below, on both sides of the river, an extraordinary conglomeration of roofs, towers, and cupolas. Solemnly, Gogol and Panov bowed to the city they were leaving. Then they set off again. At the Perkhushkov station they stopped once more, this time for refreshments. Faces were sad. Pogodin could not look Gogol in the eye, as though unable to forgive him for preferring Italy to Russia. Aksakov sighed and blew his nose; Shchepkin had tears in his eyes; the three youngsters stared at the floor. Even Gogol was moved; he promised to come back in a year without fail, bringing the first volume of *Dead Souls* ready for the printer. The sun was sinking on the horizon. A light breeze stirred in the birches across the road. The coachman was fretting. They sat down one last time for a minute of silence and meditation, the Russian custom before all departures. Then they rose, crossed themselves, and embraced. Gogol and Panov climbed back into their tarantass; it dwindled away, creaking and jolting, down the road to Warsaw. When they could no longer see it, the others turned to their coaches.

On the way back to town, Aksakov looked up: the sky was half covered by big black clouds. "Everything grew dark," he wrote, "and we were filled with a sense of foreboding. Our conversation was bleak; somehow we associated Gogol's future with these funereal clouds blocking the sun. But, less than thirty minutes later, we were surprised by a sudden change. A strong northwest wind was tearing the dark clouds apart and driving them away; and in fifteen minutes the sky was swept clean and the sun shone out again in full glory, wheeling majestically down toward the horizon. A feeling of gaiety filled our hearts."[29]

5. Second Trip to Rome

As always, the journey had a tranquilizing effect upon Gogol. He was flattered by Panov's youthful adulation; he cracked jokes, eagerly unpacked Mrs. Aksakov's provisions at every posting station, and did not appear unduly anxious to reach their destination. Traveling by short stages across the endless Russian plain, the tarantass eventually reached Warsaw. There, Gogol wrote to ask Aksakov for some legal documentation he said was necessary for the next phase of his work on *Dead Souls*. Then, after a tour of the city, he and Panov set off again, for Vienna by way of Cracow.

In Vienna they took rooms in a hotel and plunged into the colorful and noisy street scene: cafés, theaters, and beer-hall bands; but the ponderous silence of Metternich's imperial administration lay just below the sparkling surface. Gogol, who so loved Italy, might conceivably have felt uncomfortable as the guest of the oppressors of the Italian people. But he decidedly had no head for politics. White-gloved despotism, police surveillance, and a muzzled press did not disturb him. Things here were the same as in Russia; and as long as peace and order could be seen to reign, he was satisfied. He went to the opera to hear the best Italian singers and drank bottled water from Marienbad to cure his stomach, overtaxed by the lavish Muscovite dinners he had eaten.

"I am all alone here," he wrote to Aksakov; "there is no one to disturb me. To me, the Germans are like the insects one invariably finds in every Russian isba. They scurry around me and crawl all over me, but they don't bother me; and if one of them should happen to climb up my nose, a flick of the finger and it's gone! Vienna has given me an imperial welcome! The opera has been closed only twice. For two whole weeks, the finest singers of Italy have moved and transported me, producing a salutary upheaval of all my senses. Great are the divine graces. I am about to live again!"[1]

To Pogodin: "The Marienbad water has done me a great deal of good: I have begun to feel the return of youthful vigor, my nerves are awake, I have emerged from the virtually comatose intellectual idleness of these past years. . . . Ideas have begun to whirl around in my head like a swarm of bothered bees. My imagination is honed fine. Oh, what a joy it has been for me, if you could only know! The subject I had been lazily storing in my mind for some time, not daring even to tackle it, began to expand before my eyes to such proportions that an exquisite shiver ran through me . . . and I set to work, forgetting that this is precisely what one should not do when taking the waters, for complete rest is prescribed then."[2]

The subject he refers to was a theme for a Ukrainian drama, *The Shaven Mustache,* which he never completed. About this time, however, he did finish the first draft of his short story "The Overcoat," revised "Taras Bulba" once again, and completed his adaptation of an Italian comedy by Giovanni Giraud (an imitator of Goldoni) called *The Embarrassed Uncle.* The play had previously been translated in Rome by some young Russian artists he knew; it was a satire showing the consequences of an excessively strict upbringing, and he thought it might suit Shchepkin.

He also had become interested in the problem of education, after seeing his sisters. Filled with his sense of responsibility, he wrote lengthy epistles designed to provide remote-control guidance. Each of his letters was a lesson in morality. He reprimanded Elizaveta for her tendency to complain of imaginary illnesses—as though he himself had never expatiated to his mother and friends upon every detail of his mental and abdominal anguish: "What have you done, Elizaveta? Mother is almost in tears. Why did you write her that you fell from the carriage, and how your chest has been aching ever since, and how bored you are? Aren't you ashamed of such foolishness? You should be trying to calm her instead of writing letters like that!"[3]

Anna, who had followed the custom of the Vasilyevka peasants by giving up needlework during the religious holidays, earned a still more scathing rebuke. How dare she revert to those idiotic country customs? She should listen to the voices of God and her brother instead of yielding to the superstitions of an obsolete culture. "Thus, I command you to work," he wrote her, "and to keep busy especially during the holidays; except, of course, for the hours dedicated to the worship of God. And if anyone tells you you do wrong, offer no explanations and make no attempt to prove the contrary; simply say this, briefly and firmly: 'It is my brother's will. I love my brother, and therefore his smallest desires are law for me.' After that, no one will want to nag at you any more."⁴

Early in August, persuaded that the Marienbad water really was stimulating him, he decided to prolong his treatment and let Panov go on alone, arranging to meet him in Venice in September. Afterward, in his little hotel room, he suddenly felt stifled, filled with apprehension. Outside, the sun was shining, the city throbbing with life. But the light and bustle did not reach him; he was cutting himself off from life, becoming a stranger to himself. His chest flamed with a strange pain. His nerves winced under his skin. His head was burning. Impossible to think. Every step made him dizzy. And if he stretched out on his bed, all he could see was poor young Vyelgorsky panting and spitting; he felt the chill of death creep into his veins. Alone. Eternally alone. In a foreign country. None of his friends—Aksakov, Pogodin, Pletnyev, Zhukovsky—none of them could conceive his agony. Help! He called a doctor. Some German with gold-rimmed spectacles. Learned words, but no credible diagnosis. Was he to understand that he was condemned? And his work, his great work, which he had not had time to finish? And his mother, his sisters? God could not call him before he had had time to set his house in order. Other doctors came for bedside consultations.

To Pogodin he wrote: "My state of nervous hypertension became enormously aggravated; the weight on my chest was pressing upon me harder than ever. Fortunately the doctors determined that I was not consumptive, that it was some stomach disorder; I was not digesting at all and my nerves were extraordinarily overwrought, which did not help matters, because it was dangerous to give me any treatment: what was good for the stomach was bad for the nerves, and the nerves reacted upon the stomach. To this was added an indescribably irrational anguish. I was in such a state that I did not know where to put myself or what to cling to. I could not remain in the same place for ten minutes, whether in bed, or in a chair, or standing up. Oh, it was dreadful; it was the same anguish I had seen in poor Vyelgorsky at the very end. I summoned all my strength and scribbled some sort of will, so that my debts, at least, would be paid after my death. But the thought of dying sur₁ rounded by Germans seemed appalling to me."[5]

He later gave Marya Balabin this description of his affliction: "I felt an emotion growing within me that transformed every image in my mind into an enormous monster, inflated any even mildly agreeable sensation into a joy so terrifying that human nature could not bear it, and every dark thought into a dragging, tormenting grief, and this was followed by fainting spells and, at last, by a completely somnambulistic state."[6]

Just as Gogol felt that the whole world had forsaken him, a miracle occurred: into his hotel room marched a Russian who was paying a brief visit to Vienna. His name was Nikolai Petrovich Botkin; he was a friend of Pogodin and the son of a wealthy tea merchant. Seeing the degree of physical and mental distress of the author of *The Inspector General,* he took pity upon him and transformed himself into an unpaid nurse. He put up with all his patient's moods and complaints, nursed him, reasoned with him, and persuaded him that he would survive. Gogol's strength and confidence gradually returned, but he felt that he was not the same as before. He had known the horrors of the tomb in his own flesh; he was returning from the other shore. The latter-day Lazarus, still weak on his feet and dazed by the light, looked down upon his fellow men as ignorant babies. His rebirth gave him a Messianic superiority over them. If the Lord had given him back to the world for a few brief days, he thought, it must be so that he could complete his work. He decided that he would not be fully cured until he had finished his journey. Botkin desperately pointed out what a mad idea this was, but Gogol was obstinate: to hear him talk, the very lurches of the carriage would settle his nerves and the changing scenery help his digestion. Botkin anxiously consented to accompany him to Venice.

"When we reached Trieste, I was already beginning to feel better," Gogol wrote. "Travel, my only real medicine, had done its work again. Despite the suffocating heat, the air cooled my mind. Oh, how I longed to go on some very long voyage. I felt, I knew that nothing else could permanently restore my health. But I did not have enough money for that."[7]

On September 2[8] he arrived in Venice and went straight to the piazza San Marco to find himself face to face with Panov, who had also just arrived. They were joined by the celebrated Russian painter

Aivazovsky, who wrote in his *Recollections:* "Short and lean, with a long nose pointed at the tip and blond curls often falling into his tiny, squinting eyes, Gogol compensated for his unalluring appearance by the liveliness and bursts of humor that typified his conversation in a group of friends. The arrival of a new face cast a shadow over his amiable countenance, as if a cloud were passing overhead."

Although he was still very weak, Gogol explored Venice thoroughly with his companion, by gondola, visited the museums and churches, gazed at the marble homes of the patricians, sat in the piazza San Marco by moonlight and steeped himself in the universe of water, stone, and reflections, so silent and weightless that it became unreal. After ten days of this, the four men (Gogol, Botkin, Panov, and Aivazovsky) set out for Florence, stopping in Bologna. In the spacious, well-sprung carriage, the passengers played cards, using a cushion for a table. From Florence they went on to Rome, via Livorno and Civitavecchia. Panov, who was surreptitiously watching Gogol throughout the journey, wrote to Aksakov: "He was completely preoccupied with his stomach and his convalescence; yet none of us could consume as much macaroni as he put away some days. . . . On the whole, I think Gogol is mistaken in his belief that a trip abroad is all he needs to recover the strength and energy he claims to have lost. . . . Unfortunately, his trouble is unaffected by climate or locality, and cannot easily be cured. Perhaps his whole system has been gradually deteriorating for the past ten years and is now beyond treatment."

In Rome, Gogol was lucky enough to rent the same apartment he had lived in before, at strada Felice 126. He found his beloved tall writing desk, the two high windows with the inside shutters, the bed near the wall, the round table dominating the middle of the room, the narrow caned bench, the rickety wardrobe, the Roman oil lamp with the pointed beak, and the floor covered with mosaic tiles that rang so brightly underfoot. He moved Panov into a room nearby. Now would he be happy? At first he thought he would, and he hurried into the streets to renew his acquaintance with old stones and faces. Nothing had changed; yet it was another world. A world in which anguish lurked beneath the beautiful forms and glorious hues. The blue sky, the dome of St. Peter's, the ruins of the Forum and the Coliseum, the Lago d'Albano, and even Raphael's paintings—now all of them spoke of the grave. The very permanence of his setting reminded him of the brevity of man's life on earth. He tired quickly, and began to shorten his walks. Almost nothing remained of the heir apparent's four thousand-ruble loan. He had sent out another distress signal from Vienna, to see whether there was any chance of getting the job of Krivtsov's secretary at the Russian academy in Rome. This time he turned to Pletnyev, rather than Zhukovsky, to plead his case:

"I wrote to Zhukovsky asking him to use his influence with the grand duke, because Krivtsov owes his position to him; and it is quite plain that if the grand duke were to ask the emperor, the whole business would be settled. But I have thought it would be as well for you to speak to the grand duchesses too. If Grand Duchess Marya Nikolayevna could put in a word for me, it would naturally be even more effective."[9]

Perhaps the pleas of Zhukovsky and Pletnyev were insufficiently persuasive; or perhaps the grand dukes and duchesses were fed up with the eternal demands of this Russian who could not live in Russia. In any case, no order came from above. And the latest word from Krivtsov was that he desired his secretary to be "a figure of European importance, noted for his knowledge of art."[10] Realizing that this job would never be his, Gogol resigned himself to borrowing again, a little at a time, from his acquaintances. In his poverty and anxiety, he surprised himself regretting that he had left Russia. How he did love that country—from afar!

"Oh, Russia, Russia!" he wrote in *Dead Souls*. "I see you from the magnificent remoteness where I dwell. You are poor, chaotic, and inhospitable. You have no great works of art to mingle with those of nature and cheer or startle the eye. In vain does one search you for these towns with their tall palaces poised on the edges of cliffs and pierced by a thousand windows, these houses carpeted with ivy, shaded by picturesque trees, and cooled by the mist from roaring waterfalls; you do not call one to crane the neck and stare up at blocks of stone piled to dizzying heights; you have no long vistas of dark arcades where vine shoots, ivy, and dog rose tangle, through the far ends of which one can glimpse, shimmering in the remote distances, the unchanging lines of mountains drawn against a transparent, silvery sky. In you everything is open, flat, and always the same. Your towns are low and stand out like dots, like scarcely perceptible signs on your infinite plains. Nothing delights the eye; nothing holds it. But what is this mysterious and incomprehensible force that draws me to you? Why does that plaintive song, which vibrates from sea to sea throughout your vast expanse, ring endlessly in my ears? What is the meaning of this call, which sobs and catches at my soul? What are the sounds that creep like a painful caress inside my heart and haunt it continually? What do you want of me, Russia? What secret bond unites us? Why do you look at me that way? Why does everything in you turn upon me those waiting eyes?"[11]

Now when Gogol thought of Russia, his nostalgia was further aggravated by remorse. He accused himself of having been oafish, selfish, and aloof with his friends in St. Petersburg and Moscow; he wondered how he could ever live apart from them.

"Neither Rome nor the sky nor any of the things that formerly delighted me have any effect upon me now," he wrote Pogodin. "I no longer see them, I no longer feel them. I dream of a road, a muddy road in the rain, going through woods and over steppes, a road that would lead me to the ends of the earth. I left [Moscow] refreshed, full of energy and determination to work, to produce. And now—God! Friends have sacrificed so much for me. When will I ever repay them? I, who believed that this year I would finish the book that would solve all my problems and rid me of the load on my dishonest conscience! Here I am, hopeless and without the resources to restore my health. Often, in my present condition, I ask myself, 'Why did I go to Russia?' But when I remember my sisters I say, 'No, the trip was not in vain.' I swear I have done a lot for them. Madman that I was, when I went to Russia I thought, 'It is good for me to go back there but I begin to feel it fading, that little store of wrath, so necessary to the author, against the weeds invading the soil of the fatherland. In this way I shall refresh my memory and everything will become more vivid to my eyes.' But what have I brought back from my trip? All the bad things have slipped from my memory, even those I saw before, and all I have left is an idea of beauty and purity that comes from my meetings with my friends."[12]

The same day, to Mrs. Pogodin: "You cannot imagine to what extent I torment myself thinking how hard and stiff and tedious I was in Moscow, how little I expressed my true feelings and involuntarily appeared so withdrawn, hypocritical, insensitive, and cold. If you knew how fiercely I regretted, when I left Moscow, having behaved so badly! I care little for the opinion of ordinary people, but that of my friends! And they still love me, even though I was plainly insufferable!"[13]

At the same time as he was moaning over his poor health and poorer disposition, Gogol was also beginning to work—with Panov, as his secretary, diffidently recopying the pages as they fell from the master's hand. *Dead Souls* was making headway; new characters took form from one chapter to the next. To maintain himself in a sufficiently elevated state of mind, the author read Francis of Assisi, Dante, and Homer. Before completing the first volume of the novel—which he wanted to call a "poem," like the *Divine Comedy*—he began planning the second. The mere thought of it made him feel solemn and lofty. God was somehow present in the very ink in which he dipped his pen.

"Fear no more," he told Pogodin. "Divine mercy is a wondrous thing: my health is restored. Full of energy, I am making corrections and amendments to the text of *Dead Souls,* and have even started thinking about the sequel. I see the subject becoming more and more profound. I plan to publish the first volume next year, if the divine force that has revived me will allow it. Much has gone on inside me within a very short time, but I cannot talk about it yet, although I don't know why. Oh, you must understand that someone who is born to create in the depths of his soul, to live and breathe through his works, must often seem strange to those around him. But enough of that. I am at peace, so much at peace that I forget I haven't got a kopeck to my name. I don't know how I'm surviving, but I am—on credit. I don't care about anything."[14]

The same day, he sent a still more exalted letter to Aksakov: "I am now engaged in completely revising the first volume of *Dead Souls.* I am altering, abridging, and rewriting many passages and see that the book cannot be printed in my absence. The sequel, meanwhile, is growing much clearer and more majestic in my mind, and I see that something colossal can be made of it if my puny health does not fail me. It is certain, at any rate, that very few people know what powerful ideas and profound images can grow out of an insignificant theme, the modest opening chapters of which you already know."[15]

And for the sake of these "powerful ideas" and "profound images," he again summoned his friends to the rescue. God gave him inspiration; let man give him the means of putting it to work. He was preparing such a gift for them that they were all, already, indebted to him.

"I must speak to you about an important matter," he wrote to Aksakov a few months later. "But Pogodin will tell you what it's about. You can decide together what will be the best way to work it out. I am directly and openly asking for help. I have the right; I feel it in my inmost being. Yes, my friend, I am deeply happy. Despite my poor health, which has grown slightly worse again, I am experiencing divine moments. A marvelous work is growing and building in my soul, and my eyes are often moist with tears of gratitude. Here the sacred will of God is plain to see. Such inspiration does not come from man; no human would ever have imagined such a subject! Oh, if I could have another three years of it! All I demand is enough life to finish my work, not one hour more."[16]

This money, which his friends could not refuse him, he would repay as soon as the first volume of *Dead Souls* was published; in other words, in a year at most. He had even made up his mind to go back to Russia to see the book through the censor's office and supervise the printing of it. But his feeble constitution worried him.

"I am rather afraid," he went on, "to make the journey alone. It is painful, almost impossible for me to endure the anxiety and all the little annoyances of traveling. I must remain calm and keep a happy and cheerful frame of mind. Now I have to be protected from harassment, and pampered."

And he suggested, as a matter of course, that the actor Shchepkin and Aksakov's son Konstantin should come to fetch him in Rome:

"They will have to take care of me—not for me personally, oh, no, certainly not! But they will be doing something worthwhile; what they will bring back is only a vase of clay, full of cracks, it is true, and very old and scarcely hanging together, but in that vase there is a treasure. Therefore it must be taken care of."[17]

In Moscow, meanwhile, Aksakov and Pogodin were discussing the problem. Gogol's constant demands for money put them in a difficult position. Pogodin, who founded a new periodical, *The Muscovite,* in 1841, thought that in return for sums furnished, "the Italian" might send him a few unpublished pages. Aksakov timidly put forward this view in a letter; upon reading this, Gogol flew into a rage. Create to order? Whom did they take him for? His friends in Moscow clearly failed to understand the sacred nature of his mission. He replied to Aksakov:

"You write that I should send something to Pogodin for his review. God, if you only knew how that demand pains and disheartens me, how it fills me all of a sudden with gloom, how it torments me! To tear myself away, now, even for one moment, from my sacred duty, would spell disaster for me. Anyone realizing how much it would cost me would not make such a proposal a second time. I swear it is a sin, a great sin, to take me away from my work. Only a person who does not believe what I say and is incapable of entertaining sublime thoughts could act in such a way. My work is great, it can bring salvation. Henceforth I am dead to all lesser things. Embrace Pogodin and tell him I weep; I can be of no use to him with his review, and if he has any truly Russian love for his country, he must order me to send him nothing at all."[18]

In March and April 1841, Pogodin published a few scenes from a new version of *The Inspector General* and part of a letter to Pushkin in *The Muscovite*, without Gogol's authorization. In his diary he wrote: "Letter from Gogol asking for money. I would like not to send him any." But he did. Too little to suit his correspondent, who was expecting twice the amount.

"Thank you very much for the money," he wrote. "I received it. But as you well know, that is only half. I have paid my debts, but am stuck here. If you have not sent the remaining two thousand rubles by the time you get this letter, then woe, woe unto me, for I shall be forced to stay in Rome through the hottest part of the summer."[19]

Something else was worrying him: Aksakov had just lost his son Mikhail, and his other son, Konstantin, mourning his brother's death, did not want to leave his parents, not even to act as traveling companion to the author he most admired. Shchepkin, too, had said he could not go to Italy; and Panov was preparing to leave Rome for Berlin. Gogol felt that everyone was deserting him again. He could not believe it was impossible to find one Russian, somewhere, sufficiently devoted to set out with him on the day of his choice.

"I am forsaken and assailed by fears," he wrote in the same letter to Pogodin, "when I think I shall have to come back alone. The journey by stagecoach and all the problems of traveling, which even before were not so easy to bear, are especially harrowing to me now. I feel deeply for the Aksakovs, not only because they have lost a son but because an infinite and exquisite attachment to anything in this life is in itself a source of woe."

The Easter holidays, which he was preparing to spend in deep misery, brought him one great consolation, however. One day he looked up to see in the doorway a chubby little man with a mustache and goatee: his friend Annenkov, alias "Jules Janin." He was passing through Rome on his way to Paris. Gogol instantly explained to him that Paris was a sewer in comparison with the Eternal City and urged him to stay at least a few weeks, for the sake of art and friendship; and as Panov had gone to Germany, his room just happened to be free. Annenkov duly moved into it and offered to transcribe *Dead Souls* from Gogol's dictation. It was decided that they would work together for an hour every day. The rest of the time, in theory, each would go his own way. As it turned out, though, they often met elsewhere, and even when both were in the house the communicating door between their rooms remained open.

Gogol would rise early and write, standing at his desk. Now and then he would put down his pen and drink a glass of cold water. Sometimes he would finish off two or three jugs during the morning: since his illness in Vienna he had decided that water alone could relieve him. His system, he told Annenkov, was entirely unlike those of other people; in particular, he had a "deformed stomach." "You can't understand it. But that is how it is. I know myself." This did not prevent him, after filling a few sheets of paper, from going to the café del Buon Gusto and eating quite a copious little breakfast there. He was particularly fussy about the quality of the cream in his coffee. After eating and drinking, he would stretch out on the bench for a short rest. At the appointed hour, the two friends would meet in the house for their joint labors. Gogol would close the shutters, to protect them from the blazing heat of the street, seat himself at the round table, open his notebook, and begin to dictate. "He dictated," Annenkov wrote, "calmly and solemnly, with such feeling, such intensity, that the opening chapters of *Dead Souls* have remained more powerfully impressed upon my memory than all the rest. He would patiently wait for me to catch up with him, and then begin a new sentence in the same intent voice. Often the braying of some little Italian donkey would float into the room; then we would hear the sound of a stick hitting its sides and an angry woman's voice, 'Ecco, ladrone!' [Take that, you big brute!] Gogol would pause and say with a smile, 'Oh, he's grown lazy, the little dickens!' and resume his dictation with the same intensity and conviction as before."[20]

In the funniest places, Annenkov would burst out laughing and fall back in his chair. "Do try not to laugh, Jules," Gogol would sternly reprimand. Sometimes, though, even he could not restrain his hilarity.

But at other moments he would assume a positively transfigured air, staring out into space, his fluttering hands sketching some misty landscape as he spoke. It was in this semihallucinated state that he described the garden of the miser Plyushkin. When he had finished, Annenkov exclaimed: "I think that chapter is a work of genius!"

Gogol closed his notebook, rolled it into a tube, and softly replied, "Rest assured that the others are not inferior." Then, delighted at having so impressed his copyist, he took him on a walk through the city. He was in such a good mood that day that he burst into a Ukrainian folk tune in an alley behind the Palazzo Barberini, followed it with a few dance steps, and, with a flourish of his arm, broke the umbrella he had brought along in case of rain.

Usually, however, his mind took a didactic turn on their walks. He would lead Annenkov to the museums, the churches, and the Coliseum, or seat himself on a stone in the middle of the Forum, and comment in a low voice on the monuments around them or lapse into silent contemplation, sometimes lasting several hours. They took their meals in inns or at Lepre's or Falcone's, where they met the Russian painters Ivanov, Moller, and Yordan. Gogol criticized the preparation of every dish, but consumed it with startling voracity. "He bent so low over his plate," Annenkov wrote, "that his blond hair would fall into it. And he swallowed spoonful after spoonful [of rice] with the speed and intentness said to be typical of persons suffering from hypochondria." The finest coffee was then drunk, at the Buon Gusto on the piazza di Spagna. Toward seven in the evening a cool breath would come down over the city, and then it was good to go wandering through the streets. Sometimes they met a procession led by some stout abbot. The crowd would gather around an altar set up in the street. The sinking sun gilded the worshipers' faces and touched the holy banners with blood.

When night came, a myriad lights glowed in the cafés; multicolored lanterns lit up the stalls of fresh-fruit and drink vendors; young men in shirt sleeves paraded down the streets in groups, singing and laughing; a guitar thrummed beneath a balcony; women squabbled in a courtyard; every window was wide open; and Gogol was elated. When the scorching breath of the sirocco licked the city, however, he felt ill. "His skin dried out," Annenkov wrote; "his cheeks became flushed. In the evenings he would seek the cool air at street corners. Leaning on his stick, head thrown back and face uplifted to the sky, he seemed to be trying to catch the slightest stirring of cool air in the atmosphere."[21]

Sometimes, instead of going for a walk or hanging about the cafés, they would meet the painters in the apartment for a game of "boston." As no one actually knew the rules, Gogol ran the game to suit his own ideas, changing conventions to fit the circumstances and noting down tricks on a scrap of paper only to contest them later. The Roman lamp, which he lit with his own hands, was so dim the players could scarcely make out the cards in their hands. Those who complained they couldn't see were reminded that, in antiquity, that same lamp had illuminated the work and play of consuls, senators, and courtesans. To encourage them, he would seize a flask, skim off the plug of oil floating on the surface in place of a cork—another good old custom—and pour the light wine down their throats. Gradually the conversation grew animated. As long as the talk was of art and literature, everybody agreed. But as soon as it turned to politics, Gogol found himself arguing with Annenkov. As a fanatical defender of tradition, he could not tolerate his friend's view of France as the country of the future, destined to spread throughout Europe the ideas of liberty, equality, and justice, which had germinated in its soil in the time of the Encyclopedists. He looked upon that nation in horror: it was the embodiment of a principle that would destroy "the poetry of the past," and he feared it like a creeping disease. Whenever he even spoke of France his voice, according to Annenkov, became "dry, despotic, staccato." True, he had no greater love for Germany, which, in his eyes, was "a stinking whiff of bad tobacco and loathsome beer."[22] And what he chiefly admired about Italy was his own false picture of it as the nation of the carefree and content. When Annenkov pointed out one day that there were quite a few people in Rome who ardently longed for a change of government, he merely heaved a mournful sigh and said, "Yes, yes, my dear fellow, such people do exist!"

These conversations upset him so that he had difficulty going to sleep after his guests had left. Instead of getting into bed, he would lie on the narrow caned bench and spend part of the night there by the light of his oil lamp. Or he would sit by Annenkov's bed and drag out the conversation until his weary friend snuffed the candle; then he would return to his room, lie down, and wrestle with his fear of being suddenly taken ill in the dark. He was haunted by the memory of Vyelgorsky's death. A young Russian architect whom he knew had fallen seriously ill in Rome, but he would not go to see him, because he was afraid of the effect it might have upon him. Then, when he heard the young man had died, he seemed very worried by the thought that he would have to attend his funeral. The night before it was to take place, he announced to Annenkov that he himself was at death's door. "Save me, for God's sake!" he whimpered with a wild, lost look. "I know what is happening inside me. I'm dying. I nearly passed away last night, after a nervous attack. Take me somewhere, quickly. I hope it's not too late!"[23]

Annenkov rushed out in a panic to hire a coach and have himself and Gogol driven to Albano. "Both on the road and in the little town where we stayed, Gogol appeared perfectly calm and did not once allude to his desperate words, as though he had never uttered them," he wrote.

A short time later, Annenkov caught a cold after bathing in the Tiber and took to his bed with a bad case of angina. His fever would not respond to any drug. Gogol became frantic, torn between compassion for his friend and terror of catching his germs. When one carried a work as crucial as *Dead Souls* in one's head, one did not have the right to expose oneself to illness. So he rushed away to the country, leaving Annenkov in the care of a woman servant and the landlord. To the latter he wrote a letter in Italian, asking him to look after *nostro povero ammalato* [our poor patient].

"I think the sight of suffering was as unbearable to him as that of death," Annenkov wrote. "When it did not plunge him into lyrical melancholy, as was the case in 1839 with Count Joseph Vyelgorsky, the spectacle of human distress drove him away. On the whole, although he was capable of profound compassion, he had none of that gift and ability which enable some people to soothe the pain of those who are close to them. He could translate the griefs and worries of others into the reasonable language of the wise counselor, he could help a friend with advice, support, or connections, but he never really experienced the bitterness of the other's torments and never engaged in active communion with him. He could give an unhappy man his thoughts, his prayers, the warm hopes of his heart; but never himself."[24]

Annenkov soon recovered, and a relieved Gogol returned to his domicile. No word was ever spoken between them of this incident. One man's respect and the natural dissimulation of the other prevented them from saying what they really thought.

Gogol frequently went to see Ivanov in his studio, as he had done during his first stay in Italy. *Christ Appearing to the People,* begun four years before, was slowly progressing. Every face, blade of grass, and pebble was a problem. The painter had asked the writer to pose for one of the figures in the painting. Now, in a group in the background stood a thin man with sharp features and long hair, his body enveloped in a full brown robe. It was Gogol, his head tilted to one side as though he sensed the arrival of Christ behind him.[25]

Ivanov said that this figure was "nearest of all to the Saviour." He had purposely given this privileged place to his friend, who had gratefully consented to be symbolically present at the moment of Revelation. After all, he sometimes felt himself literally illuminated by God while he was working; so, in the painting, he would simply be playing the same part he played in real life. Besides, *Christ Appearing to the People* was the complement to *Dead Souls*. Like the book, the painting was intended to have a moral effect upon the populace and alter the destiny of Russia. By devoting themselves exclusively to their work, both painter and writer were fulfilling the will of God. It was no less than blasphemy to prevent them from working. "Remember that you cannot serve both God and Mammon,"[26] Gogol liked to say.

Ivanov made several other drawings and two oil portraits of Gogol. Moller, another artist, also painted him around the same time. The model always asked to be painted wearing a smile, "for a Christian must not look sad." Out of the canvas emerges a face with long silky hair falling diagonally across the forehead. The nose is pointed, the lips smiling beneath a thin blond mustache, while the small, oblique eyes gaze mournfully into space. When he looked at this painting, executed with great delicacy, Gogol might almost have fancied himself handsome.

His affection for the painters was sincere; he recommended them to influential friends and tried to get commissions for them. Learning that one of them, Shapovalov (a friend of Ivanov, Moller, and Yordan), had lost his grant without warning following a decision by the society for the promotion of the arts, he decided to hold a public reading of *The Inspector General* as a benefit performance. Princess Volkonsky loaned her villa, the price of admission was set at five scudi,[27] and when the day came, all the Russian high society in Rome gathered in the princess' drawing room.

As he sat down at a large table in front of this select public, Gogol felt as though a row of pikes were being aimed at him, and he had to struggle to keep from running out the door. There couldn't be one person in ten there who had any interest in him. He read badly, apathetically, in a monotone. His friends were dismayed. At the end of the first act there was a thin ripple of applause, the audience rose, servants in livery passed drinks and cakes. When the reading resumed, half the seats were unoccupied. At each intermission the room emptied a little more. Important gentlemen were saying offhandedly, "He's already treated us to this inanity in St. Petersburg, and now he's serving it up again here in Rome!"[28] At the end, only a few artist friends of the author stood at their posts. They clustered around to congratulate and thank him on behalf of Shapovalov. "Gogol, looking utterly frantic, remained silent,"

Yordan wrote. "He was cruelly offended and afflicted. His self-respect, so terribly sensitive, suffered exaggeratedly."

On second thought, however, this affront confirmed his opinion that he was ahead of his time. By refusing to understand him, these socialites gave him proof of his exceptional destiny. *The Inspector General,* he thought, was not a flawless play. But even so, it was "a Gogol." That is, a manifestation of a prophetic power.

He was increasingly coming to believe that he had been born to edify his fellow man. He had begun by upbraiding his mother and sisters; now he enlarged his fold to include his friends. Danilevsky had confessed that he was bored, living on his estate in the country, and was thinking of looking for work in a big city; Gogol rose up in fraternal indignation. Little did he care that Danilevsky, whom he knew better than anyone else, was an easygoing, jolly fellow who loved company, adored plays and entertainments, and was totally incapable of putting up with the monotony of rural life. He never tried to identify with his friend, or even to analyze his reasons. Unable to see beyond himself, he judged others abstractly, theoretically. His lessons were not addressed to flesh-and-blood individuals, but to entities suffering from some malady or other which needed to be forcefully denounced. And the more he cared for his correspondents, the more he believed himself empowered by God to give them the benefit of his experience. His urge to do good did not quail at the possibility of hurting the person he was proposing to heal. Truly he felt, on that hot summer day when he sent his letter to Danilevsky, that he was accomplishing a pastoral duty:

"Is it possible you have not yet seen how far superior your activity at Semeryerk [Danilevsky's property] is to any possible gaudy, official life, with all the conveniences and facilities and so forth. Listen to me! Now you must heed what I say, for my words have a double power over you and woe betide him, whoever he be, who does not listen to my words. Abandon everything for a while, absolutely everything that troubles your mind in your leisure moments, however alluring the agitation may appear. Submit; and take good care of your estate, if only for one year. One year, and you will never forget it again! I swear it will be the dawn of happiness for you. Therefore carry out my behest, without resentment and reservations. You will not be doing this only for yourself; to me, too, you will be doing a great favor. Don't seek to know what it is. It is not for you to know, but when the time is ripe you will thank Providence for giving you the opportunity of doing me that favor. Oh, believe in my word. Hereafter, it is endowed with a higher power. Everything can deceive you, lead you astray and betray you, everything except my word. I do not tell you anything of the events in Rome about which you ask. I see nothing of what is before my eyes, and I no longer look with the quivering attentiveness of the novice. Like the traveler who has closed his trunks and waits, weary but calm, for the carriage that is to take him on a long, sure, and desired voyage, so I, having undergone my time of trial and prepared myself by an inner life, withdrawn from the world, am now ready to set off, quietly and without haste, my soul fortified, on the road shown to me from above."[29]

A month and a half later it was the poet Yasykov who was honored with a sermon: "Oh, trust in my word! I can tell you no more than that: trust in my word. I myself am compelled to trust in it. There is something miraculous and incomprehensible about it. The tears that fill my grateful and inspired soul prevent me from explaining. My lips are sealed. No human thought is capable of imagining even the hundredth part of God's immense love for man. Everything is in that. Henceforth let your clear gaze be ever courageously uplifted to the sky. And if tedium gains you and, remembering me, you do not have the strength to master it, then you do not love me. And if illness suddenly lays hold of you and your spirit weakens, then you do not love me. But I pray, I pray with all my strength that that does not happen to you. And that this light by which I am wholly enveloped in this instant will shine as much as possible in your soul."[30]

To Ivanov: "Walk bravely, never lose heart, for otherwise it would mean you do not remember me and do not love me, for he who remembers me bears power and fortitude in his soul."[31]

Having relieved himself of his mystical ardor, Gogol returned to *Dead Souls* with a remarkable zest for humor; it was as though his predilections for sermonizing and for caricature ran parallel in him, without interference. The moment he turned away from actual beings to deal with imaginary characters, the comical got the upper hand. But it sometimes pained him to be condemned, by the subject he had chosen, to perform this harsh and continual mockery of his fellows. He envied Ivanov, who could paint beautiful figures of men anticipating the coming of Christ. When would he, too, be able to dip his brush in brighter pigments? For the time being, he must work in sneers and snarls and muck.

With complicated feelings of disgust, exaltation, and duty, he finished the first volume of *Dead Souls* and began to revise the whole work. Annenkov, after remaining in Rome longer than he had intended, had now finished his job as copyist and gone on to Paris. The whole manuscript was there, eleven long chapters. Gogol leafed through them in anguish. The time had come to surrender to the world the fruit of six years of work. Would his contemporaries be able to appreciate the gift? In mid-August he set out for Russia, traveling by short stages.

He went through Florence, Genoa, Düsseldorf, and, hearing that Zhukovsky was resting in Frankfurt, went on there to see him. The poet, at fifty-eight, had just married a young thing of twenty, the daughter of the painter Von Reutern, and seemed overflowing with his new joys and cares. He had grown stout, his hair was thinning, but the old benevolence still streamed from his asymmetrical black eyes. He undoubtedly told Gogol how dreadfully upset people in Russia had been over the recent death of Lermontov, killed like Pushkin, in a duel over some idiotic question of honor.[32] This was the second great Russian poet struck down by violent death in four years. And Lermontov had established himself as Pushkin's defender and successor! Fate seemed bent upon destroying anything that bore the spark of genius in Russian literature. Gogol, feeling himself continually menaced in flesh and spirit, certainly thought so; but it was not just one man challenging him to single battle: it was the whole of humanity. And he had God to satisfy as well.

Although Zhukovsky seemed somewhat preoccupied, Gogol insisted upon reading him his Ukrainian play, *The Shaven Mustache*. Dinner was over, and it was the usual hour for a siesta. Curled cozily in his armchair before the lighted fire, Zhukovsky could not help finding the play dull and verbose. He finally dozed off. When he awoke, Gogol said, "I asked you to criticize my work. Your sleep is the most eloquent criticism possible."

"Forgive me," said Zhukovsky; "all of a sudden I just had to have a little nap!"

"If you just had to have a little nap, then the play is fit to be burned!" And with one sweeping gesture Gogol flung the notebook into the fireplace. The flames were momentarily smothered by the weight of the paper, then leaped up, high, gay and dancing.

"Well done, brother!" Zhukovsky murmured.[33]

This time, the amicable bond that had always drawn the two men together was missing. It is quite likely that Zhukovsky was exasperated by Gogol's maneuvers—always after money, official support, or recommendations for himself or one of his starving painter friends in Rome. Now he was campaigning to get Ivanov's grant prolonged for another three years. He had even drafted a letter to the heir apparent about it. When, however, a position as librarian to Krivtsov was offered him, he haughtily declined on the ground that he must devote himself to his work. He was willing to be secretary to the director of the Russian academy in Rome, but not librarian. Anyway, the offer came too late.

How was it possible to have so much talent and be so insufferable? The newly wed Zhukovsky was in a hurry for his cumbersome guest to leave; Gogol sensed this and packed his bags.

"At that moment you had many worries, distractions, and an absorbing private life, and were not at all interested in me," he later wrote to the poet. "And I, weighed down by my own feelings, did not have strength to fly to you with a light spirit. I remember that I wanted to communicate to you some little part of the exquisite thoughts that filled me, but I could not find words to do so in our conversations and emitted nothing but senseless sounds, like the delirium of a madman, so that now, no doubt, you are still wondering who on earth I can be and what strange thing has taken place in me."[34]

From Frankfurt he went to Hanau, where he knew he would find Yasykov, the poet he had met two years before whose musical, rich verse, sometimes akin to that of Pushkin, he had admired. At thirty-eight, after a life of dissipation, the consumptive Yasykov was dragging himself from one watering spot to another. He was so acutely bored that he welcomed Gogol rapturously. They had the same tastes in literature, the same religious aspirations, and the same views of Russia's sacred mission to the misled peoples of Europe. The time flew by so quickly while they talked that the two men, delighted with each other, decided to live together later in Moscow. In the evening, before going to bed, they played at inventing characters and finding names for them to fit their faults. Gogol was unbeatable at this game. They also, of course, discussed their ailments. That of Gogol, to hear him talk, was even more disturbing than Yasykov's consumption.

"He told me the strange symptoms of his illness, no doubt imaginary," Yasykov wrote. "He also described to me the unique structure of his head and the abnormal position of his stomach. According to him, some famous doctors had examined him in Paris and found that his stomach was upside down. By and large, there is a great deal that is odd and weird in Gogol. Sometimes I don't understand him. But he is very nice, all the same."[35]

After three weeks with Yasykov, Gogol set out again, with the poet's elder brother, Pyotr, who was also returning to Russia.

"What a strange, captivating, enthralling charm lies in that simple word: the road!" he writes in *Dead Souls*. "And how beautiful is the thing itself, the road! A pale clear day, autumn leaves, the air pure and cold. You wrap yourself up tightly in your traveling coat, pull your hat down over your ears, and snuggle farther and more comfortably back into your corner of the coach. A last shiver runs through your limbs and is immediately replaced by a pleasant warmth. The horses canter on. A gentle drowsiness invades you, your lids close, you hear as in a dream the coachman's song, 'This is no white snow falling,' and the snorting of the horses and noise of the wheels, and you're already snoring, leaning against your neighbor. When you wake, five stations have gone by. Moonlight. A strange town. Churches surmounted by old wooden cupolas and blackened spires. Log houses, utterly black; stone houses, totally white. It is as though the moonlight had spread out white linen handkerchiefs on the walls, pavement, streets. Coal-black shadows cut slanting across them. Plank roofs, lit obliquely, shine like polished metal. And not a soul abroad. Everything sleeps. Except, perhaps, for a single light blinking in a window: some little shopkeeper mending his boots, or a baker busy about his oven—who cares? Dear God, how beautiful you can be sometimes, road, road without end! How many times, when about to perish, to drown forever, I have turned to you, and always you have saved me! And how many splendid schemes, poetic dreams, marvelous impressions you have given to my mind!"[36]

Gogol and his companion stopped in Dresden for a rest, and again in Berlin. Then they took to their coach once more, over the rough autumn roads, heading toward the Russian frontier.

6. The Fight over *Dead Souls*

In the first days of October, 1841, Gogol reached St. Petersburg. As usual, he stayed with Pletnyev, who immediately brought him up to date on the latest gossip of the capital. A novel by Kukolnik, *Sergeant Ivanov,* had displeased the emperor because it contrasted a vice-ridden high society with a virtuous lower class. Benkendorf, the chief of police, had severely reprimanded the author, while the censors had been instructed to keep a doubly close watch on manuscripts. In general, the tension seemed greater than the previous year. In his anxiety for the manuscript he was carrying in his case, he turned to his friend Alexandra Smirnov for advice. He found her evasive on all matters of importance and loquacious on the subject of society gossip. He learned from her that the "romance" between Nicholas I and a lady in waiting named Nelidov was at its apogee, that all the empress' friends were in a great tizzy over it, that the empress herself was wasting away, that old Count Vyelgorsky was playing for high stakes at whist with Count Nesselrode and Prince Lobanov, that she herself was about to go abroad again. Listening to her, Gogol had less and less desire to prolong his stay in the capital. Besides, wind and rain were conspiring to drive him out. Five days, during which he met Prokopovich to discuss a possible edition of his "Complete Works" and learned that Belinsky still thought highly of him, and he hurried on to Moscow.

A man named Peiker sat next to him in the stagecoach and, having looked at the passenger list and discovered the identity of his neighbor, tried to engage him in conversation. Gogol, however, pretended his name was Gogel and said there was no connection between himself and the author and that he had just lost his parents and desired to commune with his grief in silence. Whereupon, burying himself in his coat collar, he turned away from the undesirable person. A few days later, he met the man again at the home of some mutual friends; Peiker understood the trick and took offense.[1]

Back in Moscow, with the colorful streets, the disorder and conviviality, the mild, shifting autumnal skies and pealing bells, Gogol began to think the trip had been worthwhile after all. His room was waiting for him at the Pogodins'; a pale sun slanted through the windows, and the Virgins' Field stretched out as far as the eye could see. Not a single carriage could be heard. Nothing had changed in the house, and yet there seemed to be a kind of strain that had not existed before, as though, for the first time, his host was not pleased with his guest. Pogodin probably was still unable to forgive Gogol for refusing to write for his *Muscovite*. Nonsense: in the end, he would simply have to understand and accept!

On October 18, Gogol went to see the Aksakovs, who gave him an ecstatic welcome. He felt more at home in their huge, simple, wooden house bursting with people than he did in the Pogodins' austere residence, where every stick of furniture was a museum piece. At the Aksakovs' nothing was expected of him, he was petted and pampered without ulterior motives and loved for his faults, whereas with the Pogodins he always felt somehow indebted. It was true that he had not repaid the first kopeck of the six thousand rubles Pogodin had lent him over the years, but it was only a matter of time. Aksakov noted his delight at Gogol's return, but also, sadly, how changed he was.

"He had dried out and grown pale," he wrote, "and every word expressed his resigned submission to the will of God. His old love of gastronomy and sense of mischief had both disappeared."

For the time being, Gogol's thoughts were fully occupied by the publication of *Dead Souls*. He read out the last five chapters at the Pogodins', in the presence of Aksakov and his son Konstantin. At the end the two Aksakovs, speechless with admiration, preserved a religious silence. Pogodin, on the other hand, remarked that the "poem" did not progress, that the author "had built a long corridor along which he dragged the reader and his hero Chichikov, opening doors left and right and showing a monster seated in every room." The indignant Aksakov moved to defend Gogol's structure, but the author interrupted him. "You neither can nor will offer any criticism of your own," he told him, "and you try to prevent other people from making any!" And he continued to listen very closely to his detractor's reproaches.

He made no major alterations as a result, but became fanatically particular with details in his final, hairsplitting revision. The manuscript, transcribed first by Panov and then by Annenkov, was black with scratchings out and writings in. A new copy had to be made, so a scribe was hired and instructed to work overtime and double time.

While this was going on, his host returned to his demand for something new by Gogol for his review. Pogodin was a tall thin man with a harsh, thick-lipped face and bushy eyebrows, and his outbursts frightened Gogol. He had an authoritarian and narrow mind, and for him there was no such thing as doing someone a favor without being repaid. There were no gifts between friends: there were exchanges. Weary of the whole argument, Gogol gave Pogodin his long, unfinished story "Rome," and the editor calmed down long enough to digest this piece; but Gogol was worried that he might come back for more. He was greatly changed since taking over the review. Uvarov, the minister of education, now held him in high esteem and it had gone to his head. He had become devoted to the government and posed as a champion of Orthodoxy and the imperial order. Even the Slavophiles found his attitude retrograde, and their position was not far removed from his principles. They, too, looked to the past, but only as a better preparation for the future: they saw the country's salvation not in immobility, but in a specifically Russian form of progress inspired by the traditions of the people. They shuddered with horror at all European ideas, which were known to produce nothing but disorder, and so could not abide the "European" school, of which Belinsky was a member.*

Wherever he went, to the Pogodins', Aksakovs', Shevyrevs', all Gogol heard was fulmination against a critic who had latterly come to St. Petersburg to write for the liberal review *Annals of the Fatherland:* in their opinion this man Belinsky was "an eternal student who has quit studying," a revolutionary, a "madman," a "hothead sword waver" for

---

* The latter group thought that Russia must study the civilization of Europe before she could fulfill her own historic mission. The object was not to make a servile copy, but to take the best Europe had to offer, in administration, social reform, and separation of state and church. The Slavophiles, on the contrary, held that the cause of the country's woes lay in its neglect of spiritual resources. The Orthodox Church, they said, and the people's voluntary submission to the tsar and the *mir,* would guarantee Russia's uniqueness and her superiority to the rest of the continent.

whom nothing was sacred. Not daring to disagree with them openly, Gogol made no mention of his respect for this champion of his own work. How could one fail to loathe politics, he asked himself, when it turns equally decent, sincere men into enemies? Whenever anyone brandished a social question in front of him, he felt like sinking through the floor. He did not want to incur the anger of his friends in Moscow and he did not want to break with his friends in St. Petersburg. As he had done earlier, when faced with the Roman Catholic urgings of Princess Volkonsky, he avoided commitment, fled the issue, and swam a careful current with flexible and effective cowardice.

At last, *Dead Souls* was recopied from start to finish, in a regular and anonymous hand, in notebooks of stiff white paper, and Gogol took the manuscript with trembling hands to Snegirev, a professor at the University of Moscow and a censor whom he judged to be "more intelligent than his colleagues." Snegirev read the book in two days and announced that he personally saw no reason why it should not be published, with a few tiny alterations.

Gogol thought he had won, but Snegirev had second thoughts, changed his mind, and decided, to cover himself, that the book must be submitted to the full committee. He was presumably afraid that he would find himself in deep trouble with Benkendorf or the emperor himself if he issued an authorization entirely on his own responsibility. Censors had been suspended and even arrested for approving texts less subversive than this. Also, the author's previous works hardly militated in his favor: who could forget the upper-class outcry over *The Inspector General?*

The committee met, determined to go through the prose of this scandal raiser with a fine-tooth comb. When the title was read out, Golokhvastov, the chairman, shuddered from head to heel and exclaimed, in tones of outraged superiority: "No! Never shall I allow that! The soul is immortal. There can be no dead soul. The author is attacking the dogma of the immortality of the soul!" It was very difficult to make him understand that these "dead souls" were serfs who had died between two censuses, but then Golokhvastov burst out again, and this time with the support of most of his colleagues: "All the more reason why it is inadmissible! This is an open criticism of the institution of serfdom!" Snegirev patiently explained that the institution was never called into question in the entire book, and that Gogol merely related, in a comical fashion, the dealings of a swindler named Chichikov with a wide range of types of landowners. "Aha! Then Chichikov's actions are criminal!" exclaimed some. "But the author makes no attempt to justify him!" protested Snegirev. "Doesn't justify him!" they retorted; "why, it was all his idea! Now other people can copy Chichikov; they'll all be trying to buy dead souls!" One of the censors, Krylov, thought to display his broad "European" sympathies and coolly observed, "You may say what you like, but Chichikov's price of two and a half rubles per soul is degrading. Human conscience rebels against such a rate. True, he's only paying for a name on a piece of paper, but even so, that name represents a soul, a human soul, a soul that has lived. It would be unthinkable in France or England or anywhere else! After that, no foreigner would ever consent to set foot in Russia!" Meanwhile, another censor had opened the manuscript and chanced upon a passage in which a landowner was ruining himself to build a mansion in the modern style in Moscow. "Careful," put in the censor Kachenovsky; "the emperor is building himself a palace in Moscow!" Snegirev could think of no reply to that, and retired from the field. There were some forms of idiocy against which one's only defense was silence. After a brief discussion, the book was banned.[2]

When he heard the news, Gogol collapsed. He had not expected anything as brutal as this. The idea that a book to which he had devoted so many years should be condemned, never to see the light of day, annihilated him. By what right, he asked, could a handful of incompetents oppose the publication of a book willed by God? The censors' criticisms, which Snegirev had repeated to him, reminded him of some of the reactions of the characters in *Dead Souls* when they first heard Chichikov's proposal. Indeed, the monsters engendered by the author's imagination had their peers among his judges. He had thought he was drawing caricatures, but in fact he had painted portraits of a tragic likeness. What now? Put the manuscript away in a drawer? No; he must fight. He had lost in Moscow; he would try his luck in St. Petersburg. But this time he was determined to arm himself with all the official support he could command.

"This is a very serious matter for me," he wrote to Pletnyev. "You know that this poem represents the totality of my resources and livelihood. It seems they want to tear the last mouthful of bread from my hand, that mouthful earned by seven years of sacrifice and rejection of the world and all its pleasures. I cannot begin anything else to ensure my livelihood. My deteriorating health makes it impossible for me even to continue what I have begun. The minutes when my mind is clear are few, and now this misery has robbed me of the use of my limbs. This is what must be done: now, you should act, working all together, and get the manuscript into the emperor's own hands. I am writing the same thing to Alexandra Smirnov. Let her try to activate the grand duchesses, or find some other means. That is your business!"[3]

Belinsky, the bête noire of Pogodin and Shevyrev, happened to be in Moscow just then, staying with Botkin. Gogol could not meet him openly without arousing the wrath of his friends on *The Muscovite,* so he made a secret and surreptitious visit, informed him of his failure, and asked him to take the manuscript of *Dead Souls* to St. Petersburg and give it to Prince Odoevsky, whose word might tip the scales with the censors. Belinsky readily agreed to undertake this confidential mission.

He had come to Moscow to recruit contributors for the *Annals of the Fatherland.* He strongly berated Gogol for clinging to the little group of reactionaries in Pogodin's circle: it was his duty, as a great Russian writer, to break with the "governmental," Slavophile clique and join the proud ranks of the Europeans. Why didn't he give the *Annals* some unpublished work as proof of his devotion to the ideals of justice and freedom? Alarmed and squirming, Gogol swore he had already given everything he had ready to *The Muscovite,* in accordance with an arrangement of long standing; he was really terribly sorry; perhaps later, if there were an opportunity. Belinsky pretended to believe him.

"I am sorry *The Muscovite* has taken all you had and that you have nothing left for *Annals of the Fatherland,*" he wrote shortly thereafter, alluding to their conversation. "I am sure this is an accident of fate, not an expression of your favorable disposition to the former publication and hostility toward the latter. Fate has long played a curious part in the dealings of the great names of Russian literature: it stripped Batyushkov of his wits, Griboedov, Pushkin, and Lermontov of their lives, and has left Bulgarin, Grech, and similar scum safe and sound, in both Moscow and Petersburg; and it now bestows your work upon *The Muscovite* and ravishes it from the hands of the *Annals.*"[4]

The two men parted on good terms. When he stepped inside Pogodin's house again, however, Gogol, after diplomatically expressing sympathy for the European cause throughout his conversation with Belinsky, quickly shifted gears: here he must display respect for autocracy in all its rigidity—which, when all was said and done, it was quite easy for him to do. But what agony, the waiting! Belinsky had gone, taking the manuscript with him. His Petersburg friends were already on the alert. His connections, like so many levers, must now activate the most illustrious personalities of the realm. But the mail brought no hopeful word from the capital. It was rumored that the manuscript was being passed from hand to hand, with nobody really looking after it. He anxiously approached Prince Odoevsky:

"I am ill and can hardly stir. . . . My sole remaining possession is being torn from me. You and your friends must exert all your strength to get my manuscript to the sovereign. Read it together with Pletnyev and Alexandra Smirnov and see what is the best way to go about it. Don't speak to anyone else about this yet."[5]

A few days later, second cry of alarm: "What is wrong with you all, that you don't say anything? Why haven't I had a reply? Have you read my manuscript? Have you taken any steps about it? Don't torture me so, for God's sake!"[6]

Then, taking the plunge, he decided to act alone. He drafted two letters, one to Prince Dondukov-Korsakov, chairman of the St. Petersburg board of censors, and the other to Uvarov, the minister of education. Both were forwarded to Pletnyev with the request that he give them to the illustrious addressees at the earliest opportunity. Pletnyev wisely did nothing of the sort.

"I know you have a noble soul," Gogol had written to Dondukov-Korsakov, "and that you will let your self be guided solely by your sense of equity. You will not wish to harm a man who, in a pure outpouring of his heart, has remained several years harnessed to his work, has sacrificed everything to it, borne with unhappiness and poverty, and would never have allowed himself to write anything against a government to which he already owes so much!"

And to Uvarov: "No one will give a thought to my present position; no one will see that I am in need, that time is passing while my book might already be published and selling, and that this is depriving me of the resources I need to continue my existence and complete my work, the sole reason for my presence on earth. Is it possible that you, too, can remain unmoved by my state? Is it possible that you, too, can refuse me your protection? Perhaps, despite the hard and thorny path that is my lot in life, my poor name will be passed on to future generations. Will it then be pleasing to you to hear the tribunal of our descendants, after giving credit to you for your admirable work in the sciences, announce that, at the same time, you were indifferent to the works of Russian literature and unmoved by the condition of a poor writer in ill health who had no hole to hide in in this world, when you might have been his patron and defender? No, you will not do this, you will be magnanimous. A Russian dignitary of such high rank must have a Russian soul."[7]

He also decided to appeal to the emperor for financial assistance, however little, until his other problems could be settled. Count Stroganov, keeper of the educational institutions of the district of Moscow, supported his application in a letter to Benkendorf, the director of police:

"Having been notified by the Moscow censor's office that the publication of his work Dead Souls could not be authorized, Gogol has decided to send it to Petersburg. I do not know what decision will be taken on the manuscript there, but this approach was adopted on my advice. Pending the decision, Gogol is starving and has sunk into despair. I cannot but think that a grant from His Majesty would be extremely precious to him."[8]

Benkendorf sent a report to the emperor noting that Gogol[9] was "famous for several works, and in particular The Inspector General." He concluded, "I dare to solicit from Your Majesty's supreme benevolence the order to award a single grant of five hundred silver rubles to the above mentioned."[10] In the margin the emperor wrote "Granted."

With the money, Gogol's hopes revived: he could not be out of favor with the authorities, since the emperor had come to his rescue, and this piece of good news meant that another, more important, might be on the way: permission to publish Dead Souls. But Petersburg remained silent. At home, Pogodin was becoming increasingly irritable and insistent. Someone had "leaked" the clandestine conversation between Gogol and Belinsky, and Pogodin could not forgive this "treason." He unconsciously felt that by helping his friend on so many occasions, he had purchased the right to dispose of his output. He was eternally harrying Gogol with demands for something to put in his review, and Gogol, at the end of his tether, broke off all communication. In the end, they avoided each other except at mealtimes, and when communication was necessary they wrote notes, which a servant carried from Pogodin's study to Gogol's room and back again. Endless minor matters—invitations to dinner, payment of a copyist, questions of proofreading—were dealt with in this manner, by a few short words. The method was employed to announce and comment upon even relatively important events as well. Pogodin would scribble on a scrap of paper, "Do you know that God has given me a son and you a godson?" And on the back of the same scrap, Gogol would reply: "I congratulate you with all my heart and soul. May God's blessing be upon him."[11]

At last, Petersburg was showing signs of life. A letter from Belinsky to Shchepkin announced that "the affair" was progressing satisfactorily. Odoevsky had given the manuscript to Count Vyelgorsky, who had not been able to reach the minister of the interior but had immediately gone to work on Nikitenko, the censor. He, after looking through *Dead Souls,* had declared himself prepared to issue the imprimatur, requiring no more than thirty small amendments and the deletion of a passage entitled "The Story of Captain Kopeyekin." Shortly thereafter came a letter from Pletnyev, confirming the good news. Then a letter from Nikitenko in person:

"By now you will undoubtedly have received the manuscript of your *Dead Souls.* As you can see, the work has successfully negotiated the hurdle of the censor. The path it traveled was narrow, and it is not surprising, therefore, that one or two scratches have marked it, and that its fragile and exquisite skin has been creased here and there. We have found it absolutely impossible to pass the Kopeyekin episode. No power on earth could have prevented its deletion and I am convinced that you yourself will agree there was nothing to be done."[12]

At first Gogol was ecstatically happy, as though his beloved had escaped death before his very eyes. Then, reassured about the essentials, he began to grumble over the details. Cutting the Kopeyekin episode was like mutilating his very flesh. "It's one of the best passages in the poem," he wrote to Pletnyev, "and without it there is a hole I am incapable of either filling or camouflaging. I've decided to rewrite it rather than let it go. I have eliminated all the generals and exaggerated Kopeyekin so that it is now plain he alone is to blame for everything and has been fairly treated."[13]

Pletnyev submitted the new version of Kopeyekin to Nikitenko with the following letter: "For the love of God, help Gogol as much as you can! He is not well now and I am sure that if he is not able to publish *Dead Souls* he will die of it. Once you have taken a final decision about the manuscript, send it to me posthaste so I can transmit it to our martyr. He lies like a heavy stone on my heart."[14]

The same Nikitenko wrote, in his private diary, "The state of our literature is conducive to melancholia. . . . There is no lack of talent among us. But how can they write, when they are forbidden to think?"[15]

The board of censors, guided by Nikitenko, chose to be indulgent. Kopeyekin, in version two, ceased to be a soldier incensed by ingratitude and was instead a mere outlaw, a contemptible swine—giving evidence of the author's laudable efforts to comply with the demands of official morality.[16] Now the whole book could be laid before the public.

On the title page of the manuscript, however, above the words *Dead Souls* in Gogol's hand, Nikitenko had written, *Chichikov's Adventures, or, —,* to attenuate the macabre or possibly subversive implication of the original wording.

Gogol tamely consented to this, and made his own design for the cover of the book. In small print, he wrote the title proposed by the censors, *Chichikov's Adventures,* in minute print the conjunction *or,* and in very large print his own title, *Dead Souls,*[17] and below that, in enormous letters, white on black, the single word POEM. In this manner, he hoped to lead his readers to grasp the broad, epic significance of his task. For them, this tale must be a universal hymn in the style of Homer or Dante, a sort of Russian *Iliad* or *Divine Comedy* of the steppe. To encourage them in this direction, he surrounded title, author's name, and date (1842) with a tangle of tiny drawings alluding to the themes of the book. There is an avalanche of cranes with gaping beaks, a troika in a cloud of dust, an isba with its well and hanging bucket, bottles and glasses, barrels, hams, fish—the symbols of the good life mingled with those of death.

There remained the material problems of publishing. Gogol had no money. Pogodin agreed, with a bearish snarl or two, to furnish the paper. It was decided to have the book typeset on credit by the "University Typesetters." The size of the first edition was less than modest: on the copy visaed by the censors, Gogol wrote, "2,400 copies to be printed on paper furnished by me."

Then began the work on the proofs, rendered interminable by the author's insistence on perfection. To do the work properly, he thought, he would need complete tranquillity, whereas the whole world was clamoring at his door. Belinsky, from St. Petersburg, was insisting that he set aside "something" for the *Annals of the Fatherland.*

"*The Annals of the Fatherland* is now the only periodical in Russia," he wrote, "in which an honest, noble, and, if I may say so, intelligent mind can find a refuge. The review can in no wise be compared with the products of the underlings of that famous village of Porechy.[18] . . . You are the only one left. My moral life and my love of creative art are closely bound up with your fate. If you did not exist I should bid farewell to both the present and future of our country's artistic life. I should live only in the past."[19]

Although touched by such words of praise, Gogol still did not dare to compromise himself by a direct reply. Oh, why must he be stretched on this rack between *The Muscovite* and *Annals of the Fatherland,* Europeans and Slavophiles, conservatives and liberals, Moscow and St. Petersburg, when all he wanted was to stay out of the fight in the lulling mists of neutrality? Prudently, he wrote to Prokopovich: "I have received a letter from Belinsky. Thank him. I do not write to him because, as he knows, we must speak of this and discuss it all face to face, which we will do when I next come to Petersburg."[20]

Pogodin would not let go either. He hurled inprecations upon Belinsky and his Westernizing accomplices and urged Gogol to proclaim his allegiance to *The Muscovite* and not allow his signature to be cheapened in any other periodical. The tone of the little notes flying back and forth from second floor to library grew sharper. In regard to some dispute with the paper merchant, Pogodin wrote: "For the past month or two you have put me in the untenable position of a bankrupt to him. Yet if ever I chance to forget to look after the publication of one of your articles, you rage as though I had cut off both your legs; or at least that is how you look and sound. You have a truly limitless conceit."

"By God, leave me in peace with your tales of conceit," Gogol answered on the same scrap of paper. "Torment me no more, if only for the next two weeks. Let my soul have a moment's respite!"[21]

But Pogodin would not: now he wanted to print a chapter from *Dead Souls* in *The Muscovite* before the book went on sale at the booksellers'. That was more than Gogol could bear. Deflower his life's work by piecemeal publication? Never! His nerves at breaking point, with tears in his eyes and trembling hand, he wrote to Pogodin: "As for your proposal regarding *Dead Souls,* let me tell you that you are impudent, inflexible, cruel, and unreasonable. You may have no care for my tears, the struggles of my conscience, and my intimate convictions, which you are incapable of understanding; but do at least hear my prayer, in the name of Christ who was crucified for us: trust me even if it costs you, even if only for five or six months. God! I had hoped I could be at peace, at least until my departure. But you act only on impulse. One minute you are all generosity and three minutes later you are ready to swallow your words. If I had any money at all I should instantly give every penny of it to prevent my works from being published in periodicals before they come out in book form."[22]

His ire had abated two or three days later, however, when he informed his tormentor: "Try to be here May 9. That day [feast of St. Nicholas] is very important to me and I should like to have you beside me. Farewell. I embrace you."[23]

Thus, through storm and calm, it pained him to dislike so intensely the man who was lodging and feeding him and lending him money and yet to be too cowardly to leave him. He might have gone elsewhere, to live with more tolerant friends, but he stayed on there, exasperated, weak, demanding, vacillating, desperate for attention and incapable of giving it to anyone else. A vindictive supplicant, he somehow felt that the world owed him everything and he was entitled to give nothing in return. Bartenyev† saw him in the home of some friends, the Khomyakovs, and said of him: "He was exceptionally moody, repeatedly demanding and then rejecting a glass of tea, which was never to his liking —it was either too hot or too strong or too weak; or the glass was too full or not full enough, and Gogol was very irate. In short, everyone was most embarrassed in the end, and could only express amazement at the patience of the hosts and the great indelicacy of their guest."[24]

Even Aksakov, while continuing to admire Gogol, began to suffer from his rudeness, irascibility, and dissimulation.

"Pogodin soon began to complain bitterly of Gogol," he wrote; "of his whims, hypocrisy, even his lying, and his coldness and lack of consideration for [Pogodin], his wife, his mother and mother-in-law, none of whom could ever satisfy [Gogol] in anything. And I must admit, to my keen regret, that Pogodin's complaints and accusations seemed so plausible that both myself and my family, and Shevyrev, were very worried. To myself I interpreted Gogol's behavior—and I tried to explain it that way to others—as natural dissimulation and aloofness, and observance of a rule he had adopted in childhood, to the effect that it was sometimes necessary not only to avoid telling the truth but to invent any nonsense at all to hide that truth so that people would never find it.

† Piotr Ivanovich Bartenyev was contributing and managing editor of *Russian Archives.*

Often, when talking about Gogol's actions, I would tell myself and others that we could not judge his acts by our own, we couldn't even understand his perceptions, because he was undoubtedly put together differently from ourselves, and his nerves—probably more sensitive than ours—perceived things we did not and reacted for reasons unknown to us. To my demonstration, Pogodin replied with a wry laugh, 'Yes, that must be it!' Now I realize that Pogodin, with his rough, harsh, unpolished nature, could not behave otherwise with Gogol—who was essentially poetic, impressionable, and thin-skinned. Pogodin's intentions were always good and he could show great kindness even to a man unable to return it; but as soon as he saw that his debtor was in a position to repay him, he would tackle him without further ado, grab him by the collar, and say, 'I helped you when you were in need; now work for me.' "[25]

He went on: "Even with his friends Gogol was never entirely honest. A short time before he went abroad again, the people he saw most often said he seemed a completely different man. With one friend, for example, he was all levity, in writing or conversation; with another he talked nothing but art; with a third he would not speak at all, or even dozed or pretended to sleep. Thus it was that the first man said he was a hearty fellow, thoughtful and sympathetic, the second found him taciturn, gloomy, and proud, and the third said he cared for nothing but spiritual matters. In a word, no one knew all of Gogol."[26]

Did he know himself? He analyzed himself, at any rate, complacently and interminably. And the more he contemplated his position in Pogodin's house in Moscow, the more tragic it seemed to him, regardless of the imminent publication of *Dead Souls*. He wrote to Marya Balabin: "Ever since I first set foot on my native soil, it has seemed to me that I am in a foreign country. I see people I know and have the impression that they were not born here and that I have seen them somewhere else. There is no longer a single thought in my head. If you need a dummy to hold your hats and bonnets, I am entirely at your service. You can put your hat or whatever else you please on me, you can dust me, brush me under my nose, and I won't sneeze, I won't even move an eyelash."[27]

And to Yasykov: "I was not made for rush and bustle, and every day, every hour, I see more clearly that the best possible state in the world is that of the monk."[28]

To Pletnyev: "It is my nature to be able to picture the living world to myself only by removing myself from it. That is why it is only in Rome that I am able to write about Russia. Also, apart from external circumstances in Moscow that torment me, I feel a physical incapacity to write here. My head gives me a thousand different kinds of trouble: if it is cold in my room the nerves in my brain ache and freeze, and you cannot imagine what pain I endure every time I try, in these conditions, to master myself and compel my head to work; if the room is heated, the artificial warmth stifles me and the slightest intellectual effort produces such a coagulation in my brain that it feels about to burst. How could I guess I should have to endure such tortures upon my return to Russia?"[29]

While complaining of his health, his inertia, and Pogodin's evil machinations, he continued to frequent the "friendly houses" of Moscow, languishing at the Aksakovs', Khomyakovs', Elagins', Shchepkins', or visiting his sister, who was still living with Mrs. Raevsky. Elizaveta seemed to be growing more intelligent and cultivated. For her, at least, Moscow was beneficial. Through Mrs. Raevsky he came to know Nadezhda Nikolayevna Sheremeytyev, an old lady of sixty-seven, pious and kindly though somewhat hard of hearing, who instantly took a fervent liking to him. She delightedly detected his spiritual aspirations and urged him to forsake his solitary and somber faith for the illuminated paths of the Church. His willingness to listen to her was increased by the fact that she, at least, was not overawed by his prowess as a writer. For her, he was primarily a man in torment seeking support. She, too, was poor and lived at the expense of other people, and must therefore be in a better position to sense the direction of his spiritual quest. He said she was his "spiritual mother."[30] It was not necessary for him to explain to her his great, God-inspired undertaking: she knew.

As he worked through the proofs of *Dead Souls,* at any rate, the necessity for a radiant sequel to his grotesque prelude became increasingly clear to him. After depicting the vices of his contemporaries, he must demonstrate the virtues to which the Russian might attain. After pointing out the depths, he must now show the way to the summit. He wrote to Pletnyev: "My work is important and vast. You cannot judge it from the part I am preparing to make public now. This is no more than the portico of the palace rising within me."[31]

To purify himself before beginning this great labor, he needed a special benediction. The Archbishop Innocent, famed for his devoutness, rectitude, and simplicity, happened to be passing through Moscow.

Gogol called on him. Innocent received him kindly, encouraged his projects, blessed him, and gave him an icon. Gogol, deeply moved, hurried to the Aksakovs' bearing his holy image and collided with his friend, who was just on his way—oh, vanity!—to spend the evening at his club. Before the assembled family he announced, with moist eye and quavering voice: "I have always been waiting for someone to bless me with a holy image, but nobody ever did. At last, Innocent has given me his blessing. Now I can tell you where I intend to go next: to visit the tomb of Our Lord."

"I confess I was not well pleased, either with Gogol's inspired countenance at that moment or with his plan to visit the Holy Land," Aksakov wrote. "To my mind it all came from a state of nervous tension particularly alarming from the viewpoint of the artist. I went to my club."[32]

Left alone with Aksakov's family, Gogol was subjected to a battery of questions. Wife, daughter, and son in turn asked him to explain himself and his intentions: had he come to Russia to stay or "to bid it adieu"? "To bid it adieu," he declared with fire. How long would he be away? "Two years," he answered; "or maybe ten!" Would he send his friends a description of Palestine? "Yes," he sighed; "but first I must purify myself, make myself worthy."

He was pale, tormented, overexcited. Never before had he felt so strongly that the truth was in him and that no one understood him. His friends were forever nagging at him about literary trivia, while he bore within himself the divine word. Analyzing the gulf between them, he wrote to Alexandra Smirnov:

"My literary friends met me when I was a very young man, and even then they did not fully understand me. From my conversation they concluded that all I cared about was literature and nothing else existed for me. But since I have left Russia, a major change has taken place within me. The soul has become my only concern. When I returned, my literary friends all welcomed me with open arms. Every one of them, working at some form of journalism or other and passionately serving one idea in opposition to those of the enemy camp, was awaiting me as though I were some sort of Messiah, convinced that I would share his opinions and beliefs and uphold him in the face of his adversaries. To them this was the prime condition and first act of friendship, and in their innocence it really never occurred to them that such demands were inhuman as well as foolish. It was impossible for me to sacrifice my time and efforts to defend their pet ideas, in the first place because I did not wholly share those ideas and in the second because I had to earn enough to continue my modest existence and could not distribute my articles among their various periodicals but had to publish them separately, in their full freshness and novelty, in order to make money from them. They took my coolness toward their literary ventures as coolness toward themselves. A kind of jealousy developed in them. Everyone suspected me of betraying him for somebody else. I received strange letters in which one or another of them, after assuring me of the purity of his sentiments for me, falsely calumniated and belittled the others, insisting that their flattery was not disinterested, that they didn't know me and loved me only for my work and not for myself. At the same time, they heaped reproaches upon me and leveled accusations at me so base that never, I swear it, would I have dared to proffer them to the vilest individual in the world! These misunderstandings led to such hurtful suspicions, and the blows struck at me were so gross and reached fibers so sensitive and fragile (whose very existence was unimagined by those who struck them), that my soul was dejected and exasperated and I could take no more."[33]

Despite his feelings of resentment toward all these troublesome friends, Gogol once again decided to celebrate his patron saint's day, May 9, in their company. The chill between him and Pogodin did not prevent Gogol from organizing a luncheon in the garden behind the Virgins' Field house, as in 1840. Following the same program as before, he invited his mother to come and bring his sister Anna. They would naturally stay with him at Podogin's, and when they left, Elizaveta would go with them; after spending two years under the tutelage of Mrs. Raevsky, there was nothing more for her to do in Moscow.

As for him, he would return to Rome. There, far from the friends and enemies he had found guilty of identical crimes, he would write the second part of *Dead Souls*. A trip to Jerusalem would be his reward after this labor of religious love. He might go there first, to seek inspiration at the tomb of the Lord; but then he thought it would be better to wait until his task was done and he could go for the repose of his soul alone, without ulterior motives. To reassure his mother, who was worried by his desire to leave Russia again, he told her that the tsar, in his infinite goodness, had attached him to the embassy in Rome, where he would be earning a very respectable salary.[34] Who knows, he told himself, the lie might one day come true? God was so near that he must learn not to wonder at miracles.

The party on May 9 began on a less cheerful note than that of two years earlier. Oh, there were lots of people: the Aksakovs, Kireyevskys, Elagins, Nashchokin, Pavlov, Samarin, Professors Armfeld, Botkin, and Granovsky from the university . . . but Gogol and the master of the house were hardly on speaking terms any more, and their friends were made uncomfortable by this obvious but unavowed state of feud. The tension was eased by the fortunate arrival of Marya Ivanovna and her daughter, whose stagecoach drove them right into the courtyard. They had been delayed on the road and were sure they would miss the party. Then came the embraces, the tears of joy, signs of the cross, compliments, and urgent demands for news from Vasilyevka. Marya's son, Nikolai,[35] was doing very nicely, but Marya herself had been ill for the past year. They were afraid she might be consumptive. Olga was growing like a strong young plant, in spite of her semideafness. Anna was bored in the country. The property itself was in as disastrous a condition as ever. Well, they would talk about that later. Just now, the growing crowd of guests had to be looked after. Katerina Khomyakov and Elizaveta Chertkov made a spectacular entrance on horseback, riding sidesaddle. They dined indoors with the other ladies, while the men ate in the garden. It was a beautiful day. Gogol exuded the frantic good humor of a master of ceremonies. After the meal he made punch, as before, in the arbor. As he held a light to his mixture of rum and champagne, he poetically compared the blue flame to that of the uniform of the police and said it was their chief, Benkendorf, who would now descend into their stomachs and restore order. This innocuous impertinence raised a hearty laugh, and the party ended better than it had begun.

On the morning after this great day, Gogol began to arrange his departure. *Dead Souls* would soon be back from the printer: all the more reason for him to clear out! The mere thought of the outcry that had greeted his *Inspector General* was enough to drive him away. Good or bad, the reviews could only irritate him, and he required complete tranquillity to embark upon the sequel to the book. His friends in Petersburg and Moscow would look after the material problems of editions and sales in his absence, and defend his interests. He was already issuing his instructions, viva voce and in writing: "I have never worked on a sale-

or-return basis with booksellers, so you can tell them they will have to pay on receipt of copies; otherwise they will get nothing."[36]

He also drew up a list of his debts and instructed Shevyrev to repay them as funds became available. "The first sums are to be allocated as follows," he noted: "Sverbeyev, 1500; Shevyrev, 1900; Pavlov, 1500; Khomyakov, 1500; Pogodin, 1500. After that, pay my other debts: Pogodin, 6000 rubles; Aksakov, 2000."[37]

Panic seized him as he read through this list of names and figures: would he ever sell enough *Dead Souls* to free himself from his creditors?

He had set May 23 as his date of departure. On the twenty-first he received the first copies of his book, fresh from the binder. A solemn moment: what had been his daily dream for so long was now a commercial object, which anyone could purchase for a few rubles. He turned over the printed pages, inhaled the smell of printer's ink, and a crippling anguish mingled with his joy. So: *Dead Souls* existed outside himself. He could do nothing more for or against it. Whether he liked it or not, it would now fulfill its destiny among the host of his readers, attracting some, repelling others. He felt at once dispossessed and enriched. In number 42 of *The Muscovite News* a notice had already appeared, announcing the sale of a work entitled *Chichikov's Adventures, or, Dead Souls,* "poem by N. Gogol, large octavo, linen, 473 pages, Moscow, 1842, price in quality binding: ten rubles fifty kopecks."

On the threshold of this great experience Gogol felt a need for renewed contact with the man who had consented to bless his efforts, Archbishop Innocent. In a moment of mystical fervor he even sent him his own benediction. On May 22, he wrote to the archbishop: "Heart and soul contracted, I shake your hand by letter and, strengthened by your blessing, bless you in turn. Tread your pastoral road firmly and without faltering. We are dominated by a limitless power. Nothing happens in the world without its intervention. Our meeting was determined On High, it is the promise of a perfect communion before the tomb of the Lord. Take no steps and do not concern yourself with the manner of fulfillment. I feel in myself that a significant interview is awaiting us. Farewell. Accept the potent kiss of my soul. I am never parted from the icon you gave me!"

The next day, May 23, 1842, Gogol left the Pogodin household with feelings of mournful rancor and ill-tempered relief; and Pogodin was anxious to see him go. Much later he wrote to Gogol: "When you shut the door behind you, I crossed myself and heaved a sigh of liberation, as though a mountain had dropped from my shoulders. Everything I have learned since has added to my unhappiness and, apart from a few wonderful moments, I have seen you as an abominable person."[38]

Five years later Gogol, too, spoke of their estrangement, in a letter to Pogodin:

"Before even coming to Moscow, I wrote to S. T. Aksakov from Rome, asking him to warn you not to ask me for anything for your review. Upon reaching Moscow I entered your house in fear, sensing that trouble would come between us. On the very first day, I repeated my prayer to your face. I told you that my work would be so important that it would make you weep and that many other people all over Russia would weep because of it. With tears in my eyes I asked you to believe me. Then, you were moved and said, 'I believe you.' Again I asked you not to make me give you something for your magazine. You gave me your word. But by the third or fourth day you were beginning to waver. Two weeks later, when you announced, as though there had never been anything between us, that I had to give you an article, I was both stupefied and angered. And when you reminded me three weeks after that, saying that I ought to do as you asked because I was living in your house and your family wanted to know how it was that I was living with you and not working for your review—this ultimatum was contemptible, dishonest, and ignoble. Yes, I thought it contemptible to remind a man lodging under your roof that he was supposed to be grateful to you; I thought it dishonest, after giving your word of honor, to take it back; I thought it unworthy of a noble soul to doubt the tears of someone who has implored you; and, even more, to tell him, 'I believe you,' and then to doubt him. In a word, it all seemed so cowardly and base that I began to feel contempt for you. I did not even try to conceal my contempt. On the contrary, I displayed it openly whenever I could. Not guessing the cause, you simply took it for a sign of my pride and, seeing the disgusted expression on my face in various circumstances, even trivial, you concluded that I was nursing the demon of self-love in its most diabolical form; you thought that that was my true nature and that I behaved like that with everyone—whereas I confess to you truthfully, I have never behaved so badly with anyone as with you. From that moment I told myself, 'Go ahead and flounder, since that's the way it is!' And I began, intentionally, to act contrary to my nature, desiring to annoy you still more."[39]

It was in this frame of mind that Gogol walked away from the house on Virgins' Field. He had already said good-by to his mother and sisters, who intended to remain in Moscow a few more days. Marya Ivanovna was worried about *Dead Souls*. If the book did not have the success it most assuredly deserved, how her son would suffer! And he would be far away, without her or his friends to help him bear the blow. She pitied him; she suffered to think she could do nothing to help him. After he left, she and her daughters and Mrs. Aksakov went, in three carriages, to the Troitsa Monastery, some sixty-five versts from Moscow, to pray that God would protect her son, who was about to exile himself (but why?) to the ends of the earth.

This time Pogodin was certainly not in the group accompanying Gogol to the first posting station, as he had been two years before. But Aksakov and Shchepkin, flanked by their sons, carried on the tradition. Old Mrs. Sheremeytyev joined them at the Tverskaya barrier, made the sign of the cross over the travelers' heads, and returned home. The others continued to Khimky, thirteen versts outside Moscow. There, everyone got out. While waiting for the stagecoach, they walked along the river's edge in a little birch woods. Gogol made Aksakov promise to send him all written and verbal reactions—"especially unfavorable" —to *Dead Souls*. The main thing, he said, was to know what his enemies thought of him. He intended to stop in St. Petersburg to arrange the publication of his "Complete Works," and from there he would go on to Italy by way of Germany and Austria.

He was unusually nervous, even for him, and manifestly ill at ease with Aksakov and Shchepkin. He was delighted to be getting away from Moscow, but his joy was soured by the thought that he was leaving his best friends with an unfavorable impression. He was angry with himself for disappointing them, and with them for having forced him to disappoint them. "He felt that he had deceived us, and was going away too soon and too hastily, after promising to stay in Moscow forever," Aksakov wrote. "He realized that we, who did not know his secret thoughts and were unaware of the impossible situation in the Pogodin household, where his behavior had been justified, in his eyes—we could fairly accuse him of strangeness, capriciousness, and inconsistency, and of harboring a passion for Italy and a coldness toward Moscow and Russia."

The coach was late, so they sat down to eat; but even with the champagne Gogol had brought along, conversation languished. Nobody dared say what was really on his mind. At last the vehicle drew up, with a merry jingle of bells. Gogol leaped up to look after his luggage. His fellow passenger was a stout military man with a Germanic name. "Although I had been extremely cross with Gogol for some time," Aksakov wrote, "at that moment I forgot all that and felt only profound sorrow to see a great artist forsake his country and ourselves. I was filled with bitterness when the coach doors slammed abruptly. Gogol's face disappeared and the stagecoach moved off on the road to St. Petersburg."[40]

In St. Petersburg, Gogol stayed with Pletnyev, called on Alexandra Smirnov, and had a secret meeting with Belinsky, whose support could be invaluable in the launching of *Dead Souls*. But he spent most of his time with Prokopovich, preparing a four-volume edition of his "Collected Works" (excluding *Dead Souls*). While he was working on this scheme, his friends in Moscow were expressing their indignation that he should entrust the project to a man on the "other side."

"We did not really trust Gogol," Aksakov wrote. "His hypocritical character, his unexpected departure from Moscow without consulting us, the publication of his works in St. Petersburg, the bestowal of such an important commission upon a totally inexperienced person [Prokopovich] when Shevyrev possessed every qualification—not to mention his friendship and loyalty—to do the job well, and lastly, Gogol's meetings in St. Petersburg with people who were hostile to us and of whom he thought no more than we did (such as Belinsky, Polevoy, Kraevsky): it all added to our general mistrust, even that of Shevyrev and myself. It confirmed Pogodin's idea that Gogol was utterly false and could never be believed."[41]

In a week, Gogol finished his business in St. Petersburg. He had given virtually full responsibility for the publication to Prokopovich, who would even read and correct the proofs. He had no time to waste on such trivia. On the eve of his departure he wrote two letters, one to Mrs. Pogodin (*not* to Pogodin himself!), assuring her of his loyal friendship, in which she had to believe, he said, for "the heart of woman is less given to skepticism and mistrust than that of man"[42]; and the other to Aksakov, informing him of his latest activities in the capital and insisting that he was leaving with his soul held high: "The four volumes of "Collected Works" will certainly be out next October. The copy of *Dead Souls* has not yet been presented to the emperor. I embrace you repeatedly. Be strong and valiant in your soul, for strength and valor reign in him who writes you these lines; everything is communicated between two who love each other; that is why part of my strength must penetrate your soul too. Those who believe in the light will see the light; the shadows exist only for the faithless."[43]

The next day, June 5, 1842, Gogol strapped up his trunks once again; he had finished with Russia and the first volume of *Dead Souls*. Abroad, he would recover his true homeland, the one that is invisible to the eyes of the flesh.

7. Dead Souls

On none of his previous works had Gogol lavished as much care, worry, and hope as on *Dead Souls*. The simple anecdote of the swindler who bought up the souls of deceased muzhiks for a song and mortgaged them to the State Bank as living people quickly fired his imagination. He set to work enthusiastically, not measuring the scope or direction of his plan.

"Pushkin thought the subject of *Dead Souls* was ideally suited to me because it enabled me to travel all over Russia with my hero and create a huge cast of very different characters," he wrote in his *Confession of an Author*. "I accordingly set to work without any fixed plan, without even a clear idea of the hero's personality. All I knew was that Chichikov's activities would lead to a variety of people and characters as I went along, and that my own desire for laughter would suggest comic episodes, which I wanted to intersperse with more serious passages."

By his own admission, then, Gogol first saw Chichikov merely as an entertaining figure and his quest for dead souls as a simple device for introducing the reader to a group of exaggeratedly absurd country gentry. It was the exact formula of the picaresque novel, as illustrated by Le Sage in *Gil Blas* and copied by several Russian authors—Bulgarin in particular, whose *Ivan Vyzhigin* had been a great success—at the beginning of the century. Gogol was also thinking, of course, of Cervantes' *Don Quixote*, another migratory novel; and of the *Divine Comedy* and the *Iliad* and *Odyssey*. These illustrious models made his head swim. The more he thought about his story, the greater depth he discovered in it. He, too, wanted to write a poem, and an epic one at that. The epic of provincial platitude and tedium, for of course it was all going to take place in the provinces—those provinces Gogol knew so little about. Since the age of nineteen he had lived in St. Petersburg, Moscow, or abroad. He knew the little towns of Russia only as a traveler who stops for a few hours to change horses at the inn. And all he knew of the unchanging Russian landscape was what he had seen through the windows of his stagecoach. Nevertheless, the stories told by others, combined with his fleeting personal impressions, enabled him to conjure up a strongly convincing picture of this world of landowners and junior bureaucrats into which he had scarcely penetrated.

In *The Inspector General* he had already written about one of those muddy, drowsy towns, and in *Dead Souls* we find the same commonplace setting, the same rainy sky, and the same people, dedicated body and soul to vanity, falsehood, filth, and double-dealing. As in the play, the placid little sewer is suddenly agitated by the appearance of a mysterious figure whom nobody knows and who can hail from nowhere except that far-off, foggy capital. The first man was named Khlestakov, the second Chichikov; in *The Inspector General,* however, theatrical convention demanded that the protagonists of the comedy come to call on Khlestakov, whereas Chichikov, in the novel, can pursue each character in turn. Who is this Chichikov, whose name uncoils like a spring?

An impostor, like Khlestakov, since he never stops deceiving the people around him. But the lies of Khlestakov were light, absurd, intoxicating; those of Chichikov are heavy, calculating, and highly practical. The author soon realized that this commerce in dead souls, initially seen as a pretext for some door-to-door exploration of the ridiculous, carries a disturbing philosophical message. There is something aberrant, certainly, in the idea of buying individuals who no longer exist and temporarily resuscitating them for a bureaucratic swindle. And the man responsible for this weird resurrection must be something more than an ordinary crook. If Chichikov had swindled the owners in transactions involving live serfs, he would have been no more criminal than the rest of the world. But by purchasing dead ones, he adds a supernatural note to his skulduggery. This time, almost in defiance of the author's will, it is no longer the hero's personality that directs the action, but the action itself that gives such a peculiar cast to the hero. Gogol detected a smell of sulphur around Chichikov. He wrote to Shevyrev: "For many years now, my sole aim has been that a person who reads my work will split his sides laughing at the devil."[1]

If he had the devil in mind when he created Chichikov, however, it was no foul fiend of hell: this is a lesser demon, the spirit of pettiness and comfort. None of your flamboyant Lucifers who specialize in great negations and tragic crimes: this is his hard-working, tidy, common-place little deputy, the devil "in gray flannel," who feeds on trivial com-promise and straightforward lies. This devil never attacks anyone great or noteworthy; he is interested in neither saints nor murderers. His cus-tomers are run-of-the-mill mankind. Here, he is on an equal footing. His external appearance is reassuring, he talks like everybody else, he is phenomenally "any one of us," and that is why he does not arouse our suspicions.

Besides, unlike his grand master, he is not trying to lead mortals into temptation for the sheer pleasure of winning their souls, but simply to make a little profit for himself out of his dealings with them. This very material interest shows that Chichikov is a close cousin of the human species. When disguising himself as a mortal, he also clothes himself in all the pains and pleasures human flesh is heir to. He is both devil and man; devil to the extent that he represents what is basest in man—Devil-in-Man, as Christ is God-in-Man. For years, Ivanov had been painting Christ appearing to the people, while Gogol painted Satan ap-pearing to the people. The devil of the middle road: Chichikov is neither "handsome nor ugly, neither fat nor thin; one couldn't call him old and yet he is not very young."

The moment he takes a room in the inn of the little town of N., he be-gins to make contact with the local dignitaries, and his engaging manner wins every heart. Adapting speech and attitude to suit his audience, he proffers to everyone the language most apt to flatter his opinion of him-self and allay all suspicions.

"If stud farms were the subject, he talked stud farming," Gogol wrote; "if the conversation was of dogs, he slipped in a few sound remarks; when it turned to an investigation at the court of accounts, he showed his knowledge of the foibles of Milady Justice; when billiards and punch were the subject, he proved himself a connoisseur of both; when it was virtue, he discoursed upon the theme with brimming eyes; if cus-toms regulations came up, he handled them like an ex-customs official. In a word, he was at home everywhere."[2]

And when, close-shaven and attired in his elegant maroon frock coat,

Chichikov sets out to make the rounds of the local landowners, this adaptability begins to border upon mental gymnastics. The moment he sets foot on a property, he takes on its very color, so to speak. Nevertheless, these perpetual reptilian skin sheddings never cause him to lose sight of his objective, which is to buy up dead souls. He varies his approach to suit the circumstances, of course, when proposing his macabre deal; and the responses he receives are equally varied, and revealing. In the first moment of surprise, each landowner, crouching in his lair, spontaneously reveals his true nature. None, however, finds anything *morally* reprehensible in the idea: according to temperament, they are stupefied, suspicious, amused, cunning; they ask for time to think it over or they demand an exorbitant price, but they never express indignation. Only one man, Manilov, rather fears that the transaction might be "contrary to the institutions and subsequent views of Russia." Chichikov's task of reassuring him is made all the easier by Manilov's horror of anything complicated.

Once again it is as though some northern mist had befuddled the brains of the people Chichikov interviews. The ancient tradition of serfdom has already prepared them for the idea that everything in a man can be sold, both body and soul. They find nothing ghoulish or excessive in a contract that prolongs a serf's slavery beyond the grave. They follow a certain logic, which leads them to the confines of the preposterous. Their attachment to tangible realities prevents them from seeing that they are living in a raving dream. One after the other, Chichikov persuades them. They draw up lists of deceased peasants at so much a head. An absurdly small price—but even that is a windfall, after all, when it is paid for cadavers who can no longer do anything with their ten fingers.

As his stock of corpses grows, Chichikov's optimism similarly flowers. He will take all these phantoms that are now his property and pretend to move them to some stretch of desert land bought for a song in the Tauris or Kherson districts. He'll call his non-existent village Chichikovo; and there will be no difficulty, he is quite certain, about mortgaging the lot with the State Bank. And thus he will reap a fortune and the pleasures it procures—for Chichikov is no mere "acquirer," to use Gogol's term: for him, money is not an end in itself, but a means of gaining a comfortable position in society.

"In him," Gogol wrote, "there was no attachment, in the strict sense of the word, to money as money. Avarice and stinginess were both foreign to his nature. He dreamed of a life filled with every contentment and comfort: coaches, a handsome house, a large staff of servants, fine dinners—that was what he was after. To be able, at last, one day, to savor to the full every pleasure. Everything that smacked of opulence and ease had such a powerful effect on him that he himself could not account for it."[3]

As a true positivist, Chichikov denies anything absolute in good and evil. No lie causes him a moment's hesitation, when it is in pursuit of increased wealth and its consequence, increased comfort. He is as fussy about physical cleanliness as he is oblivious to moral cleanliness. "He changed his underclothes every other day," Gogol writes, "and in summer, every day: any even mildly unpleasant odor offended his nostrils. Whenever his man, Petrushka [a strong-smelling fellow], came to undress him or take off his boots, he held a carnation to his nose."[4] His favorite soap is a French brand, "which gave a remarkable whiteness to the skin and a clean look to the cheeks." He desires to wear none but fine Holland shirts. When he looks at himself in the mirror, he melts with affection for his face, in which everything is smooth, regular, unobtrusive, and respectable. He makes faces at himself. "Look how round my chin is!" he says as he shaves. And chortles over his great prosperity, coming after such an inauspicious start.

His whole past is one long series of sharp deals, swindles, double crosses, and bribes, beginning at school, where he fleeces his playmates, developing in the customs administration, where he levies tariffs on smugglers, and, undeterred by a few court appearances with no serious consequences, exploding into glorious fruition with the inspired idea of buying up dead souls. This time, again, he will increase his substance without actually creating anything with his own hands. He is a sleight-of-hand artist juggling air, laughing up his sleeve as he watches his tricks work. He stands in his nightshirt facing his open money box, capers for joy, and kicks up his heels to his buttocks.

These diabolical cavortings of the plump pink gentleman precede the transcription of his list of the dead. Lovingly, he ticks them off and indulges in dreams of marriage and progeniture. He is much preoccupied by the thought of paternity. He cannot admit that his "seed" should be lost and he have no sequel. Procreation is his only chance for survival. There is nothing in the other world, he thinks; so to die without having given birth to anything means that the final balance adds up to—zero. In his own words, he sees "some fresh, pink person, a pretty little scamp, a delicious little daughter, or maybe two little lads and two or even three little girls—so that everyone will know he really existed and did not simply pass over the earth like a shadow or ghost." He is afraid of "disappearing like a bubble on the surface of the water, leaving not a trace behind." His obsession is like that of the satanical old man—the chief character of the second part of "The Portrait"—who insists upon being painted for the same reason: so that he will not die altogether, so that even after his death he will be "present in the world." Chichikov says, "I want to make enough money . . . to leave some to the wife and children I would like to have for the good of the country." And when one of his swindles looks as though it might collapse, he cries out, thinking of this hypothetical spouse and descendants, "What will my children say of me? Our pig of a father, they'll say, has left us no money at all!"[5]

Thus Chichikov justifies the acquisition of dead souls in terms of souls unborn. Things that do not yet exist are his pretext for purchasing things that no longer exist. He balances himself on two voids, two lies. But his fortune, although founded on nothing and destined for nothing— his fortune itself seems real enough. A little warm place on the edge of the abyss; but nothing more. His aspirations are those of a respectable bourgeois. A comfortable residence, faithful servants, an elegant ward- robe, a well-matched team, the respect of his neighbors, and the friend- ship of a few highly placed officials. It is not in Chichikov that we will find the genius of imposture intoxicated by his own omnipotence. He may cheat at the game of life and death, but for very small stakes. He may deploy quite exceptional ingenuity, but it is in order to amass a very ordinary fortune.

By a curious trick of art, moreover, the character of Chichikov is not fundamentally repellent to the reader. We follow him on his round of visits, unconsciously hoping he will triumph over his reluctant hosts. Every time he gains a fresh herd of dead souls, we rejoice with him at his success. Whenever an obstacle looms in his path, we tremble lest he be unmasked and punished. Although we cannot excuse Chichikov, we are actually on his side. There are three reasons for this.

Firstly, when he is collecting his dead souls for a few paltry kopecks, Chichikov is not stealing from their owners, because the muzhiks themselves are lying in their graves, and represent no real value to the estate. In fact, by transferring them to Chichikov, the landowners will no longer have to pay tax on them. The State alone will suffer from the transaction, when Chichikov submits his list of phantoms as security for a large loan; and the State has no face; the State is an abstract principle. Anyone wanting to condemn Gogol's hero cannot do so in the name of a specific victim, only in the name of a principle. When he buys his abstract beings, the only thing Chichikov is attacking is an abstraction.

Secondly, how could he be blamed for buying dead souls in a country in which it is legal to buy live ones? Isn't it more reprehensible to reduce living beings to slavery than to transfer dead ones from one record book to another?

Thirdly, the succession of characters Chichikov approaches in his quest for souls are themselves so ignoble that the hero of the book emerges as pure as the driven snow by comparison. What he is making a profit on, after all, is the stupidity, vulgarity, complacency, and sloth of the dwellers in and around the little town.

This little town is clearly a symbol: for the author, it represents Russia, and Russia represents the world. In his notes about the novel, Gogol wrote: "The town and its maelstrom of gossip should be portrayed as a chaos depicting the futility of mankind in general. How to reduce the universal image of futility in all its forms until it can be embodied in the futility of that town, and how to magnify the latter until it will approximate to an image of planetary futility?"

Lined up side by side, Chichikov's victims form a remarkable gallery of monsters. The reader, like the mayor in *The Inspector General,* suddenly finds himself surrounded by "pigs' snouts," each one bearing a name that symbolizes and crowns him like a paper party hat. In Russian the name Manilov, for instance, means "honeyed" and evokes a pleasing invitation, an enticing appeal. Nozdrev, the braggart with the haughty air and curling lip, comes from the Russian word *nozdrya,* nostril. Sobakevich, of the canine temperament, is derived from the Russian *sobaka,* which means exactly that: a dog. Korobochka, that mistrustful idiot with the hermetically sealed mind, merely reproduces the Russian *korobochka,* little box. And the name Plyushkin, the hideous skinflint, comes from *Plyushka,* which could be translated as "pancake."

Furthermore, if one thinks of it that way, Plyushkin really is as much a pancake as a man, just as Korobochka is nothing but a little box dressed up as a woman, Nozdrev a gigantic nostril perched on a pair of legs, and Sobakevich a tail-thumping, hairy, clumsy dog. This is not to say that each of the characters is only a personification of some vice— Manilov of meaningless sentimentality, Nozdrev of dishonesty, Sobakevich of boorishness, Korobochka of idiocy, or Plyushkin of greed. When Gogol created his "types," he contrived to give them so much flesh that they have all the warmth and complexity of real individuals instead of remaining allegorical puppets. Plyushkin is not "the Miser" but one particular miser, very particular, identifiable among all other misers. No one could confuse Nozdrev with any other cheat; Korobochka, too, is unique, even though she is also female imbecility incarnate, and there is no one else like Sobakevich, although he is a perfect definition of masculine pomposity.

They all have one feature in common, however: they are the sellers of dead souls, and they are dead souls themselves. They speak, move, sleep, and eat like the living, but behind this semblance of humanity, no atom of conscience remains. "It seemed that this body was devoid of soul," Gogol wrote about Sobakevich. He might have said as much of every other character in the book; and this fact only sharpens the ugly contrast between the landowners' moral nullity and their privileged position as the masters of human lives.

Manilov—fair-haired, infinitely obliging, lazy, and nauseatingly inconsistent—is the first to receive a visit from Chichikov. His heart overflows with concern for the whole universe, but some curious atrophy of the will prevents him from undertaking the smallest action. Lost in his endless reveries, he tells himself that it would be "good to make an underground passage from the house to the village, or to build a stone bridge across the pond, with shops on the sides selling all the little articles in common use among the village people." In his study he keeps a book, with a bookmark on page 14, "which he had been reading for two years." He has nothing but good to say of everyone. Leaning over Chichikov's shoulder, he sighs: "How pleasant it would be to live under the same roof, or to talk philosophy under the shade of a young elm!" But when his guest reveals the object of his visit, Manilov starts: "How's that? Excuse me—I'm growing a little hard of hearing—I thought I heard something odd . . ."

"I would like to buy dead souls," Chichikov repeats, "or to be exact, those which are still listed as living on the census records. You seem rather at a loss?"

"I? No, no," stammers Manilov; "not exactly that. But I don't quite understand. Forgive me. Of course, I did not have an education anything like as fine as that which, so to say, speaks in your every gesture; I do not possess the great art of talking well. Perhaps there is some hidden meaning in your words? Perhaps the expression you used was some refinement of style?"

"No, no," says Chichikov; "I am not speaking figuratively; I mean just that, dead souls. We call them living, as they are listed as such on the census sheet. I am accustomed to using exact legal terminology. The law; I am mute before the law."

These words are enough to dispel Manilov's qualms. He will not even hear of money or prices. "How could I accept money for souls that, so to say, have ended their existence?"

The reaction of the idiotic Korobochka is very different. Manilov may be a dreamer, but she, oh, yes, has got her two feet firmly on the ground. "Dead souls?" she exclaims. "Would you be wanting to dig them up again, perchance? Really, I have never sold dead people before. I would be afraid, on this first occasion, to take a loss. Perhaps you're trying to cheat me, little father?"

"Listen; really, you're most peculiar! How much could they be worth? I mean, they're nothing but dust, you understand! Nothing but dust!"

Despite this unanswerable argument, the old woman is still suspicious. She would much rather sell honey, hemp, or live peasants, because at least she knows the going price for those commodities. "To tell the truth," she says, "I am only a poor, inexperienced widow. I would do better to wait. Who knows; maybe other buyers will come along, and then I can compare prices."

In the end, she barters all the deceased of her estate for fifteen assignation rubles, and Chichikov draws up the list.

Next we see Nozdrev, the complete braggart, with his white teeth and "jet-black side whiskers." A carousing, babbling, boasting, quarrel-seeking, guffawing brute who is your sworn friend after five minutes and spends the rest of his life saying nasty things about you and trying to ruin you. He can't hold still, is always rushing around making wagers, playing cards, plunging into adventures, or seeking to trade something for anything. "Guns, dogs, horses, everything is seen in terms of barter." Lies issue from his mouth like smoke from a chimney. As a past master of sharp dealing, he smells a rat at the first mention of dead souls, demands an explanation, and refuses to believe what he is told. "You're lying!" he chortles. And proposes, after a thousand other crazy combinations, that they play checkers for the dead souls. Chichikov, by this time utterly exhausted, agrees; but his opponent cheats, and a quarrel breaks out. Red-faced and brandishing his massive brier pipe, Nozdrev shouts for his servants to come and thrash his guest; and Chichikov only narrowly escapes, thanks to the opportune arrival of a police captain. This time he leaves empty-handed—not one dead soul in his bag.

His next move brings him face to face with the giant Sobakevich, who resembles "a medium-sized bear." "As though to complete the simile," writes Gogol, "he wore a suit of a color so like a bear's fur as to be indistinguishable from it; the garment's sleeves and trouser legs were inordinately long; he never looked where he put his feet and was constantly treading on other people's." Morose, powerful, bestial, and ill-tempered, Sobakevich—the opposite of Manilov—denigrates all his neighbors. His chief interest in life is grub. He does not eat, he devours.

"Have a taste of this saddle of mutton and kasha," he says to Chichikov. "It's an altogether different matter from the stews they cook up in those great lords' houses of yours, with the leftovers that have been lying around the market for four days! That was one fine invention of those French and German doctors! If I had anything to say about it, they'd all be hanged! They invented the diet—cure by hunger! Those little twerps who think they can dictate to Russian stomachs! No, it's all trickery. In my house things are different. When a goose or sheep or pig is served in my house, it's served whole. I'd rather have only two dishes to my meal, but have as much of them as my soul desires."

In Sobakevich's home, thus, it is the soul, not the stomach, that is restored by food. For him, physical nourishment replaces spiritual sustenance. Why should he be surprised by Chichikov's curious proposition? Dead souls? Sure, he's got some. And without batting an eyelid he asks a hundred rubles apiece for them. The goggling Chichikov protests.

"Why are you bargaining?" asks Sobakevich. "That's not much to pay. Anybody else would try to put one over on you by fobbing any old thing off on you and calling it souls, but I offer only the best-quality goods. Even the ones who aren't craftsmen are good stout fellows. See for yourself. Here, take Mikheyev the cartwright, for example. Every one of his coaches had springs. And not like they make them in Moscow, either, the ones that don't last you more than an hour. No, good solid stuff, he made! And he upholstered the insides and painted them himself, too. And Stepan Probka the joiner. I'll wager both my arms you won't find anybody like him! What strength! And Milyushkin the brickmaker, who could put up a chimney anywhere. And Maxim Telyatnikov! Why, he'd make you a pair of boots with one stroke of his awl and every pair was perfection. And never touched a drop of alcohol!"

"Yes; but permit me, please," Chichikov finally manages to protest, trying to stem the tide of the seemingly endless flood of words; "why are you giving me a list of all their good points? Since they're dead, all that's no use to me. A corpse can't even prop up a fence, as the saying goes."

"Yes, of course they're dead," replies Sobakevich, as though he had forgotten that detail. "Besides," he goes on, "what good are the ones who are still listed as living? Men? No, you might as well call them flies!"

"At least they still exist," says Chichikov, "while the others are only a memory!"

"Ah, no! Not just a memory! Let me tell you about Mikheyev. You won't find anyone to touch him. A colossus; he couldn't even get through the door to this room!"

In the end, Chichikov beats Sobakevich down from one hundred to two and a half rubles apiece.

After Sobakevich, he turns to Plyushkin the miser, whose old-woman's face, keen eye, and filthy smock rather surprise him. This man's wealth looks like poverty. His addiction to money is such that he cannot bring himself to spend a single farthing on his estate. He has become impermeable to all human sentiment, has broken with his friends and children, and lives alone with his columns of sums. He lets his peasants starve. All his servants have to share the unique pair of boots kept in the front hall. "When one was called, he would hop across the courtyard barefoot and put on the boots before entering the room," Gogol writes. Moreover, "Plyushkin had already forgotten how rich he was, but he remembered very distinctly that a decanter containing a few drops of liquor stood in a particular back corner of a shelf of the buffet, with a secret mark on it so he could tell when any of his people touched it."

The old man is delighted at the prospect of selling dead souls. Now, here is a transaction after his own heart. A bit of air in exchange for good, ringing, singing cash. He bargains fiercely, however; and Chichikov finally buys not only dead souls from him, but "souls in flight"—in other words, live peasants who have disappeared from the estate and are hiding out somewhere where no authority can find them. For Chichikov, souls dead or souls fled, it's all one to him as long as he doesn't have to feed them and their names are still on the census books.

Back at the inn, weary but rather pleased with himself, he dines on

suckling pig, goes to bed, and sleeps "with the wonderful sleep that is
the attribute of those happy mortals who have no acquaintance with
hemorrhoids, fleas, or overintelligence."[6] The next morning, he wakes
in fine fettle, sits down at his desk, and draws up deeds of sale and lists
of names so they can be notarized as quickly as possible. He performs
this piece of drudgery with the delight of an artist finishing a masterpiece.

"When he glanced over his lists," writes Gogol, "these muzhiks who
were once real muzhiks, working, plowing, getting drunk, and stealing
from their masters—or perhaps plain, honest folk—he experienced a
strange sensation which he did not understand himself. Each list seemed
to have a character of its own, transmitted to all the muzhiks constitut-
ing it. Most of Korobochka's muzhiks had both surnames and nick-
names. Plyushkin's list was remarkable for the brevity of the appella-
tions. Sobakevich's collection was exceptionally complete and detailed.
Not one peasant virtue was omitted. One was a "good joiner," another
"knew his trade and did not drink." These details gave the lists an indefinable immediacy. One could imagine that the muzhiks had been
alive only yesterday. After studying their names at length, Chichikov
felt overcome with affection, and sighed, "My good friends, how many
you are! What did you do, my good fellows, in your lifetimes? How did
you live?"

Chichikov's tenderness is short-lived. Placed at the head of a legion
of the dead, he finds himself grown rich and powerful. Also, he does
not consider himself guilty. What harm has he done? He had acted as
a good citizen, obeying the regulations contained in òfficial documents
to the letter. If the administration deems the muzhiks he has bought to
be alive, then they are alive, regardless of the masses sung for the repose
of their souls and the crucifixes in the cemeteries. Similarly, if through
some scribe's error the occasional hale and hearty peasant is entered in
the column of the defunct, then he has ceased to exist, though you may
see him plowing in the field. For Chichikov, the authority in matters of
life and death is not God's census but that of the civil service. The
passage from life to death is not a scandalous trauma, not a manifestation of the will of God, but a secretarial game directed by the hand of
an accountant. The frontier between presence and absence is blurred,
being and non-being exchange valences; and, having achieved this
monstrous confusion, Chichikov consolidates his triumph, plump, smiling, and alert.

However, the subterfuge of the honest "acquirer" is about to be revealed: Nozdrev the chatterbox accidentally lets the cat out of the bag; then Korobochka comes to town at dawn to inquire into "the current price for dead souls in the region" and to find out whether she hasn't let hers go "for a third of their value." Tongues begin to wag. Solemn civil servants are amazed. Respectable ladies begin to suspect Chichikov of hatching some dark scheme to kidnap the mayor's daughter. The whole hamlet shakes off its millennial lethargy. Disturbed by the earthquake, rustic gentry who had been hibernating in their lairs like marmots stick their noses out of doors and blink in the light of day. People appear in local drawing rooms who had not been seen for years and were presumed dead. Twice the usual number of carriages rattle through the streets. Panic mounts in men's minds. They lose weight. They try to understand. "All these investigations carried out by the civil servants," Gogol writes, "served only to establish that they knew nothing about Chichikov and that Chichikov must nevertheless be someone or something. But was he someone who should be arrested and thrown into prison for his evil intentions, or someone who could arrest and throw all of them into prison as suspects?"

Chichikov has palmed so many cards, compromised so many landowners, and duped so many civil servants that his small pink person now inflates, floats into the atmosphere, and balances perilously in the mists of minds. The apparently most rational people hold consultations to decide whether he is acting for his own or the general welfare, is an enemy of the human race or an emissary of the State on a secret mission, should be prosecuted or appealed to for protection. The postmaster is convinced he is none other than the famous bandit Captain Kopeyekin and tells the criminal's story on every occasion: the only hitch is that Kopeyekin has one arm and one leg, while Chichikov has a full set of both. Some go even further and imagine that Chichikov is Napoleon escaped from St. Helena—or even that he is Antichrist. The fable grows. The illiterate and superstitious common folk begin to mutter. The prosecuting attorney is so upset by all the fuss that he dies. When the doctor comes rushing in to bleed him, he finds himself attending an inanimate corpse. "It was only then that the lawyer was perceived to have a soul; no doubt it was modesty that had prevented him from making it known while he lived."

Doors are already beginning to be closed to Chichikov, who, sensing the gathering storm, packs his bags, and, like Khlestakov in *The In-*

spector General, runs away in a troika, leaving behind him a little world in turmoil, the result of his fantasy.

At the end of the play, the author remained in town to report on the rattled condition of his villain's prey; but in *Dead Souls* he follows his hero out onto the Russian roads. His troika rushes along so swiftly that it must be drawn by supernatural horses with hoofs of fire. The landscape streams past on either side, sliced by the wind of his headlong course. The spokes of the wheels blur, there is nothing to be seen but an empty circle.

"And you, Russia," Gogol writes; "are not you, too, hurtling along like one of those swift troikas nothing can catch? The road smokes beneath you, the bridges thunder, everything is overtaken, everything is left behind. The observer stops as though struck by a divine miracle: wasn't that a bolt of lightning that just streaked down from heaven? What is the meaning of this terrifying rush? What is the mysterious power of these courses never seen before? O coursers, sublime coursers! What tempests are hidden in your manes? Is there a listening ear in every nerve of yours? You hear, coming from above, a familiar song, and then, swelling out your chests of bronze, your hoofs hardly touching the ground, merging into three taut lines cleaving the air, off you fly as though driven by the inspiration of God. O Russia, where are you racing? Answer! There is no answer. The little bells jingle prettily. The shredded air moans and sweeps into a hurricane. Everything on earth is abandoned in your flight, and other nations, other lands, glance sidewise at the troika and leap aside to let it pass."

In reality, this lyrical outpouring, which ends the book, is a snare. It was not easy both to pluck Chichikov from the fire of his just deserts and, at the same time to conceal the heinousness of his escape from the readers. The mad speed of the troika does indeed help Chichikov to get away, but it also distracts our attention from the motives for his flight. But, after all, how could human laws pretend to punish the devil's delegate? He had to whirl away from his accusers in a cloud of dust and a jingle of bells, weightless, elusive, anonymous, and ready for his next adventure. His greatest feat, moreover, lay not in pulling the wool over the eyes of the little town of N., but in misleading the censors in St. Petersburg! Lulled by the patriotic tone of the final pages of the "poem," those gentlemen never noticed how the villain's magical disappearance undermines traditional morality. Even more amazingly, they failed to see anything odd in the parallel drawn between Russia and a troika carrying off a crook! The magic of words enables Chichikov to abscond scot free, and the author to get away with the whole escapade.

The poetic hymn to the troika is not the only flight of fancy in the book. Gogol often punctuates his narrative with explosions of eloquence, exalted meditations like musical interludes in a spoken text. It has been estimated that these digressions occupy one eighth of the book, and ten of them are wholly lyrical. In the course of Chichikov's adventures, the author celebrates, *inter alia,* the delights of stagecoach travel, the freshness of childhood memories, the mysterious bond linking him to Russia, the agonies of an author compelled to describe monsters when his whole heart yearns to sing of cherubim. He is impatiently awaiting the moment when, having finished with the hideous masks around him, he can at last, like Ivanov, paint only features illuminated by the coming of Christ. He wrote:

"Happy the author who discards the flat and repulsive figures that amaze by their painful reality, for the sake of incarnations of the nobler human virtues; who selects one or two exceptional beings from the great whirlwind of shifting images that surround him daily. He is proclaimed a great, universal poet, esteemed above all other earthly geniuses as the eagle towers above all other high-flying birds. But a hard life and a hard fate lie in store for the writer who dares to talk about the things which are continually before our eyes but which, in our indifference, we do not see: that sludge of ghastly and bothersome trivia which complicates our existences; the full horror of the cold, petty, disintegrated characters that swarm across our tedious and bitter earthly paths. He will never know public acclaim, never see eyes brimming with tears of gratitude, never arouse that unqualified admiration in human souls; it is not to him that the girl of sixteen, her head whirling with hero worship, will fly; nor will he escape the censure of his hypocritical and insensitive contemporaries, who call the creations of his mind base and ignominious, relegate him to a humiliating corner, consign him to the ranks of the authors who insult mankind, attribute his characters' morals to himself, and deny him everything: heart, soul, and the divine spark of talent. As for me: impelled by a supernatural power, I am destined to walk still many a mile with my strange hero's arm linked in mine, observing the multiple and stormy proceedings of life through the lens of a laughter evident to all, and a tear that no one sees. It is still remote, that day when, yielding to the pressure of a force surging from a different source, the formidable torrent of inspiration will burst from

my brow girt with sacred terror and light, and humans trembling in awe
will hear the majestic thunder of another language."

Having thus forewarned his readers of the moral bliss awaiting them
in the second volume of *Dead Souls,* if only they will have courage to
wade through the muck of the first, Gogol returns to his story: *"En
route! En route!* Disappear, thou wrinkle come to furrow my brow, thou
austere darkness drawn down over my face. Let us plunge back into life,
with its deafening din and jangle, and see what Chichikov is up to now."

But at the end of the same chapter[7] comes another digression, this
time marvelously prosaic. Leaving Chichikov and his dead souls in the
middle of the night, the author is suddenly fascinated by a lighted window. Behind it is a lieutenant of whom we know nothing and whom we
will never meet again, trying on a pair of boots he has just bought in
Ryazan. "It was a fact, those boots were well made, and he went on
raising his foot and studying the superbly elegant cut and fine finish of
the heel for a long time."

Similarly, just as the "Chichikov scandal" is about to break, a group
of people who seem to have wandered on stage by mistake, lost,
phantomlike, on the point of dissolving and whirling away in a gust of
wind, flow into view at the turning of a phrase: "Some Syzoy Paf-
nutyevich and MacDonald Karlovich, of whom no one had ever heard,
appeared; a tall, gaunt individual was seen in the drawing rooms, unbelievably tall, with a bullet hole in his hand." In conversation with the
mayor's daughter, Chichikov chatters away about a hundred people of
absolutely no importance, whose names clatter down like so many pearls
from a broken necklace. The apogee of verbal inanity, however, is
achieved by two voluble ladies—the "charming lady" and the "lady who
is charming in every respect"—exchanging, in total disorder, their views
on the latest fashions and Chichikov's indescribable conduct. The echoes
of their cackling soon ring through the town from end to end. Thus, two
very peripheral characters come to affect the destinies of the central
figures; and there is a swarm of such ancillary figures in the book, with
their various mugs, tics, and odors. Some are defined in a few words,
such as the mayor, who "wore the Cross of St. Anne around his neck,
was a good fellow, and sometimes even did embroidery on net," or the
lawyer, "who had thick black eyebrows and one eye—the left—that
winked as though to say, 'Just come along into the next room, old chap,
and I'll tell you something rather out of the ordinary.'"

Gogol's hallucinating deformation affects objects as well as people.

They participate in the characters' lives and help to place them. Chichikov's "silver and enamel" snuffbox, at the bottom of which lie two violets "for the scent," his "speckled maroon" coat, the roast chicken which is his traveling fare, his flask of Cologne water and his many-compartmented little chest—all of them, mysteriously, explain the man. The house of Sobakevich, the brute, is the image of its owner: solid, thickset, weatherproof; and in the drawing room hang engravings of Greek heroes, all of whom have "thighs so thick and mustaches so long that you shivered at the very sight of them." In a cage, a white-speckled blackbird "bore a strong resemblance to Sobakevich." And the longer Chichikov studies the room the more he becomes persuaded that every object in it, "by its robust, chunky, and graceless aspect, offered a similarity with the master of the place. In one corner a potbellied walnut desk sitting on four twisted feet looked very much like a flesh-and-blood bear. Table, armchairs, and chairs—all were of a hefty and un-manageable style. In a word, every object, every chair bottom seemed to be saying, 'Me too: I'm Sobakevich!' 'I look like Sobakevich too!' "

The home of Manilov, the mild-tempered idler and impotent dreamer, reveals its owner's negligence at first glance: "A gorgeous piece of silk, which must have cost a fortune, covered the handsome drawing-room furniture, but there hadn't been enough of it, so two armchairs were still covered with a piece of woven stuff. For years the master had been warning his guests every time they came: 'Don't sit on those chairs, they aren't ready yet.' Some of the rooms were still empty, although he had said to his wife on their honeymoon, 'Sweetheart, I must think of furnishing that room, at least provisionally. . . .' "

The study of Nozdrev, the braggart and playboy, is also a kind of visualisation of his soul. Not a book to be seen, no sign of a newspaper, only sabers, swords, guns, a pipe collection, a hubble-bubble with an amber mouthpiece, and a "tobacco pouch embroidered especially for him by a countess who had become infatuated with him at a posting station."

Plyushkin's overgrown grounds, the dilapidated isbas of his muzhiks, his scraps of paper, worn nibs, the bits of candle he collects, and his inkwell filled with a turbid fluid and the floating cadavers of flies, tell us more about his miserliness than any confession. And Korobochka's zany rattletrap stuffed with cushions and victuals might have been secreted by that thrifty, thickheaded female as a cocoon by some loathsome larva.

Gogol may be severe with the mighty, but he is no more indulgent to the small fry. Petrushka, Chichikov's servant, is a lazy, evil-smelling, taciturn wretch; Salifan, the coachman, has no brain at all; Uncle Mityaye and Uncle Minyaye are equally doltish; and then there are the two muzhiks in the first chapter, trying to judge the solidity of the carriage wheels; and Plyushkin's valet, Proshka, who is "as stupid as a goose," and Pelagya, the little serf girl on the Korobochka estate "who can't tell right from left": not one peasant or servant escapes the author's derision. There is no affection in his laughter. He looks down upon people of every station in life and, in a word, does not like his fellow man. His mission, he believes, is to hold up their vices to ridicule so that they will mend their ways.

He is always castigating men, but he never says a word against their institutions. For him, serfdom is a respectable and useful tradition. But although he is not aware of it, this succession of sneers points to a dire moral: by showing the bestial imbecility of the muzhiks and the patriarchal insensitivity of their masters, he has condemned the entire social structure of Russia. The Proshkas, Pelagyas, and Selifans are the pitiful products of serfdom. The full horror of their condition springs to the reader's eyes through the merry fable of *Dead Souls*.

Gogol longs to paint angels but can draw nothing but swine; Gogol is a staunch conservative but cannot help giving a subversive twist to everything he writes. He is an architect with the heart of a demolitions foreman; and he knows it, and it makes him miserable. No one ever tried harder to justify himself—in his prefaces, open letters, notices, and commentaries of every description. Speaking of the idea behind *Dead Souls,* he wrote in *Selected Passages from My Correspondence with My Friends:*

"None of my readers ever suspected that when they laughed at my heroes they were laughing at me. In me, there was no outstanding vice that overshadowed all the rest, just as I had no shining virtues that could give greater dimension to my person. I did, however, possess a complete collection of every possible nastiness, but all in small doses; there were so many of them that I have never seen the like in any human being. God gave me a personality in which there was a little of everything. As I progressed and learned my faults, a great inspiration came to me from above, a growing desire to be rid of them. I began to endow my characters with my own vilenesses, in addition to their personal turpitudes. This is how it worked: I would take one of my failings and pursue it by giving it a different shape and placing it in a different station in life; I sought to picture it in the features of some mortal enemy who had cruelly offended me; I riddled him with wrath and scathing sarcasm; I struck at him with everything I could lay hold of. If anyone had seen the monsters my pen first engendered for my own eyes, he would surely have shuddered. Do not ask me why the first part of my work had to be entirely devoted to baseness, and why every one of my characters, without exception, is lowly: the following volumes will bring you the answer, and that is all! This book is a child born prematurely. But don't imagine, after this confession, that I am the same kind of monster as my characters. No, I do not resemble them. I love the good and seek it. Already I have divested myself of many of my faults by passing them on to my heroes, have ridiculed the faults in them, and forced others to laugh at them."

The apologetics written after the book was published are assuredly subject to caution: he had no such moralizing intentions when he joyfully set out to write *Dead Souls*. It was only gradually, when he began asking himself what was the purpose of his work, that the idea of this double spiritual operation came to him. It was comforting to imagine he was working simultaneously for the regeneration of his contemporaries, by compelling them to laugh at themselves, and for his own, by embedding each of his shortcomings in an imaginary person. We may doubt whether he actually achieved his self-purification in this manner. But he is certainly telling the truth when he claims he has projected the various aspects of his own personality onto the characters of *Dead Souls*. Invested with his own sins, they become his scapegoats. Every one of them is a fragment of himself. "The history of my soul," he wrote. Its geography, rather—a pictorial *mea culpa*.

To one he gave his boastfulness, love of lying, and morbid dissimulation; to another his covetousness for material things, his vast gluttony; to a third his penchant for idleness and daydreaming. But none of his creations received his unfortunate propensity for preaching to his fellows! The one person missing from his galaxy of ghouls is the false father-confessor who believes himself at all times inspired by God. Perhaps he did not regard this feature as a weakness? Indeed he did not, since in his own words *Dead Souls* is primarily a lesson for erring mortals. In depicting all these figures, he also, of course, borrowed psychological details from friends and acquaintances, but they were details that struck him only to the extent that they reinforced his own attitudes.

He observed what was going on around him far less than what went on inside him. It is his own inner world that emerges in *Dead Souls*. Heroes and walk-ons, humans and animals, furniture and landscapes— their essential features, drawn from within himself, all have something in common: something heavy, lethargic, and rotten.

This "family" look is further accentuated by an admirable unity of style. Whether it is a face or a box he is describing, the gesture of a hand or the outline of some foliage, he does it with the same incisive precision, the same wealth of vocabulary. Naturally, no translation can render the truculence of his dense, undulating language supercharged with adjectives. However faithful the adaptation, the colors lose all their brilliance passing from Russian to French.[8]

All the metaphors the author has scattered through his book share one peculiarity: they open onto images having no direct bearing on the story. They are like glimpses into a secondary universe, thumbnail sketches all around the sides of the painting. Speaking of the mayor's party at the beginning of the book, for example, Gogol writes:

"The black frock coats swooped and buzzed, individually or in clusters, like flies on a dazzling white sugar loaf an old servant woman is breaking up and separating into sparkling white segments near an open window on a hot July day. The children gather around, peering intently at the motions of her rough hands as she raises the hammer, while a swarm of flies borne on the light air come boldly in and, as absolute masters of the place, take advantage of the old woman's acute near-sightedness and the sun that blinds her even more, to spread themselves all over the succulent morsels, sometimes alone and sometimes in throngs."[9]

The reader abruptly leaves the mayor's *soirée* and finds himself, to his amazement, in an unfamiliar country house in midsummer, watching an old woman break sugar. Or, as he is rolling along in a carriage with Chichikov in the direction of Sobakevich's home, an unlikely comparison brings a balalaika player to mind:

"When his carriage drew near the entrance, he saw two faces which had appeared at the window almost simultaneously: one was that of a woman wearing a bonnet, as long and narrow as a cucumber; the other was a man's, and as round and broad as one of those Moldavian vegetable marrows they call *gorlyanki,* which are used in Russia to make light, two-stringed balalaikas, the pride and joy of the nimble young peasant of twenty, the village cock who crows and ogles the pretty girls with the milky throats who cluster around him to listen while he scrapes away at his humble instrument."[10]

And then there are the two ladies who are turned into little girls in the same sentence. "The two ladies clutched at each other's hands, embraced, and uttered cries of joy, like two little schoolgirls whose names have not yet told them that the father of one is inferior in rank and fortune to the father of the other."[11]

Or there are Plyushkin's eyes, from which we suddenly withdraw our attention only to fasten it upon some mice. "His small eyes, still keen, ran under the tufted bar of his eyebrows like mice that venture their pointed noses out of their dark holes, watchful, ears pricked, mustaches bristling, to see whether the tomcat or some scalawag of a boy is not hiding somewhere close by, and mistrustfully sniff the air."[12]

Then there is this sky of an indefinable hue which leads us by a curious detour into a military garrison: "The weather itself had obligingly coincided with the setting: the day was neither luminous nor gloomy, it was that light gray shade seen on the threadbare uniforms of garrisoned soldiers—a peacetime army, all in all, one that only gets drunk on Sundays."[13]

This avalanche of metaphor may carry the reader away from his everyday world and bring a smile to his lips, but it is in dialogue that Gogol's brilliance gleams brightest. Chichikov, as we have seen, changes tone to suit his circumstances; but every one of the people he talks to has a language of his own. Whether they are protagonists or onlookers, whatever they say is a direct expression of their characters. Sobakevich's crude and brutal utterances have nothing in common with the mellifluous and pretentious discourse of Manilov; and that in turn is very distinct from the giddy braying of Korobochka or the sere and suspicious retorts of Plyushkin. The muzhiks, too, have their own juicy jargon, the opposite of that of the ladies of the town, whose idle prating clearly amuses the author:

"I have just sent my sister a length of material, a love of a thing, a pure wonder. I cannot begin to describe it. Imagine, my dear, stripes so thin, thin, as thin as your mind can imagine them, on a blue background, and between the stripes eyes and paws, eyes and paws, eyes and paws . . ."

"It sounds quite loud, my dear!"

"No, no; not at all loud!"

"Yes, it is, too, loud!"

"Oh, by the way: my compliments, they're not wearing ruffles any longer!"

"Impossible!"

"No; they're wearing loops instead."

"Hardly very beautiful, loops."

"Yes, it's loops now, nothing but loops; loops on capes, loops on sleeves, loops on shoulders, loops on borders, loops everywhere.' "[14]

What reader, before opening *Dead Souls,* could have imagined there were so many forms of banality? With cruel delectation the author spreads before our eyes his catalogue of triviality. But when he has reached the end, he is no longer sure exactly what he meant to say by it all. He thought he was ridiculing the devil, but has celebrated his triumph instead; he was seeking to glorify Russia's greatness, but has exhibited all her pettiness instead; he was claiming his right to instruct his brothers, but has diverted them instead, and here they are laughing instead of hanging their heads in shame.

Nevertheless, despite its blurred line, its contradictions and digressions, *Dead Souls* is Gogol's most finished work. It is a self-contained universe, hermetically sealed and bursting with mysteries. The moment one enters it, one is struck by the stifling atmosphere and artificial lighting. Objects and faces are deformed. Voices resound as though in a barrel. At every step a trap door may gape. When the reader leaves Chichikov, flying away in his troika to a hypothetical hell, he has some difficulty in reinserting himself into the real world. He will never see people or things quite the same as before. A sixth sense has been given to him, enabling him to perceive the chaos behind the screen. He has become a habitué of the irrational. Why did he like *Dead Souls?* The question has no meaning. His attachment transcends reason. This dense book with its superimposed intentions, comic on the surface and tragic underneath, epic poem and satirical pamphlet, satire and nightmare, confession and exorcism, will not let itself be defined or classified on a library shelf. Under its maleficent halo, it reigns in the highest sphere of literature, between *Don Quixote* and the *Divine Comedy.* A curious fraternity unites those people, all over the world, who have prized from its pages, of an evening, good reason to laugh, and to shift uneasily in their chairs.

Six years had passed since the first performance of *The Inspector General.* Six years of silence. Suddenly came *Dead Souls.* The publica-

tion of this book was like a hard kick at an anthill. The anonymous host
of readers were shaken to their boots. The stacks of copies shrank in the
booksellers' shops. The book's partisans and detractors met horn to
horn in the drawing rooms, with even greater violence, perhaps, than
after the opening of Gogol's play. People were for or against Chichikov,
for or against Gogol.

"An astonishing book," Herzen wrote in his diary for June 11, 1842;
"a bitter reproach to the Russia of today, but there is yet hope. Where
our eyes can pierce the dirty fog and exhalations of the dung heap, we
perceive a hardy and vigorous national spirit. His portraits are amazingly successful, life is shown in all its fullness. Sadness reigns in
Chichikov's world."

The critics were promptly divided. Gogol's habitual foes found themselves shoulder to shoulder, facing the serried ranks of the determined
champions of gogolism.

For Bulgarin, all-powerful director of the *Northern Bee, Dead Souls*
was a superficial, unpolished piece of work, a "caricature of Russian
reality," and its author a pamphleteer, "inferior to Paul de Kock." In
The Reading Library Senkovsky scoffed at Gogol for presenting this
incoherent and vulgar tale as a "poem": "Poem? Really, now! Paul de
Kock for subject, Paul de Kock for style. Poor, poor writer who mistakes Chichikov for real life!" Page after page, the critic tore the book
apart, picking up errors of syntax, solecisms, pleonasms, improprieties.

Polevoy, in *The Russian Messenger,* defending his romantic and
patriotic concept of literature, refused to qualify the novel as a "work of
art." *"Dead Souls,"* he wrote, "is a crude caricature. The characters are
all, without exception, improbable, exaggerated, and form a collection
of repulsive curs and sheer imbeciles. The book is so overloaded with
descriptions that you sometimes throw it involuntarily to the floor."

The critics who were friendly to Gogol, on the other hand—whether
of European or of Slavophile persuasion—broke into a paean of praise.
In the former clan, Belinsky hailed *Dead Souls* as an immortal masterpiece and sneered at the puny hacks who dared to criticize the author
for superficiality of portrayal or flaws of style. With his usual vehemence, he wrote:

"In the heyday of pettiness, mediocrity, nonentity, and incompetence,
among all those dried prunes and raindrops of literature, among so many
infantile outlines, puerile thoughts, and false feelings born of a patriotism
of the Pharisees and sentimental condescension, suddenly, like a cool-

ing thunderbolt in the stifling and pestilential drought, there appears a purely Russian work, national, drawn from the hidden folds of the life of the people, as true as it is patriotic, ruthlessly unveiling reality and animated by a passionate, instinctive, visceral love for that fertile seed of Russian life; a work of indefinable artistic quality in both conception and execution, in the personalities of its characters and the details of Russian behavior it describes, and lastly, in the profundity of thought on every level, social, public, historical."

And Belinsky congratulated himself, to the readers of the *Annals of the Fatherland,* upon being the first to hail the author's great gifts. The award he thus publicly bestowed upon himself was not at all to the liking of Gogol's friends in the opposite camp. In *The Muscovite,* Shevyrev began with a direct personal attack upon Belinsky, comparing him to a screeching and gesticulating pygmy: "Overjoyed to have the opportunity to pay himself a compliment by complimenting a great talent, he [Belinsky] plants himself in front of the book, puffs up his skinny body to hide it from your sight, and then shows it to you afterward as though trying to convince you that it was he who had told you about it in the first place and without him you would never even have noticed it." Shevyrev then goes on to praise the realism of *Dead Souls* and to forgive the coarseness of one or two passages for the sake of the novelist's deeper intentions, which were—he had it on good authority— moral, patriarchal, and patriotic. The lyrical digressions filled with national feeling pleased him best of all. Unlike Belinsky, he saw no social satire in the poem: it was a hymn to eternal Russia. Even the most hideous figures were pardonable to him, because they were Russian and because, behind them, one could already glimpse the promised rebirth.

"Apart from its artistic value," he wrote, "a work of this kind can also claim our attention as an act of patriotism. Besides, the negative figures of the first part will certainly be followed by more harmonious subsequent apparitions. We believe the author capable of giving far greater scope to his fancy. Then it will embrace not only Russia but all nations."

Pletnyev, writing under a pseudonym in *The Contemporary,* awarded the author the title of foremost living Russian writer, and approved his having "embodied the phenomena of his inner life in reality." He also states that the volume was only a "curtain raiser intended to elucidate the hero's strange progression."

But it was among the Aksakovs that enthusiasm reached fever pitch. Aksakov senior read *Dead Souls* twice straight through to himself and once aloud to his family. His son Konstantin, with the ardor of a neophyte Slavophile, wrote a dithyrambic article on the book, which he vainly tried to publish in *The Muscovite* and ultimately brought out as a separate leaflet at his own expense. With the awkwardness and extremism of youth, he proclaimed that *Dead Souls* was a resurrection of the classical epic and that Gogol was to be compared with Homer and Shakespeare. Preserve us from our friends! Seeking to promote his idol's fame, the virgin critic only succeeded in arousing sarcasm on all sides.

Even those who thought very highly of Gogol's ability rejected this tribute as excessive when paid to a living author. Belinsky in particular, as a European, could not bear to find himself in the company of a Slavophile where his opinion of a book was concerned. He had his own reasons for esteeming the author and would not accept anyone else's. Applause issuing from a political position other than his own was more intolerable to him than censure. Although he had already expressed his views on *Dead Souls,* he now wrote two supplementary and sarcastic articles in which he demolished Konstantin Aksakov's arguments line by line.

Dead Souls had nothing to do with classical epic poetry, or Gogol with Homer: "As a poem, *Dead Souls* is diametrically opposed to *The Iliad. The Iliad* is the apotheosis of life; *Dead Souls* the debasement, the corruption of life." But after he had praised Gogol for "denigrating" this life, or in other words, for condemning the country's iniquitous social structure, Belinsky went on to ask whether the author was not about to betray the cause of liberalism in the coming volumes: "Who knows what the sequel of *Dead Souls* will be? We are promised creatures that have never yet existed, to whom the great men of other lands will be as puppets."

Thus each person found what he wanted in the book: an attack upon serfdom, a glorification of Russia and her mission, a realistic portrayal of the landowning class, a nightmare vision with no foundation in fact, an insult to the fatherland and its government, a hilarious farce with no political overtones, a profoundly Christian poem, a work of the devil . . . Gogol's allies—liberals and conservatives, Europeans and Slavophiles—quarreled to see which should have the honor of electing him champion of their cause; while his opponents refused to call him a great

Russian author or even a respectful subject of the sovereign. Meanwhile, like Chichikov fleeing the gossip of that little town of N., the author was speeding away from St. Petersburg and the tempest he had stirred up there.

Every turn of the wheels removed him farther from the battlefield. Once across the frontier, he ceased to hear the bugle calls and backbiting of his compatriots. He might even believe *Dead Souls* had been greeted with universal indifference. Should he worry or rejoice? Happy hamlets, calm tile-roofed towns rolled past, one after the other, through the spinning dust. There were no bedbugs in the inns. What peace upon the roads of Prussia!

Part Three

1.   Squaring the Circle

When Gogol reached Berlin, on June 8, 1842,[1] his first idea was to go on to Düsseldorf, where Zhukovsky, now a father, was living quietly with his young wife and baby daughter. But Mrs. Zhukovsky's nerves were said to be very bad and the family might well have left for some health resort.

Seated in his hotel room, Gogol pored over the map and was discouraged by the distance between Berlin and Düsseldorf. He did not want to make such a journey for nothing, and decided instead to send the poet a copy of *Dead Souls* along with one of those ambiguous letters, half humility and half pride, which were his speciality.

"Every day, every hour," he wrote, "brings greater clarity and solemnity to my heart. My travels and withdrawal from society were not aimless or meaningless. They have contributed to the imperceptible edification of my being. Purer than mountain snows and clearer than the sky must be my soul: only then shall I have acquired strength to undertake my sacred journey, only then will the enigma of my life be resolved. . . . I send you *Dead Souls*. It is the first part. Compared with those that are to follow, it is as the portico a provincial architect builds hastily in front of the palace, a building that, according to the plan, will have colossal proportions. For the love of God, let me know your comments. Be as severe and ruthless as possible. You know how essential that is to me. . . . Don't read without a pencil and scrap of paper within reach, and note down your observations immediately. Then, at the end of each chapter, write down your impressions of the whole of it. Then look at the relationship between the different chapters; and in the end, when you have finished the book, judge it as a whole. All these considerations, general and particular, are to be assembled by you, enclosed and sealed in a package, and sent to my address. No more precious gift could I receive at this moment."[2]

The next day, Gogol climbed into another stagecoach and left for Gastein, three days' drive away. The journey's end brought heavily forested, forbidding mountains, wonderfully pure air, a frothing river, a comfortable resort hotel, and, in a little house off to one side, poor Yasykov, condemned to a chaise longue by consumption. In less than a year, his condition had noticeably deteriorated. Movement had become an ordeal for him. A spasm of pain crossed his juvenile, swollen face from time to time. He greeted Gogol with joy and begged him to stay.

Every morning, Gogol went to take the waters and then for a little walk in the park, breathing deeply and daydreaming as he gazed at the clouds caught on the peaks; then he returned to the house to work. While jotting down notes for the sequel to *Dead Souls,* he polished up a few texts Prokopovich needed for the "Collected Works": *The Gamblers,* extracts from *The Vladimir Cross,* and especially *Upon Leaving the Theatre After the First Performance of a New Comedy,* the idea for which had clearly been given to him by Molière's *Critique de l'École des Femmes.* In this series of scenes he told of the agony of a comic author hiding in the vestibule of a theater and listening to the audience's comments upon his play: "Not one real character! Nothing but caricatures! An odious mockery of Russia!"

Gogol did not have to invent the words; he had heard them himself or read them in the papers after *The Inspector General.* Putting them in the mouths of his characters, he revealed the spitefulness and senselessness of the reproaches aimed at him. He also gave his reply, in the voice of one "Mr. B." or another "very modestly dressed man."

"I take comfort," said the latter, "in the simple thought that ignominy among us does not remain hidden or winked at; that here, before the eyes of all wellborn persons, it is buried in scorn; that a pen has been found which does not fear to unveil our base inclinations, however unflattering they may be to our national pride; and that there exists one generous government, which allows this to be shown to all to whom it should be shown, and in the full light of day."

"Mr. B." maintained that after such a play "there was no danger of losing respect for either civil servants or their duties, except those civil servants who performed their duties badly."

After the crowd leaves, the author reads the moral he has drawn from such contradictory reactions to his play: "Odd; what a pity nobody noticed the one honest character in my play. Yes, there was one honest and noble person there all the time. The honest and noble character was laughter. Nobody came forward to defend him. As a comic author, I have served him faithfully. Laughter is more profound and significant than we suppose. Not the laughter provoked by momentary annoyance or a bilious and unhealthy humor, and not the light laughter of superficial amusements; but that which surges up from the luminous inner nature of man, the place from which his source eternally springs afresh, the laughter that goes to the heart of things. The man who no longer fears anything else in the world, fears laughter. Only a profoundly good soul has the power of fresh, clear laughter. Courage, then; onward! Who knows? Maybe one day it will become plain to all that, following the same law that makes a proud, strong man weak and helpless in adversity and a weakling swell to become a giant in the depths of his difficulties, he who sheds many tears from the bottom of his soul is the same man as he who seems to laugh more than anybody else on earth."

When Gogol wrote these sentences he was alluding to *Dead Souls* at least as much as to *The Inspector General.* He was terribly anxious about the fate of his book. He thought his friends extremely negligent, because they were not forwarding daily every echo of response to the book. Anyone who thought him a greater writer was morally obliged to abandon his own concerns and serve him. As usual, he was not interested in praise, only censure—for criticism alone could show him the "temperature" of the country, and so help him to plot his future course.

It would certainly have been simpler for him to remain in Russia if he wanted to know his countrymen's reactions; but blows struck at such close quarters would have hurt too much. Distance did not save him from insults, but it softened them. He wanted to hear every last one, but he preferred to receive them weakened by their long trajectory. In that way, the pain he clamored for so loudly remained bearable and, at the same time, salutary. He pursued Zhukovsky, whose verdict was long in coming:

"If you had written even a single line about *Dead Souls,* you would have done me so much good and made so much joy in Gastein! Thus far I have heard nothing at all about the book apart from a few vague words of praise which, I swear it, displeased and irritated me more than ever. My sins! Show me my sins, my soul thirsts to know them. If you only knew what delight it is to discover in my heart some vice that has escaped me hitherto! No one could make me a finer present. Only you can tell me all, uninhibited by shyness or the fear of offending the author's vanity. Attack me, then, in the most sensitive places of my nervous system. It is so necessary for me! But perhaps you have already read the book; if so, many impressions will have faded from your memory. Never mind; give me a little more time, read it again, or at least skim over as many parts as you can."[3]

To Prokopovich: "Things are assuredly being said about *Dead Souls*. For friendship's sake, tell me about them, whatever they are and whatever their source. All are indispensable to me. You cannot conceive to what degree! It would be good, too, to mention the mouth that pronounced them."[4]

To Marya Balabin: "Note down everything you may hear about me. Ask your brothers, too, every time they hear some judgment referring to me—whether justified or unfair, pertinent or not—to write it down that very minute, while it is still hot, on a scrap of paper, and slip the paper into your letter."[5]

To Shevyrev: "You write that I must forge boldly ahead and pay no heed to any critic. But I cannot forge boldly ahead until I know what those critics say. Criticism gives me wings. After criticism, public reaction, and contradictory opinions, I always see my work more clearly. Even the criticisms of a Bulgarin are some use to me."[6]

He humbly accepted the violent attacks of Bulgarin, Senkovsky, and Grech, who told him his style was execrable and said he was inferior to Paul de Kock; but although he agreed with them that the book contained many imperfections, his faith in the moral virtue of his undertaking remained unshaken. As the articles, hostile or flattering, came in from Moscow and St. Petersburg, he saw more clearly the need to enlarge the scope of his work. He had painted the inferno of Russian life in all its horror; now he must draw the purgatory, peopled by bright, well-balanced souls with noble aspirations. And in a third volume, by which time he should have become altogether worthy of his subject, he would introduce his readers to the luminous certainties of paradise. A scheme so grand, he thought, could not be grasped by intellectuals. The opinions of critics and colleagues mattered less to him than those of the general public, for it was to save that general public that God had placed the pen in his hand.

"What distinguishes my works from those of other authors," he told one of his correspondents, "is that the whole world can judge them, every reader without exception, because the object of my writing is the life of every day and everyone."[7]

Gogol often discussed his great project with Yasykov (a confirmed Slavophile), who also considered that it was time to abandon satire and that the second part of *Dead Souls* ought to present, through a few positive characters, the ideal Russian man, the Russian of tomorrow. From the top of heaven God was watching over the painter of this titanic patriotic tableau, and when the time was ripe He would come to his aid in a manner that could not be foreseen. For the moment, his task was to purify himself by detaching himself from worldly goods and possessions. "Only the love born of earth and attached to earth, sensual love alone, bound to human faces, to a face and being visible to us, that love alone does not see Christ," Gogol wrote to Aksakov.[8]

He went to Munich in search of inspiration, but it was so hot there, so stifling, that he quickly returned to the bedside of the sick man at Gastein, who was impatiently awaiting him. Then came the mists and rains of autumn. The landscape darkened, the mountains drew together and brooded, the resort emptied. Gogol decided the waters had done him no good. Yasykov was bored. Why remain under this heavy gray sky when the sun was shining on Italy?

The two men set forth. Yasykov took one serf with him and limped about on crutches at the posting stations in agonized contortions. Gogol patiently nursed and encouraged his friend, "as a true Christian." Venice first; then Rome. They arrived on September 27, 1842. Ivanov, alerted by letter, had been able to rent—as before, at strada Felice 126—an apartment on the third floor for Gogol and one on the second for Yasykov. Another Russian, Fyodor Vasilyevich Chizhov, associate professor of mathematics at the University of St. Petersburg, was living on the fourth floor.

The weather was sunny, the air mild, the streets full of life; brown-robed monks jostled blowzy, noisy women on the pavements, and little donkeys brayed beneath the windows. Every evening they gathered in Yasykov's apartment; he received them, slouching in his armchair, feet dangling and head hunched into his shoulders. The painters Ivanov and Yordan arrived, their pockets filled with roasted chestnuts. The servant brought out a bottle of wine and glasses. But neither wine nor chestnuts stirred Gogol; he ate and drank like a man in a dream. Now and then, when spoken to, he would pull himself together and launch into a vehement declaration on the significance of his work; or, changing tone, tell a juicy anecdote. His friends were surprised by the crudeness of his language on those occasions and could no longer recognize in him the inspired defender of art and morality.[9] Then he lapsed into gloomy silence. "Why are you so stingy with your speech?" Yordan said. "We are all workers here. We work hard all day long. We come to see you in the evening, looking for a little distraction and relaxation, and you don't utter a word. Is it possible that the only way we can get anything out of you is by buying your books?" Gogol smiled, sighed, nibbled at a chestnut, and did not answer.

"I must confess," Yordan wrote, "that our meetings were frightfully tedious. We met, I do believe, solely because we had got into the habit of meeting and could not think of anywhere else to go." One day when they were all lounging there, mute, half asleep, and gloomy, around a half-empty bottle, Gogol said, "We might be a painting of the guards sleeping outside the sepulcher of the Lord." A little later he added, "Well, gentlemen, isn't it about time we ended this raucous discussion?"[10]

Winter came on. Yasykov sat shivering in his room. He was already angry with Gogol for dragging him so far for so little.

"He adores organizing things and keeping house, but he does it in such a chaotic and irrational way," Yasykov wrote to his parents. "I curl up, shiver, and yawn with cold: Gogol, his nose blue, walks around the room insisting that we are quite warm. He is forever being duped by the Italians; he believes they are honest and has the most extraordinary respect for them. He throws his money out the window, bustles and scurries about, fully convinced that he is cleverer than everybody else and buys everything cheaper, and is painfully cross when proved wrong."[11]

A little while later, Yasykov returned to Gastein, but not before a loan of two thousand rubles was extorted from him. The money sped swiftly away, and once again Gogol faced the abyss. The cost of printing *Dead Souls* had far exceeded the estimates, and the slender profits on sales were earmarked for the repayment of the author's debts in Moscow and St. Petersburg. As for the "Collected Works," Prokopovich, who was rich in good will but poor in experience, was coping badly. He made so many corrections that the original text was weakened, paid an exorbitant price for paper, and let himself be robbed over the size of the printing. In view of the expense of putting it out, the operation was unlikely to be a commercial success. The author and his friends might even have to pay part of the cost themselves. Where was the money to be found? The second volume of *Dead Souls* was still in limbo. Gogol's entire fortune amounted to one trunk, his papers, "a little linen and three cravats." He had long since given up his share of the Vasilyevka farm. His mother and sisters were hard up and kept hoping from year to year that he would be able to help them. As usual, he was reduced to his sole resource: his friends! The Almighty had given them the good fortune to count Gogol among their number; so they ought to relieve him of all care and ensure his survival, however long it might take him to produce a new masterpiece. For the sake of their souls, they must look after his body. All they would do for him on earth would be returned to them a hundredfold in the next world. To serve him was to serve God. He explained this in a long letter to Shevyrev:

"My work is far more important and significant than might have appeared from the early beginnings. And if the first volume, covering scarcely a tenth of the substance of the second, demanded five years of work—a fact that no one, of course, has taken into account—judge for yourself how long the second will take. I shall starve to death if I must, but I shall not produce a superficial and incomplete work. Read this letter together, you [Shevyrev], Pogodin, and Sergey Timofeyevich [Aksakov]. I ask you to make a sacrifice, and this sacrifice you must bear for my sake. Take charge of all my material cares for three or even four years. There are a thousand reasons—intimate, profound ones—why I may not and must not concern myself with such details. Trust in my word, that's all. Make whatever arrangements you please as regards the second printing and any subsequent ones, but do it so that I will have six thousand rubles a year for three years. That is the tightest possible budget I can make. I could have spent less by staying in one place, but travel and changes of scene are as necessary to me as my daily bread. My head is so strangely made that I must sometimes travel several hundred versts before I can drive one image out and find another, turn any light on my mental view, or embrace and bring together all the necessary elements. The money should be sent in two installments, on October 1 and April 1, three thousand rubles each time, to the address I give you. For God's sake don't let the payments be late.

Sometimes financial difficulties can become intolerable abroad. If sales from my books don't produce enough, think up something else. I trust I have accomplished enough thus far to deserve the chance to finish my work without needing to run around and worry myself with business, now that every minute is precious. If you have no other resources, just take up a collection for me. However the money is found, I shall accept it gratefully. Every kopeck tossed my way will be a prayer for the salvation of the giver's soul. But don't accept the kopeck if the one who throws it has had to go without for my sake. I must not deprive anyone of the necessities; for that I don't yet have the right."[12]

Did that mean he would avail himself of that "right" later, when his moral superiority, had become manifest to all? Fearing that Shevyrev might disobey orders, he repeated his instructions almost word for word in a letter to Aksakov: six thousand rubles a year for three years, at fixed intervals. "Go together, the three of you—you, Shevyrev, and Pogodin, and take care of my affairs for three years. It's a question of life and death for me. If you cannot find enough money by the due date, get it by charity if you must. I am a begger and am not ashamed to be."

Not content with ordering his friends to support him, he also exhorted them to advise his mother and sisters. Marya Ivanovna wrongly imagined that the success of *Dead Souls* was bringing in fabulous sums and her son would soon be able to rescue her from her poverty.

"Let her know that money is not flowing toward me in wide rivers and that the cost of printing the book is too high for me ever to grow rich from it," Gogol continued in his letter to Aksakov. "If there is any money left over, do send it to her; but I must tell you that with all her admirable qualities, *Maman* is a very poor manager, and her demands might be renewed every year. That is why intelligent advice from you could be worth more to her than financial aid."[13]

Pogodin, who was ill-disposed toward Gogol since Gogol's last stay in his home, was revolted by these two letters, while Aksakov and Shevyrev were deeply embarrassed by them. Although the book was selling well, there could be no profits from *Dead Souls* in the immediate future, or from the "Collected Works," which had only just been passed by the censor and would sell at such a high price (twenty-five* rubles a volume) that many readers might be discouraged. In addition, none of the three Muscovite friends was sufficiently rich in himself. Really, Gogol saw everything solely from his own point of view and never gave

* Approximately $30.

a thought to other people's problems. But a man of his talent could not be allowed to starve in a foreign country. Complaining and protesting, Aksakov took fifteen hundred rubles from his savings, borrowed an equal amount from a friend, Mrs. Demidov, and sent three thousand rubles off to Rome.

The "Collected Works," in four volumes, included a few previously unpublished texts, among which were a comedy (*Marriage*), some "scenic fragments" (*The Gamblers, The Lawsuit, The Servants' Hall, Upon Leaving the Theater,* etc.) and one short story, "The Overcoat."

The first performance of *Marriage* took place in St. Petersburg, on December 9, 1842, when Gogol was already in Rome. He learned without much bitterness that the play had been badly acted and badly received. It opened in Moscow on February 5, 1843, with Shchepkin and Zhibokini in the leading roles, and once again disconcerted the audience. *The Gamblers,* on the same bill as *Marriage,* was equally unpopular.

Gogol had spent nine years on *Marriage* (the first version was written in 1833 and the last in 1842), revising a scene here and adding a character there. He took great pains to pad out the fable (a hesitant suitor whom a friend tries to force into marriage escapes at the last minute rather than let himself be caught), but attached scant importance to his labors. For him, as for his friends, *Marriage* was no more than a little pleasantry that might divert the public. And indeed there is no common measure between it and a solitary, strange, and brilliant masterpiece such as *The Inspector General.* But, as though the author could write nothing really commonplace, even *Marriage* contains comic figures representing both a weakness of character and a social milieu.

This time, the society is that of the city merchants, so successfully exploited by Ostrovsky in the second half of the century. Here again Gogol appears as an innovator, opening the way for social comedy, which aims less at weaving a skillful plot than at raising the roofs. The suitors parading before Agafya, the girl to be married off, were to meet again fifty years later in certain of Chekhov's tales, while Podkolyosin, the hero, who thinks he ought perhaps to marry, doesn't dare take the plunge, and is only truly happy stretched out on his sofa in a dressing gown smoking his pipe—he, in his massive inertia and infinite indecision, is the ancestor of Goncharov's famous Oblomov. His friend, the enterprising Kochkaryov, decides to get him married without the help of Fyokla, the professional matchmaker, who had initially agreed to take him on as a client. He drags Podkolyosin along to see the girl and maneuvers until he has convinced her she will find nothing better, while simultaneously persuading her other suitors that she would make a hopeless match. These suitors include Yayishnitsa, treasury clerk and realist, who is interested in nothing but the dowry; Anuchkin, retired infantry officer, who wants a well-educated fiancée able to speak French; and Zhevakin, former naval officer in quest of a physically well-endowed mate. All are outdistanced by Podkolyosin, forcefully backed by Kochkaryov. But in his very instant of triumph, the happy bridegroom is beset by doubts: "His whole life, his entire existence, tied to somebody, and afterward nothing, no more regrets, no more escapes, nothing, it's all over, it's all said. . . ." He spies an open window, leaps into the street, climbs into a cab and—lay on, driver!—there he goes, off at a gallop. Like Khlestakov in *The Inspector General* and Chichikov in *Dead Souls.*

Despite the feebleness of the plot, this farce is so lively and well contrived that the characters of the shilly-shallying bridegroom, smooth-spoken friend, offended matchmaker, grotesque suitors, and limply distraught bride form a bouquet whose perfume is unforgettable.

Marriage is a situation play with a virtually non-existent plot, whereas *The Gamblers,* a short curtain raiser, is almost nothing but plot. Swiftness of movement, a succession of sudden reversals, and a surprise denouement make it a model of the genre. The theme of the joke is related, to be sure, to Regnard's *Gambler; Thirty Years, or, A Gambler's Life,* by Ducange and Dinaux; an anonymous Russian novel called *A Gambler's Life Described by Himself,* and many other Russian comedies of the day; but once again, Gogol's incisive dialogue gives the work the unimpeachable stamp of originality. It was Shchepkin who told the author the basic anecdote of a remarkable cardsharp who sets out to cheat some players he thinks are quite naïve, only to find he has fallen among crooks as expert as himself, proposes an alliance with them to pull off a "big one," and is left holding the bag. Manifestly written for no other purpose than to make an innocent public laugh, this playlet is yet another illustration of the Gogolian obsession with the deceiver. Always, as though unconsciously, he returns to the theme of the liar triumphant. One man fools people by passing himself off as an important person, another by buying up dead souls, a third by cheating at cards. And, as always, the whole business ends in the villains' flight. "They've already gone. Their coach and horses were waiting downstairs a half hour ago!"[14]

Duped, despoiled, and fuming, Ikharev, the cheated cheat, speaks the moral of his mishap: "There is always a scoundrel more scoundrelly than you! A beast who with one blow will bring down the whole edifice you have been working on for years! Oh, the devil take me! What a bunch of lies is this world!"

"The Overcoat," unlike these two frankly merry comedies, is possibly the most profound and moving of Gogol's short stories; it has a human touch, a sad humor, and a mysterious and disturbing quality. Dostoevsky took inspiration from its compassion for the meek in *Poor Folk, Humiliated and Offended,* and so many of his other novels. "We all came out of Gogol's 'Overcoat,'" he wrote later, speaking of himself and his contemporaries. The tale is based on a true story told to Gogol by a group of friends around 1832: the misfortunes of a little clerk who, after many a sacrifice, can at last afford to buy a hunting rifle, loses it his first time out, and is thrown into such despair that his compassionate colleagues pool their money to buy him another one.[15] It is interesting to see how the author has transformed the tale to suit his very personal style. The gun—a luxury—is replaced by an overcoat, a prime necessity. The hero does not lose his most precious possession, it is stolen from him. He finds no compassionate friends to help him in his trouble, but meets indifference on all sides. He does not recover from the loss, he dies. And lastly, the real adventure is prolonged by a supernatural one. Thus, as the initial tale passed through Gogol's brain, it became more petty, cruel, and unreal. He began to write it in 1839 and polished it in 1840 and 1841, sharpening the character of the hero, Akaky Akakyevich Bashmachkin.

His absurd name (in Russian, *bashmak* means carpet slipper) is in itself a symbol, because everybody "walks on" Akaky Akakyevich. A pale, office-dwelling pen-pusher, he has been doing the same thing for so long and so regularly that he seems to have been there always and "to have come into the world bald-headed and in uniform." The scapegoat of his colleagues, who laugh at him and tease him, he occasionally feebly protests, "Let me alone! What have I done to you?"

His only pleasure in life is copying reports. There are some letters of the alphabet he likes better than others, and he is filled with joy when he writes them. "That was how you could read on his features the letter his pen was forming." Wholly absorbed by his gentle dream of ink and paper, he does not even desire diversion in friendly evening gatherings. But the monotonous and withdrawn existence of this aging eccentric has been disrupted by a great preoccupation: Akaky Akakyevich's overcoat is so threadbare that he must order a new one. Here, no doubt, Gogol was recalling the time of his greatest poverty, in 1830, when he was shivering with cold, and his "protector," Troshchinsky, finally gave him his own coat. In the mind of Akaky Akakyevich, the purchase of this coat assumes the proportions of a historical event. He begins to save money for the fateful day. He gives up drinking tea, no longer uses a candle, walks "on tiptoe so as not to wear out his soles," and seldom eats a square meal. "As he was continually dreaming of his future coat, the dream gave him adequate nourishment, albeit spiritual. Even more, its very existence began to count; one could feel beside him the presence of another being, like a friendly companion who had agreed to travel life's roads with him. He became more energetic and firm, as befits a man who has adopted a goal in life. Sometimes a little flame shone in his eyes, and the most daring, even insane thoughts passed through his head: what if the collar of the coat were faced with sable?"

At last, after saving his money kopeck by kopeck, he can order the coat, whose color and cut he has so often discussed with the tailor. He dons it and is stunned: perfection! The lightness of the new object on his shoulders gives him such joy that he bursts into little trills of laughter as he walks. But suddenly disaster strikes: in the midst of a large, deserted, foggy open space, thieves fall upon him and steal his coat. Wild with grief, the poor man feels as though he has lost his wife. His reason for living is gone. He lodges a complaint, then explains his situation to a rather important person, an "Excellency," whose intervention can, he has been told, accelerate the police investigation.

The Excellency receives him so icily that he thinks he will faint from fear. In the street he catches cold, and dies a few days later, abandoned by all. "They took the body away, put it in the ground, and St. Petersburg remained without Akaky Akakyevich. He vanished, that defenseless creature for whom no one had ever showed any affection, in whom no one had taken the slightest interest. He was replaced the very next day. The new clerk was much taller and his writing sloped."

Here ends the work of Gogol-the-realist; on the next line begins the work of Gogol-the-ghostly. The phantom of Akaky Akakyevich takes up where the living man left off. The phantom of a little bureaucrat begins to haunt the vicinity of Kalinkin Bridge; still looking for his lost property, he strips pedestrians of their coats, "be they quilted, lined, cat- or beaver-collared." One evening the ghost attacks the same "important person" who dismissed him before, and removes his fur-lined cape. The terrified "important person" goes home a reformed man. After this encounter, the antics of the phantom clerk cease. "His Excellency's fur-lined cape had presumably satisfied his desire."

The break between realism and the supernatural is not as sharp as appears at first glance. Even in the more "realistic" part, a swarm of slightly jarring details provide a background of the bizarre. The story of Akaky Akakyevich takes place on two levels. On the surface, we are indeed studying a portrait of an oppressed and humiliated creature colliding with the imbecilic haughtiness of his superiors, and the whole tale can be seen as a satire on Russian bureaucracy or, better still, as a protest against social injustice. But, behind this half-ironic, half-compassionate portrayal of a mini-man with ink-stained fingers, lurks the strange power of the forces of unreason. The nullity of Akaky Akakyevich is such that even in his lifetime he resembles an automaton, a "dead soul."

In this world of futility, in which chiefs and their subalterns struggle for the possession of a new toy prettier than the last one, his idea of a new overcoat fires his brain with mystical passion. And we who were just now grinning at the disproportion between the commonplace object of his desire and his excessive adoration of it, suddenly realize that our own infatuations are often no less absurd. A close look at our own lives convinces us that they are filled with irrational impulses toward this or that infinitely fascinating goal which, once attained, will disappoint us. We suppose ourselves dedicated to undertakings of essential importance, whereas in fact we move steadily, "overcoat" by "overcoat," toward a dreadful end of which we never think. Yet, now and then, the chill breath of the Beyond rends the tissue of our days. If ever we were tempted to forget that, a look at Gogol is enough to remind us. The visible world he describes in such great detail is poor camouflage for the invisible world in which his heroes have their sources. Akaky Akakyevich, like Chichikov himself, is made half of flesh and blood and half of smoke—a proof of the absurdity and futility that corrupt every human action.

The "Collected Works" caused the same division among critics as their individual parts had done. With intensified spite, Bulgarin, Senkovsky, and Polevoy renewed their attacks upon the author, comparing him to Paul de Kock and Pigault-Lebrun. On the other side, Slavophiles and Europeans—each in their own way—wove crowns of laurel for him.

"This work," Belinsky wrote in *Annals of the Fatherland* (February 1843), "is what forms at the present moment the pride and honor of Russian letters."

Such affirmations made Gogol smile: everything he had published thus far was as nothing in comparison with what he was now preparing. To make himself ready for this major creation, he was reading the Bible, *The Imitation of Christ,* and the *Meditations* of Marcus Aurelius. Of that greathearted emperor he said, "I swear before God that the only thing he lacked was to be a Christian."[16]

God, to whom he was praying so fervently, had reserved him a great joy. At the end of January 1843 his tender, peerless friend, Alexandra Osipovna Smirnov, moved to Rome, where she had rented the palazzetto Valentini on the piazza Traiana. Gogol and Arkady Osipovich Rosset, Mrs. Smirnov's brother, had made all the preparations for the young woman's arrival. When she and her children stepped out of her coach at nightfall, she found herself in front of a handsome edifice with brilliantly lighted windows. Gogol appeared on the central staircase, face aglow and arms outstretched.

"All is ready!" he cried gaily. "Supper is waiting. Arkady Osipovich and I have made all the arrangements. I'm the one who found the house. The air is excellent in this part of town. The Corso is just over the road, and the best thing of all is that you are close to the Coliseum."[17]

The next day, he returned and drew from his pocket a timetable entitled "Alexandra Osipovna's Trip," containing a day-by-day tour of the palaces, ruins, and museums of Rome. Each outing was to end with a pilgrimage to St. Peter's in the Vatican, where there was so much to see—even though, according to Gogol, the façade of the basilica looked like "a chest of drawers." Mrs. Smirnov toiled enthusiastically in the wake of her guide with the indefatigable legs and unfaltering memory. He always wore a gray hat, pale-blue vest, and trousers of a muted mauve hue, which reminded one of a dish of "strawberries in cream." He knew the city so well, his companion said, that he could have given lessons to any professor. But he demanded equally unqualified admiration. Finding her insufficiently excited by the frescoes in the Farnese, he took her indifference as a personal affront and became angry. However, he complimented her upon her gaping wonder at the Moses of Michelangelo. Seated near him on the tiers of the Coliseum, she wanted to know how Nero was attired when he appeared before the crowd. The question infuriated him. "Why do you bother me with that scum?" he snarled. Then he calmed himself and added, "Nero, the swine, came to the Coliseum and entered his box wearing a crown of laurel on his brow, a red chlamys, and golden sandals. He was very tall, very handsome, and extremely gifted. He sang and accompanied himself on a lyre. We have seen his statue, copied from nature, in the Vatican." For longer excursions they hired donkeys. Gogol gladly entrusted his person to the reassuring footsteps of these beasts beloved of Christ. In the countryside around Rome he would gather herbs, listen to the singing of the birds, or lie on the ground murmuring, "Let us forget everything and look at the sky!" or "What is the point of talking? We must breathe, breathe deeply this invigorating air and thank God that there is so much beauty in the world."[18]

In the evenings he would often call on Mrs. Smirnov in her palazzetto Valentini, and there, sitting opposite each other, they would take turns reading aloud. One day Mrs. Smirnov was reading, with feeling, from George Sand's *Letters of a Traveller;* Gogol began to show signs of impatience, sighed, cracked his knuckles, and finally interrupted to ask if she was fond of the violin. When she said she was, he went on, "And do you like to hear it played badly?" George Sand, in his opinion, littered her descriptions of nature with false notes; and nothing could move him from that opinion. In all his dealings with Mrs. Smirnov he displayed a conviction that brooked no argument. One time, he reverted to his alleged trip to Spain. She reminded him that on that particular point, she had already convicted him of falsehood. "Well," said he, "if you must know the truth, I never went to Spain, but I did go to Constantinople, and that you never knew!" And he described the capital of Turkey as minutely as if he had returned the day before, mentioning the names of streets, listing the treasures of the mosques, going into ecstasies over Turkish coffee, growing moist-eyed over the sorry state of the homeless dogs, slipping in a word about the mysteries that could be divined behind the moucharabies. He went on thus for half an hour, and Mrs. Smirnov, fascinated, let herself be persuaded. "Now I am sure you have been to Constantinople," she said. A glint of mischief appeared in Gogol's eyes. "You see how easy it is to deceive you," he said. "I have never been to Constantinople, but I have seen Spain and Portugal!" And this time Mrs. Smirnov wondered if he weren't telling the truth.[19]

Even when he was playing his little games of truth and falsehood, she still saw him as a mentor. He was her guide in life as well as in the streets of Rome. Moreover, he hardly ever teased her any more and usually adopted a paternal and sermonizing tone in his conversation that suited her perfectly. He urged her to become a better Christian, to give up the vanity of social engagements, to cultivate her soul like a precious rosebush. On the slightest provocation he would produce an *Imitation of Christ* from his pocket and reel off a passage from it.

As Easter approached he decided to keep a strict fast, but the Roman Church had lost its former appeal. In the past, his infatuation with the Apostolic Roman faith had flowed from his adoration of the Eternal City. Now, as he withdrew from the external world, the fascination of the Western religion faded and he turned toward the faith of his own country. Having dedicated his work to the glory of Russia, he must either return to the Orthodoxy of his forefathers, or betray his mission. Now he went to pray in the little Orthodox church of the Russian embassy. Mrs. Smirnov, who sometimes went with him, was surprised to see him move apart from the congregation and plunge into solitary meditations in front of some icon. He began to talk of his trip to Jerusalem again. He had written to Aksakov:

"How could you imagine that in the breast of a man who has known instants of heavenly life, who has perceived that love, there should not be born a desire to see the earth on which He stood, the first man to speak that word of love to humans—the land from which that love spread out to the rest of the world? Own that you were surprised when I first revealed my intention. A person wearing neither cowl nor miter, who has caused and is still causing his fellow men to laugh, who even now thinks it important to throw light upon insignificant things and to show the emptiness of life—it looks most strange in this person, does it not, to undertake such a trip? But is there not a great deal of strange-

ness in the world? My soul senses the beatitude to come and knows
that we need only reach out to that beatitude and divine grace will let
it descend upon our souls. That is what the man who makes men laugh
has to say to you."[20]

Gogol was always thinking about his trip to the Holy Land, but he
was in no hurry to make it. For the moment, he was planning
shorter and less devout excursions. Mrs. Smirnov had forsaken Rome
for Naples in April 1843, so he suddenly discovered that he was "bored
as an orphan" at strada Felice 126 and conveyed himself to Florence
on May 1. From Florence, via Bologna, Modena, Mantua, Verona,
Trent, Innsbruck, and Salzburg, he inched his way by stagecoach to
Gastein, where he found Yasykov. After two weeks with the sick man,
he left for Munich, where he wrote to Prokopovich, who had dared to
inquire whether the second volume of *Dead Souls* would soon be ready
for the printer:

"You sound as though *Dead Souls* were a pancake you could cook
with a flick of the wrist. Not only is the second volume not ready for
the printer, it is not even written. And it will not see the light of day
for two more years, provided my strength does not fail me during that
time."[21]

Having sent this letter, he left for Frankfurt, where Zhukovsky was
living with his young wife; lovely, melancholic, and ailing. Thence all
three proceeded to Wiesbaden and then to Ems, to take the waters.
But Mrs. Smirnov had just arrived in Baden-Baden. What are 150
miles to a passionate heart? Gogol set forth in the hottest days of July.
In Baden-Baden he drank the waters, bathed in the somber and tender
expression of Mrs. Smirnov's eyes, read her some passages from *The
Iliad,* and complained that he could write nothing of his own. A little
leap over to Karlsruhe to give a neighborly greeting to Mickiewicz, and
he was back in Düsseldorf with the Zhukovskys. This continual moving about was not inspired by a need for a change of scenery: he no
longer even looked at the landscapes he traversed.

"I would have liked," he wrote Danilevsky, "to rejoice in the fresh
scents of the spring and the sight of new places, but I am no longer
capable of feeling anything of that sort. On the contrary, I live wholly
withdrawn, absorbed in my memories, my people, my land, which I
carry around within me, and they all become nearer to myself with
every passing minute."[22]

Later he wrote, also to Danilevsky: "I am perfectly indifferent to my surroundings. Most of the time, I travel only to meet the people whose presence my soul requires."[23]

One of these people was definitely the wise, kindly Zhukovsky, struggling with his worries about his wife's health and his verse translation of *The Odyssey*. In Düsseldorf, Gogol began to want to emulate him, and set seriously to work on *Dead Souls*. But his head was heavy as lead. He was utterly disheartened by the "Collected Works," of which he had at last received a few copies. The paper was too thin, the print too small, the volumes too thin and light for the price. Was that really all he had written in eleven years?

His present phase of inertia, brought about "by divine will," did not prevent him from passing authoritative judgment upon his friends and relations. Although unable to continue his "poem," he suffered no lack of energy when his object was to admonish someone by letter. He exhorted his correspondents to mend their ways, to read the Fathers of the Church, and to trust in his word. He chided Danilevsky for yielding to the glittering seductions of society, while he, Gogol, trod the narrow path of righteousness. "You have not yet begun to live an inner life. No; you have not yet felt the mysterious and terrifying significance of the word "Christ."[24]

To Shevyrev he proclaimed, "Woe unto him who, placed to stand guard over the flame of truth, lets himself be drawn into the agitation around him!"[25]

It was his mother and sisters, however, who received his sternest sermons: "I turn now to my sisters: one of them imagines that she has no obligations or occupations, that she was born for the express purpose of sitting idle, that she is useless and incompetent, . . . and that her sole duty is to protect herself from harm. The other abandons herself to daydreaming, looks upon reality with disdain, and unreasonably supposes that she can find happiness only in some other place than where she is. The third has taken it into her head that she is stupid and good for nothing but trivial tasks, and that she knows nothing, whereas she might actually perform some deed that would please God and save the family. Has even one among you ever so much as asked God to help you to understand the sense and meaning of the misfortunes He has visited upon us, so that you could see what was good and necessary about them? Know that there is no misfortune in the world, and that our happiness lies at the very heart of all unhappiness. I advise you to pray so that all will be, not as you desire, but as His holy will desires."[26]

Gogol's mother and sisters replied to this sermon with protestations of innocence and complaints of his harshness. He magnanimously agreed not to continue the discussion, but on one condition: his letter must remain a breviary for the whole family.

"Give me your word," he wrote, "that throughout the entire first week of Lent (I would like you to fast during that week), you will read my letter, going through it once every day in order to understand the exact meaning of it, for this cannot be grasped at one reading. Whoever loves me must perform what I demand. Afterward, that is to say after the fast, if any of you should feel a sincere need to write to me about that letter, she may do so, passing on to me whatever her soul dictates to her."[27]

With the first autumn rains, the atmosphere in Zhukovsky's little house, so comfortable and quiet, suddenly became stifling to Gogol. He began to dream once again of blue skies, sun, and Italy. He decided to go to Nice to see Countess Vyelgorsky and Mrs. Smirnov, who planned to spend the winter there.

Part of Germany and the whole of France to cross. He reached Marseilles exhausted, spent a night at the hotel, and felt so ill that he began to fear his last hour had come. Once more he prepared himself, praying, for death. But the attack ended with the night and he climbed back into the stagecoach. He was in a hurry to get to Nice, the Piedmontese town[28] whose beauty, climate, and tranquillity he had often heard vaunted.

At first he was charmed. An azure sky above the shoreline with its slow, calm surf, the drifting caress of springtime in midwinter, the savorous mixture of Italian and French tongues in the streets. "Nice is a paradise," he wrote to Zhukovsky upon his arrival. "The sun spreads over everything like a layer of oil; butterflies and flies abound in countless swarms; the air is summery. Utter peace. . . ."[29]

He stayed with Countess Louisa Karlovna Vyelgorsky, who had rented the home of a lady named Paradise in the center of town not far from the sea and was living there with her two daughters, Sofya (Countess Sollogub), and Anna. A cold, pious society woman, much preoccupied with her family life, she had preserved a deep sense of gratitude to Gogol for nursing her dying son in Rome four years before. For her, he was more than an admirable writer: he was the man most likely to understand her sorrow. However, he never felt entirely at ease with her, found her lamentations tedious, and took advantage of every opportunity to escape.

His happiness was in his meetings with Alexandra Smirnov, although she, too, was often draped in gloom. She lived in a luxurious house in the Croix de la Marbre district and seemed to be suffering from everything, even the opulence of her establishment. Weary of her drawing-room triumphs, but unable to find peace alone, seeking God but forever looking at herself in mirrors, this unsatisfied, anxious woman of thirty-two was unable either to give up the world or to live in it. In four months, her condition had deteriorated to the point of neurosis. Watching her now, it was hard to recall the mischievous girl with the flashing eyes and sharp tongue who had once made a collection of the hearts of statesmen and writers. True, she was still beautiful; her dark eyes glowed with intensity; but her complexion had grown sallow, her eyelids were wrinkled, the line of her throat had imperceptibly thickened. An expression of melancholy, of sickly uncertainty sometimes darkened her face. She prayed a great deal and kept the sermons of Bossuet at her bedside. Then she would suffer an attack of frivolity and want to put on all her finery, to show herself, shine, seduce. She would dazzle her audience with her witticisms, her flashing eyes, the slightly faded grace of her smile; and suddenly all the light would go out, she would be overcome with horror at her own superficiality, return to her morbid thoughts, and have no further traffic with anyone but God.

They met every day without fail. After a morning spent working in his room in Countess Vyelgorsky's house, Gogol would go for a solitary walk along the shore, sniff the fortifying spray, buy some candied fruits, and turn up, package in hand, in time for lunch with Mrs. Smirnov. The French cook, knowing he was a gourmet, would call out at the top of her lungs as soon as she caught sight of him, announcing the special features of the day's menu: "Monsieur Gogo, Monsieur Gogo!" (as she called him), "radishes and Pères français salad!"

After the meal, Gogol would draw out a large notebook, into which he had transcribed extracts from the Church Fathers, and read them aloud while his hostess listened, rapt and tearful. He had also copied out fourteen psalms of David, which she promised to memorize. At his command she would recite, her head erect, staring fixedly into his eyes. If she made a mistake he sternly chided, "That is not right." And ordered her to prepare her lesson more carefully for the morrow. One day, concerned by his extreme poverty, she wanted to know what was in his wardrobe. Did he have enough shirts and cravats? "I see you have no subtlety at all," he told her. "I am a dandy, particularly where cravats and vests are concerned. I own three cravats: one for special occasions, one for every day, and a warmer one for traveling." And he urged her to give away most of her gowns and gewgaws and, like him, keep only the strict minimum. She rather halfheartedly promised to bear his counsel in mind. Sometimes, if she had been good, he would read her a few pages of the second volume of *Dead Souls,* which he had finally started. On one of these occasions, a storm was gathering outside; suddenly he closed his notebook, and at the same instant there came a thunderclap overhead. He paled, closed his eyes, and began to tremble. The storm passed. Mrs. Smirnov asked him to continue reading. "No," he said, "God himself did not want me to read something unfinished which has not been given my inner approval. Admit that you were frightened!" "It was not I who was afraid, my little Ukrainian," she replied. "It was you!" "I was not afraid of the storm," he sighed, "but of the fact that I had read you something I should not have read to anyone; and you see? God has threatened me!"[30]

Despite this reproof from heaven, he continued to scratch away at his novel. "I am resolutely rowing against the current, going against myself; that is to say, against the idleness and throbbing anxiety that are invading me,"[31] he wrote to Yasykov. He told his friends: "You must make a rule for yourself to spend at least two hours a day at your desk, and order yourself to write." "But what if inspiration doesn't come?" Sollogub objected. "Never mind; pick up your pen and write," he answered.[32]

For the time being, notwithstanding this self-discipline, the second volume remained, in his own words, in a state of "chaos." A similar chaos reigned in his head. He could see clearly into neither the future of his book nor that of his life. He was disturbed by the pleasure he felt in Mrs. Smirnov's company. No other woman had ever exerted such attraction upon him. He wanted to love her for her soul alone, but he had to admit that she was also extremely nice to look at. Still, he did not think he was in any real danger. As before, when he had watched at the bedside of Joseph Vyelgorsky, the sacred nature of his mission was protecting him from the weaknesses of the flesh. He was so sure of this that he savored in complete security the little spice of a temptation he knew could lead to nothing. Day after day, as he confessed and berated his penitent, he undressed her morally while rapturously forbidding himself the slightest physical contact, the briefest meaningful gaze. And she abandoned herself, opened herself to him with a kind of Christian coyness, weighing and rationing her confessions, imploring counsel, moaning over her life "without a future." In this ecstatic dialogue, she was always the more imprudent of the two: one day she ventured to say, in half-serious, half-jesting tone: "Listen, you are in love with me!" He turned white with anger, shot away like an arrow, and did not see her for three days.[33]

When he reappeared, the little sentence had apparently been forgotten. But he thought about it incessantly, with anguish and delight. His relationship with Mrs. Smirnov became even more intimate than before, yet remained entirely platonic. Even had he wanted to cross the line, he would almost certainly have been prevented from doing so by a sudden inadequacy. Some of the people in his circle whispered that he had indulged in solitary consolations in his youth and that these bad habits had made him hostile to women. Others maintained that he remained chaste on principle. He himself always proffered moral and religious grounds for condemning the slavery of the flesh. But in that case, he ought to have rejected every other physical pleasure, whereas he was a very greedy eater and had a passion for bright colors, brilliant spectacles, and eccentric clothes. His sense of smell was so keen that he was always talking about his nose; he loved to tell dirty stories; he sought the company of pretty women, but was instantly on the defensive in their presence.

Incapable of uniting with them, he appealed to God for justification; and if ever they tried to entice him, they became devils incarnate, vessels of sin. Backing away from their carnal forms, he would retreat into his reassuring myth of the ethereal creature. The force of his imagination revenged him upon reality when it became too insistent: he comforted himself with a cloud. Mrs. Smirnov knew how to be the cloud and yet remain alive and accessible, at least to his eyes. The better he knew her, the more he loved her. In his enthusiasm he wrote to Yasykov: "She is a pearl among Russian women; I have never known another like her, and nevertheless I have known many who had noble souls. I wonder if anyone possesses sufficient moral strength to esteem her at her true worth. She became my consolation at a time when no one else could have comforted me with words. Our two souls were as close as twin brothers."[34]

Surprised by this lyrical outpouring, Yasykov wrote to his brother:

"You must have noticed how Gogol praises Mrs. Smirnov in his letter. All of us here have been amazed by it. Khomyakov, who used to write of her as "The Stranger" or the "Pink Girl," thinks she is not at all like Gogol's idea of her. From everything else I have heard about her, she is nothing but a siren swimming in the transparent waters of seduction."[35]

Aksakov noted: "He loved Mrs. Smirnov passionately, perhaps because he saw her as a repentent Magdalen and himself as the savior of her soul. In my humble opinion, he was not insensitive to the still attractive brilliance and vivacity of the lady, despite his highmindedness and purity."[36]

Intrigued by these echoes from Nice, Danilevsky ventured to request an explanation, but Gogol couched his reply in very lofty tones: "You ask me why I am in Nice and you fabricate all manner of suppositions concerning my sentimental weaknesses. I think you must be joking, for you know me well enough on that account. Besides, even if you didn't know me, you could find the answer for yourself if you put together all the aspects of the problem."[37]

There was one person in Moscow who was seeking that answer frantically: Mrs. Sheremeytyev, who considered herself to be Gogol's spiritual mother. Upon hearing the talk of his inclination for Mrs. Smirnov, she decided that he must be lost to religion. A man of his quality, caught in a woman's snares! What a loss! She owed it to the world to intervene. But what could she do, at that distance, to combat such an attractive rival? After making a tour of the churches, she was emboldened to express her anxiety in a letter to Gogol:

"You wish me to inform you of my fears about you: so be it. Having prayed, I shall satisfy you. Know, my friend—in this moment I speak before God, Who will one day summon us all—that rumors, perhaps unfounded, are going around concerning you. Those returning from abroad and those writing us from there all say the same thing: that you have dedicated yourself to a person who has lived the life of a socialite and has only lately given it up. Can this constant companion be useful to your soul? I fear that in her society you may stray from the path which, by the grace of God, you had chosen."[38]

The amazed Gogol told his correspondent she had a morbid curiosity and ordered her to name the person who was alleged to have turned him from God. Mrs. Sheremeytyev would say no more and declared herself fully satisfied by her great friend's reply, but had she continued to issue her warnings, he would have paid no heed.

Mrs. Smirnov, moreover, was not his only penitent, and this gave him all the more reason to persist in his course; for he left her house only to find other admiring and respectful female faces, in the Vyelgorsky home. Around a table set for high tea sat Countess Louisa Karlovna Vyelgorsky, devout, haughty, and tormented, living on the memory of her dead son; her elder daughter, the mournful and mild Sofya, who had been abandoned by her impenitent playboy husband, Count Sollogub; and the younger daughter, Anna, then eighteen years old, called Annoline or Nosi—a fresh-faced, graceful child who had spent so much of her life traveling abroad with her mother that she could scarcely speak a word of Russian. Other ladies of the Russian colony in Nice occasionally joined the group, sharing its concern for their souls and its fondness for literature, so they were attracted quite as much by Gogol's fame as by his reputation as a spiritual guide. Uprooted, idle, and estatic, they surrounded him with their beflowered hats and warblings. In their midst he became more deeply conscious of his messianic role. They devoured him with their eyes, they drank in his words, they shuddered in fear of his wrath. The most touching, the most confiding, he thought, was Anna Vyelgorsky, the little Nosi, whose candid gaze pierced him to the core. He compared her youthful innocence with the riper beauty of Mrs. Smirnov, and found each a mysterious complement to the other.

Perhaps his true destiny was not to write novels, but to edify his contemporaries with word and letter. Some evenings, after a heart-to-heart talk with one or another of his admirers, he told himself that God had placed him on earth to explain the meaning of life to others and help them to overcome their misfortunes. He had pious recipes, moreover, for combating every conceivable woe. One had to use Holy Scripture like a cookbook, and prepare one's future as one would prepare a fine dish. It was in this spirit that he conveyed his recommendations to Aksakov, Shevyrev, and Pogodin in a letter to all three, in early 1844:

"I feel that your souls are often in torment. If so, reciprocal brotherly help is needed. I send you my advice. Devote one hour each day to meditation on yourselves. Live that hour inwardly, in deep concentration. Some book of high spiritual value can bring you to the desired state. I am sending you *The Imitation of Christ* (by Thomas à Kempis).

Read one chapter every day, no more. If the chapter is long and complex, read it twice. After reading it, meditate upon it. Try to understand how it can be applied to life amongst the noise and cares of the world. Choose a free hour for these spiritual activities, one in which you have no business to attend to, and let it serve as the foundation for your day. The best moment is immediately after your tea or coffee so that you will not be distracted by appetite. Always set aside the same hour and do not use it for any other purpose. May God help you!"[39]

He did not actually send his friends *The Imitation of Christ,* for he did not have enough money to buy the book; he instructed Shevyrev, however, to purchase four copies of the book at the French bookshop in Moscow—to be paid for, naturally, out of his friend's pocket. "It will be my new-year present," was his ingenuous comment.

After lengthy hesitation, Aksakov, unable to contain his annoyance, replied; "I am fifty-three years old and, I read Thomas à Kempis before you were born. I will dispute no man's convictions, provided they are sincere. But here you are ordering me, like a schoolboy, to read Thomas à Kempis without even seeking to know my opinions; and telling me when to do it—after my coffee, and to divide it up into chapters, like lessons! It's laughable and distressing. I fear mysticism like the plague, and it is my impression that it is rearing its head in you. I loathe moral recipes and everything resembling faith wrapped up in talismans. You are walking on a razor's edge. I fear the artist will suffer."[40]

Gogol, unperturbed, continued to dish out his prescriptions by letter and by voice. He even wrote out a sort of little spiritual guide for the Vyelgorsky ladies: *Rules for living at peace: Concerning our faults and the states of mind that cause unrest in us and prevent us from remaining at peace.*[41]

For the Russian new year, there was a fireworks display on the quai du Midi.[42] Carnival came and went merrily, with its confetti, tootings, and masks. Then quiet returned. Gogol walked along the shore by the mouth of the Paillon and admired the changing hues of the distant mountains. A large number of tourists, mostly English and Russian strolled along the road at the top of the pebble beach.[43] Everything seemed easy in this land of warmth, moderation and clarity. But in March Mrs. Smirnov, wearied by so much mildness, left Nice for Paris, and the sun instantly shone less brightly on Gogol's head. His illnesses returned, along with his need for a change of scene. He decided to go back to Zhukovsky, in Frankfurt. His flock need not fear, however: he would continue to shed his light upon them from afar. Before he even reached his destination he wrote to Countess Vyelgorsky, from Strasbourg:

"You gave me your word (you and your two daughters), whenever you should find yourselves in a bitter and painful state of mind, that you would pray within yourselves, fervently and honestly, and then read the rules I left you [*Rules for living at peace,* etc.], filling yourselves with the meaning of every word, because every word is heavy with meaning and it is impossible to understand it all in one reading. Have you kept your promise? It is no accident that those rules have been placed in your hands. The will of the Almighty put them there."[44]

With Mrs. Smirnov he must be even more exacting, for he regarded her as closer to himself, a model of his own making.

"You are still too ready to let yourself be drawn by passion; do not forget that," he wrote her. "Flee all things tainted with passion; avoid introducing it even into religious observances. God demands total impassiveness of us and will reveal Himself only in serenity."[45]

Again: "Remember that we have only very recently discovered the language that enables us to understand each other; remember how much patience was required of me to make our relations what they are now. You have often told me in deepest confidence things you afterward revealed to the first gossip you saw, or to some man of the world. This is only a mild rebuke, and do not take offense at it, for more severe shall follow. A time will come when your soul will thirst for reproach as for fresh water, reproach and only reproach."[46]

A few days later: "Tell me how it is that, according to a widely held opinion, it is impossible to speak of carnal matters in your presence without your feeling the need to speak of them as well? Examine yourself attentively and without indulgence; ask yourself whether you have not sometimes provoked such talk rather than putting an end to it. Have you not even incited others to engage in this type of conversation; did you not say to them, 'Fine, carry on!' I have twice witnessed the manner in which you threw oil upon a fire that was almost out."[47]

She, for her part, wrote him letters filled with tenderness and ecstatic gratitude: "My soul is open to no one as to you. You have seen it in all its black nakedness. May God preserve me from showing it to anyone else."[48]

Or: "Pray for Russia, pray for all who need your prayers, pray for me, a sinner, who loves you so much, so much, with life-giving gratitude. You have given me back my lightheartedness. But have I told you all my sins? I have ceased to pray at all except on Sundays. Is that very bad, in your opinion, for in other ways I am constantly turning to God, sometimes freely, sometimes under duress? You know the human heart. Look at the bottom of mine and tell me if you do not see some baseness there, lurking in the guise of a good deed or fine sentiment. As yet I am only on the bottom rung and you will not be able to abandon me so soon; on the contrary, you are more necessary than ever to me."[49]

And again: "I am bored, I am sad. I am bored because there is no one around me with whom I can think and feel aloud as I can with you. I am bored because I have grown used to having Nikolai Vasilyevich (Gogol) beside me, because there is no man like him here, and because it is not very likely that another Nikolai Vasilyevich can be found in this life."[50]

The chaste recipient of these feverish epistles read and reread them with a mixture of pride, gravity, and fear. The gratitude of his female correspondents incited him to enlarge his congregation. He could no longer write any of his friends without slipping some pious word of advice into his letter.

Almost as soon as he reached Zhukovsky in Frankfurt, sad tidings came: his eldest sister, Marya, had died, after a long illness. News of this importance called for a funeral oration in the manner of Bossuet.

"My sister has paid for her earthly errors with suffering," he coldly wrote to his mother, "and God sent suffering into her life in order to lighten her burden in the next world. Therefore, drive all sorrow from your heart, or you will commit a sin. Pray for her and do not grieve. I am saying this for you, Mother. And you, my sisters, never fail to cherish the dead one in your hearts and always pray for her. Also, never forget this terrible event, this death, which took place at the very time of your fast. Misfortune never strikes without reason. It is sent to us in order that we shall look into ourselves and observe ourselves closely. Be therefore more vigilant toward yourselves. Our enemy, our tempter, never sleeps."[51]

The epistle continues in this vein page after page, and no note of honest pain ever interrupts the spate of rhetoric. For Gogol, Marya's death was first and foremost an opportunity to say how badly she had lived and how his other sisters must take heed not to follow her example. Why, she had even, in a moment of exasperation, asked her brother not to write any more admonitory letters! For two years, thus, she had gone without his instructions; and see what happens when he turns away from a soul! Ah, thought he, the Lord knew full well upon whom His blow fell. In his anxiety to justify God he forgot to ask about the orphan, little Nikolai Trushkovsky, then aged eleven.[52]

As far as he himself was concerned, Providence, on the whole, was showing clemency. Living with other people reduced his expenses to almost nothing. His host, Zhukovsky, had now invented a friendly fiction that he owed Gogol four thousand rubles—the amount he had previously borrowed from the heir apparent, who was now refusing repayment. At first Gogol haughtily declined the gift, then consented to have it sent to him in four annuities.

Zhukovsky's little house in the outskirts of Frankfurt was well heated, quiet, and comfortable. But despite all the advantages of his retreat, *Dead Souls* was not advancing. By turns, its author blamed his moral imperfection, his poor health, and the political situation for disturbing his meditations. All over Europe, maniacs were inciting the masses to rebellion, workers were going on strike, people were forgetting that the social order was the will of God. In June, a ray of sunlight: the unexpected arrival of Mrs. Smirnov, who came to spend two weeks with her spiritual guide. She was as defenseless, capricious, and charming as ever. He bombarded her with good advice and was sorry to see her leave.

For the previous few days he had felt his nerves all on edge and a strange weight in his chest. A physician recommended salt baths at Ostend. Thither he ran. The town was half empty. A scattering of tourists ventured out onto the beach. The waves rolled up at Gogol's feet as he sat shivering, his bare bony knees squeezed together, nose upwind and hair flying. When he first stood in the raging surf, he thought the shock would kill him.

"But afterward," he wrote, "your whole skin burns. The moment you come out of the water you feel as though you're standing in a steam bath. You must not stay in the water more than five minutes. The worse the weather, the icier the water, the harder the wind blows and the fiercer the storm, the better it all is. I feared the contact of cold water and wore a flannel garment next to my skin, but bore it bravely."[53]

Back in Frankfurt, he claimed that the treatment had revived him;

but when he sat down at his desk, it was not to work on *Dead Souls* but to write more letters to his friends, letters that were growing longer and longer, more and more solemn, and more and more hortatory. When he wrote, he felt that he was reaching past his correspondents' heads to address the entire country. The more he thought about it, the more it seemed to him that an anthology of these epistles could compose a work of art and morality of unequaled importance. He began choosing his subjects, polishing his style, keeping his rough drafts. He tirelessly exhorted his mother, his sisters, Alexandra Smirnov, Countess Vyelgorsky and her two daughters, Danilevsky, Annenkov, Yasykov, Mrs. Sheremeytyev, Pletnyev, Shevyrev, Aksakov. And when the last-named balked at his sermonizing mania, he advised him to guard against the devil:

"All your trouble is nothing but the devil's work. Slap him across the muzzle, the nasty animal, and do not worry. He is just a low-grade bureaucrat who has sneaked into town pretending to be an inspector. He tries to fool everyone with his shouting and threatening. One moment of hesitation, one step back, and he begins to grow bolder. But walk straight up to him, and down droops his tail. We magnify him into a giant when all he really is, is 'the devil knows what.' His tactics are well known: if he sees that he cannot tempt you into some evil deed, he scampers away, then comes back in another disguise, from another angle, and tries to demoralize you that way. I have never swerved, inside myself, from my main principles. From the age of twelve, perhaps, I have been following the same path as I am now. I call the devil devil, I do not clothe him in some splendid Byronic garb, I know he struts about in a dress coat made of shit and that the proper thing to do is to cover his conceit with shit, once and for all."[54]

He denounced that same "low-grade" devil's sly tricks to his mother and sisters: "He slips by unnoticed, and that makes him all the more to be feared. He will not tempt you right away, or lead you to commit some bad and criminal act, knowing that your soul is not yet perverted and that you can, in the twinkling of an eye, recognize him and drive him away. No, he knows a better way: he will open up a path to your heart by appealing to your little weaknesses—sloth, idleness; so that at first you will not think of trying to change and will tell yourself, 'It's the way I am, I can't help it!' or 'It must be something unhealthy, something involuntary that is part of me!' I see weaknesses in you that could very easily give the evil spirit access to your soul."[55]

At the same time as he was preaching to his circle, Gogol also recognized his own imperfections. He thought they helped him to understand his fellow men, and he wished that, in return for the help he gave them by alerting them to their failings, they would point out his shortcomings to him. It was by flagellating one another that they might best drive out the devil—just like in the Russian steam baths. But one had to proceed methodically. Shevyrev, Aksakov, and Pogodin ought, he said, for friendship's sake, to keep a sort of diary in which they would record their misdeeds.

"Every time you think of me, write down then and there, in a few short words, the thought that has come to you," he wrote to Shevyrev. "Very simply, like a diary—day, date, and month. 'Today I saw you thus and so.' Day, date, and month. 'Today I was furious with you for such and such reason.' Day, date, and month. 'This is what I find inexplicable in your character or behavior.' Day, date, and month. 'Here the following rumors are going around concerning you, but a doubt came to me about them.' Day, date, and month. 'At the bottom of my heart I nurse a grievance against you for such and such reason.' When you have filled even a half page with these observations, send it to me in your letter. In this way you will be doing me a greater service than ever before. Help me now, and when I have grown stronger and more intelligent, it will be my turn to help you."[56]

He tried to impose upon Pletnyev the same "frankness" he had recommended to his Muscovite friends; but what was to him an invigorating moral hygiene, Pletnyev considered a morbid game. Exasperated by Gogol's insistence, he wrote back with stinging quill:

"What are you? As a man, you are a devious, selfish, arrogant and suspicious creature who will do anything for fame.

"As a friend, what are you? And can you have any friends? If you ever did have, they would long since have laid before you what you now read from my pen. You have two kinds of friends: some love you truly, for your talent, and have not grasped anything of your inner self. Such are Zhukovsky, the Balabins, Mrs. Smirnov; and such was Pushkin. The others—are the Moscow fraternity [Shevyrev, Pogodin, Aksakov, the Slavophiles, etc.]: schismatics, pleased to have enlisted a man of genius on their side, by making him drunk with flattery in their big tavern. Not only are they schismatics who hate truth and enlightenment: they are also businessmen, completely engrossed in the houses they are building, villages they are buying, and orchards they are planting. And you, who judge everything by words and not by lives or actions, believe in them. It is for them you betrayed me when, in place of my silent sympathy and pure affection, you heard their grandiloquent exclamations and insipid public acclaim ringing in your ears. You came to my house as to an inn; you went to them as though to your own home.

"But now let us see what you are as a man of letters. An individual endowed with a brilliant creative faculty, who intuitively divines the secrets of the language, the secrets of art itself, the foremost comic author of our time by virtue of your way of looking at man and nature and your ability to extract their most comical aspects and situations; but a monotonous writer, unwilling to take the trouble to acquire a conscious mastery of all the treasures of the language and your art and, when your fancy turns from the comic to the serious, improper to the point of bad taste, and pompous to the point of absurdity. You are nothing but a self-taught genius, whose creative faculty dazzles but whose artistic illiteracy and ignorance inspire only pity."[57]

Gogol took this tongue-lashing with a mixture of pain and pleasure, gratitude edged with indignation. His answer was humble. He thanked Pletnyev for the "gift." But although he fully agreed that he was riddled with dreadful faults, he also gave his detractor a point-by-point rebuttal. From line to line, his *mea culpa* was metamorphosed into a plea *pro domo sua*. Forgetting that he himself handed out advice to all and sundry, he wrote: "How can one say of someone like me, 'You do wrong?' A sick animal seeks the one herb that will relieve it, finds it, and is better off than if it had eaten the one prescribed by the wisest doctors. Friend, I was right to remove myself to a distance, for a time, from a place in which I could not live. You can see for yourself that a premature renewal of contact with the world is enough to cause a storm. Why, after agreeing that I was an odd, peculiar man, do people demand that I behave like everybody else? Why, before reaching his conclusion about me on the basis of two or three actions, did my judge, in a moment of doubt, not say to himself: 'I see such and such a sign in that man. In others, such signs are evidence of this and that. But this man is not like other men, his life is not that of other men, and also, he does not reveal himself. Perhaps—God knows!—the wise doctors were mistaken in basing their diagnosis on these symptoms, and have taken one illness for another.' "[58]

Thus, he insisted upon being attacked, and as soon as he was attacked he parried every thrust. Like those discontented citizens who are forever demolishing their country but will not hear a word said against it by a foreigner, Gogol was very willing to denigrate himself but found his friends' reservations quite out of place, although he thanked them all the while for thrashing him so soundly.

After justifying himself, Gogol turned, in this letter to Pletnyev, to another matter. Since he had caused his friends so much worry, he ought to impose a penance upon himself, and therefore he was giving up all the income from his books, starting immediately:

"I shall punish myself by refusing any money from the sale of my works. My soul demands this sacrifice, for it is fair, and I should be sorely afflicted if I did not make it. Every ruble and kopeck stands for my friends' displeasure and offense, and as there is no man whom I have not injured, the money would weigh too heavily upon my conscience. For this reason, both in Moscow and St. Petersburg, I am handing over this money to poor and deserving students. It must not be given to them indiscriminately, but only in reward for their efforts. Neither you nor Prokopovich must tell anyone about this, either while I live or after my death. Similarly, I must not know to whom or for what reasons you have awarded the money. You can say the gift comes from some rich man and tell the emperor it is someone who wishes to remain anonymous."[59]

The same day, he issued almost identical instructions to Shevyrev and Aksakov in Moscow. From them, too, he required an oath not to reveal the donor's name to the recipient, or that of the recipient to the donor.

"Although you may find these arrangements strange," he wrote, "you must understand that *a person's will is sacred,* and give me only one word in reply to this request: yes."

It never crossed his mind that he was considerably in debt to the very men he was now calling upon to distribute his earnings to "poor and deserving" students. No more did he think of the assistance such money might have given to his mother and sisters. As for his personal expenses, he always counted on his friends to look after him. With truly grandiose inconsistency, he made gestures of largess in the same breath as he asked other people to keep him, treating himself to a good deed by reaching into his neighbor's pocket, and rendering himself agreeable to God without untying his purse strings. A little sleight-of-hand, a moral swindle worthy of Chichikov. Ten days after having so touchingly forsworn the income from his books, he wrote to Mrs. Smirnov for funds. She was now back in Russia. She was rich. She owed Gogol so much for all his good counsel. After lengthy pages of religious dissertation, the students' benefactor came unblushingly to the point:

"You have often spoken to me about money, so I have made up my mind to turn to you. Since it pleases you to be useful to me and to help me, I am going to ask you for a loan. I will need between three and six thousand rubles next year. If you can, send three thousand rubles by bill of exchange to Frankfurt, either to Betman the banker or to Zhukovsky and myself. The other three thousand should be sent to me at the end of 1845."[60]

Having settled that small matter, he confidently anticipated his friends' congratulations upon his initiative on behalf of the academic world. To his great amazement, from both Moscow and St. Petersburg came nothing but abuse. Shevyrev would do nothing until Gogol had at least repaid his debt to Aksakov, who was then in difficulties, and he added that the whole idea was incompatible with the most elementary notion of justice; Pletnyev reminded him that he should think of his mother and sisters before he began to play philanthropist; both agents, moreover, despite their principal's instructions, had let the secret out. Worst of all, Pletnyev had informed Mrs. Smirnov of the intentions of her spiritual adviser who was applying to her for a long-term loan. She girded her loins and wrote:

"You are responsible for your old mother and your sisters. You have tried to provide for them, but what if, through their mismanagement or some unforeseen event, they remain dependent upon you. Your duty, immediately upon receiving Prokopovich's accounts and without further thought of aid to students, is to relieve your mother. This is how we have decided, with Pletnyev, to act—assuming, of course, that Prokopovich has any money for you."[61]

When Gogol read this, he felt that his sacerdotal majesty had been slighted. Since when did penitents criticize their confessor? They'd got it all wrong! Seizing his pen, he tartly retorted:

"Pletnyev was wrong to tell you what ought to have remained secret in the name of friendship. You were wrong to listen to what was not meant for you to hear. You have even had the audacity to take decisions in this matter, to tell me that I was acting foolishly, that I must do this instead of that, and without even obtaining my consent you were going to change the whole plan and make arrangements to suit yourself. Your reproaches and comments relating to the fact that I have a mother and sisters and should think of them rather than of giving help to strangers are cruel, unfair, and cause me great bitterness. They might have lived decently with the money I gave them. But although my mother is the best of women and our mutual affection deepens with the years, I cannot deny that she is a rather poor businesswoman. It has become very clear to me that financial aid is not what she requires, and that all the money I could ever give her would only sink into a bottomless well. This money [coming from the sale of his books] was earned by pain and is sacred; it would be a sin to use it for any other purpose [than the grants to students]. If my good mother knew what moral torture this whole business is for her son, her hand would not touch one kopeck of the funds amassed. On the contrary, she would sell some possession to add to the sum. Once again I ask and I demand in the name of friendship that you comply with my request. Pletnyev can take two thousand rubles of his own and send them to my mother; I'll settle with him later."[62]

Notwithstanding these adjurations, the friends in Moscow and St. Petersburg were adamant, the starving students went without their grants, and Gogol himself temporarily forgot his passion for liberality.

Something else was bothering him now. Pogodin had published a lithograph of the author of *Dead Souls,* in the November 1843 issue (no. 11) of his periodical *The Muscovite,* taken from Ivanov's portrait. Gogol, who had given the painting to his host in Moscow as a token of friendship, choked with fury to see it used without his permission. In his mind, that portrait must remain hidden from all eyes until the completion of his major work. To throw it to the crowd now was to betray and ridicule the writer, especially as Ivanov had painted him in a dressing gown and with his hair in disorder. Blind with rancor, his quill spouting insults, Gogol wrote to Yasykov:

"No man in the entire world, I think, from the beginning of time, has ever been victim of such lack of tact and propriety, or such utter want of delicacy. You write some stupid piece of nonsense in your youth that you would never dream of publishing: the moment he sees it, bang! he [Pogodin] flings it into his paper without rhyme or reason, without anybody asking him to do it and without asking anybody's permission to do it. That's like a pig that can't even let a decent man s____ in peace: the moment he sees him squat down in the shadow of a hummock, he has to shove his snout under the man's a____ to catch the first lump that falls. Pick up a stone and chuck it at his snout, he couldn't care less. He just gives a little grunt and sticks his snout back under your a____."[63]

A little later, to Shevyrev: "Think a little: what is achieved by picturing me to the entire world, unkempt, with long, wild hair and mustache, in a dressing gown? Couldn't you guess, perchance, how people are going to interpret it? But it is not for myself that I so resent being portrayed as dissipated roisterer—for I know full well, my friend, people will cut that picture out of the review. Believe me, youth is silly. Many young people have pure aspirations, but they all feel the need to create idols."[64]

And, thought Gogol, you never see an "idol" preserved for posterity in an unflattering pose. Instead of putting him up on a pedestal, Pogodin had flung him into the mire. If anything was to be published, he would, reasonably enough, have preferred Moller's syrupy and prettified portrait to Ivanov's crude attempt at the truth.

As a well-timed diversion from these problems, Count Alexander Petrovich Tolstoy and Countess Vyelgorsky invited him to spend a few days in Paris, all expenses paid. Dr. Kopp was consulted and recommended the trip for his health; and Zhukovsky, who may possibly have been weary of him, urged him to seize the opportunity. He left, his "nerves irritated" and his body "completely broken," in the first days of January, 1845. In Paris a warm, cozy room was awaiting him at the Hotel Westminster, 9, rue de la Paix, where Count Tolstoy's family were also living. Gogol had met the Count in Nice during the winter of 1843–44 and felt deep respect for this high official of the imperial administration. After a brilliant debut as a guards officer, Alexander Petrovich Tolstoy had dabbled in diplomacy in the embassies of Paris and Constantinople and even become a secret agent in the Near East, and was appointed governor of Tver and then military governor of Odessa before retiring, in 1840, to devote himself to the study of religion. His knowledge of Scripture was universally admired. Russian and Greek priests often came to see him, and he would converse with them in either language with equal fluency. Slender, elegant, with a military bearing and solemn expression, he was a fierce champion of church and throne, who detested the liberal ideas that had inflamed the youth of Europe and were now threatening to spread to the young people of Russia. Gogol was in complete agreement with him on this point. He arrived in Paris to find that quarrelsome, disorderly, demanding, arrogant atmosphere he so disliked. Prices were higher, people in the cafés made improper jokes about Louis-Philippe and Guizot, the newspapers were filled with caricatures and polemics, and all France, resentful, vindictive, and bohemian, seemed to be infested with the itch. Without question, this people carried the germs of anarchy, and ought to be quarantined off.

"Paris," Gogol wrote to Mrs. Smirnov, "or rather the air of Paris, or rather the exhalations of the inhabitants of Paris, which, here, take the place of air, can hardly be said to have done me any good and have even undone the benefits of the trip."[65]

To Yasykov: "All I can tell you about Paris is that I have not seen Paris at all. Even before, I had precious little affection for the city; now it's worse. By that I mean the material side, the commodities: it is an unclean place and the air is so thick you could cut it with a knife. I have seen no one except the people dear to my heart, that is to say the countesses Vyelgorsky and Count Alexander Petrovich Tolstoy."[66]

There was no more touring of restaurants and theaters or lounging in the Tuileries or visiting museums, as on his previous trip. Some bleak inertia kept him out of the stream of life. His only pleasure was in preaching to Countess Vyelgorsky and the sharp-eyed Nosi, or discussing a passage from Holy Scripture with Count Tolstoy. Most of the time, he kept to his room, reading and annotating St. John Chrysostum, St. Basil, Bossuet, treatises on ancient theology, and modern liturgical works. Outside his window he heard the rumble of carriages, clop of hoofs on the pavement, vendors' cries, the whole joyous unbearable din.

When he had to go out, he viewed the Frenchmen in the streets with sharp distaste. It never occurred to him to engage one of them in conversation. Even their cuisine had lost its appeal. On the other hand, almost every day, he went to hear services in the Russian church of Paris at 4, rue Neuve-de-Berri.[67] The priest, Dmitri Stepanovich Vershinsky, had taken a liking to him and lent him religious books to read. Immersed in his lofty meditations, he was quite unmoved to hear that he— and Pogodin—had just been elected to honorary membership of the University of Moscow. He did not learn that a man named Louis Viardot, a French man of letters, director of the Italian Theater of Paris, and husband of the celebrated soprano Pauline Garcia-Viardot, was just translating some of his stories for publication under the title *Nouvelles Russes*[68]; and had he been aware of the fact, he would assuredly not have bestirred himself to meet his translator. His incognito was far too precious. To pass unseen and yet be admired by all was his dream.

He soon tired of Paris and took a stagecoach back to Frankfurt. Four days and nights on the road. Twelve hours outside Paris, they met snow. "My nose alone reached Frankfurt," he wrote Countess Vyelgorsky, "together with two or three bones basted together by muscles like bits of string."[69]

The Zhukovskys were alarmed to see how much weight he had lost and how nervous he was. A walking skeleton with long hair and a mournful expression. He announced that he was tired of living off his friends. Zhukovsky wrote to Mrs. Smirnov asking her to approach the emperor for a subsidy for a writer who was the glory of Russia. Knowing the tsar, she decided to postpone her petition until she was sure he was in a good mood. The opportunity finally came at a palace reception. Mrs. Smirnov, perfumed and smiling, spoke to Nicholas I and transmitted Zhukovsky's request concerning Gogol. "Gogol has a great talent for the theater," the monarch said, "but I cannot forgive him his coarse and vulgar expressions." "Have you read *Dead Souls?*" she inquired. "Why, is it his? I thought it was by Sollogub!" Mrs. Smirnov advised him to read the book, many pages of which, she said, were infused with an ardent patriotism. He looked at her more than he listened, and finally promised to assist the impecunious author for the sake of the person who was so graciously pleading his cause. She went straight to Orlov, the chief of police, and informed him of the imperial decision. "Who's this Gogol?" muttered the suspicious Orlov. "You ought to be ashamed of yourself, a Russian, not knowing who Gogol is!" she snapped. Then he: "What odd ideas you have, looking after all these naked poets!" Choking with indignation, Mrs. Smirnov was groping for some sufficiently shattering retort when the emperor, having moved near, laid his big arm familiarly across her shoulders and said to Orlov, "It's all my fault. I forgot to tell you that Gogol must have a pension."[70]

Soon Uvarov, the minister of education, was submitting a resolution to be signed by the emperor awarding a gift of three thousand silver rubles (or ten thousand assignation rubles), payable in three annual installments of one thousand silver rubles each, to the writer Nikolai Vasilyevich Gogol, "whose state of health, in the opinion of the doctors, necessitates a period of residence abroad in a temperate climate and treatment with mineral waters."

For Gogol the sky began to clear. Touched by the imperial solicitude, he wished to express his gratitude to Uvarov; but, as always, he exaggerated: "I can only express my gratitude [to the emperor] by praying for him," he wrote to Uvarov. "To you I shall merely say that I was saddened by your letter, because everything I have produced thus far is not deserving of attention. Although praiseworthy thoughts have dictated what I wrote, the actual result was said so poorly and inadequately, in such an unpolished and mediocre manner, that most of my readers quite rightly see my books as containing more harm than good. I swear it was in no way my intention to ask anything of the emperor. I was silently preparing a work that would have been far more useful to my fellow countrymen than all my previous scribblings. I should like to thank you for all you have done to further knowledge and the study of our country's past; and, what is more, to base our educational system on firmly Russian principles.[71]

Uvarov proudly displayed this letter to various people, who promptly revealed its contents. The new word in liberal circles was that Gogol would sell himself to the authorities for a lump of sugar. Nikitenko, the censor, wrote in his diary, "What a regrettable self-abasement on Gogol's part—a man who had made it his aspiration to denounce the abuses of our society and has indeed thrown much light upon them, not only with accuracy and precision but tactfully, with the talent of a great painter. What a pity, a pity! But it suits Uvarov and a few others very well."[72]

Meanwhile, in Frankfurt, Gogol knew nothing of the effects of his letter, preoccupied as he was by his health. His nervous attacks were occurring more and more frequently; his pastoral epistles were interrupted by long laments over the corporal miseries that made it impossible for him to create. In thanking Mrs. Smirnov for the money he had requested, he said she need no longer worry about his material needs, but rather about his health.

"My whole body trembles, I am constantly chilled, nothing can warm me, not to mention the fact that I have become thin as a shaving, utterly without strength, and am very much afraid I may die before I can go to the Holy Land."[73]

A little later it was Count Tolstoy's turn to receive the SOS: "My health goes from bad to worse. The symptoms tell me that the time has finally come to know what must be, and, thanking God for all things, to make room, perhaps, for the living."[74]

During a short remission he analyzed his ailment for the same correspondent: "My face had gone quite yellow, my hands, swollen and black, were no more than lumps of ice; merely touching them made me afraid."[75]

Almost at the same moment, he was telling Mrs. Smirnov: "God has long deprived me of the creative faculty. I am only too well aware that until I have been to Jerusalem I shall be incapable of saying anything comforting to anyone in Russia."[76]

When Mrs. Smirnov's duly mournful reply came, he allowed his tenderness for her to appear: "My friend, my soul, do not sorrow. One year more, and I shall be with you, and you will no longer have to suffer from loneliness. When life becomes too bitter, too harsh for you, I shall fly through space and appear before you and you will be comforted, for there will be a third person beside us: Christ."[77]

After another lull his pains returned, and his anxiety, and the sensation of a cold wave running through his veins, creeping toward his heart. Thinking his last hour had come, he wrote his testament[78]:

"1. I ask that my body not be wrapped in a shroud until it shows definite signs of decomposition.

"2. I ask that no monument be placed over my grave.

"3. I ask that no one should mourn for me.

"4. I bequeath to all my fellow countrymen: the best that my pen has produced. O my countrymen, I am afraid! My soul fails with terror at the very thought of the majesty of the hereafter.

"5. I ask that after my death no one should run either to praise or condemn my works in newspapers and periodicals."

In the next paragraph he adjured his mother and sisters to share whatever income there might be from his books with the poor. Having expressed his last will, he scribbled a note to Father Bazarov, Superior of the Orthodox Church in Germany: "Come quickly to give me communion, I am dying."

The priest harnessed his horses and hurried to the side of the dying man, whom he found firmly on his feet. In surprise he inquired what his illness was. "Look!" Gogol replied, holding out his hands. "They are all cold." He insisted that extreme unction be administered. Father Bazarov refused. "I managed to convince him that he was not so ill that he needed to take communion at home," he wrote in his memoirs, "and advised him to go to Wiesbaden and make his Lenten devotions there."

To Wiesbaden, then, he obediently went, with Zhukovsky, to fast and hear the Easter service in the local Orthodox church; and returned to Frankfurt more distraught than ever. Now the doctors were recommending a treatment in Homburg, which was not far away. Thither he limped. An elegant little town filled with idle people who divided their time between the waters and the roulette wheel, with an orchestra playing in a pavilion, sun, German pastries, an easy life—and him, in the midst of all that, gnawed by his black obsession of the void. To Aksakov, who was gradually losing his sight, he recommended resignation, in the name of his own ailments: "You are ill, I am ill. Let us commend ourselves to Him who knows better than we what we need and what is best for us. When He takes away the sight of the *senses,* He gives us that of the *spirit,* and makes us see things that render those of this earth as dust."[79]

He told Mrs. Sheremeytyev: "My health is very bad, I am losing my strength and expect nothing further from either physicians or art, for that is physically impossible; but all things are possible for God."[80]

To Danilevsky: "Nothing but a divine miracle can save me. In any event, my life on earth could not have been long. My father also had a weak constitution and died young; he was carried off by his own lack of strength, not by any specific malady. I am losing weight, melting away—hourly, now, and not from day to day; my hands are never warm and are all swollen with water in the tissues."[81]

Now too weary to write, he reread the few chapters of the second part of *Dead Souls,* which he had painfully strugged to write in the previous few years, and was startled by their mediocrity. His new characters— the noble thinker Tentetnikov, the pious and generous distiller and ideal landowner Kostanzhoglo—were colorless and conventional. Even Chichikov was undistinguished in this reincarnation. It was unworthy of the author's grand design, which was to seduce his fellow countrymen by his portrayal of noble sentiments. There was only one solution, the same as for *Hans Kuechelgarten:* immolation. One calm day in July 1845 he threw his manuscript into the fire and watched it burn, as though witnessing a birth.

"It was hard to burn the work of five years, achieved at the price of such morbid tension, every line of which cost me a nervous disorder, and some of them were the fruit of my finest meditations," he wrote a little while later. "But all was burned—and at an hour when, looking death in the face, I so longed to leave at least one thing that would give a better idea of me. I thank God for the strength to accomplish this. The moment the flames had consumed the last sheet of my book, its contents were reborn, luminous and purified, as the phoenix from its ashes, and I suddenly saw how chaotic was all I had supposed to be orderly and harmonious. The publication of the second volume, as it was then, would have done more harm than good. I have no need to hurry; let others do that. I burn when burning is necessary, and with no hesitation; and what I do is right, for I do nothing without prayer. As to your apprehensions regarding my poor health, they are futile. It is my body that is infirm, not my soul. On the contrary, everything in my soul is gaining in strength and firmness. And my body will grow stronger too. I am convinced that when the time comes a few weeks will be enough to finish what five years of illness could not do."[82]

The pain of this ordeal by fire was made still easier to bear by another scheme—one easier to carry out and, in his view, more useful to Russia—by which his thoughts had recently been absorbed: that of collecting, completing, and binding into a volume the interminable letters he had been writing to all and sundry. On April 2, 1845, he told Mrs. Smirnov: "Pray God give me the possibility to prepare what I must before my departure [for Jerusalem]. It will be a small book with a very modest title, as the world goes, but necessary for many people, and in addition it will bring me the money for the trip."

This "small" opus also had the advantage of writing itself, so to speak. Painless creation. It would carry on where the faltering *Dead Souls* left off. What a relief for the author! But now, even his correspondence exhausted him. He must try a different spa. The local doctors could not agree upon a treatment to recommend. The best thing would be to go to Berlin and consult the famous Dr. Schoenlein. Gogol went, with Count Tolstoy. On their way they stopped at Halle to seek enlightenment from a Dr. Krukkenberg. After thoroughly examining the patient, he declared that he was suffering from a serious nervous derangement and recommended a three-month stay on the island of Helgoland, which had a most invigorating climate. Gogol was skeptical and wished to have Dr. Schoenlein's opinion before making up his mind. But he reached Berlin just after the great man had left. After dithering for a few days, he decided upon a Dr. Carus, of Dresden, as a second choice. Interrogated, palpated, and thumped by this pinnacle, he was informed that his nerves had nothing whatever to do with his condition. It was his liver, his liver alone, that was at fault; it had grown too large and was pressing upon his lungs, hence a nervous imbalance and poor oxygenation of the blood. The sole remedy in such cases was a prolonged term of treatment in Karlsbad.

Gogol obeyed. In his life, one watering place drove out another. He was a veritable connoisseur of waters, swallowing glass after glass, comparing springs, questioning his body's mysterious twitchings and hummings in the hope of detecting some sign of improvement. But despite his scrupulous adherence to the doctors' orders, he kept losing strength. Karlsbad was no good for him. His only joy there was a letter from Mrs. Smirnov telling him that her husband had just been appointed governor of Kaluga, whereupon the professor of morality in him instantly awoke and he sent his penitent instructions on the proper conduct of a conscientious governor's wife:

"Contrive always to be simply dressed, with the smallest possible number of gowns; repeat often how modestly the empress and court dress. Whenever you hear that some lady in your society has fallen ill, or is sad, or has had some difficulty or simply that something has happened to her, go instantly to her side. Pay attention to your husband's work and duties so that you will know exactly what it means to be a governor, what achievements are expected of him, and what are the limits of his power. Reread this letter and ponder, at the proper time, all it contains, even if this seems of little importance to you now."[83]

Convinced that he possessed all wisdom by intuition, he did not doubt that, thanks to his good counsel, Mrs. Smirnov would inspire her husband to fulfill his official functions for the general welfare and the glory of God. Perhaps the new governor of Kaluga would become an example for all governors in Russia. Perhaps the country's spiritual regeneration would begin in this provincial outpost. Then Gogol's work would not have been entirely in vain. If only the doctors had been able to care for his body as well as he cared for the souls of his friends! But none of these Teutonic practitioners was capable of understanding him.

The lukewarm, sulphurous, sodium-filled water of Karlsbad revolted him, but gave no relief. Weak, nauseated, and shivering, he decided to try his luck at Gräfenberg, in Silesia, where Dr. Vincent Priessnitz officiated, a champion of energetic cold-water baths. This very fashionable healer was said to put his patients back on their feet in a few sessions. But although he was eager to try out the effects of a new type of therapy, Gogol broke his journey in Prague, where, dazzled by the beauty of the ancient city, he forgot his fatigue and ran to admire the Royal Palace, St. Vitus Cathedral, the Church of the Assumption, the clock of the seasons, the bridge over the Vltava with its statues of the saints, and the national museum, whose curator, Ganka, welcomed him enthusiastically. When he clambered back into the stagecoach, his anxieties and shivers repossessed him. At Gräfenberg Priessnitz's staff took him in hand with a vengeance. Their hydrotherapeutic discipline scarcely left him time to gasp.

"I haven't a minute here to think about anything at all or write a two-line letter," he told Zhukovsky. "I am living in a dream, now swaddled in damp sheets, now stuffed into a bathtub, then rubbed, then sprinkled, then running convulsively around to warm myself up. I feel nothing but the contact of cold water on my skin and am incapable of any other sensation or cerebration at all."[84]

At first the treatment seemed to be having some effect. His extremities grew warmer, he was sleeping better and breathing more comfortably. But he did not have the courage to take his punishment to the end. Surfeited with water, he returned to Berlin, where Dr. Schoenlein was said to be again. The illustrious physician received him, burst out laughing when he learned that his colleague Carus had diagnosed a hypertrophied liver, and announced that the patient was suffering from a nervous ailment of the digestive system and, as soon as the weather permitted, he must bathe in salt water. In the meantime he prescribed pills, homeopathic drops, and cold-water massage; meat and vegetables should form the basis of his diet. Coffee instead of milk . . .

Supplied with these new instructions, Gogol went to Rome, whose climate, he claimed, had always "vivified" him. At his request, Ivanov rented a little apartment for him at via della Croce 81, near the piazza di Spagna. Now the brotherhood of painters disappointed him. Ivanov seemed less sincerely devout than before. How could the man continue to paint *Christ Appearing to the People* when he didn't go to church? Gogol often went to the embassy Orthodox chapel to make his devotions, and met some fellow Russians there whose regularity of attendance was more reassuring—including the pietist author Alexander Sturdza and Countess Sofya Apraxin, Count Tolstoy's sister. Late that year this little world was wildly agitated by the visit of Tsar Nicholas I. The tsar had come to negotiate a concordat with the pope governing the status of Roman Catholic clergy in Russia, and to seek his benediction for a possible "mixed" marriage between Grand Duchess Olga and Archduke Stephen, the son of the Hungarian palatine (Archduke Joseph). Since the quelling of the Polish uprising of 1830–31, in which the Polish Catholic clergy had taken an active part, Nicholas I had passed for a sworn enemy of Rome. The sovereign pontiff's entourage took a dim view of the invasion of the sacred walls of the Vatican by the head of the Orthodox Church. His cardinals are even said to have advised Gregory XVI to feign illness in order to avoid such an embarrassing quest. Gregory did nothing of the sort, however; he received Nicholas very amicably and discussed the terms of the agreement with him. In the Russian colony it was rumored that the tsar had been very firm and had denounced the lack of discipline of the Russian Catholic clergy, most of whose members, neglectful of the apostolic character of their mission,were preaching rebellion against the authorities. In Italian ecclesiastical circles, however, it was affirmed that the pope had dominated his visitor and talked him into submission.[85]

Nicholas I refused to hold a reception for the diplomatic corps and Roman aristocracy, and devoted his leisure to the monuments, basilicas, ruins, and museums. He also made a whirlwind visit to the Russian painters' studios, admired Ivanov's vast canvas, and commissioned copies of a few pieces of classical sculpture. Gogol might easily have arranged to be presented to him but was paralyzed by timidity. He had written nothing important for years and was afraid of being seen as an idler or an ungrateful wretch by the person who had so recently honored him with a pension. Deeply stirred, he mingled with the crowd and watched the monarch's carriage moving along the Monte Pincio road. He found the features of Nicholas I "inspired" and felt proud to be Russian.

"Like everyone here, I saw the emperor only three times, and each time only for an instant," he wrote to his mother. "He stayed four days in Rome and was too busy to receive the small fry, which includes me. I was happy to know he was in good health and good spirits, and I prayed for him sincerely."[86]

As the tsar was his benefactor, so he desired ever more intensely to be the benefactor of somebody else. Lack of money need not stand in his way. In a pinch, one could give away what one did not possess. His old idea returned, that of gratifying poor and deserving students. Since Shevyrev would not do as he was told, then Aksakov, already half blind, would have to take over. "Let not one kopeck of that money be spent for any other purpose," he wrote. "Let the money be put all in one place and guarded as a sacred trust; so I have sworn before God."[87]

He reiterated all his injunctions, but had no great hope of seeing them obeyed in his lifetime. His friends always managed, or so he fancied, to keep his money in their own desk drawers. What a misery that one could never get along without them! His weakened condition put him at their mercy.[88]

"Although there has been some faint improvement, my health still refuses to return for good," he wrote to Aksakov. "I am terribly weak, and, what is yet more incomprehensible, so chilled that I cannot remain seated in my room. I am continually obliged to run around to warm myself, and the instant I am warm and come in again, I can feel the cold, even though the room is quite warm; and so I have to go back out and run. The whole day goes by in these incessant races, and I no longer have enough time even to write a letter. But why speak of one's physical miseries? It is even a sin to do so: they are given to us for our own good."[89]

Three days later, to Zhukovsky: "My weakened mind can already see what great benefit is to be gained from all these illnesses: in the end, they ripen one's ideas, and what appears to be slowing down one's work is in reality accelerating it. I am sharpening my pen. Pray strongly to God for me."[90]

And to Pletnyev on the same day: "Blessed be, for all the centuries to come, the will of Him Who has sent these afflictions. Without them my soul should not have been properly educated for the task ahead, and dead and buried would be all that must be living in life itself, beautiful and true as truth itself."[91]

It now seemed to him that in his former works he had betrayed that *truth,* toward which he was straining with all his strength, through want of artistry and want of heart.

"My friend," he wrote to Mrs. Smirnov, "I do not like the works I have published thus far, and most of all *Dead Souls.* But it would be unjust of you to blame the author on the ground that he ridiculed the provinces by caricaturing them, just as it was unjust of you to extol him before. It is not provincial life, nor a few ghastly landowners, nor what is imputed to them, that is the subject of *Dead Souls.* For the time being it is still a secret, which will suddenly be revealed to the stupefaction of one and all (for not a single reader has guessed!) in the following volumes, if it please God to prolong my life and send his blessing upon my work. I repeat to you that it is a secret, and the key to it still lies in the author's soul."[92]

Sometimes he would have preferred that no one should speak of his old books in his presence. One of the reasons he liked living abroad was that nobody knew him there. But now Sainte-Beuve, in Paris, was publishing a eulogistic review of Louis Viardot's translation of Gogol's *Nouvelles Russes,* in the December 1845 issue of the *Revue des Deux Mondes*[93]:

"In short, it will be thanks to this publication by Mr. Viardot that the name of Mr. Gogol will become known in France as that of a man of real talent, a sagacious and implacable observer of human nature." Then came another article, in *L'Illustration;* and a third, in *Les Débats.* A German translation of *Dead Souls* appeared in Leipzig. Where must a man flee to escape his notoriety? As if the idiotic sneerings and maunderings of the Russian public weren't enough! Now he must await the screechings of the French and Germans, and tomorrow, who knows, the English and the Italians! Peace, peace; he had no desire to become an international figure. Above all, he was afraid of giving an unfavorable impression of Russia abroad.

"I was much displeased by the news of the German translation of *Dead Souls,*" he wrote to Yasykov. "Apart from the fact that I am not eager for Europeans to know anything about me at all for some time yet, I consider it unfortunate that this work should appear in a translation before it is finished. I should not like foreigners to read it and make the same mistake as the majority of my fellow countrymen, who took *Dead Souls* to be the portrait of Russia. I have already read something in French about my short stories in the *Revue des Deux Mondes* and in *Les Débats.* So far, there is no danger. It will sink into oblivion along with the newspaper advertisements of the latest pills or pommade to dye the hair, and that will be the end of it."[94]

As the new year (1846) approached, he drew up his usual balance sheet of his endeavors and was, as usual, terrified to see how little he had done in relation to all that remained to do. Without God's help he would never reach his goal. But God was there, at his back. He could sense the divine presence even in his aches, even in his fainting spells. An ejaculatory prayer rose up in his feverish brain. He seized his notebook and wrote, with shaking hand:

"Lord, bless me at the dawn of this new year. Let me devote it entirely to fertile and beneficient effort, and dedicate it all to Your service and the salvation of souls. May the Holy Spirit descend upon me, may It speak through my lips, may It sanctify my being by destroying my impurities, my vices, my baseness, and transform me into a temple worthy of Your presence, Lord! My God, my God, do not forsake me! My God, my God, remember Your former love for me! Bless me, my

God! Give me strength to love You, to celebrate You, to exalt You, and to bring my neighbor to glorify Your Holy Name!"

After such an outpouring, his face bathed in tears, he felt equal to the task of writing either the sequel to *Dead Souls* or a collection of really splendid letters to his friends.

2. *Selected Passages from My Correspondence with My Friends*

Despite the strong desire for renewed energy shown in the prayer he had dashed off during the night of December 31, 1845, the new year brought no change. Still Rome, the cold winter sun, the shivering, anguish, stomach cramps, and still the difficulty in settling down to *Dead Souls*. To soothe his conscience he persuaded himself that an even more important and urgent task was awaiting him now: to finish off the *Selected Passages* from his correspondence.

"About my letters: do keep them," he wrote to Yasykov. "After looking over all I have written of late to various people, and especially to those in need of spiritual assistance who were asking me for succor, I see that a book can be made out of this that will be of some use to suffering men in many walks. The sufferings I have endured myself have been profitable to me, and thanks to them I have been able to help others. I shall try to edit this material and add a few general considerations on literature."[1]

While he was preparing to transform his private letters into public correspondence, echoes of stormy literary currents were reaching him from Russia. New young authors were making names for themselves, as he had done before. It was as though the wave that had heaved him aloft was slowly subsiding before the next swell. "In St. Petersburg, according to *Annals of the Fatherland,* a new genius has just appeared, somebody called Dostoevsky,"[2] Yasykov wrote.

"Belinsky and Krayevsky are all in an uproar over someone named Dostoevsky,"[3] Pletnyev chimed in. Some saw the newcomer as "a second Gogol." *Poor Folk,* his first book, was a homage to the humble, like "The Overcoat."

Gogol had to know. After looking at the novel, he wrote to Anna Vyelgorsky: "The author of *Poor Folk* shows talent, his choice of subject is proof of his spiritual qualities, but one can also see that he is still young. There is a great deal of verbiage and very little inner concentration. I would have found the book more lively and stronger if his text had been tightened up."[4]

In the same letter, he ordered his correspondent to pray for him, for he had need, "in the midst of my torments," of a few "lucid minutes" in which to say everything that was on his mind. These "lucid minutes," which Rome was inexplicably denying him, he suddenly decided to seek in Paris, with Count Tolstoy.

Back in a room in the Hotel Westminster, on the rue de la Paix, he paid no more heed than before to French intellectual and political life. Paris was wearing its Sunday best: King Louis Philippe was entertaining Ibrahim Pasha. Alexandre Dumas was publishing *The Count of Monte Cristo* and George Sand *La Mare au Diable.* Nothing worth noticing in all that. Annenkov called on Gogol and found him wan and aged. "A profound inner process had stamped the marks of wear and fatigue upon his features, but his general mood seemed brighter and more serene than in the past," he wrote. "It was the face of a philosopher."[5]

A few days later, the same Annenkov, having left Paris for Bamberg, in Bavaria, was mightily surprised, out walking one day, to meet a person whose nose was too long and whose coat was too short and who resembled in every particular the author of *Dead Souls.* Gogol was on his way to Ostend and had emerged from the stagecoach with the other passengers to stretch his legs. The coach would not be leaving for another hour. The two friends visited the famous thirteenth-century basilica, and Gogol exhibited his architectural expertise. Coming out of the church he told Annenkov that he intended to publish his *Selected Passages* soon and that the book would be like a gust of fresh air through the smog and fumes of modern life. His eyes gleamed with the intransigent light of certainty. On an impulse, he enjoined his friend to spend the winter in Naples. "I'll be there myself," he added. "In Naples you will hear things you are not expecting. I will tell you things concerning yourself. Yes, concerning you personally. Man cannot foresee from what quarter his help will come. I tell you, go to Naples and there

I shall reveal to you a secret for which you will thank me." Then he turned to the current upheavals of Europe: "People are beginning to fear that the European trouble—the proletariat—will come to us. They ask why the muzhiks can't be changed into German farmers. Why is this? Can the muzhik be parted from the land? What sort of a proletariat do you see there? Think how our muzhik weeps for joy when he sees the earth. Some lie down and cover it with kisses like a beloved woman. That means something!" He spoke with restrained passion, his eyes on the ground, looking at no one and nothing.

"Gogol was convinced," Annenkov wrote, "that Russia was something unique, subject to special laws, of which no one in Europe had any idea."[6]

When they got back to the stagecoach, the postilion was already sounding his horn. Gogol climbed into the vehicle, wedged himself diagonally against the shoulder of an elderly, overfed German, and said to Annenkov: "Farewell. Remember my words. Think of Naples." The next moment, he was lurching, lost in his meditations, along a road that could tell him nothing new.

After another cold-water cure at Grafenberg following the Priessnitz method, he rejoined the Zhukovskys at Schwalbach. In the meantime, at the posting stations and in his hotel rooms, he had written the first notebooks for his *Selected Passages*. For once, he experienced no difficulty in giving form to these texts based on his pet ideas, those he had so often had occasion to expatiate upon in his letters and conversations; the ease with which he was producing his material persuaded him of its excellence. Divine approbation alone could explain this untroubled flow of his pen across the paper. On July 30, 1846,[7] he sent off the first six chapters to Pletnyev in a notebook written in his own hand, with a few peremptory suggestions:

"Lastly, here is my request! You are to obey it as the most faithful friend obeys that of his friend. Drop all your other affairs and look after the printing of this book, to be called *Selected Passages from My Correspondence with My Friends*. The book is necessary, too necessary to all; that is what I can tell you now; the book itself will explain the rest. When the printing is finished, all will become clear and the misunderstandings that torment you will vanish at once. The printing must take place quietly. Apart from the censor and yourself, no one must know about it. Choose Nikitenko as censor. He is better disposed toward me than the rest. I will write a note to him. Prepare paper for a second printing now; I'm sure it will follow immediately. This book will go better than all my previous ones, because it is my only sane book."[8]

Two days later he wrote to Nikitenko: "I am not at all anxious about this, assured as I am of your kindly disposition and also of the innocence of the book, which I wrote with myself as the sternest of censors. Even supposing that some expression might give you pause at first glance, I am sure that the end of the book will explain its meaning more fully and that you will recognize, in a word, the necessity for it."[9]

He now set off for Ostend, to build up his strength by bathing in the sea during the hot weather. After a shuddering dip in the waves, he would shut himself into his hotel, pick up his pen, and issue lessons in morality, religion, literature, administration, political economy, justice, and patriotism to his contemporaries. Three further notebooks left Ostend by post, addressed to Pletnyev. The fifth, and final, one was sent from Frankfurt, where Gogol had gone at the beginning of October to stay with Zhukovsky again. Nikitenko, however, seemed in no hurry to give his opinion.

"For the love of heaven, use all your strength and resources to hasten the printing of the book," Gogol wrote to Pletnyev. "You must, for me and for the others; you must, in a word, for the good of all. As soon as it is published, prepare as many copies as are necessary and offer them to all the members of the imperial family, including even the children who are not yet of age—all the grand dukes. But accept no gifts from anyone. However, should anyone offer you money for the numerous pilgrims I may chance to encounter on the road to the Holy Land, take it without hesitation."[10]

While he was awaiting the publication of *Selected Passages*, another edifying idea took root in Gogol's mind. On the occasion of a revival of *The Inspector General* in St. Petersburg and Moscow, he thought of adding an act entitled *The Denouement of The Inspector General*. It would be included in the fourth edition of the comedy, and profits from sales would be given to the poor by a committee appointed in an author's preface: Princess Odoevsky, Countess Vyelgorsky, Countess Dashkov, Arkady Rosset (Mrs. Smirnov's brother), Mrs. Aksakov, Mrs. Elagin, Alexis Khomyakov, Peter Kireyevsky, etc. The theme of the *Denouement* was simplicity itself: Gogol had to demonstrate that his comedy was not just a psychological and social satire, but had a mystical significance that no one—including himself, no doubt—had hitherto perceived. When the curtain rose, the "foremost comic actor,"

Shchepkin, would be crowned with a laurel wreath by the other actors, for having well served his art. But in expressing their admiration, the people wanted to know what was the deeper meaning of this play, *The Inspector General,* in which the great actor had triumphed again: no doubt, the author had merely wanted to poke fun at his contemporaries. To his blind flock, Shchepkin would now give the key to the comedy.

"Think carefully of the town we have seen in the play," he would say. "Everybody agrees that there is no such town in Russia. But what if it were the town of our soul, lying within each of us? Let us examine ourselves, if possible with the eyes of Him who will one day summon all men to appear, before Whom even the best among us, do not forget, will lower his gaze in shame. Whatever else you may say, the *inspector general* who waits at the door of the tomb is terrifying. Do you claim not to know who he is? Why pretend? This *inspector general* is our awakened conscience, compelling us, suddenly and at one flash, to see ourselves as we are. From that *inspector general* nothing can be hidden, for he acts on higher orders, knocking at every door by name but not sending in his card until it is too late to change. And then suddenly you will discover such horrors in yourself that your hair will stand on end. When we start out in life, we must hire an *inspector general,* and examine, together with him, what is in us—a real *inspector general,* not a false one, not a Khlestakov. Khlestakov is a snatch-and-grab thief, Khlestakov is the conscience of society. I swear to you that the city of your soul is worth all the trouble you take over it, as a good king does over his domain. And just as he drives out dishonest officials from his land, so must we, nobly and sternly, drive out our inner cheats and swindlers. There is one means, one flail with which we can scourge them all: laughter, my openhearted fellow citizens! The laughter our base passions so dread. The laughter created to ridicule everything that degrades the true beauty of man!"

Clearly, Gogol was trying to convince himself *a posteriori* that *The Inspector General* was a scenic representation of an internal drama. He wanted to see his characters as comic symbols of our personal struggle with our passions, enacted before the eyes of the Judge. He had cherished this idea ever since the revelation that had come to him as he was writing *Dead Souls.* His concern with morality was so all-consuming that he now sought to transform all his past works into an allegorical conflict between vice and virtue, abstract terms in his ethical equation.

Without pausing an instant to think that this fleshless interpretation of the play might not be altogether to an actor's taste, he sent off his *Denouement* to Shchepkin (in Moscow) and Sosnitsky (St. Petersburg), with instructions to perform it at the end of the play. His orders were that the two men were to be crowned on stage at the close of a performance given for their benefit, and were then to explain the work to a grateful audience. Apprised of this latest folly, Gogol's friends were panic-stricken.

"Now I come to this new *Denouement of The Inspector General,*" Aksakov wrote him. "I won't even mention the fact that there is no denouement in it, let alone the other fact that there is no need of one. But have you actually envisaged how, after playing *The Inspector General* for his own benefit, Shchepkin would go about crowning himself with heaven knows what laurels presented by the rest of the cast? You have lost every shred of human modesty. And that is not all. Tell me, honestly and truly, is it possible that your explanation of *The Inspector General* is sincere? Can it be that the idiotic utterances of imbeciles and ignoramuses have frightened you into committing the sacrilege of disfiguring your own creations, treating them as allegorical figures? Is it possible that you do not see how irrelevant is this allegory of the 'city within,' or how nonsensical it is to call Khlestakov a 'social conscience'?"[11]

Gedeonov, director of the imperial theaters, would not allow the *Denouement* to be performed, because "the regulations forbid any expression of an actor's approval of other actors, and even more, the crowning of one of them on stage."[12]

Shchepkin wrote to Gogol a few months later: "After reading your *Denouement,* I became absolutely furious with my short-sightedness, for until then I had studied all the heroes of the play as though they were living persons. All I have seen in them is so familiar and so dear to me, and I have grown so attached to the mayor and Bobchinsky and Dobchinsky, after associating with them for ten years, that it would be dishonesty to tear myself away from them. What will you give me in their place? Let me keep them as they are. I love them, I love them with all their weaknesses. Don't come telling me they are passions instead of government officials. No; I don't want any revisions of that sort. These are real, living men, among whom I have grown up and almost old. I will not give them back to you. I will not give them back as long as I am alive. After me, make them into billy goats, if that's your fancy. But until then, I will not give up even Derzhimorda [the constable], because he, too, is dear to me."[13]

In the face of this concert of expostulations, Gogol gave up the idea of publishing or performing the *Denouement*.[14] "The time is not yet ripe," he wrote to Anna Vyelgorsky.[15] He did not in fact attach any real importance to this little theatrical scheme, in comparison with the *Selected Passages,* which were about to emerge from the censor's office. In the meantime he conveyed himself to Nice, Florence, and Rome— but the Eternal City was not what it had used to be. The new pope, Pius IX, was said to have liberal ideas. The climate had deteriorated. It was cold beneath the blue sky. The venerable monuments had lost their souls. In search of both solar and human warmth, Gogol took himself to Naples, where Count Tolstoy's sister, the devout, mournful, and unctuous Sofya Petrovna Apraxin, was calling him.

In the Apraxin villa, the flames of scores of vigil lights flickered in semidarkness beneath the icons; outside lay the dazzling landscape, the bay of Naples, Vesuvius, the boats at anchor, and the steep twisting streets bedecked with multicolored washing.

"Naples is admirable," Gogol wrote to Zhukovsky, "but I feel that the city would not have seemed so beautiful if God had not prepared my soul to receive the impressions its beauty makes upon me."[16]

"My health has suddenly improved, I am returning to life, my soul and my whole being are refreshed. Before me lies Naples the magnificent! The air is mild and soothing. I have halted here as at some splendid crossroads, awaiting the breeze of divine will that will carry me away to the Holy Land."[17]

In St. Petersburg, meanwhile, Pletnyev was still struggling to get permission to publish the *Selected Passages*. As some of the letters dealt with the Orthodox Church, they had to be submitted to the ecclesiastical censor and so on up to the chief administrator of the Holy Synod, who eventually gave his imprimatur. There remained the ordinary censor, who was being recalcitrant, even though the entire text was infused with respect for the government. Harassed by Gogol, Pletnyev turned to the heir apparent, Grand Duke Alexander Nikolayevich.[18] He agreed with Nikitenko, the censor, who had suggested some lengthy cuts in the book despite "the excellent attitude" displayed by its author.

Gogol was stupefied to learn how his text had been mutilated. Several letters were deleted altogether, others rephrased or ruthlessly cut. Had they not seen, up there, how pure his intentions were? There was something fishy somewhere: his first idea was that Nikitenko and the liberals had connived to disfigure a work whose reactionary tendencies offended them.

"No more than a third of the book has been printed, and even that was truncated and all muddled up; it is some kind of weird stump of a limb, but no book," he wrote to Mrs. Smirnov with some exaggeration. "The most important passages, which were to form the heart of the volume, are not in it—letters designed for the very purpose of making people more familiar with the evils that come from within us in Russia, and showing how to set many things right; letters in which I sincerely thought I was serving the sovereign and all my compatriots! I have just written to Vyelgorsky to ask him to submit those letters to the emperor. My heart tells me he will honor them with his attention and have them printed."[19]

Pletnyev would not ask the monarch to arbitrate, however, and explained his decision to his impetuous employer as follows: "We must not even think of submitting your book recopied in full to the emperor. How could I face the grand duke [Alexander Nikolayevich], when he himself advised me not to publish the passages barred by the censor. I would look as though I were trying to humiliate him by going over his head."[20]

The emperor and his entourage did not trust their overzealous defender. In a country ruled by absolute monarchy it was always dangerous to allow a writer to discuss political, social, and religious issues: even a declared partisan of the established order might all too easily attract the attention of ill-disposed minds to some flaw in the regime. A loyal subject must not concern himself with the conduct of public affairs, not even to praise it. Gogol consoled himself with the thought that the *Selected Passages,* even as pruned by Nikitenko, would give the world a body of truth that would act like yeast upon the formless dough of its soul. For the first time in his life, no doubt, he felt, in that month of January 1847, that he was publishing something he could be proud of. "By this act I desired to pay for the futility of everything I had published before," he wrote in the Preface; "the persons to whom my letters were written say that they contain far more of what men need than do my books. I ask the more prosperous of my readers to buy several copies and give them to those who cannot afford one. I ask all the inhabitants of Russia to pray for me, beginning with the pontiffs of our Church, whose whole lives are spent in prayer."

Some of the thirty-two letters in the original edition of the *Selected Passages* were written especially for the book, others were based on actual correspondence, which had been modified, revised, and reworked. The chapter entitled "A Governor's Wife," for example, reproduced almost verbatim the advice Gogol had given to Mrs. Smirnov; his discourse "To a Person in High Office" and that on "Church and Clergy" were initially addressed to Count A. P. Tolstoy; passages from his exhortations to his mother and sisters and to Danilevsky found their way, joined end to end, into his study of "The Landowner."

The author's ambition was vast. He wanted to regenerate Russia, but without altering the institutions. After reflecting so long upon the problem of good and evil, he had come to think that the salvation of the world lay with individuals and not with governments. So far as each person amended his ways, without seeking to alter his station in life, only so far would mankind as a whole draw nearer to God. Every governor, hence, should strive to be a model for all governors, every society woman a model for society women, and every serf a model for all serfs. And the rule for improvement at every level of the hierarchy was the same; listen to the teachings of the Church and exert a good influence on your neighbor. If each individual would consent to serve Christ in his assigned place, society would progress. In short, the author was opposed to a Christian religion of meditation and denial; he preached a social faith, concrete and incarnate, present in every moment of everyday life. For him, no action, however trivial, was too insignificant to be performed with faith. Religion boiled in the water in the samovar, foamed in the shaving cream, and clinked in the coins tossed down on the counter. The kingdom of heaven filled the kingdom on earth—whence this mixture, in the Gogolian sermons, of flights of mysticism and handy religious recipes to be used in the everyday kitchen. Years later, Leo Tolstoy returned to this theory that the sole remedy for the ailing universe was the spiritual reform of every individual in it. But, for Tolstoy, spiritual reform would end in the negation of State and Church alike. Once he had established the principle of human perfectibility, he refused tsar, courts, army, clergy, police, and every other manifestation of the authority of the few over the many. Gogol, on the other hand, was quite content with the Russia he saw before his eyes. His aim was not to create a new order, but to teach his fellow countrymen how best to serve the existing one. Using the Gospels to back him up, he meant to convert government officials, both great and small, to honesty, socialites to charity, artists to a true understanding of their art, and peasants to the love of labor under the enlightened tutelage of their master, the owner of their persons and of the soil they tilled. In this ideal Orthodox State, each person would perform his duty joyfully, virtue would blossom in the serest of hearts, the wheels of administration would bathe in oil; yet, paradoxically, there would still be police, judges, prisons, rich and poor, and serfs to be sold with the land they stood on. Nicholas I must have felt some satisfaction when he read phrases such as this:

"A State without an absolute monarch is an orchestra without its conductor."[21]

Or: "Each of us, while saving his soul without leaving the State, must save himself within the State. A few decades more and you will see Europe coming to buy not hemp or tallow from us, but wisdom, a commodity no longer to be found on European markets."[22]

Elsewhere: "The more deeply one looks into the workings of the administration, the more one admires the wisdom of its founders: one feels that God himself, unseen by us, built it through the hands of the sovereigns. Everything is perfect, everything is sufficient unto itself. I cannot conceive what use could be found for even one more official."[23]

Gogol's awed reverence for the virtually divine excellence of the imperial administration merely increased the confidence with which he handed out his more banal instructions to the various categories of his readers. Not content with his role as the prophet of a new religious civilization, he also proposed to solve the personal problems of its citizens. The fact that he had lived half his adult life outside Russia and was a bachelor, a peripatetic parasite begging his subsistence from friends or grand dukes, who had never dealt directly with either muzhiks or land and was totally ignorant of the problems of both household management and government administration, did not prevent him from believing himself elected to teach rules of conduct to husbands, society women, governors, landowners, peasants, artists, priests, and judges. As he saw it, his authority upon such matters did not come from experience, but from meditation. A man inspired by God, as he was, could know without learning and teach without knowing. In fact, remaining outside society put him in a better position to direct it.

It emerged from his advice to his contemporaries that whoever would enrich himself morally was almost certain to enrich himself materially as well. Property was not theft: it was the anteroom of paradise. "In a village where the Christian way of life reigns supreme, the peasants positively coin money,"[24] the author wrote. He ordered the landowner never to forget that he held his power in trust from God: "Call your peasants together and tell them who you are and who they are. That if you are their owner and placed above them it was not because you wanted to give orders or to become a landowner but because you are a landowner, you were born a landowner, and God would call you to account if you exchanged your station for some other, for all men must serve God in their own place and not in someone else's; just as they, born under a master's power, must submit to that power. Then tell them that if you make them work and labor hard, it is not at all because you need money for your pleasure—and to prove it, burn some bank-notes then and there while they are watching, so they can see that money is nothing to you—but if you make them work it is because God himself wanted man to earn his bread by work and the sweat of his brow."[25]

If a serf was lazy or a drunkard, his master must not flog him himself, but have "the canton police officer or village elder" do it for him. The guilty one might also be admonished in front of the assembled peasantry "in such a way that everyone would laugh at him." The best thing would be to call him "an unwashed mug." As for universal education, what nonsense! "It is absurd," Gogol wrote, "to teach a peasant to read and write so that he will be able to read the empty nonsense European philanthropists publish for the people!"

His recommendations to a married woman conscious of her duties were equally curious, to say the least. He exhorted her to divide her money "into seven roughly equal piles," the first for household expenses and the seventh for the poor. But love of charity must never get the upper hand of sound bookkeeping: "Even if it were necessary to give aid to some poor person, you cannot use more money for that purpose than there is in the pile set aside for it. Even were you to witness some heartrending misfortune, and you saw that financial assistance would help, even then be careful not to touch the other piles."[26]

The vocation of the governor's wife was to save the souls of officials removed from office by her husband. "Never abandon an official discharged from his duties, however bad he may be: he is unhappy. He should leave your husband's tutelage for yours; he belongs to you."[27]

The author paid a passing compliment to the Russian aristocracy, whose qualities had been displayed in 1812, lavished praise upon the tsar, who was God's representative on earth, set the Orthodox Church above any other, insisted that Pushkin had always revered the authorities, ridiculed his friend Pogodin for being "as busy as an ant," reviled "the mendacious periodicals published in Europe," anathematized "the Decembrists," who had dared, some twenty years before, to rebel in the name of some so-called liberal ideas ("But, thank God, the time is past when a few madmen can disturb the entire State."[28]), and, forgetting all he had suffered himself at the censor's hands, proclaimed, in a letter on Karamzin, "He was the first to declare that the censors could in no way impede a writer and that if the writer is motivated by the purest desire to do good, to such a degree that this desire, invading his whole soul, becomes its flesh and nourishment, then no censor seems harsh to him and he is at ease everywhere! After that, see how ridiculous are those who claim it is impossible to speak the full and complete truth in Russia and say it can only cause trouble!"[29]

There were also, to be sure, some admirable pages on Russian literature in the *Selected Passages,* a perceptive analysis of the works of Zhukovsky, Batyushkov, Griboedov, Pushkin, and Lermontov; but the dominant key of the book was ponderously moralistic. In writing it, Gogol tried to appear absolutely honest. The secretive, withdrawn, dissimulating liar had turned his most hidden pockets inside out. Having made this attempt at openness, he was convinced that his contemporaries, enlightened about him and themselves at last, would thank him for taking such pains to edify them.

And it is true that, immediately after publication of the *Selected Passages,* he received a few encouraging letters:

"This book will increase your influence upon an elite only; the rest will not find sustenance in it," Pletnyev wrote to him. "But, in my opinion, it is the true beginning of Russian literature. Everything that went before was nothing but schoolboy essays culled from a grammar book. You are the first to have extracted ideas from the depths and brought them to light. Whatever anyone else may say, follow your own path. In the little group in which I have lived for the past six years, you are now looked upon as a genius of thought and deed."[30]

Mrs. Smirnov, in transports of enthusiasm, bought twenty copies of the book to distribute to her husband's associates and wrote to the author: "Your book came into the shops in time for the new year. I congratulate you upon its appearance, and Russia as well, for the treasure you have presented to it. Everything you have written thus far, even *Dead Souls,* pales before my eyes as I read it."[31]

But the hymns of praise were soon lost in a blare of invective. Attacks upon *Selected Passages* came from all sides. The liberals accused Gogol of defending a brutal and obsolete absolutism, the reactionaries of presuming to dictate how those in command should perform their duties, and the moderates of abasing himself to get a pension from the emperor. His closest friends were dismayed. Was this madness, a hypocritical maneuver, or sheer stupidity? The latest drawing-room witticism was, "His name should be Tartuffe Vasilyevich, not Nikolai Vasilyevich."[32] Belinsky called him "a Talleyrand, a Cardinal Fesch, who cheated God all his life and cheated Satan at his death."[33] Aksakov, aghast, wrote to his son: "Alas! This exceeds the fondest dreams of Gogol's enemies and the most anguished fears of his friends. The best that can be done now is to call him a madman."

Later in the letter, he wrote: "His entire book is permeated with servility and terrifying conceit parading as humility. He flatters women and their beauty, he flatters Zhukovsky, he flatters those in power. He is not ashamed to write that the truth could be more freely told here than in any other country. Can there be pride more insane than that which drove him to demand that his last will be published in every newspaper immediately upon his death, that no statue be dedicated to him, that everyone must seek to improve himself for love of him?"[34]

A few days later, unable to master his spite, his anger, and his sorrow, Aksakov wrote directly to Gogol: "My friend, if your aim was to cause a scandal, to make your friends and foes stand up and declare themselves—they have now changed places, moreover—then you have amply achieved it. If this publication was one of your jokes, it has succeeded beyond anyone's wildest dreams: everyone is totally mystified. But, alas, I cannot be mistaken: you honestly believed it was your vocation to proclaim great moral truths to mankind in the guise of meditations and sermons. You were grossly and pitifully mistaken. You have confused everything, become hopelessly muddled, you contradict yourself from start to finish, and, thinking to serve heaven and earth, you have offended God and man alike. It was a dark day and hour when you first thought of going abroad to that Rome, the perdition of Russian minds and talents. They will have to answer to God, your blind fanatical friends, the high-class Manilovs who have not only allowed you to go your way but positively encouraged you to fall into the traps of your own mind, of the diabolical conceit which you take to be Christian humility. I cannot pass in silence over the thing that saddens and vexes me most: your ugly attacks upon Pogodin. I could not believe my eyes when I saw how you mocked and dishonored a man you used to call your friend, a man who was indeed your friend, in his fashion. At first, Pogodin was deeply wounded; I was told he even wept."[35]

Shevyrev added his voice to the chorus of reproach: "You have been spoiled by all Russia. By offering you fame, it fed your conceit. And that conceit has showed itself in your book to be colossal, in some places monstrous. Conceit is never so hideous as when it is coupled with faith. In faith, pride is a monstrosity."[36]

Even Father Matthew Konstantinovsky, archpriest of Rzhev and confessor of Count A. P. Tolstoy, who had recommended the priest to Gogol, accused the author of writing a harmful book that would turn people away from the Church, toward the false pleasures of the theater and poetry. Every day brought the writer some fresh outburst of indignation or aggrieved astonishment. And, as usual, the heavier the blows rained down upon his head, the more he wanted.

"Do not fail to pass on every opinion, your own and those of other people," he wrote Shevyrev. "Ask other people, too, to find out what is being said about my book at every level of society, not excluding the servant class, and for this purpose ask people who like to perform acts of charity to buy copies of the book and give them to simple and needy persons."[37]

His reaction to the criticism was, as always, a mixture of pride and humility. At first he acknowledged his error, but justified it immediately afterward. This swing from total admission of defeat to arrogant retort was so natural in him that the same letter, begun as an act of contrition, would end in a sermon.

"The publication of my book has resounded like a slap in the face," he wrote to Zhukovsky. "In the face of the public, in those of my friends, and even more stingingly in my own. When it struck me, it was like someone waking after a dream, feeling like a guilty schoolboy, as though I had done more than I had bargained for. In this book I had laid about me with my cudgel like a Khlestakov, so fiercely that I haven't the courage to look at it any more. Never mind; it will remain upon my table like a faithful mirror in which I must look to see all my uncleanness, and sin less hereafter."

But the next line reads, "Nevertheless, it is a useful book. Every copy was sold in a week (and I had ordered two printings). In itself, it is not a major work in our literature, but it can engender many major works."[38]

The same day, he wrote back to Aksakov, who had so violently called him to account: "Thank you, good and honest friend, for your reproaches. They made me sneeze, but sneeze for my health." This is immediately followed by: "I would merely point out to you that a man who seeks so avidly to know himself, who welcomes every judgment, and sets such great store by the comments of intelligent people—even when they are harsh and cruel—such a man cannot be *utterly* and *completely* blind about himself."[39]

He adopted the same attitude with Anna Vyelgorsky, who had reluctantly passed on to him some of the reactions to *Selected Passages* in St. Petersburg: "I know that nasty things are being said about me in society, about my duplicity, my hypocritical principles, and my ulterior motives of personal interest or favoritism. I need to know all that, and also who speaks of me and in what terms. Believe me, my next books will be as universally approved as this one has been universally contested. But first, I needed to become more intelligent. And to become more intelligent I absolutely had to publish this work and hear what everyone had to say about it, especially those who were hostile to it."[40]

Prince Vladimir Vladimirovich Lvov wrote a melancholy letter in which he reproached Gogol for yielding to the "spirit of pride," whereupon Gogol tried to explain the origins of that pride and the reasons why he was both proud and ashamed of having published his book: "When I think of the impropriety and complacency of many passages of my book, I burn with shame. That shame is useful to me. If my book had not been published, I should not know the half of my condition, I should not have discovered in their full nakedness all those flaws that were so obvious to you, for there would have been no one to point them out to me. The people I see nowadays are seriously convinced of my perfection. Where, then, was I to find a voice condemning me? If the book had not been published, I should have remained blind to myself."[41]

Later he produced a different version of the genesis of his work, for the critic Nikolai Pavlov: "At that time there was no friend nearby to prevent me. But I think that if my closest friend had been there, I should not have listened even to him, so strongly did I feel that I was at the summit of my development and that I saw all things clearly. I did not even show some of the letters to Zhukovsky, who could have objected to them."[42]

Thus, although he gave way before the flood of criticism, Gogol remained convinced of three things: firstly, that his book, however imperfect, was useful to others and to himself; secondly, that if he had written it, God had willed it so; and thirdly, that his past experience, his long meditations, and his natural inclination to pedagogy qualified him to instruct his fellow men. What he did not dare say to some of his disdainful correspondents he wrote to Mrs. Smirnov, whose admiration was unreserved: "God is merciful. Was it not He Who gave me the desire to serve Him by my work? Who else could have done so? Or am I forbidden to glorify His name, when every other creature glorifies it? I am criticized for daring to speak of God; it is said that I had no right, because I am cursed with insane self-love and conceit. How can I help it if, in spite of these failings, I still want to talk about God? How could I be silent when the very stones are ready to shout the name of God? No, you wise gentlemen, you will not make me lose heart with your claims that I am unworthy, that I do not have the right, that it is not my business. Every one of us, even the lowliest, has that right and must teach his fellow by showing him the way, in accordance with the will of Christ and the Apostles."[43]

The mail from Russia brought more than letters: sometimes Gogol would find a newspaper or a periodical waiting for him at the Naples post office, with a story about himself outlined in pencil. Apart from a few tolerant notices, the press was also comminatory. Belinsky, leader of the "European" movement, ranted and raved in *The Contemporary:*

"Gogol instructs, edifies, stigmatizes, vituperates, pardons. He takes himself for some sort of village priest, or for the pope of his little Catholic world."

Belinsky's ire was clearly intensified by the fact that he had long regarded Gogol as a great realistic writer whose duty was to denounce the wretchedness of the poor. For him, this bombastic, servile, incense-reeking book was more than a failure: it was treason. Gogol was exasperated to find himself so misunderstood by the man who had formerly sung his praises, and replied: "I was aggrieved by your article in the second issue of *The Contemporary*—not because I was pained by the abuse you wished to heap upon me publicly, but because I could hear, underneath it, the voice of a man who was angry with me. At no point in my book did I wish to cause you pain. How is it that everyone in Russia, without exception, is angry with me? I am still unable to understand it: Easterners, Westerners, and neutrals, all are indignant. You read my book with the eyes of a furious man, and that is why you have taken against it so. Believe me, it is no easy matter to judge a book that is impregnated with the inner life of someone very different from the rest of the world, someone very withdrawn, moreover, who has been living away from society for a long time, and suffers from an inability to express himself. Write the harshest rebukes, choose the words most likely to humiliate, help to make me ridiculous in the eyes of your readers, and do not spare the most sensitive fibers of a particularly tender heart —all that I will bear, albeit in pain. But it is hard, very hard indeed, I tell you honestly, to know that someone nurses a personal grievance against me—even someone evil, and I thought you were good."[44]

Gogol sent this letter to Belinsky in St. Petersburg, but the critic received it at Salzbrunn, in Silesia, where he had gone for treatment. Consumed by tuberculosis and very conscious of his approaching death,[45] he attached even more importance than before to the ideas he had defended throughout his life: his hatred of despotism, mistrust of the Church, hopes for scientific and social progress culminating in a luminous republic in which all citizens would be perfectly equal. Gogol's self-justifications only revived the critic's initial irritation with the book. The censor had prevented him from saying a tenth of what he thought in his article; here was an opportunity to make up for it. So! Gogol doesn't understand why people are angry with him, he said to Annenkov, who shared his lodgings. Well, it will have to be explained to him, then. I shall answer him.

His skin was pale, his cheeks hollow, his expression seething with hatred. Wrapping a shawl around his shoulders, he sat at his round table and began jotting down his thoughts with a pencil on scraps of paper. Then he drafted his letter. It took him three days. When he had finished, he read it to Annenkov, who was alarmed by the ferocity of the diatribe and begged him not to send it. But Belinsky was adamant: "Everything must be done to protect people from a man who has lost his mind, were that man Homer himself. As for the question of offending Gogol, I could never offend him as deeply as he has offended me, by destroying my trust in him."[46]

And so the letter was sent: a heavy wad of closely written sheets. Gogol received it in Ostend, where he had gone to bathe in the sea. The first lines stunned him. The blow was so violent that the blood rushed to his head, and he pursued his reading through a mist of tears, skipping sentences to reach the end more quickly:

"Yes, I did love you with all the passion a man profoundly attached to his country can feel for someone who was its hope, honor, glory, one of its great guides toward knowledge, evolution, and progress. I cannot give you any idea at all of the anger your book aroused in every noble heart. You know Russia in depth only as an artist, not as a thinker—the role you so disastrously appropriate to yourself in your demented book. It has long been your habit to look out upon Russia from your lofty remoteness! But everyone knows that it is easy to see things however one likes, from afar. And so you never noticed that Russia itself, far from looking to mysticism, asceticism, and pietism for salvation, saw it in the increase of civilization, education, and human understanding. It does not need sermons (it has heard quite enough of them) or prayers (it has uttered quite enough of them too); it needs the people to become aware of human dignity, a sense that has been lost in the mire and manure for so many centuries. The most acute, the most pressing national problems for Russia are the abolition of serfdom and corporal punishment, and the strict observance of at least those laws we have. And this is the moment chosen by a great writer to bring out a book in which he instructs a barbarian landowner, in the name of Christ and the Church, how to make more money out of his muzhiks and humiliate them more adroitly. If you had made an attempt upon my life, I should not have loathed you more than I do for the ignoble lines you have written there! And to say a book like that is the result of arduous inner struggles and divine illumination of the soul? It's impossible! Either you are ill and need care, or—I dare not say what I think. Preacher of the knout, apostle of ignorance, champion of obscurantism, panegyrist of barbarism, what are you doing? Look at your feet. You are standing at the edge of an abyss. How could you, the author of *The Inspector General* and *Dead Souls,* begin singing hymns to the glory of the disgusting Russian clergy, setting it even higher than the Catholic priesthood? I remember even now how you present the idea that education is not necessary for the people, is actually harmful to it, as some great and unarguable truth. May your Byzantine God forgive you that Byzantine thought! Behind the seemingly incidental demonstrations of your book a deliberate conviction can be seen, and your hymns in praise of the authorities are so convenient to the earthly needs of their devout author. That is why it was said all over St. Petersburg that you wrote the book because you hope to be appointed tutor to the heir apparent. What can be so surprising, then, in the fact that your book has lowered you in the eyes of the public both as a writer and, what is even more serious, as a man? In literature alone, despite the tyrannical censor, is there still any life or forward movement among us. The public looks to Russian authors as its sole guides, defenders, saviors from Russian autocracy and orthodoxy. That is why it is always ready to forgive an author for writing a bad book, but it will never forgive him for writing a pernicious one. If you love Russia, you ought to join me in rejoicing at the failure of your book. Prayer is possible anywhere, and the only people who seek Christ in Jerusalem are those who have never found him in their hearts, or have lost him. There is nothing new, to begin with, in the humility you preach, and in addition, it exudes a truly terrifying conceit and ignominious abasement of your own human dignity. A man who slaps his neighbor's face arouses indignation, but one who strikes himself arouses contempt. It is not the truth of Christian doctrine that can be found in your book, but rather a morbid fear of death, the devil, and hell. . . ."[47]

Gogol remained dazed by this tongue-lashing for several days. He, who had thought to serve the cause of his fellow men by opening his heart to them—here he was being suspected of the vilest crimes. His love for the tsar, his respect for the Church, his affection for the people, his devotion to ancestral tradition, his passion for the Russian land, for Russian history, his thirst for charity: everything was misinterpreted. Covered with abuse, he did not know what attitude to adopt. Christian humility dictated that he submit to the ordeal, but his self-respect as a writer rebelled at the injustice. He wrote out several drafts for a reply to Belinsky. Bitter phrases flowed from his pen: "Why is there such hatred in you? It is not the conceited fatuousness and superficiality of the journalist that can judge truly of such matters." But no; such protestations were unworthy of the author of the Selected Passages. In the end, he mastered his spleen and wrote, with the sorrowful tranquillity that befitted a reviled prophet:

"My soul is exhausted, everything in me is overwhelmed. I read your letter in a state of near unconsciousness. What to reply? God knows, perhaps there is some truth in what you say. I can only tell you that I have received nearly fifty letters about my book and no two of them were alike. No two men exist who can agree upon the same subject. What one denies, the other asserts. And yet there are honest and intelligent people on both sides. What does seem to be beyond question is that I know nothing of Russia, that many things have changed since I have been living abroad, and that I must learn, starting almost from scratch, what is there now. The coming century is a century of rational awakening. Do believe it: you and I are equally guilty in the eyes of this century. You and I have both gone too far. I at least admit it, but do you? Just as I have too much *concentrated* myself upon myself, so have you *dispersed* yourself too much. Just as I need to learn many things that you know and I do not, so you ought to learn at least a fraction of what I know and you mistakenly scorn."[48]

He hoped that this justification would disarm Belinsky, but it was not enough to relieve him. Sorrow, disgust, and discouragement weighed upon his breast. Shortly after the publication of the *Selected Passages,* he learned of the death of his friend Yasykov.[49] He had not been exaggeratedly cast down at the time, but now it added a funereal note to the disillusionment caused by the failure of his book. All his letters sang the same refrain, monotonous as the moan of a wounded man.

"How is it that my wits are not completely gone; why have I not gone stark mad in this crazy tumult? I cannot understand it," he wrote to Aksakov. "If you put ycurself in my position, you would see that I am more unhappy than any I may have offended. It is hard to find oneself in the center of this hurricane of misunderstanding. I see that I am going to have to give up the pen for a long time, and go far away from everything."[50]

But, Aksakov having written, "By your book you have dealt yourself a terrible blow and that is why I have attacked you so—as I should have attacked anyone else dealing such a blow to you," Gogol recovered his majesty long enough to reply: "I have never been particularly frank with you; I have hardly ever spoken to you of what was nearest my soul, so that you can hardly have known me otherwise than as an author, not as a man. True, my book dealt me a blow, but it was the will of God. Without that blow I should not have come back to myself or seen so clearly what I lack. How can you repeat the nonsense babbled by shortsighted people after reading my book? My book is in the straight and steady line of my inner formation, essential if I am to become anything more than a superficial, empty writer, if I am to become fully conscious of the sacredness of my profession. I will say it again: you may be right in your analysis of my book, but by passing a final judgment upon it you betray your own pride."[51]

Later, as his bitterness toward his overhonest and exacting friend increased, he decided to tell him exactly how he felt about him. When he reviewed his relations with the rest of the world, he had to admit that only those persons who could give him material or moral assistance were of any interest to him. He could not imagine having any dealings with someone who was of no use to either his daily or his literary life. Loving people not for themselves but as they related to himself, he saw them chiefly as servants to his cause—which could be served, moreover, in a multitude of ways: by offering him hospitality, by confessing to him, by giving him material for his books, by doing favors for him, by praising his works, and even by criticizing them, respectfully.

"I cared far less for you than you for me," he coldly informed Aksakov. "Besides, it seems to me that I have always been disposed to like everyone, for I am incapable of hatred; but I can only like a person in particular, in preference to anyone else, out of *interest*.[52] If anyone can truly *advance*[52] me, and if through him my mind is enriched, if he has made me see something new about himself or others; if, in a word, I have increased my knowledge as a result of his acquaintance, then I like that person, even if he is less worthy of love than another, and even if he cares less for me. What can I do about it? You see what a strange creature is man: what counts most with him is his personal interest. How can one say? Perhaps I would have liked you better if you had given something to my mind, even notes on your own life, something that might have told me what kind of people I ought not to put in my books and what features of the Russian personality I ought to immortalize in public memory. But you did nothing of this kind for me. That being so, can I help it if I have not loved you as much as I ought to have done?"[53]

Relations between the two men were temporarily broken off as a result of this exchange, but without bitterness on Gogol's part. True, he was incapable of caring for Aksakov, in spite of the man's loyalty and past devotion to him. When he looked back over his life, he found that he had known but three deep affections: Pushkin the phoenix, whose poetry he had admired; Ivanov the ascetic, whose painting he had admired; and Joseph Vyelgorsky the fair boy, whose youth, now eternally frozen in death, he had admired. Aksakov had as yet written nothing spectacular and could hardly be compared with these stars in the firmament.[54] For Gogol, he was a nice chap, well educated and hospitable. An obliging friend. A singer of praises. A singer who had joined the enemy camp. A curious seesaw movement had taken place in the literary world, with onetime detractors hailing his return to "sensible ideas" and former admirers covering him with opprobrium. After defending himself in individual answers to his new "enemies," he resolved to justify himself to the public at large by writing an "author's confession."[55] In this long-winded argument he sought once again to clear himself of the charge of servility toward the authorities and contempt for the people.

"This book [*Selected Passages*] is the faithful mirror of human nature," he wrote. "In it can be found what is found in every man. First, the desire for the good, then an honest awareness of one's own faults, and beside it a high estimation of one's merits; a sincere desire to learn, and with it the certainty that one is capable of teaching others; humility and, with it, pride, and perhaps pride in that very humility. In short, in this book there is what is in each of us, with the difference that there it is all said, without any concern for conventions or proprieties, and everything ordinarily hidden by men is seen naked, all the more striking and blatant because it is an author displaying it."

Having to some degree relieved himself in this explanatory memorandum, Gogol left the manuscript in his drawer. He was afraid that publishing it would stir up a painful quarrel. It would be wiser to let the fuss die down. It was also around this time he wrote his *Meditations upon Divine Liturgy,* which he envisaged as an aid to the faithful in understanding the different phases of the religious service. But he could not bring himself to publish this text either.[56] He vaguely felt that, for the time being at least, he should not engage in any more didacticism. Russian readers were not ready for his thought. They were put off by abstraction. Like children, they needed concrete examples, a story. The good the author had been unable to do in his letters, he would achieve with his next novel.

"Instead of speaking to society in the language of impassioned reasoning," he said, "let the writer use the language of living images!" However, for Gogol those "living images" had to correspond to Russian reality, and he had humbly confessed that he had only the vaguest of ideas of that Russian reality. In his preface to a new edition of *Dead Souls,* he had already appealed to all his readers for notes, reminiscences, personality traits, or descriptions of specifically Russian events: "I send this urgent prayer to all who will kindly give me the fruit of their thoughts. I beg them not to think that they are writing to a man as well educated as they or who has the same tastes and thoughts and could understand many things without explanations, but to behave as though, on the contrary, they were talking to someone far less learned than themselves, or even totally untaught."

To his great surprise, no one answered. The public refused to help him in his task. But, now more than before, he needed these "details and odds and ends that prove that the person actually existed."[57] Having decided to take up the sequel to his "poem," he reopened his heroes' files. It was up to his friends to provide the information and anecdotes; no excuses, please; off to work, everybody!

"It would be no trouble for you to begin a sort of diary," he wrote to Arkady Rosset, "and take notes like this every day: 'Today I heard such-and-such opinion; it was expressed by Soandso; his life style, his personality (in a word, his portrait in broad outline)! If you don't know him, write, 'I don't know how he lives, but I presume etc. etc.; he seems to be a respectable type (or otherwise); this is how he holds his hands, blows his nose, takes his snuff, etc.' In short, omit nothing, either essentials or insignificant characteristics. Believe me, this will not be a boring task. You will not need to make any outline or follow any particular order. Just a few lines scribbled on the paper before you go to wash."[58]

His instructions to Arkady Rosset's sister, Mrs. Smirnov, were even more explicit. If she had faith in his word and his talent, she should include a portrait of someone in her circle in every letter: "For instance, today you might take the title *A Provincial Lioness*[52] and, choosing a woman you take to be typical of such persons, describe her, giving me details of her mannerisms, how she sits, how she speaks, what she wears, what manner of men have their heads turned by her. . . . Tomorrow you might choose *A Misunderstood Woman* and paint her for me in the same way. Then *A Lady of Charity* and then *An Honest Prevaricator,* then *A District Bigwig.*[52] In short, any character that seems able to give an exact idea of the class to which he belongs. I think you will enjoy this task, for as you are sketching these portraits you will imagine me before you and feel that you are doing it for me."[59]

In his insouciance, he did not hesitate to set the same task for his friend Danilevsky's wife, whom he had never seen: "Whenever you have a free moment at home, I ask you to draw for me, as lightly and briefly as possible, little portraits of people you knew before, or still see.

Don't get it into your head that this will be difficult. All you need do is think of someone and imagine him in your mind. Do not be annoyed with me for importuning you in this way, before I have even had a chance to deserve your consideration; but I have a great need to know the Russian, wherever he may be and whatever his place in society. These life studies are as necessary to me as to a painter about to embark upon a great painting. He includes none of them in his final work, but they are all in his mind and he refers to them constantly in order not to get muddled, not to cheat or stray from reality. Also, if God has given you a special gift and if, when you are in company, you are able to perceive the grotesque or insipid sides of those around you, you can create *types*[52] for me, that is, characters who in themselves represent a whole category of people, such as *The Lion of Kiev, A Misunderstood Provincial Lady, A European-style Civil Servant, An Old-Believer Civil Servant,*[52] etc. And if you are of a sympathetic nature and are touched by your fellow men, describe for me the pains and injuries of your society. By doing this you will be performing a Christian action, for with God's help I shall make a good work out of it all. My poem can be a necessary and very useful thing, for no sermon can affect minds as strongly as a gallery of *living portraits,*[52] arising out of the same earth and modeled in the same flesh as ourselves."[60]

In spite of his weekly reiterated appeals, his friends in Russia, whether out of laziness or out of frivolity, failed to send him the information he required. It was as though nobody took his request seriously. But, without information, he could not set to work. Or, at least, that was the excuse he gave himself for doing nothing. After a short burst of reanimation, he again began to doubt his creative powers. It was all so vague in his weary brain! Would he still know how to shape a plot and manipulate characters? Wasn't his impotence a sign that God had lost patience with him? And if that was the case, shouldn't he give up literature altogether? He wrote to Father Matthew Konstantinovsky for reassurance:

"Christ's law can also be obeyed by an author. If an author has been given talent, it was surely not for nothing, or to be used for evil. Could not an author show, in a compelling novel, living examples of better men than those portrayed by other authors? Examples are more effective than arguments. Before he begins, he need only have learned to be good himself, and to please God, however little, in his life. As for myself, having talent and knowing how to make vivid portraits of people and nature, am I not morally obliged to depict good people, who believe in and live according to the law of God? That is the reason why I am a writer, not for fame or profit."[61]

To Zhukovsky: "Let the writer, if he has been endowed with that creative power which enables him to create images, first accomplish his education as a man and a citizen of his country, and only afterward take up his pen. In any genuine work of art, there is something soothing and conciliating. Reading it, the soul fills with harmonious acquiescence and, at the end, is satisfied. Art brings order and harmony into the soul, not upheaval and disorder. If you find this letter worthy of consideration, keep it. When a new edition of the *Selected Passages* is prepared, it could be placed at the beginning of the book instead of the *Testament,* with a title such as *Art Is Reconciliation with Life.*"[62]

Artistic perfection and moral perfection having become one and indivisible in his eyes, his trip to the Holy Land beckoned more insistently than ever. He had previously thought of the pilgrimage as an expression of gratitude to God, after completion of the second volume of *Dead Souls.* As that book was still in limbo, he now envisaged going to the tomb of the Lord in search of inspiration. Submission to a state of grace had unconsciously become a call for help. In his present state of uncertainty, this was his last resort. If Christ would consent to bless his work, he would be saved. Otherwise . . . The mere thought of failure chilled his blood. He was torn between his longing to go and his dread of returning empty-handed. What was more, he had found no one to join him on the trip. The crossing was said to be dangerous. He was afraid of the sea, afraid of all those sordid Eastern towns in which he would have to sleep, afraid of leaving the Holy Sepulcher as cold as he was when he found it. Back in 1846, when he thought he was about to go, he had written to his mother: "All the time I shall be traveling, I ask you not to leave your house, to stay at Vasilyevka. I need you to pray for me at Vasilyevka and nowhere else. Anyone who wants to see you can come there. Tell everyone that you do not think it proper to go to anyone else or think of other things while your son is making a pilgrimage."[63]

Now he was even more anxious. To put off his departure, he had had recourse to his poor health, lack of money, some vague work in progress; then, suddenly, he ran to Paris, Frankfurt, Ems, Ostend, and back to Naples by way of Marseilles, Nice, Genoa, Florence, and Rome. These jerky, hurried journeys filled up the time of preparation for the great adventure. He would rather have occupied it in prayer, but the harder he prayed, the more upset he grew. In spite of his determination to achieve excellence, his soul simply would not rise from the earth.

"To you I can confess," he wrote to Mrs. Smirnov, "that my prayers are dry. Before, I used to think I prayed well, I knew how to pray. And now I see that if He to Whom we pray does not desire it, it is impossible to pray. Nevertheless I pronounce my poor powerless words, however arid my soul, however sluggish and heavy my tongue."[64]

To Shevyrev: "I often wonder what I am going to do in Jerusalem. If my pilgrimage pleased God, I should be fired with longing to go, my whole being would be reaching toward that goal, and I should have no regard for the difficulties of the voyage. But my soul is filled with indifference and drought."[65]

To Mrs. Smirnov: "I am more cowardly than I thought: everything frightens me. Perhaps it all comes from my nerves. I am going to have to go all by myself. There is no companion here to sustain me in moments of crisis. I shall have to go in the season when the sea is rough too, and the slightest roll or pitch makes me seasick. My soul is troubled by it all, and this is so, of course, because my zeal is spineless and my faith weak."[66]

Should he give it up? Sometimes he thought he would. But he had talked about the trip so much that he could not back out now. And, then, the Almighty would certainly hold it against him if he defaulted. As the days went by, he felt increasingly uncertain of his personal relations with the celestial powers; it was as though, God having lost confidence in him, he could no longer have confidence in God, as though there was the same estrangement between God and himself as between him and his fellow men. A sign: he implored Providence to give him a sign.

His solitude was total, irreparable, terrifying. He was alone in the world and alone in the Church. He had set himself up as a father-confessor without consulting a single spiritual authority. Self-taught in all things, his sole sources of inspiration had been his haphazard reading and silent meditations. But now, suddenly, he needed to lean upon someone. Count Tolstoy had recommended to him that archpriest of Rzhev, Father Matthew Konstantinovsky—a half-ignorant ascetic whose faith was exacting, narrow, and unshakable. Gogol's only knowledge of him was by letter; but he had been impressed by Father Matthew's brutal certainty. In the agony of his doubt, he turned to him again.

"It is hard to pray," he wrote. "How can one pray if God does not want it? Oh, my friend, my God-given confessor! I burn with shame and do not know where to hide in the infinite multitude of my weaknesses and vices, whose existence I had not even dreamed of. I am not even sure I still believe. If I see God-made-Man into Christ, it is my reason, and not my faith, that commands me to do so. I do not believe, but I want to believe. And even so, I am going off to worship at the Holy Sepulcher! Oh, pray for me; pray that God will not chastise me for my unworthiness and will deign to allow me to pray."[67]

Paradoxically, the "sign" he wanted before setting out came from the Italian rebels. As though on command, uprisings broke out in most of the big towns. The part of the peninsula not directly subject to Austrian rule was demanding a "constitution." That fashionable word made Gogol's hackles rise. Even in Naples the streets no longer seemed safe. He was amazed that the least serious people on earth should allow themselves to be dragged into politics like everyone else. When all was said and done, he told himself, the raging of the masses was even more distasteful than the raging of the sea. Fearing fresh disturbances, he hastened his preparations for departure. Before leaving Italy, he composed a prayer and sent it to his mother and friends with the request that they read it themselves and have it read by a priest during a series of services said for his sake: "God, let his voyage be without danger, his stay in the Holy Land beneficial, and his return to his homeland happy and untroubled. Restore the sea's calm and soothe the tempestuous roar of the wind. Fill his soul with lofty thoughts throughout his trip. Help him to leave the Holy Sepulcher with renewed strength, courage, and ardor, and to return to his work for the good of his native land and the elevation of all our hearts, who celebrate Thy Holy Name."

After taking these precautions, he embarked, sick with anguish, on a little steamboat, the *Capri*, bound for Malta.

3. Jerusalem

The sea was relatively calm, but the monotonous sway of the ship eventually conquered Gogol, whose heaving stomach tied his insides in knots. Icy sweat bathed his face. "Without exception, all the passengers showed compassion for me, saying they had never seen anyone suffer so much," he wrote Count Tolstoy when he disembarked at Malta.[1] His limp legs could hardly carry him through the streets. Lying nerveless in a wretched hotel room, both smaller and dirtier even than his cabin on the *Capri,* he waited in terror to board another ship five days later. He scribbled a few more letters to friends, informing them that he was dying and exhorting them to select particularly fervent priests to perform the propitiatory services essential to the success of his voyage.

On January 27, 1848, he left Malta for Constantinople, where he boarded a third ship, a vessel of Lloyd's of Austria, for Smyrna. There he changed to yet another craft, the *Istambul,* a steamboat belonging to the same company, bound for Beirut. This time the sea was so calm that even Gogol did not suffer. A crowd of pilgrims of every nationality thronged the deck, all going to the tomb of the Lord. Among them was a Russian general named Krutov, in a white uniform and scarlet fez, and a shy, bearded little pope, Father Peter Solovyev. Gogol was wearing a broad-brimmed white hat and an Italian cape. "He was small," Father Peter wrote, "with a long nose, thin black mustaches, and long hair worn in the artists' fashion; he stooped slightly and was always looking at his feet."[2] After becoming acquainted with the priest, Gogol showed him a little icon of St. Nicholas of Myra, which was, he said, an exact replica of an old miniature of the bishop-martyr preserved at Bari. He said that St. Nicholas was both his patron saint and the protector of travelers on land and at sea. He had had some misgivings about the powers of the holy image between Naples and Malta, but all his confidence was restored by the time the ship came in sight of Beirut.

The Russian consul general there was none other than Konstantin Bazili, an old classmate of Gogol's from Nyezhin. A skillful diplomat, great connoisseur of the Near East, and author of books on Turkey and Greece, he had remained faithful to the friendships of his youth and joyfully welcomed the man his comrades used to call "the mysterious dwarf." He invited Gogol to stay with him, and there the author spent a few days recovering from his trip. Then he set out with Bazili, who wanted to be his guide, across the Syrian desert toward Jerusalem.

The journey, at a monotonous snail's pace, put his mind to sleep. His curiosity waned daily. "I saw this country as though in a dream," he wrote.[3] They rose before dawn, climbed onto their mules, and the caravan stretched along the shore between guides mounted and on foot. On one side, the blue waves of the Mediterranean; on the other, gray sand; and beyond, the bony slopes of the mountains. At noon, a halt beside a well shaded by dusty olive trees or sycamores. Then the lulling gait of the mules again, dry heat of the sky, dazzle of the desert, feeble green of thistles, three scrawny camels kneeling in front of a tent, and so it went until "on the horizon, burnt copper by the setting sun, would appear five or six palm trees and a little hamlet standing out from the iridescent shadows, picturesque from afar, sordid at close range."[4]

Thanks to Bazili, who, as representative of the "Grand Padishah" of Russia, enjoyed the esteem of the Arab chiefs, their lodgings were relatively comfortable. But even in the best houses, the divan cushions harbored bushels of fleas; and swarms of mosquitoes hummed, and the desert wind parched the throat and scorched the eyes. Gogol lay sleepless and cursing night after night, and Bazili begged him not to show his ill humor. They crossed sun-gutted Sidon, Tyre sleeping behind its medieval ramparts, Acre with its suffocating bazaars, and scores of nameless, dead villages. The trail moved back from the coast, the arid ground began to rise. Stone, brazen light, patches of moss. They were approaching Jerusalem. Gogol, his back aching from the jogging of his mule, prepared himself for the revelation. From the summit of a hill he saw the holy city, dull white, fragmented, in a transparent vapor. The travelers entered by the Jaffa Gate and stopped in front of the house of the Orthodox patriarch.

The next morning, Gogol edged out into the narrow, twisting streets, between low houses joined by overhead archways, visited the noisy markets, mingled with the slow-moving, dense crowd around the stalls: the Jews, Turks, Armenians, Arabs, and Greeks; and returned from his walk aghast at the dirt, indifference, and disorder that reigned in this site sanctified by the memory of Christ. That Jerusalem should be under Ottoman domination seemed to him an insult to the memory of Our Lord.

After fasting and prayer, he went to the Holy Sepulcher. Five or six Turkish guards, squatting among cushions on a rug-covered platform, were smoking and playing chess as they watched the entrance. The massive doors stood open. Gogol crossed himself and entered. The first thing he saw, in the light of the lanterns and tapers, was a large pink marble slab called the "Unction Stone," on which, tradition says, Christ was embalmed after being taken down from the Cross. Under the central apse stood the sanctuary venerated above all others: the Holy Sepulcher, divided into two parts. The first was a sort of anteroom, where the angel had stood to announce the Resurrection; the second was where the body of the Lord had lain. The ceiling of the latter was so low that one could not stand upright in it, and it was so small that no more than three people could be inside it at the same time. The walls were sheathed in marble, and there was a marble table over the tombstone that served as an altar. How much more moving the crypt would have been, starkly bare: the naked rock, the gaping hole, without all this glossy, sumptuous decoration. Gogol paid to have a service sung by an Orthodox priest. "I was alone," he wrote. "In front of me there was no one but the priest performing the service. The deacon calling the people to worship was behind me, outside the Sepulcher walls. I could hear his voice in the distance, and the answering voices of the people and choir echoed still farther away. The mingled chanting of the Russians repeating, 'Lord, have mercy on us!' and the other religious hymns were barely audible, as though coming from another world. It was all wonderful! But I can't remember praying. I think I was only rejoicing to find myself in a place so propitious for prayer, so suitable for worship; but, to tell the truth, I didn't have time to pray. At least I think that was so. The liturgy sped by so quickly that the most winged prayers could not have flown after it. Before I had time to pull my wits together, I found myself facing the chalice which the priest had fetched and was holding out to my unworthy self for communion."[5]

He confirmed this deplorable impression in a letter to Count Tolstoy: "Not only were my prayers unable to rise up to heaven, I could not even tear them loose from my breast. Never before had I felt so keenly my insensitivity, and how dry and hard I was, like a block of wood."[6]

He left the Holy Sepulcher in a state of total prostration. His heart was oppressed by the feeling that there had been some dreadful mis-understanding. The person he had come all this way to meet had missed the rendezvous. He dragged himself, cold and mute, to the walled Garden of Gethsemane. He struggled manfully, but could not imagine either Christ or the Apostles in the shadow of these pale leaves quivering in the breeze. Elsewhere he was shown Jesus' footprint in a stone, where he had leaped up to heaven; and Pilate's palace, now a barracks. And the house of Veronica. The metropolitan even gave him a little piece of the tombstone and a bit of wood from the door of the Church of the Resurrection, which had burned in the fire of 1808. He accepted the relics with feigned delight. He talked, prayed, crossed him-self; but solitude reigned within. His only emotions came from the land-scape, as when he admired the shores of the Dead Sea.

"Not a tree, not one bush, a wide unchanging plain," he said. "At the foot of this plain, or rather this mountain, down below, shone the Dead Sea. I cannot describe the loveliness of that sea in the setting sun. The water was not blue or green or sapphire, it was purple."[7]

He was no longer expecting anything from his pilgrimage. Time had erased all traces of the footsteps of the Lord on this stony, sun-scorched earth. His true presence was in the books he had inspired, not in the ground he had trod. Jerusalem, Bethlehem, Nazareth, the Mount of Olives, Golgotha, the Jordan—they were so many names to beguile the traveler's imagination before he came; now, emptied of their mys-tery, they represented only a squalid, vermin-ridden, Oriental gloom.

"What have all these Stations of the Cross of Our Saviour got to say to us now," he wrote to Zhukovsky; "the Holy Sepulcher, Golgotha, the place where Christ was shown to the people by Pontius Pilate, the residence of the High Priest, where he was taken, the site of the Holy Cross—when all these places have been gathered together under the roof of a single church? What is there for artist or poet in the landscapes of Judea with their monotonous hills, like the gray waves of the sea in a gale? No doubt, it was all very picturesque in the Saviour's lifetime, when Judea was nothing but gardens and every Jew sat in the shade of the tree he had planted himself; but today, when you met five or six olive trees straggling up the mountain slope, gray and dusty as the rocks themselves, when a thin membrane of moss and a few tufts of grass showed green in the middle of a barren, irregular plain strewn with stones, when after five or six hours' travel you saw some tiny Arab hut glued somewhere to the hillside, looking less like a human habitation than a terra-cotta pot, an oven, or some animal's lair—where in this could you see the land of milk and honey? Imagine Jerusalem, Bethlehem, and all the Eastern towns, like so many heaps of stone and toppling brick in the middle of this desert; imagine the Jordan as a meager trickle among bald mountains dotted here and there by a few bushes and willows; imagine, in the midst of this same desolation, the valley of Jehoshaphat beneath Jerusalem, with a few boulders and one or two grottoes alleged to be the tombs of the kings of Judea. What can such places tell you, unless your mind's eyes see, above Bethlehem—the star; above the ripples of the Jordan—the dove descending from the gaping skies; inside the walls of Jerusalem—the awesome day of the Crucifixion, the darkness and quaking earth, or the luminous day of the Resurrection, its brilliance outshining anything before or since? My drowsing soul saw nothing else. Somewhere in Samaria I picked a wild flower; another one, somewhere in Galilee; caught by a downpour in Nazareth I stayed there two days, no more knowing I was in Nazareth than if I had been in some Russian posting station."[8]

Was he a bad Christian? Sometimes his lucidity seemed positively diabolical. The great corruptor was guiding his steps. He was Chichikov, come to call on Christ. He was in a hurry to go back, as though caught in some embarrassing false identity. But Bazili had to stay on in Jerusalem for his business. Gogol left alone. During the journey, he had plenty of time to masticate his disappointment. His awareness of his unworthiness tormented him all the way to Beirut, where Mrs. Bazili, alarmed by his morose expression, tried to divert him by introducing him to the local grandees. He refused. How could one disperse oneself in social drivel after such an overwhelming experience?

Soon afterward, he took a ship for Constantinople, where a letter from Father Matthew was being kept for him by the councilor of the Russian mission. He told no lies in his answer: "I must say that I have never been so little content with the state of my heart as in Jerusalem and afterward. The only result for me has been an even stronger awareness of my dryness and selfishness."[9]

Now he was certain that Father Matthew deserved to be his spiritual guide: no lesser priest would ever have extended his solicitude so far as to send him a message of peace in Constantinople. Filled with gratitude, Gogol wrote to Count Tolstoy: "What can I say of him [Father Matthew]? He is the most intelligent man I have ever known, and if I am ever to be saved, it will assuredly be through his precepts."[10]

The *Chersonesus,* lying at anchor outside Constantinople, was soon to sail for Odessa. Gogol boarded it, feeling that the true Holy Land might, after all, be Russia.

4. Last Travels

His homeland welcomed him coolly: all passengers from Constantinople had to remain in quarantine for a fortnight after reaching Odessa. It was through a double-barred window that Gogol's friends first perceived him. He appeared to be in good health and smiled at them from behind the bars, telling the beads of a rosary. Once released, he went to call on a few acquaintances—Princess Repnin, old Sturdza, Leo Pushkin (the poet's younger brother), Andrey Troshchinsky—and left again. He set out on May 7, 1848, hoping to celebrate his feast day, May 9, in the family house at Vasilyevka.

He was touched by the thought of seeing those places where he had dreamed his childhood dreams of glory. Nearly twenty years had passed since he had left his mother and sisters for the capital, burning with ambition—twenty years of struggle, disappointment, poverty, and stagecoaches. Twenty years, and he did not know whether he was nearer his goal or farther from it than ever. The prairie grass was a soft green, the horses cantered apace; with a little luck he would reach home in time for the traditional felicitations. He had told his family of his intention to celebrate the great day in their company. Everything must be ready: cakes, flowers, champagne.

The sun was sinking when the carriage came in sight of the house. Gogol told the driver to stop, leaped down, and walked the rest of the way. He used to love to follow this path that circled the church and disappeared into the undergrowth. Some of the trees in the wood had grown so tall he did not recognize them; others had been cut down. To return to the scenes of the past was to invite the melancholy of impossible resurrections. "You ask me what impression these sights so long forsaken made upon me," Gogol wrote to Danilevsky. "It was rather sad, that's all."[1]

His mother was waiting for him at the door; she embraced him, weeping. He had changed so much since their last meeting, in Moscow: so pale, so thin, so serious! Whereas she seemed to have grown younger. Not a single gray hair, rosy-cheeked, her features firm and her glance sharp, with a shadow of a mustache above her thick upper lip. He told her she was looking very handsome, and turned to examine his sisters: two stiff, tall girls with a provincial air and fleeting eyes, who came shyly forward and kissed his hand. Everyone moved into the dining room. A few neighbors had invited themselves. The conversation lurched and halted. The traveler was plied with questions about Jerusalem, which he answered briefly and as though against his will. "So many different pilgrims have already been to the Holy Land at so many different times and so much has been written about it that I can tell you nothing new," he grumbled.[2] Everyone agreed that the party was not a success.

That evening, Gogol's sister Elizaveta wrote in her diary: "How changed he is! He has become so serious! Nothing, it seems, can cheer him up. And he is so indifferent and cold to us. It was very painful for me."[3]

Later she wrote:

"May 10. We were not able to see our brother at all this morning. It is sad. We have not seen each other for six years and he is avoiding us.

"May 11. This morning we called together all the people of the village. We gave them food and they drank to my brother's health. I was very touched to observe how happy they were to see him. They sang and danced in the courtyard. Everybody was drunk.

"May 13. We have guests every day. My brother is still as cold and serious as before. He seldom smiles. Today he talked more than before."[4]

To preserve his privacy, Gogol moved into the little pavilion to the right of the main house. The room he worked in was furnished with a bed, a few chairs, and a tall black pearwood desk, behind which he stood, as always, to write. Between the two windows, a mirror. On a gaming table, a mountain of books. Gogol rose early, worked a little, took a turn in the garden, and sat down for lunch under the respectful eye of his mother and sisters. After the meal, he moved to the drawing room, where he uttered pious aphorisms and colored Bible pictures in the company of the rest of the family. His sister Olga was given the job of distributing these pictures to the muzhiks, explaining the scenes and stressing the moral value of the gift. Another digestive walk, a little meditation, and it was time for evening tea, after which the mysterious brother would withdraw to his study, where the heroes of the second volume of *Dead Souls* were awaiting him. To please him, his sisters prepared all his favorite dishes. "Every time he noticed that I had fixed something he liked, he would nod at me and smile," wrote Olga, the youngest. "I was transported by that smile. My only wish, for all time, has been to do everything to please him."[5]

Mildly nauseated, at length, by this atmosphere of quiescent adoration, Gogol went to spend a few days in Kiev with Danilevsky; but the meeting was a disappointment. He was too hot and Danilevsky too busy. A soiree had been arranged in honor of the illustrious writer, at the home of the vice-chancellor of the University of Kiev. All the young university professors, buttoned up to the neck in their new uniforms, excitedly awaited the arrival of the author of *Dead Souls*. At last he appeared, wearing a plum-colored coat and a green velvet vest spotted with red and yellow like the skin of a frog. With drooping nose, lank hair, and dull eye, he nodded with boredom throughout the presentations, and was untouched by the timidly proffered compliments. He seemed incommoded by the glare of the setting sun, so one young man leaped up at the behest of the master of the house, and stood on the balcony to intercept its rays. Gogol did not even thank him. He was offered a light snack, but would not go near the table. Everybody remained standing, uncertain and embarrassed. Suddenly the great author spoke to a professor, his eyes fixed on a spot somewhere beneath the man's nose: "I think I saw you in a restaurant once. You were eating onion soup." Then, with a circular bow, he moved to the door. "Everybody fell silent," relates one witness to the scene; "we watched the writer go, moving his legs very oddly, as though they were slightly paralyzed—but, in fact, they were fettered by his gray trousers, which were too tight and had very wide foot straps."[6]

Gogol returned to Vasilyevka to find the family in an uproar. A cholera epidemic had broken out in the district, and five muzhiks from the village were dead. Prayers were ordered. A torrid heat fell from the inexorably blue sky. Even the nights were sweltering. The soil cracked, the wheat did not grow, the crops would be ruined. Men and beasts, parched and anxious, shuffled through a cursed scene of glare and drought.

"I am writing from my bed, barely recovered from an exhausting diarrhaea, which has left me a shadow of myself after three days," Gogol wrote to Pletnyev. "In fact, thank God, it isn't cholera, simply diarrhaea caused by heat of such intensity that even Africa, I think, can offer nothing worse."[7]

To Aksakov: "What mortally unhealthy weather, the air is sickeningly stifling! Continual stomach upsets, headaches, nervous ailments. What with cholera and all sorts of diarrhaeas, I haven't a moment's peace. What makes me even more unhappy is that my head is incapable of the slightest intellectual work, the simplest book is more than I can manage."[8]

The distribution of edifying images designed to encourage the muzhiks to love their labor in the fields was now deemed insufficient, and Gogol decided to visit them "in order to see how they lived." He took his sister Olga on a tour of inspection. In the first isba they entered, a stout peasant woman invited them to be seated and made them an omelet, which they could hardly refuse. Gogol liked this hospitality; it expressed, he thought, the submissive and smiling gratitude that should typify the relations between a good master and a good serf. A few yards beyond, the scrubbed tidiness of another isba caught his eye. He congratulated the muzhik and concluded, "One can see that the people who live here are workers." The third isba, however, was dirty and dilapidated, and he sternly remarked, "You must work, you must take trouble; only thus can you obtain all you need." Thereupon, he judged that it was time to go home. "Three isbas were enough for him to see how the muzhiks lived," marveled his sister.

Another day, he went out to the fields with her to watch the peasants work. The wheat had been so stunted by the drought that it could not be cut and had to be pulled up, roots and all, by each puny short stem. Gogol stepped out of the calèche, smiled at the sun-baked men and women, and cheerfully observed: "It's harder to pull than to reap, isn't it?"

The peasants showed him their black, blistered hands and agreed that it was not an easy task.

"Work hard, that you may win the kingdom of heaven!"[9] Gogol exclaimed.

He had the exhilarating impression that he was actually living the chapter of his *Selected Passages* entitled "A Russian Landowner." Yes: cultivation of the soil, serfdom, Holy Scripture, they all went together. And at the end, prosperity for the owner and well-being for the muzhik. Gogol would have liked to convince his mother; but she did not know how to manage her estate, went a little deeper into debt every year, and would not change her ways. He loved her, but he was weary of her lamentations. Besides, he had better things to do in life than put the farm in order. Even the education of his sisters interested him less, now that they were actually there. They were so afraid of displeasing him that they were positively stupid. Their fearful glances and whispered consultations irritated him. Trivial arguments, rustling skirts, provincial gossip, starched conversations with the neighbors . . . he thought nostalgically of his friends in Moscow—both those who had remained faithful, such as Shevyrev, and those with whom he had quarreled, such as Pogodin and Aksakov. With them, his desire to work would return. At the end of August he informed his family that he could remain no longer at Vasilyevka.

"We all wept," Elizaveta wrote in her diary on August 22. "Dreadful sadness. I love him so much! Even though he is often unpleasant, I love him like a father!"[10]

Gogol reached Moscow on September 12, 1848, and went directly to stay with Aksakov, with whom he had meanwhile been reconciled by letter. They embraced in the joy of friendship renewed and grievances forgotten. Time to catch his breath, have his clothes brushed, and write a few letters, and the inveterate traveler set out again, for St. Petersburg. There he stayed with the Vyelgorskys, ran to see Pletnyev, who gave him some money from the sale of *Dead Souls,* and looked up a few friends, including Annenkov, who had just returned from France. He had been in Paris during the revolution of 1848 and related the story of the fighting at the barricades in great detail. Much good it has done them, Gogol thought, to proclaim that shameful French Republic in gunpowder, blood, and mire! All Europe was intoxicated with the idea of freedom, lurching about brandishing guns and proclamations. Ah, it made one proud to be a Russian, when one saw the corruption of those Western nations!

"Everything he [Annenkov] tells in his eyewitness accounts of the events in Paris is simply horrifying: a complete disintegration of society," Gogol wrote to Danilevsky. "What makes it even more deplorable is that nobody there can see any way out, any solution, and people are rushing madly into battle solely in order to be hit on the head. No one can bear the awful sadness of this transitional period and everyone is surrounded by night and darkness. Not one person has yet thought to pronounce the word: prayer."[11]

To Zhukovsky: "However revolting may be the events taking place around us, however likely to deprive us of the peace and silence we require for our work, still we must remain true to our chief task; God will take care of the rest."[12]

The more strongly he condemned the upheavals in Europe, the more he longed to be in touch again with the intellectual life of his country. He asked Professor Alexander Komarov, a friend of the late Belinsky, to gather together a few of the new writers, whom he thought he wanted to meet. Komarov was delighted, and arranged a supper to which he invited the flower of young Russian literature. At nine o'clock they were already there: the slow-moving, bulky Goncharov, author of *A Simple Story;* the elegant journalist Panaev; the young poet Nekrasov; the amiable, curly-headed Grigorovich, whose *Village* and *Anton Goremyka* had aroused so many readers' compassion for the serfs; Druzhnin the critic. At ten, the guest of honor still had not arrived; the host served tea. Thirty minutes later, Gogol appeared. From the start, he was as stiff and uncomfortable with his young colleagues as he had been with the professors of the University of Kiev. Refusing to swallow a single drop of tea, he sank onto a sofa far from the table. They clustered around him. He could think of nothing to say. His admirers looked at him in silence, politely dismayed. After a long pause, with visible effort, he began to talk to them about their works: "But it was clear," Panaev noted, "he had not read them."[13] Then, as though fearing an attack on *Selected Passages,* he tried to forestall it by declaring that he had written the texts in a state of "partial illness" and now regretted having published them. "It was as though he was trying to justify himself to us" (Panaev). Komarov took advantage of a lull in the conversation to remind Gogol that supper had been served. To everyone's surprise, Gogol would eat nothing. Not even a swallow of wine. "But, then, what can I offer you?" moaned Komarov. After due thought, the guest of honor declared: "Well, I shall take a little glass of malaga." There was every imaginable beverage in the house, of course, except that one. It was past one in the morning; all the shops would be shut. Komarov's honor was at stake. He sent his servants to scour the city for the precious liquid. The moment they had gone out the door, Gogol announced that he was leaving too. "Just two minutes; the malaga will be served in just two minutes!" Komarov stammered. "Wait at least two minutes!" "No, I don't really want it any more," Gogol replied. "It is too late for me to be up." However, at the sight of his host's woebegone countenance, he consented to stay. A breathless servant soon returned with a bottle thrust out at the end of his arm. Komarov poured some into a glass. Gogol wet his lips in it, seized his hat, and marched toward the door. "I don't know how the others felt," Panaev wrote, "but I personally breathed more freely after he had gone."[14]

Gogol, too, no doubt, breathed more freely after leaving his flabbergasted colleagues. How could he have wanted to associate with these writers, with whom he had nothing in common? His way was not theirs. They sought the acclaim of the mass, he the applause of God. They dreamed of increasing their readership, he of saving souls. And how many of those souls, alas, whose edification he had pursued for years, were now slipping out of his net and plunging back into worldly distractions! The most distressing instance, perhaps, was Mrs. Smirnov, who was too taken up with her husband's career and increasingly escaping Gogol's influence.

The sweet young Anna Vyelgorsky, on the other hand, abandoned herself to him with heart-rending trustfulness. His feelings for this pure, honest, simple, natural girl were a complex mixture of tenderness and delight in power. Perhaps he saw in her the same charm her brother Joseph had possessed, when he watched over his dying moments so long ago in Rome. Sometimes, looking at her, he thought he saw the dear features of the dead boy forming in her face. Now, as before at the bedside of the sick youth, he was utterly disarmed by the gentle questioning of a pair of eyes. What spell did the members of this Vyelgorsky family cast upon him? He became possessed by the desire to guide this docile child, to leave a thumbprint in the soft clay. One moment, Anna Vyelgorsky's delicate health, her doubts and melancholy drove him distraught; the next, he found intolerable the idea that, at her age, she might wish to go out and enjoy herself in society. He would have liked her to be more homely, so that no one would want to pay court to her; but at the same time he dissolved in delight at the sight of her graceful gestures. How could he persuade her that she must seek to please none but himself?

"For the love of God, don't sit in one place for more than an hour and a half at a time, and don't lean over tables: you have a weak chest, you must know it," he wrote with stern concern. "Try always to be in bed by half past eleven. And do not dance at all, especially not these wild dances! They stir up the blood but do not allow the body to move as it should. Besides, dancing does not suit you; your figure is not good enough, and you are not light enough on your feet. You are not pretty. Are you quite sure you know that? You are only pretty when your face expresses some elevated emotion. Your features were patently made to express the nobility of your soul; as soon as you lose that expression, you become plain. Therefore, give up all social functions, however modest. You must see that society can give you nothing. Keep your childlike innocence; that is worth more than everything else."[15]

Gogol issued advice to his favorite pupil in person as well as by letter. She, surprised by the vehemence of his sermons, trembled with admiration and fear before this great man who deigned to concern himself with her unworthy person. To her he seemed sure of himself, violent, unhappy, vulnerable, ill, lonely, selfish, and overflowing with holy rage. She respected and pitied him. For her, he was something like a doctor and priest combined. At his command, she read sacred books, the *History of the Church,* the works of Philaretus of Riga. One day she told him she would like to forget all her European learning and become more profoundly Russian. "Not only Russian in my heart," she said, "but in my knowledge of the country and the language." Her brother-in-law, Count Sollogub, had decided to introduce her to the culture riches of her fatherland by reading her lectures on contemporary literature. Gogol immediately offered to do so too. But, in his opinion, this type of "Russification" must needs be superficial.

"It is far easier to become Russian by learning about the country and language than it is to acquire a Russian soul," he wrote. "What does it mean, to become *a true Russian?* Wherein resides the attraction of our race, which we are now so assiduously cultivating, casting off everything foreign, incongruous, unseemly? What is our essential quality? The greatest merit of the Russian people is that it understands more profoundly than anyone else the sublime words of the Gospel, which alone can raise man to perfection. The seeds of the Heavenly Sower were cast everywhere with the same prodigality; but some fell upon the highway and were devoured by the birds; some fell among stones and dried up before the harvest; some fell among thorns and sprouted, but were soon choked by the weeds; and still others fell upon fertile soil and bore fruit. That fertile soil is our warm, welcoming Russian nature. The seeds of Christ, well sheltered in our hearts, gave all the best features of the Russian character. And so, in order to become Russian, you must go to the source."[16]

Obviously, the best way to show the girl a Russian soul, he said, was to read her what he had written on the subject: "I should have preferred to begin my lessons with you with the second volume of *Dead Souls*. Afterward it would have been easier for me to talk to you about many things."[17]

Anna's parents were finally alarmed by all these letters and conversations. Without questioning the purity of Gogol's intentions, they thought his constant association with their daughter might—regardless of the difference in their ages—give rise to unkind comment. They became cooler toward him. They no longer urged him to prolong his stay. Conversation languished at table and in the drawing room. At her mother's request, Anna often kept to her room. Gogol irritatedly wondered what he had done to deserve this cold shoulder, but preferred not to demand an explanation. Disappointed, he went back to Moscow.

There he was faced with another housing problem. Now that winter was coming on, with whom was he going to live? He had certainly not spared his old friend Pogodin; he had insulted and mocked him and belittled his hospitality, which he qualified as "the opposite of disinterested"; he had made a public target of him in Chapter IV of his *Selected Passages*. "His whole life long," he wrote, "P. [Pogodin] has hurried and rushed to tell his readers everything he hears, never looking to see whether his thoughts have sufficiently matured in his mind. What has been the result? The readers have found nothing but carelessness and dross in him."

The copy of *Selected Passages* he had sent to Pogodin, moreover, was adorned with the following dedication: "To Pogodin, an untidy and rumpled soul who remembers nothing, notices nothing, is constantly causing pain without even realizing it; to Doubting Thomas, this book is given so that he may forever remember his sins, by a man as sinning as himself and, in many respects, even more untidy." Pogodin had cut out the dedication and pasted it in his diary. Such a harsh judgment, one would have thought, had settled the matter and sealed the break for all time. But that, Gogol considered, was all in the past. The house on

Virgins' Field was by far the most comfortable place he knew. He must go back to it, even at the price of a reconciliation.

The Russian likes to open his doors, increase his family, share his possessions. For him, no offense is final, the culprit can always buy his pardon, heart will prevail over mind, and naïveté and charity go hand in hand. Pogodin, "the egotist," the "hangman," did not bear grudges. He had already agreed with Gogol, by letter, to bury the hatchet. He welcomed him and installed him in his old rooms on the second floor overlooking the gallery. But the guest's lack of consideration soon reopened his host's wounds. Gogol, decidedly incorrigible, behaved as though the world owed him everything. For him, his friends were his servants and their homes his hotel.

"I've been thinking about Gogol," Pogodin wrote in his diary on November 1, 1848; "he is still the same. Only his clothes are different. People mean nothing to him."

And the following day: "No sight of Gogol for the past two days. It never occurs to him to ask how I manage to feed 25 people."[18]

The young poet Berg met Gogol one evening at the Shevyrevs' and wrote in his *Recollections:* "It is hard to imagine a man of letters more spoiled and pretentious than Gogol was in those days. His Muscovite friends (acquaintances would be a better word, for Gogol never had a friend in his entire life) treated him with incredible veneration. Whenever he came to Moscow he could find, in one home or another, everything he needed for a peaceful and comfortable life: his favorite food, a calm and private place to work in, servants ready to do his bidding at every instant. The friends of Gogol's host of the moment had to learn exactly how to behave in his presence. They were taught, for instance, that Gogol could not bear to talk about literature, especially his own work, and that therefore on no account must he be importuned with questions such as, 'What are you writing now?' Nor must one ask, 'Where do you plan to go?' or 'Where have you been?' He didn't like that either. Besides, such questions were said to be futile in a conversation with him. If he meant to go to the Ukraine he would say, 'I am going to Rome,' and if he was on his way to Rome he would answer, 'I am going to stay with Soandso in the country.'"

Berg also supplied this candid portrait: "A man short in stature, in a black frock coat and full trousers, his hair falling like two commas on either side of his face, with a small mustache, dark, quick, piercing eyes, a pale complexion. He would pace the room from corner to corner with his hands in his pockets, and talk. He had a unique, jerky irregular walk. There was in his whole demeanor something forced, constrained, tense as a fist. No reaching out, nothing open, either in gesture or look. On the contrary, his eyes glanced up from below, obliquely, furtively, with an air of cunning, never straight at the face of the person to whom he was speaking."[19]

In the course of these semiliterary, semisocial gatherings, Gogol usually appeared somnolent and taciturn, uttering only commonplaces or such obvious falsehoods that his friends were embarrassed for him. Privately, however, he was posing increasingly as a heaven-inspired prophet. On November 19 he had a mass sung in his rooms. The smell of incense spread through the house. Irritated by this excessive devoutness, Pogodin wrote in his diary: "Orthodoxy and autocracy have entered my house: Gogol has just had a mass sung. In preparation for his accession to the throne?"[20]

Some time later, another priest came to call: his spiritual guide, Father Matthew Konstantinovsky, who was passing through Moscow. Gogol was thrilled to meet the person in whom he had so often confided in his letters. Paper and ink became flesh and blood: a man some sixty years old, of average height, slightly stooped, with a reddish beard and hair streaked with white, a broad nose, little gray eyes, and the general look and bearing of a peasant, in spite of his cassock and glittering cross.[21] From his very first utterance, Gogol was enchanted by his caller's crude eloquence. Father Matthew did not mince words: whatever was not Orthodox religion belonged to the Devil. Christ, he said, must be followed step by step without looking either right or left. Even art was suspect in his eyes. In Rzhev and the outlying districts he hunted down all forms of heresy and was feared by muzhiks and landowners alike. He occasionally came to Moscow to confess and enlighten his great admirer Count Tolstoy. Gogol told the priest that he had decided to place all his talent at the service of the Church, that the second volume of *Dead Souls* would be a hymn to Russian Orthodoxy, and that he desired to improve himself in order to be worthy of the task God had assigned to him on earth. And he kissed the strong hand that blessed him. Father Matthew promised to return.

After he had gone, Gogol wondered whether he should rejoice or tremble at this ominous guardian he had acquired for the salvation of his soul. However, when he met the archimandrite Theodore, at about the same time, he reiterated his decision to subordinate his art to the imperatives of religion. When the holy man inquired what was to be the fate of his heroes in the second part of *Dead Souls,* he replied that the poem would end with Chichikov's conversion to viture, with "the tsar himself participating in that conversion."[22]

It pained Pogodin to see Gogol falling into the clutches of the priests, and on occasion he frankly said so. Fresh storm clouds began to gather between the two men. There were no outbursts, but the strain was exhausting. Also, Gogol claimed that the house was poorly heated. Now that winter had come in earnest, he could not contain himself. Count Tolstoy had just offered him unlimited hospitality, with every possible convenience, in surroundings of exemplary devoutness. There could be no hesitation. Gogol transferred his clothes and papers to the count's house in time for Christmas.

The Tolstoys had just rented a two-story house on Nikitsky Boulevard near the Arbat Gate.[23] It was a spacious Empire mansion dating from the beginning of the century. The count and countess lived upstairs and Gogol moved into two ground-floor rooms to the right of the entrance. One room was his bedroom, the other his study. The latter was relentlessly green. A green rug on the floor, green taffeta screen in front of the stove, green cloth covering the two book-littered tables. Two sofas against the walls completed the furnishings. An icon stood in a corner, glowing in the light of the vigil lamp.

Aksakov said that the atmosphere in the Tolstoy home was one of "popes, monks, bigotry, superstition, and mysticism." Fasting, prayer, masses celebrated in the house every Saturday, frequent visits from priests, devout readings annotated at the dinner table. After longing for a life steeped in religion, Gogol now felt stifled and bored, owing, no doubt, to the exaggerated number of external manifestations of faith. At least he had no more material problems: lodged, boarded, laundered, and otherwise maintained by the count, at last he could forget about money. There was no longer any obstacle to his plan of turning over all his royalties, administered by Pletnyev in Petersburg and Shevyrev in Moscow, to his mother and his fund for needy students. His dream was coming true: he was becoming generous through the generosity of someone else. And yet, never had he felt so little like working. A victim of intellectual torpor, he gaped in front of his blank sheets of paper.

"I cannot understand why I am unable to write and why I have no desire to speak of anything," he confessed to Zhukovsky. "My literary activities are at a complete standstill."[24]

Oddly enough, this defection of his creative faculties was accompanied by a definite improvement in his health. He was sleeping better and complained less of his upset stomach. Aksakov, embracing him, observed that he had put on weight. "I rejoiced and thanked God," he wrote.

On May 9, 1849, for his feast day, Gogol arranged the traditional "garden party" at Pogodin's house. But the friends' he had invited seemed to greet one another reluctantly. What had united them in the past now separated them. They had aged, both physically and spiritually; they had become caricatures of themselves.

"A great deal had happened during those years," Aksakov wrote after the party. "Almost everyone there had quarreled in the meantime; they belonged to opposing camps and had already expressed their opinions many times. In a word, the dinner was gloomy, strained, sad, and boring. When the gathering grew livelier, after the wine, some of the guests exchanged insults."[25]

This meeting with the ghosts of his youth intensified Gogol's sense that time was fleeting. "The days fly past so quickly that I cannot keep track of them, and almost nothing is accomplished," he wrote to Danilevsky. "I am less absent-minded, I live more alone than ever before, and yet I have never worked so little."[26]

He turned to his old, tried-and-true remedy, travel. But, this time, he was not drawn to foreign parts: he wanted to explore Russia, the better to see, understand, and portray it. Mrs. Smirnov, on a visit to Moscow, introduced him to her half brother, young Leo Arnoldi, and invited them both to join her in July on her estate outside Kaluga. After his friend's departure, Gogol was surprised to find that he could no longer think of her except with sorrow. How she had aged! Careworn and dried, her dark, glowing eyes were all that was left of her youth. Her half brother was a nice young fellow; steeped in admiration for the author of *Dead Souls*, he nevertheless knew better than to vex him with misplaced compliments or indiscreet questions. Together they made preparations for the trip. One evening, Arnoldi was escorting his future traveling companion back to the Tolstoy home when they met some prostitutes on Nikitsky Boulevard, who were strolling along with undulating hips and provocative glances. Gogol clutched the young man's arm and murmured:

"Do you know what happened to me just a short while ago? I was out walking late one evening in a deserted alleyway when I heard religious chanting coming from the ground floor of a sordid-looking house. The windows were open but covered with those light muslin curtains one usually sees in that type of residence. I stopped, glanced through the casement, and discovered a dreadful sight. Six or seven bloated and faded young women, whose shameful profession could be divined by the white and pink paint on their faces, and a frightful old crone who was with them were praying in front of an icon standing on a rickety table in the corner. The little room, furnished like every other room in such establishments, was brightly lighted by tapers. A priest was celebrating mass in his vestments, a deacon was singing the responses. The sinners prostrated themselves with fervor. I remained at the window more than a quarter of an hour. There was no one in the street, and I prayed, with them, to the end. It was awful, awful. That cluttered room, with its particular purpose, its particular smell, those depraved, painted puppets, that horrible fat old woman, and in that same place the icons, a priest, the Gospel, the chants."[27]

That nightmare vision was Russia too, of course. But of that Russia there would be no work in the second volume of *Dead Souls*. His Russia would be all virtue, hope, hard work, discipline, and faith. Other writers might mine the vein of base sensuality coupled with Christmas exaltation—a Dostoevsky, for instance, would have felt right at home in a scene like the one Gogol had witnessed. But he, unfortunately, had been arrested the previous April for his part in a political plot, and imprisoned, with dozens of other conspirators, in the Peter and Paul Fortress. An investigating committee was deliberating the case of these poor wretches, who, led by someone named Petrashevsky, had allowed themselves to be infected by the European revolutionaries. It was whispered that they would probably be sent to the salt mines. The tsar saw them as the spiritual descendants of those "Decembrists" he had put down on his accession twenty-five years before. By punishing them, he undoubtedly hoped to set an example for all those warped minds who were seeking to overthrow the imperial regime in the name of liberty. And in this particular, Gogol could not disagree. He felt sorry for these young men who were the victims of their ideas, when their number included an author of such promise as Dostoevsky; but a fatherly spanking was sometimes necessary to preserve the unity and health of the great Russian family. Besides, there was little talk of the case in the circles he frequented: society was so compartmentalized that life flowed gently on for some, while others were writhing in the depths of despair ten feet away.

While Dostoevsky was moldering in his cell in St. Petersburg, Gogol was preparing to leave heat-prostrated Moscow. On July 6, 1849, he appeared at Arnoldi's door with his little expanding-flap suitcase and his fat leather briefcase containing the manuscript of the second volume of *Dead Souls*. "That briefcase," Arnoldi wrote, "was never to leave Gogol throughout the entire voyage. He took it into his room in the posting stations and always set it next to him in the tarantass, covering it with his hand." The tarantass sped along, jolting roughly. Bouncing up and down with every rut, Gogol was in an excellent mood, talked about literature, reminisced about his friends, or told risqué anecdotes that made his companion laugh until he cried. He was not even annoyed when the coach broke down as they came into Maloyaroslavets. Luckily the mayor happened to be passing by and gave orders for its immediate repair. Upon learning that Gogol was one of the passengers, he might have expressed indignation on behalf of his colleagues, who had been so maligned in the character of Skvoznik-Dmukhanovsky, in *The Inspector General;* on the contrary, he congratulated the author upon his brilliant exposé of the administrative abuses and ennui of a provincial town. Gogol, heartened by such understanding in a government official, questioned him about his fellow officials and the local merchants and landowners, begging him for details. As he leaned toward the mayor, he looked, Arnoldi said, like a "bloodsucker" glued to a patient's skin and drinking down his blood in little gulps. He would have stayed there for hours, sucking the mayor's substance, but the tarantass was soon repaired and they had to set out again. At the following stop his curiosity returned. As he had done with the mayor, he began to interrogate the station master and waiters in the inn about the local inhabitants, the dishes they liked to eat, how they got along with the administration, the latest scandals, what was good and what was wrong in the neighborhood. Notebook in hand, he wrote down every piece of information with an air of famished jubilation. Stage by stage, they eventually reached Begichevo, the Smirnov estate: a white stone building, a park and pond, and the affable Mrs. Smirnov. After four days of exploring the countryside, the entire family left for Kaluga. The governor's house was just outside the city, near a pine forest above the Yachenka River. Gogol and Arnoldi moved into a separate pavilion in which two connecting rooms had been set aside for them.

In the mornings, Gogol withdrew to write; then he walked in the grounds and joined his hosts at lunchtime, nattily attired in yellow nankeen trousers and a short turquoise vest. During the meal he eagerly discoursed on matters of which he knew nothing, disposing of every topic in turn with irrefutable pronouncements. If hunting were the subject, he who had never once engaged in the sport freely contradicted Smirnov, the owner of kennels famous throughout Russia. If the conversation turned to agriculture, he who can hardly be said to have managed his own little farm proffered advice to his host, who owned five thousand serfs and huge estates in six different governments.

"His tone was dictatorial, taking no note of any objection," Arnoldi noted, "and on the whole I thought him thoroughly imbued with conceit, exaggeratedly self-assured, vain, and even stupid. Then, and later also, I saw in Gogol a pretension to know more about everything than anyone else. True, he did sometimes question specialists, but always contrived to make their information and explanations confirm his own preconceived ideas on the subject. He did not like to learn anything from another person."[28]

And although her admiration of Gogol was unqualified, Mrs. Smirnov added: "When he was introduced to someone who interested him, he would listen attentively or begin enunciating eternal truths. On occasion he would loudly proclaim such commonplaces that his listeners were exasperated with him. Some of them never forgave him for forcing lessons upon them that they had not asked for."[29]

On Sundays he liked to see all the senior officials sitting stiff and starched, on their best behavior, at the governor's table. It gave him a sense of the strength of the administrative hierarchy and the solidity of the Russian Empire. He himself would make a special effort for the occasion: black frock coat and snowy shirt, with a heavy gold chain across his vest. "On feast days," he said, "everything must be out of the ordinary. The fresh cream in the coffee should be especially thick, the dinner exceptionally fine, and around the table should be presidents and judges, all sorts of important people, and even the expressions on their faces should be more solemn than usual."[30]

One morning, he consented to read the first chapter of the second volume of *Dead Souls* to Mrs. Smirnov and Arnoldi. When he had finished, they both professed themselves overwhelmed. Arnoldi remarked, however, that he found the character of the author's pure young girl Ulenka rather conventional. "Perhaps," murmured Gogol, "but she will have more depth in the later chapters."[31]

To Mrs. Smirnov he repeated that *Dead Souls* was being written at

God's command. "I am sure that when I have finished my service and completed the work I have been called to do, I shall die," he said. "And if I give the world an immature or imperfect work I shall die sooner, because I will not have performed the task for which I was put on earth."[32]

Listening to him—by turns humble and boastful, preaching to others when he had so much to learn himself, complaining of a thousand difficulties and living off others, referring everything to God and treating himself as the center of the universe, proffering brilliant ideas and sheer nonsense in the same breath—Arnoldi felt as though he were trying to contend with ten people in one. "My brother," he wrote, "made a remark that struck me as highly pertinent at the time: he thought Gogol had a great deal in common with Jean-Jacques Rousseau."[33]

By the end of July, Gogol was fidgeting again. Hearing that Prince Dmitri Obolensky, then in Kaluga, was on his way to Moscow, he decided to join him. Once inside the prince's "sleeper," he began looking for a safe place to put the precious leather briefcase containing his manuscript. He finally put it under his feet, and never took his eyes off it. As he dozed, he kept feeling for it with the tip of his shoe. At dawn, the carriage stopped at an inn for tea. Gogol carried his briefcase with him. He was in high spirits and had a hearty appetite. In the posting-station complaint book the prince showed him a rather amusing entry by some stranger. Gogol's eyes instantly sparkled mischievously. "'And what do you imagine this gentleman looks like?' he asked. 'His qualities, his character?' 'I've no idea,' I answered. 'Well, then, I shall tell you!' And he proceeded to give the most comical and original description imaginable of the unknown gentleman's physiognomy, then related his entire career in the civil service down to the smallest details of his private life. I was laughing myself silly as he pursued his demonstration in utter seriousness."[34]

Once he had reached Moscow, Gogol decided that he could not possibly stay there during the hottest month of the year; but whose roof to shelter under this time? Living off others had become such a habit to him that he wrote, immediately upon his arrival, to Anna Vyelgorsky: "For my upkeep and daily needs I pay nothing to anyone. I spend today with this person, tomorrow with another. If I come to see you, I shall move in and live there without paying a kopeck for my keep."[35]

But it was not to the Vyelgorskys he went, in the end. First he stayed with Shevyrev at Abramtsevo, and then he went to the Aksakov estate, sixty versts from Moscow. Sergey Timofeyevich Aksakov, now half blind, had decided to live there permanently while continuing to write his *Recollections of a Hunter* in rural tranquillity. The entire family welcomed their guest in raptures and led him ceremoniously to the spacious, sunny room that had been set aside for him on the second floor overlooking the garden. Work, walks in the woods with the family, mushroom picking, long conversations by lamplight or readings from the old authors—the time passed quickly and Gogol congratulated himself on his choice of summer residence. On August 18 he offered to read his hosts a chapter from *Dead Souls*. Thinking he meant the first volume, Aksakov's elder son, Konstantin, rose to fetch it from the library. But Gogol caught his sleeve: it was the beginning of the second volume he meant. "I cannot explain what I felt," Aksakov related. "I was utterly paralyzed. Rather than joy, it was dread that I felt, dread of hearing something unworthy of Gogol."[36] The author pulled a thick notebook from his pocket, the family drew their chairs around him, and Chichikov rolled back on stage. Aksakov's misgivings vanished at the first words. Their author's mystical affliction had not asphyxiated his talent. In many passages of that opening chapter, his verve burst forth as in the days of his inventive youth. Congratulated and touched, he nevertheless refused to read on, saying that the next part was not ready. The following day he went to Moscow, promising to return.

He kept his word. Early in January 1850 the Aksakov family heard a second reading of the first chapter, now revised. Although the text was no longer a novelty, they were even more impressed than before. Gogol, delighted by their reaction, said, "You see what happens when the artist puts the final touches to his work. The changes are almost unnoticeable —a word removed here, another added there, a third relocated somewhere else—and the whole thing seems different. I shall not give my book to the printer until every chapter has been worked over in the same way."[37]

A few days later, he asked Aksakov to read him a section from his *Recollections of a Hunter*. The good man, touched by this sudden interest in his work, asked his son to read for him. While Konstantin was performing, Gogol fidgeted in his chair and could hardly contain his impatience. He could not have paid less attention if he had been listening to a list of Russian county seats. With a preoccupied air, he kept feeling a fat notebook in his pocket. The moment Konstantin stopped speaking, he exclaimed, "Well, now it is my turn to read!" Everybody understood his little ploy: he had wanted to hear the *Recollections of a Hunter* in order to prepare his listeners for the sequel to *Dead Souls.* Aksakov thought too highly of him not to forgive his little trick, and found the second chapter even better than the first. "In three places I could not restrain my tears," he wrote to his son Ivan. "Art of that level, which shows something sublimely human in the most vulgar individuals, exists in Homer alone. Only now am I finally convinced that Gogol is actually capable of accomplishing the task he speaks of with such confidence and boastfulness in the first volume."[38]

As he accepted his old friend's congratulations, Gogol assumed an inspired air and said, as though speaking of somebody else: "Yes, yes, let God grant health and strength to His servant. Some great good must come of all this, for man cannot know himself without the help of his fellows." He would have liked to read the third chapter, which was also finished, but he was too weak and his voice was gone.

Even with all his friends' encouragement, he made little progress. Just after his triumphant reading to Aksakov, he wrote to Pletnyev: "I don't understand what is going on in me. Is it the onset of old age that impels us to be weak and idle, is it my poor health, is it the climate? I simply cannot find the time to get anything done. I get up early, take pen in hand first thing in the morning, allow no one to enter, reject everything that is not of the first importance, do not even write letters to my family and friends, and in spite of all this, very few lines are coming out of me. I think I have worked hardly an hour, I look at my watch, and it's dinnertime. The end of the thing, that is, the end of *Dead Souls,* is by no means in sight. I don't even understand how it is possible to create a work of art in haste."[39]

He proceeded to give the following analysis of his view of the slow process of creation: "To begin with, you must jot down your ideas as they come, any old how, without worrying about the form, but also without omitting anything, and then forget the very existence of the notebook. After a month or two (sometimes longer), you take out your notes and read them over. Right away you will notice that there are many inaccuracies, other things are superfluous, and still others missing. Correct your text, make notes in the margins, and forget the notebook again. Reading it over once more after some time has gone by, make more corrections in the margins, and, if there is not enough space, glue a piece of paper to the bottom of the sheet. When everything has been written and rewritten in this way, copy the notebook over yourself. That will give you new ideas, you will cut some things and add others, and purify your style. After that, forget the notebook yet again. Travel, enjoy yourself, do nothing or write something different. A day will come when suddenly you will remember your manuscript. Pick it up, read it over, correct as before, and when that notebook is as dirty as the first, copy it once more. Then you will see that your hand, so to speak, is becoming firmer as your style itself grows firmer and the sentences are being decanted. This work must be done, in my opinion, eight times. Finally, the eighth time, the work, which must absolutely be copied always by the author himself, has become artistically finished and approaches perfection. Further amendment and revision will be likely to spoil it—painters call it overtouching. One can't always follow these rules to the letter, of course. I am talking about an ideal case. Occasionally one writes quickly. Man is not a machine."[40]

He repeated the last sentence over and over to excuse the stagnation of his own work. Before, he might have held his material circumstances to blame; but in Count Tolstoy's house, where he had returned for the winter, everything seemed conceived on purpose to safeguard his peace of mind and sanctify his soul. A devout atmosphere, decent cooking, glowing-hot stoves, a comfortable study, abundant servants—what more could be needed for the spawning of ideas? "Here," Berg related, "Gogol was spoiled like a child and given complete freedom in every respect. He did not have to worry about anything. Breakfast, dinner, supper, and tea were brought to him wherever he commanded. His linen was washed and laid in drawers by invisible hands. Other invisible hands dressed him. His chambers were unbelievably silent. Gogol would pace from one corner to the other, or write while he rolled bits of white bread into pellets with his fingers: he maintained that this helped him to solve the most arduous and complicated problems. When his work wearied or bored him, he would go upstairs to see the master of the house, or put on an overcoat and take a walk along Nikitsky Boulevard."[41]

Around this time he had a curious idea: perhaps he would produce better if he were married. Initially appalled by the thought, he acknowledged on further reflection that it was not totally absurd. A loving wife, the quietude of a Christian household, the sweet permanence of conjugal routine—that was what he had been needing, his whole life long, in order to write a masterpiece. He had raced along the highways, eating up the miles, leaping frontiers, while all the time, perhaps, the solution lay here, in a tender face lit by the flame of the vigil light.

Oh, there was nothing sensual in his abrupt desire for union. His age (he was forty-one) would save him, he told himself, from the repulsive lusts of the flesh. If he could even think of a possible association with a person of the opposite sex, it was precisely because he aspired solely to a communion of souls. Just as he had loved Joseph Vyelgorsky because the poor boy had already ceased to be wholly alive, so he loved Joseph's sister Anna because he knew that between that very young girl and himself there could never be the least physical contact, the smallest stain of uncleanliness. By dint of writing to her as her guide and adviser, he had come to feel responsible for her, as for a God-given companion. Perhaps this alliance that existed between them in heaven should be made manifest on earth. She could, it was true, have been his daughter. And, it was true, he had no money. And true, too, he possessed no title, whereas the Vyelgorskys belonged to the highest Russian aristocracy. But happy marriages are not founded upon human reasoning. They are decided by the Almighty, for motives we are not given to know. Pure, irrational encounters, inexplicable and shattering as the cataclysms of nature. Gogol meditated upon his scheme for a time, half delighted and half in terror, and eventually confided in Venevitinov, the husband of the Vyelgorskys' elder daughter. He, long since forewarned by his parents-in-law of the writer's inclination for their younger girl, flatly rejected such a misalliance in their name. The reasons he gave were the very ones Gogol had banished from his thoughts: the difference in age, and, above all, the difference in social rank. Speaking on behalf of Count and Countess Vyelgorsky, he asked the suitor to curtail his visits and refrain from writing to the girl any more.

What would have happened if the count and countess had said yes? Terrified by his own audacity and appalled by his good fortune, he would undoubtedly have fled, like Podkolyosin in *Marriage,* by leaping out the window. But heaven was protecting him. After this rebuff, he could be miserable without reservations. What a dismal world! How could people who had taken such good care of him when he was in their house slam the door in his face merely because he loved their daughter? Class prejudice, he thought, was decidedly stronger than the Christian spirit in the great Russian families. By seeking to take Anna for his wife, he had lost her as a disciple and penitent! And would she even mind this enforced rupture? She was so young, so vulnerable, so devoutly obedient

to her parents! She would forget him. In his dismay, he sent her a letter
of farewell, which he imagined to be quite clear, but which revealed the
extreme confusion of his mind and heart:

"I thought it essential to write to you if only a part of my confession.
Before beginning, I prayed that God would help me to express the pure
truth. I wrote, corrected, crossed out, and began again, and I saw that I
must tear it all up. Do you really need my confession? Perhaps you will
look coldly on what is at the bottom of my heart, or you will have some
other point of view, and then it will all seem different and what has been
written to make things clear can only confuse them. All I will tell you of
that confession is this: I have greatly suffered since we parted in St.
Petersburg. My soul languished utterly, and I have been in a sorry state,
so distressful that I could not describe it to you. What made it even
worse was that there was no one to whom I could explain it, no one to
whom I could go for advice or sympathy. I could not confide in my
closest friend, for there my relations with your family interfered, and
everything touching your house is sacred to me. You will sin if you continue to resent my surrounding you with a troubled cloud of misunderstanding. There was something very strange about it and I could not
now tell you how it all came about. I think the fault was that we did not
know each other well enough and thought of many *very important* things
lightly, or at least less seriously than we should have done. You would
all have known me better if we had lived together for a long time somewhere, not in idleness but working. Then you would have seen, as plainly
as I do, what I must be to you. For, after all, I must be something to
you! It is not for nothing that God brings beings so miraculously together. Perhaps I am to be no more to you than a faithful dog guarding
its master's possessions in a corner. All the same, our relations are not
such that you have cause to look upon me as a stranger."[42]

Deeply disturbed by this break with the Vyelgorsky family, Gogol's
spirits were already very low when he learned, on May 11, that Mrs.
Sheremeytyev had died. What upset him most in her demise was that the
old lady, continually haunted by the thought of her approaching end,
had paid an unexpected call on him that same day. Finding him out, she
vainly returned twice more and told the servants: "Inform Nikolai

Vasilyevich that I came to bid him farewell." Then she went home, lay
down, and passed away. "I lived with her, soul in soul," Gogol said.
"Her death leaves a great gap in my life."[43]

Thus, one after the other, two people—one very young and the other
very old—had left him forever. Why had God inflicted this double blow
on him? It would not matter so much if he had recovered in his art what
he was losing in his life. But the Lord, Whose intentions he had sworn to
carry out, was no longer helping him to find his words. In his confusion,
he sought someone to intercede with the Almighty on his behalf, and the
voice he found was that of Father Matthew, however hostile to literature
of any description Gogol knew him to be. Instead of avoiding the fanatical monk for whom poetry was a temptation of the Devil, he humbly
tried to win him to his cause. He thought that if he could only convince
him, the wellsprings of his inspiration, miraculously released, would gush
forth again in his head.

"Never have I been so conscious of my helplessness," he wrote to him.
"I have so many things to say, but simply picking up my pen is enough
to hold them all back. I await the refreshing dew from above like manna.
As God is my witness, I want to say nothing that will not glorify His
Holy Name. I would like to show, in a living way, by living examples,
for all my unknown brothers inhabiting the world, that this life, which
they treat as a plaything, is no pleasantry. I feel that everything has been
thought of and made ready, but still my pen will not move. What I
lack is the freshness of spirit. I will not conceal from you that this impotence is becoming a kind of secret suffering for me: it is, in a way, my
cross. I have been ill all winter. Our climate does not suit my cold-
blooded nature. I need the South."[44]

Plans for new trips began to whirl in his head: Vasilyevka, then on to
Odessa, and then Greece and maybe Constantinople. For the Russian
part of the trip, he thought the wisest course would be to take the back
roads and lodge in monasteries: that way, he would see more of the
country. Maximovich, a philologist and ethnographer, offered to accompany him. They set out on June 13, 1850, after lunch at Aksakov's.
Gogol had ordered the meal by letter: "Maximovich and I will stop by
your place around two o'clock, that is to say the dinner hour, to have a
bite with you: one dish, no more. Meatballs or maybe curd dumplings
with some bouillon."[45] After stopping at Podolsk, Maloyaroslavets, and
at Mrs. Smirnov's in Kaluga, on June 19 the travelers reached the famous hermitage of Optina.

Gogol, his throat contracting as they drew near the holy site, got out of the carriage, followed by Maximovich, to finish the journey on foot. On the way, they met a little girl carrying a bowl of strawberries. They wanted to buy them from her, but she gave them the fruit with a smile, saying, "One can't take money from travelers!" "This hermitage spreads goodness among the people," was Gogol's comment.[46]

With its white walls, flower-strewn meadows, stream, ringing bells, and chapels with their gilded cupolas nestling under the forest, the monastery seemed like a doll's kingdom. The moment he entered it, the cares of profane life fell from the traveler's shoulders and time ceased to exist. A little way from the main building, lost among the trees, were the cells of the "staretz," the wisest of the wise, to whom troubled souls went for counsel and solace. The most remarkable of these exceptional beings was "staretz" Makarios, a highly cultivated man of noble family who exuded humility and mildness. Day and night, prayers rose up like smoke from the little forest community with the icon-crowned palisades. Even the most hardened visitor had to acknowledge that a supernatural peace reigned over the place, as though, by sheer force of meditation, the monks' spirit had come to dominate matter. Gogol came away from his conversations with some of them convinced that they were literally midway between heaven and earth.

"I stopped at the hermitage of Optina," he wrote to Count Tolstoy, "and took away with me a memory that will never fade. Clearly, grace dwells in that place. You can feel it even in the external manifestations of worship. Nowhere have I seen monks like those. Through every one of them I seemed to converse with the whole of heaven. I did not ask how they lived: their faces told me everything. Even the servants amazed me with their luminous expressions, so pleasant and angelic, and the radiant simplicity of their manners; and the workmen in the monastery too, and the peasants and people living in the neighborhood. . . . A few versts away from the hermitage, one can already smell the perfume of its virtues in the air: everything becomes hospitable, people bow more deeply, brotherly love increases."[47]

The evening of his visit to the hermitage, he told himself that if only this community of monks would pray for him, their combined orisons must ultimately reach the ear of the Lord. In a desperate case such as his, every devout soul must be mobilized, the drums must beat, they must all join together. Sitting in the home of a friend, the Slavophile

Kireyevsky, where he was spending the night (at Dolbina, not far from the monastery), he wrote to Father Philaretos, priest-monk of Optina:

"In the name of Christ, pray for me, Father Philaretos. Ask your good prior, ask your whole brotherhood, ask all those among you who pray most fervently and love to pray, to do it for me. My way is hard, my work is such that, without the explicit help of God every hour and every minute, my pen is unable to move. Show this letter to the Father Superior and beg him to send up his prayers for this sinner, so that God will find me worthy, in spite of my unworthiness, to glorify His Name. In his generosity, he can obtain all things, can whiten me, who am black as coal, can uplift me to the cleanliness a writer must achieve if he would be bold enough to speak of things holy and sublime. In the name of Christ, pray! I must always, I repeat, be above the pettiness of this world, and able, wherever my travels carry me, to return in thought to the hermitage of Optina."[48]

Less than two weeks later, Gogol reached Vasilyevka, and on July 18 was writing to another Optina monk, Peter Grigorov (in the Church, Father Porfyry), and including ten silver rubles in his letter "for prayers to facilitate my future trip and prepare for the successful completion of my work."

Back in his family, he resumed his former habits of work and leisure. In the mornings he would write, draw, or garden, read religious books, daydream, bathe, or ask his sister Olga to play Ukrainian songs on the piano for him. One day, he called some passing beggars into his room and listened with delight while they sang folk refrains. He was discovering Russia late in life, and it was growing increasingly dear to his heart. He saw it as a country loved possessively by God. "As though this land were closer to our celestial fatherland," he wrote to Sturdza; but immediately added, "Unfortunately, I cannot live here, as it is bad for my health."[49] And as autumn was drawing near, he began to mull over his plans to set out for sunnier shores. On Mrs. Smirnov's advice, he even sent a letter to Count Orlov, chief of police, requesting both a passport and some money. His health and the smooth progress of his work required, he said, that he spend the winter months in hot countries. And his work was essential to Russia, because it was the sequel to *Dead Souls,* "in which it is no longer the trivial side of the Russian character that is shown, but the full depth of its nature and the vast riches of its inner resources.

"For all these reasons," Gogol went on, "it seems to me that I am entitled to husband my strength and have regard for my material security. I have no fortune, receive no salary, and the small pension that the emperor generously granted to me while I was living abroad for my health stopped upon my return to Russia. Of course, I could earn money if I would publish my work in an unfinished and imperfect form, but I shall never stoop to that. With age, I feel all too strongly that for every word I utter *here* I shall have to answer *hereafter*."

As the clinching argument in his plea to his eminent correspondent, Gogol added that in addition to the second volume of *Dead Souls,* he was thinking of writing a geography of Russia in a "vivid and expressive" style, designed to show children, from their earliest years, their country's magnificent features and the "qualities and particularities of the Russian people."[50]

He wrote similar letters to the heir apparent and Count Olsufyev, but it is not known whether they reached their destinations; in any event, no money was forthcoming, and his passport was made valid only for the southern provinces of Russia. Meanwhile he had decided to spend the winter in Odessa, where he went around mid-October.

The journey was endless, through an unending downpour.

"With great difficulty I rode, or rather navigated, to Odessa," Gogol wrote to his mother. "Driving rain accompanied me all the way. The road was intolerable. I dragged on for a week, clutching the warped carriage door in one hand and my coat, torn open by the wind, in the other."[51]

The weather improved, however, soon after his arrival. The wide streets and broad tree-lined boulevards, the noisy port, the sun, and the blue sea reconciled him to Odessa. The housing problem was, as always, settled promptly and to his satisfaction. As though by miracle, there was always a house ready to take him in, in every city on earth. This time he moved into the residence of his distant cousins the Troshchinskys, on the far side of the Sabaneyev Bridge. The owners happened to be away at the time, so he lived alone in a pavilion they had placed at his disposal. For his meals, he paid a daily visit to Prince Repnin. The prince had even fitted out a study for him with—how very thoughtful!—a high desk so he could write standing up. Another commodity: old

Princess Repnin (the prince's mother) had a private chapel, in which Gogol liked to hear mass. The servants told how he prayed "like a muzhik," lying flat on his face on the ground and "shaking his hair" when he rose. He always wore a dark-brown jacket and a dark vest with a floral design. When he went out, he would tie a loud-patterned scarf or a black silk foulard around his neck, crossing the points and pinning them down on his chest. His coat, also brown, had a velvet collar, and on very cold days he would wrap himself in a muskrat cape. A top hat and black gloves completed his attire.

"Pale, thin, with his long nose like the beak of a bird, his unique appearance and eccentric manners produced a curious impression, something like a bogeyman," said a student of the Richelieu Grammar School after his first meeting with Gogol.[52] The Odessa friends he saw most often were the Repnins; the reactionary pietist Sturdza; Pushkin's brother Leo, a jolly, superficial, skirt-chasing officer; Prince Gagarin; the Orlaev brothers; the Titovs, and Troyinitsky.

He also made friends with some actors from the local repertory company, and would often meet them for dinner at César Automne's French restaurant, formerly frequented by Pushkin. Whenever he came, César Automne, in bulging belly and white chef's cap, would try to tempt him with some succulent rarity, but Gogol invariably insisted upon his own menu—mainly meat, something plain and simple. He would drink one glass of vodka before the meal, a glass of sherry during it, and a drop of champagne at the end. Then the actors would ask him to make punch according to his special recipe, and he would comply, gesticulating like a witch as he bent over the chafing dish. The conversation would grow animated. Warmed by the enthusiasm of the little company, Gogol would expand and let himself go. Although unwilling to talk about modern literature, he condescended to observe that a certain Ivan Turgenev, a few of whose stories had been printed in *The Contemporary,* showed promise. He also advised the actors on how to bring a play to life. They were impressed, and asked him to read them the Russian translation of Molière's *School for Wives,* which was soon to go into rehearsal. He did so with such vivacity and simplicity that even those who thought they had understood their parts suddenly saw unsuspected depths in them. "His reading," one witness said, "differed sharply from the accepted theatrical usage of the day, by the absence of all effects, or any tendency toward declamation. It was astonishing in its simplicity, its lack of artifice."[53] Yielding to the actors' prayers, he agreed to watch a rehearsal, and again made valid criticisms, encouraged, and gave advice. But he would not attend a performance—his old fear of crowds!

He may have shone among the actors, but in society he wilted. His listlessness, and the triteness, even foolishness, of his statements pained his hearers. During one after-dinner conversation on recent scientific discoveries, he deplored the use of the oil lamp.

One of his lady admirers in Odessa, who wrote down every word he uttered, explained: "So many novelties to remember: the highway, stagecoaches between Moscow and St. Petersburg, stearin, daguerreotypes! 'And what's the good of it all?' grumbled Gogol, yawning. 'Does it make people better? No; worse.'" In reply to a question by the same lady concerning his taste in art, he sighed, "I used to be fond of colors, when I was very young." "Yes," said she; "you could have been a painter. And before that, what did you like?" "Before that, when I was just a child, I liked cards." "That signifies intellectual activity," simpered the lady, trying to raise the tone of the exchange. "What intellectual activity?" muttered Gogol. "Half the people in Russia don't know how to do anything else. That's intellectual inertia!" Another lady ventured to ask when the second volume of *Dead Souls* would be published. He yawned again from ear to ear and said in a blurry voice, "In a year, I think." "Then you didn't burn it?" "Ye-e-es, but only the beginn-nn-nn-ing!" "The dinner, with a Russian menu, had made him sleepy," the good lady benignly noted.[54]

His drowsiness, however, was not exclusively digestive. Even on an empty stomach, inspiration was deserting him increasingly often. A fog had invaded his brain and was drowning everything in gray mist. The fog of boredom, pettiness, and laziness. Turn your head this way or that. What for? His curiosity was extinct. Writing was no longer a liberation for him, it was an obligation, the consequence of a promise made long ago to God. Come what may, he must deliver his essay to the waiting professor. Grimly, he blackened pages, joined chapter to chapter. As far as quantity was concerned, he couldn't complain. But quality? Doubt stabbed at his heart. Then, the next moment, he was strutting: his fears were absurd, God was guiding his hand across the paper, and he would give Russia the masterpiece she was expecting of him.

"My strength does not fail me," he wrote Zhukovsky. "My work is progressing regularly, as before; it is not finished, but the end is near. When a writer is young, he works abundantly and quickly. Imagination is constantly goading him on. He creates, he builds splendid castles in the air. But when truth has become the sole object of this work and his need is to depict the highest dignity of life with exactitude, then imagination can hardly touch the writer; he must struggle to draw every line out of himself."⁵⁵

To the painter Ivanov: "It would be good if your painting [*Christ Appearing to the People*] and my poem could come to the world at the same time."⁵⁶

To Mrs. Smirnov: "As far as I am concerned, I can say that God is keeping me and giving me strength to work. I spend the whole morning writing, unhurriedly, taking time to reread. Artistic creation is the same in literature as in painting. Sometimes you must back away, sometimes come very close to your work, examining it all the time to see if there is not something in it that sticks out too sharply, if the over-all harmony is not spoiled by some discordant line. The winter here is almost pleasant this year. Sometimes the sun shines brightly, like in the South of France. Now and then I can recall some corner of Nice."⁵⁷

When spring came, he decided to return to Vasilyevka and spend the Easter holiday with his family. Before he left, his friends gave him a farewell dinner at César Automne's, and then another at Matteo's restaurant. There were champagne toasts to the writer's health and the successful completion of his work. Even this raucous homage could not cheer him; he left regretfully, on March 27, 1851, as though some higher force had compelled him to vacate the town.

The first days of his stay at Vasilyevka were enlivened by the presence of Danilevsky and his very pregnant wife. The guest lived in the same pavilion as he, to the right of the main house. One night he was awakened by dreadful shrieks. He thought someone was being murdered: it was Mrs. Danilevsky, giving birth to a boy. He was called Nikolai, of course. The baptism took place at the village church. During the ceremony, the somewhat tipsy priest had difficulty in pronouncing the ritual phrases. Marya Ivanovna indignantly whispered to her son: "How is it possible that a priest should officiate in that condition?" "It would be an odd thing to demand that a priest be sober on Sunday," Gogol replied with a grin. "You must excuse him. . . ."

After the Danilevskys' departure, he reverted to his melancholy. He had become a little hard of hearing. He often sighed, as though talking to himself, "It is all absurd! It makes no sense at all!" His companions disappointed him. Illuminated by his advice, his mother and sisters ought to have formed an ideal Christian family; yet, at Vasilyevka, he was preaching in the desert. He was respectfully listened to, he was approved, and the moment he turned his back, the old, futile habits were resumed. Marya Ivanovna complained from dawn to dusk, neglected the management of the farm, borrowed from the neighbors without knowing if she could every pay them back; and her daughters thought of nothing but fads and fancies. They whispered, bickered, dreamed of dresses and "meetings," besieged an itinerant peddler with a wagon full of "magnificent fabrics for next to nothing." Gogol tried to interest them in useful occupations such as gardening or rugmaking. He himself prepared patterns for them to work on the loom. He also asked his sisters to transcribe any Ukrainian songs they might hear from the peasants. They actually wrote down 228 of them in a notebook. "This," Kulish said, "was the only literary link that existed between them and their brother."

He spent most of his time in his study, standing at his tall desk beneath the picture of the Saviour he had brought back from Italy. Flies, drunk with the heat, hummed in through the open window. The bittersweet smell of the garden tickled his nostrils. He felt in the mood for work, but the sentences wouldn't come. He distractedly doodled churches all prickly with bell towers in the margins of his manuscript. Sometimes, however, a tide of ideas would sweep over him and he would write several pages at once. Then he would appear in the dining room more cheerful than usual, smiling at his sisters and speaking tenderly to his mother. But, even then, he seemed somehow absent. He took less and less interest in material things. Surrounded by these four women, all filled with their tiny, everyday worries, he affected the serenity of the apostle who has time for nothing but essentials. "Before," his sister Olga wrote, "when my brother came to the village, he would always manage to introduce some innovation in the running of the estate: he would plant fruit trees, or oaks and beech and birch; often he changed the serfs' program of work, or ate with them, or gave them advice on how to run their homes. Now all that has been relegated to the past. My brother no longer takes a hand in anything, and when my mother complains that the property yields so little income, he simply makes a pained face, changes the subject, and starts talking about religion."[58]

He would find no peace at Vasilyevka, that was certain. Spending the whole summer there was more than he could contemplate. He only liked women who consented to be his pupils, and neither his mother nor his sisters were true penitents. Oh, how he missed the sweet submissiveness of Anna Vyelgorsky! Several times he made up his mind to go, but his mother tearfully implored him to postpone his departure. "Stay!" she whimpered. "Who knows when we will see each other again?"[59] At last, on May 22, 1851, he found strength to pack his bags. His mother and youngest sister, Olga, accompanied him as far as Poltava, where they stayed with some friends named Skalon.

Almost as soon as they set down their suitcases, three letters were brought by express courier from Vasilyevka. The first was from one Vladimir Ivanovich Bykov, captain of sappers, asking for Elizaveta's hand; the second was from Elizaveta, expressing her delight with the proposal; and the third was from Anna, approving her sister's choice. Clearly, Bykov's intentions had long been known to the sisters, who, fearing their brother's opposition to the marriage, had kept the plan secret while he was at Vasilyevka. Marya Ivanovna herself, although feigning total surprise, may well have been following every step in the matrimonial negotiations. They were so afraid of him at home! A spoilsport was all he was for his family. He obviously could not prevent the marriage, as Elizaveta was twenty-eight years old! But this captain—a penniless sword waver with no expectations—would be dragging her off to a life of bivouacs. Why did they all have to go throwing themselves into some man's arms? Both sisters deserved a proper talking-to; and Anna, the confidante, most of all. Gogol wrote in anger:

"I do not know if you and your sister were right, after arranging this whole thing in secret, not to tell our mother or, at least, me. Personally I see no cause for rejoicing: neither of them has any money. True, poverty would be no hardship if my sister Elizaveta had prepared herself for an active, laborious life, if she were able to adjust and accept; if, in a word, she had that equable and radiant nature that enables a person to live and be happy wherever fate may deposit him. I can, of course, take consolation by telling myself that I will not be responsible for either my sister's happiness or her misery, since nobody asked my advice. We hardly know the man. All I can say is that on the two or three occasions I have seen him, I observed no evil in him. But you, you're no sort of judges. Go to Dikanka on foot and pray to God; ask him to make this marriage happy. Let your lips utter no word that is not a prayer the whole way, and speak nothing trivial, and no word of argument."[60]

The second letter was addressed to the chief protagonist in the drama, Elizaveta: "The step you have taken is terrifying: it will lead you either to happiness or the abyss. Go to the church [at Dikanka] on foot, fall on your knees before the effigy of Nicholas Thaumaturge, and implore Christ our Saviour to make this marriage beneficial despite the fact that you have planned it without even asking your mother's advice, without thinking of the future, and without any notion of the importance of such a decision. The mere thought of the difficulties you will face in trying to be a good wife, all obedience and heavenly gentleness, fills my soul with terror—especially when I think that you have never listened to me, although the advice I gave you was for your own good. It is true: your sisters tried, as far as they were able, to carry out some fragment of my instructions, but no prayer or exhortation was ever able to bring you to take the measure of yourself."[61]

A few weeks later, he decided it was his duty to teach his future brother-in-law, Bykov, how to run a marriage: "In your letter to my mother you write that you have known poverty and are used to a simple life. For the love of God, never alter that way of life; love poverty more than ever before and guide your wife into that path from the first days of your marriage. You must strike while the iron is hot: a wife, in the first year of marriage, is like wax, she can be molded in your hands; if you wait any longer, it will be too late!"[62]

Well, after all, maybe this army man would know how to train Elizaveta. The thought finally reconciled Gogol to the idea of her marriage. He left his mother and sister Olga to make their way back to Vasilyevka, and set off for Moscow. More tears, kisses, and signs of the cross at the door. He could not wait to escape from this swamp of sentiment. His real family would be right beside him in the coach, in his leather briefcase.

5.   The End of *Dead Souls*

Upon his arrival in Moscow, Gogol received a letter from Elizaveta inviting him to her wedding, which was to take place in late September or early October, and asking him to buy her a traveling vehicle, "coach" style—she badly needed it, she said, to follow her husband from post to post. Gogol was aghast at her audacity. In his brain, the vehicle assumed the fantastical proportions of a fairy queen's chariot. How dare she ask such a favor of him without a thought for the cost?

"Do please realize my condition," he retorted. "I tell you that, if I die, I shall undoubtedly not leave enough to pay for my own funeral. It is clearly God's will that we should remain poor. Besides, I must admit that total penury is preferable to semiprosperity. When you have a little, you become obsessed by all sorts of desires that are beyond your means: a 'coach'-style vehicle, a fit of temper if it cannot be purchased, and some new desire at every step. When one is really poor, on the other hand, one tells oneself: 'I cannot afford that,' and one is content. Dear sister, love poverty. Whoever loves poverty is no longer poor, but he is rich."[1]

He further recommended that, for economy's sake, the wedding be celebrated simply, inviting no one outside the family. And there was no point in fussing about a trousseau: as the future wife of an officer, Elizaveta should disdain fashionable clothes, reduce her possessions to the minimum, and be prepared to live anywhere. "I have seen countesses who, after marrying army men, went off with nothing but a bundle and a money box," he said in his letter. His sister would not get a kopeck from him. But, the same day he delivered this stern lesson in economy to her, he sent twenty-five silver rubles[2] to the archimandrite of the Optina monastery with the request that it be used to furnish the holy dwelling of the monks: "I earnestly beg you to pray for this sinner!"[3] Money was better invested in religion than in a carriage. Prayers took you farther than wheels.

Moscow was torrid and choked with dust. All who could were fleeing to the country in search of cooler air. Gogol accepted an invitation from Mrs. Smirnov to visit her estate at Spasskoye, seventy *versts* from town, on the banks of the Moskva. The main house, with its luminous windows and colonnade, the pavilions linked to it by a covered gallery, and the terrace adorned with marble statues, stood at the top of a hill like a miniature palace. On the right, a French garden, raked and trimmed; on the left, the English garden, a carefully tended wilderness with brooks, grottoes, and ruins; and beyond, the fields of wheat, a few hamlets, the peaceful and laborious world of the muzhiks.

In this beatific setting a phantom was awaiting Gogol: worn, gaunt, her skin tinged with yellow and her eyes filled with anxiety, Mrs. Smirnov seemed at the end of her strength. "I am annihilated," she told him. "Nerves, insomnia, worries." "Nothing to be done," Gogol replied. "I've got troubles with my nerves too!"

She told him about all her husband's setbacks, how he had been a victim of infamous slander, how he had been summoned to appear before a Senate investigating committee, how he had just been compelled to resign as governor of Kaluga. Gogol pretended to sympathize with her many misfortunes, while privately thinking that his own problems were far more worthy of interest. Mrs. Smirnov had set aside two rooms for him (a bedroom and a study) in a pavilion. Servants were assigned to wait on him, but he would not let them wash or dress him. He arose at dawn and went, prayer book in hand, for a walk in the English garden. Then he drank his coffee and worked until eleven, standing at a desk he had raised on logs. Whenever Mrs. Smirnov came to see him, he would lay a handkerchief over his manuscript, for he knew she was curious, and he did not want anyone to see the book until he had made his last revision.

Every day, for her edification, he read out some pages from the *Lives of the Saints*. In the afternoon they would sit side by side in the open carriage and trot gently through the forests and over the prairies, exchanging mournful memories: Pushkin, Rome, Nice. All the wealth of their lives seemed to belong to the past. After so many shining hours, could they hope for any more happiness in the future? Mrs. Smirnov thought not. And although Gogol contradicted her, in his heart of hearts he agreed. Sometimes, unable to bear the heat, he would order the carriage to stop at the bathhouse by the river's edge. In the water he would crouch down, jump up, and hop about on one leg, convinced that these exercises would fortify his system. At the end of their daily outings, he liked to watch the flocks brought in at sundown, surrounded by clouds of dust. It reminded him, he said, of his Ukrainian childhood. More and more often, now, he would sink into a semilethargy: sometimes Mrs. Smirnov would surprise him lying on a sofa, his eyes lost in the mists of his mind, with the *Lives of the Saints* open on his knees. "What are you doing there, Nikolai Vasilyevich?" He would start, as though suddenly awakened. "Nothing, nothing; I was reading the lives of Saint Comus and Saint Damien."[4]

One evening, he wanted to read her a few chapters of the second part of *Dead Souls,* but she was too tired to listen. He was annoyed, but concealed his displeasure. They sat and talked about their illnesses. "He complained of his shattered nerves," she wrote; "of his pulse that was too slow and his stomach that was too lazy. No more gaiety, no more humor in his words. He was completely immersed in himself." Out of the blue he asked, "Do you ever think about death?" She said she did. That pleased him, and he blessed her with an icon; but no sanctifying gesture could comfort her. Prayers or no prayers, she felt her strength waning day by day, and decided, toward the end of July, to go to Moscow for treatment.

Gogol had no choice but to abandon the country too, but not for long. The Shevyrevs were spending the summer in a villa twenty versts from Moscow. Without a word of warning—no formality among friends, after all—Gogol hired a coach and horses and set out. The arrival of this unexpected traveler, in a broad-brimmed gray hat with a Spanish cape over his shoulders, took everyone by surprise. Shevyrev quickly asked the young poet Berg, who was staying in a pavilion, to give up his room and move into the main house with them. The servants were instructed to keep quiet and out of the way. Wide-eyed with respect, the entire family forgot their carefree holiday atmosphere and adapted their lives to suit the author's requirements.

He worked in his little cottage surrounded by tall, dark pines. In the evening, Shevyrev would glide through the half-open door like a shadow, and Gogol, after making certain that no one was spying on them, would read aloud what he had written. "It was all so mysterious," Berg observed, "that one could have taken them for conspirators meeting to concoct bombs for a revolution." Gogol revealed seven long chapters to Shevyrev, some of them still only roughed out. After each session, he would say to this overawed listener: "I earnestly beg you not to tell anyone what you have heard, to make no allusion to even the smallest scenes, nor to speak the names of the characters."[5] Shevyrev was flattered by such trust, and promised that he would allow his tongue to be torn out before betraying the secret. In his opinion, the second volume was even better than the first; he did not understand the author's misgivings and tried to draw him back to life. But even when he was at table with his hosts, Gogol remained apathetic and distant. He ate almost nothing, consumed quantities of pills, and drank only water. "His stomach was troubling him," Berg wrote; "he was boring; his gestures were slow; but his face was not thin. He spoke little, listlessly and reluctantly; seldom did a smile widen his lips; his eyes had lost their former fire and swiftness; in a word, this was no longer Gogol, but a ruin of Gogol."[6]

While engaged in the laborious composition of the sequel to *Dead Souls,* he was also preparing a second edition of his "Collected Works." To save time, he sent each volume to be set up by a different printer. Meanwhile, the booksellers had spread the rumor that the work would be banned, and remaindered their stocks of the 1842 edition at black-market prices: one hundred rubles each. As though on purpose, moreover, the Moscow censor was delaying authorization of the new publication. In despair, Gogol begged Pletnyev to sacrifice his own copy of the "Collected Works" so that a visa could be obtained in St. Petersburg, at least.

"At first I wanted to add a few passages and make some changes," he wrote, "but now I've abandoned the idea. Let it stay the way it was in the first edition. Otherwise we'll have even more fuss with the censors."[7]

Shevyrev's hospitality was flawless, but Gogol's need for distraction was so acute that he could not long look at the same faces. Suddenly he was restless again. Where could he go now, to renew his vision of the world? Plenty of choice: a few days in the villa of the actor Shchepkin, a few days at Abramtsevo with the Aksakovs, and, with the first autumn rain, back to the Tolstoy house.

There he received a letter from M. S. Skurdin, a Petersburg friend, telling him of the charges made against him by the exiled political writer Herzen in his French publication *Sur le développement des idées révolutionnaires en Russie.* Inured as he was to the insults of the liberal press, Gogol was nevertheless upset by an indictment from this man of the highest intelligence, who accused him of betraying, in *Selected Passages,* the generous principles of his youth. He was dimly aware that he had lost part of his public, whereas what he wanted was to win the whole world to his side. Preaching universal love, how could he be an object of hatred to anyone? His sincerity, he thought, should have disarmed all critics.

Annenkov came to see him and found him worried about the consequences of his book but also completely ignorant of political realities. "He did not know, or did not want to know, what was going on around him," he wrote. "He talked about deportations and similar administrative measures as though they were moderate decisions showing clemency to the convicted. When he ushered me out, he stood in the doorway and said in an emotional voice, 'Do not think evil of me, and defend me to your friends [the European and liberal groups]. I care about their opinion.' "[8]

At Vasilyevka, meanwhile, Marya Ivanovna and her daughters were making energetic preparations for the wedding. Gogol had promised to be there but somehow could not bring himself to go. Every decision was mental torment. His only comfort was in contradiction, flight, and inconsistency. Also, he was afraid he would not be able to put up with the idiotic pretensions of his sister Elizaveta. Moved by a feeling of manly alliance with his future brother-in-law, he wrote a second precautionary letter:

"My mother and sisters are running about like besotted cats, trying to amass the largest possible pile of linen and clothes for the fiancée. They will spend a great deal of money doing this—if they can find any, that is; and you will be incommoded by all these rags. I beg you to make them understand that you will be living the life of an army camp and will have no use for all that stuff and there will be plenty of time to worry about it later."[9]

Thereupon Gogol received a letter from his mother telling him she was ill and begging him to come to Vasilyevka to see her, as well as to bless his sister on the threshold of her new life. He could no longer hesitate.

"I have made up my mind to come," he wrote his mother, "but do not put off the wedding and don't wait for me to celebrate it. I cannot travel quickly. My nerves have been so strained by this indecision, not knowing whether I would be with you or not, that it will take me some time to get there; I am afraid it will do nothing but harm to my health. In any event, I shall make only a brief visit and must hurry on to the Crimea; so please do not try to keep me. It would be more painful for me to spend the winter in the Ukraine than to stay here in Moscow. I would fall prey to melancholy and hypochondria. I need a climate in which I can get out and walk every day. In Moscow, at least, the houses are large and well heated and there are streets and sidewalks."[10]

He left Moscow on September 22, 1851, and had a fresh attack of uncertainty upon reaching Kaluga. Should he go on or turn back? His fraternal and filial affection was in conflict with his loathing for family affairs. One moment, he told himself this silly trip was surely going to destroy his peace of mind, and the next, he thought of his mother and sisters impatiently awaiting him at Vasilyevka and felt he could not disappoint them.

His dilemma was making him ill, so he went to the Optina monastery to consult a "staretz." Father Makarios patiently heard him out and advised him to continue his voyage. Half convinced, Gogol returned to see him the following day, to list all his excellent reasons for going back to Moscow. After a sharp look at his visitor, the monk agreed that perhaps this would be the best solution after all; but instead of calming Gogol, these conciliatory words only increased his torment. He visited the holy man a third time, to tell him how miserable his family would be if he did not go. Father Makarios, exasperated, told him rather curtly that if that was the case he had better attend the wedding, and dismissed him.

Gogol immediately wrote a note explaining all the anguish he felt at the idea of the journey: "My nerves are deranged, I am very much afraid the trip would finish me. The thought of falling ill in the middle of it frightens me, especially when I know I am far from Moscow, where I would not be allowed to succumb to melancholy. Tell me, does your heart not whisper to you that I would have done better to remain in Moscow?"[11]

Father Makarios scribbled his answer on the back: "I feel great pity for your state of torment and uncertainty. Of course, had you known what was in store you would have been wiser to stay in Moscow. As things are now, you yourself must decide what to do. If the thought of going back to Moscow gives you peace, then such is the will of God."

And he made him a present of a little icon of Saint Sergius. Praying to it, Gogol managed to convince himself that he should retrace his steps. However, just as he was about to do so, he was suddenly filled with panic and rushed to see the monk, who angrily ordered him to obey the inspiration he had received from the Almighty and closed the door in his face.[12]

Feeling both humiliated and relieved, Gogol returned to Moscow, but only to leave it again. He went to stay with the Aksakovs at Abramtsevo, where, as he sat beside his old friend with the graying beard, he continued to be gnawed by remorse for having disappointed his family. To lighten his heavy heart, he went to pray at the convent of Trinity St. Sergius on his mother's feast day, October 1. The priest in charge of the theological school introduced him to some students. He stood, speechless with timidity, in front of the cassocked young men, who were watching him with admiring eyes. At last he said, "You and I are performing the same task; we have the same goal and serve the same master."

He was back at the Tolstoys', in Moscow, on October 3, the day of his sister's wedding. He wrote to his mother to explain his absence: "When I reached Kaluga I fell ill and was obliged to turn around and come back. My nerves are so irritated by these worries and uncertainties that travel, which always used to be beneficial to me, now makes me suffer. It is evidently God's will that I should spend the winter in Moscow. I am sorry my circumstances are such that I cannot send even a tiny gift to the newlyweds."[13]

A few days later, on October 10 to be precise, the censor's office authorized a new edition of the "Collected Works," unmodified. Gogol brightened enough to accompany Arnoldi to a performance of *The Inspector General,* with Shumsky playing Khlestakov and Shchepkin as the mayor, on October 13. Tensely craning his neck, he anxiously followed the actors' movements from his box. On the whole, he thought Shumsky made an acceptable Khlestakov, but the other actors had not yet understood their parts. The pace dragged. The audience laughed too often and in the wrong places. Gogol was annoyed and began to fidget. Some spectators recognized him and started aiming their opera glasses at him. He was afraid of their applause, or of being asked to go on stage at the curtain call, so he slipped through the door. Arnoldi found him at

Mrs. Smirnov's, drinking sweetened wine diluted in warm water to recover from his emotions.

A week after the performance, Shchepkin went to see Gogol, and
brought along a young author who was extremely anxious to meet him:
Ivan Sergeyevich Turgenev.

"Shchepkin and I arrived at one o'clock and were received immediately," wrote Turgenev. "Gogol's room was to the right of the entrance
hall. We went in and found him standing at his desk, pen in hand. He
was wearing a dark coat, green velvet vest, and brown trousers. I was
struck to see how he had changed since 1841, when I had twice met him
at the home of Avdotya Petrovna Elagin. Then, he had been a short,
stocky Little-Russian; now there stood before me a gaunt creature whose
flesh hung on his bones. Some secret sorrow, preoccupation or morbid
anxiety I could not identify mingled with his ever-alert expression. He
came to greet us looking quite gay, and said as he shook my hand, 'We
should have met long before this.' I sat beside him on a large divan.
Mikhail Semyonovich [Shchepkin] sat in an armchair near us. I
scrutinized Gogol closely. His fair hair hung straight down, Cossack
style, and still kept its youthful tint but had grown sparse; his pale,
domed forehead still exuded intelligence; his little brown eyes sometimes
sparkled with merriment—and I mean merriment, not irony—but most
of the time his expression was one of weariness. His long, sharp nose
somehow imparted a cunning look to his whole face, reminiscent of a
fox. That disagreeable impression was further accentuated by the soft,
thick lips beneath his mustache, which he wore short: their indefinite
curve (it seemed to me than) revealed that hidden, darker side of his
nature. When he spoke, they parted unpleasantly to disclose his bad
teeth. His little chin was buried in a wide, black-velvet cravat. Gogol's
attitudes and gestures made one think not of a professor but of some
little provincial village schoolmaster. 'What an intelligent, strange, and
unhealthy person!' I said to myself as I watched him. I recall that
Shchepkin and I had set out as though to visit some extraordinary person, a genius whose mind was somewhat deranged. That was the general
opinion of him in Moscow. Shchepkin had warned me that Gogol did
not speak much. But, that day, he was very loquacious, speaking ani-
matedly and enunciating every word carefully; not only did this not
seem affected, but it bestowed special weight and meaning upon his
words. He talked about the importance of literature, the writer's role,
about how the author should look at his work, about the physiology, so

to say, of artistic creation, always employing unusual phrases and terms."

Turgenev's enthusiasm cooled, however, when Gogol, on the wings of his eloquence, began defending the necessity for the censor. He said this institution forced an author to decant his thoughts and weigh his words —in short, to give only his best.

"In these comments and in this reasoning," Turgenev noted, "the influence of those exalted personages to whom most of the *Selected Passages* were dedicated became clearly apparent. I very soon felt that there was an abyss between my view of the world and Gogol's. We did not hate the same things and we did not love the same things. But, just then, none of that mattered to me. I was in the presence of a great poet, a great artist, and I listened to him reverently even when I did not agree with him. He was presumably aware of my connection with Belinsky and Iskander [Herzen's pseudonym]. He made no mention of the former or of his letter[14]; the name would have seared his lips. But Iskander had just published an article abroad in which, referring to *Selected Passages,* he accused Gogol of betraying his former allegiance. Gogol spoke of this article. We know, from his letters, how deeply Gogol had been wounded by the total failure of his *Selected Passages,* and that day Shchepkin and I could see how badly that wound still smarted. His voice had changed, he was gasping, as he began to assure us that he did not understand what they could have against him, for he had always remained loyal to his religious and conservative principles and was ready to prove it by showing us passages from his early works. He leaped up in childish haste and ran into the next room, returning with a copy of *Arabesques.* He read out some passages from one of the puerilely grandiose and desperately vapid articles in which the volume abounds. I recall that it had to do with the need for strict order and unconditional obedience to the authorities, etc. 'You see?' Gogol repeated; 'I have always said the same thing, I haven't changed! How could they accuse me of treason?' And this was the author of *The Inspector General* speaking, the author of one of the most destructive works ever seen on the stage!"[15]

After this outburst, and as though tired of defending himself, Gogol went on in a murmur, "Why does Herzen take such liberties denouncing me in foreign papers?" Then he admitted that *Selected Passages* was a mistake. "I am guilty," he stammered, "guilty of having listened to the friends I was seeing in those days. If I could turn back the clock, and take back what I said, I would destroy all of *Correspondence with My Friends*. I would burn it."[16] Turgenev and Shchepkin sat in strained silence. Then, changing the subject, Gogol began to speak of his latest revival of *The Inspector General* and to criticize the interpretation. He said the actors had "lost the tone." Shchepkin persuaded him to read the whole play to them, to clarify his characters' psychology.

The reading was held two weeks later, on November 5, 1851, and Turgenev was present. To his great surprise, he saw that a few of the more temperamental actors, unwilling to be given a lesson by the author, had not accepted the invitation, and not a single one of the women in the company had bothered to come. The listeners sat at a round table and Gogol on a divan. His features were wooden and his expression morose. But as he uttered the opening lines of the play, his eyes began to shine and his cheeks flushed as though he had been drinking. "Gogol read admirably," Turgenev wrote. "I was struck by his great simplicity of tone, a kind of sincerity that was at once grave and naïve; he seemed totally uninterested in his listeners and their opinions. The effect was remarkable, particularly in the comic passages. It was impossible not to burst out laughing for the sheer fun of it."[17]

Another young author, Grigori Danilevsky,[18] met Gogol around this time, and spoke of his astonishing resemblance to those storks one saw in the Ukraine, perched on one leg on a rooftop "with an appealing and thoughtful expression on their faces." Gogol complained to Danilevsky of the trouble he was having with the sequel to *Dead Souls*. "I have to wrench the words out of my head with pliers!" he sighed. He told Mrs. Aksakov that he now found the second part of his work inferior to the first and would have to start all over again, or perhaps even abandon the book. But to other people, he said his work was progressing— eleven chapters completed—and might be published in the summer of 1852, "maybe even early in the spring."

Often, sitting in his study, he would read his manuscript aloud to himself. Was this really the second part of *Dead Souls?* He was having such difficulty in following his reincarnated characters that he sometimes doubted it.

The fragments of the second part of the book that have survived bear witness to Gogol's desperate attempt to goad his talent into line with his conscience. Believing that if a work of art reached a certain level of perfection it could become a moral force, he saw it as his duty to muster all the resources of his intellect for the regeneration of his fellow man. To be worthy of the task God had assigned him at birth by giving him the gift of writing, he thought he had to show virtue fair and vice foul in his books. However, he was only at ease painting physical and spiritual ugliness; his muse deserted him when he tried to create a pure face. He was wonderfully able to capture human foibles, to transform features into grimaces and decompose ordinary gestures into a grotesque dance, but his skill collapsed whenever he sought to portray the new, just, and vigorous men who were going to "save Russia." His imagination balked in pursuit of his dream of excellence; and his hand, which was made for the thick black line of caricature, became cramped and awkward when he tried to etch a smooth-featured profile. Working against his true nature, he writhed and wrestled, praying God to help him—and nothing but unctuous triteness flowed from his pen. He wanted to be Raphael, but he *was* Hieronymus Bosch.

There are a few comic characters in the second part of *Dead Souls,* it is true, who bear some relationship to those of the first, but they are paler and smaller. There is the lazy, ponderous, superficial Tentetnikov, a blissfully immobile landowner with a butterfly brain; and General Betrishchev, ambitious and majestic, who is fond of "incense and opulence"; and the hospitable Pyetukh, dedicated heart and soul to swilling; and the monumental imbecile Koshkarev, whose great idea is that "all you needed was to give the muzhiks European trousers, and knowledge would advance, commerce would flourish, and a golden age begin in Russia"; and Khlobuev, who is Russian chaos incarnate, giving dinner parties when he doesn't have a kopeck to pay for them, praying instead of working, and living happily off his friends. Drawn up across from these mediocrities are the ranks of the luminous. The supposed inmates of Purgatory (Volume II), they are not yet "wholly virtuous" as those of Paradise (Volume III) will be—but they are "important." In other words, to Gogol they represented the finer qualities of the Russian people. At the head of these happy mortals stands Kostanzhoglo, landowner and industrialist, possessing equal shares of common sense and sense of duty; he teaches Chichikov how to get rich while remaining true to Christian principles.

In short, what the author set out in theory in his *Selected Passages,* he now illustrates with "living images" in the sequel to *Dead Souls:* honesty leads to prosperity, and the Bible gives birth to the bank account. As if Kostanzhoglo was not enough to prove his point, he offers us another edifying character, called Murazov, an openhanded manufacturer of spirits who started with nothing and made millions "without engaging in any devious practices" and is growing wealthier every day because he conducts all his business with his thoughts fixed on God. The third hero to be given as an example to the Russian public is the governor general, in whom the title of Excellency acquires full significance, this senior official being at once firm, farsighted, and filled with integrity. At his side shines the honest scribe, the young bureaucrat "unacquainted with ambition, cupidity, or the habit of copying others, who works solely because he feels he should be where he is and nowhere else, that that was what life was given him for." Also noteworthy is the charming Olga, an ideal Russian virgin, whimsical but so truthful and pure that in her presence "the wicked lose countenance," "the boldest talker falls silent," and "the shy man can speak at last."[19]

Light emanates from these celestial beings and, little by little, shows Chichikov his own unworthiness. The words of Murazov, Kostanzhoglo, and, most of all, the governor general, turn his soul inside out. The punishment hanging over his head prepares the way for his moral resurrection, which, in the mind of the author, should justify the entire work in the eyes of God.

Unfortunately, the "positive" heroes Gogol has conceived here are so conventionally drawn that, instead of making us long for virtue, they give us a yearning for vice. With all their profoundly human failings, it is still the grimacing monsters of the first part who are alive, whereas the honorable puppets of the second are truly dead souls.

Only a few fragments of the work have survived. But what we have gathered of the over-all scheme seems to indicate that the Purgatorio and Paradiso of the trilogy would have been weak studio compositions in comparison with the admirable Inferno we have.

Gogol was aware of his failure but refused to admit it. The friends to whom he would occasionally read a chapter encouraged him to go on with the book. It did seem to them that these bright figures were not at home in the malevolent and grotesque world of Chichikov, that the virtuous landowner, the distiller overflowing with high sentiment, the angelic girl, and the governor general as just as God the Father had got into the wrong book by mistake, but they trusted the author's genius to rectify these imperfections and give the needed spice to the work.

Some even thought the second volume, once it was really finished, would be better than the first.

At the same time, he was also completing his *Meditations upon Divine Liturgy* and correcting the proofs of his "Collected Works." Toward the end of January, 1852, one of his Ukrainian friends, a professor of history and literature called Bodyansky, came to visit. Finding Gogol immersed in his papers, he asked: "What are you working on, Nikolai Vasilyevich?"

"Just scribbling," Gogol replied, "and looking over the proofs of my old books, which are to be reprinted now."

"Will they all be reprinted?"

"No, I may omit some of my early things."

"Which in particular?"

"Evenings on a Farm."

"What?" Bodyansky exclaimed. "You want to do away with one of your most effective pieces of work?"

"That volume contains many immature passages. I would like to give the public a collection of my works with which I myself am satisfied now, at this moment. After I die, they can do as they please."[20]

He spoke the last words with a sort of funereal detachment, then added, shaking his head, "How dismal the world is, when you look at it! Do you know, Zhukovsky writes me that he is going blind?" Gogol's face fell; then he suddenly brightened again and offered to take Bodyansky the following Sunday to hear a recital of Ukrainian songs at Aksakov's home. The Ukraine—its songs, customs, cooking—seemed the only thing able to revive him these days.

The gathering at the Aksakov home could not take place, however, because of the sudden death, on January 29, 1852, after a short illness, of Katerina Mikhailovna Khomyakov, the sister of the poet Yasykov. Gogol had been very fond of the gracious and lively young woman; she reminded him of Yasykov, his friend and confidant, who had died six years before. Her death penetrated his own flesh. This was not the first time he had felt himself being nudged toward the precipice, but never until that day had the call seemed so imperative. This time it was not a warning, it was a summons. He had an icy premonition, which paralyzed his body and numbed his mind. After seeing the young woman in her coffin, he murmured, "Nothing could be more solemn than death. Life would lose all its beauty if there were no death." During the first part of the funeral, which took place in the dead woman's home, his courage failed him. "It's all over for me," he said. Dizzy with fatigue and sorrow, he could hardly bear to stay until the service ended.

The next day, November 30, he did not go to the formal funeral, but ordered a requiem sung for her in Count Tolstoy's private chapel. That evening, he was at the Aksakovs' and said, "Terrible is the moment of death." "Why terrible?" somebody challenged; "you need only believe in God's mercy upon all suffering creatures, and the thought of death ceases to hold any terror." "On that point, one would need to ask those who have been there!" Gogol snapped.[21]

The effect of this event upon him was to make him worry about himself even more than before; his first idea was to wrap himself in a cold, wet sheet every morning, to increase his resistance. This treatment was not a success. Every day, he was looking more like a walking cadaver. After a chance meeting at the Aksakovs', the Moscow physician Dr. Alexander Sanovich Over took Vera Sergeyevna Aksakov aside and whispered to her, "The poor man!" "Who do you mean?" she asked. "Gogol." "Why do you call him a poor man?" "Because he's a hypochondriac. Pray God I never have him as a patient! It's dreadful!" "He has one consolation," the girl said; "he is a true believer." "That is not saving him from being miserable!" Dr. Over concluded as he moved toward the door.

Returning to Gogol in the drawing room, Vera Sergeyevna invited him to stay for dinner. He refused. His expression was serene. Cold winter sunshine filled the room.

"You haven't done any work today!" Vera Sergeyevna said to him. "You've walked enough now; you must go back to work!"

"So I should, you're right," he said with a smile; "but I don't know whether I shall be able to. My work is such that wanting to do it isn't enough to make it happen."[22]

He put on his overcoat and went out into the white, empty street. Gaunt, stooped, and twisted, he plodded through the snow like a crow. Vera Sergeyevna's heart contracted as she watched him go.

"Ask God to make my work conscientious," he wrote to Zhukovsky the next day, "and to find in me some degree, however tiny, of worthiness to sing a hymn to heavenly beauty."[23]

To elevate himself to that degree of "worthiness," he intensified his perusal of pious books, prayed, fasted, and carried Father Matthew's latest letters in a secret pocket, like relics.

"I thank you again and again for keeping me in your memory," he wrote to the priest. "The mere thought that you are praying for me gives my soul hope that God will find me worthy to serve Him better than I have in the past in my impotence, laziness, and weakness. Your last two letters never leave me. Every time I read them again, I find fresh illumination in them and thank God, Who helped you to write them. Do not forget me, good soul, in your prayers."[24]

Father Matthew's letters to Gogol have not been preserved, but their style can be imagined from those he sent to other penitents:

"Do not trade God for the devil and the kingdom of heaven for this world," he wrote to a widower who wanted to remarry. "You will have one moment of pleasure here and then weep for all eternity. Do not enter into conflict with God; do not marry again. You know well that the Lord Himself requires you to struggle against the flesh. Think of death, and it will be easier for you to live. If you forget death, you will forget God. If you adorn your soul here below with fasting and abstinence, it will be pure when it reaches the hereafter. You know what to do in order to calm your passions: eat little and as seldom as possible, avoid gluttony, give up tea, drink cold water instead, with a piece of bread, and that only when you need them. Sleep less, speak less, and work more."[25]

Father Matthew practiced the harsh regimen he preached: neither wine nor meat, no reading other than that necessary to shore up the faith, the most abject poverty, abhorrence of any pleasures; in the villages under his ecclesiastical authority he was said to have so terrorized the faithful that even in their own homes they no longer dared show their naturally lighthearted dispositions. No more laughter, no more song. Even the children's faces were sad. In compliance with the archpriest's recommendations, their parents permitted them to amuse themselves only if they hummed psalms while playing.[26]

A landowner named Markov, who knew Father Matthew well, tried to warn Gogol against the influence of the archpriest of Rzhev, and wrote to him: "As a man, he assuredly deserves respect; as a preacher, he is most remarkable; but as a theologian, he is weak, being totally uneducated. I do not believe he would be capable of solving your problems if they have to do with fine points of theology. Father Matthew can discourse upon the importance of fasting and the need for repentance, which are well-worn topics, but he will scrupulously avoid any discussion of matters of pure religious philosophy."[27]

Disregarding this lucid opinion, Gogol would not break off relations with his spiritual guide. It seemed to him that Father Matthew's simplicity and rough-hewn manner were just the kind of soul hygiene he needed; for now, that was the only idea in his head: to uplift his soul until the nascent work would be worthy, no longer merely of its human creator, but of the Creator himself. From small to capital letter he would ascend. Forget the body. Mortify the flesh with fasting.

Hope surged within him when he heard that Father Matthew had come to Moscow at the invitation of Count Tolstoy. At last he would be able to unburden his soul and fortify his courage in the presence of a man of God.

He gave the priest a few chapters of the second volume of *Dead Souls*. After glancing through them, the Father expressed disappointment and advised the author to delete the passages alluding to "a priest more Catholic than Orthodox in manner" and "a governor whose like was never seen." Such portraits, he said, would provoke even more criticism than the *Selected Passages*. How could a man who claimed to have turned to God waste his time in such scribbling? He must think of purifying his heart, not lining up sentences on paper. Facing an appalled Gogol, the red-bearded priest with the big nose and the iron-gray eyes gave voice as from the pulpit. "The divine rule is written for all," he said. "All must follow it without murmur. The defection of the body cannot keep us from fasting. What work have we to worry about? What need have we of strength? Many are called, but few are chosen."[28]

When Gogol tried to explain that art and holiness were not irreconcilable, the priest, on the crest of his wave of oratory, ordered him to abjure his beloved Pushkin. "Deny Pushkin!" he cried. "He was a sinner and a pagan!" And he described to his prostrated and sobbing penitent the awesome ceremony of the Last Judgment. Long ago, in childhood, Gogol had been deeply affected by his mother's portrayal of the torments of hell; this time, he thought his head would explode with the horror of it. "Enough! I can't listen to you any more!" he moaned. "It's too awful!"[29] He begged Father Matthew to leave him.

The priest withdrew in anger, and the next day, February 5, 1852, he returned to Rzhev. A contrite Gogol accompanied him to the railway station, but their parting was extremely cool. Gogol was consumed by remorse and rushed home to write to his spiritual father: "Yesterday I wrote to ask you to forgive me for having offended you. But divine grace, guided by someone's prayers, suddenly illuminated me, whose heart is so dry, and I then wanted to thank you with all my strength.

But why speak of that? I owe you eternal gratitude, here and beyond the grave. Wholly yours, Nickolai."[30]

Upon receiving this, Father Matthew could tell himself that his eloquence had finally won the day. Russia might have lost a great writer, but God had surely gained a beautiful soul. Sometime later, the publicist Philippov questioned the priest about his last conversation with Gogol, and Father Matthew gave the following account: "Gogol was seeking inner peace and purification." "Why inner purification?" asked Philippov. "There was an unclean place in him." "What unclean place?" "An unclean place, I tell you. He was trying to get rid of it and couldn't. I helped him to purify himself. What's wrong with my having made a true Christian of Gogol?" "You are accused, as his spiritual father, of having forbidden him to write profane works." "It's not true! An artist's talent is God-given. No gift of God can be forbidden. I certainly advised him, it is true, to describe good people, that is, to show positive rather than negative characters as he had done so successfully in the past. He tried, but it didn't work." And then, annoyed by the persistence of these literary men who were charging him with obscurantism, the priest added, in a growl: "You don't blame a doctor for prescribing surgery when he diagnoses a serious disease!"[31]

Gogol, meanwhile, could not forget his conversation with Father Matthew. As long as he had been in good health, he had regarded the devil as a sort of ghoulish charlatan, a third-rate juggler, a Khlestakov or Chichikov who could be disarmed with laughter. But now that his strength was failing and his mind filling with mist, it seemed to him that the devil was not content with tempting flabby and defenseless souls: even apparently lofty undertakings such as the completion of a work of art could be put into their authors' heads by the Evil One. Perhaps, all the time he had thought he was serving God, he was really working for the Tempter. Maybe that was what Father Matthew had meant when he urged him to put down his pen and deny Pushkin. Perhaps he had only a few days left in which to repair the error of a lifetime.

On the morning of Shrove Tuesday he went to see a priest at the other end of the city and asked when he could take communion. The priest advised him to wait until the first week of Lent, but upon seeing the writer's distress, he agreed to an appointment in church two days later.

In the meantime, Gogol renounced all forms of literary activity.

Surrounded by pious works, he tried to impose upon himself a discipline even more harsh than that prescribed by the church: he began to fast during carnival week. Struggling with the loathsome demands of his stomach, he ate less and less: a few spoonfuls of kasha or borsht, a piece of holy bread, a glass of water. His legs could hardly carry him, and still he called himself a gluttonous pig. He tried to sleep as little as possible at night to resist the fiendish temptation of dreaming. He wrote to his mother, imploring her to pray for him: "I always feel great tenderness in the moments when you pray for me. Oh, how much a mother's prayer can do for us!"[32]

On Thursday, February 7, he went to church very early, confessed and took communion, and prostrated himself upon the ground and wept. Shevyrev, who came to see him shortly afterward, found him so thin and listless that he went down on his knees and begged him to eat. Gogol claimed he wasn't hungry. Then, as though suddenly inspired, he had himself driven to the Preobrazhensky Hospital, to see one of the innocents, the "crazy men of Christ," who was there. His name was Ivan Koreysha, and he was much loved by the people. When he got to the hospital he could not make up his mind to go inside and paced up and down in the snow, then stood, motionless, in the wind, for several minutes; then climbed back into the coach and went home. What had he hoped to hear from the visionary's mouth? A confirmation of Father Matthew's commandments, or a different opinion that would release him and give him back to life and literature?

He seemed so haggard and lost when he returned that Count Tolstoy asked him to see the family physician, Dr. Inozemtsev. The perplexed doctor finally declared that he was suffering from intestinal catarrh and told the patient to rub his stomach with alcohol, drink cherry-laurel water, and take rhubarb pills to relieve constipation. Scornful of such physical palliatives, Gogol preferred to treat himself, by multiplying his genuflections in front of the icons with which Count Tolstoy's home was amply provided.

In the night of February 8–9 he was dozing, exhausted, on his sofa, when he heard a voice from the grave. His eyes staring into the darkness, he felt as though he were already dead, uttered a dreadful shriek, awakened his servant, and sent him to fetch a priest, any priest. When the half-sleeping pope came stumbling in, Gogol told him that he was suffering from the same illness as his father, that he felt himself about to give up the ghost, and wanted to take communion again because the previous day's sacrament had not given him peace. The priest, noting that the allegedly dying man had risen to greet him, assured him that there was no need for alarm; it was not yet time for him to prepare to meet his Maker. Temporarily reassured, Gogol consented to lie down again and sleep. But on Sunday, February 10, he summoned Count Tolstoy and asked him to hand over all his works, after his death, to the metropolitan of Moscow, Philaretos, so that the supreme ecclesiastical authority could judge what should be made public and what left in darkness: "Whatever he finds useless, let him ruthlessly strike it out!" The count refused, trying to make Gogol think he was not seriously ill.

During the whole of the following day, Gogol's sole nourishment was water with a little wine diluted in it. It was the beginning of Lent. The city entered a period of abstinence and privation. The church bells rang seldom, and when they did they sounded like death knells. Priests officiated in mourning vestments. The imperial theaters closed. Dried mushrooms, pickles in brine, bitter cabbage, and marinades presided gloomily over the market stalls. In some devout homes, the furniture was shrouded and sheets were hung over profane paintings. Through the walls of his room, Gogol sensed the universal repentance. His thoughts, dwelling unremittingly on the shadows, fitted well with the solemn mood of Christianity. A few anxious friends came to see him: Pogodin, Shevyrev, Shchepkin. He made it clear he did not want to see them, lying on his sofa listening but making no reply; and after a minute he would whisper, "Forgive me, I'm sleepy."

"When I consider his state," Shevyrev wrote after leaving him, "I think there is more of sorrow in it than true illness."

On the evening of Monday, February 11, Count Tolstoy had a mass sung at home. Gogol dragged himself from chair to chair until he reached the front row. Then, with an enormous effort, he straightened up and remained standing through the service, murmuring prayers, crossing himself, and swaying from side to side, his eyes filled with tears.

In the night of February 11–12, he continued to pray alone in his room in front of the icons. He could not close his eyes. At three in the morning he called the Ukrainian servant, who was sleeping, curled on the floor, behind the partition, and asked him if the other rooms in the house were still warm.

"No," the boy said. "They're cold."

"Then give me my cape. I have to go down there to take care of some business."

With his cape on his shoulders and a candle in his hand, stooped and faltering, he crept into the next room as furtively as a thief. At every step, he crossed himself. His humpbacked shadow broke at the angles of wall and ceiling. When he reached the stove, he ordered the boy to open it as silently as possible and to bring him his leather briefcase. From it he withdrew a sheaf of notebooks tied with a string: the manuscript of the second part of *Dead Souls,* a few chapters of the third part, and some minor pieces. The packet weighed heavy in his hands. As heavy as some inexpiable sin. He must get rid of it as soon as possible. In order to come before God pure. He threw the mass of paper onto the hearth and held his candle to it. The flame nibbled at the edge of a sheet, then leaped up, bright, joyful, insolent.

"Sir! What are you doing?" the boy cried out. "Stop! You might still be able to use these papers!"

"It is none of your concern," Gogol said. "Be content to pray."

The boy, sensing a tragedy, burst into tears and continued imploring his master to take the papers out of the fire. Gogol would not listen. Was he thinking, in that moment, of the far-off time when he had burned every copy of *Hans Kuechelgarten?* There was nothing like fire to cover all traces of an error. But, this time, the pages were too close together. After consuming the edges of the notebooks, the flame died. Gogol vexedly extracted the wedge, half carbonized and peppered with sparks, untied the string, and spread the pages so they would burn more easily. Then he put his candle into the stove a second time and set fire to his manuscripts. At last they caught.

He started back from the sudden glare; facing the hole, he watched the lines of his writing writhe and fade. Chichikov was returning to the hell he ought never to have left. But so many years' work, destroyed in a few minutes! God had willed it. Unless it was the devil. Lost in his thoughts, Gogol sat nailed to his chair, staring in fascination, nose drooping, hands on his knees, like a bird with its wings folded, until all that remained of the notebooks was a pile of ashes. Then he crossed himself, embraced the little servant, and began to weep.[33] A little later, he sent for Count Tolstoy and said, pointing to the pile of ashes and choking on his words:

"See what I have done! I wanted to burn some things I had got ready beforehand and instead I've burned the lot! How powerful is the Evil One! See what he's driven me to do! Now everything is lost!"

"It's a good sign," the count answered, his only wish being to comfort Gogol. "You have burned manuscripts three or four times already, only to do better the next time. Besides, you must remember what you've written!"

"Yes, yes," Gogol said, touching his brow, "I can, I can; I have it all in my head."[34]

He stopped crying. His face cleared. Why had he lied to the count, telling him he had burned the manuscript by mistake? He knew perfectly well what was in the notebooks he had thrown into the stove. But he had never been able to tell the truth about his intentions and actions. Every time he uttered a falsehood, he felt protected against the crushing threat of—evidence.

In any case, the problem that was tormenting him could hardly have been solved by the holocaust. He hoped he had severed the bonds that linked him to his fellow man, but the old doubts still whirled in his head: Had he been obeying God, by destroying a useless pile of paper; or the devil, by depriving mankind of a work—however imperfect— in which his contemporaries could have found inspiration to escape from their bad instincts? Wasn't it offering insult to the Almighty, by refusing the world as He had made it, with all the sleet and mud? Did a Christian called to earth to bear witness by his writing have the right to reject the divine gift for the sake of asceticism? Who could answer his questions? Neither Father Matthew, nor the metropolitan Philaretos, nor the "staretz" of the Optina monastery could enlighten Gogol. Wrenched and torn, unable to understand what God was asking of him, he could no longer see any reason to remain among men. Death attracted and terrified him, by turns. Sometimes it seemed as if a voice was calling him from very far away, as in his childhood.

In the ensuing days, he sank into a lethargy. Sitting in one armchair with his legs propped on another and his eyes closed, he took no interest in the compassionate fuss his friends were making around him. "Everyone has to die; I am ready; I will die," he said to Khomyakov one evening. And when Count Tolstoy tried to divert him by talking of his mother and sisters, he muttered crossly, "What are you talking about? How can you talk of such things when I am preparing myself for such a terrible event?" Then he emptied his pockets and ordered that part of the money be given to the poor and the remainder be used to buy candles.

Doctor Inozemtzev was also ill, so Count Tolstoy called in Doctor Tarasenkov to replace him—a sensitive, considerate, and cultivated man for whom Gogol had some affection. "When I saw him, I was afraid," Tarasenkov said. "His whole body had grown excessively thin, his eyes were dull and had sunk into their sockets, his features were blurred, his cheeks hollow, his voice weak; it was even hard for him to move his tongue in his dehydrated mouth, and the expression on his face was indefinite, inexplicable. At first glance, I thought he was dead. He was sitting down, with his legs stretched in front of him; his head, thrown slightly back, was leaning against the back of the armchair. When I came toward him, he raised his head but, despite a visible effort, was unable to hold it upright. His look was that of a man for whom all problems are solved, all feelings deadened, all words pointless, and whose resolution is unshakable."

In a clearheaded moment, however, Gogol consented to answer a few personal questions the doctor put to him. "He had had no relations with women for a very long time," Tarasenkov wrote. "He said himself, moreover, that he felt no urge in that direction and had never derived the slightest pleasure from it; nor did he practice onanism."[35] But how much credit should one give to this type of confession, made by a person as devious as Gogol? At the end of the interrogation he let himself be handled, opened his mouth to show his tongue, listened to Tarasenkov's urgings that he drink some hot milk to keep up his strength, and suddenly yielded to his exhaustion and let his head fall on his chest.

In the meantime the metropolitan Philaretos, who was ill himself, had sent a message to Gogol telling him that he must obey the doctors, "for salvation is in obedience, not in fasting." Gogol replied that he would abandon himself to the will of God. He had, in fact, given up the fight. In a trembling hand he drafted his will:

"In the name of the Father, the Son, and the Holy Ghost, I bequeath everything I possess to my mother and my sisters. I advise them to live all together, united by love, in the village. The servants who have waited on me must be rewarded. Give Yakim his freedom. And Simon, too. I should like, after my death, our village to become a haven for any unmarried girls who want to bring up orphans. Their education should be very simple: catechism and outdoor work. In time our house might become a monastery, if my sisters decided to take the veil. I would like to be buried either in the church or, failing that, in the churchyard outside, and requiems to be sung without interruption. Be living souls, not dead souls. There is no door but the one we were shown by Jesus Christ. Whoever tries to reach heaven by any other route is a scoundrel and a thief."

Then, on long strips of paper, he added:

"If you do not become as little children, you will not enter into the kingdom of heaven."

"Lord, throw Satan in chains again by the power of Thy Cross!"

"What can I do to keep in my heart, with gratitude, the memory of the lesson I received?"

His stiff fingers were too weak to propel the quill. He pushed the writing case away. It was clear to him now that he would never write another word of literature. But that did not bother him. The visible world had, at last, ceased to have any importance. He murmured, "Leave me alone. I am fine as I am." Wrapped in his dressing gown, he no longer washed, or combed the long hair that hung slanting across his forehead, or trimmed his mustache. Trying to encourage him to eat, the parish priest came every day and earnestly munched prunes under his nose or swallowed gruel with a beguiling expression. Reluctantly, the sick man began to imitate him, but at the first mouthful he pushed the dish away with his bony hand. "What prayer do you wish me to read?" asked the priest. "They're all good," Gogol gasped. "Read, read." On Sunday the priest persuaded him to swallow a spoonful of castor oil. After gulping it down, Gogol made a face and declared that he would take no more nourishment. His bewildered friends had the impression that they were watching a slow suicide, not a natural death. And the patient was committing his suicide, a crime in the eyes of religion, in order to obey what he saw as the will of God.

On Monday of the second week of Lent, the priest asked if he wished to take communion and receive extreme unction. Gogol joyfully consented and listened greedily while the Gospel was read. He was holding a lighted candle in his hands, and big tears rolled from his eyes. In the evening they tried to give him some medicine. "Leave me alone!" he cried. "Why are you tormenting me?" A few friends came to see him. He would not open his eyes when they entered, but would ask them to help him drink or change his position in the armchair. Although he was longing for death, he was afraid to lie down in his bed, for, he said, once he was down he would never get up again. However, as he continued to grow weaker, he finally agreed to lie on top of the bed. "If God wants me to live, I shall live!" he sighed as he let his head fall to the pillow.

On Tuesday, February 19, Count Tolstoy decided that doctors should have priority over priests in this battle against Gogol's mysterious ailment. From the exorcisms of the Orthodox Church they moved to the exorcisms of modern science, from idealism to positivism, from prayers to potions. Dr. Tarasenkov, summoned to Count Tolstoy's home, found the entrance hall jammed with a crowd of dismayed faces. "How is Gogol?" he asked. "Bad," the count said. "Go look at him. You can go straight into his room."

Gogol was lying in his dressing gown on his sofa, his boots on his feet, his nose to the wall and his eyes closed. A rosary hung from his fingers. He was facing a lighted icon of the Holy Virgin. When Dr. Tarasenkov took the patient's pulse, Gogol grumbled, "Don't touch me, please!" His pulse was weak and rapid, his hands cold, his breathing regular. Dr. Tarasenkov was soon joined by two colleagues, Drs. Alfonsky and Over. The newcomers agreed to try mesmerism to overcome the patient's aversion to food. That evening, a noted hypnotist, Dr. Sokologorsky, stood, resplendent with confidence and concentration, at the dying man's side. He placed one hand on his forehead, another in the hollow of his stomach; he frowned; but the fluid was not coming through. Irritated by the physician's esoteric gestures, Gogol twisted and turned, moaning, "Leave me alone!" Dr. Sokologorsky abandoned the case in a huff; he was replaced by a colleague famous for his tenacity— Dr. Klimentov—who favored a more aggressive approach and began shouting at Gogol as though talking to a deaf man:

"Does your head hurt?"

"No."

"Your stomach?"

"No."

The interrogation had no effect. However, the doctors did manage to force a cup of bouillon down the sick man's throat, and, despite his howls, administered a soap suppository.

Around noon the following day, February 20, they met for a consultation: Dr. Over, Dr. Evenius, Dr. Klimentov, Dr. Sokologorsky, Dr. Tarasenkov, Dr. Vorvinsky. These six pinnacles of learning, having reviewed the causes of their patient's state of prostration (prolonged and intense mental effort, no nourishment, refusal of all medication), reached the conclusion that he was probably no longer altogether sane. Dr. Over put the question straight: "Ought we to abandon the case, or should we treat him as irresponsible and prevent him from letting himself die?" Dr. Evenius replied without hesitation, "Yes! We must feed him by force." Thereupon, all hands returned to the sickroom. Leaning over Gogol, they took turns asking him questions and feeling him. "His stomach was so soft and hollow," Tarasenkov wrote, "that his vertebrae could easily be felt through it." With hands all over him, assailed by prying questions, penetrated by learned eyes, the poor man howled and writhed on his couch: "Stop tormenting me, for the love of God!" Latin formulae were blossoming on all sides: *mania religiosa, gastroenteritis ex inanitione*, . . . Somebody even mentioned typhus. There was a long doctoral frown. A resonance of learned words. Gogol, past master of the transformation of ugliness into the fantastic, looked on in horror at this insane dance of doctors in his bedroom. Could he, in that distant past when he had written "Diary of a Madman," have dreamed that one day, at the end of his life, he would be subjected to the same torture as his pitiable hero? "No, I cannot endure it," he had written. "What are they doing to me, my God? They are pouring cold water on my head! They don't listen to me, they don't see me, they don't hear me! What have I done to them? Why are they tormenting me? What do they want from me, miserable me? What can I give them? I have nothing."[36]

As though following the author's stage directions, Dr. Over, after consulting his colleagues, prescribed bloodletting and warm baths alternating with dousings of cold water on the head. Then the physicians gravely withdrew, leaving their most energetic member, Dr. Klimentov, to supervise the careful execution of their orders. Gogol was seized bodily and thrust into a tub of hot water, while a servant poured ice water over his head. Then he was put naked into his bed, and Dr. Klimentov applied a half dozen leeches to his nose; and thus that nose, the subject of so much of Gogol's writing, now became the pretext for yet another nightmare. Fat creatures were hanging from his nostrils, gorging on his blood. They squirmed and writhed, they touched his lips. He yelped, "You mustn't! Take the leeches away! Get the leeches out of my mouth!" But nobody listened. His hands were pinned down so he could not tear the cluster of worms with the voracious suckers from his nose.

Around seven in the evening, Dr. Over returned to Gogol's bedside and decided, with Dr. Klimentov's approval, to put plasters on his extremities, blister the nape of his neck, and put ice on his head and, in his stomach, a mixture of marshmallow root and cherry-laurel water. Dr. Tarasenkov, who watched the proceedings, was offended by his colleagues' rough handling of the patient.

"They were treating him like a madman," he wrote, "shouting in his presence as though he were already a corpse. Klimentov would not leave him alone for a second, kept kneading him, turning him over, pouring I don't know what kind of corrosive alcohol on his head, and when the patient moaned the doctor would ask, without ceasing his ablutions: 'Well, now. Does that hurt, Nikolai Vasilyevich? Eh? Say something.' But he only whimpered and did not answer."[37]

At last Over and Klimentov went away, leaving Dr. Tarasenkov alone with the dying man. Gogol's pulse had grown weaker and his breathing began to be congested. Lying on one side, incapable of moving, he meekly complained that the plasters were burning him. The insertion of another suppository tore a groan of pain from him. Then he asked for something to drink. A swallow of broth. His head dropped back almost immediately. Clearly, he was no longer fully conscious. Around eleven, he uttered a loud cry:

"The ladder! Quick! Pass me the ladder!"

In the final chapter of his *Selected Passages from My Correspondence with My Friends* Gogol had written: "God alone knows, but perhaps, because of this unique desire [love of one's fellow man, through God], a ladder stands ready to be thrown down to us from heaven, and a hand is outstretched toward us, to help us mount in one bound."

Desperately he was seeking that ladder and that hand by the wavering light of the vigil lamp; but all he saw was a pair of spectacles leaning over his shoulder, the gilding of an icon, and flasks of medicine on a table. Since the ladder was not coming down to him, he would have to reach up to it. He made one attempt to get up. His legs would not carry him. He was dizzy. Dr. Tarasenkov and a servant seated him in an armchair. He could no longer hold up his head. It dropped back "like that of a newborn baby," Tarasenkov wrote. They put him to bed again, slipped a shirt on him. He lost consciousness, then regained it but without opening his eyes. His feet were icy. Tarasenkov slid a hot-water bottle into the bed, but it had no effect: he was shivering. Cold sweat covered his emaciated face. Blue circles appeared under his eyes. At midnight Dr. Klimentov relieved Dr. Tarasenkov. To ease the dying man, he administered a dose of calomel and placed loaves of hot bread around his body. Gogol began to moan again. His mind wandered, quietly, all night long. "Go on!" he whispered. "Rise up, charge, charge the mill!" Then he became still weaker, his face hollowed and darkened, his breathing became imperceptible. He seemed to grow calm; at least he was no longer suffering. At eight in the morning of February 21, 1852, he breathed his last. He was not yet forty-three years old.[38]

When the first mourners arrived, Gogol was lying on the table, dressed in his old frock coat. In his face, hollowed by illness, his nose seemed longer than ever and sharp as a knife blade; his mustache drooped over a serenely composed mouth; his domed, sepia eyelids seemed to be guarding a convalescent sleep; a crown of laurel rested on his long locks. A priest was murmuring prayers, a sculptor modeled a death mask. Later the painter Mamonov sketched the little, shrunken body in its coffin.

After seeing him, Sergey Timofeyevich Aksakov exclaimed, "To me, Gogol had scarcely been human, so although I was always very frightened of dead people in my youth, last night I did not have that feeling at all."[39]

How did Father Matthew react to Gogol's death? Did he feel pity for the martyr torn between his art and his faith? Was he sorry he had so sternly dissuaded him from his life's work? Or did he feel the soothing satisfaction of having performed his duty?

It was apparently written in heaven that Gogol would cause friction between his friends until the bitter end. At Count Tolstoy's, the Slavophiles, led by Aksakov, insisted that the funeral service should be held in the parish church where the writer used to worship; Professor Granovsky, a "European," demanded on the contrary that it take place in the university church, for, said he, the dead man belonged in the great tradition of educators. "Absolutely not," retorted the Slavophiles. "He was never a member of the university. He belonged to the people, and therefore the funeral must be held in the parish church, where any footman or coachman can come, or any person who wants to pay his last respects; and ordinary people are not allowed in the university church."[40]

The coffinside quarrel was growing heated, so it was Count Zakrevsky who settled it: the body would be removed to the university church, and, for the occasion, that church would be declared open to all. The angry Slavophiles decided to boycott the funeral. On February 22 the coffin—open, according to custom was carried into the university church by a group of men of letters, including Ostrovsky. For two days, horses and carriages struggled in and out of Nikitskaya Street, which was congested by the crowd that was waiting to file past the author's mortal remains. People of every station went to bow down before the laurel-wreathed waxen head that had so often made them laugh. Constables and plain-clothes policemen stood by to see that there was no disturbance: whoever and whatever the author, one could never be sure there was not some suspicious motive behind the admiration of the populace.

On Sunday, February 24, Count Zakrevsky in person attended the High Mass in dress uniform. The coffin was covered with camellias, and a bouquet of immortelles lay in the dead man's hands. There had not been enough time to notify Gogol's mother and sisters in their remote Ukrainian village, so they were not in Moscow for the funeral; but the church was full. When the last leave-taking came, the press of admirers nearly overturned the catafalque. Everyone wanted to kiss the dead man's hand or snip a leaf from his crown. To curtail these effusions, the organizers firmly closed the coffin lid, removing the dead man's unconcerned face from the prying eyes of the multitude. Professors Granovsky, Kudryavtsev, Ankoy, Moroshkin, and Solovyev hoisted the coffin onto their shoulders; outside, they were relieved by students. A straggling cortege moved down the snow-covered street, the men walking, the women following in their carriages. The burial took place in the cemetery of the monastery of St. Daniel. It was a cold, bright day; the snow sparkled in the sun. The grave had been dug not far from the tombs of Yasykov and Mrs. Khomyakov, his sister who had died two weeks before.[41]

The list of the deceased's belongings included a gold watch that had once been Pushkin's, a black woolen overcoat with a velvet collar, two old black woolen frock coats, three well-worn pairs of linen trousers, four old cravats (two in taffeta and two in silk), two sets of underclothes, and three handkerchiefs. No money, no jewels, no important papers. The wardrobe of a pauper. But there was the work.

How was it viewed by the authorities? Gogol had certainly never attacked them or the church in his writings. But he had made fun of officials and landowners, the great and humble servants of the system. And as everyone knows, even the most seemingly innocuous literature is an ideal culture medium, in which the germs of subversion are often found swimming. Prudence dictated that the lamentations of the intellectual elite should be muted. *The Muscovite* ran a black-framed obituary, which provoked the following sour response from paid police agent Bulgarin in his *Northern Bee:* "Every detail of this man's illness has been laid before us as though he were some person of consequence, a benefactor of mankind!"

Despite this warning, Ivan Turgenev wrote a brief eulogy and expression of sorrow, shortly after the funeral, and submitted it to the St. Petersburg censor, who refused to pass it. Undeterred, he sent off his story to the Moscow *News,* and the censor there absent-mindedly approved it.

"Gogol is dead," Turgenev wrote. "What Russian soul could not be stricken by those three words? Our loss is so cruel and so sudden that we cannot yet accept it. He is dead, the man we now have the bitter right to call a great man. The man whose name has been given to this period in our literary history, the man of whom we are as proud as of a national hero. Like the most noble of his antecedents, he was struck down in the prime of his life and the fullness of his strength, his life's work unfinished."[42]

The publication of this article infuriated the chief of police; and lumping Gogol together with Pushkin, Lermontov, and Griboedov made him all the more suspect to the authorities. An official of the III Section wrote a report on the schemings of the literary world, "which is today the active agent of all the trouble we are witnessing in the Empire." It was proposed that Turgenev be called in and reprimanded, and placed under police supervision. Nicholas I thought this was not enough. This Turgenev fellow: hadn't he dared to express sympathy for the serfs in his stories in *The Contemporary?*[43] He deserved a lesson. With a firm hand, the tsar wrote in the margin of the report: "I consider this insufficient. To punish Turgenev for his disobedience, let him be placed under arrest for a month and then exiled to his estate." There was no appeal from this sentence; Turgenev was incarcerated on the spot and subsequently dispatched to his family home at Spasskoye-Lutovinovo.

Now the imperial administration had to deal with another problem. Should it allow the publication of the "Collected Works" of this author

of whom the public seemed so excessively fond? They were already at
the printer's. No. It would be wiser to postpone such homage. The
censors were instructed to reject categorically any lines bearing the
dead man's signature. In death, the authorities' incense bearer became
a suspect to the very people he had flattered. In a report on "the
case," Dubelt, chief of staff of the constabulary, declared: "Among the
works of Gogol previously printed and in manuscript, the censors have
found a large number of passages—on almost every page—which,
taken on their own, are to be condemned not because they contain
pernicious ideas, but because they can be wrongly interpreted by readers and thereby lead to reprehensible conclusions." Gogol's friends had
to wage war with the censors for three and one half years before obtaining permission to publish.[44]

The newspapers and periodicals maintained their obedient discretion;
nevertheless, as the months went by, Gogol's name, far from sinking
into oblivion, assumed proportions beyond the expectations of even
his fondest friends. While flesh decayed in the grave, name and work
grew greater. His contemporaries vaguely sensed that the sick, devious,
tortured, vain, mendacious, outrageous little man had been more than
the extraordinary creator of *The Inspector General* and *Dead Souls:* he
had set some force in motion in his country's literature that nothing
could ever stop.

The prodigious development of the novel in nineteenth-century Russia began on two notes, one bright and one dark: Pushkin and Gogol.
The realism of Pushkin, concise, limpid, poetic; the realism of Gogol,
distorted, fantastic, satirical, funereal. The moderation of Pushkin; the
exaggeration of Gogol.

All the Russian writers who came after them combined, in varying
proportions, those two original elements. The embryos of the successors'
boldest innovations are to be found in the two great precursors. At the
very moment when they think they have found something new, they
are unconsciously dipping into those two vast reservoirs of ideas and
characters. From Gogol came the compassion for the lowly and the
meek that runs through all the works of Dostoevsky and Tolstoy. From
Pushkin came the feeling for direct, objective narration that animates
the best parts of *War and Peace.* The Tentetnikov of the second part of
Dead Souls gave birth to Levin in *Anna Karenina.* Podkolyosin of
Marriage turns up again as Goncharov's Oblomov. The heroes of

Turgenev, Saltykov-Shchedrin, Leskov, Chekhov, Gorky, Remizov, and so many others are the illustrious offspring of the characters of *The Inspector General* and "The Overcoat." Even before those authors' books appeared, the readers had been informed by some mysterious premonition that it was Gogol they had to thank for the great renaissance of Russian literature. The man who had complained all his life of being so ill-loved became doubly precious to his countrymen after death—for what he had written himself and for what others, inspired by him, wrote afterward.

In May 1852, two and one half months after Gogol's death, young Grigori Danilevsky made a pilgrimage to Vasilyevka. A few versts from the village, he told the driver to stop so that he could ask directions from a peasant woman holding a baby in her arms.

"They say Gogol is dead," she said, "but it's not true. A devout 'staretz' was buried in his place. It seems he has gone to pray for us in Jerusalem. He has left, but he'll be back."[45]

Danilevsky got into his coach. Soon a little church with a green cupola appeared between two hills, then some whitewashed isbas, and finally, the family home of the author of *Dead Souls*—a low wooden building with a red roof. To the right stood a pavilion, to the left the outbuildings, then a garden, ponds; and all around, tall, ancient trees. Behind, stretching to infinity, the Ukrainian steppe.

Suddenly three women in black appeared in front of the traveler: Gogol's mother and two of his sisters, Anna and Olga. Elizaveta, the third surviving sister (the one who had married Bykov), lived in Kiev. Grigori Danilevsky was struck by the remarkable youthfulness of Marya Ivanovna Gogol: robust, stout, not one wrinkle in the rosy, determined face under the white bonnet. Grief made her thick lips quiver under the shadow of down. After leading the visitor into the drawing room, she began to speak of her son in tones of exalted reverence.

"The tsar himself knew my son," she said, wiping away the tears that flowed from her heavy eyelids. "He regarded him as a member of his staff because of his writing. He gave him a salary!"

"Your son lived many years abroad."

"Yes, almost ten years, but even there he served his country with his pen!"

Grigori Danilevsky was shown the author's study in the pavilion, his tall pearwood desk, his bed, his icons, his books in a cupboard; he was taken to walk in the garden behind the church, and around the pond where Gogol had used to dream of his characters.

The three black skirts snagged on the rough weeds; Marya Ivanovna sighed and wept; but it made her so happy to talk about her son to this gentleman who had come from so far away, that Grigori Danilevsky did not have the heart to tear himself away.[46]

Bibliography

The bibliography is immense, so I have mentioned only the main works consulted. Unless otherwise indicated, all the titles below refer to works in Russian.

Gogol, N. V. *Complete Works,* new edition by the USSR Academy of Sciences in 14 volumes, 1940–52.

——. *Complete Works* (in French), Édition de la Pléiade, N.R.F., Gallimard, 1966.

——. *Correspondence,* ed. Shenrok, 4 vols., St. Petersburg, 1902.

Aksakov, S. T. *History of My Relations with Gogol,* Russian Archives, 1890, and Moscow, 1960.

Aksakov, Vera. *Gogol's Last Days,* Moscow, 1918.

Annenkov, P. V. *Literary Recollections,* St. Petersburg, 1909, and Moscow, 1960.

Barsukov, N. P. *Life and Works of M. P. Pogodin,* St. Petersburg, 1888–1910.

Belinsky, V. G. *On Gogol,* Moscow, 1949.

Botkin, M. P. *Ivanov, Life and Letters,* St. Petersburg, 1880.

Bukharev. *Three Letters to Nikolai Gogol,* 1861.

Ermilov, V. V. *The Genius of Gogol,* Moscow, 1959.

Europe (periodical, in French). Special issue on Gogol, Paris, July 1952.

Evdokimov, P. *Gogol and Dostoevsky, or, the Descent into Hell* (in French), Desolée de Brouwer, Paris, 1961.

Gaetsky, I. *Gogol,* Moscow, 1956.

Gerbel, N. V. *Prince Bezborodko's School,* St. Petersburg, 1881.

Gogol, N. V. *Material and Studies*, Leningrad, 1936.

――――. *Literary Heritage*, Vol. LVIII, Moscow, 1952.

――――. *Gogol Seen by His Contemporaries*, Moscow, 1952.

Gogol-Golovnya, O. V. *Gogol Family Chronicle*, Kiev, 1909.

Gourfinkle, Nina. *Gogol*, "Les grands dramaturges" series (in French), L'Arche, Paris, 1956.

Gukovsky, G. *Gogol's Realism*, Moscow-Leningrad, 1959.

Guss, M. *Gogol and Russia at the Time of Nicholas I*, Moscow, 1957.

Hippius, V. *Gogol*, Leningrad, 1924.

――――. *Gogol from Recollections and Documents*, Moscow, 1938.

Hofmann, M. and R. *The Life and Works of Gogol* (in French), Corréa, Paris, 1946.

Khrapchenko, M. B. *The Works of Gogol*, Moscow, 1959.

Kirpichnikov, A. I. *Chronological Survey*, Moscow, 1902.

Kotylarevsky, N. A. *N. V. Gogol*, 4th ed., Petrograd, 1915.

Kulish, P. A. *Notes on the Life of N. V. Gogol*, 2 vols., St. Petersburg, 1856.

Leger, L. *N. Gogol* (in French), Paris, 1914.

Mandelstam, I. *On Gogol's Style*, Helsingfors, 1902.

Mashinsky, S. *Gogol*, Moscow, 1951.

――――. *Gogol and the Question of Freethinking*, Moscow, 1959.

――――. *Gogol in Russian Criticism*, Moscow, 1952.

――――. *Gogol and Belinsky*, Moscow, 1952.

Mashovtsev, N. G. *Gogol Among the Artists*, Moscow, 1957.

Merezhkovsky, D. *Gogol and the Devil*, Moscow, 1906; (in French) Gallimard, Paris, 1939.

Mochulsky, K. *Gogol's Spiritual Progression*, Paris, 1934.

Nabokov, V. *Nikolay Gogol* (in English), London, 1947; (in French) Éditions de la Table Ronde, Paris, 1953.

Nikitenko, A. V. *Notes and Diary*, St. Petersburg, 1905.

Ovsyaniko-Kulikovsky. *Gogol*, Moscow, 1902.

Panaev, I. I. *Literary Recollections*, in *Complete Works*, Vol. VI, St. Petersburg, 1888.

Poltoratsky, A. *Gogol in St. Petersburg*, Moscow, 1962.

Pospelov, G. N. *The Works of Gogol*, Moscow, 1953.

Schick, A. *Nicholas Gogol* (in French), S.E.I., Sceaux, 1949.

――――. *Gogol in Nice*, Paris, 1946.

Schloezer, B. de. *Gogol* (in French), Plon, Paris, 1932.

Shenrok, V. I. *Material for a Biography of Gogol*, 4 vols., Moscow, 1892–97.

Smirnov, Mrs. A. O. *Autobiography*, Moscow, 1931.

――――. *Notes, Diary, Recollections, Letters*, Moscow, 1929.

Sollogub, V. A. *Recollections*, St. Petersburg, 1887.

Stepanov, N. L. *Gogol's Creative Method,* Moscow, 1959, 2nd edition.

Tarasenkov, Dr. A. T. *Gogol's Last Days,* St. Petersburg, 1857.

Veresaev, V. *Gogol Alive,* Moscow-Leningrad, 1933.

———. *How Gogol Worked,* Moscow, 1932.

Yofanov, D. *N. V. Gogol, Childhood and Youth,* Kiev, 1951.

Yordan, F. I. *Notes,* Moscow, 1918.

Zemenkov, V. S. *Gogol in Moscow,* Moscow, 1954.

Zenkovsky, V. *N. V. Gogol,* YMCA Press, Paris, 1961.

Chronology

1809   March 20: birth of Nikolai Gogol, son of Vasily Afanasyevich Gogol-Yanovsky and Marya Ivanovna, nee Kosyarovsky.

1811   Birth of his sister Marya.

1812   Birth of his brother, Ivan.

1819   Attends Poltava boarding school; death of Ivan.

1821   Enters Nyezhin high school; birth of his sister Anna.

1823   Birth of his sister Elizaveta.

1825   Death of his father, Vasily Afanasyevich Gogol; birth of his sister Olga.

1827   Inquiry concerning four teachers at the Nyezhin School suspected of "freethinking."

1828   Leaves school, spends holiday on the family estate of Vasilyevka, then moves to St. Petersburg.

1829   June: publishes his first work, *Hans Kuechelgarten,* at his own expense. July: leaves for Lübeck. September: returns to St. Petersburg. November: obtains position in department of public buildings, ministry of interior.

1830   Transfers to ministry of the court.

1831   January: publishes under the name of Gogol for the first time, in the *Literary Gazette.* February: appointed professor of history at the Patriotic Institute. May: first meeting with Pushkin. September: publication of first volume of *Evenings on a Farm near Dikanka.*

1832 March: second volume of *Evenings on a Farm.* June: trip to
      Moscow; holiday at Vasilyevka.

1834 July: appointed assistant professor of history at University of
      St. Petersburg. September: inaugural lecture.

1835 January: *Arabesques.* March: *Mirgorod,* two volumes. Septem-
      ber: relieved of duties at Patriotic Institute, after which he re-
      signs from the university; Pushkin gives him the subject for
      Dead Souls. October: begins *Dead Souls.* December: finishes
      The Inspector General, also on a theme supplied by Pushkin.

1836 April 19: first performance of *The Inspector General,* at the
      Alexandra Theater, St. Petersburg. May 25: first performance at
      the Maly Theater, Moscow. June: leaves for Europe. Travels
      through Germany and Switzerland. November: arrives in Paris.

1837 February: learns of Pushkin's death. March: leaves Paris for
      Italy; settles in Rome.

1838 Living in Rome, associating with expatriate Russian artists;
      flirtation with Roman Catholic Church; intense friendship with
      Joseph Vyelgorsky.

1839 May 21: Joseph Vyelgorsky dies in Rome. June–September:
      travels in France and Germany. September: leaves for Russia.
      End of October: after visiting Moscow, returns to St. Petersburg.
      December: to Moscow again.

1840 May: travels from Moscow to Rome with Vasily Panov.
      September: visits Vienna, goes to Venice, then returns to Rome
      via Florence.

1841 August: after completing the first volume of *Dead Souls,* sets out
      for Russia. December: in Moscow the censor's office forbids
      publication.

1842 April: the St. Petersburg censor authorizes publication of *Dead
      Souls.* May: *Dead Souls* on sale. Gogol leaves for Rome,
      stopping in Gastein. September: reaches Rome. September 9:
      first performance of *Marriage,* in St. Petersburg.

1843 February: *Marriage* performed in Moscow (with *The Gamblers*
      as curtain raiser). Publication of "Collected Works" in four
      volumes. May–December: visiting in Germany, then to Nice to
      see Mrs. Smirnov. November: destroys first version of sequel to
      Dead Souls.

1844 March: visits Zhukovsky in Frankfurt. Death of eldest sister,
      Marya.

1845   January: to Paris. February: returns to Frankfurt. July: burns new version of second volume of *Dead Souls*. Publication of *Nouvelles Russes* in France, in a translation by Louis Viardot. October: to Rome.

1846   July: sends first six chapters of *Selected Passages from My Correspondence with My Friends* to St. Petersburg. October: in Frankfurt again. November: returns to Italy.

1847   Publications of *Selected Passages;* beginning of his association with Father Matthew Konstantinovsky, for ten years the confessor and spiritual adviser of Count A. P. Tolstoy. Gogol drafts *Confession of an Author* and *Meditations upon Divine Liturgy*.

1848   January: sets out for Jerusalem. April–May: after a brief visit to the Holy Land, returns to Russia and moves into the family home at Vasilyevka. September: to St. Petersburg. October: Moscow.

1849   July: travels across Russia, then returns to Moscow, where he lives with Count Tolstoy and works on the second volume of *Dead Souls*.

1850   June: leaves for Vasilyevka. October: sets out for Odessa, where he remains for some time.

1851   Winter: in Odessa. March: back to Vasilyevka. May: in Moscow. October 3: his sister Elizaveta marries. October 10: censor authorizes second edition of "Collected Works."

1852   February 4: final, highly emotional interview with Father Matthew. February 11: burns third version of the second volume of *Dead Souls*. February 21: death. February 24: funeral, in Moscow.

Biographical Notes

Brief identifications of some of the people mentioned in the book:

AIVAZOVSKY Ivan Konstantinovich (1817–1900); famous painter of seascapes.

AKSAKOV Sergey Timofeyevich (1791–1859); in his youth, poet and theater critic; translated Boileau and Molière. Later, half blind, wrote *On Fishing* (1847), *Recollections of a Hunter* (1855), *Chronicles of a Russian Family* (1856), and *Years of Childhood* (1858), which provide an excellent picture of Russian character and a description of the life of the landowning class. These books have become classics, and his recollections of Gogol are our most important source of information on that author. He was an ardent nationalist, strongly attached to patriarchal tradition.

AKSAKOV Konstantin Sergeyevich (1817–60); elder son of the above. Poet, historian, philologist, and critic, and a founder of the Slavophile movement.

AKSAKOV Ivan Sergeyevich (1823–66); brother of the above. Poet and publicist, champion of the Panslavists; founder of the review *Russia*.

AKSAKOV Olga Semyonovna (1793–1878); wife of S. T. Aksakov.

AKSAKOV Vera Sergeyevna (1819–64); daughter of S. T. Aksakov.

AKSAKOV Nadezhda Sergeyevna (1829–69); daughter of S. T. Aksakov.

ANNENKOV Pavel Vasilyevich (1812–87); literary critic, author of biographical work on Pushkin and, most important, of *Recollections* of Belinsky and Gogol, whose secretary he was in Rome. Prepared first critical edition of Pushkin's works. An ardent "European," member of Belinsky's circle.

APRAXIN   Sofya Petrovna (1802–86); nee Tolstoy, sister of Gogol's friend
Count A. P. Tolstoy.

ARMFELD   Alexander Osipovich (1806–68); professor of history of medicine
at the University of Moscow.

ARNOLDI   Leo Ivanovich (1822–60); half brother (on his mother's side) of
Mrs. Smirnov; worked with her husband in Kaluga for a time.

BALABIN   Varvara Osipovna. Of French origin; married ex-general Pyotr
Ivanovich Balabin. Friend of Gogol.

BALABIN   Marya Petrovna, daughter of the above. Pupil of Gogol, with
whom she corresponded regularly.

BALABIN   Elizaveta Petrovna, elder sister of the above and wife of Prince
Repnin, with whom Gogol lived in Odessa.

BAZILI   Konstantin Mikhailovich (1809–84); classmate of Gogol at the
Nyezhin School. Official in the foreign ministry from 1844 to 1853;
Consul General of Russia in Syria and Palestine. Author of works on
Turkey and Greece.

BELINSKY   Vissarion Grigoryevich (1811–48); famous literary critic, who
became known through his articles in the *Annals of the Fatherland,* and
later in *The Contemporary.* He championed the doctrine of literary
realism. His somewhat unsystematic philosophy inclined toward materialism, his politics toward utopian socialism. He belonged to the
"European" movement, and his ideas influenced Russian thought
throughout the nineteenth century.

BENKENDORF   Alexander Christoforovich (1783–1844); from 1826, chief of
national police and director of the III Section; established a ruthless
police state in Russia; ennobled in 1832.

BERG   Nikolai Vasilyevich (1823–84); poet and translator; an editor of *The
Muscovite.* Firm Slavophile.

BODYANSKY   Osip Maximovich (1808–77); professor of history and Slavic
literature at the University of Moscow.

BOTKIN   Nikolai Petrovich (1813–69); member of a rich Moscow merchant
family; generous patron of impoverished artists throughout his life.

BULGARIN   Thaddeus Venedictovich (1789–1859); publicist and critic, edi-
tor-in-chief of the periodical *Northern Bee.* Employed by police to act as
informer in the literary world.

BYKOV   Vladimir Ivanovich (? –1862); officer in the army field engineers,
husband of Gogol's sister Elizaveta.

CHERTKOV   Elizaveta Grigoryevna, nee Chernychev (1805–58); wife of
archaeologist and numismatist A. V. Chertkov, founder of the Chertkov
Library. A cultivated and original woman, she received Gogol in her
Moscow *salon.*

DANILEVSKY   Alexander Semyonovich (1809–88); childhood friend of Gogol.

After leaving the Nyezhin School, entered the guards officers' school in St. Petersburg. Spent some time in the Caucasus before returning to the capital and a position in the foreign ministry; resigned to accompany Gogol abroad. At his mother's death sometime later, he returned to Russia, married, and held a position in the provincial administration, then retired to his estate. In their correspondence, he doggedly resisted Gogol's religious exhortations, despite his affection for the author.

DANILEVSKY   Grigori Petrovich (1829–90); author of extremely popular historical novels; in the '50s, worked in the ministry of education.

DELVIG   Anton Antonovich (1798–1831); intimate friend of Pushkin; wrote romantic poetry. Director of a literary periodical, *Northern Flowers;* then, from 1830 until his death, director of the *Literary Gazette.*

DMITRYEV   Ivan Ivanovich (1760–1837); poet, author of elegies in the sentimental manner of his day and of several collections of tales. Minister of justice from 1810 to 1814. Gogol made his acquaintance in Moscow in 1832.

DOSTOEVSKY   Fyodor Mikhailovich (1821–81); deeply marked at an early age by his father's death at the hands of his own muzhiks, he became a mediocre student at the St. Petersburg School of Engineering but received immense and immediate acclaim for his novel *Poor Folk,* in 1845; around the same time, joined a group of liberal youths led by Petrashevsky who detested the tsarist regime and wanted to abolish serfdom. Denounced by a double agent and arrested with his companions in 1849, he was imprisoned, sentenced to the firing squad, led out to be executed, and, just before being bound to the stake, was told that his sentence had been commuted to four years' hard labor in Siberia. His first epileptic fits occurred there. He was not allowed to return to Russia until 1859. Undermined by disease but impelled by an indomitable will, he published, in rapid succession, *The Insulted and the Injured, The House of the Dead, Letters from the Underworld, Crime and Punishment, The Gambler.* Deeply in debt, he fled abroad with his second wife to escape his creditors, and there, defying want, exhaustion, and anxiety, wrote his most remarkable masterpieces: *The Idiot, The Eternal Husband, The Possessed.* At the age of fifty he returned to Russia, and wrote and published his *Diary of a Writer,* in which he adopted a nationalistic and resolutely orthodox position toward the major issues of the day. This labor of Hercules did not prevent him from producing two more great works: *A Raw Youth* and *The Brothers Karamazov.* His celebrity was crowned by a speech he made at the unveiling of a Pushkin monument; he died shortly thereafter.

ELAGIN   Avdotya Petrovna, nee Yushkov, (1789–1877); a clever and cultivated woman whose *salon* in Moscow became a center of intellectual exchange. Her sympathies lay with the Slavophiles. She was the mother of the Kireyevsky brothers and a niece of Zhukovsky.

GOGOL Vasily Afanasyevich (1777–1825); father of Nikolai Gogol.

GOGOL Marya Ivanovna, nee Kosyarovsky (1791–1868); mother of Nikolai Gogol.

GOGOL Marya Vasilyevna (1811–44); eldest sister of Nikolai. Married, in 1832, to a surveyor named Trushkovsky. Widowed in 1836. Mother of Nikolai Trushkovsky, future editor of the complete works of Gogol.

GOGOL Anna Vasilyevna (1821–93); sister of Nikolai; remained single.

GOGOL Elizaveta Vasilyevna (1823–64); sister of Nikolai; married Bykov, engineer-corps officer, in 1851; widowed 1862. Her eldest son, Nikolai, married Pushkin's granddaughter.

GOGOL Olga Vasilyevna (1825–1907); youngest sister of Nikolai; married retired Major Golovnya.

GOGOL Ivan Vasilyevich (1812–19); brother of Nikolai; died aged seven.

GONCHAROV Ivan Alexandrovich (1812–91); great Russian novelist; his first work, published in 1847, was a short psychological novel, *A Common Story;* traveled to Japan, then produced his masterpiece, *Oblomov,* in 1859. Ten years later, published *The Precipice.* Gogol met him in 1848, in St. Petersburg. In his country, Goncharov is considered a master of the realistic novel.

GRECH Nikolai Ivanovich (1787–1867); journalist of the Bulgarin group, editor of *Son of the Fatherland* and contributor to the *Northern Bee.* Sworn enemy of Gogol.

HERZEN Alexander Ivanovich (1812–70); a man of acute intelligence, wide culture, and great literary ability; remarkable philosopher and critic. Fiercely opposed to the tsarist regime, he believed in an "agrarian socialism" of specifically Russian character. After being imprisoned and exiled in Russia, he succeeded in leaving the country in 1847 and settled first in Paris, then in London and Geneva. Founded a free Russian press abroad and edited two periodicals, *The Polar Star* and *The Bell,* in which he relentlessly attacked autocracy. Published numerous works, including a book of recollections: *My Past and Thoughts,* an important and unclassifiable work.

INNOCENT Ivan Alexeyevich Borisov (1800–57); bishop of Kharkov, then (from 1848) archbishop of Kherson and Tauris.

INOZEMTSEV Fyodor Ivanovich (1802–83); professor of surgery at the University of Moscow. One of the foremost physicians of his day.

IVANOV Alexander Andreyevich (1806–58); painter, friend of Gogol. Sent to Rome in 1830 by the St. Petersburg Academy of Fine Arts for three years, but remained in Italy twenty-seven years. It was in 1833 that he first conceived the idea for his great painting *Christ Appearing to the*

People. After numerous preliminary sketches, he began work on the actual canvas in 1837 and devoted the rest of his life to it. Gogol and he met in Rome and quickly became close friends. Gogol thought *Christ Appearing to the People* and *Dead Souls* had a common ideal and demanded total self-sacrifice on the part of their creators in its pursuit. Only in 1858, after the painting was at last finished, did Ivanov return to St. Petersburg. The exhibited work was very successful, but the painter died of cholera the same year. The canvas is now in the Tretyakov Gallery, in Moscow; Gogol figures in the crowd.

KARAMZIN Andrey Nikolayevich (1814–54); son of the historian. Artillery officer, killed in a battle with the Turks.

KARATYGIN Pyotr Andreyevich (1805–79); actor at the Alexandra Theater, in St. Petersburg. Persistently hostile to Gogol; there is a watercolor by him showing Gogol at a rehearsal of *The Inspector General*.

KHOMYAKOV Alexis Stepanovich (1804–60); poet, playwright, theologian, and philosopher. An outstanding public speaker and one of the most brilliant personalities of the Slavophile circle.

KHOMYAKOV Katerina Mikhailovna (1817–52); wife of the above and sister of the poet Yasykov. Mrs. Khomyakov's death, on January 26, 1852, powerfully affected Gogol, who saw it as a personal summons from the afterworld.

KIREYEVSKY Ivan Vasilyevich (1806–56); critic and publicist. Met Gogol in Moscow in 1832. A Founder, with Khomyakov and the Aksakov brothers, of the Slavophile movement.

KIREYEVSKY Pyotr Vasilyevich (1808–56); brother of the above. Also helped to start the Slavophile movement. Throughout his life he collected folksongs and Russian *byliny*.

KONSTANTINOVSKY Matvey Alexandrovich (1791–1857); Father Matthew, archpriest of Rzhev, was a churchman of impassioned eloquence and rigid narrow-mindedness. Was introduced to Gogol by Count A. P. Tolstoy, whose spiritual adviser he was; toward the end, he exhorted the author to practice asceticism and abjure the temptations of art.

LERMONTOV Mikhail Yuryevich (1814–41); one of the greatest names in Russian poetry. A career officer, he was exiled to the Caucasus for writing a poem (*Death of a Poet*) in 1837 calling for the punishment of Pushkin's assassin. Recalled in 1838 and again exiled in 1840 on account of a duel he fought with the French ambassador's son, Ernest de Brabante. The following year, he was killed in another duel, with a former classmate named Martynov, over an absurd question of honor. His most famous works are the poems *The Demon* and *The Novice* and a short novel, *A Hero of Our Time,* written in a disenchanted tone and an elegant, smooth-flowing style.

LYUBICH-ROMANOVICH—Vasily Ignatyevich (1805–88); schoolmate of Gogol; a poet, translator (of Byron and Mickiewicz), and historian.

MAXIMOVICH Mikhail Alexandrovich (1804–73); botanist, ethnographer, and historian. Professor of botany at the University of Moscow, then of Russian literature at the University of Kiev. In 1845 abandoned the academic world and retired to his estate on the banks of the Dnieper, to follow his own pursuits. Author of numerous studies of the language, songs, customs, and history of the Ukraine. Showed great affection for Gogol until the author's death.

MICKIEWICZ Adam (1798–1855); great Polish poet and patriot, the author, *inter alia*, of *Forefathers' Eve, Konrad Wallenrod, Pan Tadeusz*. In 1823 arrested for his part in a Polish student uprising and sent to Russia. Living in Moscow and St. Petersburg, he became friendly with many Russian writers, including Pushkin. He went abroad in 1829, and in 1839 took a chair of Latin literature at the University of Lausanne; in 1840 began teaching Slavic languages and literature to the Collège de France, in Paris. His teaching was influenced by the dangerous mysticism of the "prophet" and "magnetizer" Towiansky, and in 1845, when his classes were discontinued, he found himself librarian of the Arsenal. In 1848 he set up a Polish legion in Italy. Gogol admired and loved Mickiewicz, although he did not share the Polish poet's nationalistic and revolutionary ideas.

MOLLER Fyodor Antonovich (1812–75); historical painter and famous portraitist. Settled in Rome in 1830. A friend of Gogol, whose portrait he painted.

NASHCHOKIN Pavel Voyinovich (1800–54); an intimate friend of Pushkin and an intelligent and educated man although incapable of managing his own affairs. He dilapidated his vast fortune and died in penury. Gogol is said to have based the character of Khlobuev, in the second part of *Dead Souls,* on Nashchokin.

NADEZHDIN Nikolai Ivanovich (1804–56); journalist and critic, editor of *The Telescope* and *Renown* (periodicals) and professor at the University of Moscow.

NEKRASOV Nikolai Alexeyevich (1821–77); great poet and famous publicist. In 1847 he purchased *The Contemporary,* founded by Pushkin and Pletnyev in 1836. With the help of Ivan Panaev, he quickly turned it into the most prominent Russian literary review; the tone was progressive and liberal. The authorities stopped publication in 1866. His manner was assertive, and in his most famous works (*Who Can Be Happy and Free in Russia, The Red-Nosed Frost, Russian Women*) he portrayed the misery and aspirations of the common people and helped to prepare public opinion for the abolition of serfdom.

Biographical Notes 451

NIKITENKO Alexander Vasilyevich (1805–77); writer and censor. Professor of Russian literature at the University of St. Petersburg.

ODOEVSKY Prince Vladimir Fyodorovich (1803–69); great friend of Pushkin. Writer and journalist, author of fantasies in the style of the tales of Hoffmann. The center of a literary circle in St. Petersburg.

ORLOV Alexis Fyodorovich (1787–1862); after Benkendorf's death, in 1844, Orlov took over as chief of police and director of the III Section. Given the title of prince in 1851; became chairman of the Council of Empire and the Cabinet.

OSTROVSKY Alexander Nikolayevich (1823–86); a playwright who wrote over fifty plays, most of which, conceived as "slices of life," satirize the customs of the merchant middle class.

OVER Alexander Ivanovich (1804–64); Moscow physician.

PASHCHENKO Ivan Grigoryevich (? –1848); classmate of Gogol at the Nyezhin School. Official in the ministry of justice.

PANAEV Ivan Ivanovich (1812–62); socialite journalist and novelist of Belinsky's circle. In 1847 he became coeditor, with Nekrasov, of *The Contemporary*.

PANAEV Avdotya Yakovlevna, nee Bryansky (1820–93); a famous beauty, wife of the above. Afterward lived with Nekrasov as his common-law wife and wrote novels with him. She also produced interesting *Literary Recollections*.

PANOV Vasily Alexeyevich (1819–49); Gogol's traveling companion in 1840. Belonged to the Moscow Slavophile group; later became editor in chief of the *Muscovite Review*.

PHILARETOS (Mikhail Vasilyevich Drozdov) (1782–1862); metropolitan of Moscow: a deeply devout, authoritarian churchman, who believed in the imperial regime, serfdom, and corporal punishment.

PLETNYEV Pyotr Alexandrovich (1792–1865); a critic and poet, friend of Pushkin and Gogol. While inspector at the Patriotic Institute, secured a post as teacher there for Gogol. Professor of Russian literature at the University of St. Petersburg, then rector of that university. Taught Russian literature to the heir apparent and various members of the imperial family. Directed *The Contemporary* after Pushkin's death.

POGODIN Mikhail Petrovich (1800–75); historian, archaeologist, journalist. Professor of history at the University of Moscow. Editor of the *Moscow Messenger* and *Muscovite* (periodicals). Staunch defender of autocracy, Russian nationalism, and patriarchal tradition. Compiled a large collection of manuscripts relating to the history of Russia. Gogol was a friend of his and stayed in his home at Virgins' Field on several occasions, but Pogodin tried to exact unpublished copy in return for his hospitality and their friendship was traversed by frequent storms.

POLEVOY Nikolai Alexeyevich (1796–1846); journalist and, until 1834, editor of the *Moscow* Telegraph. At first he was favorably disposed toward Gogol, but soon went over to the enemy camp: Bulgarin, Grech, and Senkovsky.

PROKOPOVICH Nikolai Yakovlevich (1810–57); fellow student of Gogol. Poet and professor of Russian literature at the St. Petersburg cadet corps training school. Gogol asked him to publish his "collected works," but Prokopovich performed the task very unsatisfactorily.

PUSHKIN Alexander Sergeyevich (1799–1837); poet and prose author of genius, he endowed every area of Russian literature with models that have seldom been equaled for perfection of form, harmony, measure, and taste. His early, liberal poems brought about his exile, by order of Alexander I, to Yekaterinoslav, Kishinev in the Caucasus, and Odessa. After further escapades, he was placed under supervised residence (1824–26) on his farm at Mikhailovskoye, where he wrote most of his verse novel *Eugene Onegin*. In 1825 he produced the historical drama *Boris Godunov*. The new tsar, Nicholas I, finally allowed him to return to St. Petersburg, where he enjoyed great fame and prestige and, without quite abandoning his liberal ideas, refrained from open criticism of the authorities. After marrying Natalya Nikolayevna Goncharov, a young Moscow beauty, in 1831, he divided his time between literature and the social obligations that so exasperated him. With the exception of *The Bronze Horseman*, his works after this date were in prose: *The Tales of Byelkin, The Queen of Spades, The Captain's Daughter*. A young French officer serving in the Russian army, Georges d'Anthès de Heckeren, began flirting ostentatiously with Natalya Pushkin. Ugly rumors circulated, Pushkin received insulting anonymous letters; he challenged d'Anthès to a duel and was mortally wounded. Gogol, who literally worshiped him, was grief-stricken at the news of his tragic end.

PUSHKIN Leo Sergeyevich (1805–52); brother of the above. A reckless, womanizing army officer. Spent the last years of his life as a customs official in Odessa.

REPNIN Princess Varvara Nikolayevna (1809–91); met Gogol in Baden-Baden in 1836 and remained on friendly terms with him until his death.

ROSSET Alexandra Osipovna. See under Smirnov.

ROSSET Arkady Osipovich (1811–81); brother of the above. Friend of Gogol; gave considerable assistance with the publication of *The Inspector General* and *Selected Passages*. Later became an important government official and finally a senator of the empire.

SAMARIN Yury Fyodorovich (1819–76); essayist and critic. A convinced Slavophile who became acquainted with Gogol in the '40s and was much esteemed by him.

SENKOVSKY Osip Ivanovich (1800–58); columnist and literary critic, professor of Oriental languages at the University of St. Petersburg, editor in chief of the *Reading Library*, member of the "triumvirate" (Bulgarin, Grech, Senkovsky), which reigned over the Russian press. Consistently hostile to Gogol.

SHCHEPKIN Mikhail Semyonovich (1788–1863); born a serf. Brilliant actor in Moscow theater and founder of the national theater; he met Gogol in 1832, became a close friend, and acted in his plays.

SHEREMEYTYEV Nadezhda Nikolayevna, nee Tyuchev (1775–1850); devout lady friend of Gogol, who regarded her as his "spiritual mother." He often wrote to her. Mrs. Sheremetyev's death was a painful blow to him at a time when he was much preoccupied by thoughts of his own death. She was the aunt of the poet Tyuchev.

SHEVYREV Stepan Petrovich (1806–64); Slavophile, conservative critic, and professor at the University of Moscow. Met Gogol in Rome in 1838. A friend of Pogodin and regular contributor to *The Muscovite*, he was a supporter of patriarchal tradition and Russian "populism" who decried European "putrescence" and loathed Belinsky. He admired Gogol and was always ready to help him. He did him innumerable favors, chiefly in connection with the publication of his works.

SMIRDIN Alexander Philipovich (·1799–1857); St. Petersburg publisher and bookseller.

SMIRNOV Alexandra Osipovna, nee Rosset (1809–82); maid of honor to the empress; a graceful, cultivated, witty, sparkling girl who charmed all the best minds of the day. Pushkin and Lermontov wrote poems in her honor. In 1832 she made a marriage of convenience with a wealthy young diplomat, N. M. Smirnov. Gogol, who had met her in St. Petersburg, developed a deep platonic affection for her in Paris, and then, during the winter of 1842–43, in Nice. At that time she had lost the freshness of her youth and was traversing a moral crisis. Gogol became her self-appointed confessor, and she listened to his sermons and heeded his advice. In 1845 her husband was named governor of Kaluga, where she lived until 1851, when he was forced to resign. She then returned to St. Petersburg. Mrs. Smirnov died in Paris, a victim of chronic melancholy and no longer entirely in her right mind.

SMIRNOV Nikolai Mikhailovich (1807–70); husband of the above. Heir to a great fortune, which he eventually lost through extravagant overspending and a passion for cards and roulette. Member of several diplomatic missions abroad, governor of Kaluga from 1845 to 1851, then civil governor of St. Petersburg from 1855 until 1861.

SOLLOGUB Vladimir Alexandrovich (1814–82); socialite writer, author, *inter alia,* of *Tarantass* (1845), a travelogue and study of provincial customs. Married to Sofya Vyelgorsky.

SOLLOGUB Countess Sofya Mikhailovna; wife of the above. (See Vyelgorsky)

SOSNITSKY Ivan Ivanovich (1794–1871); comic actor in St. Petersburg, created the part of the mayor in *The Inspector General.*

STURDZA Alexander Skarlatovich (1791–1854); author, of religious and reactionary inspiration. At the request of Alexander I, he prepared a report on German universities for the Aachen Congress of 1818 in which he demonstrated that the instruction there dispensed was atheistic and revolutionary and therefore dangerous for the future of Europe. After serving for some time in the foreign ministry, he retired to Odessa, where Gogol was a frequent caller during his visits to that town.

TARASENKOV Alexis Terentyevich (1816–73); a prominent physician of Gogol's day; author of medical treatises and an essay, *Gogol's Last Days.*

TOLSTOY Count Alexander Petrovich (1801–74); close friend of Gogol in the last years of his life. Governor of Tver in 1834, military governor of Odessa in 1837. Between 1840 and 1855, he held no official position and spent most of his time in Moscow. He had a religious and reactionary mind. Gogol's last residence was his house on Nikitsky Boulevard (now 7, Suvorov Boulevard).

TOLSTOY Count Fyodor Ivanovich, nicknamed "the American" (1782–1846); notorious gambler, duelist, and womanizer who was for many years a chief source of copy for Moscow and Petersburg gossips.

TURGENEV Ivan Sergeyevich (1818–83); famous novelist. Studied in Moscow and St. Petersburg, later in Berlin; immediately upon publication (in *The Contemporary*) of his first short stories, was hailed as a realistic portrayer of nature and a defender of the serfs. These stories were published in a collection entitled *A Sportsman's Sketches.* He met Gogol on several occasions and wrote a stirring obituary of the author, for which he was imprisoned and later exiled to his estate. Pardoned in 1854, he spent most of his time thereafter abroad, mainly in France, where he lived with the family of Pauline Viardot-Garcia, Malibran's sister and a famous soprano herself. His talent, brilliance, and erudition earned him the friendship of George Sand, Mérimée, and Flaubert. He became something of an ambassador of Russian literature to France, and of French literature to Russia; he was responsible for French translations of Gogol and Tolstoy, and although he lived outside Russia, he never ceased to write about it in his novels, which have great psychological subtlety and a highly polished style: *Rudin, A Nest of Gentlefolk, Fathers and Sons, Smoke, Virgin Soil,* etc.

TROSHCHINSKY Dmitri Prokofyevich (1754–1829); distant relative of Gogol.

After completing his studies at the Kiev Theological Seminary, he entered government service and was senator under Paul I, member of the Council of Empire and postmaster general under Alexander I, then minister of appanages and marshal of nobility of Poltava, and lastly, from 1814 to 1817, minister of justice. In 1817 he retired to his estate at Kibinsk, where he lived as an opulent despot. He often entertained the Gogols, who were very much in his debt.

TROSHCHINSKY Andrey Andreyevich (1792–1878); nephew and heir of the above. A retired general, he gave material assistance to Gogol at the beginning of his career, in St. Petersburg.

VYAZEMSKY Prince Pyotr Andreyevich (1792–1878); poet and critic; a subtle and cultivated man, friend of Pushkin (their correspondence is fascinating and important), and admirer of Gogol. In his youth he was an avowed liberal, but with age he grew closer to the reactionaries and became a fierce enemy of Belinsky and the "Europeans."

VYELGORSKY Count Mikhail Yuryevich (1788–1856); wealthy and highly respected courtier, gifted amateur musician, and friend of a large number of artists and writers, including Pushkin, Zhukovsky, and Gogol.

VYELGORSKY Louise Karlovna (1791–1853); his wife. Authoritarian, proud, and discriminating in her choice of associates, she accepted Gogol as her spiritual adviser.

VYELGORSKY Joseph Mikhailovich (1817–39); son of the above. A talented youth, fellow student of the heir apparent (Grand Duke Alexander, the future Alexander II). Died of consumption in Rome, in Gogol's arms.

VYELGORSKY Apolina Mikhailovna; sister of the above. Married the brother of the poet Venevitinov.

VYELGORSKY Sofya Mikhailovna (1820–78); sister of the above. In 1840 married the author Sollogub (author of *Tarantass*). Her husband's roving disposition rendered her marriage unhappy. She was mild and modest, and listened trustingly to Gogol's lessons in morality.

VYELGORSKY Anna Mikhailovna, nicknamed Anoline or Nosi (1823–61); younger sister of the above. Gogol treated her as a penitent but was said to be in love with her and once even ventured to ask for her hand. She later married Prince A. I. Shakovskoy.

VOLKONSKY Princess Zenaida Alexandrovna, nee Princess Beloselsky-Belozersky (1792–1862); poet, musician, and singer. Her beauty and intelligence established her as queen of the circle responsible for the political reconstruction of Europe after Napoleon's downfall. Alexander I admired her, and she was a friend of Pushkin, Mickiewicz, Vyazemsky, Venevitinov, Chaadaev, Shevyrev, Pogodin, etc. In 1829 she became a convert to the Roman Catholic Church. Nicholas I was so displeased by this that she found herself compelled to leave Moscow and settled in

Rome, where for many years she presided over a brilliant and much-frequented *salon*. She was totally committed to her new faith, sought to convert all her friends, devoted herself to pious works, and died in penury.

VYSOTSKY   Gerasim Ivanovich; two classes ahead of Gogol at the Nyezhin School. Became a civil servant in St. Petersburg, then retired to live on his land (government of Poltava) and died there around 1870.

YASYKOV   Nikolai Mikhailovich (1803–46); gifted poet and follower of Pushkin. In 1837, suffering from consumption, left Russia for medical treatment abroad. Met Gogol in Hanau and accompanied him to Rome in 1842. Returned to Moscow in 1843, in critical condition. He never went out and saw only his most intimate friends, until his death. His later poems were mystical, patriotic, and reactionary, and he encouraged Gogol's penchant for religion and the established order. Gogol admired him as both man and poet.

YORDAN   Fyodor Ivanovich (1800–83); Russian engraver. After studying at the St. Petersburg Academy of Fine Arts he settled in Rome and spent more than twelve years there, working on an engraving of Raphael's *Transfiguration*. A friend of Gogol.

ZHUKOVSKY   Vasily Andreyevich (1783–1852); gifted poet and translator, entrusted by Nicholas I with the education of the heir apparent, Grand Duke Alexander, the future Alexander II. He moved into the Winter Palace in 1827 and taught the tsarevich until 1837. From him Alexander acquired a sense of justice, a desire to improve the lot of the poor, and a respect for public opinion. His credit with the court enabled him to intervene in many instances on behalf of other authors, such as Pushkin and Gogol. In 1842, at the age of fifty-eight, he married an eighteen-year-old girl, daughter of the painter Von Reutern, and went to live in Germany—first in Düsseldorf, then Frankfurt. He was always well disposed toward Gogol and was generous with admiration, advice, and hospitality. Toward the end of his life he turned to mysticism and died soon after Gogol, in Germany, but his remains were ceremoniously transported to St. Petersburg. His translations of Goethe, Schiller, and Byron revealed European literature to his compatriots. He is regarded as "the father of Russian romanticism."

Notes

PART I, CHAPTER 1

1. The estate was originally called Yanovshchina; its name was changed after the birth of Afanasy Damyanovich's son.
2. Marya Ivanovna Gogol-Yanovsky, *Recollections;* Shenrok, *Material*, Vol. I.
3. Marya Ivanovna Gogol-Yanovsky, *Autobiographical Notes.*
4. Gogol himself always celebrated his birthday on March 19.
5. Letter, October 2, 1833.
6. Ibid.
7. Ibid.
8. Told to Mrs. Smirnov by Nikolai Gogol.
9. As in a comedy by Vasily Afanasyevich Gogol-Yanovsky entitled *The Innocent,* or *The Vixen Outfoxed by a Soldier.*
10. For details of life at Kibinsk, see Shenrok, *Material* (Vol. I), Pashchenko, and Marya Ivanovna Gogol-Yanovsky in her communication to Aksakov (The *Contemporary,* 1913).
11. Marya Ivanovna Gogol-Yanovsky, letter to Aksakov, April 3, 1856. (*The Contemporary,* 1913).
12. Letter from Gogol to his parents, 1820.

PART I, CHAPTER 2

1. Letter of September 6, 1821.
2. Letter from Gogol to his mother, February 26, 1827.
3. Letter from Gogol to Vysotsky, June 26, 1827.
4. Letter, May 26, 1825.
5. Letter, June 3, 1825.
6. Kukolnik subsequently became an author of patriotic tragedies.
7. Grebenka later wrote poetry in Little Russian.
8. Bazili became a diplomat and wrote books on Turkey and Greece.

9. Prokopovich subsequently became a teacher and poet.

10. Lyubich-Romanovich became a poet and historian, and translator of Mickiewicz and Byron.

11. Letter, April 6, 1827.

12. *Historical Messenger,* 1892, no. 12.

13. Told by Lyubich-Romanovich, *Historical Messenger,* 1892.

14. Letter from Nikolai Gogol to his mother, January 22, 1824.

15. Voice teacher at the Nyezhin School.

16. Letter, March 19, 1827.

17. Kulzhinsky, "Recollections of a Teacher," *The Muscovite,* 1854.

18. Kulzhinsky, *Autobiography.*

19. Letter, August 20, 1826.

20. Letter, October 15, 1826.

21. Ibid.

22. Letter, October 2, 1827.

23. Kulzhinsky, *Recollections of a Teacher.*

24. Shenrok, *Gogol's Letters,* p. 109.

25. Sofya Vasilyevna Skalon, "Recollections," *Historical Messenger,* 1891.

PART I, CHAPTER 3

1. Letter to his mother, April 30, 1829.

2. Letter to his mother, January 3, 1829.

3. Letter, April 30, 1829.

4. Letter, May 22, 1829.

5. Letter to his mother, April 30, 1829.

6. Ibid.

7. Letter to his mother, May 22, 1829.

8. Letter to his mother, April 30, 1829.

9. Letter, September 24, 1829.

PART I, CHAPTER 4

1. Details of the scene as related by N. P. Mundt, Gagarin's secretary, in St. Petersburg *News,* 1861, no. 235.

2. Letter, April 2, 1830.

3. Letter, June 3, 1830.

4. In particular, of a French article on Russian trade in the late-sixteenth and early-seventeenth centuries.

5. Considerably revised, this story reappeared in Gogol's *Evenings on a Farm near Dikanka.*

6. Letter, January 10, 1848.

7. Gogol's essay on *Woman* was published in the January 16 issue of the *Literary Gazette,* two days after Delvig's death.

8. Letter, April 16, 1831.

9. Letter from Pletnyev to Pushkin, February 22, 1831.

10. Longinov, *Recollections of Gogol.*

11. In French in the original.

12. Letter from Gogol, July 24, 1831.
13. *Recollections* of A. A. Vasilchikov.
14. In French in the original.
15. In French in the original.
16. Letter, August 21, 1831.
17. Letter, September 19, 1831.
18. Ibid.
19. Letter, October 17, 1831.
20. Letter, October 30, 1831.
21. Letter, March 10, 1832.
22. Belinsky, *Literary Reveries*, 1834.

PART I, CHAPTER 5

1. "A May Night, or, The Drowned Maiden."
2. Ibid.
3. "The Fair at Sorochinsk."
4. "A Terrible Vengeance."
5. "St. John's Eve."
6. "The Fair at Sorochinsk."
7. Lobanov, "Smirdin's Dinner" (*Pushkin and His Contemporaries*), and Terpigorev, "A Note on Pushkin" (*Russian Antiquity*, 1870).
8. Contrary to Gogol's affirmation in his letter to his mother of February 6, 1832, some people still knew him as Gogol-Yanovsky.
9. Nikitenko, *Notes and Diary*, April 22, 1832.
10. Where he had gone for treatment (leaving St. Petersburg on April 19, 1831).
11. A gifted Russian poet (1803–46) much admired by Pushkin.
12. Letter, March 30, 1832.
13. Letter, December 20, 1832; here Gogol himself denies the tale of his mad passion for a fair stranger, the story he told his mother in his letter of July 24, 1829.
14. Letter, March 25, 1832.
15. Letter, March 10, 1832.
16. Letter, January 4, 1832.

PART I, CHAPTER 6

1. Aksakov's most important work, showing an acute sensitivity to nature, was published much later (*Recollections of a Hunter, Chronicles of a Russian Family, Years of Childhood*).
2. *History of My Relations with Gogol.*
3. Ibid.
4. Undated letter, July 1832.
5. Letter, September 2, 1832.
6. Letter, July 20, 1832.
7. *Notes* of Elizaveta Vasilyevna Gogol.
8. Told by Anna Vasilyevna Gogol (*Russia*, 1885, no. 26).
9. Letter, September 23, 1832.
10. Undated letter, summer 1832.

11. Letter, October 9, 1832.

12. Letter, October 10, 1832.

13. Letter to his mother, October 21, 1832.

14. Letter, November 22, 1832.

15. Annenkov, *Literary Recollections.*

16. Fashionable French woman novelist-playwright of the period (1776–1852).

17. Successful French writer, chiefly a drama critic, now seldom read (1804–74).

18. Annenkov, *Literary Recollections.*

19. First sentence of "Nevsky Prospect."

20. Letter, February 1, 1833.

21. Letter to Pogodin, November 25, 1832.

22. Letter to his mother, February 8, 1833.

23. Letter to Maximovich, July 2, 1833.

24. Letter to his mother, August 9, 1833.

25. He subsequently reworked and published these scenes, changing the characters' names in every fragment. They are: "An Official's Morning," "The Lawsuit," and "The Servants' Hall."

26. In English, "The Tale of How Ivan Ivanovich Quarreled with Ivan Nikiforovich."

27. Letter, previously cited, February 20, 1833.

28. Letter, March 6, 1834.

29. Subsequently published in *Arabesques.*

30. Letter, December 1833.

31. No such proposal was made to him, either in 1830 or 1831.

32. Letter, December 23, 1833.

33. Letter, February 12, 1834.

34. Letter, May 13, 1834.

35. Letter, March 9, 1834.

36. Letter, July 20, 1834.

37. Letter, July 23, 1834.

38. Letter, August 1, 1834.

39. Letter, August 14, 1834.

40. Letter, June 27, 1834.

PART I, CHAPTER 7

1. The text of this first lecture was subsequently published in *Arabesques.*

2. Ivanitsky, "Mixtures" (*Annals of the Fatherland,* 1853).

3. Kolmakov, *Recollections.*

4. I. S. Turgenev, *Recollections of Life and Literature.*

5. Grigoryev, *Recollections.*

6. "The Nose" was not published until October 1836, in *The Contemporary.*

7. Letter, April 12, 1835.

8. Letter, July 20, 1835.

9. Letter, July 15, 1835.

10. V. A. Nashchokin, *Recollections of Pushkin and Gogol.*

11. Letter, December 6, 1835.

12. This play was never finished.

13. Dahl himself used the idea in a short story, "Vakh Sidorov Chaikin," which was published after *Dead Souls* but undoubtedly written before it.
14. Gogol, *Confession of an Author.*
15. Mrs. Smirnov, *Diary.*

PART I, CHAPTER 8

1. Letter, January 22, 1835.
2. The full title, in the Modern Library edition, is "The Tale of How Ivan Ivanovich Quarreled with Ivan Nikiforovich."
3. Chiefly in 1839 and 1840.
4. *The Contemporary,* October 1836.

PART I, CHAPTER 9

1. The man, in fact, with whom Gogol had had trouble over "Saint John's Eve," in 1830.
2. Annenkov, *Literary Recollections.*
3. The latter play, written around 1827 in the Ukrainian dialect, had not been published, but manuscript copies were circulating and Gogol had probably read it.
4. Poet and critic, and friend of Pushkin; an important figure in the literary world.
5. Letter by Vyazemsky, January 19, 1836.
6. Karatygin in the *Historical Messenger,* 1883.
7. The verb *khlestat* means to lash or whip.
8. *Tryapichkin,* in Russian, means ragpicker.
9. Gogol, *Confession of an Author.*
10. This line was originally cut by the censor.

PART I, CHAPTER 10

1. Annenkov, *Literary Recollections.*
2. Ibid.
3. This letter is thought to have been intended for Pushkin; Gogol kept it in his desk and published it in 1841 as a "Letter to a Writer."
4. Letter, August 29, 1836.
5. Letter, May 15, 1836.
6. Letter, May 10, 1836.
7. Letter, May 15, 1836.
8. V. V. Stasov, *The Law School,* years 1836–42.
9. *Selected Passages from My Correspondence with My Friends,* Chapter XVIII.

PART II, CHAPTER 1

1. Letter, June 28/16, 1836. Gogol's letters from abroad usually bear two dates, that of the Gregorian calendar, used in Western Europe, and that of the Julian calendar, used in Russia; in the nineteenth century the latter was twelve days be-

hind the former, and thirteen in the twentieth century until 1918, when the Soviet Union adopted the Gregorian calendar.

2. Letter, July 17/5, 1836.
3. Told by Zolotarev, *Historical Messenger,* 1893, no. 1.
4. Letter, July 17/5, 1836.
5. Letter, July 26/14, 1836.
6. Letter, August 14/2, 1836.
7. Letter, September 27/15, 1836.
8. Letter, October 6 / September 24, 1836.
9. Letter, September 27/15, 1836.
10. Letter, September 22/10, 1836.
11. Letter, September 21/9, 1836.
12. Ibid.
13. Gogol's eldest sister, Marya, had had a son by Trushkovsky, named Nikolai, in 1833.
14. Letter, January 14/2, 1837.
15. Letter, September 27/15, 1836.
16. Letter, November 12 / October 31, 1836.

PART II, CHAPTER 2

1. Gogol's autobiographical short story "Rome," containing his impressions of Paris.
2. Letter, January 25/13, 1837.
3. Ibid.
4. Ibid.
5. Letter, November 12 / October 31, 1836.
6. Shenrok, *Material,* Vol. III.
7. Letter, March 28/16, 1837.
8. Letter, March 28/16, 1837.
9. Letter, March 30/18, 1837.
10. Letter, April 18/6, 1837.
11. Letter, April 30/18, 1837.

PART II, CHAPTER 3

1. Letter, March 30/18, 1837.
2. Letter to Prokopovich, March 30/18, 1837.
3. Letter to Danilevsky, April 15/3, 1837.
4. Letter to Varvara Balabin, July 16/4, 1837.
5. Letter to Zhukovsky, October 30/18, 1837.
6. Letter to Pletnyev, November 2 / October 21, 1837.
7. Letter to Marya Balabin, April 1838.
8. Ibid.
9. Letter, April 15/3, 1837.
10. "Rome."
11. Ibid.
12. Ibid.

13. Letter, April 1838.
14. Strada Felice has since been renamed via Sistina. A marble plaque on the front of the house (still number 126) states that Gogol lived there.
15. Letter, April 1838.
16. Letter, December 22/10, 1837.
17. Letter to Bogdan Yansky, March 17, 1838.
18. Letter from Semenenko to Bogdan Yansky, April 22, 1838.
19. Ibid.
20. Gospel according to St. John, 1:29.
21. For the description of Ivanov's studio, see Pogodin, *A Year Abroad*.
22. *Selected Passages from My Correspondence with My Friends*, Chapter XXIII.
23. Letter, April 18/6, 1837.
24. Letter, October 30, 1837.
25. Letter, August 20, 1838.
26. Letter, December 1, 1838.
27. Letter, September 19/7, 1837.
28. Letter, May 16/4, 1838.
29. Letter, June 25/13, 1838.
30. Letter, December 31/19, 1838.
31. Told by Zolotarev, transcribed by Odoevsky.
32. Letter, November 24, 1837.
33. "Rome."
34. Letter to his mother, July 30, 1838.
35. Told by Gogol, reported by Berg, *Russian Antiquity*, 1872.
36. Letter, second half of October 1838.
37. Letter, February 12, 1839.
38. Pogodin, *Selected Memoirs*.
39. Letter, April 14, 1839.
40. Letter, May 5 / April 23, 1839.
41. Letter, May 30 / 18, 1839.
42. A. O. Smirnov, *Notes*.
43. Princess Repnin; reported by Shenrok in his *Material*.
44. Letter, June 5 / May 24, 1839.
45. *Revue des Deux Mondes*, 1845, XII. Mentioned by Sophie Lafitte in *Oxford Slavonic Papers*, Vol. XI, 1964.
46. Letter by Sainte-Beuve, dated March 16, 1857, also noted by Sophie Lafitte op. cit.
47. And did, as Kostanzhoglo, in the second part of *Dead Souls*.
48. Letter, September 5 / August 24, 1839.
49. Ibid.
50. Letter to Shevyrev, September 10 / August 29, 1839.
51. Ibid.
52. Letter, December 22/10, 1837.
53. Letter, February 5 / January 24, 1838.
54. Letter, September 10 / August 29, 1839.
55. Letter, September 15/3, 1839.
56. Letter, December 11 / November 29, 1838.
57. Letter, June 1839.
58. Letter, spring 1839.
59. Letter, June 1839.

60. Or September 10, Old Style.
61. Letter, September 28/16, 1839.
62. Old Style.

PART II, CHAPTER 4

1. Letter, September 26, 1839.
2. Letter, October 26, 1839.
3. Letter, September 27, 1839.
4. D. M. Pogodin, "Gogol in My Father's House" (from *Gogol Seen by His Contemporaries*).
5. Aksakov, *History of My Relations with Gogol*.
6. Avdotya Yakovlevna Panaev, later the mistress of Nekrasov; she wrote mediocre novels and interesting literary memoirs.
7. Avdotya Yakovlevna Panaev, *Recollections*.
8. Ivan Ivanovich Panaev, *Literary Recollections*. Panaev was a journalist and member of Belinsky's circle.
9. Ibid.
10. Details of the scene are given in Panaev's *Literary Recollections*.
11. Ibid.
12. Chertkov was a distinguished archaeologist, whom Gogol had met in Rome.
13. Panaev, *Literary Recollections;* Aksakov, *History of My Relations with Gogol*.
14. Chopped-chicken croquettes.
15. Told by Elizaveta Vasilyevna Gogol, *Russia*, 1885, no. 26.
16. Aksakov, *History of My Relations with Gogol*.
17. Letter, November 27, 1839.
18. Aksakov, *History of My Relations with Gogol*.
19. Khomyakov, one of the leaders of the Slavophile movement; Kireyevsky, a Slavophile critic; Mrs. Elagin, mother of Kireyevsky and niece of Zhukovsky, held a literary salon in Moscow.
20. Letter, December 29, 1839.
21. Aksakov, *History of My Relations with Gogol*.
22. Letter, January 25, 1840.
23. Letter, beginning of January 1840.
24. Zhukovsky's letter to Mrs. Elagin is dated February 26, 1840.
25. Letter, May 3, 1840.
26. Meshchersky, *Recollections*.
27. See Henri Troyat, *The Strange Destiny of Lermontov* (published in French by Plon).
28. Letter to Elizaveta, May 1840.
29. Aksakov, *History of My Relations with Gogol*.

PART II, CHAPTER 5

1. Letter, July 7 / June 25, 1840.
2. Letter, October 17/5, 1840.
3. Letter, August 10 / July 29, 1840.
4. Letter, October 13/1, 1840.
5. Letter, October 17/5, 1840.

6. Letter, February 17, 1842.

7. Letter to Pogodin, October 17/5, 1840.

8. August 21, Old Style.

9. Letter, June 25, 1840.

10. Letter to Pogodin, October 17, 1840.

11. *Dead Souls,* Part I, Chapter 11.

12. Letter, October 17/5, 1840.

13. Letter, October 17/5, 1840.

14. Letter, December 28/16, 1840.

15. Letter, December 28/16, 1840.

16. Letter, March 5, 1841.

17. Ibid.

18. Letter, March 13/1, 1841.

19. Letter, May 15/3, 1841.

20. Annenkov, "Gogol in Rome," from *Literary Recollections.*

21. Ibid.

22. Ibid.

23. Ibid.

24. Ibid.

25. The painting, begun in 1837, was not completed until 1856; it is now in the Tretyakov Gallery, in Moscow.

26. Letter to Ivanov, January 10, 1844.

27. Old Italian silver coin.

28. Yordan, *Recollections.*

29. Letter, August 7 / July 26, 1841.

30. Letter, September 27/15, 1841.

31. Letter, December 25, 1841.

32. Mikhail Lermontov was killed in the Caucasus on July 15, 1841, in a duel with a former schoolfellow named Martynov.

33. Told by Zhukovsky, taken down by Chizhov, and confirmed by Nikitenko.

34. Letter, June 26, 1841.

35. Letter, September 1841.

36. *Dead Souls,* Part I, Chapter 11.

PART II, CHAPTER 6

1. Aksakov, *History of My Relations with Gogol.*

2. This scene is reproduced verbatim in Nikolai Gogol's letter to Pletnyev dated January 7, 1842.

3. Ibid.

4. Letter from Belinsky to Gogol, April 20, 1842.

5. Letter, early January 1842.

6. Letter, mid-January 1842.

7. Letters written in late February 1842.

8. Letter from Count Stroganov to Benkendorf, January 29, 1842.

9. In the report, Benkendorf wrote "Gogel."

10. Or 1,660 assignation rubles.

11. Note sent on February 24, 1842; the birth was that of Pogodin's third son, Ivan.

12. *Russian Antiquity,* August 1889.

13. Letter, April 10, 1842.
14. Letter from Pletnyev to Nikitenko, April 12, 1842.
15. *Russian Antiquity,* 1889, Vol. 9; and *Gogol in Moscow,* by V. S. Zemenkov.
16. In recent editions, of course, the original text has been used.
17. Recent editions use the double title.
18. Porechy was the estate belonging to Uvarov, minister of education, where Pogodin and Shevyrev were among the most assiduous guests.
19. Letter from Belinsky to Nikolai Gogol, April 20, 1842.
20. Letter, May 11, 1842.
21. Note, early April 1842.
22. Note, second half of April 1842.
23. Note, April 30, 1842.
24. Bartenyev, story reported by Shenrok in *Material,* Vol. IV.
25. Aksakov, *History of My Relations with Gogol.*
26. Ibid.
27. Letter, January 1842.
28. Letter, February 10, 1842.
29. Letter, March 17, 1842.
30. Anna Vasilyevna Gogol, recorded by Shenrok, *Material,* Vol. IV.
31. Letter, March 17, 1842.
32. Aksakov, *History of My Relations with Gogol.*
33. Letter from Gogol to Mrs. Smirnov, cf. Veresaev, *Gogol Alive,* pp. 288–89.
34. Letter to his mother, March 22, 1842.
35. Nikolai Trushkovsky, son of the eldest of Nikolai Gogol's sisters.
36. Letter to Prokopovich, May 15, 1842.
37. *Gogol in Moscow,* by Zemenkov, p. 67.
38. Letter from Pogodin to Gogol, September 1843. Cf. Veresaev, *Gogol Alive,* p. 294.
39. Letter, July 5, 1847.
40. Aksakov, *History of My Relations with Gogol.*
41. Ibid.
42. Letter, June 4, 1842.
43. Letter, June 4, 1842.

PART II, CHAPTER 7

1. Letter, April 27, 1847.
2. *Dead Souls,* Chapter 1.
3. Chapter 11.
4. Ibid.
5. Chapter 11.
6. Chapter 6.
7. Chapter 7.
8. Translator's note: Troyat bases his remark, of course, on translations into French.
9. *Dead Souls,* Chapter 1.
10. Chapter 5.
11. Chapter 9.

12. Chapter 6.
13. Chapter 2.
14. Chapter 9.

PART III, CHAPTER 1

1. June 20, 1842, New Style.
2. Letter, June 26/14, 1842.
3. Letter, July 20/8, 1842.
4. Letter, September 10 / August 29, 1842.
5. Letter, November 2 / October 21, 1842.
6. Letter, November 12 / October 31, 1842.
7. Letter to someone unknown (possibly Benardaki), July 20, 1842.
8. Letter, August 18/6, 1842.
9. Chizhov, *Recollections.*
10. Ibid.
11. Letter by Yasykov, January 9, 1843 / December 28, 1842.
12. Letter, February 28/16, 1843.
13. Letter, March 18/6, 1843.
14. *The Gamblers.*
15. See Chapter 6, Part I, of this book.
16. Kulish, from Mrs. Smirnov's account, in *Notes on the Life of N. V. Gogol.*
17. Ibid.
18. Ibid.
19. Ibid.
20. Letter, August 18/6, 1842.
21. Letter, May 28/16, 1843.
22. Letter, June 20/8, 1843.
23. Letter, April 13/1, 1844.
24. Letter, June 20/8, 1844.
25. Letter, September 20/8, 1843.
26. Letter, April 1843.
27. Letter, October 1 / September 19, 1844.
28. Nice was not finally reannexed by France until 1860.
29. Letter, December 2 / November 20, 1843.
30. Mrs. Smirnov, noted by Viskovaty (*Russian Antiquity,* 1902).
31. Letter, January 2, 1844 / December 21, 1843.
32. Sollogub, *Recollections.*
33. Aksakov, *History of My Relations with Gogol.*
34. Letter, June 5 / May 24, 1845.
35. Letter, June 25, 1845.
36. Aksakov, *History of My Relations with Gogol.*
37. Letter, April 13/1, 1844.
38. Shenrok, *Material,* Vol. IV.
39. Letter, January 1844.
40. Letter, April 1844.
41. This manuscript was not discovered and published until 1965.
42. Now the quai des États-Unis.
43. Now the Promenade des Anglais.
44. Letter, March 26/14, 1844.

45. Letter, April 7 / March 26, 1844.

46. Letter, April 20/8, 1844.

47. Letter, May 16/4, 1844.

48. Quoted in the letter from Nikolai Gogol, May 16/4, 1844.

49. Letter to Gogol, November 26, 1844.

50. Letter to Gogol, December 12, 1844.

51. Letter, June 12 / May 31, 1844.

52. Nikolai Trushkovsky (1833–65) became the first editor of Gogol's complete works after his death.

53. Letter to Yasykov, 1844.

54. Letter, May 16/4, 1844.

55. Previously cited letter of June 12 / May 31, 1844.

56. Letter March 11 / February 28, 1844.

57. Letter, October 27, 1844.

58. Letter, December 14/2, 1844.

59. Ibid.

60. Letter, December 24/12, 1844.

61. Letter, December 18, 1844.

62. Letter, December 28/16, 1844.

63. Letter, October 26/14, 1844.

64. Letter, December 14/2, 1844.

65. Letter, February 24/12, 1845.

66. Letter, February 12 / January 31, 1845.

67. Now 12, rue de Berri: the site of a Russian chapel since 1820, which was replaced in 1881 by the Russian church on the rue Daru.

68. This volume eventually contained "Taras Bulba," "Diary of a Madman," "The Coach," "Old World Landowners," and "The King of the Gnomes" (i.e. "Viy"); it was published in the summer of 1845.

69. Letter, March 5 / February 21, 1845.

70. Scene related by Mrs. Smirnov in her *Diary*, March 11, 1845, and in her *Autobiography* and in Lorer's *Memoirs*.

71. Letter, late April 1845.

72. Nikitenko, *Diary*, May 8, 1845.

73. Letter, March 15/3, 1845.

74. Letter written between March 20 and 28, 1845 (New Style).

75. Letter, March 28/16, 1845.

76. Letter, April 2 / March 21, 1845.

77. Letter, May 11 / April 29, 1845.

78. Which he then placed at the front of his *Selected Passages from My Correspondence with My Friends.*

79. Letter, May 2 / April 20, 1845.

80. Letter, June 5 / May 24, 1845.

81. Letter, June 5 / May 24, 1845.

82. *Selected Passages from My Correspondence with My Friends,* Chapter XVIII.

83. Letter, July 28/16, 1845.

84. Letter, September 12 / August 31, 1845.

85. The concordat, based on terms laid down in December 1845, was signed on August 3, 1847, and denounced in 1866.

86. Letter, December 8 / November 26, 1845.

87. Letter, November 25/13, 1845.

88. It was ultimately Shevyrev who acted for him in Moscow, and Pletnyev in St. Petersburg.
89. Letter, November 25/13, 1845.
90. Letter, November 28/16, 1845.
91. Letter, November 28/16, 1845.
92. Letter, July 25/13, 1845.
93. Viardot received considerable help with his translation from I. S. Turgenev.
94. Letter, January 8, 1846 / December 27, 1845.

PART III, CHAPTER 2

1. Letter, April 21/9, 1846.
2. Letter from Yasykov, February 18, 1846.
3. Letter from Pletnyev, March 4, 1846.
4. Letter, May 14/2, 1846.
5. Annenkov, *Gogol in Rome.*
6. Ibid.
7. July 18, Old Style.
8. Letter, July 30/18, 1846.
9. Letter, August 1 / July 20, 1846.
10. Letter, October 20/8, 1846.
11. Letter from Aksakov, December 9, 1846.
12. Letter from Gedeonov to Pletnyev, November 1846.
13. Letter from Shchepkin, May 22, 1847.
14. It was not published until after Gogol's death.
15. Letter, December 8 / November 26, 1846.
16. Letter, November 24/12, 1846.
17. Letter, November 24/12, 1846.
18. The future Alexander II.
19. Letter, January 30/18, 1847.
20. Letter from Pletnyev, January 17, 1847.
21. *Selected Passages,* Chapter X.
22. Chapter XXVI.
23. Chapter XXVIII.
24. Chapter XXII.
25. Ibid.
26. Chapter XXIV.
27. Chapter XXI.
28. Chapter XXVIII.
29. Chapter XIII.
30. Letter, January 13/1, 1847.
31. Letter to Gogol, January 11, 1847.
32. Letter from Sverbeyev to Aksakov, February 16, 1847.
33. Letter from Belinsky to Botkin, February 28, 1847.
34. Letter from Aksakov to his son, January 16, 1847.
35. Letter from Aksakov, January 27, 1847.
36. Letter from Shevyrev, March 22, 1847.
37. Letter, February 11 / January 30, 1847.
38. Letter, March 6 / February 22, 1847.

39. Letter, March 6 / February 22, 1847.
40. Letter, March 16/4, 1847.
41. Letter, March 20/8, 1847.
42. Letter, summer 1848.
43. Letter, April 20, 1847.
44. Letter, June 20/8, 1847.
45. He died a year later.
46. Annenkov, *Literary Recollections.*
47. Letter from Belinsky to Gogol, July 15/3, 1847. Handwritten copies of this letter were soon being circulated among the public, passed furtively from hand to hand. It became a sort of breviary for liberals. The government, alerted of its existence, forbade both its publication and its possession. Twenty-five years went by before a Russian periodical, *The European Messenger,* was authorized to print extracts from it, and it was only after 1905 that the whole of the document was made public in Russia. Herzen, however, published the complete text in 1855, in his review *Polar Star,* printed in London.
48. Letter, August 10 / July 29, 1847.
49. On January 7, 1847.
50. Letter, July 10 / June 28, 1847.
51. Letter, August 28/16, 1847.
52. Gogol's italics.
53. Letter, December 18/6, 1847.
54. The major part of his work was published late in life, after Gogol's death.
55. The *Confession of an Author* (the title is not Gogol's) was found among the author's papers after his death.
56. The *Meditations upon Divine Liturgy,* like the *Confession,* were not published until 1857, after the author's death.
57. *Confession of an Author.*
58. Letter, April 15/3, 1847.
59. Letter, February 22/10, 1847.
60. Letter, March 18/6, 1847.
61. Letter, September 24/12, 1847.
62. Letter of January 10, 1848 / December 29, 1847.

   N. B. Gogol expressed the same idea, in almost the same words, five years earlier, in the second version of "The Portrait" (1842): "It is for the consolation and reconciliation of all, that the divine creation of art comes down to earth. It cannot implant protest or rebellion in the soul."
63. Letter, November 14/2, 1846.
64. Letter, November 20/8, 1847.
65. Letter, December 2 / November 20, 1847.
66. Letter, early December / late November 1847.
67. Letter, January 12, 1848 / December 31, 1847.

PART III, CHAPTER 3

1. Letter, January 22/10, 1848.
2. Father Peter Solovyev, "Meeting with Gogol," (*Russian Antiquity,* 1883).
3. Letter to Zhukovsky, February 28/16, 1850.
4. Ibid.
5. Letter to Zhukovsky, April 6 / March 25, 1848.

6. Letter, April 25/13, 1848.
7. *Gogol,* from Arnoldi's notes.
8. Letter, February 28/16, 1850.
9. Letter, April 21, 1848.
10. Letter, April 25/13, 1848.

PART III, CHAPTER 4

1. Letter, May 16, 1848.
2. Pashchenko, from notes by V. Pashkov.
3. Elizaveta Vasilyevna Gogol, *Diary* (Shenrok, *Material,* Vol. IV).
4. Ibid.
5. *Recollections* of Olga Vasilyevna Gogol.
6. Yasinsky, based on Mikholsky's account; "A Gogol Anecdote" (*The Historical Messenger,* June 1891).
7. Letter, July 7, 1848.
8. Letter, July 12, 1848.
9. *Recollections* of Olga Vasilyevna Gogol.
10. Elizaveta Vasilyevna Gogol, *Diary* (Shenrok, *Material,* Vol. IV).
11. Letter, September 24, 1848.
12. Letter, June 15, 1848.
13. Panaev, *Recollections.*
14. Ibid.
15. Letter, October 29, 1848.
16. Letter, March 30, 1849.
17. Letter, October 29, 1848.
18. Pogodin, *Diary.*
19. N. V. Berg, *Recollections of Gogol.*
20. Pogodin, *Diary.*
21. N. Barsukov, *Pogodin's Life and Work.*
22. Archimandrite Theodore (A. M. Bukharev), *Three Letters to Gogol.*
23. Now no. 7, Suvorov Boulevard.
24. Letter, April 3, 1849.
25. Letter from Aksakov to Mrs. Smirnov, May 16, 1849.
26. Letter, July 1, 1849.
27. Arnoldi, *My Relations with Gogol.*
28. Ibid.
29. Mrs. Smirnov; from Viskovaty's notes (*Russian Antiquity,* 1902).
30. Kulish, from Mrs. Smirnov's account: *Notes on Gogol's Life.*
31. Arnoldi, *My Relations with Gogol.*
32. Mrs. Smirnov; from Viskovaty's notes (*Russian Antiquity,* 1902).
33. Arnoldi, *My Relations with Gogol.*
34. Prince D. A. Obolensky, "On the First Edition of Gogol's Posthumous Works" (*Russian Antiquity,* 1873).
35. Letter, July 30, 1849.
36. Aksakov's account as noted by Kulish.
37. Ibid.
38. Letter From Sergey Aksakov to his son Ivan, January 20, 1850.
39. Letter, January 21, 1850.
40. N. V. Berg, *Recollections of Gogol.*

41. Ibid.
42. Letter, spring 1850.
43. Mrs. Smirnov, *Recollections.*
44. Letter, 1850.
45. Letter, June 13, 1850.
46. Told to Kulish by Maximovich, *Notes on Gogol's Life.*
47. Letter, July 10, 1850.
48. Letter, June 19, 1850.
49. Letter, September 15, 1850.
50. Letter, second half of July 1850.
51. Letter, October 28, 1850.
52. Lerner, based on Demenitru's account; *Russian Antiquity,* 1901.
53. Tolchenov, *Gogol in Odessa.*
54. *Diary of an Unknown Lady. Russian Archives,* 1902.
55. Letter, October 16, 1850.
56. Letter, December 16, 1850.
57. Letter, December 23, 1850.
58. Olga Vasilyevna Gogol, *Recollections.*
59. Shenrok, *Material,* from an account by Danilevsky.
60. Undated letter, written after May 22, 1851.
61. Undated letter, written after May 22, 1851.
62. Letter, July 14, 1851.

PART III, CHAPTER 5

1. Letter, July 14, 1851.
2. 83.25 assignation rubles.
3. Letter, mid-July 1851.
4. Mrs. Smirnov, *Notes.*
5. Letter to Shevyrev, late July 1851.
6. N. V. Berg, *Recollections of Gogol.*
7. Letter to Pletnyev, July 15, 1851.
8. Annenkov, *Last Meeting with Gogol.*
9. Letter, early September 1851.
10. Letter, September 22, 1851.
11. Letter, September 25, 1851.
12. Letter from Pletnyev to Zhukovsky, February 24, 1851; and Mrs. Smirnov, *Autobiography.*
13. Letter, October 3, 1851.
14. Belinsky's vehement letter about *Selected Passages,* mentioned above (Part III, Chapter 2).
15. I. S. Turgenev, *Recollections of Literature and Life.*
16. From Shchepkin's memoirs.
17. Turgenev, *Recollections of Literature and Life.*
18. No connection with Gogol's childhood friend Alexander Semyonovich Danilevsky.
19. The model for this paragon is said to be Anna Mikhailovna Vyelgorsky.
20. Conversation told by Bodyansky to Kulish, in the latter's *Notes on Gogol's Life.*
21. Vera Sergeyevna Aksakov (Aksakov's daughter), *Diary.*

22. Ibid.

23. Letter, February 2, 1852.

24. Letter, November 28, 1851.

25. *The Letters of Father Matthew Konstantinovsky,* cf. Veresayev, *Gogol Alive.*

26. Greshishchev, *Account of the Life of the Deceased Archpriest of Rzhev, Matthew Konstantinovsky.*

27. Letter from K. I. Markov to Gogol, quoted in Shenrok, *Material,* Vol. IV.

28. Tarasenkov, *Gogol's Last Days.*

29. Ibid.

30. Letter, February 6, 1852.

31. Related by Obraztsov, a monk who was present at the interview.

32. Letter, early February 1852.

33. As told by Pogodin, *The Muscovite,* no. 5, 1852. The second part of *Dead Souls* is known only through a few fragments, drafts, and plans found by Shevyrev among Gogol's papers, and by the accounts of the few friends to whom he had read extracts before he died.

34. Told by Tarasenkov, *Gogol's Last Days.*

35. Tarasenkov, *Gogol's Last Days.*

36. "Diary of a Madman."

37. Tarasenkov, *Gogol's Last Days.*

38. To account for the death of Nikolai Gogol, the doctors talked of intestinal catarrh, typhus, gastroenteritis; but he had always been a neuropath. His long fast, complicated by anemia, had brought his physical resistance to the lowest possible point. According to Dr. Bazhenov, "The treatment should have been the exact opposite of that administered: he should have been fed by force and given hypodermic injections of saline solution, instead of bled." (Bazhenov, *Gogol's Illness and Death,* Moscow, 1902.)

39. Letter from Aksakov to his sons, February 23, 1852.

40. Report to Orlov, the chief of police, from Count Zakrevsky, governor general of Moscow, February 29, 1852.

41. On May 31, 1931, Gogol's tomb was transferred to the monastery of the New Virgins.

42. He is alluding to Pushkin, Lermontov, and Griboedov, all of whom died violent deaths while still young.

43. These stories were collected and published the same year in a volume entitled *A Sportman's Sketches.*

44. Nikolai Gogol's nephew Trushkovsky reprinted the complete works in 1855–56. The first four volumes (1855) reproduced the 1842 edition; the following two contained later works.

45. G. P. Danilevsky, *My Relations with Gogol.*

46. Gogol's mother died at Vasilyevka in 1868, at the age of seventy-seven. His youngest sister, Olga (1825–1907), married Major Golovnya, retired, and had two sons and a daughter by him. Anna (1821–93) never married. Trushkovsky, son of Gogol's eldest sister, Marya (died 1844), assumed responsibility for editing his uncle's complete works (1855–56) and died insane in 1865. By a strange coincidence, another of Gogol's nephews, Elizaveta's son by Bykov (she was widowed in 1862, died in 1864), married Pushkin's granddaughter Marya Alexandrovna.

Index

Index